NATURAL RESOURCE DAMAGES

A Guide to Litigating and Resolving NRD Cases

Brian D. Israel, Brett Marston, and Lauren Daniel

NATURAL RESOURCE DAMAGES

A Guide to Litigating and Resolving NRD Cases

Brian D. Israel, Brett Marston, and Lauren Daniel

AMERICAN**BAR**ASSOCIATION

ABA Publishing

Cover design by Anthony Nuccio/ABA Design

The materials contained herein represent the opinions of the authors and/or the editors, and should not be construed to be the views or opinions of the law firms or companies with whom such persons are in partnership with, associated with, or employed by, nor of the American Bar Association or the Section of Environment, Energy, and Resources unless adopted pursuant to the bylaws of the Association.

Nothing contained in this book is to be considered as the rendering of legal advice for specific cases, and readers are responsible for obtaining such advice from their own legal counsel. This book is intended for educational and informational purposes only.

Printed in the United States of America.

23 22 21 20 19 5 4 3 2 1

ISBN: 978-1-64105-438-6
e-ISBN: 978-1-64105-439-3

Library of Congress Cataloging-in-Publication Data
Names: Israel, Brian D., author. | Marston, Brett, author. | Daniel, Lauren, author. | American Bar Association. Section of Environment, Energy, and Resources, sponsoring body.
Title: Natural resource damages : a guide to litigating and resolving NRD cases / by Brian D. Israel, Brett Marston, and Lauren Daniel.
Description: First edition. | Chicago : American Bar Association, 2019. | Includes index.
Identifiers: LCCN 2019012578 | ISBN 9781641054386 (print) | ISBN 9781641054393 (epub)
Subjects: LCSH: Liability for environmental damages—United States. | Conservation of natural resources—Law and legislation—United States. | Damages—United States.
Classification: LCC KF1298 .I87 2019 | DDC 344.7304/6—dc23
LC record available at https://lccn.loc.gov/2019012578

Discounts are available for books ordered in bulk. Special consideration is given to state bars, CLE programs, and other bar-related organizations. Inquire at Book Publishing, ABA Publishing, American Bar Association, 321 N. Clark Street, Chicago, Illinois 60654-7598.

www.ShopABA.org

Contents

Index of Expert Insights

Acknowledgments

The authors gratefully acknowledge the assistance of Leigh Logan, senior legal assistant, and Margaret Barry, environmental law writer, at Arnold & Porter. Leigh and Margaret have provided invaluable support and assistance in the development of this manuscript. The authors also thank the 18 expert contributors who have provided their insight on particular issues related to NRD.

Finally, the authors are deeply grateful for the steadfast love and support of our families: Tsila, Miriam, Abigail, Einav, Jonathan, and Aiden (Brian); Anita and Leela (Brett); Ben and Eleanor (Lauren).

About the Authors

Brian D. Israel is the chair of the Environmental Practice Group at Arnold & Porter and is a partner in the firm's Washington, D.C., office. Mr. Israel's practice focuses broadly on environmental litigation and counseling, and he is one of the nation's leading lawyers for Natural Resource Damages (NRD) claims. Mr. Israel is lead counsel to BP in relation to the *Deepwater Horizon* NRD claim; he was also one of the trial attorneys at the *Deepwater Horizon* Clean Water Act penalty trial. Mr. Israel represents several Fortune 500 companies in some of the largest and most complex NRD matters across the country. He also represents clients in regulatory enforcement matters and contaminated properties, including toxic tort lawsuits.

Mr. Israel has spoken and written extensively about environmental law issues, including NRD, and he serves as co-chair of the annual NRD conference hosted by Law Seminars International. In 2017, he was recognized as an Energy & Environmental Trailblazer by the *National Law Journal*. Prior to joining Arnold & Porter, Mr. Israel was an honors trial attorney in the Environmental Enforcement Section of the U.S. Department of Justice, where he handled several high-profile environmental cases, including a large NRD claim related to the impacts of DDT disposal. In 1998, Mr. Israel was awarded the Distinguished Service Award for his accomplishments in a Clean Air Act jury trial. Mr. Israel received his BA in environmental philosophy from New College, University of South Florida, in 1991, and received his JD from New York University in 1995, where he graduated cum laude.

Lauren Daniel is a senior associate in Arnold & Porter's Washington, D.C., office and handles a wide range of environmental disputes, including actions under the Comprehensive Environmental Response, Compensation, and Liability Act (CERCLA); the Oil Pollution Act (OPA); the Clean Water Act (CWA); and a variety of state environmental laws. Ms. Daniel has particular expertise in NRD litigation and cost recovery and contribution actions under these statutes. In addition, Ms. Daniel helps advise clients with respect to a variety of environmental regulatory, permitting, and enforcement issues under various federal and state environmental statutes, with a focus on environmental remediation issues.

Ms. Daniel currently serves as co-chair of the American Bar Association Committee on Superfund and Natural Resource Damages Litigation. She graduated cum laude from Claremont McKenna College in 2008, where she received a BA in philosophy and international relations and was awarded departmental honors in both philosophy and government. Ms. Daniel received her JD from Columbia Law School in 2012, where she was a Harlan Fiske Stone Scholar, the recipient of the 2012 Alfred A. Forsyth Prize for Qualities of Intellect and Self Dedication to the Advancement of Environmental Law, and acted as president of the Columbia Environmental Law Society.

Brett Marston is a senior associate in the Washington, D.C., office of Arnold & Porter and focuses his practice on all aspects of environmental enforcement and counseling, including contaminated site remediation, NRD, and regulatory counseling and litigation under CERCLA, OPA, CWA, the Clean Air Act, and other state and federal environmental statutes. He has extensive experience with aspects of environmental liability related to property transactions. In addition, Mr. Marston also has experience with litigation under the Administrative Procedure Act.

Mr. Marston received his AB with First Honor (valedictorian) from Davidson College in 1994, and he earned his MA and MPhil degrees in political science from Yale University in 2007. He graduated magna cum laude and Order of the Coif from Georgetown University Law Center in 2009, where he served as editor in chief for the *Georgetown International Environmental Law Review*.

Abbreviations

Administrative Procedure Act	APA
Authorized Official	AO
Bureau of Land Management	BLM
Clean Water Act	CWA
Comprehensive Environmental Response, Compensation, and Liability Act	CERCLA
Contingent Valuation	CV
Cooperative Assessment Project	CAP
Criteria for Reporting and Evaluating Ecotoxicity Data	CRED
Damage Assessment and Restoration Plan/Environmental Assessment	DARP/EA or DARP
Data Quality Objectives	DQO
Department of Veterans Affairs	VA
Discounted Service Acre Year	DSAY
Engineering Evaluation and Cost Analysis	EE/CA
Environmental Assessment	EA
Environmental Impact Statement	EIS
Environmental Liability Directive	ELD
European Union	EU
Good Laboratory Practice	GLP
Gulf Coast Claims Facility	GCCF
Habitat Equivalency Analysis	HEA
Local Government Entities	LGE
Memorandum of Understanding	MOU
National Contingency Plan	NCP
Multi-Annual ELD Work Programme	MAWP
National Environmental Policy Act	NEPA
National Highway Traffic Safety Administration	NHTSA
National Historic Preservation Act	NHPA
National Oceanic and Atmospheric Administration	NOAA
National Pollutant Discharge Elimination System	NPDES
National Pollution Funds Center	NPFC

National Priorities List	NPL
Natural Resource Damage(s)	NRD
Natural Resource Damage(s) Assessment(s)	NRDA
Natural Resource Damage Assessment Model for Coastal and Marine Environments	NRDAM/CME
Natural Resource Damage Assessment Model for Great Lakes Environments	NRDAM/GLE
New Jersey Department of Environmental Protection	NJDEP
Nongovernmental Organization(s)	NGO(s)
Notice of Intent	NOI
Oil Pollution Act	OPA
Operable Unit(s)	OU(s)
Organisation for Economic Co-operation and Development	OECD
Potentially Responsible Party	PRP
Programmatic Environmental Impact Statement	PEIS
Puerto Rico Department of Natural and Environmental Resources	DNER
Quality Assurance	QA
Quality Control	QC
Random Utility Model	RUM
Recreational Equivalency Analysis	REA
Remedial Design/Remedial Action	RD/RA
Remedial Investigation/Feasibility Study	RI/FS
Resource Conservation and Recovery Act	RCRA
Restoration and Compensation Determination Plan	RCDP
Submerged Lands Act	SLA
Superfund Amendments and Reauthorization Act	SARA
Technical Working Groups	TWGs
Texas General Land Office	TGLO
Total Economic Value	TEV
Trans-Atlantic Pipeline Authorization Act	TAPAA
Travel Cost Model	TCM
Trip Equivalency Analysis	TEA
U.S. Coast Guard	USCG
U.S. Department of the Interior	DOI
U.S. Department of Energy	DOE
U.S. Environmental Protection Agency	EPA
U.S. Food and Drug Administration	FDA
U.S. Virgin Islands	USVI
U.S. Virgin Islands Department of Planning and Natural Resources	DPNR
Value-to-Value	VtV
Willingness-to-Pay	WTP

Chapter 1
Introduction

Natural resource damage claims are claims asserted by federal, state, or tribal governments seeking restoration of injuries to natural resources resulting from certain types of industrial contamination and oil spills. The practice of natural resource damages (NRD) is highly complex, and the stakes can be huge. The magnitude of NRD claims can sometimes far exceed the cost of cleaning up the contamination at issue. Furthermore, NRD claims involve a constellation of complicated legal questions, ranging from overlapping governmental oversight to uncertain standards of proof to a myriad of untested legal defenses. Similarly, NRD claims present difficult evidentiary issues involving biology, chemistry, ecology, economics, engineering, statistics, toxicology, and numerous other academic disciplines. Superimposed on top of all of these legal and evidentiary problems are formidable strategic questions implicit in any NRD claim. These strategic considerations include whether (and how) to cooperate with the government; whether to pursue a settlement path or a litigation path; how to involve community input; whether to involve other potentially liable parties; how best to achieve cost-effective restoration based on sound science and actual legal exposure, while also minimizing transaction costs; and how to negotiate reasonable NRD settlements.

This book presents a comprehensive guide to the legal, evidentiary, and strategic issues associated with litigating and resolving NRD claims. Collectively, the authors (including many contributing experts) have many decades of experience litigating NRD claims, both for the government and for companies. The authors themselves have successfully resolved some of the largest, most difficult NRD claims of the last decade, including the NRD claims stemming from the *Deepwater Horizon* oil spill, among others.

Following is an overview of the book and its organization.

Chapter 2: NRD Statutes and Regulations. This chapter explains some of the basics of NRD law, including an in-depth discussion of the key federal statutes authorizing NRD claims. This chapter also provides an overview and history of the NRD regulations, promulgated under the Oil Pollution Act (OPA) and the Comprehensive Environmental Response, Compensation, and Liability Act (CERCLA).

Chapter 3: NRD Defenses. While there are many defenses to NRD claims, there is precious little jurisprudence interpreting those defenses. This chapter provides a critical overview of the key NRD defenses, including legal (e.g., statutes of limitations, retroactive application, standing, ripeness, federally permitted releases, and the bar against double recovery), evidentiary (e.g., causation and baseline), and procedural (e.g., the standard of review, the scope of review, the rebuttable presumption, and the right to a jury).

Chapter 4: NRD Assessments. This chapter provides a detailed explanation of the regulatory guidelines applicable to NRD assessments (NRDA), including concepts of baseline, injury determination, damages calculations, restoration planning, and public input. While the NRD regulations are not mandatory, if the government conducts a NRDA pursuant to the regulations, they will enjoy a rebuttable presumption that their assessment is accurate. Accordingly, the government often makes every effort to follow these regulations, and it is important for stakeholders to understand precisely how these regulations are structured.

Chapter 5: Valuation Methods. A finding that a hazardous substance or oil has injured a natural resource is only the first step in evaluating an NRD claim. The next step, and one of the thorniest, is determining the monetary value of that injury. The question really asks: how much is nature worth, and the answer is not merely philosophical but also legal, economic, and scientific. This chapter delves into the common methodologies and approaches used to value injured natural resources. Moreover, this chapter provides a strategic discussion of the advantages and disadvantages of various approaches, including a restoration-based approach, a survey approach, and an ecosystem approach. Finally, this chapter includes "expert insights" related to habitat equivalency assessments for measuring ecological damages, travel cost methods for calculating recreational losses, and a novel approach for measuring recreational damages called "trip equivalency" assessments.

Chapter 6: Cooperative Assessments. Unlike other environmental laws, there is no requirement that companies cooperate with the government as it conducts a NRDA. On the other hand, the government is obligated to offer companies the opportunity to cooperate. This leads to a strategic conundrum: when faced with a potential NRD claim, should a potentially responsible party cooperate in the assessment process, and if so, how? This chapter explores the strategic advantages and disadvantages to participation in a cooperative NRDA with the government. Finally, the chapter discusses the mechanics of cooperation, including the elements of a cooperative assessment agreement.

Chapter 7: Litigation Strategy. This chapter provides key suggestions for developing and implementing a successful NRD litigation strategy. The heart of this chapter is a discussion of ten large NRD trials and key lessons learned from those trials. In addition, this chapter discusses many of the pre-trial motions and other procedural aspects of litigating a large NRD matter.

Chapter 8: Restoration Strategy. Good restoration projects can often resolve hard NRD cases. This is true because a suite of popular and visible restoration projects can pave the way for a case to settle even when the parties do not agree on the injury assessment or damages calculation. This chapter explores the contours of a restoration strategy, including the interplay between restoration planning and litigation planning; the advantages, disadvantages, and mechanics of early restoration; and the challenges and opportunities presented by involving third parties (including environmental organizations) in restoration planning.

Chapter 9: Settlement Strategy. Similar to other areas of environmental law, at the end of the day, most NRD cases settle. The strategic questions surrounding an NRD settlement are immense and complicated, including finality, work performance, and timing, among other considerations. This chapter discusses these issues and provides several examples of how parties have addressed them in prior consent decrees.

Chapter 10: Complex and Novel Situations. NRD cases, already complicated and challenging, can be made more so by unusual circumstances. This chapter describes five such circumstances and provides strategic considerations for handling them. The five complex situations discussed in this chapter are (1) sites with multiple trustees; (2) third-party practice and contribution claims; (3) insurance disputes in the NRD context; (4) claims for damages to historic or cultural resources; and (5) the implications of climate change for NRD.

Chapter 11: The European NRD Regime. This final chapter describes the NRD regime in the European Union (EU), called the Environmental Liability Directive (ELD). In addition, this chapter compares the ELD to the NRD programs in the United States and describes some of the challenges the ELD has faced as it has been transcribed into the laws of the EU member states.

It is worth noting that the world of NRD is anything but static. There are numerous trends and developments, ranging from potential NRD regulatory reform to greater prominence by state and tribal trustees. There is also an increasing interest in novel restoration approaches, including restoration banking and early restoration. Finally, parties are increasingly looking for greater efficiency in the NRD process, including through the use of existing data, stipulations, partial settlements, and shared experts. Throughout this NRD guide, we discuss these emerging trends, including predictions for the future.

Of particular importance in the short term is the possibility for regulatory reform. This book comprehensively sets forth considerations under the existing NRDA regulations that, as is elucidated further throughout the book, propagate many inefficiencies and much confusion. In light of the current political climate at the time of publication of this book, NRD is an area that is ripe for regulatory reform.

In its first year, the Trump administration initiated a comprehensive regulatory reform effort. Through various executive orders, including Executive Order 13771, Reducing Regulation and Controlling Regulatory Costs, and Executive Order 13777, Enforcing the Regulatory Reform Agenda, the administration has set forth the goals of reducing unnecessary regulatory burden and improving federal program efficiency. Various executive agencies, including the U.S. Department of the Interior (DOI) and the U.S. Department of Commerce, the two most important federal NRD trustee agencies, are currently seeking stakeholder input on identifying priorities for regulatory reform.

On August 27, 2018, DOI promulgated an Advance Notice of Proposed Rulemaking (ANPRM), requesting comments related to possible revision of the NRDA regulations promulgated pursuant to CERCLA.[1] Details about the ANPRM process are discussed in Chapter 2.

---

1. Natural Resource Damages for Hazardous Substances, 83 Fed. Reg. 43,611 (proposed Aug. 27, 2018) (to be codified at 43 C.F.R. pt. 11).

Chapter 2
NRD Statutes and Regulations[1]

A. Basic Legal Framework

Federal, state, territorial, and tribal governments may seek compensation for natural resources that are injured or destroyed when property becomes contaminated with certain pollutants, including hazardous substances and petroleum. The compensation for natural resource damages (NRD) is intended to restore the natural environment to its prior condition and compensate the public for the interim lost use from the time of contamination until restoration.

Most NRD claims are brought pursuant to federal or state environmental statutes. The primary federal statutory authorities are the Comprehensive Environmental Response, Compensation, and Liability Act (CERCLA) and the Oil Pollution Act of 1990 (OPA), but the Clean Water Act (CWA) and several other federal statutes also provide avenues for recovery of NRD in certain circumstances.

Authority to seek NRD compensation is rooted in common law principles, including the public trust doctrine and others. A "central motivation" for establishing statutory authority to recover NRD was dissatisfaction with the common law, which restricted the scope of available damages.[2]

The modern statutory frameworks authorizing NRD compensation provide the relevant government agencies with a significant enforcement mechanism for obtaining monetary damages at contaminated properties.

---

1. Portions of this chapter are adapted from "Natural Resource Damages," of the *Environmental Law Practice Guide: State and Federal Law*, with permission. Copyright 2017 Matthew Bender & Company, Inc., a LexisNexis company. All rights reserved.

2. *See* Ohio v. U.S. Dep't of the Interior, 880 F.2d 432, 446 n.14, 455, 470 (D.C. Cir. 1989) (discussing dissatisfaction with common law and concern for liberalizing common law standards as motivation for CERCLA NRD provisions).

B. Context for NRD Claims: The Life Cycle of a Contaminated Site

The "life cycle" of a contaminated site is important to understand, as it provides the context for an NRD claim. Specifically, the typical contaminated site has five overlapping stages: (1) insurance, (2) allocation, (3) remedy, (4) toxic tort, and (5) NRD. Each of these stages addresses a separate issue, and resolution in one stage will not resolve the others. Also, these stages are not necessarily linear and may occur in different orders or simultaneously. Many sites do not feature all five of these stages.

The insurance stage simply refers to the effort by a liable party to enforce a contractual indemnity owed to it for its environmental liabilities at the site.[3] The allocation stage refers to the ability of a liable party to allocate responsibility for a site among itself and other liable parties.

The last three stages of the contaminated site—remedy, toxic tort, and NRD—are closely interrelated. The remedy refers to the remedial investigation, selection, and implementation. The main objective of the remedy stage is the protection of human health and the environment. Although the remedial cleanup may have collateral ecological benefits, the principal focus is on removing or isolating contaminants, not restoring natural resources. Further, there are no remedy "damages," only costs.

Conversely, the toxic tort stage is usually focused on damages, not cleanup. This is true for a number of reasons, but one is that some statutes preclude a toxic tort plaintiff from seeking injunctive relief if the site is already the subject of a government cleanup order or investigation.[4] The toxic tort plaintiff usually seeks private damages associated with the contamination, including diminution in property value, unjust enrichment, pain and suffering, personal injury, and the like.

Finally, the NRD stage generally seeks both cleanup and damages, although it is sometimes framed as related only to damages. In that sense, the NRD stage is a hybrid of the remedy and the toxic tort stages. Yet, an NRD claim should be duplicative of neither. The cleanup that is sought in an NRD matter is focused on restoring natural resources, not protecting human health and the environment. One way to describe the distinction is that the remedy removes or isolates the contaminants, whereas the restoration replaces the lost natural resources. In this way, the NRD "cleanup" is sometimes described as the residual work needed after implementation of the remedy.

---

3. Insurance issues as they relate to NRD are discussed in Chapter 10.
4. *See, e.g.*, 42 U.S.C. § 9622(e)(6).

The distinction between the NRD stage and the toxic tort stage is also important. The toxic tort claimant is an individual or class. The NRD claimant is the public through a governmental trustee. Furthermore, the damages sought in an NRD matter are tied to the lost resources, whereas the damages in a toxic tort matter are tied to the injury to the plaintiff and the culpability of the defendant.

During the life cycle of a contaminated site, the distinctions among these five stages are often unclear and there is frequently overlap. For example, the extent of liability impacts the ability to allocate, and the nature of the remedy often impacts NRD or toxic tort liability. Furthermore, there may be numerous other factors at play, such as bankruptcy, compliance with regulatory laws, and community relations. Nonetheless, considering these five stages in the life cycle of a contaminated site helps to place NRD in the proper context.

C. Trusteeship

The key figure at the NRD stage of a contaminated site is the trustee. In many or most cases, other entities will be responsible for the remediation of a spill, discharge, or release of hazardous substances.

Under CERCLA, "[a] 'trustee' is a federal, state or Indian tribal official who, in accordance with 42 U.S.C. § 9607(f)(2), is designated to 'act on behalf of the public as [a] trustee[] for natural resources.'"[5] Trustee officials have the duty to "assess damages for injury to, destruction of, or loss of natural resources . . . for those resources under their trusteeship."[6] OPA similarly provides that trustees shall assess NRD and develop and implement plans "for the restoration, rehabilitation, replacement, or acquisition of the equivalent, of the natural resources under their trusteeship."[7] Trusteeship and standing to bring NRD claims can be pivotal aspects of NRD litigation, an issue discussed in Chapter 3.

CERCLA and OPA required the president to designate federal trustees. In executive orders, the following were identified as federal trustees for natural

---

5. Nat'l Ass'n of Mfrs. v. U.S. Dep't of the Interior, 134 F.3d 1095, 1098 n.1 (D.C. Cir. 1998) (quoting 42 U.S.C. § 9607(f)(2)). OPA contemplates foreign trustees as well. *See* 40 C.F.R. § 300.612 ("Pursuant to section 1006 of the OPA, foreign trustees shall act on behalf of the head of a foreign government as trustees for natural resources belonging to, managed by, controlled by, or appertaining to such foreign government.").

6. 42 U.S.C. § 9607(f)(2)(A) and (B). Federal trustees may also assess damages for natural resources under a state's trusteeship, if requested by the state and subject to reimbursement by the state. *Id.* § 9607(f)(2)(A).

7. 33 U.S.C. § 2706(c)(1)(C).

resources: (1) Secretary of Defense, (2) Secretary of the Interior, (3) Secretary of Agriculture, (4) Secretary of Commerce, and (5) Secretary of Energy.[8] The National Contingency Plan (NCP) further provides:

- The Secretary of the Interior shall be the "trustee for natural resources managed or controlled by [the U.S. Department of the Interior (DOI)]," and for "natural resources for which an Indian tribe would otherwise act as trustee in those cases where the United States acts on behalf of the Indian tribe."[9]
- The Secretary of Commerce shall be the trustee for natural resources managed or controlled by the Department of Commerce, and for natural resources managed or controlled by other agencies where those natural resources are found "in, under, or using" water bodies such as navigable waters and waters of the contiguous zone.[10]
- The head of the relevant department—such as DOI, the U.S. Department of Agriculture, the U.S. Department of Defense, or the U.S. Department of Energy (DOE)—will be the trustee for natural resources "located on, over, or under land administered by the United States."[11]

The regulations also provide that, notwithstanding these stated designations, the Secretaries of Commerce and Interior are to "act as trustees of those resources subject to their respective management or control."[12]

CERCLA and OPA make state governors responsible for appointing state trustees. The NCP encourages the governor to designate a state lead trustee to coordinate all state trustee responsibilities with other trustee agencies and with the U.S. Environmental Protection Agency's (EPA's) response activities.[13]

The NCP further provides that tribal trustees shall be "tribal chairmen (or heads of the governing bodies) of Indian tribes . . . or a person designated by the tribal officials."[14] Tribal trustees, like state trustees, are authorized to act

---

8. Exec. Order No. 12,580, 52 Fed. Reg. 2923 (Jan. 23, 1987), *as amended by* Exec. Order No. 12,777, 56 Fed. Reg. 54,757 (Oct. 22, 1991). The NCP provides the organizational structure and procedures for preparing for and responding to releases of hazardous substances under CERCLA.

9. 40 C.F.R. § 300.600(b)(2).

10. *Id.* § 300.600(b)(1).

11. *Id.* § 300.600(b)(3).

12. *Id.* § 300.600(b).

13. *Id.* § 300.605. The designated trustees for the states are identified and state NRD programs are discussed in more detail in BRIAN D. ISRAEL, STATE-BY-STATE GUIDE TO NRD PROGRAMS IN ALL 50 STATES AND PUERTO RICO (Mar. 1, 2018), https://www.arnoldporter.com/-/media/files /perspectives/publications/2018/03/state-by-state-nrd-guide.pdf.

14. 40 C.F.R. § 300.610.

for resources, including "supporting ecosystems."[15] Historically, many tribes have been very successful in pursuing NRD claims, either in conjunction with other trustees or as the lead trustee.

The territories and commonwealths of the United States are also trustees for purposes of NRD claims.[16] There are currently two commonwealths—Puerto Rico and the Northern Marianas—and 12 territories or possessions (e.g., Guam, American Samoa, and the U.S. Virgin Islands (USVI)). The territories have indeed pursued NRD claims, most often in coordination with federal trustees. For example, in 2001, the Puerto Rico Department of Natural and Environmental Resources (DNER), along with the federal trustees, settled claims related to an 800,000 gallon oil spill off the coast of Puerto Rico. The settlement—over $80 million—included compensation for injuries to natural resources and assessment costs.[17] In 2016, DNER, along with federal trustees, agreed to a $2.75 million settlement (with $83,265.24 payable to DNER) of NRD claims stemming from a spill of 45,000 gallons from an oil tanker.[18]

Prior to the Superfund Amendments and Reauthorization Act (SARA) in 1986,[19] case law permitted municipalities to bring NRD claims, relying in part on the reference to "local government" in CERCLA's definition of "natural resources."[20] Since SARA, however, courts have consistently held that a municipality may bring an NRD claim under CERCLA only if specifically authorized by the governor of the state in which it is located.[21] SARA specified a mechanism for appointing a state representative (through the governor of the state), where no such mechanism previously existed. Courts interpreted this addition as affording the sole mechanism by which municipalities may act.[22] The absence of any reference to municipalities within the definition of

---

15. *Id.*

16. *See, e.g.*, 15 C.F.R. § 990.30.

17. Press Release, U.S. Dep't of Justice, $83.5 Million Settlement Reached in 1994 Puerto Rico Oil Spill (Jan. 19, 2001).

18. *See* Consent Decree, United States v. GMR Progress LLC, No. 3:16-cv-1507-PAD (D.P.R. Sept. 15, 2016), ECF No. 6.

19. Pub. L. No. 99-499, 100 Stat. 1613 (1986).

20. *See, e.g.*, Mayor of Boonton v. Drew Chem. Corp., 621 F. Supp. 663, 668 (D.N.J. 1985).

21. *See* Mayor of Rockaway v. Klockner & Klockner, 811 F. Supp. 1039, 1049 (D.N.J. 1993); City of Portland v. Boeing Co., 179 F. Supp. 2d 1190, 1202–04 (D. Or. 2001); City of Toledo v. Beazer Materials & Servs., Inc., 833 F. Supp. 646, 652 (N.D. Ohio 1993). The court in *Werlein v. United States*, while it ruled against the municipality, appears to have done so because the resource in question was not within the management of the city, but rather the state. 746 F. Supp. 887, 910 (D. Minn. 1990), *vacated*, 793 F. Supp. 898 (D. Minn. 1992).

22. *See* Town of Bedford v. Raytheon Co., 755 F. Supp. 469, 473 (D. Mass. 1991).

"state"—especially because SARA did not change the definition of "state," even as the amendments introduced a mechanism for appointing state trustees—led courts to conclude that Congress intended to preclude cities from bringing independent NRD claims under CERCLA.[23]

Although municipalities lack independent authority to bring NRD claims under CERCLA, the Ninth Circuit has held that a municipality may enact local ordinances that permit it to recover for damages to natural resources held in its trust.[24]

OPA authorizes foreign governments to recover NRD for natural resources belonging to, managed by, controlled by, or appertaining to their countries.[25] The heads of the foreign governments may designate trustees to act on their behalf.[26]

The extent to which trusteeship can be asserted over privately owned resources to obtain NRD for injuries to such resources is not entirely clear. The D.C. Circuit noted that "Congress quite deliberately excluded purely private property from the ambit of the natural resource damage provisions," but that "a substantial degree of government regulation, management or other form of control over the property would be sufficient to make" CERCLA's NRD provisions applicable.[27] The court offered the example of "a state law requiring owners of tideland property to permit public access" as a situation that might bring privately owned property within the ambit of CERCLA's NRD provisions.[28] Although the D.C. Circuit directed DOI to clarify the extent to which its NRD regulations extended to lands not owned by the government, DOI opted not to offer a regulatory gloss on this issue, though DOI acknowledged that the scope of NRD claims can cover "more than just resources owned by the government."[29] CERCLA NRD trustees must prepare statements to

---

23. *Mayor of Rockaway*, 811 F. Supp. at 1049; *Town of Bedford*, 755 F. Supp. at 473. *But see* Michael J. Wittke, *Municipal Recovery of Natural Resource Damages under CERCLA*, 23 B.C. Envtl. Aff. L. Rev. 921, 930–31 (1996) (suggesting that SARA's legislative history demonstrated an intent to uphold decisions allowing municipalities to serve as trustees independent of state authorization).

24. *See* Fireman's Fund Ins. Co. v. City of Lodi, 302 F.3d 928, 943–45 (9th Cir. 2002) ("Notwithstanding any authority under CERCLA or HSAA that Lodi may acquire by delegation, Lodi retains its independent authority to protect its proprietary interest in natural resources held in trust by the City.").

25. 33 U.S.C. § 2706(a)(4).

26. *Id.* § 2706(b)(5).

27. Ohio v. U.S. Dep't of the Interior, 880 F.2d 432, 460–61 (D.C. Cir. 1989).

28. *Id.* at 461.

29. Natural Resource Damage Assessments, 59 Fed. Reg. 14,262, 14,265 (Mar. 25, 1994) (to be codified at 43 C.F.R. pt. 11).

explain the basis for their assertions of trusteeship on a case-by-case basis, and DOI indicated that the basis must be grounded in a relationship of ownership, management, trust, or control created by other federal, state, local, or tribal laws.[30] One district court rejected the argument that "mere statutory authority" was sufficient to establish trusteeship over a natural resource, stating that "[p]ower that is not exercised is not management or control even though in a legal sense the resource may belong in part or appertain to that party."[31] Another district court distinguished between private ownership of land, a canal upon the relevant land, and groundwater below the relevant land, holding that although the land was privately held and the trustees' NRD claims with regard to the land were therefore foreclosed, without clear evidence of exclusively private ownership of the canal water and groundwater, the trustees' NRD claims with regard to those resources could proceed.[32]

D. Federal NRD Statutes

The principal statutory authorities for recovery of NRD are CERCLA and OPA, which are the primary focus of this chapter and this book. In the next section, we provide an overview of these two statutes and NRD regulations promulgated under them. Aside from CERCLA and OPA, the following federal authorities may also provide avenues for recovery of NRD in certain circumstances.[33]

1. Clean Water Act

The CWA contains a right of action for NRD for spills of oil and hazardous substances that decreased in use after OPA's enactment and due to the more frequent use of CERCLA.

---

30. *Id.* at 14,268.

31. Coeur d'Alene Tribe v. ASARCO Inc., 280 F. Supp. 2d 1094, 1115–16 (D. Idaho 2003).

32. Comm'r of the Dep't of Planning & Nat. Res. v. Century Alumina Co., No. 05-62, 2011 WL 882547, at *6 (D.V.I. Mar. 11, 2011); Comm'r of the Dep't of Planning & Nat. Res. v. Century Aluminum Co., No. 05-62, 2012 WL 1901297, at *11 (D.V.I. May 24, 2012).

33. This section describes authorities under which NRD may be recovered. Other statutes, regulations, and executive orders can influence how NRD matters proceed. For example, Executive Order 12898 (Federal Actions to Address Environmental Justice in Minority Populations and Low-Income Populations) requires federal natural resource trustees, like other federal agencies, to determine whether a restoration action will have disproportionate, adverse health or environmental impacts on members of a tribal or other minority or low-income population. Trustees are to ensure that no low-income or ethnic minority communities would be adversely affected by the proposed restoration activities.

Section 311 of the CWA allows the federal government to remove oil or hazardous substances discharged into or upon the navigable waters, adjoining shorelines, or waters of the contiguous zone, and to assess the costs of removal against the owner, operator, or person in charge of the vessel or facility responsible for the unlawful spill or release.[34] These costs include the cost of "restoration or replacement" of injured resources.[35] Money recovered under the NRD provisions of the CWA must be used by trustees "to restore, rehabilitate, or acquire the equivalent of such natural resources."[36] The CWA establishes restoration cost as the standard measure of damages.

NRD assessments (NRDA) under the CWA are conducted in accordance with both CERCLA regulations and OPA regulations: the CERCLA regulations are followed in the event of a hazardous substance discharge, and the OPA regulations are followed in the event of an oil spill.

2. National Marine Sanctuaries Act

This statute, formerly Title III of the Marine Protection, Research and Sanctuaries Act, creates liability for injury to any sanctuary resource, regardless of the substance that caused the injury.[37] The statute defines "sanctuary resource" to include "any living or nonliving resource of a national marine sanctuary that contributes to the conservation, recreational, ecological, historical, educational, cultural, archaeological, scientific, or aesthetic value of the sanctuary."[38] The measure of damages is the cost of restoration, replacement, or acquisition of the resource.[39] Funds left over after reimbursement of response costs must be used for restoration.[40]

3. Park System Resource Protection Act

This law allows the federal government to commence a civil action for response costs and damages against a person responsible for injury to park system resources, subject to certain defenses.[41] Recovered damages may be used only to reimburse response costs and damage assessments, as well as to restore,

---

34. *See* 33 U.S.C. § 1321(f)(1)–(3).

35. *Id.* § 1321(f)(4).

36. *Id.* § 1321(f)(5).

37. *See* 16 U.S.C. § 1443.

38. *Id.* § 1432(8).

39. *See id.* § 1432(6)(A).

40. *See id.* § 1443(d)(1)(B).

41. *See* 54 U.S.C. §§ 100721–100725; Pub. L. No. 101-337, 104 Stat. 379 (1990) (as recodified by Pub. L. No. 113-287, § 3, 128 Stat. 3094, 3106–08 (2014)).

replace, or acquire the equivalent of the injured or lost resources.[42] Excess funds are deposited in the general treasury.[43]

E. CERCLA

1. Overview of the Statute

CERCLA makes parties responsible for the release of a hazardous substance liable for "damages for injury to, destruction of, or loss of natural resources, including the reasonable costs of assessing such injury, destruction, or loss resulting from such a release."[44] CERCLA defines "natural resources" broadly as "land, fish, wildlife, biota, air, water, ground water, drinking water supplies, and other such resources belonging to, managed by, held in trust by, appertaining to, or otherwise controlled by the United States . . . , any State or local government, any foreign government, [or] any Indian tribe."[45]

To prevail on a CERCLA NRD claim, a trustee must prove that

(1) the defendants are responsible parties under CERCLA (i.e., a current owner or operator of a vessel or facility, a former owner or operator at the time of a release, a transporter, or an arranger);

(2) there has been a release or threat of release of a hazardous substance; and

(3) the release has caused the injury to, destruction of, or loss of natural resources.[46]

The categories of damages recoverable in a CERCLA NRD claim include damages determined in accordance with the NRD regulations and calculated "based on injuries occurring from the onset of the release through the recovery period, less any mitigation of those injuries by response actions taken or anticipated, plus any increase in injuries that are reasonably unavoidable as a result of response actions taken or anticipated."[47] Damages include the costs necessary to restore the natural resources to their baseline condition and may also include "interim losses," the compensable value of the services to the public

---

42. *See* 54 U.S.C. § 100724(a).

43. *Id.* § 100724(b).

44. 42 U.S.C. § 9607(a)(4)(C).

45. *Id.* § 9601(16). In addition, such resources are a CERCLA "natural resource" if "subject to a trust restriction on alienation" and controlled by "any member of an Indian tribe." *Id.*

46. *Id.* § 9607(a)(4)(c).

47. 43 C.F.R. § 11.15(a)(1).

lost during the period beginning at the time of the release until restoration of the baseline conditions is achieved.[48] Recoverable costs also include costs of emergency restoration efforts, reasonable and necessary costs of assessment, and interest.[49]

CERCLA directs that the amounts recovered by federal and state trustees are "available for use only to restore, replace, or acquire the equivalent of such natural resources."[50] CERCLA goes on to provide that the measure of damages in an NRD action "shall not be limited by the sums which can be used to restore or replace such resources."[51] In the litigation over the NRDA regulations, the D.C. Circuit said that these provisions contain the "strongest linguistic evidence" of Congress's intent to establish "a distinct preference for restoration costs as the measure of damages."[52] The D.C. Circuit also conceded that "at first glance" these two provisions might seem inconsistent, but the court found that read together the provisions indicated that "damages recovered in excess of restoration or replacement costs must be spent on acquiring the equivalent of lost resources."[53] The court also said the "shall not be limited by" language "carries in it an implicit assumption that restoration cost will serve as the basic measure of damages in many if not most CERCLA cases" and that restoration cost was not a damages "ceiling."[54]

As the following overview of the CERCLA's NRD regulatory history reveals, however, it took time to implement this restoration purpose.

2. The Protracted Regulatory History of CERCLA's NRDA Rules

a. The Statutory Mandate

As enacted in 1980, CERCLA required the president, acting through designated officials, to promulgate regulations for assessing damages to natural resources by December 11, 1982.[55]

Congress provided that the NRDA regulations should take into account "direct and indirect injury, destruction, or loss and shall take into consideration factors including, but not limited to, replacement value, use value, and

---

48. *Id.* § 11.80(b).
49. *Id.* § 11.15(a)(2)–(4).
50. 42 U.S.C. § 9607(f)(1).
51. *Id.*
52. Ohio v. U.S. Dep't of the Interior, 880 F.2d 432, 444 (D.C. Cir. 1989).
53. *Id.* at 444 n.8.
54. *Id.* at 445–46.
55. *See* 42 U.S.C. § 9651(c).

ability of the ecosystem or resource to recover."[56] Further, Congress mandated the creation of two types of procedures for conducting NRDAs. First, the regulations were to specify "standard procedures for simplified assessments requiring minimal field observation" (eventually known as the "Type A" rules). Second, the regulations were to provide "alternative protocols for conducting assessments in individual cases" (the "Type B" rules). Both Type A and Type B rules were to "identify the best available procedures to determine such damages." This final requirement was an ongoing mandate facilitated (at least in theory) by the statute's provision for a biennial review.[57] To encourage the use of the regulatory procedures, Congress further provided that any trustee assessment conducted pursuant to these procedures would enjoy a rebuttable presumption of legitimacy.[58]

As it turned out, implementing Congress's mandate was a far trickier proposition than Congress may have imagined. Instead of the two years envisaged by Congress in 1980, the development of the NRD regulations extended over two decades and three administrations and multiple trips to the D.C. Circuit.

b. Round 1: The Reagan-Era NRDA Regulations

Following CERCLA's enactment, President Reagan delegated responsibility for promulgating the NRDA rules to DOI via executive order.[59] As Chief Judge Wald of the U.S. Court of Appeals for the District of Columbia later stated, however, "Interior's response to its assigned task of promulgating regulations for assessing natural resource damages was, to put it charitably, relaxed."[60]

DOI took its first formal but still preliminary step towards developing the NRDA rules—an advance notice of proposed rulemaking—in January 1983, one month after CERCLA's statutory deadline for having final rules in place.[61] After issuing two additional notices seeking comments and facing three lawsuits to compel it to issue regulations, DOI issued a proposed rule in 1985 that

---

56. *Id.* § 9651(c)(2).

57. *Id.*

58. *See id.* § 9607(f)(2)(C). The provision for a rebuttable presumption was added as part of SARA. The trustee is not obligated to utilize the NRDA procedures in order to maintain an NRD case. However, any assessment that is not done pursuant to these regulations will not enjoy the statutory rebuttable presumption.

59. Exec. Order No. 12,316, 46 Fed. Reg. 42,237 (Aug. 14, 1981); *see also* Exec. Order No. 12,580, 52 Fed. Reg. 2923 (Jan. 23, 1987).

60. Ohio v. U.S. Dep't of the Interior, 880 F.2d 432, 440 (D.C. Cir. 1989).

61. Natural Resources Damage Assessment, 48 Fed. Reg. 1084 (proposed Jan. 10, 1983) (to be codified at 40 C.F.R. Ch. II).

set forth regulations concerning the assessment process generally and the Type B procedures (to be utilized in most NRDAs).[62]

DOI published the final rule in 1986[63] and issued final Type A regulations (simplified assessment procedures to be utilized in a limited number of specific circumstances) in 1987.[64] In 1988, DOI revised the regulations promulgated in 1986 to conform them to SARA, which was enacted in 1986.[65]

Both the Type A and Type B regulations were challenged by multiple factions in the D.C. Circuit. In July 1989, the court issued two opinions, upholding many aspects of the regulations, but remanding a key element concerning the relative weight the rules were required to give to restoration costs versus diminution in use values in the calculation of damages.[66] Specifically, the D.C. Circuit rejected DOI's adoption of the "lesser of" rule, that is, the regulation providing that damages for destruction to natural resources shall be the "lesser of: restoration or replacement costs; or diminution of use values."[67] The court found that the equal presumptive legitimacy the regulation accorded to use value and restoration cost (and the resultant likelihood that use value would end up being the measure of damages, as it would more often be less than restoration cost) contravened Congress's stated preference for restoration costs to be the minimum measure of damages in natural resource cases. The D.C. Circuit said the practical import of the "lesser of" rule was enormous because there would be a "minuscule" number of cases where restoration would be cheaper than paying for lost use[68] and that its application would "in a majority of cases risk underfunded, half-finished restoration projects."[69]

The D.C. Circuit struck down two other aspects of DOI's Type B rules. First, the court rejected DOI's hierarchy of methods for determining "use values," which limited recovery to the market price of the resource unless the

---

62. *See* Natural Resource Damage Assessments, 50 Fed. Reg. 52,126 (proposed Dec. 20, 1985) (to be codified at 43 C.F.R. pt. 11); Natural Resource Damage Assessment, 50 Fed. Reg. 1550 (notice requesting additional comment on the development of regulations Jan. 11, 1985); Natural Resources Damage Assessment, 48 Fed. Reg. at 1084; *see also* Colorado v. U.S. Dep't of the Interior, 880 F.2d 481, 484 (D.C. Cir. 1989) (recounting history).

63. Natural Resource Damage Assessments, 51 Fed. Reg. 27,674 (Aug. 1, 1986) (to be codified at 43 C.F.R. pt. 11).

64. Natural Resource Damage Assessments, 52 Fed. Reg. 9042 (Mar. 20, 1987) (to be codified at 43 C.F.R. pt. 11).

65. Natural Resource Damage Assessments, 53 Fed. Reg. 5166 (Feb. 22, 1988) (to be codified at 43 C.F.R. pt. 11); *see* Pub. L. No. 99-499, 100 Stat. 1613 (1986).

66. Ohio v. U.S. Dep't of the Interior, 880 F.2d 432, 440 (D.C. Cir. 1989).

67. *Id.* at 441.

68. *Id.* at 446.

69. *Id.* at 454.

market for that resource was not competitive. The court found this preference for market value as a methodology to be an unreasonable interpretation of the statute, because natural resources invariably have values that are not fully captured by the market system, and because CERCLA evinced an intent to capture all aspects of loss, not just those reflected in the market value.[70] Second, the court struck down DOI's interpretation that option and existence values be estimated in lieu of use values only when use values cannot be determined.[71] The court found, instead, that "[o]ption and existence values may represent 'passive' use, but they nonetheless reflect utility derived by humans from a resource, and thus, *prima facie*, ought to be included in a damage assessment."[72]

In its opinion addressing the Type A regulations, the D.C. Circuit held that DOI could not base the Type A regulations exclusively on lost use values to measure NRD.[73] The court acknowledged that limited restoration cost data might hinder creation of standardized models for calculating NRD but said the limitations could not justify ignoring the congressional mandate to focus on restoration.

To be sure, the D.C. Circuit's decisions were not a total loss for the government, and indeed, numerous important principles of NRD law were established or clarified. For example, as mentioned previously, the court confirmed that damages were not recoverable for "purely private" resources.[74] In addition, the court rejected the notion that DOI's regulations gave preferential treatment to potentially responsible parties (PRPs) by authorizing PRPs to undertake assessment tasks and by providing for notice to PRPs at certain stages of the assessment process when members of the public do not have the right to receive notice.[75] The court affirmed DOI's use of "acceptance criteria"—which provide the framework for determining whether a release of a hazardous substance actually caused injury to a resource—over claims that the acceptance

---

70. *Id.* at 464. The court thus remanded for DOI to consider a rule that "would permit trustees to derive use values for natural resources by summing up all reliably calculated use values, however measured, so long as the trustee does not double count." *Id.*

71. "Existence values" are the intrinsic, noneconomic values derived from the mere existence of the natural resource. "Option values" are the dollar amounts individuals are willing to pay although they are not currently using the resource but wish to reserve the option to use that resource in a certain state of being in the future. *Id.* at 476 n.72.

72. *Id.* at 464 (citing Frank B. Cross, *Natural Resource Damage Valuation*, 42 Vand. L. Rev. 269, 285–89 (1989)).

73. Colorado v. U.S. Dep't of the Interior, 880 F.2d 481, 491 (D.C. Cir. 1989).

74. *See Ohio*, 880 F.2d at 460–61.

75. *See id.* at 465–68; *see also* Brian D. Israel, *Natural Resource Damage Claims: Strategies for Responding to Increased Federal and State Enforcement*, 38 A.B.A. Trends 4 (2006).

criteria imposed an unreasonably stringent causation standard.[76] The court also rejected the main challenge asserted by industry representatives, namely that the contingent valuation method of calculating nonuse values was arbitrary and capricious.[77] In addition, the court affirmed DOI's limited use of the Type A rules.[78] The court said the limited scope of the rules was "a sustainable response to an ambiguous statutory mandate in an area of scientific uncertainty," but that it expected DOI "to continue to promulgate, as expeditiously as possible, further type A regulations to cover as many types of releases in as many different kinds of environments as feasible."[79]

Thus, nine years after the enactment of the statute and seven years after DOI was initially to have promulgated the rules, the process was far from complete. While the 1980s regulations caused the most profound concern from environmental groups and some states, the regulations that emerged from the next round would provoke an outcry principally from industry.

c. Round 2: The Clinton-Era NRDA Regulations

In April 1991, during the George H.W. Bush administration, DOI issued a proposed Type B rule in response to the D.C. Circuit's opinion and sent a final—and different—rule to the Office of the Federal Register on the last full day of the administration. On the first full day of the Clinton administration, DOI withdrew the document. In July 1993, DOI reissued the April 1991 proposed rule,[80] with suggested revisions. DOI finalized the revised regulations in March 1994.[81] Revisions to the Type A regulations were finalized in 1996.[82]

---

76. *See Ohio*, 880 F.2d at 472.

77. *Id.* at 479.

78. *See* Colorado v. U.S. Dep't of the Interior, 880 F.2d 481, 486–87, 489 (D.C. Cir. 1989) ("[I]n light of DOI's subsequent determinations of data and resource inadequacies, we find that DOI acted reasonably in limiting the scope of the final rules as it did. . . . [D]espite its footdragging, DOI appears to have made a technically reasonable and responsible determination that the data to produce a suitable computer model for assessing natural resource damages in noncoastal and nonmarine environments were inadequate or insufficiently reliable.").

79. *Colorado*, 880 F.2d at 483, 486.

80. Natural Resource Damage Assessments, 58 Fed. Reg. 39,328 (proposed July 22, 1993) (to be codified at 43 C.F.R. pt. 11).

81. Natural Resource Damage Assessments, 59 Fed. Reg. 14,262 (Mar. 25, 1994) (to be codified at 43 C.F.R. pt. 11).

82. Natural Resource Damage Assessments—Type A Procedures, 61 Fed. Reg. 20,560 (May 7, 1996) (to be codified at 43 C.F.R. pt. 11). DOI promulgated technical corrections in 1997. Natural Resource Damage Assessments—Type A Procedures, 62 Fed. Reg. 60,457 (correcting amendments Nov. 10, 1997) (to be codified at 43 C.F.R. pt. 11).

The D.C. Circuit upheld the bulk of the Type B rules (and rejected claims regarding the unusual procedural history) in 1996[83] and upheld the Type A rules in 1998 (though the court was implicitly critical of DOI's delay in responding to its 1989 directive to "act as expeditiously as possible" to promulgate new Type A regulations).[84] However, the D.C. Circuit invalidated language in the Type B rules that appeared to measure damages both "in terms of 'the cost of restoration, rehabilitation, replacement, and/or acquisition of the equivalent of the injured natural resources *and* the services those resources provide.'"[85] The court said this regulatory language appeared to require trustees "to restore *both* the services *and* the resource itself," which it said was not consistent with language in the regulatory preamble defending the services approach. The court said this inconsistency made the "resources and services" provisions of the regulation arbitrary and capricious.[86]

d. Round 3: Responding to D.C. Circuit and Increasing Restoration Focus

The D.C. Circuit's decisions on the Type B rules as well as the promulgation of NRDA rules under OPA in 1996 spurred the next regulatory development in DOI's assessment rules. As with the earlier rounds of rulemaking, these regulatory developments took place over a number of years.

The OPA rules, discussed later in this chapter, sought to focus NRD claims on the costs of restoration not only for determining the costs to restore injured resources to the baseline but also for compensating for interim losses, that is, public losses pending restoration. A concern emerged that the DOI regulations for assessment of interim losses lacked a restoration-based approach similar to the OPA rules approach. Instead, the DOI rules calculated interim losses based on "the *economic value* the public loses until the baseline condition is re-established."[87]

DOI chartered a federal advisory committee in 2005 to consider how to optimize NRDA and restoration activities.[88] The issue of compensation for interim losses was one concern before the committee. Other issues concerned

---

83. Kennecott Utah Copper Corp. v. U.S. Dep't of the Interior, 88 F.3d 1191 (D.C. Cir. 1996).

84. Nat'l Ass'n of Mfrs. v. U.S. Dep't of the Interior, 134 F.3d 1095 (D.C. Cir. 1998).

85. *Kennecott*, 88 F.3d at 1220 (quoting 43 C.F.R. § 11.80(b)).

86. *Id.*

87. U.S. Dep't of the Interior, Natural Resource Damage Assessment and Restoration Federal Advisory Committee Final Report to the Secretary 14 (2007).

88. *Id.* at 5.

natural resource injury determination and quantification, restoration action selection, and timely and effective restoration after NRD claims are resolved.

In 2007, the committee issued a report recommending that DOI revise its regulations to explicitly allow calculation of interim losses based on the cost of restoration projects that provide services equivalent to the lost services, rather than requiring that damages be measured based on the monetary value of lost services.[89] The committee indicated that such an approach would be more consistent with the restoration-based goals of NRD.[90]

DOI adopted narrowly targeted amendments in 2008 in response to the federal advisory committee's recommendation regarding interim losses, leaving other recommendations of the federal advisory committee to be addressed at a later time.[91] The 2008 amendments also eliminated a limitation in the Type B regulations on the estimation of option and existence values, as required by the D.C. Circuit's 1989 decision. In addition, in response to the D.C. Circuit's 1996 decision, DOI indicated that it had never intended to abandon a services-based approach to measuring damages. DOI clarified that the measure of damages was either the cost of restoring or rehabilitating the injured resources to a condition where they provide a level of services provided in the baseline condition or replacing or acquiring equivalent natural resources capable of providing baseline services.[92]

e. Round 4: Regulatory Reform Efforts in the Trump Administration

On August 27, 2018, DOI promulgated an Advance Notice of Proposed Rulemaking (ANPRM), requesting comments related to possible revision of the NRDA regulations promulgated pursuant to CERCLA.[93] In the ANPRM, DOI specifically requested comments on the following categories of potential reforms:

- Simplification and "plain language"—According to DOI, the CERCLA NRD regulations "are arguably complicated, overly prescriptive, repetitive,

---

89. *Id.* at 14.

90. *Id.* at 5; *see also* Natural Resource Damages for Hazardous Substances, 73 Fed. Reg. 57,259, 57,260 (Oct. 2, 2008) (to be codified at 43 C.F.R. pt. 11). The shift to a focus on restoration in the CERCLA NRD regulations is discussed in Chapter IV.D, *infra.*

91. 73 Fed. Reg. at 57,259; *see also* Natural Resource Damages for Hazardous Substances, 73 Fed. Reg. 11,081 (proposed Feb. 29, 2008) (to be codified at 43 C.F.R. pt. 11).

92. 73 Fed. Reg. at 57,261.

93. Natural Resource Damages for Hazardous Substances, 83 Fed. Reg. 43,611 (proposed Aug. 27, 2018) (to be codified at 43 C.F.R. pt. 11).

and dense. . . . A number of stakeholders have suggested that DOI should consider a comprehensive 'plain English' revision to the CERCLA . . . Regulations that closely aligns with the structure of the existing OPA . . . Regulations."[94]

- Type A regulations—As DOI noted, Type A regulations were designed "to result in efficient, cost effective, standardized assessments." However, "it has been challenging . . . to develop workable Type A Regulations that are streamlined and utilize minimal actual field observations but are still relevant and reliable enough to be entitled to a rebuttable presumption of correctness. Accordingly, DOI is seeking comments or suggestions regarding revision to and utilization of the . . . Type A Regulations."[95]

- Early emphasis on restoration over damages—Prior reports have "recommended that DOI could encourage a restoration focus and negotiated agreements by revising the regulations to encourage early scoping of restoration opportunities at [NRD] sites." Accordingly, DOI is requesting "comments or suggestions on where specifically in the assessment process restoration scoping may be cost effective and appropriate and how that could best be addressed in the regulations."[96]

- Procedures to further encourage negotiated settlements and early restoration—DOI noted that "a number of [NRD] matters have utilized partial negotiated settlements early in the assessment process to cost effectively resolve discrete [NRD] claims and re-inforce an overall restoration focus for ultimate comprehensive resolution. However, the current regulations offer little guidance on how to align early restoration settlements with existing statutory and regulatory requirements for assessment and restoration planning."[97]

- Advance restoration and restoration banking—DOI noted that "[r]estoration 'banking' and advance restoration—where restoration is undertaken in anticipation of marketing portions of such restoration to responsible parties to address natural resource injury caused by releases of hazardous substances—has been considered at a number of sites since the last revision of the CERCLA [NRD] regulations. Some states (such as Louisiana) have enacted specific statutory provisions and promulgated regulations on

---

94. *Id.* at 43,612.
95. *Id.*
96. *Id.*
97. *Id.*

[NRD] banking. The existing CERCLA . . . regulations do not provide any guidance on the use of advance restoration and restoration banking techniques."[98]

- National Environmental Policy Act (NEPA) compliance—The DOI has been encouraged "to adopt Department-wide categorical exclusions from NEPA as appropriate and to ensure that compliance with NEPA requirements occurs concurrently with . . . restoration planning." DOI is interested in comments or suggestions on this topic.[99]

In response to the ANPRM, 54 comments were submitted, including by various state and tribal trustees, several nongovernmental organizations (NGOs), NRD practitioners, and industry stakeholders. Industry comments provided many novel reform ideas, generally aimed at expediting the process and reducing transaction costs. The authors of this book submitted a single set of comments on behalf of the vast majority of American industry, including the U.S. Chamber of Commerce, the American Chemistry Council, the American Petroleum Institute, the National Association of Manufacturers, the Association of American Railroads, and the Western States Petroleum Association. Many state, tribal, and NGO commenters expressed that no revisions need be made to the existing CERCLA NRDA regulations, but several recommended particular reforms and/or endorsed reforms proposed by industry. While revision to the regulations is far from certain at this stage, based on the authors' review of all comments, we anticipate the most likely reforms to succeed are the following:

- Elimination of redundant NEPA review in restoration planning;
- Overhaul of the existing Type A assessment regulations to apply to a broader set of NRD cases; and
- Formalization of process for pursuing early restoration (i.e., before all injuries are assessed).

At the time of this writing in January 2019, DOI's efforts have been temporarily stalled by a government shutdown, and DOI has not yet indicated its intended next steps in the regulatory reform process.

---

98. *Id.* at 43,612–13.
99. *Id.* at 43,613.

F. Oil Pollution Act

1. Overview of the Statute

Since 1990, OPA has provided an avenue for trustees to recover NRD. OPA—which was enacted in response to the *Exxon Valdez* tanker spill in 1989—makes parties who are responsible for oil spills liable for the damage to natural resources resulting from those spills.[100] A trustee must prove that a defendant is a responsible party under OPA for a vessel or facility from which there was a discharge, or substantial threat of a discharge, of oil into navigable waters or adjoining shorelines or the exclusive economic zone, and that removal costs and damages resulted.[101] NRD claims are barred where a discharge was authorized by a federal, state, or local permit, and for discharges from public vessels or onshore facilities subject to the Trans-Alaska Pipeline Authorization Act.[102]

The measure of NRD under OPA includes the cost of restoring, rehabilitating, replacing, or acquiring the equivalent of the damaged resources; the diminution in value of those natural resources pending restoration; and the reasonable cost of assessing those damages.[103] Responsible parties are also liable for interest calculated from 30 days after presentation of a claim until the date a claim is paid.[104]

2. OPA Regulatory History

OPA directed the president, acting through the National Oceanic and Atmospheric Administration (NOAA), to promulgate regulations for assessment of NRD.[105] Like CERCLA, OPA states that assessments made in accordance with the regulations enjoy a rebuttable presumption on behalf of the trustee in an administrative or judicial proceeding.[106] NOAA promulgated final NRDA rules in 1996 after publishing 11 notices in the *Federal Register* between 1990 and 1995 requesting information and comments on approaches to assessments.[107]

---

100. *See* 33 U.S.C. § 2702(a), (b)(2)(A); Oil Pollution Act of 1990, Pub. L. No. 101-380, 104 Stat. 484.

101. 33 U.S.C. § 2702(a).

102. *Id.* § 2702(c).

103. *Id.* § 2702(d).

104. *Id.* § 2713.

105. *Id.* § 2706(e)(1).

106. *Id.* § 2706(e)(2).

107. Natural Resource Damage Assessments, 61 Fed. Reg. 440 (Jan. 5, 1996) (to be codified at 15 C.F.R. pt. 990).

The explicit focus of the NOAA regulations and the methodology they created was restoration. In the preamble to the final rule, NOAA wrote:

> The goal of the Oil Pollution Act of 1990 (OPA) is to make the environment and public whole for injuries to natural resources and natural resource services resulting from an incident involving a discharge or substantial threat of a discharge of oil (incident). This goal is achieved through returning injured natural resources and services to baseline and compensating for interim losses of such natural resources and services through the restoration, rehabilitation, replacement or acquisition of equivalent natural resources and/or services. The purpose of this rule is to provide a framework for conducting sound natural resource damage assessments that achieve restoration under OPA.
>
> Under the rule, restoration plans developed with input from the public and responsible parties form the basis of a claim for natural resource damages.

The OPA regulations therefore involved assessment of the injury followed by development of a plan for restoring the injured resources.[108]

In 1997, the D.C. Circuit upheld all but two provisions of the NOAA regulations.[109] The court's notable holdings related to contingent valuation, residual removal authority, and monitoring costs.

With regard to contingent valuation, the court followed its 1989 decision on the Type B CERCLA regulations and held that NOAA had not acted arbitrarily or capriciously by authorizing trustees to use contingent valuation to measure passive-use losses. The court also rejected petitioners' procedural arguments and held that NOAA did not ignore comments an expert panel had made on contingent valuation, but "simply gave trustees discretion to use contingent valuation, so long as the technique produces . . . valid and reliable results for the particular incident."[110]

With regard to residual removal authority, industry petitioners challenged a provision that authorized trustees to "[r]emove conditions that would prevent or limit the effectiveness of any restoration action (e.g., residual sources of contamination)."[111] Petitioners argued that NOAA exceeded its statutory authority because OPA delegated sole responsibility for oil removal to the president, acting through EPA or the U.S. Coast Guard (USCG). The court ultimately did not resolve the dispute but vacated the section and remanded for further agency action because it found that NOAA had failed to exercise

---

108. *Id.*
109. Gen. Elec. Co. v. U.S. Dep't of Commerce, 128 F.3d 767 (D.C. Cir. 1997).
110. *Id.* at 773.
111. *Id.* at 774 (quoting 15 C.F.R. § 990.53(b)(3)(i) (1996)).

reasoned decision making. Specifically, the court found that NOAA had failed to explain the difference between the language in its proposed rule versus the final rule, the relationship between the trustees' removal authority and the primary removal authority of EPA and USCG, and whether the three agencies concurred as to how they would coordinate removal authorities.

With regard to monitoring costs, the court held that costs associated with monitoring restoration projects could be included in the definition of reasonable assessment costs, for which trustees could recover. The court vacated, however, a provision allowing recovery of attorneys' fees, a point that NOAA conceded without challenge. Still, because the parties disagreed about the extent to which trustees could recover for certain other legal work, the court left it to NOAA to draw a "precise line between recoverable and nonrecoverable" legal costs.[112] In 2002, NOAA revised its rule to respond to the court's concerns. With regard to legal costs, the agency set forth various criteria for determining whether trustees' legal costs were "reasonable assessment costs." The rule provided examples of attorney action performed for the purpose of assessment or development of a restoration plan.[113]

---

112. *Id.* at 776.

113. *See* Natural Resource Damage Assessments, 67 Fed. Reg. 61,483, 61,490–91 (Oct. 1, 2002) (to be codified at 15 C.F.R. pt. 990).

Chapter 3
NRD Defenses: Legal, Evidentiary, and Procedural[1]

This chapter provides an overview of the key NRD defenses, including legal (e.g., statute of limitations, ripeness, and the bar against double recovery), evidentiary (e.g., causation standard and baseline), and procedural (e.g., right to a jury). The number of litigated NRD cases is relatively small, and many of the issues discussed in this chapter are unsettled.[2] Where parties are seeking to resolve NRD liability short of litigation, as they do in most cases, the lack of clarity on many key defenses is an important consideration for all sides, since the parties face substantial risk that they could lose one or more arguments relating to a defense, potentially affecting their entire case. Practitioners should familiarize themselves with the key concepts in this chapter as early as possible in the life cycle of an NRD matter, since thinking about how to defend against an NRD claim (or thinking about how to overcome defenses) can help to guide other steps in the process, starting with the assessment.

A. Statute of Limitations

Given that many NRD matters involve inactive sites that are well-known and quite old, defendants often look to the statute of limitations as an available defense. Although the limitations period does provide an important statutory defense to many claims, there are numerous obstacles to the successful assertion of this affirmative defense.

---

1. Portions of this chapter are adapted from *Natural Resource Damages*, of the ENVIRONMENTAL LAW PRACTICE GUIDE: STATE AND FEDERAL LAW, with permission. Copyright 2017 Matthew Bender & Company, Inc., a LexisNexis company. All rights reserved.

2. Chapter 7, NRD Litigation: Strategy, Procedures, and Preparation, includes a close look at ten NRD cases that illustrate the unsettled nature of these defenses.

1. The NRD Statute of Limitations under CERCLA

The Comprehensive Environmental Response, Compensation, and Liability Act (CERCLA) provides multiple limitations periods depending on the status of the site at issue, including whether it is listed on the National Priorities List (NPL). CERCLA section 113(g)(1) contains the limitations period for most NRD claims.

a. General (Non-NPL) Limitations Period

Generally, a damages claim must be commenced within three years after the later of the following: "(A) [t]he date of the discovery of the loss and its connection with the release in question [or] (B) [t]he date on which regulations are promulgated under [301(c) of CERCLA]."[3]

In *California v. Montrose Chemical Corp.*, the Ninth Circuit established that the "date on which the regulations are . . . promulgated" was March 20, 1987, the date on which DOI promulgated the Type A regulations.[4] Since most cases arising now are brought more than three years after that date, whether the limitations period has run would depend on the date of discovery, as required by the first prong of the provision.[5]

There is little case law interpreting section (A) of this provision. However, when and how much a trustee must know before being deemed to have "discovered the loss" appears to be a fact-intensive inquiry. In *Montrose*, the district court found that the "discovery" prong had been triggered where trustee agencies had conducted several site investigations and generated reports describing the extent of the contamination, some of the resource injuries, and the pollution by defendants.[6] The court also found that defendant responsible parties bear the burden of demonstrating that trustees have knowledge of the loss and connection of that loss to the release, although that knowledge may be established by demonstrating knowledge on the part of low-level employees.[7]

---

3. 42 U.S.C. § 9613(g)(1). The statute explicitly excepts contribution and subrogation claims from this provision.

4. 104 F.3d 1507, 1514 (9th Cir. 1997). This case is discussed in detail in Chapter 7, Section D.4.

5. In Kennecott Utah Copper Corp. v. U.S. Dep't of the Interior, the court held that DOI's subsequent revisions of the regulations did not postpone the limitations period. 88 F.3d 1191 (D.C. Cir. 1996).

6. United States v. Montrose Chem. Corp. of Cal., 883 F. Supp. 1396 (C.D. Cal. 1995), *rev'd on other grounds*, California v. Montrose Chem. Corp. of Cal., 104 F.3d 1507 (9th Cir. 1997); *see also* Kelley v. United States, 23 ERC 1503, 1985 WL 61, at *1 (W.D. Mich. Sept. 12, 1985) (holding that date of discovery was not until the state's hydrogeologic investigation was completed).

7. *Montrose*, 883 F. Supp. 1396; *see also* Comm'r of the Dep't of Planning & Nat. Res. v. Century Alumina Co., No. 2005/0062, 2008 WL 4809897 (D.V.I. Oct. 31, 2008) (where complaint did

In *Commissioner of the Department of Planning & Natural Resources v. Century Alumina Co.*, the district court rejected the trustee's argument that the test for discovery should be one of actual knowledge.[8] The court concluded that the statute of limitations embodied a constructive knowledge standard and that the trustee's claims accrued when he discovered or should have discovered any loss to natural resources and the loss's connection to a particular release.[9] The court then engaged in a fact-intensive inquiry to determine whether the trustee had constructive knowledge of injuries to particular resources and of each injury's connection to a particular release. As in *Montrose*, the court found that the trustee's receipt of notices of the releases and reports and work plans regarding investigation at the sites gave rise to constructive knowledge.[10] The court was not persuaded by the trustee's argument that the statute of limitations had not been triggered in relation to ongoing arsenic contamination in groundwater because there were questions regarding the arsenic's source; the court said that "[t]he lack of specificity regarding the pinpoint source location" should not bar the trustee from discovering the loss and did not prevent the NRD claim from accruing.[11] In some situations, however, the court found that there were genuine issues of material fact as to when the trustee should have known of alleged losses due to the absence of discharge monitoring reports in the record and the inclusion of undated reports,[12] or as to when the trustee should have been aware of injuries to particular natural resources caused by releases of which the trustee had long been aware.[13]

In *New York v. General Electric Co.*, the defendants argued (as part of a non-limitations issue) that plaintiffs' limitations period had expired three years after the enactment of CERCLA because the activities in question "took place in the early 1960's, and . . . there is no allegation in the complaint that

---

not contain sufficient information on its face to find that claim accrued more than three years before action was filed, denying motion to dismiss on statute of limitations grounds and calling for expansion of record to include trustee's evidence concerning when losses of natural resources were actionable).

8. No. 05-0062, 2010 WL 2772695 (D.V.I. July 13, 2010) (granting summary judgment in favor of defendants with respect to some NRD claims but not others); *see also* Chapter 7, Section D.8 (overview of this case).

9. *Century Alumina Co.*, 2010 WL 2772695, at *6.

10. *See id.* at *7–9.

11. *Id.* at *9.

12. *See id.* at *11.

13. *See id.* at *14 (no trustee could be expected to discover losses to natural resources based on a report that "as a whole" conveyed that there was "minimal, if any, loss to the mangroves or other natural resources caused by this release of red mud").

the alleged loss was not discovered until some later time."[14] The court rejected the defendant's argument, stating that, given the procedural posture (motion to dismiss), the court was required to construe the complaint's allegations in favor of the plaintiff, and, as the complaint alleged that sampling had taken place in 1982 and 1983, "as a pleading matter, it appear[ed] that the statute of limitations would not expire until some time in 1985."[15] Perhaps more pertinently, the court was also persuaded by the plaintiff's argument that the action would be timely, based on the "theory of continuing nuisance. That is, even if the injury was discovered more than three years ago, because the injurious activity has not yet abated, the wrong is a continuous one and the cause of action must therefore continue to accrue."[16]

b. Limitations Period for NPL and Scheduled Remedial Sites

In addition to section 113's two-pronged limitations period for non-NPL sites, the statute also provides an alternative longer limitations period[17] for (1) "any facility listed on the National Priorities List," (2) certain federal facilities, or (3) "any vessel or facility at which a remedial action under [CERCLA] is otherwise scheduled."[18] With respect to these facilities, an NRD action must be commenced within three years of "completion of the remedial action (excluding operation and maintenance activities)."[19]

This provision was litigated in *United States v. ASARCO Inc.,*[20] in which federal trustees sought damages for injury to natural resources at the Bunker Hill facility, a site listed on the NPL. In their complaint, the trustees stated that the NPL site included the Coeur d'Alene basin, an area that happened to be outside the original listing. The defendants moved for summary judgment on a statute of limitations defense, arguing that the area outside the original NPL site fell under the shorter section 113(g)(1) limitations period and that EPA could not now expand the site's boundaries without engaging in notice-and-comment rulemaking.

---

14. 592 F. Supp. 291, 300 (N.D.N.Y. 1984) (citing defendant's brief).

15. *Id.* at 300.

16. *Id.* at 300 n.17.

17. One commentator has termed these two aspects of CERCLA related to limitations the "conventional" limitations period and "special" limitations period. *See* David G. Mandelbaum, *The Timing Provisions of CERCLA for Natural Resource Damage Claims,* 19 TOXIC L. REP. (BNA) 22 (2004); *see also* MICHAEL R. THORP, HANDBOOK OF THE LAW OF NATURAL RESOURCE DAMAGES 18–22 (2004).

18. 42 U.S.C. § 9613(g)(1)(B).

19. *Id.*

20. 214 F.3d 1104 (9th Cir. 2000); *see also* Chapter 7, Section D.1 (discussing other aspects of this case).

The Ninth Circuit noted that EPA's own policy stated that it could revise NPL site boundaries at any time and that the D.C. Circuit had previously indicated that EPA need not engage in notice-and-comment rulemaking for revisions to site boundaries, as long as it gave sufficient notice of the revision, which the *ASARCO* court suggested was provided in this case.[21] Nonetheless, the court did not answer the ultimate question, deeming itself without jurisdiction to hear a review of the Bunker Hill site designation, a review CERCLA vested in the D.C. Circuit alone.

Although the Ninth Circuit's decision left open the question whether an existing site's boundaries could be revised to the benefit of plaintiff trustees opposing a statute of limitations defense, the district court's statement in the case indicates more generally that an otherwise expired NRD claim can be revived if EPA decides to designate a not-yet-listed site to the NPL: "If the trustee fails to file a NRD action within 3 years of the date of the discovery of the loss and its connection with the release in question . . . then the trustee can still timely file a NRD action for the loss if the facility is [subsequently] listed by the EPA on the NPL."[22]

In addition to the revival of an NRD claim by EPA action, a trustee could potentially reinstate an otherwise expired action. In August 1996, President Clinton delegated limited authority to trustees to issue section 106 orders to compel remedial action.[23] This authority could allow trustees such as DOI to order remedial action for a particular site, thereby, in theory at least, tolling the statute of limitations for NRD claims. There are, however, no cases in which trustees have used their section 106 authority to defeat an otherwise expired claim.[24]

A related question pertains to NPL sites that involve multiple operable units (OUs). No court has addressed the effect of multiple remedial actions on the CERCLA NRD statute of limitations for NPL-listed sites. Multiple courts have, however, addressed this question in the context of the CERCLA

21. *ASARCO Inc.*, 214 F.3d at 1107 (citing Wash. State Dep't of Transp. v. EPA, 917 F.2d 1309, 1311 (D.C. Cir. 1990) and Eagle-Picher Indus. v. EPA, 822 F.2d 132, 144 n.59 (D.C. Cir. 1987)).

22. United States v. ASARCO Inc., 28 F. Supp. 2d 1170, 1179 (D. Idaho 1998), *vacated and remanded with instructions to stay proceedings*, 214 F.3d 1104; *see also* New York v. Next Millennium Realty, LLC, 160 F. Supp. 3d 485, 520 (E.D.N.Y. 2016) ("[I]t is clear that once a facility is listed on the NPL, only the '3 years after the completion of the remedial action' limitations period applies.").

23. Exec. Order No. 13,016, 61 Fed. Reg. 45,871 (Aug. 30, 1996).

24. *See* Michael R. Thorp, Handbook of the Law of Natural Resource Damages 23 (2004).

statute of limitations for third-party cost recovery actions.[25] The courts are not unanimous in their view of the effect of multiple remedial actions on this limitations period, and indeed, the United States has argued that OUs should be severable from one another for purposes of this limitations period.[26] However, the Second Circuit Court of Appeals has held that, under this provision, "there can only be one remedial action at a site," and a cost recovery action must be filed within six years of the initiation of physical on-site construction of the first remedial action undertaken at the site as a whole.[27]

Finally, the longer statute of limitations period also applies to sites at which a remedial action is "otherwise scheduled." The statute does not specify in what context a remedial action may be "otherwise scheduled" and thus trigger the extended limitations period. The term cannot be intended to apply only to EPA-financed remedial actions because such actions can only occur at NPL-listed sites, which, as just discussed, are already eligible for the longer limitations period pursuant to a different phrase in the same sentence of the provision. One possibility is that a remedial action may be "otherwise scheduled" at state-financed sites and sites financed by responsible parties, such as where EPA has issued a section 106 order,[28] or where a responsible party has entered into a remedial design/remedial action (RD/RA) consent decree with the United States. Further, a remedial action would arguably be "otherwise scheduled" if a trustee agency were to issue a section 106 order pursuant to President Clinton's Executive Order 13016 delegating section 106 authority, although the contrary argument could be made that section 106 orders do not give rise to "remedial actions." Other than *ASARCO*, where the district court

---

25. The CERCLA cost-recovery statute of limitations differs from the CERCLA statute of limitations for NRD at NPL-listed sites. It states in relevant part: "An initial action for recovery of the costs referred to in section 9607 of this title must be commenced . . . for a remedial action, within 6 years after initiation of physical on-site construction of the remedial action. . . . A subsequent action or actions under section 9607 of this title for further response costs at the vessel or facility may be maintained at any time during the response action, but must be commenced no later than 3 years after the date of completion of all response action." 42 U.S.C. § 9613(g)(2)(B).

26. *See* United States v. Manzo, 182 F. Supp. 2d 385, 402–03 (D.N.J. 2000) ("The United States asserts that, because of the complexity of Superfund sites, it is beneficial to divide response actions into different operable units and RODs because EPA is therefore able to move quickly to reduce health and environmental risks while continuing the process of studying other matters on the site."); Brief of United States as Amicus Curiae at 25, Colorado v. Sunoco, Inc., No. 02-1014, 2002 WL 34593241, at *25 (10th Cir. May 2002) ("A necessary corollary of EPA's authority to conduct multiple remedial actions is that a separate limitations period runs for each remedial action at a site.").

27. N.Y. State Elec. & Gas Corp. v. FirstEnergy Corp., 766 F.3d 212, 236 (2d Cir. 2014). *But see Manzo*, 182 F. Supp. 2d at 402 (finding different statutes of limitations for different OUs).

28. *See* United States v. ASARCO Inc., 28 F. Supp. 2d 1170, 1179 n.23 (D. Idaho 1998).

found that an ongoing remedial investigation/feasibility study (RI/FS) did not constitute the scheduling of a remedial action, no published decisions have interpreted this provision.

2. The NRD Statute of Limitations under OPA

Under OPA, the three-year statute of limitations begins to run on the later of: (1) "the date on which the loss and the connection of the loss with the discharge in question are reasonably discoverable with the exercise of due care"; or (2) "the date of completion of the natural resources damage assessment under section [1006(c) of OPA]."[29]

B. Ripeness under CERCLA

Pursuant to CERCLA section 113(g), a trustee's NRD claims at an NPL site, a federal facility, or "any vessel or facility at which a remedial action . . . is otherwise scheduled" are not ripe until the remedial action has been selected at the site. Section 113(g)(1) provides in relevant part:

> In no event may an action for damages under this chapter with respect to such a vessel or facility be commenced (i) prior to 60 days after the Federal or State natural resource trustee provides to the President and the potentially responsible party a notice of intent to file suit, or (ii) before selection of the remedial action if the President is diligently proceeding with a remedial investigation and feasibility study under section 9604(b) of this title or section 9620 of this title (relating to Federal facilities).[30]

This provision does not appear in OPA.

There is limited judicial authority bearing directly on the issue of the ripeness of CERCLA NRD claims. In an unpublished decision, a federal district court in Oklahoma held that CERCLA's timing limitation for NRD claims applied not only to claims for restoration or replacement damages but also to claims for interim and lost use damages.[31] The court also considered the issue of whether the trustee's NRD claim was exempt from the timing requirement

---

29. 33 U.S.C. § 2717(f)(1). No explicit date is given for when a trustee must conduct an assessment. *See* 33 U.S.C. § 2706.

30. 42 U.S.C. § 9613(g)(1)(B); *see* New York v. Next Millennium Realty, LLC, 160 F. Supp. 3d 485, 520 (E.D.N.Y. 2016) (rejecting defendants' argument that NRD claim was premature because amount of damages could not be measured until EPA completed its remedial work in approximately 30 years).

31. Quapaw Tribe of Okla. v. Blue Tee Corp., No. 03-CV-0846-CVE-PJC, 2008 WL 2704482 (N.D. Okla. July 7, 2008).

because EPA was not "diligently proceeding" with the RI/FS. In particular, the court considered the trustee's argument that the court should look at EPA's activities at the site over more than 20 years to determine whether EPA was proceeding diligently and the government's counterargument that the court should consider only EPA's activities at the time the action was filed and up to the present day. Considering the statutory language's plain meaning, the statutory scheme as a whole, and legislative history, the court concluded that "a limited review of the EPA's pre-suit activities may be permissible" but that "Congress intended for courts to focus on the EPA's present activities to determine if the EPA is diligently proceeding."[32] The court found that the evidence showed that EPA was proceeding with an RI/FS for an OU at the site at the time the trustee filed its NRD action and that EPA diligently worked toward selecting a final remedy at that OU. The court also noted that EPA was proceeding with a separate OU. The court viewed the trustee's arguments that EPA had failed to prioritize certain hazards that posed health risks as inappropriate challenges to EPA's selected remedial action. The court indicated it was "not in a position to second-guess the EPA's choices."[33]

Ripeness to recover NRDA costs has received slightly different treatment. The court in *Confederated Tribes & Bands of the Yakama Nation v. United States* distinguished between *damages*, which it defined as the compensation for injury, and assessment *costs*, finding that CERCLA's ripeness provision did not apply to the latter because the provision explicitly only applies to "damages."[34] Instead, the court found a claim for assessment costs becomes ripe as those costs are incurred. The Yakama Nation was allowed to proceed with a claim for declaratory relief with respect to the defendants' liability for assessment costs already incurred despite the holding, discussed later, that its NRD claims were not yet ripe.[35] Notably, in the *Yakama Nation* case (and, to our knowledge, in every case in which it has weighed in since), the United States advocated for the opposite result, arguing that no claims under CERCLA, including those for assessment costs, are ripe until a remedy has been selected for the site.[36]

---

32. *Id.* at *19.

33. *Id.* at *20.

34. 616 F. Supp. 2d 1094 (E.D. Wash. 2007).

35. *Id.*

36. U.S.'s Memorandum in Support of Motion to Partially Dismiss Plaintiffs' Second Amended Complaint and Complaints in Intervention at 14, *Yakama Nation*, 616 F. Supp. 2d 1094 (No. 2:02-cv-03105), 2006 WL 5925294, ECF No. 126.

Several other courts have also disagreed with the *Yakama Nation* court's holding on the question of whether the ripeness provision applies to assessment costs. In *New York v. Next Millennium Realty, LLC*, the Eastern District of New York stated that "I find the district court's reasoning in [*Yakama Nation*] to be unpersuasive. Under the plain language of Section 107(a)(4)(C) of CERCLA, under which the State asserts its NRD claim, natural resource damages expressly 'includ[e] the reasonable costs of assessing such injury.'"[37] In *Quapaw Tribe of Oklahoma v. Blue Tee Corp.*, the federal district court for the Northern District of Oklahoma expressed doubt regarding the *Yakama Nation* court's interpretation of the ripeness provision but ultimately dismissed the tribal trustee's assessment cost claims based on a failure to plead that any had been incurred.[38]

There is no court decision in any jurisdiction bearing directly on the question of whether a CERCLA NRD claim is ripe when a remedial action is selected for a single OU rather than the entire site. The United States (arguably the most important NRD trustees) has weighed in, arguing that an NRD claim is not ripe until a remedial action has been selected at all OUs designated within a site. In the *Yakama Nation* case, just discussed, the Yakama Nation sought to recover from the United States NRD related to the Hanford Nuclear Reservation. The Hanford Nuclear Reservation was divided into four separately listed NPL sites (each referred to as an "area"). Each site, or area, had multiple OUs. At the time of the complaint, all the areas for which the Nation claimed NRD had at least one OU where a remedial action had not yet been selected and at least one OU where a remedial action had been selected. The United States filed a motion to dismiss these claims, arguing that "at an NPL site . . . that is divided into multiple OUs, the claim for natural resource damages is not ripe until selection of the remedial action at all of the OUs within the Area."[39] It stated that

> [d]elaying the assertion of claims for natural resource damages reflects Congress's recognition that the remediation of a site may address natural resource injuries, and that any residual loss that is not addressed during the remediation can be better assessed after the remedial action is selected so that the likely effects of the remedial action on the natural resources have been taken into account.[40]

---

37. 160 F. Supp. 3d 485, 522 (E.D.N.Y. 2016).

38. No. 03-CV-0846-CVE-PJC, 2008 WL 2704482, at *22–23 (N.D. Okla. July 7, 2008).

39. U.S.'s Memorandum in Support of Motion to Partially Dismiss Plaintiffs' Second Amended Complaint and Complaints in Intervention, *supra* note 36, at 14.

40. *Id*. at 12.

The court ultimately declined to reach the question of ripeness of an NRD claim at a multiphased site, finding that consideration of the question was unnecessary in light of the fact that the case had already been stayed. While it is possible that, given a different procedural posture, the United States might change its view on this question, it has made similar arguments in other cases.[41] As such, if an NRD case is filed before a remedy is selected for all OUs at a site, it will likely be driven by a state or tribal trustee, not the United States.

C. "Wholly Before" Exemption and Retroactivity

Section 107(f) of CERCLA provides that "[t]here shall be no recovery [for natural resource damages] where such damages and the release of a hazardous substance from which such damages resulted have occurred wholly before December 11, 1980."[42] There is very little case law discussing what in particular is exempted by this section. One issue that is central to this inquiry is when "damages" "occur" under this section—whether they occur when the actual injury to natural resources occurs, or when monetary expenses to assess or restore them are incurred. Two cases that discussed this issue in depth reached opposite conclusions.

The court in *In re Acushnet River*[43] noted the lack of legislative history and relevant case law and concluded that "'damages'—*i.e.*, monetary quantification of the injury done to the natural resources—'occur' as a general rule when the property owner . . . [or other party] incurs expenses due to the injury to natural resources."[44] Other cases have buttressed the *Acushnet River* opinion.

---

41. *See, e.g.*, Memorandum in Support of Federal Defendants' Motion For Judgment on the Pleadings at 19, Quapaw Tribe of Oklahoma v. Blue Tee Corp., No. 03-CV-0846-CVE-PJC, 2008 WL 2704482 (N.D. Okla. July 7, 2008), 2007 WL 4717048, ECF No. 427-2 (arguing that "the Court should aggregate OUs for purposes of Section 113(g)"); Brief of the Appellant at 56, United States v. ASARCO Inc., 214 F.3d 1104 (9th Cir. 2000) (No. 98-36247), 1999 WL 33611857 ("Congress adopted the special limitations period for natural resource damage claims with respect to NPL facilities in recognition of the fact that the remedial action is likely to reduce the amount of natural resource injury, and therefore may reduce or even eliminate the natural resource damages claim. For that reason, section 113(g)(1)(B)(ii) bans the filing of a damages claim with respect to this type of facility until after the remedial action has been selected and its potential effects on the extent of damages can be assessed. Thus, Congress determined that a natural resource damage claim that may be affected by an ongoing remedial investigation is premature until the remedy has been selected.").

42. 42 U.S.C. § 9607(f)(1).

43. *In re* Acushnet River & New Bedford Harbor Proceedings re Alleged PCB Pollution, 716 F. Supp. 676 (D. Mass. 1989).

44. *Id.* at 683; *see also* Coeur d'Alene Tribe v. ASARCO Inc., 280 F. Supp. 2d 1094, 1114 (D. Idaho 2003) (damages generally occur when some entity incurs expenses due to injury to natural resources).

In *Coeur d'Alene Tribe v. ASARCO Inc.*, the court cited the DOI regulations, which define "damages" as "*the amount of money* sought by the natural resource trustee as compensation for injury, destruction, or loss of natural resources."[45] In *Aetna Casualty & Surety Co. v. Pintlar Corp.*,[46] the Ninth Circuit favorably cited the *Acushnet River* analysis of the definition of damages. The court stated: "The statutory definition, although somewhat circular, does not appear to support [an] interpretation." that "equate[s] the term 'damages' . . . with injury to the natural resources."[47] In *Alabama v. Alabama Wood Treating Corp.*, the court said it was persuaded by *Acushnet River* and its progeny that "damages" occur "when expenses are incurred due to an injury to natural resources."[48]

In contrast to these cases, the court in *Montana v. Atlantic Richfield Co.*[49] (*ARCO*) expressly rejected the *Acushnet River* interpretation of what constitutes "damages" under section 107(f)(1) of CERCLA,[50] finding instead that damages occur when the underlying injury occurs. To hold that damages occur only when a trustee incurs expenses or the court quantifies restoration costs, reasoned the court, would be to render the "wholly before" limitation meaningless. The court thus found plaintiff trustee's claims barred because the "injuries to, or destruction or loss of natural resources" occurred before CERCLA's date of enactment.[51] The court stated: "Absent proof that injuries, destruction or loss of natural resource damages occurred after December 11, 1980, the essential element of causation required by Section 107(f) is missing."[52]

Given the opposite conclusions reached in *Acushnet River* and *ARCO*, the issue of when "damages" "occur" for purposes of the "wholly before" defense remains unsettled.

In addition to discussing when "damages" occur under section 107(f), the court in *Acushnet River* considered the larger issue of the scope of recovery where releases started pre-enactment but continued post-enactment, or where

---

45. *Coeur d'Alene*, 280 F. Supp. 2d at 1114 (quoting 43 C.F.R. 11.14(l)) (emphasis added).

46. 948 F.2d 1507 (9th Cir. 1991).

47. *Id.* at 1515; *see also* United States v. ASARCO Inc., No. CV 96-0122-N-EJL, CV 91-342-N-EJL, 1999 WL 33313132, at *9–10 (D. Idaho Sept. 30, 1999) (indicating that court will apply *Acushnet River* definition of "damages" and "occurred").

48. Alabama v. Ala. Wood Treating Corp., No. 85-0642-CG-C, 2006 WL 8431771 (S.D. Ala. June 6, 2006) (also noting that burden fell on defendant to prove that damages are barred by the "wholly before" exemption). The court dismissed the plaintiffs' NRD claims because the complaint alleged only "injury" to natural resources but granted the plaintiffs leave to amend to allege proper "damages."

49. 266 F. Supp. 2d 1238, 1242, 1244 (D. Mont. 2003); *see also* Chapter 7, Section D.2 (in-depth discussion of this case).

50. *Atl. Richfield Co.*, 266 F. Supp. 2d at 1244 n.2.

51. *Id.* at 1244–45.

52. *Id.* at 1244.

a release that started pre-enactment resulted in both pre- and post-enactment damages. As the court noted, the parties did not dispute that incremental post-enactment damages caused by pre- and post-enactment releases are recoverable.[53] The court held that if damages are not divisible and either the damages or the release that caused them continue after December 11, 1980, the government can recover such damages in their entirety.[54] In contrast, where the damages are readily divisible, the government can recover only for damages occurring after the date of enactment.[55] In determining what damages are recoverable, the party seeking to rely upon the exemption in section 107(f) bears the burden of demonstrating that certain damages occurring before the date of enactment are divisible from post-enactment damages.[56]

Even though some courts have limited the scope of the "wholly before" defense's limitation on retroactive liability, it appears that the courts have not had opportunities to fully test the constitutionality of retroactive NRD liability. Cases addressing the constitutionality of such liability have almost always concerned response costs, not NRD. Appellate cases have uniformly allowed retroactive application of CERCLA liability for response costs over claims that such liability violated due process or constituted a taking.[57]

Courts have noted, however, that CERCLA treats response costs and NRD differently, citing the "wholly before" provision, among other things.[58] A frequently cited district court opinion that upheld retroactive application of CERCLA liability for pre-enactment response costs described the basis for the statute's different treatment of response costs and NRD, noting that the sites exempted from liability by the "wholly before" defense were "stable sites, that

---

53. *In re* Acushnet River & New Bedford Harbor Proceedings re Alleged PCB Pollution, 716 F. Supp. 676, 679 (D. Mass. 1989).

54. *Id.* at 686.

55. *Id.* at 685.

56. *Id.* at 687–88.

57. *See* Franklin Cty. Convention Facilities Auth. v. Am. Premier Underwriters, Inc., 240 F.3d 534, 553 (6th Cir. 2001) ("it is reasonable here to impose retroactive liability for possibly unforeseen costs of responding to environmental harms resulting from a party's disposal of waste"); United States v. Monsanto Co., 858 F.2d 160, 174 (4th Cir. 1988) ("CERCLA operates remedially to spread the costs of responding to improper waste disposal among all parties that played a role in creating the hazardous conditions."); United States v. Ne. Pharm. & Chem. Co., 810 F.2d 726, 734 (8th Cir. 1986) ("Cleaning up inactive and abandoned hazardous waste disposal sites is a legitimate legislative purpose, and Congress acted in a rational manner in imposing liability for the cost of cleaning up such sites upon those parties who created and profited from the sites and upon the chemical industry as a whole. . . .").

58. *See, e.g.*, Nevada *ex rel.* Dep't of Transp. v. United States, 925 F. Supp. 691, 694–95 (D. Nev. 1996) (CERCLA contemplated retroactive liability for response costs but not for NRD).

is, the environment, though damaged, will not deteriorate further."[59] The court said that "[a]t the opposite end of the spectrum" from these "stable sites" were sites "where the danger to the public health and welfare and to the environment was so imminent" that the United States had proceeded—pre-CERCLA—with cleanup without assurance that it would be repaid.[60] The court concluded that retroactive liability for the cleanup of such sites was appropriate.

The one case that has substantively addressed the constitutionality of retroactive NRD liability is the *Coeur d'Alene* case, which involved claims by the United States for $970 million in damages that the United States said resulted from releases related to the dumping of mining wastes both before (up to 100 years earlier) and after CERCLA's enactment.[61] A defendant mining company argued that it could not be held responsible for more than $700 million in damages that related to lawful conduct that took place significantly before CERCLA's enactment and that such liability would violate due process or constitute an unconstitutional taking.[62] The district court held that CERCLA allowed retroactive liability for NRD claims. The court said, among other things, that the "wholly before" provision "does not clearly prohibit all scenarios of retroactive liability."[63] The court also held that retroactive CERCLA liability was not a violation of the Takings Clause—finding that the economic impact of liability was not so severe as to be objectionable and that retroactivity would not interfere with reasonable investment-backed expectations.[64] In addition, the court said there was no facial violation of the Due Process Clause.[65] The court concluded, however, that the as-applied due process argument could not be resolved at the summary judgment stage. The court stated:

> [E]ven in cases in which retroactivity is generally tolerated, some limits have been suggested by the Supreme Court in the interest of fairness and justice. Distance into the past that [CERCLA] reaches back to impose liability can raise substantial questions of fairness. Additionally, the dollar amount of liability in comparison to a parties involvement for retroactive conduct may

---

59. United States v. Shell Oil Co., 605 F. Supp. 1064, 1076 (D. Colo. 1985).

60. *Id.* at 1075–77 (concluding from CERCLA's "explicit limitation on recovery of certain natural resources damages, and its failure to limit retroactive recovery of response costs, that CERCLA authorizes recovery of response costs whether incurred before or after its enactment").

61. *See* United States v. ASARCO Inc., No. CV 96-0122-N-EJL, CV 91-342-N-EJL, 1999 WL 33313132 (D. Idaho Sept. 30, 1999).

62. *Id.* at *2.

63. *Id.* at *5–6.

64. *Id.* at *6–7.

65. *Id.* at *8.

also raise questions of fairness. Congress in passing CERCLA recognized the principle of retroactive laws are generally unjust by providing that releases and damages wholly occurring prior to 1980 cannot be recovered. . . . Since the Court does not know the exact nature of the evidence supporting the Plaintiffs claims of injury to natural resources, the Court is unable to determine if the retroactive application in this case will be so severe as to violate the Due Process Clause. . . . If the term "wholly" in § 107(f) is interpreted to mean that if there are any releases and/or damages that continue beyond 1980, regardless of how small, then all similar injuries and/or damages predating 1980 are recoverable, the legislation would appear to potentially run afoul of the Constitution as applied in this case if the injuries and/or damages could not be apportioned or made divisible. Under the general principles of tort law, there is no rational basis for holding a party responsible for the entire amount of damages simply because some small portion of the damages continues beyond the arbitrary date of December 1980.[66]

The court indicated that if the mining company was determined to be liable, the "severity and overall fairness" of the liability would have to be reviewed.[67] The court also said the burden of proving a due process violation would "fall on the shoulders" of the defendants.[68]

Four years later, after the first phase of a trial, the court ruled that the trustees had established the defendants' liability.[69] The court found that the "wholly before" exemption did not apply both because passive movement and migration of hazardous substances constituted post-enactment "releases" and because the "the bulk of the damages have occurred post-enactment."[70] The court said the issue of the constitutionality of retroactive application of CERCLA would be reserved until the dollar amount of damages was established in the trial's second phase,[71] but the issue was never addressed because the parties subsequently settled the case.[72]

---

66. *Id.* at *9.

67. *Id.* at *10.

68. *Id.*

69. Coeur d'Alene Tribe v. ASARCO Inc., 280 F. Supp. 2d 1094, 1135 (D. Idaho 2003).

70. *Id.* at 1111–14.

71. *Id.* at 1111. In the 2003 order, the court appeared to leave open the possibility that retroactive liability could constitute a taking, although the court's 1999 order seemed to foreclose this possibility. *See ASARCO Inc.*, 1999 WL 33313132, at *6–7 (finding that a takings analysis was not applicable to CERCLA liability and, alternatively, finding that CERCLA liability survived the test for a regulatory takings challenge).

72. *See* discussion *infra* at Chapter 7, Section D.1.

The logic of this case indicates that an argument can be made that retro-active joint and several NRD liability may violate due process where the liabil-ity is tied to minor post-enactment releases and damages.

Therefore, to the extent that the pre-enactment bar is held to be inap-plicable in a particular case, a PRP may still be able to argue that the retro-active application of CERCLA to NRD is unconstitutional. In essence, in the appropriate case, a PRP could argue that the damages the trustees seek to recover relate to pre-enactment business operations that were beneficial to the economic development of the area, open and obvious, and lawful at the time. Accordingly, a large claim resulting from such conduct is fundamentally unfair and, in the words of the United States Supreme Court, "disproportionate to the parties' experience."[73]

D. Double Recovery

CERCLA prohibits double recovery of NRD[74]—that is, "damages or assess-ment costs may only be recovered once, for the same discharge or release and natural resource."[75] Congress added the prohibition on double recovery to the statute in the Superfund Amendments and Reauthorization Act of 1986.[76] The statute does, however, permit "different claims or actions for *different* damages stemming from the same injury to the same natural resource."[77] Sim-ilarly, OPA provides that "[t]here shall be no double recovery . . . for natural resource damages, including with respect to the costs of damage assessment or restoration, rehabilitation, replacement, or acquisition for the same incident and natural resource."[78]

In *Coeur d'Alene Tribe v. ASARCO Inc.*, the district court agreed with the government's argument that "there is not a double recovery until the total

---

73. E. Enters. v. Apfel, 524 U.S. 498, 528–29 (1998).

74. 42 U.S.C. § 9607(f)(1).

75. 43 C.F.R. § 11.15(d). CERCLA contains other provisions that reinforce the bar on double recovery, including one providing that if a trustee has already received damages under a different state or federal law, it is precluded from recovering for the same damages under CERCLA. Conversely, if a trustee has already received compensation for damages under CERCLA, it may not recover for the same damages under any other federal or state law. 42 U.S.C. § 9614(b). Courts do not appear to have applied this provision in the NRD context.

76. Pub. L. No. 99-499, § 107(d)(2), 100 Stat. 1613, 1630.

77. H.R. Rep. No. 99-962, at 221 (1986), *reprinted in* 1986 U.S.C.C.A.N. 3276, 3314 (emphasis added) (discussing Pub. L. No. 99-499).

78. 33 U.S.C. § 2706(d)(3); *see also* 15 C.F.R. § 990.22.

value of the damaged or injured resource has been recovered."[79] Although the court then went on to hold that CERCLA's bar against double recovery limited individual trustees' recovery to their "stewardship percentage" in a particular resource,[80] the court later reversed itself, sua sponte, finding that CERCLA in fact permitted any trustee to recover the full amount of damages, less any amount already paid in settlement.[81]

In another case, the defendant sought to join the state of Colorado as plaintiff, arguing that it might face multiple or inconsistent obligations to the United States and Colorado because both could be awarded damages for injury to natural resources. The court found this concern unfounded, as the double recovery bar would prevent the two co-trustees from separately recovering for the same resource. The court stated: "When the total amount of Shell's liability for injury to natural resources is determined, that amount will be apportioned between the Army and Colorado."[82]

Where private parties with commercial enterprises on public land—such as harvesting of public fish and game stocks—sue and recover the public's imputed rent as part of lost profits, a trustee is barred from including such losses in its calculation of NRD.[83] Similarly, if a trustee recovers such damages, "a private party will be barred by *res judicata* from later seeking recovery for the same public losses."[84] In addition, when the calculation of penalties is based on the "value" of an injured resource, the assessment of such penalties may count as recovery of NRD for purposes of determining whether there has been double recovery.[85]

---

79. 280 F. Supp. 2d 1094, 1117 (D. Idaho 2003); *see also* Chapter 7, Section D.1 (in-depth discussion of this case).

80. 280 F. Supp. 2d at 1117.

81. United States v. ASARCO Inc., 471 F. Supp. 2d 1063, 1068–69 (D. Idaho 2005). This ruling is also discussed later in the discussion of standing.

82. United States v. Shell Oil Co., 605 F. Supp. 1064, 1081 (D. Colo. 1985).

83. Nat'l Ass'n of Mfrs. v. U.S. Dep't of the Interior, 134 F.3d 1095, 1114–15 (D.C. Cir. 1998) (citing 43 C.F.R. § 11.44(d) (1996)).

84. *Id.* at 1114–15 (citing Alaska Sport Fishing Ass'n v. Exxon Corp., 34 F.3d 769, 774 (9th Cir. 1994).

85. *In re* Oil Spill by the Oil Rig "Deepwater Horizon" in the Gulf of Mexico, on April 20, 2010, 835 F. Supp. 2d 175 (E.D. La. 2011) (noting that penalties sought under Louisiana state law that were based on value of animals injured or killed "appear potentially duplicative" of NRD under OPA).

E. Irreversible or Irretrievable Commitment of Resources

CERCLA provides that trustees may not recover for losses to natural resources where a responsible party demonstrates that those losses were identified in an environmental impact statement (EIS) or similar analysis as an "irreversible and irretrievable commitment of natural resources . . . and the decision to grant a permit or license authorizes such commitment of natural resources."[86] OPA does not contain a similar provision.

CERCLA does not define the terms "irreversible" or "irretrievable," but the Ninth Circuit has pointed out in *Idaho v. Hanna Mining Co.* that the phrase "irreversible or irretrievable commitment of natural resources" originates in the National Environmental Policy Act (NEPA), which requires EISs to disclose "any irreversible and irretrievable commitments of resources which would be involved in the proposed action should it be implemented."[87] The generally applicable NEPA regulations issued by the Council on Environmental Quality do not define "irreversible" or "irretrievable," but at the time of the Ninth Circuit's decision, the Forest Service NEPA guidelines defined "irreversible" as applying "primarily to the use of nonrenewable resources, such as minerals or cultural resources or to those factors which are renewable only over long time spans, such as soil productivity."[88] The same guidelines defined "irretrievable" as applying to "losses of production, harvest or use for renewable natural resources," such as might happen in the case of timber production in an area temporarily used as a winter sports site.[89] The National Highway Traffic Safety Administration (NHTSA) NEPA regulations provide that identification of irreversible or irretrievable commitments of resources "requires identification of unavoidable impacts and the extent to which the action irreversibly curtails the range of potential uses of the environment."[90] The NHTSA regulations note that "resources" includes "the natural and cultural resources lost or destroyed."[91]

---

86. 42 U.S.C. § 9607(f)(1). In addition, the facility or project must be shown to have been operating within the terms of its permit or license, and, where tribal resources are involved, the permit or license must have been issued consistent with the fiduciary duty of the tribe and the United States. 42 U.S.C. § 9607(f)(1).

87. 882 F.2d 392, 396 (9th Cir. 1989) (citing 42 U.S.C. § 4332(C)(v)).

88. National Environmental Policy Act; Revised Implementing Procedures, 46 Fed. Reg. 56,998, 57,013 (Nov. 19, 1981).

89. *Id.*

90. 40 C.F.R. pt. 520, att. 1.

91. *Id.*

In *Hanna Mining*, the Ninth Circuit held that the exclusion was not meant to excuse liability for historical activities and injuries that took place before the EIS was prepared and before a permit for a project was issued.[92] The court said the waiver of liability only applied to pollution caused by the project, and not to preexisting pollution or releases that would occur regardless of whether the project goes forward.[93]

Potential trustees may fear that potentially responsible parties (PRPs) will attempt to preemptively qualify themselves for this waiver of liability. For instance, the State of Washington—in a NEPA challenge to DOE's plan to ship radioactive waste to Hanford Nuclear Reservation—argued that DOE had identified groundwater contaminated by historical releases from the Hanford site as "irretrievably committed" in an attempt to unilaterally avail itself of the exception to NRD liability. The district court found that language later included in DOE's record of decision along with other public representations "should be sufficient to preclude" DOE from asserting the defense.[94]

In *Hanna Mining*, the Ninth Circuit also indicated that while it was preferable for the EIS to include the words "irreversible and irretrievable," no such "formulaic recitation" was required by the statute, and thus a party could still successfully assert the defense by showing "an agency finding that does not employ [the statute's] specific terms [but is] otherwise clear and unambiguous."[95]

F. Federally Permitted Release

A defense is available to litigants who can show that some part of the damage to natural resources was caused by federally permitted discharges. CERCLA states: "Recovery by any person . . . for response costs or damages resulting from a federally permitted release shall be pursuant to existing law in lieu of this section."[96] CERCLA defines "federally permitted release" as discharges or emissions undertaken in compliance with permits or licenses issued pursuant to any of 11 listed federal programs.[97]

---

92. 882 F.2d at 395.

93. *Id.*

94. Washington v. Bodman, No. CV-03-5018-AAM, 2005 WL 1130294, at *15 (E.D. Wash. May 13, 2005).

95. 882 F.2d at 396.

96. 42 U.S.C. § 9607(j). Thus, "resort must be made to state common law in order to recover for any damages resulting from permitted releases." Idaho v. Bunker Hill Co., 635 F. Supp. 665, 673 (D. Idaho 1986).

97. 42 U.S.C. § 9601(10).

Under OPA, NRD cannot be recovered if the injury to the resource resulted from a discharge permitted by a permit issued under federal, state, or local law; a discharge from a public vessel; or a discharge from an onshore facility subject to the Trans-Alaska Pipeline Authorization Act.[98]

Courts have narrowly interpreted the federally permitted release exemption. For example, in *Idaho v. Bunker Hill Co.*, the court held that the exemption does not offer protection in the case of releases not expressly covered by the permit, releases that exceeded the limits of the permit, or releases that occurred outside the time period of the permit.[99] Another court noted that CERCLA's definition of "federally permitted release" was "extraordinarily detailed" and clearly addressed only releases made pursuant to a final permit.[100] In *In re Acushnet River & New Bedford Harbor: Proceedings re Alleged PCB Pollution*, the court held that the defendant claiming the exemption bore the burden of proving, "by a fair preponderance of the evidence, which releases were federally permitted and, if possible, what portion of the natural resource damages are allocable to federally permitted releases."[101] In another case (which involved claims for response costs, not NRD), the court indicated that *Acushnet River* "suggests that plaintiffs have the burden to prove that non-permitted releases contributed to the harm" but "places on defendants the burden to prove that the injury is divisible . . . so that the award . . . may be reduced to reflect the unrecoverable portion attributable to a permitted release."[102]

---

98. 33 U.S.C. § 2702(c). A "public vessel" is "a vessel owned or bareboat chartered and operated by the United States, or by a State or political subdivision thereof, or by a foreign nation, except when the vessel is engaged in commerce." 33 U.S.C. § 2701(29).

99. 635 F. Supp. at 674; *see also* Pennsylvania v. Lockheed Martin Corp., 684 F. Supp. 2d 564, 583 (M.D. Pa. 2010) (noting that agency's authorization to "leave behind" some quantities of substance "does not mean that it authorized the later release of that substance" and finding that factual questions regarding whether releases were in compliance with license precluded ruling in defendant's favor on validity of federally permitted release defense); United States v. Wash. State Dep't of Transp., 716 F. Supp. 2d 1009, 1016 (W.D. Wash. 2010) (no summary judgment for plaintiff or defendant on federally permitted release defense because of disputes as to defendant's compliance with permits, scope of permits, whether there were releases outside that scope, and whether injury was divisible).

100. Reading Co. v. City of Philadelphia, 823 F. Supp. 1218, 1231 (E.D. Pa. 1993) (rejecting argument that PCB releases from railcars qualified as "federally permitted releases" because railcar transformers qualified for exemption from Safe Drinking Water Act permit requirements based on compliance with Toxic Substances Control Act procedures).

101. 722 F. Supp. 893, 901 (D. Mass. 1989); *see also* United States v. Shell Oil Co., No. CV 91-0589-RJK, 1992 WL 144296 (C.D. Cal. Jan. 16, 1992) (finding that defendants failed to refer to any federally approved permit and did not allege what portion of damages were covered by such permit and requesting that defendants allege defense with greater specificity).

102. United States v. Iron Mountain Mines, Inc., 812 F. Supp. 1528, 1540–41 (E.D. Cal. 1992).

G. Standing

State, federal, and tribal trustees often must confront the issue of standing to sue, which turns on whether a resource is under the trusteeship of a given agency, state, or tribe. CERCLA and OPA both use the phrase "under their trusteeship" to describe the scope of trustees' obligations but do not define the phrase's meaning.[103] In describing the scope of NRD liability, however, CERCLA does state that

> liability shall be to the United States Government and to any State for natural resources *within the State* or *belonging to, managed by, controlled by, or appertaining to such State* and to *any Indian tribe* for natural resources *belonging to, managed by, controlled by, or appertaining to such tribe,* or held in trust for the benefit of such tribe, or belonging to a member of such tribe if such resources are subject to a trust restriction on alienation.[104]

OPA includes the same "belonging to, managed by, controlled by, or appertaining to" language to limit the scope of natural resources for which trustees may seek NRD.[105]

It is important to note, however, that a trustee need not "own" the resource in order to bring an NRD claim.[106] Nor, in some cases, does the resource necessarily have to be within the geographical jurisdiction of the trustee, as long as trusteeship is otherwise established.[107] Although purely private resources are excluded from the definition of natural resources, damages for such resources may be recovered if there is a "substantial degree of government regulation, management or other form of control over the property."[108]

Both DOI and the National Oceanic and Atmospheric Administration (NOAA) have implicitly discussed the scope of trusteeship over resources that are not publicly owned in their promulgation of the CERCLA and OPA regulations. In the preamble to its final rule in 1994, DOI interpreted the CERCLA liability provision to mean that "trustee officials can only recover

---

103. *See* 33 U.S.C. § 2706(c); 42 U.S.C. § 9607(f)(2).

104. 42 U.S.C. § 9607(f)(1) (emphasis added).

105. 33 U.S.C. § 2706(a).

106. Ohio v. U.S. Dep't of the Interior, 880 F.2d 432 (D.C. Cir. 1989).

107. *See* Natural Resource Damage Assessments, 59 Fed. Reg. 14,262 (Mar. 25, 1994) (to be codified at 43 C.F.R. pt. 11) (preamble to final rule) (discussing tribes); *see also* 40 C.F.R. § 300.605 (National Contingency Plan provision regarding state trustees that provides that "[s]tate trustees shall act on behalf of the public as trustees for natural resources, including their supporting ecosystems, within the boundary of a state *or* belonging to, managed by, controlled by, or appertaining to such state" (emphasis added)).

108. 880 F.2d at 461.

damages for injuries to those resources that are related to them through ownership, management, trust, or control. These relationships are created by other Federal, State, local, and tribal laws."[109]

NOAA's discussion relevant to the scope of trustee standing involved the definition of "natural resources." In the preamble to its proposed OPA regulations, NOAA indicated that it was "using . . . the OPA definition of natural resources that provides for various degrees of government regulation, management or other form of control over the natural resources to make the OPA natural resource damage provisions applicable."[110] The statutory definition encompasses "land, fish, wildlife, biota, air, water, ground water, drinking water supplies, and other such resources belonging to, managed by, held in trust by, appertaining to, or otherwise controlled by"[111] the United States, a state or local government, an Indian tribe, or a foreign government. NOAA indicated that this language "covers a broad range of government interest in natural resources on behalf of the public" and that "general sources of authority for recovery under the rule could include, but not necessarily be limited to, relevant treaty or other provision of international law, constitution, statute, common law, regulation, order, deed or other conveyance, permit, or agreement."[112] NOAA said the definition of natural resources ensured "a wide range of legitimate government interest in natural resources that may, in fact, be held in private ownership."[113]

In *Coeur d'Alene Tribe v. ASARCO Inc.*,[114] the court addressed the issue of trusteeship. The defendant responsible parties argued that the United States and tribe were not trustees over—and therefore had no standing to recover damages for—certain natural resources at issue. The defendants argued that the trustees lacked "*actual* stewardship" over the resources.[115] The tribe and

---

109. 59 Fed. Reg. at 14,269.

110. Natural Resource Damage Assessments, 59 Fed. Reg. 1062, 1075 (proposed Jan. 7, 1994) (to be codified at 15 C.F.R. pt. 990).

111. 33 U.S.C. § 2701(20).

112. 59 Fed. Reg. at 1075.

113. *Id.* In response to a comment related to potential disputes between federal, state, tribal, and foreign trustees over which trustee could exert trusteeship over specific resources, NOAA expressly declined to "clarify which resources should be appropriately claimed by which trustee." NOAA indicated that the focus should be on conducting assessments and preparing restoration plans to address affected natural resources as a whole, not in a trustee-specific piecemeal process. *Id.* at 1106.

114. 280 F. Supp. 2d 1094 (D. Idaho 2003); *see also* Chapter 7, Section D.1 (in-depth discussion of this case).

115. *Coeur d'Alene*, 280 F. Supp. 2d. at 1114.

U.S. government argued that trusteeship was a matter of statutory authority, regardless of the actual actions taken by sovereign governments.

The court rejected the tribe's and government's argument, finding that trusteeship was a "question of both fact and law."[116] The court stated:

> The factual predicate of trusteeship . . . is to be determined on a case by case basis depending on who the resource belongs to, who is it managed by, who controls the same and how the resource appertains to other resources. Resources must be under the stewardship of a trustee before damages can be assessed for their injury, loss or destruction.[117]

Because the court further held that a trustee could recover only the percentage of damages that accorded with its stewardship over a resource, the court postponed a determination of trusteeship over certain resources until the second phase of the trial, when evidence could be presented on such stewardship percentages.[118]

Significantly, however, in a later order, the court sua sponte reversed itself on the issue of trusteeship divisibility. Determining that any trustee could indeed recover the full amount of damage, less any amount already paid in settlement to another trustee, the court decided that it need not wait for Phase 2 of the trial to determine trusteeship. Based on the plaintiffs' "involvement in the management and control" of the migratory natural resources in question (fish, wildlife, biota, water, and groundwater), and based on the fact that "applicable federal statutes [gave] the United States trusteeship duties over fish, wildlife[,] and birds," the court found that the United States and tribe were indeed trustees over those resources.[119]

---

116. *Id.* at 1115.

117. *Id.*

118. The resources were fish, wildlife, biota, water, and groundwater. *Id.* at 1117. With regard to other resources, the court found that "the federal government is a trustee over 100% of federal lands in the Basin and the Tribe is trustee over 100% of the lands within the reservation boundaries." *Id.*

119. United States v. ASARCO Inc., 471 F. Supp. 2d 1063, 1069 (D. Idaho 2005). It is not clear whether the district court's sua sponte reversal affects its analysis of cultural resources and trusteeship. In its original opinion, the court held that use of natural resources in "the exercise of . . . cultural activities . . . does not rise to the level of making a natural resource 'belong or be connected as a rightful part or attribute' for purposes of trusteeship analysis." 280 F. Supp. 2d at 1117 (quoting Webster's New Collegiate Dictionary, 54 (1979)). The court's analysis here differs from the position taken by one commentator, who advises readers that where land is concerned, parties should consider, inter alia, whether "any tribal cultural resources or tribal uses of resources protected by treaties" have been affected, in determining which trustees are likely to be involved in a NRDA. *See* Valerie Ann Lee & P.J. Bridgen, The Natural Resource Damage Assessment Deskbook: A Legal and Technical Analysis 23–24 (Envtl. Law Inst. ed., 2002).

In *New Mexico v. General Electric Co.*, the parties litigated the issue of trusteeship over natural resources, although in the context of state law-based claims rather than as a federal NRD claim. The district court narrowed the state's interest as a trustee over groundwater, thus limiting the scope of the state's recovery for damages.[120] More specifically, the court held that New Mexico's sole interest was in making water available for appropriation by others, not in the use of the water itself.[121] Accordingly, the court held that the state could recover damages only to the extent that the injury prevented the groundwater from being appropriated.[122]

The Tenth Circuit subsequently affirmed judgment against New Mexico, holding that CERCLA's NRD scheme preempted state law remedies designed to achieve something other than restoration and further holding that the district court was without jurisdiction to hear the remaining narrower claims for NRD for groundwater contamination because the claims were in effect a challenge to an ongoing CERCLA remedy.[123] Although the Tenth Circuit affirmed the judgment against New Mexico on different grounds, the district court's decision should remind responsible parties of the importance of clearly defining the trustee's interest and the injury to it, as the resolution of that issue will inform the choice of assessment methodology and the measure of damages.

H. Causation

1. CERCLA

Under section 107(a)(4)(C) of CERCLA, responsible parties are responsible for damages for injury to natural resources "resulting from" a release of hazardous substances or oil. Otherwise, however, the statutory text is silent with respect to the degree of causation that is required and whether proof of causation of injury should be less strict than required by common law. Moreover, the legislative history sheds limited light on the issues.[124]

---

120. 322 F. Supp. 2d 1237, 1260–61 (D.N.M. 2004); *see also* Chapter 7, Section D.9 (in-depth discussion of this case).

121. *Gen. Elec. Co.*, 322 F. Supp. 2d at 1240–41.

122. *Id.* at 1261.

123. New Mexico v. Gen. Elec. Co., 467 F.3d 1223, 1247, 1249–50 (10th Cir. 2006) (citing 42 U.S.C. § 9613(h)).

124. *See* Ohio v. U.S. Dep't of the Interior, 880 F.2d 432 (D.C. Cir. 1989) (discussion of legislative history).

The leading CERCLA case analyzing the applicable causation standard, *Ohio v. U.S. Department of the Interior*,[125] involved challenges by various entities to the "acceptance criteria" promulgated by DOI as a method for determining whether a release of hazardous substances caused injury to a biological resource. One challenge, brought by environmental groups, alleged that the standard reflected in the acceptance criteria was too stringent, and "contrary to the statutory command that the standard of proof of causation-of-injury under CERCLA be less strict than that required by the common law."[126] The *Ohio* court looked to the legislative history of CERCLA and found that Congress's *"general* concern for liberalizing the standards of the common law" was counterbalanced by the presence of "little evidence" that it "specifically intended to ease the standard of proof for showing that a particular spill caused a particular biological injury."[127] Concluding that the legislative history was ambiguous, the court upheld DOI's interpretation—that CERCLA retained "traditional causation analysis"—as "permissible under *Chevron* Step Two."[128]

Subsequently, in *Kennecott Utah Copper Corp. v. U.S. Department of the Interior*,[129] industry petitioners argued the opposite, that DOI's rules for calculating damages (which they had re-promulgated after *Ohio*) were too lax, inasmuch as they defined costs to include indirect costs (such as overhead), which petitioners argued could not "result from" the release of hazardous substances.[130] The court reiterated that "CERCLA left it to Interior to define the measure of damages in natural resources damage assessment cases."[131] From there it reasoned that "while the statutory language requires some causal connection between the element of damages and the injury—the damages must be 'for' an injury 'resulting from a release of oil or a hazardous substance'—Congress has not specified precisely what that causal relationship should be."[132] As a

125. *Id.*

126. *Id.* at 470. The "acceptance criteria," set forth at 43 C.F.R. § 11.62(f)(2), required a showing that (1) the "biological response" alleged to have been precipitated by the hazardous substance release is a "commonly documented" response to oil or hazardous substance spills, (2) oil or hazardous substances are "known to cause" such a response in field studies, (3) oil or hazardous substances are "known to cause" such a response in controlled experiments, and (4) the biological response can be measured by a technique that is practical to perform and has been "adequately documented in scientific literature." *See id.* at 469–70.

127. *Id.* at 470.

128. *Id.*

129. 88 F.3d 1191 (D.C. Cir. 1996).

130. *Id.* at 1223.

131. *Id.* at 1224.

132. *Id.*

result, the court again found that the regulations were based on a permissible reading of CERCLA.[133]

Due to the statutory ambiguity, courts have continued to grapple in a somewhat inconsistent fashion with the appropriate causation standard for NRD claims. For example, in the *Montrose* case—which is now well-known by NRD practitioners—the court held that a trustee "must show that a defendant's release of a hazardous substance was the sole or substantially contributing cause of each alleged injury to natural resources."[134] This test—referred to the "sole or substantially contributing cause" standard—has a somewhat colorful history, which is less well-known. Here is that history in a nutshell:

The United States and State of California originally filed the *Montrose* case in June 1990. The complaint alleged injury to birds, fish, and marine mammals as a result of DDT and PCB contamination on the Palos Verdes shelf off the coast of California. On March 18, 1991, Judge Hauk of the U.S. District Court for the Central District of California held a hearing for various motions not related to the causation standard. During the hearing, the defendants asserted that the trustee's complaint contained vague allegations. Judge Hauk orally, without briefing, dismissed the trustee's complaint with leave to amend and instructed defendant's counsel to draft a proposed order. A week later, on March 27, 1991, counsel for one of the defendants submitted the proposed dismissal order, which was signed by Judge Hauk on the same day.[135]

Judge Hauk's order, which cites to no authority and resulted from an unnoticed, unbriefed oral motion, is even more remarkable in its elaboration of the trustees' burden. The order went on to say that the plaintiffs must allege the following elements:

> (1) WHAT natural resources have been injured; *i.e.*, plaintiffs shall identify each alleged injury to natural resources for which plaintiffs seek to recover natural resource damages, and shall identify the specific natural resource injured (*e.g.*, the particular species of fish, bird, mammal or other natural resource in issue); (2) the specific locations WHERE each such injury has occurred and where the releases of hazardous substances alleged to be

---

133. *See also, e.g.*, Nat'l. Ass'n of Mfrs. v. U.S. Dep't. of the Interior, 134 F.3d 1095, 1105–08 (D.C. Cir. 1998) ("Regarding causation, this court has repeatedly held that CERCLA is ambiguous on the precise question of *what standard of proof is required to demonstrate that natural resource injuries were caused by, or 'result[] from,' a particular release.*") (emphasis added).

134. United States v. Montrose Chem. Corp. of Cal., No. CV 90-3122, 1991 WL 183147, at *1 (C.D. Cal. Mar. 29, 1991); *see also* Chapter 7, Section D.4 (in-depth discussion of this case).

135. [Proposed] Order Dismissing Plaintiffs' First Claim for Relief, United States v. Montrose Chem. Corp. of Cal., No. CV 90-3122 (C.D. Cal. Mar. 27, 1991). The court handwrote on the order "[n]o objection by any plaintiff to form of order."

the sole or substantially contributing cause of each such injury occurred; . . . (3) WHEN each such injury occurred and the releases occurred; and (4) WHICH defendant's release(s) of WHAT hazardous substance was the sole or substantially contributing cause of each such injury, and by what pathway exposure to the hazardous substance occurred.[136]

The *Montrose* order, therefore, does more than impose a "substantially contributing" factor test. The *Montrose* order arguably eviscerates joint and several liability for NRD claims. A plaintiff under this standard must identify the specific release by each defendant that caused each injury. The requirement that the trustee track each hazardous substance from release to injury for each defendant means that NRD liability is several, not joint.

Later decisions have criticized the court's conclusion in *Montrose*, however. For example, in *Coeur d'Alene Tribe v. ASARCO Inc.*, the court rejected defendants' reliance on this standard, noting that the court in *Montrose* did not explain the reasoning behind its decision.[137]

In *Coeur d'Alene*, the court indicated that proximate cause was the appropriate NRD causation standard under CERCLA where multiple releases had not commingled.[138] Where waste from multiple defendants was commingled, however, *Coeur d'Alene* found that the correct causation standard was a contributing factor test, defined as "more than a de minimis amount—to an extent that at least some of the injury would have occurred if only the Defendant's amount of release had occurred."[139] *Coeur d'Alene* and other cases citing the general proposition that CERCLA requires something less than proximate cause appear to involve either the causal connection between the defendant and the spill as opposed to between the spill and the injury[140] or incidents involving multiple spillers and the question of who caused the spill.[141]

---

136. *Montrose*, 1991 WL 183147, at *1.

137. Coeur d'Alene Tribe v. ASARCO Inc., No. CV91-0342NEJL, 2001 WL 34139603, at *3 n.4 (D. Idaho Mar. 30, 2001); *see also* Chapter 7, Section D.1 (in-depth discussion of this case).

138. *See, e.g., Coeur d'Alene*, 2001 WL 34139603, at *5 (The trustee must "show that such release was the sole or proximate cause to the injury to the natural resources.").

139. *Id.*; *see also* Coeur d'Alene Tribe v. ASARCO Inc., 280 F. Supp. 2d 1094, 1124 (D. Idaho 2003).

140. *See, e.g.*, New York v. Shore Realty Corp., 759 F.2d 1032 (2d Cir. 1985).

141. *See, e.g., Coeur d'Alene*, 280 F. Supp. 2d at 1124 (holding that where hazardous waste has commingled, the trustee must show that each defendant's release is more than a contributing factor to the NRD); *In re* Acushnet River & New Bedford Harbor: Proceedings re Alleged PCB Pollution, 722 F. Supp. 893, 897 (D. Mass. 1989) (holding that where some discharges were permitted and others were not, liability was established if the non-permitted release was a "contributing factor" to the natural resource injury or loss).

In *Coeur d'Alene*, the court applied the contributing factor test and found that the plaintiffs had established the requisite level of causation where the mining waste released by the defendants "contained hazardous substances that were in such quantity as to be contributing factors to the injuries to natural resources" where one of the defendants had contributed 22 percent of the waste and another had contributed 31 percent. The court said "each Defendant's quantity alone was large enough to be considered a contributing factor."[142]

A federal district court in New York cited *Coeur d'Alene* and DOI's regulations in finding that an injury to groundwater had resulted from defendants' release of hazardous substances.[143] The court indicated that the fact that hazardous substances of the type generated by the defendants were present in groundwater at levels exceeding state drinking water standards was sufficient to establish liability. The court found, however, that questions remained as to the divisibility of the harm.

A final question related to causation is one of choice of law—namely, whether the courts should look to state or federal law for evaluating the causation standard. In at least one instance, the U.S. Department of Justice appears to have taken the position that state, not federal, common law should guide this determination.[144] Of course, the application of state decisional law in this context may present an opportunity for defendants to assert common law defenses.

2. OPA

OPA provides that a responsible party for an oil spill is "liable for the removal costs and damages . . . that *result from* such incident."[145] No court has specifically addressed what causation standard this language incorporates in the NRD context under OPA. The statutory language is almost identical to CERCLA's, however, and so the foregoing discussion of case law under CERCLA is potentially relevant. As discussed later, the learnings from *Deepwater Horizon* may also be relevant to this issue.

Other clues to the appropriate causation standard for NRD under OPA can be gleaned based on principles of statutory construction. Two related

---

142. *Coeur d'Alene*, 280 F. Supp. 2d at 1124.

143. New York v. Next Millennium Realty, LLC, 160 F. Supp. 3d 485, 524–26 (finding that defendants were liable for NRD but finding that there were triable issues of fact with respect to the affirmative defense of divisibility of harm).

144. Memo of Contentions of Law & Fact of Plaintiffs United States & State of California, at 18, United States v. Montrose Chem. Corp. of Cal., No. CV 903122-R (C.D. Cal. Aug 7, 2000) (citing to the Supreme Court of California's interpretation of the "substantial factor" test).

145. 33 U.S.C. § 2702(a) (emphasis added).

principles would indicate that the "result from" language in OPA imposes a proximate cause requirement. First, when Congress enacts statutes establishing civil liability, it does so against a background of common law principles, including proximate cause.[146] Second, and correspondingly, courts do not find that Congress intended to abrogate long-standing common law doctrines unless there is clear evidence of such intent, or extend statutes by construction or implication any further than the language of the statute requires, if such extension would contravene common law.[147] It is therefore significant that in addition to employing causal language generally understood to connote proximate cause, OPA does not suggest that any lesser standard of causation is applicable.

Judicial decisions in cases presenting economic claims under OPA—to which the same "result[ing] from" causal language applies—also are relevant to the appropriate causation standard for OPA NRD claims. The relatively few economic claims cases reflect a recognition that OPA incorporates causation requirements that should be applied rigorously. In *In re Taira Lynn Marine Ltd. No. 5*,[148] a barge accident and subsequent release of propane and gas forced the temporary evacuation of businesses from the area and the shutdown of electricity.[149] Businesses experiencing disruptions filed suit under OPA, maritime law, CERCLA, and state statutes.[150] The court bifurcated the proceedings to consider claims of "purely economic loss" prior to and separately from claims of personal injury, physical damage, or the claims of commercial fishermen.[151] The claims for economic loss included claims for "loss of revenues and sales from a convenience store as a result of the evacuation," "lost charter revenues . . . due to the evacuation," and damages from business "forced to halt work in progress for two construction projects."[152]

---

146. *See, e.g.*, Holmes v. Sec. Inv'r Prot. Corp., 503 U.S. 258, 287 (1992) ("[I]t has always been the practice of common-law courts (and probably of all courts, under all legal systems) to require as a condition of recovery, unless the legislature specifically prescribes otherwise, that the injury [must] have been proximately caused by the offending conduct.") (Scalia, J., concurring); Babbitt v. Sweet Home Chapter of Cmtys. for a Great Or., 515 U.S. 687, 712 (1995) (O'Connor, J., concurring) ("I would not lightly assume that Congress, in enacting a strict liability statute that is silent on the causation question, has dispensed with this well-entrenched principle [of proximate cause].").

147. *See* Norfolk S. Ry. Co. v. Sorrell, 549 U.S. 158, 164–65 (2007).

148. 444 F.3d 371 (5th Cir. 2006).

149. *Id.* at 375–76.

150. *Id.* at 376.

151. *Id.*

152. *Id.* at 377.

The court analyzed the text of OPA § 2702(b)(2)(E) and a Fourth Circuit case (discussed later) and concluded that "[a] party is liable under OPA if, inter alia, the claimant's damages 'result from such incident,' *i.e.*, the discharge or threatened discharge of oil."[153] The court concluded that, because plaintiff did not raise an issue of fact as to whether any property damage was caused by the release of oil, that "Claimants cannot recover under OPA and the district court erred in denying Appellant's motions for partial summary judgment."[154] The court thereby recognized a requirement that a causal link exist between the incident and the injured resource or property, and between the injured resource or property and the claimed damages.

Similarly, the Fourth Circuit upheld a finding by USCG that fire damage to a warehouse was not compensable under OPA where vandals had opened aboveground storage tanks and vapors released from the tanks ignited the fire.[155] The USCG argued, and the Fourth Circuit affirmed, that OPA only permits recovery where the damages result from a discharge of oil into navigable waters. Although the opening of the aboveground tanks did result in a discharge of oil to navigable waters, the fire did not result from such discharge to navigable waters (it was caused by the vapors), and thus, the fire damage was not compensable under OPA.[156] Although the Fourth Circuit did not interpret the NRD or economic injury prongs of § 2702(b)(2), its decision nonetheless demonstrates that courts are loathe to permit recovery under OPA unless the causation requirements are satisfied.

The Gulf Coast Claims Facility (GCCF)—which was established to receive and process claims by individuals and businesses for costs and damages as a result of the oil discharges from the April 20, 2010, *Deepwater Horizon* incident—applied proximate cause to economic claims in its interim and final protocols.[157] The GCCF's guidance on how it would determine eligibility also described a proximate cause standard, focusing on "geographic proximity to the Spill, the nature of the claimant's job or business, and the extent to which

---

153. *Id.* at 383 (quoting 33 U.S.C. § 2702(a) and citing Gatlin Oil Co. v. United States, 169 F.3d 207, 210–11 (4th Cir. 1999)).

154. *Id.*

155. *Gatlin Oil Co.*, 169 F.3d 207.

156. *Id.* at 210–11.

157. *See* Gulf Coast Claims Facility, Protocol for Interim and Final Claims (Nov. 22, 2010) ("The GCCF will only pay for harm or damage that is proximately caused by the Spill."); Gulf Coast Claims Facility, Protocol for Emergency Advance Payments 5 (Aug. 23, 2010) ("The GCCF will only pay for harm or damage that is proximately caused by the Spill.").

the claimant's job or business is dependent upon injured property or natural resources."[158]

The GCCF's application of proximate cause was not without its critics. In a letter to GCCF administrator Kenneth Feinberg, Florida's then-attorney general, Bill McCollum, wrote that the proximate cause requirement "increases the burden of proof imposed upon Claimants."[159] Mr. McCollum wrote that the "result of" language imposed "a less onerous standard of causation, reflective of the fact that OPA is a strict liability statute."[160] He concluded that the ambiguity created by deviating from the "result of" language and including references to proximate causation in the claim protocol "disserves the public, is contrary to the goal of creating a means of obtaining compensation for damages without the need for litigation, and violates OPA."[161]

A report drafted by Harvard law professor John Goldberg, commissioned by the GCCF in response to its critics, concluded that a showing of proximate cause is required for economic claims under OPA.[162] Professor Goldberg focused in large part on the intersection of what he called "OPA's liability trigger"—the strict liability provision at 33 U.S.C. § 2702(a)—and the provision that specifies when the event generates liability for economic damages—33 U.S.C. § 2702(b)(2)(E). He concluded that Congress's limitation of economic damages in § 2702(b)(2)(E) to those "*due to* the injury, destruction, or loss of real property, personal property, or natural resources" added another layer of causation in addition to the "result from" provision.[163]

---

158. Gulf Coast Claims Facility, Understanding the GCCF's Eligibility Criteria for Emergency Advance Payments (Aug. 23, 2010). Geographic proximity was primarily based on whether the loss occurred "adjacent to a beach, shoreline, marsh, bay or tributary of the Gulf where oil or oil residues came ashore or appeared in the waters," indicating the claims for losses in areas with no oil would need to make a stronger showing in other ways to recover. *Id.*

159. Letter from Bill McCollum, Florida Attorney General, to Kenneth R. Feinberg, Gulf Coast Claims Facility Administrator, at 2 (Aug. 20, 2010), https://perma.cc/B6X7-K4JZ.

160. *Id.*

161. *Id.*

162. *See* John C.P. Goldberg, Liability for Economic Loss in Connection with the Deepwater Horizon Spill (2010), https://dash.harvard.edu/handle/1/4595438 ("This report is instead intended to provide an assessment of the legal liability BP and/or its subsidiaries can be expected to face if certain claims against it are pursued in courts of law—specifically, claims seeking compensation for economic loss not predicated on personal injury or physical damage to the claimant's property.").

163. *See* 33 U.S.C. § 2702(b)(2)(E) (emphasis added). "[I]t is entirely natural to read Section 2702(b)(2)(E)'s 'due to' clause as requiring as a condition of recovery for lost profits or impaired earning capacity a nexus beyond bare causation between the lost profits or impaired earning capacity (on the one hand) and the damage to, or loss of, property or natural resources (on the other). . . . [O]ne need only treat the phrase 'due to' as refining the actual causation requirement

The NRD provisions do not contain similar "due to" language, meaning that Professor Goldberg's analysis of economic damages may be of limited relevance in the NRD context. His analysis could imply that the omission of "due to" in the other categories of damages, including NRD, implies that Congress intended a lower causation threshold for such claims. Professor Goldberg also found, however, that courts have interpreted other statutes with similar language (e.g., CERCLA and the Trans-Atlantic Pipeline Authorization Act (TAPAA)) as not abrogating principles of proximate causation. Professor Goldberg therefore concluded that the "result from" language alone would impose a proximate cause requirement. That Congress would add an "additional layer of causation" for claimants whose property was not oiled would make sense in light of the historic bar against purely economic claims.

What that additional layer means in practice and how that compares to causation of NRD claims remains to be seen. District courts that have considered OPA claims for economic loss in recent years have not considered § 2702(a)'s "result from" language in isolation. For example, the U.S. District Court for the Eastern District of Louisiana dismissed claims brought by companies seeking to recover under OPA for economic losses sustained as a result of the federal moratorium on offshore drilling activities after the *Deepwater Horizon* incident.[164] The court expressly stated that it "need not and does not decide whether or not § 2702(a) and/or § 2702(b)(2)(E) incorporates a proximate causation standard, etc."[165] Reading those provisions together, the court held that the companies' moratorium-related claims did not satisfy OPA's causation standard because even though the government would not have imposed the moratorium had the *Deepwater Horizon* incident not occurred, the moratorium addressed perceived future risks and risk at other wells, not incident-related risks.[166] The losses therefore did not "result from" the *Deepwater Horizon* incident.[167]

---

already specified by the 'result from' language of Section 2702(a)." GOLDBERG, *supra* note 161, at 20.

164. *In re* Oil Spill by the Oil Rig "Deepwater Horizon" in the Gulf of Mexico, on April 20, 2010, 168 F. Supp. 3d 908 (E.D. La. 2016).

165. *Id.* at 918; *see also* Blue Water Boating Inc. v. Plains All American Pipeline, L.P., 2017 WL 405425 (C.D. Cal. Jan. 26, 2017) (to recover economic losses under OPA, plaintiff must link harm to specific allegations of property damage caused by oil spill).

166. *Id.* at 916.

167. *But see* United States v. Am. Comm. Lines, LLC, 2016 WL 4987208, at *6 (E.D. La. Sept. 19, 2016) (rejecting argument that damages resulting from closure of Mississippi River were improper under OPA because closure of river was "a response to and a direct result of the oil spill").

Courts' interpretations of similar causal language in other statutes support the incorporation of traditional concepts of causation in OPA. The mostly closely related parallel language is in CERCLA's NRD provisions, which, as discussed previously, has been interpreted by different courts to incorporate traditional causation standards and is generally consistent with a proximate cause requirement, particularly where contamination is not commingled.

In other statutes with similar causal language, courts have identified proximate cause as the appropriate standard. In *Benefiel v. Exxon Corp.*,[168] for example, the Ninth Circuit considered whether the claims of certain businesses alleging economic losses for the *Exxon Valdez* oil spill under TAPAA were barred by a bright-line rule enunciated in a case known as *Robins Dry Dock* that prevented recovery of pure economic losses in maritime law.[169] Interpreting TAPAA's causation provision, which provides that "the owner and operator of the vessel . . . shall be strictly liable without regard to fault . . . for all damages . . . sustained . . . as the result of discharges of oil from such vessel," the Ninth Circuit concluded that "[w]e do not need to reach the specific issue of *Robins Dry Dock* abrogation, for we are confident that Congress in enacting TAPAA did not intend to abrogate all principles of proximate cause."[170]

Similarly, in *Ballard Shipping Co. v. Beach Shellfish*,[171] a group of fishermen brought suit under the Rhode Island Environmental Injury and Compensation Act (Compensation Act)[172] seeking to recover economic losses after an oil spill. The defendants responded by arguing that the claims were barred by *Robins Dry Dock*.[173] The court found that the Compensation Act's extension of liability was circumscribed by the limitation to losses that are "as a result of damage to the natural resources."[174] This language, the court concluded, "incorporates the familiar tort limitations of foreseeability and proximate cause."[175]

Other courts, including the U.S. Supreme Court, have interpreted similar causal language to refer to proximate cause.[176]

---

168. 959 F.2d 805 (9th Cir. 1992).

169. *See* Robins Dry Dock & Repair Co. v. Flint, 275 U.S. 303 (1927).

170. *Benefiel*, 959 F.2d at 807.

171. 32 F.3d 623 (1st Cir. 1994).

172. R.I. Gen. Laws §§ 46-12.3–46-12.8.

173. 32 F.3d at 624–25.

174. *Id.* at 630 (emphasis in original and citations omitted).

175. *Id.*

176. *See, e.g.*, Babbitt v. Sweet Home Chapter of Cmtys. for a Great Or., 515 U.S. 687 (1995) (interpreting general causation language in the Endangered Species Act to incorporate proximate cause); Jerome B. Grubart, Inc. v. Great Lakes Dredge & Dock Co., 513 U.S. 527, 536 (1995) ("The [Admiralty Extension] Act uses the phrase 'caused by,' which more than one Court of

One conceivable view of OPA's NRD provisions is that by employing generic causation language, Congress "left a gap" for the implementing agency—NOAA—to fill regarding the amount of causation required for NRD, and that courts should defer to any "permissible" agency interpretation of the required level of causation. In the CERCLA context, the D.C. Circuit held that Congress left open the question of whether the statute affected the causation standard and that "[DOI's] reading of the Act—as retaining traditional causation analysis for determining whether a hazardous substance release caused a particular injury—is therefore permissible under *Chevron* Step Two."[177]

As applied to OPA, similar considerations support the application of proximate cause because NOAA considered and rejected lower standards of causation, and has also affirmatively stated in litigation that its regulations do not alter traditional legal standards of causation.[178]

For example, NOAA considered and rejected "but for" and "contributing cause" standards of causation during the rulemaking process. On January 7, 1994, NOAA issued a proposed rule that included a definition of "injury resulting from a discharge of oil."[179] For instances involving "direct exposure" to oil, NOAA proposed that the trustee show exposure, a pathway, and an adverse effect.[180] For instances of "indirect exposure," the proposed rule required the trustee to show an adverse effect (which could be diminished services) and provide that the adverse effect "would not have occurred *but for* the fact of the discharge or threat of a discharge."[181] In addition, the proposed rule stated that "where multiple factors may have contributed to an indivisible

---

Appeals has read as requiring what tort law has traditionally called 'proximate causation.'"); Brown v. Gardner, 513 U.S. 115, 119 (1994) (interpreting statute requiring the Department of Veterans Affairs (VA) to compensate veterans for injuries that occur "as result of" VA treatment as incorporating proximate cause "so as to narrow the class of compensable cases" and explaining that the "narrowing occurs by eliminating remote consequences").

177. Ohio v. U.S. Dep't of the Interior, 880 F.2d 432, 472–73 ("CERCLA is at best ambiguous on the question of whether the causation-of-injury standard under § 107(a)(C) must be less demanding than that of the common law. Consequently, we uphold Interior's plausible reading of CERCLA as adopting traditional causation standards in this context."); *see also* Kelley v. Envtl. Prot. Agency, 15 F.3d 1100, 1111 (D.C. Cir. 1994).

178. *See* Brief for Respondent at 25, Gen. Elec. Co. v. U.S. Dep't of Commerce, 128 F.3d 767 (1997) (No. 96-1096) 1997 WL 34647675, at *25 (stating that petitioners' "contention that NOAA has somehow altered traditional legal standards of causation is unfounded").

179. *See* Natural Resource Damage Assessments, 59 Fed. Reg. 1062, 1169 (proposed Jan. 7, 1994) (to be codified at 15 C.F.R. pt. 990).

180. *Id.* at 1169, 1178.

181. *Id.* (emphasis added).

injury to a natural resource and/or service, the discharge of oil may be considered a *contributing factor* to the injury."[182]

On June 22, 1994, NOAA issued a summary of public comments responding to the proposed rule.[183] It noted that questions had arisen about "the distinction between establishing 'liability' under OPA and proving 'damages,'" and sought additional comments regarding its definition of injuries "that result from such incident."[184] In particular, NOAA sought comments on whether its proposed rule "mingle[d] the concepts of 'injury' with 'causation,'" whether it should "provide a regulatory definition of 'injury resulting from . . . such incident,'" and whether "the 'contributing factor' test [should] be included in either 'acceptance criteria' or a definition of 'injury' or some other appropriate place in the regulations?"[185]

A year later, NOAA re-proposed the rule.[186] The re-proposed rule retained the standard for determining injury in cases of an actual discharge—that is, exposure, pathway, and adverse effect—but replaced the "but for" test for indirect exposure with the requirement that "for injuries resulting from response actions or incidents involving a substantial threat of a discharge, an injury to a natural resource or an impairment of use of a natural resource service has occurred as a result of the incident."[187] The re-proposed rule also eliminated the reference to the "contributing factor" test.

NOAA published the final rule on January 5, 1996;[188] it retained the same causation language as the re-proposed rule, but included responses to certain comments. In particular, NOAA noted that "[o]ne commenter requested that the rule state that an incident should be deemed the cause of an injury if the incident was a contributing factor to an indivisible injury, as provided in the 1994 proposal."[189] NOAA responded that it "*does not believe it is appropriate to advocate legal standards of causation in the rule.* Injuries must be determined to have occurred, then quantified relative to baseline, to be in accordance with the rule."[190]

---

182. *Id.* at 1178 (emphasis added).

183. *See* Natural Resource Damage Assessments, 59 Fed. Reg. 32,148 (summary of public comment June 22, 1994) (to be codified at 15 C.F.R. pt. 990).

184. *Id.* at 32,150.

185. *Id.*

186. *See* Natural Resource Damage Assessments, 60 Fed. Reg. 39,804 (proposed Aug. 3, 1995) (to be codified at 15 C.F.R. pt. 990).

187. *Id.* at 39,810; *see also id.* at 39,813, 39,831.

188. Natural Resource Damage Assessments, 61 Fed. Reg. 440 (Jan. 5, 1996) (to be codified at 15 C.F.R. pt. 990).

189. *Id.* at 479.

190. *Id.* (emphasis added).

The injury assessment procedures in the final rule require a trustee to establish whether there has been an injury ("an observable or measurable adverse change in a natural resource or impairment of a natural resource service") *and* either (1) "an injured natural resource has been *exposed* to the discharged oil, and a pathway can be established from the discharge to the exposed natural resource" *or* (2) "an injury to a natural resource or impairment of a natural resource service has occurred as a result of response actions or a substantial threat of a discharge of oil."[191] In cases of exposure, a "pathway" must "link[] the incident to the injuries," such as by showing "the sequence of events by which the discharged oil was transported from the incident and either came into direct physical contact with a natural resource, or caused an indirect injury."[192] The regulations do not define what is meant by an indirect injury, but NOAA's guidance documents state that an example would be a reduction in growth or reproduction in a population of fish-eating birds when their prey is reduced because of direct injury from the oil.[193]

In subsequent litigation, NOAA has taken the position that "traditional standards of causation" apply to NRDAs under OPA. Shortly after the final rule was promulgated, it was challenged by various entities on multiple grounds, including that it would allow trustees to assess liability without evidence that the responsible party actually caused the discharge, in violation of § 2702(a).[194] Petitioners challenging NOAA's regulations were concerned that NOAA simply required that trustees demonstrate that an injury exists, that the injured resource has been exposed directly or indirectly to the discharged oil, and that there is a pathway linking the discharge to the exposed resource, but that the "injury, exposure, pathway" requirements would not require a showing that the injury was actually caused by the discharged oil.[195] In its brief to the D.C. Circuit, NOAA asserted that one petitioner's "contention that

---

191. 15 C.F.R. § 990.51(b) (emphasis added).

192. *Id.* § 990.51(d).

193. *See* Damage Assessment & Restoration Program, Nat'l Oceanic & Atmospheric Admin., Injury Assessment Guidance Document for Natural Resource Damage Assessment Under the Oil Pollution Act of 1990 2–4 (1996).

194. *See* Gen. Elec. Co. v. U.S. Dep't of Commerce, 128 F.3d 767, 776 (D.C. Cir. 1997) (citing Brief for Industry Petitioners, 1997 WL 34647673, at *41 (June 24, 1997)).

195. *See* Joint Opening Brief of All Petitioners (Except American Institute of Marine Underwriters and the Water Quality Insurance Syndicate) and Supporting Intervenors at 41–42, *Gen. Elec. Co.*, 128 F.3d 767 (No. 96-1096), 1997 WL 34647673, at *41–42. This was the argument made by the Natural Resources Defense Council, as an intervenor in *Gen. Elec. Co. See* Brief for Intervenor Natural Resources Defense Council, Inc. at 10, *Gen. Elec. Co.*, 128 F.3d 767 (No. 96-1096), 1997 WL 34647677, at *10.

NOAA has altered traditional legal standards of causation is unfounded."[196] NOAA argued that "[t]hroughout the Preamble" it had "emphasized the importance of determining whether the injury resulted from the oil spill at issue," but that it was not appropriate for NOAA "to advocate legal standards of causation in the rule."[197]

NOAA also pointed out that the regulations require the trustee to "evaluate the linkage between the oil spill and injuries in order to determine which injuries should be included in the assessment."[198] The regulations' definition of injury would "prevent[] the inclusion of speculative injuries in an assessment by requiring that the effect in question be measurable or observable."[199] The exposure and pathway requirements "require[] the trustee to establish the physical connection between the incident and the injured resource," thereby "prevent[ing] the trustee from including in the assessment any injuries to resources not affected by the oil."[200] In addition, the injury determination requirements require that the trustees show, beyond exposure and pathway, "the mechanism by which injury occurred," which "emphasizes that the trustee must be able to document the connection between the oil and the injury."[201] Finally, the comparison to baseline "serves to screen out causes other than the oil spill as the spill is the only variable excluded from the baseline."[202]

Beyond these regulatory requirements, NOAA concluded that "[r]egardless of compliance with the Final Rule, . . . the trustee must establish causation to the satisfaction of the district court before liability can be imposed."[203] At oral argument, NOAA's counsel reiterated her understanding that trustees must prove causation and acknowledged that this interpretation of the final rule would bind the agency in any future proceedings.[204] Based on these binding representations, the D.C. Circuit held that the issue had been resolved.[205]

---

196. Brief for Respondent at 54, *Gen. Elec. Co.*, 128 F.3d 767 (No. 96-1096), 1997 WL 34647675, at *54.

197. *Id.* at *55 (citing and quoting 61 Fed. Reg. at 449, 479) ("Evidence supporting the linkage between the incident and injury must be established to demonstrate injury."); *see also id.* at *55 n.44 (citing 61 Fed. Reg. at 467) ("NOAA agrees that OPA intends that responsible parties be held liable only for restoration needed to redress the injuries *caused by* specific incidents." (emphasis added)).

198. *Id.* at *55 (citing 15 C.F.R. § 990.51(f)).

199. *Id.* at *56.

200. *Id.* at *56–57.

201. *Id.* at *57.

202. *Id.*

203. *Id.* at *59.

204. *See* Gen. Elec. Co. v. U.S. Dep't of Commerce, 128 F.3d 767, 780–81 (app. to the opinion) (D.C. Cir. 1997).

205. *See id.* at 776–77.

In light of the foregoing, even if a court were to determine that Congress left a gap for NOAA to fill with respect to the causation requirements for NRD, NOAA has affirmatively declined to fill that gap with a new causation standard, and instead has taken the position that common law causation standards apply unaffected by the implementing regulations. Moreover, because NOAA has (1) taken the position that traditional common law causation standards apply, and (2) specifically withdrawn regulations that would have imposed "but for" or "contributing factor" causation standards, the regulatory history supports the application of proximate cause to OPA NRD claims.

I. Baseline

A primary objective of the NRD regime is restoration to baseline: namely, the return of injured natural resources to a condition that would have existed had the release or discharge not occurred.[206] The apparent simplicity of this objective, however, is betrayed by the complexities of the natural world, and further complicated by the reality that natural resources endure insults from numerous human and non-human sources. As a result, the evaluation of baseline frequently is extraordinarily difficult and time-consuming. For a trustee, the baseline analysis is critical for measuring damages and complying with the assessment regulations. For a PRP wishing to limit its exposure to the actual damage that it caused, the baseline analysis presents one of the most promising areas for defending an NRD claim.

The "baseline" concept, like the issue of causation, is rooted in the language of CERCLA and OPA, which impose liability only where damages "result from" a release or incident.[207] While causation relates to a defendant's liability, baseline relates to the quantification of damages—baseline does not ask about the cause of a current impaired condition, but about the condition of the resources absent the release.

As defined in the CERCLA regulations, baseline is "the condition or conditions that would have existed at the assessment area had the . . . release . . . not occurred."[208] OPA's regulations define baseline as "the condition of the natural resources and services that would have existed had the incident not

---

206. *See, e.g.*, 15 C.F.R. § 990.10 (the goal of OPA "is achieved through the return of the injured natural resources and services to baseline and compensation for interim losses"); 15 C.F.R. § 990.30 ("Baseline means the condition of the natural resources and services that would have existed had the incident not occurred."); *see also* 43 C.F.R. § 11.14(e).

207. *See* 33 U.S.C. § 2702(a); 42 U.S.C. § 9607(a)(C).

208. 43 C.F.R. § 11.14(e).

occurred."[209] In other words, the baseline analysis forces the trustee to tease out those injuries that would have existed independent of the release. As discussed later in the chapter (and also in Chapter 5), this analysis is complicated by the need to evaluate injuries caused by natural forces, human actions, and changes over time. For example, in the case of a spill of chemicals into an urban river and a subsequent fish kill, it is not enough to say the release was the "but for" cause of the fish kill. In addition, the trustees must measure the state of the fish population prior to the release, usually in terms of services provided, as well as the expected condition of the population now had the release not occurred.[210] Then, pursuant to the regulations, the trustees should claim damages only for the difference between the baseline condition and the post-release condition.

The most obvious obstacle to defining baseline is the fact that other human activity likely impacted the assessment area. In addition, the trustee must work to ascertain not only the condition of the natural resources prior to the release but also what condition the resources would be in had the release not occurred.

In order to understand the baseline, therefore, a trustee must consider other environmental and human forces that may have caused the observed injury, as well as how the services would have changed over time. As stated eloquently by the court in *Coeur d'Alene Tribe v. ASARCO Inc.* (although not while discussing baseline):

> To put this case in proper perspective, one has to review the history of over 100 years of mining in the Coeur d'Alene Basin, what efforts were made to deal with the problems as they became evident, what direction the Courts and the State of Idaho legislature gave to interested parties, what contribution, if any, the Federal Government and Tribe made to the conditions, how urbanization, forest fires and floods also impacted the environment, how settlements between certain parties may have changed the landscape and what are the observations and experiences of the people who live in the Coeur d'Alene Basin today.[211]

---

209. 15 C.F.R. § 990.30.

210. The CERCLA regulations define services as "the physical and biological functions performed by the resource including the human uses of those functions. These services are the result of the physical, chemical, or biological quality of the resource." 43 C.F.R. § 11.14(nn). The OPA regulations define services as "the functions performed by a natural resource for the benefit of another natural resource and/or the public." 15 C.F.R. § 990.30.

211. 280 F. Supp. 2d 1094, 1101 (D. Idaho 2003).

While the challenges to defining baseline are enormous, trustees have a potentially potent countermeasure: they may choose not to define it at all. As discussed later, the statute does not explicitly require a baseline assessment. The trustees may argue that the regulatory hurdles described previously are voluntary and are "not intended to affect the recoverability of natural resource damages when recoveries are sought other than in accordance with [the regulations]."[212] On the other hand, if trustees decline to follow the regulations, they will also waive their right to rely upon the rebuttable presumption, discussed in the next section. Furthermore, as a practical matter, given that the trustees have so often informally relied upon the regulations, they may not be able to distance themselves from the baseline requirements.

The viability of the strategy of choosing not to define the baseline has not been judicially tested. In a case involving a challenge by a defendant's insurers to a consent decree that resolved the defendant's NRD liability, one of the insurers, Exxon Mobil Corporation, argued that the settlement was unreasonable because the NRD estimate was flawed due to the EPA consultant's failure to conduct a baseline analysis.[213] The court was not persuaded—instead finding that "the Government's estimate for NRD sensibly derives from a plausible interpretation of the record."[214] The court noted that the government had reduced the amount of NRD "[i]n light of the uncertainty and significant risks involved in litigating the case" and that the record indicated that the consultants had considered baseline conditions.[215]

Although there are no court decisions scrutinizing a trustee's baseline calculation, a bankruptcy court has approved a settlement that resolved NRD claims over the debtor's parent's baseline-related objections.[216] The parent company had argued, among other things, that the trustees had overstated damages because they had not considered certain habitat characteristics in the development of the baseline for aquatic injuries. The bankruptcy court appeared to find it unnecessary to wade into the record, noting that whether the settlement was substantively fair did not require "that a responsible party bear no more than some mathematical calculation of harm."[217] The court

---

212. 15 C.F.R. § 990.11; *see also* 43 C.F.R. § 11.10.

213. United States v. Cornell-Dubilier Elecs., Inc., No. 12–5407 (JLL), 2014 WL 4978635, at *11 (D.N.J. Oct. 3, 2014).

214. *Id.*

215. *Id.*

216. Findings of Fact and Conclusions of Law on Debtors' Motion for Order Approving Settlement of Environmental Claims, *In re* ASARCO LLC, No. 05-21207, 2009 WL 8176641 (Bankr. S.D. Tex. June 5, 2009).

217. *Id.* at *42.

noted that the parent company was not a responsible party and therefore did not have any risk of disproportionate liability under environmental law.

The regulatory frameworks and mechanics for calculating baseline are discussed in more depth in Chapters 4 and 5.

J. The Rebuttable Presumption

Trustees need not follow the assessment procedures prescribed in the CERCLA and OPA regulations. Should trustees choose to adhere to these regulations, however, both CERCLA and OPA accord their assessments the force and effect of a rebuttable presumption.[218] One district court has said the presumption "applies to the assessment of damages by the Trustees and not just the damages demand allocations."[219] In other words, according to this court, the rebuttable presumption extends not only to the trustees' valuation assigned to the damage that did occur but also to the trustees' assessment of what injuries resulted from responsible parties' actions.

A rebuttable presumption does not alter the burden of proof, but "merely operates to shift the burden of production to the opposing party to rebut the presumption, by offering evidence which would support a finding that the presumed fact does not exist."[220] Thus, the burden of proof in an NRD challenge remains with the plaintiff trustee.[221]

The questions—as yet largely untested in the courts—remain: How does the rebuttable presumption work in practice? How closely must the trustee follow the regulations in order to gain the benefit of the presumption? This

---

218. 42 U.S.C. § 9607(f)(2)(C); 33 U.S.C. § 2706(e)(2); *see* New York v. Next Millennium Realty, LLC, 160 F. Supp. 3d 485, 523 (E.D.N.Y. 2016) (New York State not entitled to rebuttable presumption where it had not performed a NRDA in accordance with the regulations, but "the absence of the rebuttable presumption neither requires dismissal of the State's NRD Claim, nor precludes granting summary judgment in favor of the State on its claim seeking judgment declaring that [defendants] are liable").

219. United States v. ASARCO Inc., No. CV 96-0122-N-EJL, CV 91-342-N-EJL, 1998 WL 1799392 (D. Idaho Mar. 31, 1998).

220. Montana v. Atl. Richfield Co., No. 6:83-cv-00317-SEH, slip op. at 15–16 (D. Mont. Mar. 3, 1997) (citing St. Mary's Honor Center v. Hicks, 509 U.S. 502, 506–09 (1993)). The preamble to NOAA's final rule interpreted the presumption to impose on responsible parties "the burdens of presenting alternative evidence on damages and of persuading the fact finder that the damages presented by the trustees are not an appropriate measure of damages." Gen. Elec. Co. v. U.S. Dep't of Commerce, 128 F.3d 767, 772 (D.C. Cir. 1997) (quoting 61 Fed. Reg. 440, 443 (Jan. 5, 1996)).

221. *Gen. Elec. Co.*, 128 F.3d at 772; *see also* 29 C.F.R. § 18.301 (presumption "does not shift . . . the burden of proof in the sense of the risk of nonpersuasion, which remains throughout the trial upon the party on whom it was originally cast.").

question is not academic, since observers in the government have conceded that "there are few instances where there has been strict adherence to the steps outlined therein."[222]

A related question is whether the trustees may rely on selected parts of the regulations while ignoring others. For example, it is not clear whether trustees can rely upon the per se criteria for injury in the NRD regulations,[223] if they are not otherwise applying the NRDA regulations. While this issue has not been adequately tested in the courts, a responsible party may be able to argue that it is inappropriate for a trustee to "cherry pick" the parts of the regulations that help its case while choosing to avoid the other parts of the regulations, including public participation, baseline determination, and other requirements. In *Coeur d'Alene Tribe v. ASARCO Inc.*, the court relied, in part, on exceedances of water quality criteria for finding the existence of an injury while explicitly withholding judgment on whether the trustees' assessments were conducted in accordance with the regulations.[224] Specifically, Judge Lodge stated: "While the Court will grant due deference to the agency's definitions [of injury], the Court does not find it is bound to such definitions. . . ."[225]

Another practical question related to the presumption is whether it matters at all. Since contested NRD cases are scientifically complex and since the presumption is rebuttable, the court will have to hear and weigh competing expert testimony. Further, under the NOAA regulations, trustees must first prove that their damage assessments are "reliable and valid for the particular incident"[226] before they may take advantage of the presumption.[227] Moreover, there are no reported cases where the trustee has successfully relied upon the presumption to overcome a litigated dispute.

In two cases, however, courts have noted the absence of evidence of compliance with NRD regulations in their rejections of NRD settlement agreements. In one case, the district court noted that the State of Utah had chosen not to follow federal regulations, noting that its "failure to do so eliminates the presumption of validity and correctness which otherwise the State would enjoy."[228] The court went on to find that the settlement was not just and fair or consistent with CERCLA. In the other case, a district court found that the

---

222. Nat'l Res. Damage Assessment & Restoration Advisory Comm., Question 1 Subcommittee Initial Response for Presentation 2 (Mar. 2, 2006).

223. *See, e.g.*, 43 C.F.R. §§ 11.62(b)(1)(i), (iii); (c)(1)(i), (iii); (d)(1); (e)(1); (f)(1)(ii).

224. 280 F. Supp. 2d 1094, 1122–23.

225. *Id.* at 1122 n.22.

226. 15 C.F.R. § 990.27(a)(3).

227. Gen. Elec. Co. v. U.S. Dep't of Commerce, 128 F.3d 767, 772 (D.C. Cir. 1997).

228. Utah v. Kennecott Corp., 801 F. Supp. 553, 567–68 (D. Utah 1992).

proponents of an NRD settlement had failed to meet their burden of producing evidence that would enable the court to determine whether the settlement agreement was fair, reasonable, and consistent with the goals of CERCLA.[229] The court said it would not presume the validity or correctness of the trustee's quantification of damages since there was no evidence that the assessment was performed in accordance with the NRD regulations.[230]

Notwithstanding these judicial rejections of settlements where trustees had not complied with the NRD regulations, the statutory presumption has had little impact in NRD litigation to date even though the NRD regulations continue to play a large role in the development of NRDAs.[231]

Nonetheless, as part of litigation preparation, a prospective defendant should systematically evaluate all trustee actions for compliance with both the procedural and substantive requirements of the regulations pursuant to which their assessment is proceeding. Where the trustee has failed to comply, the defendant should be prepared to assert a case accordingly. Potential *substantive* areas of noncompliance by the trustees include data collection (using methods not reasonably expected to assist in an injury assessment); baseline determination (failing to robustly compare resource losses to baseline conditions); injury quantification (improperly determining injury based upon extrapolation or assumption as opposed to an "observable or measurable" adverse change); and restoration assessment (failing to account for natural recovery and/or selecting restoration options that are not cost-effective). Potential *procedural* areas of noncompliance by the trustees include failure to properly maintain an administrative record; failure to meaningfully coordinate with the defendant; failure to sufficiently document assessment decisions; and failure to provide adequate opportunities for public comment.

---

229. Comm'r of the Dep't of Planning & Nat. Res. v. Century Alumina Co., 2008 WL 4693550, at *7 (D.V.I. Oct. 22, 2008).

230. *Id.* at *4. The court had other concerns, however, beyond the absence of the rebuttable presumption, including that the amount the defendant would pay was only approximately 1 percent of the damages the trustee had preliminarily quantified.

231. *See* United States v. Montrose Chem. Corp. of Cal., 835 F. Supp. 534, 541 (C.D. Cal. 1993) (case in which defendant sought to compel trustees' full compliance with the NRD regulations or force them to forgo rebuttable presumption but where trustees ultimately decided not to avail themselves of rebuttable presumption), *rev'd on other grounds*, 104 F.3d 1507 (9th Cir. 1997); Idaho v. S. Refrigerated Transp., Inc., No. 88-1279, 1991 WL 22479 (D. Idaho Jan. 24, 1991) (post-trial ruling did not mention rebuttable presumption in discussion of burden of proof, perhaps because DOI's assessment regulations were still very new at the time this action was initiated in the fall of 1988, and the plaintiff was a state, not a federal, trustee).

K. Standard of Review

Neither CERCLA nor OPA has a provision addressing the standard or scope of judicial review of trustees' NRDAs. Trustee agencies have argued that the statute requires judges to limit their review to the administrative record, employing an arbitrary and capricious standard.[232] Courts who have addressed this issue have rejected the agencies' argument, relying in part on the provision for a rebuttable presumption and holding that trustees' assessments are subject to de novo review and that that review encompasses the entire evidentiary record, not just the record before the agency.

In *Montana v. ARCO*, the court held that administrative record review was incompatible with (1) CERCLA's statutory scheme, particularly the statute's provision of a rebuttable presumption, and (2) the defendants' right to a jury trial. The court reasoned that record review and the rebuttable presumption were incompatible, insofar as the two employ "divergent rules of evidence": Record review shifts the burden of proof to the defendant to prove that the trustees' determination is arbitrary and capricious, while the rebuttable presumption keeps the ultimate burden of proof with the plaintiff.[233] Moreover, stated the court, record review would render the rebuttable presumption superfluous, as utilizing record review "would automatically presume the validity of the NRD assessment."[234] Besides the rebuttable presumption, the court noted that when Congress amended CERCLA, it provided for administrative record review for selection of remediation alternatives, yet did not add such a provision for NRD. This omission, according to the court, signified that Congress

---

232. *See* Montana v. Atl. Richfield Co. (*ARCO*), No. 6:83-cv-00317-SEH (D. Mont. Mar. 3, 1997); United States v. ASARCO Inc., No. CV 96-0122-N-EJL, CV 91-342-N-EJL, 1998 WL 1799392 (D. Idaho Mar. 31, 1998). As the court in *ARCO* explained:

> Under an administrative record review, the court would review the administrative record created by the [government] under the traditional administrative model embodied in the Administrative Procedure Act, 5 U.S.C. §§ 701–706, giving substantial deference to the [government's] selection of appropriate restoration alternatives and determination of recoverable damages.
>
> [The defendant] could challenge the [government's] selection of restoration alternatives and determination of damages based only on the information compiled in the administrative record. The [government's] determination of damages would be set aside only if it was found to be arbitrary and capricious.

ARCO, slip op. at 8 n.11.

233. *Id.* at 15–16; *see also* Chapter 7, Section D.2 (in-depth discussion of this case).

234. *ARCO*, slip op. at 16.

intended de novo review of trustees' damage assessments—review not limited to the administrative record but including all evidence presentable at trial.[235]

Finally, the court found that record review under an arbitrary and capricious standard was contrary to the right to a jury trial, which the court established NRD defendants could assert. The court reasoned:

> The record review mandates that courts give substantial deference to the pretrial factual determinations of the administrative agency, whereas the right to a jury trial guaranteed under the Seventh Amendment "reserves the weighing of evidence and the finding of facts exclusively to the jury." Because a record review infringes upon the jury's role as the ultimate and independent fact finder, it necessarily violates the Seventh Amendment.[236]

In *United States v. ASARCO Inc.*, the court rejected plaintiffs' arguments regarding the scope and standard of review on similar grounds.[237] In addition, the court found that record review under the Administrative Procedure Act (APA) was not warranted, as plaintiffs United States and Coeur d'Alene Tribe were not "agencies" within the meaning of the APA, and an assessment was not a final "agency action" as defined by the statute.[238]

After the *Deepwater Horizon* incident, the Obama administration proposed legislation that would have replaced OPA's rebuttable presumption with a provision for judicial review based on the administrative record applying the standards of the APA. The House of Representatives approved a bill containing the provision, but it was not taken up by the Senate.[239] The application of APA standards to NRD claims would face legal and practical hurdles,[240] including possibly interference with defendants' right to a jury trial, the next and final topic discussed in this chapter.

---

235. *Id.* at 16–17.

236. *Id.* at 23 (citations omitted).

237. United States v. ASARCO Inc., No. CV 96-0122-N-EJL, CV 91-342-N-EJL, 1998 WL 1799392, at *1–3 (D. Idaho Mar. 31, 1998).

238. *Id.* at *4.

239. Consolidated Land, Energy, and Aquatic Resources Act of 2010, H.R. 3534, 111th Cong. § 706 (2010).

240. *See generally* Craig H. Allen, *Proving Natural Resource Damage under OPA 90: Out with the Rebuttable Presumption, in with APA-Style Judicial Review?*, 85 Tul. L. Rev. 1039 (2011).

L. The Right to a Jury in an NRD Case

1. Seventh Amendment

A party in a civil case only has a jury right if a statute confers the right or if the Seventh Amendment to the U.S. Constitution applies. OPA does not grant the right to a jury trial.[241] Nor does CERCLA.[242] The right to a jury trial in an NRD case therefore turns on whether the parties have a constitutional right to a jury.

The Seventh Amendment provides that "[i]n suits at common law, where the value in controversy shall exceed twenty dollars, the right of trial by jury shall be preserved."[243] The Supreme Court has found that the amendment preserves the right to a jury as it existed when the amendment was ratified, and also provides the right to a jury for statutory claims if the statute "creates legal rights and remedies, enforceable in an action for damages in the ordinary courts of law."[244] To determine whether a right to a jury exists under a statute, courts (1) compare the action "to 18th-century actions brought in the courts of England prior to the merger of the courts of law and equity,"[245] and (2) determine whether the remedy sought is legal or equitable in nature.[246] Where there are issues common to both legal and equitable claims, the court's discretion is narrow and must be exercised to preserve the jury right wherever possible.[247]

2. NRD under OPA and CERCLA

How CERCLA and OPA define the scope of NRD is important to whether there is a right to a jury trial.

As a reminder, under OPA, NRD includes "[d]amages for injury to, destruction of, loss of, or loss of use of, natural resources, including the reasonable costs of assessing the damage."[248] The damages are calculated by adding

---

241. S. Port Marine, LLC v. Gulf Oil Ltd. P'ship, 234 F.3d 58, 62 (1st Cir. 2000).

242. *In re* Acushnet River & New Bedford Harbor: Proceedings re Alleged PCB Pollution, 712 F. Supp. 994, 996 (D. Mass. 1989) ("It is clear that Congress, in enacting the Comprehensive Environmental Compensation and Liability Act . . . , did not statutorily provide individuals charged under its provisions with a right to a jury trial.").

243. U.S. Const. amend. VII.

244. Curtis v. Loether, 415 U.S. 189, 194 (1974).

245. Tull v. United States, 481 U.S. 412, 417 (1987).

246. *Id.* at 417–18.

247. Beacon Theatres, Inc. v. Westover, 359 U.S. 500, 510 (1959).

248. 33 U.S.C. § 2702(b)(2)(A).

together (1) "the cost of restoring, rehabilitating, replacing, or acquiring the equivalent of, the damaged natural resources"; (2) "the diminution in value of those natural resources pending restoration"; and (3) "the reasonable cost of assessing those damages."[249] OPA limits the use of damages collected, such that the money "shall be retained by the trustee in a revolving trust account, without further appropriation, for use only to reimburse or pay costs incurred by the trustee under subsection (c) [of this section] with respect to the damaged natural resources."[250]

The NRD provisions of CERCLA are similar, providing for recovery of "damages for injury to, destruction of, or loss of natural resources, including the reasonable costs of assessing such injury, destruction, or loss."[251] The use of damages collected is also limited in scope; they may only be used "to restore, replace, or acquire the equivalent of such natural resources."[252]

3. Federal NRD Jury Trial Precedent[253]

The only court to address whether NRD claims under OPA trigger the right to a jury upheld the defendant's request for a jury trial.[254] In *Viking*, the United States sought NRD arising from the cleanup of a tank battery oil spill near Galveston, Texas. The defendant sought a jury, and the United States filed a motion to strike the jury demand.[255] The United States argued that NRD claims are restitutionary, and therefore the remedy is equitable in nature, and that there was no right to a jury trial.[256] The court ruled that at least one component of NRD—diminution in value of impacted natural resources pending restoration—was legal in nature because it amounts to compensating the plaintiff for injury to property and is similar to recoveries in the classically

---

249. *Id.* § 2706(d)(1).

250. *Id.* § 2706(f).

251. 42 U.S.C. § 9607(a)(4)(C).

252. *Id.* § 9607(f)(1).

253. Chapter 7 includes discussion about one state court jury trial, the *American Trader Spill* case, as well as one federal case in which jury instructions were submitted (but a trial never occurred), the *Elkem Metals/Ohio River* case.

254. *See* United States v. Viking Res., Inc., 607 F. Supp. 2d 808 (S.D. Tex. 2009).

255. *Id.* at 828; *see also* Chapter 7, Section D.5 (in-depth discussion of this case).

256. With respect to removal costs, which the United States also sought, the court found that CERCLA cases consistently held them to be a form of restitution—an equitable remedy—for which the right to a jury trial is not preserved. *Viking*, 607 F. Supp. at 829 (citing Hatco Corp. v. W.R. Grace & Co. Conn., 59 F.3d 400, 412 (3d Cir. 1995); United States v. Ne. Pharm. & Chem. Co., 810 F.2d 726, 749 (8th Cir. 1986); United States v. Lang, 870 F. Supp. 722, 723 (E.D. Tex. 1994)); *see also* Int'l Marine Carriers v. Oil Spill Liab. Trust Fund, 903 F. Supp. 1097, 1102–03 (S.D. Tex. 1994) (suit to recover removal costs under OPA constitutes an equitable action).

legal causes of action in nuisance or trespass.[257] The *Viking* court determined that even if the other elements of NRD (e.g., the costs to restore, rehabilitate, replace, or acquire the equivalent of lost resources, and costs of assessment) are equitable, the one legal component triggers the Seventh Amendment's right to jury trial.[258] It also held that the factual issues of a legal nature must be tried to a jury, even if they were also relevant to the equitable components of NRD.[259] The court therefore held that the entire case would be tried to a jury for purposes of efficiency, but the jury's verdict would be considered advisory for the equitable issues.[260]

No appellate courts have addressed the NRD jury trial issue under the analogous provisions of CERCLA, but several district courts have. And the *Viking* court's ruling is consistent with the holdings of all but one of the district courts to address the jury trial issue in the context of NRD claims under CERCLA. For example, in *In re Acushnet River*,[261] the court concluded that NRD are essentially equivalent to money damages recoverable in tort for injury to property which at common law would be pursued under either a nuisance or trespass theory, and for which damages would be the diminution in value and loss of use.[262] But the court adopted a narrow definition of NRD as consisting only of "the value of the resources that are forever lost . . . ; the lost use of such resources over time; and the costs of assessing how much is lost forever or how much lost use over time there has been."[263] It considered the costs expended to restore, replace, or rehabilitate natural resources to be response costs, not NRD.[264] The court in *Viking* noted that under OPA, NRD explicitly includes the costs of restoring, rehabilitating, replacing, or acquiring the equivalent of damaged resources.[265]

---

257. *Viking*, 607 F. Supp. at 832.

258. *Id.*

259. *Id.*

260. *Id.*

261. *In re* Acushnet River & New Bedford Harbor: Proceedings re Alleged PCB Pollution, 712 F. Supp. 994 (D. Mass. 1989).

262. *Id.* at 999.

263. *Id.*

264. *Id.*

265. United States v. Viking Res., Inc., 607 F. Supp. 2d 808, 830–31; *accord* Montana v. Atl. Richfield Co. (*ARCO*), No. 6:83-cv-00317-SEH, slip op. at 18 (D. Mont. Mar. 3, 1997) (holding that the rights and remedies involved in NRD actions are characteristic of an action at law and thus invoke the right to a trial by jury); New York v. Lashins Arcade Co., 881 F. Supp. 101, 104 (S.D.N.Y. 1995) (finding that recovery for loss of natural resources is similar to an action in tort or trespass, and therefore the jury trial right was preserved for NRD actions under CERCLA).

However, in one CERCLA case decided in the 1980s, the district court concluded that NRD relief was equitable "for the same reasons that recovery of . . . response costs is considered equitable relief," which is that they were "in the nature of restitution."[266]

4. Potential Reasons Why a Jury Demand Could Be Denied

In a large NRD trial, there are many reasons why a court might conclude that a jury trial is not appropriate. This section outlines four such reasons.

a. NRD Are Restitutionary

One of the exceptions to the general rule that money damages constitute legal relief is when the relief is restitutionary.[267] Legal remedies provide a plaintiff with "substitutionary relief" in the form of compensation for an injury that was not originally monetary.[268] Restitutionary relief, in contrast, is awarded to restore the plaintiff to the status quo and prevent unjust enrichment of the defendant, and is measured by the defendant's unjust gains.[269]

In applying this distinction, the *ARCO* court concluded that CERCLA NRD actions are legal because they focus on the loss suffered by the public, and the claim is quantified from the standpoint of the plaintiff (the trustee).[270] In addition, unlike restitutionary awards of response costs that cover expenses that have already been incurred, a trustee may recover money for future restoration.[271]

There is an argument, however, that the *ARCO* court's analysis undervalues the significance of the provision of CERCLA (which is similar to the one found in OPA) restricting the use of damage awards to restorative purposes. The United States argued (unsuccessfully) in the *ARCO* and *Viking* cases that because the recovered funds are exclusively used for the restoration, replacement, or acquisition of the equivalent of natural resources, the claims are fundamentally restitutionary in nature. The damages essentially provide in-kind relief to the public.

The legislative histories of both CERCLA and OPA also support the restitutionary nature of NRD. With respect to CERCLA, the record states that

---

266. United States v. Wade, 653 F. Supp. 11, 13 (E.D. Pa. 1984).
267. *See ARCO*, slip op. at 18 (quoting Chauffeurs, Teamsters & Helpers, Local 391 v. Terry, 494 U.S. 558, 564 (1990)).
268. *ARCO*, slip op. at 20.
269. *Id.*
270. *Id.* at 21.
271. *Id.* (citing 42 U.S.C. § 9607(f)(1)).

"[t]estimony also indicated that it was appropriate and necessary for . . . trustee[s] . . . to seek restitution for such damages or restoration of such resources."[272] With respect to OPA, the legislative history suggests that Congress was dissatisfied with the traditional measure of "legal" damages, emphasizing that the bill made "clear that forests are more than board feet of lumber, and that seals and sea otters are more than just commodities traded on the market."[273]

The costs of assessing damages and the costs of restoring, rehabilitating, replacing, or acquiring the equivalent of the injured resources are also remarkably similar to response or removal costs, which multiple courts have held to be equitable under CERCLA. Awards for response costs and NRD both fund projects to restore the environment.

b. Public Rights Doctrine

The public rights doctrine involves an inquiry into whether Congress has the power to remove a suit from the jurisdiction of Article III courts (and therefore from the Seventh Amendment's applicability) and whether Congress has done so in a particular case.[274] The Supreme Court has long held that the Seventh Amendment does not apply to administrative agencies:

> At least in cases in which "public rights" are being litigated [—] *e.g.*, cases in which the Government sues in its sovereign capacity to enforce public rights created by statutes within the power of Congress to enact [—] the Seventh Amendment does not prohibit Congress from assigning the factfinding function and initial adjudication to an administrative forum with which the jury would be incompatible.[275]

As explained by the Supreme Court in *Granfinanciera*, public rights "arise between the Government and persons subject to its authority in connection with the performance of the constitutional functions of the executive or legislative departments."[276]

---

272. S. Rep. No. 848, at 518, 96th Cong., 2d Sess. 84 (1980); *see* Ohio v. United States Dep't of the Interior, 880 F.2d 432, 444 (D.C. Cir. 1989) (stating there is a "paramount restorative purpose for imposing damages").

273. S. Rep. No. 94, 101st Cong., 1st Sess. 15 (1989), *reprinted in* 1990 U.S.C.C.A.N. 722, 737.

274. *See* Granfinanciera, S.A. v. Nordberg, 492 U.S. 33, 42 (1989).

275. Atlas Roofing Co. v. Occupational Safety & Health Review Comm'n, 430 U.S. 442, 450 (1977); *see also* Sasser v. Adm'r, U.S. Envtl. Prot. Agency, 990 F.2d 127, 130 (4th Cir. 1993) ("[g]enerally speaking, the Seventh Amendment does not apply to disputes over statutory public rights").

276. *Granfinanciera*, 492 U.S. at 51 n.8 (quoting Crowell v. Benson, 285 U.S. 22, 50 (1932)).

In addition, the court in *Granfinanciera* ruled that public rights for which Congress *may* assign adjudication to administrative agencies or courts of equity are also excluded from the Seventh Amendment:

> [I]f the action *must be* tried under the auspices of an Article III court, then the Seventh Amendment affords the parties a right to a jury trial whenever the cause of action is legal in nature. Conversely, if Congress *may* assign the adjudication of a statutory cause of action to a non-Article III tribunal, then the Seventh Amendment poses no independent bar to the adjudication of that action by a nonjury factfinder.[277]

In NRD actions, there is no "private right" at stake. The trustees act on behalf of the public to obtain money that must be used to restore the environment for the benefit of the public. Congress arguably *could* have assigned claims involving NRD to non-Article III courts, as public lands and public health are among the matters for which Congress may create administrative agencies.[278] Even though Congress has not so assigned the NRD process, the fact that it *may* do so could potentially be sufficient pursuant to the Supreme Court's reasoning in *Granfinanciera*.

In *ARCO*, however, the court expressly rejected this argument in the context of CERCLA because Congress did not, in fact, delegate authority to the administrative agencies. Instead, Congress vested the federal district courts with exclusive jurisdiction over all claims under CERCLA.[279] OPA also provides that federal district courts have exclusive original jurisdiction over all cases under the statute, save in limited circumstances when state courts have jurisdiction.[280] Other than *ARCO*, no other courts have addressed how the public rights doctrine may affect the right to a jury trial of NRD claims.

c. Admiralty Jurisdiction

The Seventh Amendment does not preserve the right to a jury trial for cases in admiralty.[281] To determine if the government's NRD claims would fall under admiralty jurisdiction, the court would evaluate whether the claims were analogous to historical causes of action in admiralty.[282] The crux of the

---

277. *Id.* at 53–54 (emphasis added).

278. Austin v. Shalala, 994 F.2d 1170, 1177 (5th Cir. 1993) (striking jury demand based on public rights doctrine).

279. *See* Montana v. Atl. Richfield Co., No. CV-83-317-HLN-PGH, 1997 U.S. Dist. LEXIS 24671, at *34 n.28 (D. Mont. Feb. 28, 1997 (decided), Mar. 3, 1997 (filed)).

280. 33 U.S.C. § 2717(b)–(c).

281. Tull v. United States, 481 U.S. 412, 417 (1987).

282. *See* S. Port Marine, LLC v. Gulf Oil Ltd. P'ship, 234 F.3d 58, 62 (1st Cir. 2000).

analysis is the "locality test," which asks if the tort occurred "wholly" in navigable waters.[283] Admiralty jurisdiction historically only applied to injuries that occurred entirely in navigable waters.[284]

No court has addressed whether NRD claims satisfy this standard. In *South Port Marine*, the First Circuit held that the plaintiff dock owner was entitled to a jury trial of claims under OPA for damages to a marina stemming from a gasoline spill.[285] The court reasoned that the marina was an "extension of land" to which traditional admiralty jurisdiction would not apply. Relying on the locality test, the court in *Clausen v. M/V New Carissa* held that owners of oyster beds were entitled to a jury trial under OPA for damages resulting from the death of several million oysters following an oil spill.[286] The court reasoned that the oyster operation was more similar to farming than fishing, a traditional maritime activity.[287]

d. Complexity of NRD Cases

A trial of a large NRD claim is extraordinarily complex, in some cases lasting for several weeks, if not longer. When confronted with similarly byzantine issues, some courts, but not all, have held that the Seventh Amendment does not guarantee a right to trial by jury.

The Supreme Court, in *Ross v. Bernhard*,[288] provided the primary basis for considering complexity in a jury determination. The case involved a derivative suit brought by corporate stockholders seeking an accounting by the defendant directors and brokers for their alleged conversion of corporation assets. The court stated in a footnote that as a tertiary issue, a court could consider "the practical abilities and limitations of juries" in determining the applicability of the Seventh Amendment right to trial by jury.[289] In deciding *Ross*, however, the Supreme Court did not refer to this factor as playing a part in the ultimate decision.

---

283. *Id.* at 63.

284. *Id.*

285. *Id.* at 63–64.

286. 171 F. Supp. 2d 1127, 1135 (D. Or. 2001).

287. *Id.* Because of the uncertainty regarding whether damages to an oyster farm sound in law or in admiralty, the court made separate findings and conclusions, noting that if its "findings coincide with the jury's, the issue will be moot. If the findings differ, and the Court of Appeals agrees with defendants that the plaintiffs were not entitled to a jury trial, there will be no need for a new trial or a remand." *Id.* at 1135 n.6.

288. 396 U.S. 531 (1970).

289. *Id.* at 538 n.10.

Following *Ross*, the Third Circuit, in *In re Japanese Electronic Products Antitrust Litigation*, a complex antitrust matter filed by various electronics manufacturers against competing Japanese and American corporations, balanced arguments regarding Fifth Amendment due process and Seventh Amendment right to trial by jury, ultimately holding that "the most reasonable accommodation between the requirements of the [two amendments is] a denial of jury trial when a jury will not be able to perform its task of rational decisionmaking with a reasonable understanding of the evidence and the relevant legal standards."[290]

Similarly, the Sixth Circuit, in *Hyde Properties v. McCoy*,[291] an interpleader action that turned on the accounting procedures used to list the assets and liabilities of a corporation, held that due to the complexity of the case "a jury is not especially well-qualified to dispose of such issues and that a nonjury trial of the issues is both more efficient and more likely to produce a just result."[292]

A related consideration, adopted by a limited number of courts, is that if the complexity of a case would lead to an unacceptably long trial for purposes of impaneling a jury, the jury demand should be denied.[293]

---

290. *In re* Japanese Elec. Products Antitrust Litig., 631 F.2d 1069, 1086 (3d Cir. 1980).

291. 507 F.2d 301 (6th Cir. 1974).

292. *Id.* at 306; *see also* Bernstein v. Universal Pictures, Inc., 79 F.R.D. 59 (S.D.N.Y. 1978); Sec. & Exch. Comm'n v. Associated Minerals, Inc., 75 F.R.D. 724, 726 (E.D. Mich. 1977) ("the issues of fraud and noncompliance with the registration provisions of the securities laws presented in this action are indeed complex and for this reason are not especially suited for resolution by a jury."). Note, however, that the Ninth Circuit has explicitly rejected this argument. *See In re* U.S. Fin. Sec. Litig., 609 F.2d 411, 431 (9th Cir. 1979) (refusing "to read a complexity exception into the Seventh Amendment").

293. *See* Bernstein v. Universal Pictures, Inc., 79 F.R.D. 59 (S.D.N.Y. 1978); Rosen v. Dick, 83 F.R.D. 540 (S.D.N.Y. 1979).

Chapter 4

NRD Assessments: Regulatory Framework

A. Introduction

This chapter discusses the precise regulatory steps for conducting an NRD assessment under both CERCLA and OPA.[1] The NRDA regulations have three principal functions. First, while they are not required to follow the NRDA regulatory procedures, trustees are entitled to a rebuttable presumption that their damage assessment is accurate in any future judicial or administrative proceedings if they do follow the regulations.[2] Second, the NRDA regulations supplement the procedures for identifying and responding to oil discharges or hazardous substances releases established by the NCP. And third, the NRDA regulations aim to provide standardized and cost-effective procedures trustees can use to expeditiously determine compensation for injuries to natural resources that NCP response actions would not address.[3]

This chapter provides an overview of applicable regulations, while subsequent chapters provide more detailed discussions of how these regulations work in practice, including the types of injuries for which NRD may be sought, the techniques for valuing such injuries, associated real-world strategic questions

---

1. In Chapter 2, we explained the history of the NRDA regulations, including the fierce litigation associated with their promulgation. In this chapter, we provide an in-depth discussion of the regulatory steps for both CERCLA and OPA. In Chapters 5 and 6, we discuss the practical application of the NRDA regulations, as well as some of the ways parties assess damages outside of the strict regulatory protocols.

2. *See* Chapter 3, Section J.

3. *See* 15 C.F.R. § 990.10; 43 C.F.R. §§ 11.10, 11.11.

(Chapter 5), and the mechanics of cooperative NRDAs (Chapter 6). Finally, this chapter describes some past efforts to align and improve the NRDA regulations, as well as possible future regulatory reform initiatives.

B. NRDAs under CERCLA

1. Overview

"Damages" under the CERCLA regulations refers to "the amount of money sought by the natural resource trustee as compensation for injury, destruction, or loss of natural resources."[4] "Loss" refers to a measurable reduction in quality or viability of a natural resource,[5] whereas "destruction" is the total and irreversible loss of such a resource.[6] "Injury" encompasses both loss and destruction and refers generally to a "measurable adverse change . . . in the chemical or physical quality or the viability of a natural resource" that results from "exposure to a discharge of oil or release of a hazardous substance, or exposure to a product of reactions resulting from the discharge . . . or release."[7] Once an assessment is complete, the damages a trustee may seek include damages calculated from injuries occurring from the release of hazardous substances through the end of the recovery period, and the "reasonable and necessary costs of the assessment."[8] The calculated injury is reduced by any mitigation of injuries by response actions taken or anticipated and increased to reflect additional injuries that are "reasonably unavoidable" as a result of such response actions.[9] The regulations prohibit double recovery of damages or assessment costs from the same discharge or release and impacted natural resource.[10]

Under CERCLA, there are three phases of the NRDA process: (1) preassessment, during which trustees determine whether a NRDA can and should be performed; (2) development and implementation of an Assessment Plan of either Type A (a rarely used, simplified procedure) or Type B (the more common, case-specific procedure); and (3) post-assessment, which includes reporting requirements and steps for obtaining assessed damages from responsible

---

4. 43 C.F.R. § 11.14(l).

5. *Id.* § 11.14(x).

6. *Id.* § 11.14(m).

7. *Id.* § 11.14(v).

8. *Id.* § 11.15(a). The trustee may also seek damages for any costs for emergency restoration efforts under § 11.21 and interest on the amounts recoverable. *Id.*

9. *Id.*

10. *Id.* § 11.15(d).

parties.[11] Both Type A and Type B procedures have three stages: injury determination, quantification, and damage determination.[12]

2. Preassessment

A preassessment may begin either after an agency acting under the NCP notifies trustees of potential NRD (as required by CERCLA) or when a trustee identifies or learns of apparent injuries to natural resources from a previously unreported discharge or release.[13] The trustee then must complete a preassessment screen—a preliminary review of information on the impacted natural resources—to determine whether an NRD claim would have a reasonable probability of success.[14] The review, which has two stages, is conducted by an "authorized official," a federal or state employee delegated authority to act on the trustee's behalf.[15] In the first stage of the screen, the trustee must review six types of information about the impacted site and the discharge or release: (1) "[t]he time, quantity, duration, and frequency of the discharge or release"; (2) "[t]he name of the hazardous substance" (as listed in a table codified at 40 C.F.R. § 302.4); (3) "[t]he history of the current and past use of the site identified as the source" of the discharge or release; (4) "[r]elevant operations occurring at or near the site"; (5) "[a]dditional oil or hazardous substances potentially discharged or released from the site"; and (6) "[p]otentially responsible parties."[16] The trustee must also determine whether CERCLA or the CWA excludes the damages from liability.[17]

The second stage of the preassessment screen is identification of the resources potentially at risk. This inquiry has multiple steps. The first is a preliminary identification of potential exposure pathways, which could include "direct contact, surface water, ground water, air, food chains, and particulate movement."[18] In considering whether those pathways may have led to exposure, the trustee should consider (1) "the circumstances of the discharge or release"; (2) "the characteristics of the terrain or body of water

---

11. 43 C.F.R. § 11.13; *see also id.* § 11.33 (describing Type A and Type B procedures).

12. *See id.* §§ 11.40, 11.60.

13. *Id.* § 11.20. The trustee should also assist the individual or agencies operating under the NCP in identifying and notifying other potentially affected trustees. *Id.*

14. *Id.* § 11.23. For a sample preassessment screen, see https://www.fws.gov/southwest/es /Documents/R2ES/Phelps_Dodge_Mines-FINAL_PAS.pdf.

15. *Id.* §§ 11.24, 11.14(d) (defining authorized official).

16. *Id.* § 11.24.

17. *Id.*

18. *Id.* § 11.25.

involved"; (3) "weather conditions"; and (4) the known physical, chemical, and toxicological properties of the oil or hazardous substance."[19] The trustee must also make an estimate of the areas where exposure or effects have occurred or are likely to occur, including areas where the oil or hazardous substance is visible, where oil or the substance has likely been spread through exposure pathways, or where animal movement into or through the site may have led to effects from the discharge or release on biological populations.[20] Finally, the trustee must estimate the area of groundwater or surface water that may be or has been exposed, and the concentration of oil or the hazardous substance in areas of potential exposure.[21] Based on those estimates, the trustee should identify the natural resources potentially affected by the discharge or release and make a preliminary estimate of the services of those resources.[22]

When the preassessment screen is complete, the trustee makes a preliminary determination of whether an assessment is warranted. The trustee must determine that five criteria are met: (1) "[a] discharge of oil or a release of a hazardous substance has occurred"; (2) "[n]atural resources for which the [f]ederal or [s]tate agency or Indian tribe may assert trusteeship under CERCLA have been or are likely to have been adversely affected by the discharge or release"; (3) "[t]he quantity and concentration of the discharged oil or released hazardous substance is sufficient to potentially cause injury . . . to those natural resources"; (4) "[d]ata sufficient to pursue an assessment are readily available or likely to be obtained at reasonable cost"; and (5) "[r]esponse actions, if any, carried out or planned do not or will not sufficiently remedy the injury to natural resources without further action."[23] If the trustee decides an assessment is appropriate, the final step is preparation of a Preassessment Screen Determination, which must describe the decision to proceed in terms of those five criteria.[24]

---

19. *Id.*

20. *Id.*

21. *Id.* The regulations include an appendix to assist with the estimation of groundwater or surface water resource exposure. 43 C.F.R. pt. 11, app. I.

22. *Id.* § 11.25. "Services" of a natural resource are defined as "the physical and biological functions performed by the resource including the human uses of those functions." *Id.* § 11.14(nn). Services "are the result of the physical, chemical, or biological quality of the resource." *Id.*

23. *Id.* § 11.23(e).

24. *Id.* § 11.23(c).

3. Assessment

a. Assessment Plan

The assessment phase of the NRDA begins with development of an Assessment Plan that describes the procedures that the trustees will use for the assessment, as well as their costs.[25] The plan must describe the natural resources and geographical areas involved and provide a statement of each trustee's authority over those resources,[26] and must include procedures and schedules for sharing data, samples, and analysis results with PRPs and other trustees.[27] The Assessment Plan must also specify whether the trustee will use Type A procedures, Type B, or a combination, and must explain the choice of procedure.[28] If the plan specifies that the trustee will use Type B procedures, several other items must also be included. The plan must describe in detail the trustee's strategy for collecting and analyzing samples from the subject geographical areas and provide any other information required to perform the chosen assessment methodologies.[29] A Type B Assessment Plan must also include the objectives of testing and sampling,[30] analysis of initial samples to confirm natural resource exposure,[31] and a Restoration and Compensation Determination Plan (RCDP) identifying restoration alternatives if existing data are sufficient to produce it at that time.[32]

Before commencing the Assessment Plan, however, the trustee must fulfill several procedural requirements. First, the trustee must publicize that the Assessment Plan is in development to any trustees who share responsibility because of coexisting or contiguous natural resources or concurrent

---

25. *Id.* §§ 11.30, 11.31.

26. *Id.* § 11.31(a)(2). Notably, the regulations state that the statement of authority is not entitled to a rebuttable presumption. *Id.*

27. *Id.* § 11.31(a)(4).

28. *Id.* § 11.31(b); *see* Section B.3.b in this chapter (describing the requirements for choosing Type A or a combination of Type A and Type B).

29. 43 C.F.R. § 11.31(b).

30. *Id.* § 11.31(c)(3); *see also id.* § 11.64(a)(2) (expanding on this requirement).

31. *Id.* § 11.31(c)(1); *see also id.* § 11.37 (establishing the sampling and analysis procedure for confirming exposure).

32. *Id.* § 11.31(c)(4). If sufficient data does not exist to create the RCDP, it may be developed after completion of the injury determination or quantification phases. *Id.*; *see also id.* § 11.81(d)(1). The 2008 amendments to the regulations modified previous language requiring development of the RCDP prior to completion of the injury determination and quantification phases of the assessment. *See* Natural Resource Damages for Hazardous Substances, 73 Fed. Reg. 57,259, 57,261–62 (Oct. 2, 2008) (to be codified at 43 C.F.R. pt. 11).

jurisdiction.[33] Second, and importantly, the trustee must make reasonable efforts to identify any PRPs if the lead agency under the NCP has not done so already.[34] If there are a large number of potential PRPs or if some PRPs cannot be located, the trustee may proceed "against any one or more" identified PRPs, using reasonable efforts to "proceed against most known [PRPs] or at least against all those [PRPs] responsible for significant portions of the potential injury."[35] The trustee must send to all identified PRPs a Notice of Intent to Perform an Assessment that invites their participation, or the participation of their designee, in the development of the type and scope of the assessment and its implementation. The notice must describe the site, vessel, or facility involved; the oil discharge or hazardous substance release at issue; the resources potentially at risk; and the trustee's statement of authority. The trustee must allow at least 30 calendar days for a response before proceeding with the development of the Assessment Plan or any other assessment actions.[36]

Once the trustee has developed the draft Assessment Plan, the final step is opening it for a public review and comment period of at least 30 days.[37] The trustee must include in the Report of Assessment all comments to the Assessment Plan from identified PRPs, other trustees, other affected federal or state agencies or Indian tribes, and the public.[38] After the review period concludes, the trustee may begin implementing the Assessment Plan.[39] Notably, the trustee has the option to allow any PRP or group of PRPs to implement all or part of the plan, although the plan must document any decision by the trustee to allow or deny PRP implementation.[40] During implementation, the

---

33. 43 C.F.R. § 11.32(a)(1). The notification must include the results of the preassessment screen determination. Authorized officials (AOs) for different trustees are encouraged to divide responsibilities for such assessments, although one must serve as lead AO. An official from a federal agency or Indian tribe will be the lead AO when the natural resources at issue are under the jurisdiction of either type of entity. For all other natural resources over which a state may be a trustee, a state official will be the lead. *Id.* § 11.32(a). If there is a reasonable basis to do so, however, the trustees may divide the assessment and claims that arise as long as they do not overlap. *Id.* § 11.32(a)(1)(iii).

34. *Id.* § 11.32(a)(2).

35. *Id.* § 11.32(a)(2)(ii).

36. *Id.* § 11.32(a)(2)(iii)(A). For an example notice, see https://www.fws.gov/northeast/nj fieldoffice/pdf/20140918_Dupont_Pompton_Lakes_NOI_Lukas_Letter.pdf. For a sample draft Assessment Plan, see http://www.hanfordnrda.org/wp-content/uploads/2012/11/Draft-Hanford -Injury-Assessment-Plan_November-15-2012.pdf.

37. 43 C.F.R. § 11.32(c).

38. For a sample response to public comments, see https://www.fws.gov/midwest/es/ec/nrda /SEMONRDA/documents/semodapresponsecommentfinaljan609.pdf.

39. 43 C.F.R. § 11.32(c).

40. *Id.* § 11.32(d).

trustee may modify the Assessment Plan at any time in light of new information.[41] If the trustee determines that a modification is "significant," it must be made available for public review for 30 days before the tasks called for in the modified plan can begin; if not significant, the modification may go into effect immediately, although there still must be a review period for comments.[42] A final requirement for Type B assessments is that the trustee must conduct a review of the entire Assessment Plan at the completion of the injury determination phase to ensure that the methodologies selected for the subsequent phases are consistent with the results of the first phase and that the cost remains reasonable.[43]

b. Choice of Procedure

Although trustees use the Type A assessment procedure only for a relatively constrained set of cases, the choice between Type A and Type B merits brief discussion. First, in order to use Type A, several conditions must be met: (1) the released substance must have entered one of two areas for which the computer models that generate Type A assessments are designed; (2) the models must apply to the released substance; (3) the substance must have entered water at or near its surface; (4) at the time of the release, wind conditions must have been such that wind would not "significantly affect the level or extent of injures"; (5) the trustee must not be aware of reliable evidence that there is insufficient biomass of the affected species for the computer models to process; and (6) currents below the affected water's surface must be sufficiently uniform or limited such that they are not expected to significantly affect the level or extent of injuries.[44] Even if these conditions are met, the trustee has discretion to use Type B procedures if the cost will be reasonable and the increase in accuracy over Type A outweighs the cost increase.[45] The trustee must use Type B, however, whenever Type A is not available, and whenever a PRP files a request for Type B with supporting documentation, or advances all reasonable costs for a Type B procedure within a time frame that the trustee finds acceptable.[46] The trustee may change the type of procedure in light of comments to the Assessment Plan, but may not switch to Type A after choosing Type B but

---

41. *Id.* § 11.32(e).
42. *Id.*
43. *Id.* § 11.32(f).
44. *Id.* § 11.34.
45. *Id.* § 11.35(a).
46. *Id.* § 11.35(b).

failing to confirm exposure through the analysis of samples.[47] The trustee may also use both Type A and Type B procedures for the same release if the costs are reasonable, there is no double recovery, and the Type B procedures are used only to determine damages for injuries and compensable values to which Type A procedures do not apply.[48]

i. Type A Procedures

There are two Type A procedures, each of which employs a computer model as part of a standardized methodology to perform an Injury Determination, Quantification, and Damage Determination. One procedure is used strictly for Great Lakes environments and incorporates the Natural Resource Damage Assessment Model for Great Lakes Environments (NRDAM/GLE). The other is available for coastal or marine environments and incorporates the Natural Resource Damage Assessment Model for Coastal and Marine Environments (NRDAM/CME). Because the procedures rely on the computer models, minimal field observation is necessary.[49] Both models require certain data inputs, however, including the identity of the released substance, the mass or volume released, the time and location of the release, and the extent of any response actions, among other data points.[50]

The trustee must first perform a preliminary application of the applicable model. Critically, damage assessments under Type A are limited to $100,000. If a preliminary application of the computer model indicates damages that are greater, the trustee must either limit the portion of the claim calculated with Type A procedures to $100,000, or calculate all damages using Type B procedures instead.[51]

A trustee that decides to proceed with Type A after the preliminary application must next issue an Assessment Plan for public comment.[52] The trustee must review and respond to all comments, modify the plan as appropriate, and then perform a final application of the model using updated data inputs

---

47. *Id.* § 11.35(d).

48. *Id.* § 11.36. The AO must follow all other requirements for using Type B procedures to use them for injuries not covered by Type A; for merely calculating compensable values resulting from injuries addressed in the Type A procedure, the requirements are relaxed. *See id.* § 11.36(d).

49. *Id.* § 11.40. For a discussion of several cases in which the NRDAM/CME model was used in Florida, see Jill Rowe, Deborah French McCay & Nicole Whittier, *Estimation of Natural Resource Damages for 23 Florida Cases Using Physical Fates and Biological Modeling*, 12 Proc. of the Ann. Int'l Conf. on Soils, Sediments, Water & Energy 335 (2010).

50. 43 C.F.R. § 11.41. The regulations include appendices that specify the format for data inputs and modifications to the models. 43 C.F.R. pt. 11, apps. II, III.

51. *Id.* § 11.42.

52. *Id.* § 11.43.

and any reliable information from the comments.[53] Although the final application may calculate damages greater than $100,000, the trustee may not proceed with a claim of any greater than that amount for damages calculated under a Type A procedure.[54]

ii. Type B Procedures

Trustees use Type B procedures to conduct damage assessments in individual cases to which Type A procedures do not apply. Unlike Type A, Type B procedures involve extensive field observations and may be used in any environment. Each of the three main stages of the Type B assessment involves highly detailed methodologies. Before proceeding to the first stage, however, the trustee must develop a preliminary assessment of damages. This estimate comprises assessments of (1) "the anticipated costs of restoration, rehabilitation, replacement, and/or acquisition of equivalent resources for the injured natural resources"; and (2) the "compensable value" of the injured natural resources, if the trustee intends to include compensable value in the damage claim.[55] The trustee should make the preliminary damage estimate before the completion of the Assessment Plan, but if insufficient data is available at that time, may do so following injury determination.[56] The purpose of the estimate is to ensure that methodologies chosen in the Assessment Plan do not exceed a reasonable cost.[57] In making the preliminary estimate, the trustee must consider a range of alternatives to accomplish rehabilitation, restoration, or acquisition of equivalent resources, as well as the effect of any response actions.[58]

---

53. *Id.* § 11.44.

54. *Id.* § 11.44(f).

55. *Id.* § 11.38(a). "Compensable value is the amount of money required to compensate the public for the loss in services provided by the injured resources between . . . the discharge or release and the time the resources are fully returned to their baseline conditions, or until the resources are replaced and/or equivalent natural resources are acquired." *Id.* § 11.83(c)(1).

56. 43 C.F.R. § 11.38(d)(2).

57. *Id.* § 11.38(b).

58. *Id.* § 11.38(c). The 2008 amendments to the regulations made a small revision to the procedure for the compensable value component of the preliminary estimate to more clearly distinguish between estimates for restoration or rehabilitation of the injured natural resources and estimates for replacement or acquisition of equivalent resources. The amendments made similar clarifying changes in the regulations concerning the damage determination phase. Each of these related amendments was in response to a 1996 D.C. Circuit decision, *Kennecott Utah Copper Corp. v. U.S. Department of the Interior*, which invalidated the NRDA regulations' definition of damages. *See* Natural Resource Damages for Hazardous Substances, 73 Fed. Reg. 57,259, 57,261, 57,266 (to be codified at 43 C.F.R. pt. 11); *see also* Chapter 2, Section E.2, in this book (describing the *Kennecott* holding and the regulatory response).

(a) Injury Determination

The first main phase of a Type B assessment is the injury determination, in which the trustee determines whether an injury has occurred to one or more of the natural resources at issue, and if so, whether the injury resulted from the oil discharge or hazardous substance release in question.[59] The process proceeds in several steps. First, the trustee determines whether the potentially injured resource falls into one of the five categories of natural resources subject to CERCLA NRDAs, each of which has a separate definition of injury.[60] Next, the trustee must select a methodology to gather evidence to determine whether such injury has occurred. Finally, the trustee must determine the route through which the oil or hazardous substance is or was transported from its source to the resource.[61] If the trustee at the conclusion of the injury determination finds that the discharge or release caused injury to the resource, the trustee may proceed to the quantification and damage determination phases.[62] If the trustee does not reach such a conclusion, the assessment ends.[63]

(i) Injury Definition

The NRDA regulations provide detailed guidelines for determining whether injury has occurred for each of the five categories of natural resources.[64] For a finding of injury to surface water, groundwater, air resources, and geologic resources, the test results from applying the trustee's chosen methodology must show certain levels of change in the physical or chemical quality of the resource.[65] For surface water, such changes include concentrations and duration of oil or the hazardous substance in excess of maximums set by federal or state policies for drinking water, public water supplies, or water quality in general.[66] The trustee must find sufficient concentrations in two water samples taken at different locations or times, a directive called the "acceptance criterion" for surface water resource injury methodologies.[67] The required changes

---

59. 43 C.F.R. § 11.61(a).

60. The categories are surface water, groundwater, air, geologic, and biological resources. *Id.* § 11.61(c)(1); *see also id.* § 11.14(z) (defining the five categories). Section 11.62 provides guidance for determining whether injury has occurred to each resource category.

61. 43 C.F.R. § 11.61(c). If more than one resource has potentially been injured, the AO must conduct an injury determination through this process for each resource. *Id.* § 11.61(c)(4).

62. *Id.* § 11.61(e).

63. *Id.*

64. *See id.* § 11.62.

65. *See id.*

66. *Id.* § 11.62(b).

67. *Id.* § 11.62(b)(2).

in physical or chemical quality and the acceptance criterion are highly similar for groundwater resources.[68] For air resources, an injury occurs if concentrations of emissions exceed Clean Air Act or other federal or state air standards for protection of public health or natural resources.[69] For geologic resources, an injury results if concentrations of substances are found in the resource sufficient to change its pH or salinity past specified levels, or if the concentration impacts certain biological processes and resources, including plant, microbial, or invertebrate populations.[70]

In contrast, an injury results to a biological resource if the oil discharge or hazardous substance release causes at least one of a set of biological responses in a resource or its offspring, including death, cancer, other diseases, behavioral abnormalities, genetic mutations, physiological malfunctions, or physical deformations.[71] The biological response measured must satisfy four acceptance criteria: (1) the response must be "a commonly documented response resulting from exposure to oil or hazardous substances" rather than other factors; (2) "[e]xposure to oil or hazardous substances [must be] known to cause this biological response in free-ranging organisms" living "in a natural ecosystem"; (3) exposure to oil or hazardous substances must be known to also cause the response in controlled experiments; and (4) the measurement of the response must be "practical to perform and produce[] scientifically valid results," which in turn means the measurement "must be adequately documented in scientific literature, must produce reproducible and verifiable results, and must have well defined and accepted statistical criteria for interpreting as well as rejecting results."[72] The regulations list several types of responses within each response category that "have been evaluated and found to satisfy the acceptance criteria," including, for example, thinning of eggshells in an impacted bird population.[73]

---

68. *See id.* § 11.62(c).

69. *Id.* § 11.62(d).

70. *Id.* § 11.62(e). Also included are findings of substance concentration "sufficient to restrict the ability to access, develop, or use mineral resources within or beneath the geologic resource." *Id.* § 11.62(e)(7).

71. *See id.* § 11.62(f)(1)(i). Injury is also sufficient if the level of the substance present in an edible organism exceeds limits in the federal Food, Drug and Cosmetic Act or analogous state directives. *See id.* § 11.62(f)(1)(ii).

72. *Id.* § 11.62(f)(2). Additionally, the inquiry must establish a statistically significant difference in the biological response between samples from populations in the area under assessment and a control area. *See id.* § 11.62(f)(3).

73. *Id.* § 11.62(f)(4).

(ii) Methodology Selection

The second stage of injury determination is selection of a testing and sampling methodology that meets the objectives identified in the Assessment Plan.[74] Selected methodologies must meet four criteria: (1) they must have performed effectively in conditions similar to those anticipated at the assessment area; (2) they must be cost-effective; (3) they must produce data that were previously unavailable and are needed to make the injury determination; and (4) they must provide data that is usable for the quantification phase of the assessment.[75]

The trustee should consider several specific factors when selecting methodologies, including the physical state of the oil or hazardous substance; the duration, frequency, season, and time of the discharge or release; the time required and potential safety hazards of obtaining and testing samples; and the costs, limits, accuracy, and time required for alternative methods, among other factors.[76] The regulations also provide specific methodological requirements for each of the five resource categories. For example, if a methodology for assessing injury to surface water or groundwater uses a computer model, the model's general validity and applicability to the specific assessment must be demonstrated through citation or description of the model's inputs and the physical, chemical, or biological process it simulates.[77] For air resources, the regulations specify particular methodologies that the trustee may use, including those developed by EPA and certain other government and nongovernmental organizations.[78] The regulations also identify specific methodologies for testing and sampling geologic and biological resources.[79]

EXPERT INSIGHTS: Statistics and Modeling in NRDA
William Warren-Hicks, PhD, and Steven Bartell, PhD[80]

Analysis and evaluation of available data is clearly a critical aspect of most NRDA cases. Unfortunately, large scale NRDA cases have many problematic issues with respect to data availability and data quality, even before statistical analysis is attempted. In many

---

74. *See id.* § 11.64(a)(2); *see also id.* § 11.31(c)(3).

75. *Id.* § 11.64(a)(3).

76. *Id.* § 11.64(a)(4).

77. *Id.* §§ 11.64(b)(6), 11.64(c)(8).

78. *Id.* § 11.64(d)(3).

79. *Id.* § 11.64(e), 11.64(f).

80. Dr. William Warren-Hicks is the CEO of EcoStat, Inc., in North Carolina. He holds a PhD in environmental statistics from Duke University. Dr. Steven Bartell is the CEO of Highwood, Inc., in Tennessee. He holds a PhD from the University of Wisconsin, Madison.

cases, information critical for supporting damage claims is sparse, or both spatially and temporally dispersed. Assessments may require additional sampling activities, and the availability of historical or reference site data may be nonexistent or severely limited. However, even given this diversity of data issues, statisticians are charged with employing statistical hypothesis testing approaches and statistical probability modeling approaches that are intended to differentiate the true state of environmental damage from background noise and natural variability. The degree to which "signal to noise" can be determined is confounded with many sources of variability, including measurement error, natural changes over space, and natural changes over time. In most NRDA cases, separating the effect of actual environmental impact from natural changes over space and time is a challenging endeavor, and advanced statistical methods are required. Attorneys should carefully recruit statisticians with the appropriate skills and training.

From an attorney's perspective, discerning an appropriate use of statistical analysis from inappropriate approaches can be difficult. Most attorneys are not trained in statistics, probability, and modeling. However, awareness of a few key issues could provide attorneys with insight into identifying issues in expert report findings. Next we discuss a few of the many issues that attorneys should consider when reading expert reports and documents, and provide illustrations with lessons learned from historical NRDA cases.

A key issue that frequently arises is the application of statistical models to non-representative data. There are two elements of concern: the first is the relationship of data collection strategies to questions of interest, and the second is the degree to which available data represent the biological and hydrological processes under evaluation. As an example, during the initial phases of the *Deepwater Horizon* oil spill, ships were sent to locations around the wellhead and within the predicted oil pathway to the beaches to collect water data, but in most cases without a statistically robust sampling design for data collection. The majority of the data on oil concentrations in the Gulf were taken by what was termed "adaptive sampling." Meaning that instrumentation on the ship would identify oil in the water, and samples were taken. A small proportion of data was collected with a prespecified statistical survey design. While the question of "is there oil in the Gulf" can be answered with adaptive designs, questions like "what is the distribution and concentration of oil over large spatial regions in the Gulf" are best addressed with data collected using a well thought out statistical design. The water samples were "statistically biased" toward non-zero samples of oil. There are statistical approaches to minimizing the degree of statistical bias in data collected without an appropriate and well-designed sampling strategy, like post-stratification weighting approaches. And, sophisticated statistical models can be implemented that measure the degree of bias and appropriately adjust the available measured data. During the NRDA analysis phase, the lack of statistical sampling rigor inhibited direct interpretation of the extent and severity of oil within the Gulf. The lesson here is that attorneys should be aware of the possible lack of linkage between questions of interest and data collection, but understand that while sophisticated statistical methods are available to aid with statistical inference, the degree of confidence in the assessment result may be limited. If at all possible, attorneys and their experts should discuss any data collection tasks prior to implementation, and during those discussions ensure that the data are collected with questions of interest in mind. At that time, statistical models intended for answering the questions should be fully detailed, and written out in equation form to ensure effective communication.

Statistical analysis should begin using graphical approaches, and build to more complicated mathematical approaches if required. In most cases, inference based on statistical models should be evident in graphical output. Combining both statistical outputs with graphics enhances communication of sometimes complex findings, and provides a degree of insurance that the statistical model outputs are believable. Expert reports that only supply statements akin to the following, "the p-value was < 0.05, therefore avian reproduction was evident," should be taken with caution. Good statistical practice requires that the hypothesis test be clearly stated, and the underlying statistical model be written in equation form. Otherwise, the methods and approaches used to generate the statistical inference are unknown to the reader. As an example, peer-reviewed publications on the effect of dioxin and furans on egg survival at an NRD site (private client) were lacking in graphical depictions of the data, and only simple statements like the one preceding were supplied in arguing that avian reproduction and survival was reduced. The author examined the original data using both graphics and models, and was easily able to show that the apparent decrease in egg survival was due to nest predation, and not the discharge or release of the chemicals of concern. Attorneys should be aware that a lack of sufficient support in expert reports and papers is a warning sign that should lead to further exploration. The lack of data graphics and mathematical rigor in this case and others is a lesson to attorneys when reviewing expert reports or other documents.

Due to the advancement in statistical software, and acceptance of sophisticated statistical approaches, it is now easier to correctly select an appropriate sampling distribution prior to building a statistical model. Attorneys should be aware that selection of a sampling distribution representing the endpoint of interest is critical to the statistical findings. For example, peer-reviewed publications evaluating shrimp survival in the *Deepwater Horizon* case assumed that the number of shrimp per trawl were normally distributed, even though the data are "counts" of shrimp per trawl. Sampling distributions appropriate for count data, include in part, Poisson and Negative Binomial distributions. Attorneys should pay careful attention to the default selection of sampling distributions when reading reports and documents. Incorrect selection of sampling distribution can result in both false positive and false negative findings.

Causality is a critical piece of the NRDA. Linking statistical methods with biological systems models can be a productive approach to establishing the true cause of changes to the environment, which may not necessarily be caused by an environmental stressor (e.g., toxic chemicals).

NRDAs routinely entail assessing direct and indirect effects of environmental stressors in complex ecological systems. Establishing unequivocal relationships between environmental stressors and measured responses (e.g., changes in the distribution or abundance of valued resources or habitat) is often made challenging by spatial and temporal variability characteristics of dynamic ecosystems that are unrelated to the stressor(s) of concern. This complication is particularly evident in quantifying indirect (e.g., food web) effects from data.

The stated challenges can be addressed through the integration of statistical analysis and mechanistic food web/ecosystem modeling. One relatively common practice uses the power of statistical analysis to (1) facilitate implementation of ecosystem models and (2) evaluate the accuracy and reliability of model results in relation to available data. Straightforward statistical approaches can be used to help derive and quantify model input values based on sources of data that range from site-specific values to published relevant data and even extending to professional judgment (e.g., expert elicitation). Statistical analysis can characterize and describe (e.g., statistical distributions) the uncertainty associated with estimated model input values. Similarly, standard methods can be used to develop time series of environmental inputs (e.g., temperature, nutrients) from available data that might be used by the ecosystem model in computing biological production. These kinds of statistical analyses can prove instrumental in developing model applications for actual use in assessments, including NRDAs. Attorneys might benefit from utilizing the skills of experienced ecological modelers to help identify the strengths and limitations of modeling approaches and evaluate the robustness of model parameter values.

Statistical methods can also be used to evaluate the accuracy and reliability of model results. Standard methods are available to quantify the degree of agreement between model outputs and available data. Importantly, these kinds of analyses can be used to determine if the model is performing in a manner consistent with criteria specified at the outset of model development. Combined with methods of numerical sensitivity and uncertainty analysis, statistical evaluation of model performance can identify the key model parameters that are contributing to model accuracy or bias. Importantly, the results of these kinds of analyses can guide the continued refinement of the model until performance criteria are met. Additionally, application of statistical methods in evaluating model accuracy and reliability can focus data collection efforts (e.g., monitoring) to obtain high-value information for refining and further evaluating the model. These kinds of analyses can also help lawyers pinpoint the key components of models and evaluate quality of model results used in environmental assessments.

A more recent and novel integration of statistics and models in support of environmental assessment reverses the typical use of statistical analysis to inform and evaluate the model. Now, the complex ecosystem model generates time series of model outputs (e.g., biomass of valued resources) that are subsequently explored using techniques of analysis derived from "complexity theory" to define causal relationships between model outputs (e.g., trophic interactions), and, importantly, quantify any impacts of environmental stressors on these relationships. Complexity theory posits that a time series of a causally connected measurable quantity should contain some attributes of the dynamics described by variables to which it is functionally connected (i.e., causal relationships). In more tangible terms, a time series of a prey species abundance ought to include some temporal characteristics of an associated time series of the abundance of its predator. Complexity theory implies that causality can be rigorously defined from statistical analysis of time series data without the necessity of developing and implementing complex ecological models and their attendant challenges—this approach has been termed "equation-free modeling." One key obstacle in developing the needed arsenal of complexity-based analytical tools is the paucity of adequate time series data for resources of interest, for both baseline (reference) conditions and conditions subsequent to environmental stress. This obstacle can be usefully addressed by using food web/ecosystem models (with known accuracy and reliability) to generate the time series.

Food web/ecosystem models (e.g., CASM, Ecopath/ecosim, Atlantis, AQUATOX) are deterministic models, and the causal connections among modeled state variables are explicitly defined (e.g., predator-prey relations, effects of light, temperature, and nutrients on biological production) in the structure and implementation of the models. Time series of causally connected state variables produced by these deterministic models will be highly correlated and provide the opportunity to derive and apply complexity-based statistical analyses to reconstruct the causal relations. In addition, the models can be set up to vary the strength of deterministic causal connections between state variables (e.g., relative preference of a predator for potential prey species) to vary the signal noise characteristics of the resulting modeled time series. The statistical analyses can be applied to determine how much "noise" in the time series can be tolerated while still reconstructing the known causal relations defined by the model. Iterations of modeled time series and corresponding complexity-based analysis can importantly be used to develop a set of empirical tools that can be used with known confidence to infer causal relations and impacts on causal connections from comparatively sparse data sets commonly encountered in environmental assessments (i.e., NRDA). The continued development and improvement of complex food web/ecosystem models can be leveraged toward the innovation of sophisticated complexity-based analytics for valuable applications in real-world assessments. Attorneys might increase their awareness and familiarity with complexity-based analytics because these methods will increasingly be encountered in environmental assessments aimed at establishing causal relationships between stressors of concern and impacts on valued ecological resources.

In summary, statistical analysis of information in NRDAs is a critical piece of the total project, providing insights useful for determining the extent and nature of any injury that may have occurred. Lessons based on historical NRDA cases, revolving around complex issues in survey design, data analysis, and modeling may be helpful to attorneys involved in future studies.

(iii) Pathway Determination

The final stage of the injury determination phase is determination of the exposure pathways of the oil or hazardous substance: "the route[s] or medi[a] through which oil or a hazardous substance is or was transported from the source of the discharge or release to the injured resource."[81] The regulations refer to the five natural resource categories as "media" or "pathway resources" that can each serve as exposure pathways.[82] The trustee can determine the pathway "by either demonstrating the presence of the oil or hazardous substance in sufficient concentrations in the pathway resource," or by using a model that demonstrates that the route served as the pathway.[83] As with methodology selection, the regulations also provide detailed procedures for determining whether each type of resource served as an exposure pathway, which in some cases includes use of the methodologies provided for determining injury to those resource categories.[84] Additionally, the trustee must also consider three general criteria: (1) the chemical and physical characteristics of the discharged oil or released substance when transported by natural processes or present in natural media; (2) the rate or mechanism of transport by natural processes of the oil or substance; and (3) combinations of pathways that together could transport the oil or substance to the impacted resource.[85] The trustee may also conduct tests and collect data as necessary to complete the requirements for the pathway determination.[86]

(b) Quantification

Once the trustee has determined that a discharge or release caused an injury to a natural resource, the next phase of the assessment is to quantify the effect

---

81. 43 C.F.R. § 11.14(dd).
82. *Id.* § 11.63(a).
83. *Id.* § 11.63(a)(2).
84. *See id.* § 11.63(b)–(f).
85. *Id.* § 11.63(a)(1).
86. *Id.* § 11.63(a)(3).

of the injury. The measurement is made "in terms of the reduction from the baseline condition in the quantity and quality of services . . . provided by the injured resource."[87] There are three components of the quantification phase. First, the trustee measures the reduction in the natural resource services due to the injuries caused by the discharge or release. Second, the trustee must determine the baseline conditions for the resource at the assessment area and compare the baseline to the present conditions. Finally, the trustee must estimate the time that will be required for the injured resource to recover to the baseline conditions through restoration, rehabilitation, replacement, or acquisition of an equivalent.[88] At the completion of quantification, the trustee will use the final determination of the reduction in services resulting from the discharge or release to determine the appropriate amount of compensation at the damage determination phase.[89]

(i) Service Reduction Quantification

The quantification of the effects of an oil discharge or hazardous substance release measures the extent to which the injury from the discharge or release reduced the natural resource's services.[90] In most circumstances, this involves five steps. The trustee must (1) "[m]easure the extent to which the injury demonstrated in the Injury Determination phase has occurred in the assessment area"; (2) determine the "change" to the injured resource by measuring the extent to which it differs from baseline conditions; (3) determine the baseline services (the services normally produced by the injured resource); (4) identify "interdependent services" to avoid double counting and to discover any secondary services disrupted by the injury; and (5) measure the disruption of services resulting from the discharge or release.[91] The trustee must also consider several factors in determining the "[s]pecific resources or services to quantify and the methodology for doing so," including the degree to which a resource

---

87. *Id.* § 11.70(a)(1). For additional discussion of baseline as an important area of dispute between trustees and responsible parties, see Chapter 3, Section I, and Chapter 5, Section A.2.

88. *Id.* § 11.70(c).

89. *Id.* § 11.70(d).

90. *Id.* § 11.71(a). Certain effects of injuries from releases and discharges are exempt from this process by statute. *See id.* § 11.71(g). "[N]atural resource services" include "provision of habitat, food and other needs of biological resources, recreation, other products or services used by humans, flood control, ground water recharge, waste assimilation, and other such functions that may be provided by natural resources." *Id.* § 11.71(e).

91. *Id.* § 11.71(b). In certain cases, the effects of a discharge or release on a resource may be quantified by directly measuring changes in the resource's services rather than the changes in the resource itself. *See id.* § 11.71(f).

or service can represent related resources or services and the technical feasibility of quantifying changes in a resource or service at reasonable cost.[92]

Beyond the five main steps, the regulations identify several other general factors for the trustee to take into account when conducting the quantification, including the "[t]otal area, volume, or numbers affected of the resource in question" and the resource's ability to recover, "expressed as the time required for restoration of baseline services."[93] The regulations also provide category-specific methods and guidelines to determine the area or extent to which each type of affected resource differs from its baseline. For example, in addition to specifying mechanisms for estimating the area of surface water and groundwater resources exposed to oil or hazardous substances, the regulations identify specific methods for water sampling and analysis.[94] For biological resources, the extent to which a resource differs from baseline must be analyzed and expressed "as either a population change or a habitat or ecosystem change."[95] Analysis of populations, habitats, or ecosystems is limited to those identified as injured during the injury determination phase, or those that can be linked directly through services to resources identified as injured.[96] Methods for obtaining data for these analyses must allow the data to be interpreted in terms of services and permit numerical comparison between the assessment area and a control area or baseline data.[97]

(ii) Baseline Services Determination
As part of the quantification of the effects of the discharge of oil or release of a hazardous substance, the trustee must determine "the physical, chemical, and biological baseline conditions and the associated baseline services for injured resources at the assessment area."[98] The regulations specify five general guidelines for selecting data to determine the baseline: (1) the data should reflect conditions at the assessment area in the absence of the discharge or release, considering natural and anthropogenic processes impacting the site; (2) the data should recognize the normal variations in the "physical, chemical, or biological conditions for the assessment area or injured resource"; (3) the data

---

92. *Id.* § 11.71(d). This emphasis on using only procedures with a reasonable cost is a common theme throughout the NRDA regulations.

93. *Id.* § 11.71(c).

94. *Id.* §§ 11.71(h)(3), 11.71(i)(3).

95. *Id.* § 11.71(l)(1).

96. *Id.* § 11.71(l)(3).

97. *Id.* § 11.71(l)(4).

98. *Id.* § 11.72(a); *see also id.* § 11.72(e) (requiring the AO to determine baseline services associated with the baseline data).

should be as accurate, complete, and representative of the resource as the data used or obtained for the service reduction quantification stage and collected by comparable methods or accompanied by an explanation of comparability; (4) the data collection must be restricted to the data necessary for conducting the assessment at a reasonable cost; and (5) the trustee may use baseline data that may not fully represent the baseline conditions if the data are as close to the actual baseline conditions as can be obtained due to technical or cost limitations.[99]

To help establish the baseline data, the trustee should also use any available historical or existing data for the assessment area or injured resource, including statements and assessments prepared under NEPA or similar federal or state laws, scientific literature, information from landowners in or near the assessment area, or similar data.[100] If historical data for the assessment area are unavailable, the trustee should designate and collect baseline data from control areas, including any historical data for those areas, if available, or field data if not. The trustee should select control areas based on their demonstrable similarity to the assessment area and lack of exposure to the discharge or release.[101] The regulations provide several guidelines for gathering and analyzing data from the selected control areas, including collection of data over a long enough time period to account for normal variability, use of collection methods comparable to those used at the assessment area, and comparison to values reported in existing literature to show the data represent a normal range.[102]

Although the regulations make clear that the trustee should follow these general guidelines for determining baseline conditions and services, they also provide specific directions for each of the five resource categories.[103] For example, for air resources, the trustee should gather applicable and available historical data on ambient air quality and source emissions, although certain conditions must be met to use the data.[104] If historical data are insufficient, the trustee may designate one or more control areas, guided by additional considerations specific to air resources, including that the areas be "spatially

---

99. *Id.* § 11.72(b).

100. *Id.* § 11.72(c).

101. *Id.* § 11.72(d)(1).

102. *Id.* § 11.72(d).

103. *Id.* § 11.72(f).

104. *Id.* § 11.72(i). Such conditions include that "[t]he historical data show that normal concentrations of the oil or hazardous substance are sufficiently predictable that changes as a result of the discharge or release are likely to be detectable." *Id.* § 11.72(i)(2)(iii).

representative of the range of air quality and meteorological conditions likely to have occurred at the assessment area during the discharge or release into the atmosphere."[105] For biological resources, the trustee should determine baseline conditions that include both population and habitat data if available. The trustee may derive such data from aerial photographs or maps, biological specimens in museums and similar facilities, and photographs.[106] The trustee should select control areas based on comparability to the habitat or ecosystem at the assessment area.[107]

(iii) Resource Recoverability Analysis

The last stage of the quantification phase is resource recoverability analysis. The main focus of this stage is an estimate of the time needed for the injured resources to recover such that the trustee may determine that the services are restored, rehabilitated, or replaced, or that an equivalent has been acquired.[108] The trustee must also estimate the "no action-natural recovery" period, a span of time needed for recovery if no restoration or other activities are undertaken beyond response actions.[109] For estimates of recovery time, the trustee must use the "best available information" and may use models when appropriate.[110] In general, the trustee may use information from several types of sources, including published studies on the same or similar resources, any data sources available for the baseline services determination stage, accounts of individuals with experience with the injured resource or restoration of a similar resource, and field and lab data from the assessment and control areas.[111] The trustee should also consider several factors when estimating recovery times, including ecological succession patterns in the area, life cycles and reproductive patterns of biological species involved, and natural removal rates of the oil or hazardous substance from the media involved.[112] Finally, if the trustee determines restoration is not technically feasible, the basis for that decision must be documented as part of the justification for any alternatives involving replacement that may be considered or proposed.[113]

---

105. *Id.* § 11.72(i)(3)(ii).
106. *Id.* § 11.72(k)(2).
107. *Id.* § 11.72(k)(3).
108. *Id.* § 11.73(a).
109. *Id.* § 11.73(a)(1).
110. *Id.* § 11.73(c).
111. *Id.*
112. *Id.* § 11.73(c)(2).
113. *Id.* § 11.73(b).

(c) Damage Determination

The final phase of the Type B procedure is damage determination, in which the trustee makes a determination of NRD by using the information from the quantification phase to estimate the monetary damages resulting from the oil discharge or hazardous substance release.[114] The purpose of the phase is to establish the amount of money the trustees will seek in compensation for the damages.[115] The main feature of the damage determination phase is the RCDP, a written product in which the trustee lists alternative proposals for restoration, rehabilitation, replacement, or acquisition of equivalent resources and selects the most appropriate option.[116] Importantly, the trustee should complete the RCDP at the time of the Assessment Plan, but may do so whenever sufficient data becomes available.[117] Regardless of the timing, however, the trustee must develop the RCDP pursuant to the guidelines in the sections of the regulations concerning damage determination.[118] Further, if the trustee completes the RCDP separately from the Assessment Plan, it must be made available for public review for at least 30 calendar days.[119] Following the review, the trustee must implement the RCDP, concluding the damage determination phase and the Type B assessment.[120]

(i) Restoration and Compensation Determination Plan

An RCDP must have several elements. First, it must develop and list "a reasonable number of possible alternatives for (i) the restoration or rehabilitation of the injured natural resources to a condition where they can provide the level of services available at baseline, or (ii) the replacement and/or acquisition of

---

114. *Id.* § 11.80(a)(1).

115. *Id.* § 11.80(b). Similar to their changes to the procedure for preliminary estimates of compensable value, the 2008 amendments to the regulations made two small revisions to more clearly distinguish this phase's measure of damages for restoration or rehabilitation of the injured natural resources from measures for replacement or acquisition of equivalent resources. The revision was in response to the D.C. Circuit's 1996 holding in *Kennecott Utah Copper Corp. v. U.S. Dep't of the Interior. See* Natural Resource Damages for Hazardous Substances, 73 Fed. Reg. 57,259, 57,261, 57,264 (Oct. 2, 2008) (to be codified at 43 C.F.R. pt. 11); *see also* Chapter 2, Section E.2 (discussing *Kennecott*).

116. For a sample RCDP, *see* Nat. Res. Trustees of the St. Lawrence River Env't, St. Lawrence River Environment Natural Resource Damage Assessment: Restoration and Compensation Determination Plan and Environmental Assessment (2013), https://casedocuments.darrp.noaa.gov/greatlakes/lawrence/pdf/ENV_ENFORCEMENT-2371812-v1-Alcoa__Final_May_2013_RCDP__FILED.pdf.

117. 43 C.F.R. § 11.81(d)(1).

118. *Id.* § 11.80(c).

119. *Id.* § 11.81(d)(2).

120. *Id.* §§ 11.80(c), 11.80(d).

equivalent natural resources capable of providing such services, and, where relevant, the compensable value."[121] It must also select one of the alternatives and give the rationale for the selection.[122] Finally, it must identify the methodologies the trustee will use to determine the costs of the selected alternative, as well as the methodologies for calculating compensable value associated with the selected alternative if the trustee plans to include it in the damages claim.[123] The RCDP may also be expanded to incorporate requirements from procedures required under other portions of CERCLA, the CWA, or other applicable federal, state, or tribal laws, as long as the trustee fulfills the NRDA requirements.[124]

(ii) Development and Selection of Alternatives

The regulations provide further guidance on development and selection of alternatives in the RCDP. In broad terms, the trustee must list a number of alternatives to "restore" or "rehabilitate," or "replace and/or acquire the equivalent of" the injured resources.[125] "Restoration or rehabilitation actions" are actions to return injured resources to the baseline conditions so that the resources exhibit the properties and provide the services that they would have exhibited and provided in the absence of the discharge or release.[126] Replacement or acquisition of an equivalent, in contrast, refers to the substitution of injured resources with resources that provide the same or substantially similar services.[127] Both types of actions must be additional to or extend beyond the actions completed, anticipated, or determined to be appropriate under the

---

121. *Id.* § 11.81(a). Similar to the revisions to § 11.80, the 2008 amendments modified this language to more clearly distinguish between the two categories of restoration actions, as well as the use of such alternatives when described in an RCDP. *See* Natural Resource Damages for Hazardous Substances, 73 Fed. Reg. 57,259, 57,264, 57,266 (Oct. 2, 2008) (to be codified at 43 C.F.R. pt. 11).

122. 43 C.F.R. § 11.81(a).

123. *Id.* §§ 11.81(a), 11.81(c).

124. *Id.* § 11.81(e).

125. *Id.* § 11.82(b)(1). One alternative considered must be based on the no action-natural recovery determination. *Id.* § 11.82(c)(2); *see* § 11.73(a)(1). The scope of possible alternatives is limited to only those actions that restore or rehabilitate the injured natural resources or "replace and/or acquire equivalent natural resources capable of providing such services." *Id.* § 11.82(b)(1)(iii). Both the general description of types of alternatives and the provision limiting the scope of possibilities were adjusted slightly by the 2008 amendments to more clearly distinguish restoration and rehabilitation from replacement and acquisition of equivalents. *See* 73 Fed. Reg. at 57,264, 57,266.

126. 43 C.F.R. § 11.82(b)(1)(i).

127. *Id.* § 11.82(b)(1)(ii).

NCP.[128] To select the course to pursue, the trustee must evaluate each alternative based on all relevant considerations, including ten enumerated factors. These include each alternative's technical feasibility; the relationship of the expected costs to the expected benefits; the results of any actual or planned response actions; the potential for additional injury resulting from the proposed actions; the natural recovery period; potential effects of the action on human health and safety; and consistency with relevant and applicable federal, state, and tribal policies and laws.[129]

(iii) Cost Estimation and Valuation Methodologies

Selecting a methodology to determine the costs of a chosen alternative, and the compensable value of the services lost to the public between the discharge or release and the completion of the restoration activities, is another key component of the RCDP for which the regulations provide guidelines.[130] Generally, estimation and valuation methodologies must meet four criteria: they must (1) be "feasible and reliable for a particular incident and the type of damage to be measured"; (2) be usable at a reasonable cost; (3) avoid double counting or allow any double counting to be estimated and eliminated; and (4) be cost-effective.[131] To evaluate feasibility and reliability, trustees may consider factors including whether a methodology addresses a particular natural resource injury in light of its nature, degree, and scope; whether it is peer reviewed; whether it has general or widespread acceptance in the field; whether it is subject to standards; and whether its inputs and assumptions are rationally supported.[132]

---

128. *Id.* § 11.82(b)(1). The 2008 amendments also clarified that the possible alternatives for returning the injured resources to their baseline level of services may range from intensive action by the AO to return the resources and services they provide to baseline conditions as quickly as possible, to natural recovery with minimal action by the trustees. The amendments further explained that the alternatives in this range may vary in their rates of recovery, level of management action, and needs for resource replacements or acquisitions. *Id.* § 11.82(c)(1); *see* 73 Fed. Reg. at 57,262, 57,266.

129. 43 C.F.R. § 11.82(d).

130. *Id.* § 11.83(a)(1). As with the preceding sections, revised in response to the *Kennecott* decision, the 2008 amendments revised the wording of this section to more clearly distinguish restoration and rehabilitation from replacement and acquisition of alternatives. *See* 73 Fed. Reg. at 57,262, 57,266.

131. 43 C.F.R. § 11.83(a)(3).

132. *Id.* § 11.83(a)(4). Not all factors are applicable in every case, but the AO must document consideration of the factors applied in the Report of Assessment. *Id.* § 11.83(a)(5). The 2008 amendments added the factors to help trustees better evaluate the feasibility and reliability of selected methodologies. The addition reflected the amendments' overall goal of emphasizing restoration activities over economic damages in NRDAs. Such prioritization was a

The regulations also provide definitions for costs and compensable value in addition to offering suggested methodologies for deriving them. Costs for restoration, rehabilitation, replacement, and acquisition of equivalent resources are defined as "the amount of money determined by the [trustee] as necessary to complete all actions identified" in the alternative selected in the RCDP.[133] Direct costs are costs of performing the selected alternative, including payment of employees, acquisition or consumption of materials, purchase of equipment or other capital expenditures, and other items the trustee identifies in carrying out the alternative.[134] Indirect costs, in contrast, are costs of activities or items that support the selected alternative "but that cannot practically be directly accounted for as [its] costs," including traditional overhead, as well as other costs "not readily assignable to the selected alternative."[135] The regulations provide several types of potential methodologies for cost estimation, including extrapolation from the cost of a particular item, probability-based methodologies, and cost- and time-estimating regressions. The trustee may combine cost estimation methodologies as long as the selections do not result in double counting.[136] The trustee may also use any other methodologies besides those listed as long as they are "based upon standard and accepted cost estimating practices and are cost effective."[137]

Compensable value is defined as the amount of money required to compensate the public for the loss of an injured resource's services between the time of the discharge or release and the resource's restoration to baseline, or until the resource is replaced or an equivalent is acquired.[138] The section of the regulations concerning compensable value was the subject of the most significant changes in the 2008 amendments, a major goal of which was to increase trustees' focus on restoration actions rather than simply economic damages.[139] To that end, the amendments state that compensable value can be determined

---

key recommendation of DOI's Natural Resource Damage Assessment and Restoration Federal Advisory Committee. *See* Natural Resource Damages for Hazardous Substances, 73 Fed. Reg. 11,081, 11,082–83 (proposed Feb. 29, 2008) (to be codified at 43 C.F.R. pt. 11).

133. 43 C.F.R. § 11.83(b)(1).

134. *Id.* § 11.83(b)(1)(i).

135. *Id.* § 11.83(b)(1)(ii). The AO may also use an indirect cost rate rather than estimating the actual indirect costs as long as the assumptions underlying the rate are documented. *Id.* § 11.83(b)(1)(iii).

136. *Id.* § 11.83(b)(2).

137. *Id.* § 11.83(b)(3).

138. *Id.* § 11.83(c)(1). The 2008 amendments added replacement and acquisition of equivalents to this section.

139. *See* Natural Resource Damages for Hazardous Substances, 73 Fed. Reg. 57,259, 57,260 (to be codified at 43 C.F.R. pt. 11).

not only in terms of economic value, but also through a "restoration cost approach," which measures the cost of implementing projects to restore a natural resource's services pending restoration to baseline.[140] The amendments also clarified the meanings of the terms "use value" and "nonuse value" in economic terms, defining use value as "the economic value of the resources to the public attributable to the direct use" of the natural resource's services.[141] That contrasts with nonuse value, defined as "the economic value the public derives from natural resources that is independent of any direct use of the services provided."[142] Finally, the amendments removed a provision limiting estimates of "option and existence values," which the D.C. Circuit had invalidated in 1989, and replaced it with a definition of "[r]estoration cost": "the cost of a project or projects that restore, replace, or acquire the equivalent of natural resource services lost pending restoration to baseline."[143]

The 2008 amendments also revised the set of valuation methodologies the trustee may select from to add four methodologies relating to restoration activities rather than economic value.[144] The trustee may now choose from a list of 11 methodologies to determine the compensable value of the injured resources.[145] Among the original seven methodologies were techniques to assess the diminution in market price of injured resources or lost services that are traded in a competitive market, as well as "contingent valuation" techniques to establish hypothetical markets that can "directly elicit an individual's economic valuation of a natural resource."[146] The four newer methodologies include conjoint analysis, which compares natural resource losses to "natural resource service gains produced by restoration projects," and resource equivalency analysis, which "compare[s] the effects of restoration actions on specifically identified resources that are injured or destroyed."[147] Finally, the 2008 amendments also revised the explanation of when a trustee may use a nonlisted methodology for compensable value. The regulations now specify that the trustee may use methodologies that measure compensable value in

---

140. 43 C.F.R. § 11.83(c)(1); *see* 73 Fed. Reg. at 57,260–61.

141. 43 C.F.R. § 11.83(c)(1)(i).

142. *Id.* § 11.83(c)(1)(ii).

143. *Id.* § 11.83(c)(iii); *see* 73 Fed. Reg. at 57,261. The D.C. Circuit found the earlier version of § 11.83(c)(iii) to be inconsistent with CERCLA in *Ohio v. U.S. Department of the Interior,* 880 F.2d 432 (D.C. Cir. 1989); *see* Chapter 2, Section E.2.

144. *See* 73 Fed. Reg. at 57,261.

145. 43 C.F.R. § 11.83(c)(2). The 2008 amendments also reorganized the methodologies into a table rather than textual paragraphs. *See id.*

146. *Id.* For additional discussion of "contingent valuation," see Chapter 5, Section C.5.

147. 43 C.F.R. § 11.83(c)(2).

a cost-effective manner, "in accordance with the public's willingness to pay for the lost service, or [in accordance] with the cost of a project that restores, replaces, or acquires services equivalent of natural resource services lost" between the discharge or release and the restoration to baseline.[148]

(iv) Implementation Guidance

The regulations for the damage determination phase conclude with guidance for the trustee on using the selected methodologies to estimate costs and determine compensable value. The first step is to "determine the uses made of the resource services identified in the Quantification phase."[149] The trustee may only use "committed uses" of the resource or services over the recovery period to measure the change from the baseline due to injury.[150] These baseline uses must be "reasonably probable"; the trustee may not consider "[p]urely speculative uses" in estimating damages.[151] The trustee should also avoid double counting of damages, one strategy for which is factoring the effects of past or anticipated response actions into the damage analysis.[152] If there are "significant uncertainties" concerning the assumptions made during all phases of the assessment, the trustee should examine reasonable alternatives. The trustee should also document the uncertainty and incorporate it into the estimates of benefits and costs by "deriv[ing] a range of probability estimates for the important assumptions used to determine damages."[153] In such cases, the damage estimate is "the net expected present value of the costs of restoration, rehabilitation, replacement, and/or acquisition of equivalent resources, and, if relevant, compensable value."[154] Generally, the final damages estimate should be an expected present value dollar amount calculated using a specified discount rate.[155]

The regulations further specify several notable points of guidance for calculating compensable value. First, the trustee should incorporate estimates of the public's ability to substitute resource services or uses for those

---

148. *Id.* § 11.83(c)(3).

149. *Id.* § 11.84(b)(1).

150. *Id.* § 11.84(b)(2). A "committed use" is either a current public use or a planned public use of a natural resource "for which there is a documented legal, administrative, budgetary, or financial commitment established" before the discharge or release. *Id.* § 11.14(h).

151. *Id.* § 11.84(b)(2).

152. *Id.* § 11.84(c).

153. *Id.* § 11.84(d).

154. *Id.*

155. *Id.* § 11.84(e). The AO should use a rate published by the Office of Management and Budget in a 1972 circular. *See id.*

of the injured resources.[156] The authorized official also has discretion to calculate and include in the amount of damages the compensable value for the time that elapses during restoration activities. If compensable value will be included, the trustee should make sure the calculation follows a five-part procedure. First, the trustee should estimate the ability of the injured resources to recover over the recovery period, considering both natural recovery rates and the rate reflecting management actions or resource acquisitions. Second, the trustee should select a recovery rate for the analysis, taking into consideration cost-effect management actions or resource acquisitions, as well as a no action-natural recovery alternative. The trustee should then estimate compensable value. Third, the trustee should estimate the rate at which the uses of the injured resources and their services will be restored, discounting compensable value based on the likelihood that the restored services will not be utilized at their full capacity through the entire period. Fourth, the trustee should estimate the use of the resources that would have occurred in the absence of the discharge or release, drawing on the baseline services determination in the quantification phase; that estimate constitutes the expected present value of uses forgone. Finally, the trustee should subtract the present value of uses obtained through restoration or replacement from the expected present value of uses forgone, which produces the amount of compensation to include in the measure of damages.[157]

4. Post-Assessment

After the assessment is complete, the trustee must prepare a Report of Assessment that includes the Preassessment Screen Determination and the Assessment Plan.[158] For Type A assessments, the report must also include all information specified in the regulations governing Type A procedure.[159] For Type B, the report must include all documentation supporting the determinations made in each of the three phases, test results of all methodologies the trustee performed, the preliminary estimate of damages, and the RCDP and its public comments and responses.[160] In order to seek recovery of the assessed damages for either assessment type, the authorized official must present to the

---

156. *Id.* § 11.84(f).

157. *Id.* § 11.84(g). These steps need not be taken in sequence. *Id.* § 11.84(g)(2).

158. *Id.* § 11.90(a).

159. *Id.* § 11.90(b); *see* this chapter, Section B.3.b.i (describing the Type A assessment procedure).

160. 43 C.F.R. § 11.90(c).

PRP or PRPs a written demand for damages with the Report of Assessment attached. The demand must adequately identify the federal or state agency or tribe asserting the claim, the general location and a description of the injured resource, the type of discharge or release that allegedly caused the injuries, and the damages sought.[161] The trustee must allow the PRP at least 60 days from receipt of the demand to acknowledge and respond before filing suit, granting reasonable extensions as appropriate.[162]

If a federal trustee brings a successful claim under section 107(f) of CERCLA or sections 311(f)(4) and (5) of the CWA, the trustee must prepare a Restoration Plan.[163] The Restoration Plan must be based on the RCDP and must describe how the trustee will use the damage award for restoration, rehabilitation, replacement, or acquisition of equivalent resources. If damages for compensable value have also been awarded, the Restoration Plan must also describe how the funds will be used to address services lost to the public until the restoration is complete. The trustee should follow the regulations' guidance for RCDPs in designing the Restoration Plan.[164] Notably, federal agencies may not incur any expenses for restoration activities besides those awarded unless funds are separately appropriated.[165] No type of trustee may use the award funds for any actions not described in the Restoration Plan.[166] The trustee may modify the Restoration Plan as the restoration proceeds, however, although significant modifications must be made available for review by PRPs and the public for at least 30 days before tasks called for may begin.[167]

---

161. *Id.* §§ 11.91(a), 11.91(b). The AO must also deliver the demand "in a manner that establishes the date of receipt." *Id.* § 11.91(a).

162. *Id.* § 11.91(d). In cases governed by section 113(g) of CERCLA, the AO may also include a notice of intent to file suit with the demand for damages. *Id.*

163. For a sample Restoration Plan, see Indus. Econ. Inc., Onondaga Lake Natural Resource Damage Assessment Restoration Plan and Environmental Assessment, https://www.fws.gov/northeast/nyfo/ec/files/onondaga/Onondaga%20RP%20EA%20and%20 Appendices%208-11-2017_reduced%20(2).pdf.

164. 43 C.F.R. § 11.93(a).

165. *Id.* § 11.93(b). The damage award funds must be placed in a separate account in the U.S. treasury if a federal agency is the trustee, or either an account in a state or tribal treasury or an interest-bearing account payable in trust to the trustee if the trustee is a state agency or tribe. *Id.* §§ 11.92(a)(2), 11.92(a)(3). If funds are placed in a non-interest-bearing account, the amount must be adjusted for inflation while restoration activities are completed. *Id.* § 11.92(b).

166. *Id.* § 11.92(c). For Type A assessments, however, the Restoration Plan may describe actions to be taken with funds from more than one damage award as long as the actions are intended to address the same or similar resource injuries. *Id.* § 11.93(d).

167. *Id.* § 11.93(c).

C. NRDAs under OPA

1. Overview

The OPA regulations divide the NRDA process into three phases: (1) preassessment; (2) restoration planning; and (3) restoration implementation. Each phase is discussed in more detail in the following subsections.

2. Preassessment

In the preassessment phase, the trustees determine the likelihood that a natural resource—land, fish, wildlife, biota, air, water, and other resources—has been, or will be, injured (in accordance with the regulatory definition of "injury" in 15 C.F.R. § 990.30) as a result of a spill. More specifically, during preassessment, OPA regulations require trustees to evaluate if "[a]n injured natural resource has been exposed to the discharged oil, and a pathway can be established from the discharge to the exposed natural resource,"[168] or "[a]n injury to a natural resource or impairment of a natural resource service has occurred as a result of response actions or a substantial threat of a discharge of oil."[169]

The preassessment phase allows trustees to determine whether they have jurisdiction to undertake a full injury assessment and to begin to determine whether there is a need for restoration planning.[170] The first step in a NRDA under OPA is the potential trustees' notification by the on-scene coordinator of a potential incident affecting natural resources, pursuant to the NCP.[171] Before undertaking a NRDA under OPA, potential trustees must first determine whether (1) there has been an unpermitted discharge of oil, or substantial threat of a discharge of oil; (2) into or upon navigable waters or adjoining shorelines; (3) not from a public vessel (or onshore facility if covered by the Trans-Alaska Pipeline Authority Act); and (4) as a result of that discharge, "[n]atural resources under the trusteeship of the trustee[s] may have been, or may be, injured as a result" of the discharge.[172] Only when all four conditions are met do trustees have jurisdiction to engage in a NRDA and pursue restoration.[173]

If the trustees determine that they have jurisdiction to pursue restoration, they must then determine whether (1) injuries have resulted or are likely to

---

168. 15 C.F.R. § 990.51(b)(2)(i).
169. *Id.* § 990.51(b)(2)(ii).
170. *Id.* § 990.41(a).
171. 40 C.F.R. § 300.320(a)(5).
172. 15 C.F.R. § 990.41(a).
173. *Id.* § 990.41(b).

result from the incident; (2) response actions have not adequately addressed, or are not expected to address, the injuries resulting from the incident; and (3) feasible primary and/or compensatory restoration actions exist to address the potential injury.[174]

If the preceding conditions are met, then trustees may proceed with injury assessment and restoration planning.[175]

3. Restoration Planning

a. Organization

To initiate the injury assessment and restoration planning phase of a NRDA, trustees must issue a Notice of Intent to Conduct Restoration Planning (NOI) that includes the trustees' "proposed strategy to address injury and determine the type and scale of restoration."[176] The NOI is often published in the Federal Register. Trustees are generally required to "make a copy of the [NOI] publicly available," but "[t]he means by which the notice is made publicly available and whether public comments are solicited on the notice will depend on the nature and extent of the incident and various information requirements, and is left to the discretion of the trustees."[177]

Regardless of whether and how trustees publicize the NOI, they are required to "open a publicly available administrative record to document the basis for their decisions pertaining to restoration."[178] Trustees are required to "maintain the administrative record in a manner consistent with the Administrative Procedure Act, 5 U.S.C. § 551-59, 701-06."[179]

Under the OPA regulations, trustees are required to "invite the responsible parties to participate in the natural resource damage assessment."[180] Trustees must document the invitation in the administrative record and "briefly describe the nature and extent of the responsible parties' participation."[181] The OPA regulations state further that "[t]rustees and responsible parties should consider entering into binding agreements to facilitate their interactions and

---

174. *Id.* § 990.42(a).

175. *Id.* § 990.42(b).

176. *Id.* §§ 990.44(a), 990.44(b). For an example, see the NOI published for the *Deepwater Horizon* NRDA, http://www.gulfspillrestoration.noaa.gov/sites/default/files/wp-content/uploads/2010/10/Deepwater_Horizon_Final_NOI1.pdf.

177. 15 C.F.R. § 990.44(c).

178. *Id.* § 990.45(a).

179. *Id.* § 990.45(b).

180. *Id.* § 990.14(c)(1).

181. *Id.* § 990.14(c)(7).

resolve any disputes during the assessment," and "attempt to develop a set of agreed-upon facts concerning the incident and/or assessment."[182]

Although trustees and any responsible party may agree to greater levels of participation by the companies, trustees must, at a minimum, provide "notice of trustee determinations . . . and [an] opportunity [for the responsible party] to comment on documents or plans that significantly affect the nature and extent of the assessment."[183] Trustees are required to "objectively consider all written comments provided by the responsible parties, as well as any other recommendations or proposals that the responsible parties submit in writing."[184] The OPA regulations state further that "[s]ubmissions by the responsible parties will be included in the administrative record."[185]

If multiple trustees' interests are affected by a discharge of oil, the trustees "should act jointly . . . to ensure that full restoration is achieved without double recovery of damages."[186] If their activities coincide with response activities, trustees must coordinate with response agencies consistent with the NCP.[187] In many cases, the trustees will have a Memorandum of Understanding (MOU) that addresses coordination and decision making.[188] NOAA guidance specifies that the following activities may be included in establishing an administrative structure for the NRDA: (1) forming a co-trustee council and selecting a lead administrative trustee; (2) establishing a budget and a schedule; (3) allocating assessment activities among the trustees; and (4) determining responsible party participation.[189]

In complex cases with many trustees, in addition to one or more responsible parties, the NRDA process is often governed by a set of technical working groups (TWGs) with different areas of expertise. The TWGs are often organized by reference to natural resource categories, which may be based on habitat (e.g., shoreline) or animal species (e.g., birds or turtles). The process of developing plans is often iterative as different stakeholders provide input into the overall strategy and specific research and restoration plans. Although much

---

182. *Id.* § 990.14(c)(3).

183. *Id.* § 990.14(c)(4).

184. *Id.*

185. *Id.*

186. *Id.* § 990.14(a)(1).

187. *Id.* § 990.14(b).

188. For an example, see the Trustees' MOU for the Enbridge Spill, https://www.fws.gov/midwest/es/ec/nrda/MichiganEnbridge/adminrecord/FinalEnbridgeTrusteeMOU.pdf.

189. Damage Assessment & Restoration Program, Nat'l Oceanic & Atmospheric Admin., Injury Assessment Guidance Document for Natural Resource Damage Assessment under the Oil Pollution Act of 1990 3-3 (1996) [hereinafter DARRP Injury Assessment Guidance].

of the work creating NRD plans is TWG-specific, injury assessments and restoration plans may intersect with multiple TWG groups. In addition, as NRD plans develop, different TWG groupings may evolve along with them.

b. Assessment Procedures

According to the OPA regulations, NRDA procedures must be "reliable and valid for the particular incident," and "capable of providing assessment information for use in determining the type and scale of restoration appropriate for a particular injury."[190] Costs of a more complex procedure "must be reasonably related to the expected increase in the quantity and/or quality of relevant information provided by the more complex procedure."[191]

OPA regulations allow for a wide range of assessment procedures to be used in a NRDA, including modeling, field studies, literature-based procedures, and laboratory-based procedures.[192] In selecting the procedures to use, trustees must take the following factors into consideration: (1) the range of procedures available; (2) the time and cost necessary to implement the procedures; (3) the potential nature, degree, and spatial and temporal extent of the injury; (4) the potential restoration actions for the injury; and (5) the relevance and adequacy of information generated by the procedures to meet information requirements of restoration planning.[193] If a range of procedures "providing the same type and quality of information is available," the trustees must use "the most cost-effective procedure."[194]

A participating responsible party may request alternative assessment procedures, but the process for doing so is cumbersome under the existing OPA regulations. According to the regulations, a responsible party may request an alternative assessment procedure by doing the following:

- Identify procedures that meet the requirements governing all NRDA procedures in 15 C.F.R. § 990.27, and provide reasons supporting the technical adequacy and appropriateness of such procedures for the incident and associated injuries;
- Advance to the trustees the trustees' reasonable estimate of the cost of using the proposed procedures; and
- Agree not to challenge the results of the proposed procedures.[195]

---

190. 15 C.F.R. § 990.27(a)(1), (3).
191. *Id.* § 990.27(a)(2).
192. *Id.* § 990.27(b).
193. *Id.* § 990.27(c)(1).
194. *Id.* § 990.27(c)(2).
195. *Id.* § 990.14(c)(6)(i).

The trustees may reject the proposed alternative assessment procedures if the trustees determine that the procedures are not technically feasible, are not scientifically or technically sound, or could not be completed within a reasonable time frame, among other reasons.[196]

c. Injury Characterization

Once trustees have determined that an injury has occurred to a natural resource, they must then "identify the nature of the injury."[197] The OPA regulations identify several potential categories of injury, including "adverse changes in: survival, growth, and reproduction; health, physiology and biological condition; behavior; community composition, ecological processes and functions; physical and chemical habitat quality or structure; and public services."[198] When considering which injuries to include in the assessment, trustees are instructed to consider several factors, including the evidence indicating injury and the potential degree, and spatial and temporal extent of the injury.[199] Trustees are not limited in the types of data they may collect, except that "data collection and analysis should be reasonable in light of the characteristics of the incident and the natural resources and/or services potentially affected."[200] NOAA guidance states further that "[c]onstructing the inventory of possible injuries should not require an extensive research effort, but should instead be based on the knowledge of the trustees and outside experts, and the information collected during response and preassessment."[201]

Trustees must also "estimate the amount or concentration and spatial and temporal extent of the exposure" and "determine whether there is a pathway linking the incident to the injuries."[202] Potential pathways include "the sequence of events by which the discharged oil was transported from the incident and either came into direct physical contact with a natural resource, or caused an indirect injury."[203] NOAA guidance discusses criteria trustees

---

196. *Id.* § 990.14(c)(6)(ii).

197. *Id.* § 990.51(c).

198. *Id.*

199. *Id.* § 990.51(f).

200. Damage Assessment & Restoration Program, Nat'l Oceanic & Atmospheric Admin., Preassessment Phase Guidance Document for Natural Resource Damage Assessment under the Oil Pollution Act of 1990 3-10 (1996).

201. DARRP Injury Assessment Guidance, *supra* note 189, at 2-12.

202. 15 C.F.R. § 990.51(d).

203. *Id.*

should use in evaluating the causal pathway between the incident and injury to each specific resource.[204]

d. Injury Quantification

Trustees must determine the extent to which natural resources have been injured relative to baseline conditions.[205] NOAA guidance lists information that may be used in determining baseline, including:

- Information collected on a regular basis and for a period of time from and prior to the incident;
- Information identifying historical patterns or trends for the area of the incident and injured natural resources and services;
- Information from areas unaffected by the incident, that are sufficiently similar to the area of the incident with respect to the parameter being measured; and
- Information from the area of the incident after particular natural resources or services have been judged to have recovered.[206]

OPA regulations allow trustees to quantify injury in terms of the "degree, and spatial and temporal extent of the injury to a natural resource," and to translate that injury to a reduction of services provided by that resource.[207] Trustees are also obligated, however, to estimate the time for natural recovery without restoration when quantifying injury.[208] Factors to consider when estimating natural recovery times include (1) the sensitivity of the natural resource; (2) natural variability; (3) reproductive and recruitment potential; and (4) physical/chemical processes of the environment.[209]

---

204. DARRP INJURY ASSESSMENT GUIDANCE, *supra* note 189, at 2-5.

205. 15 C.F.R. § 990.52(a).

206. DARRP INJURY ASSESSMENT GUIDANCE, *supra* note 189, at 1–7. As discussed previously, under the OPA regulations, "baseline" means "the condition of the natural resources and services that would have existed had the incident not occurred." 15 C.F.R. § 990.30. The goal of the trustees (by law) is not to return the ecosystem to a pristine condition but rather to return the ecosystem to the condition it would be in had the release never occurred. It is critical to understand quantitatively what the baseline condition was for each injured resource. Baseline conditions may be impacted by many things including hurricanes, commercial fishing, other contamination sources, climate change, stormwater run-off, urbanization, sewage discharge and overflows, invasive species, and floods. The impacts from all of these must be subtracted from the injury calculation.

207. 15 C.F.R. § 990.52(b).

208. *Id.* § 990.52(c).

209. DARRP INJURY ASSESSMENT GUIDANCE, *supra* note 189, at 2-15.

e. Developing and Evaluating Restoration Alternatives

If trustees have determined that injuries to natural resources have occurred as a result of the incident, and have quantified those injuries, the trustees may then develop a plan for restoration of the affected resources.[210] Restoration plans are either "primary" (actions to return injured natural resources and services to baseline) or "compensatory" (actions to compensate for interim losses or resources or services pending recovery). Trustees must consider a range of restoration alternatives comprising combinations of primary and/or compensatory restoration to restore the environment and make the public whole.[211]

Primary restoration is aimed at restoring the resource itself. Among the primary restoration options, the trustees must consider a natural recovery alternative in which the resource would be allowed to recover on its own without human intervention.[212] The trustees may also consider active restoration options, including removing contaminants, replacing or modifying habitat, or otherwise facilitating a return to baseline conditions. Trustees are also required to determine what scale of restoration is required to return an injured natural resource to baseline levels.[213]

To compensate for interim losses to the public of the use or enjoyment of the natural resource services, the trustees must consider compensatory restoration actions to provide natural resource services of similar type, quality, and value to the public.[214] If no services of comparable quality are available, the trustees may consider whether, and to what extent, to scale the compensatory restoration actions to make the environment and public whole. Scaling includes actions "involving replacement and/or acquisition of equivalent of natural resources and/or services."[215] Trustees are required to consider both a resource-to-resource and a service-to-service scaling approach. The trustees must also discount for risk and uncertainty in scaling a restoration option. In other words, a scaled restoration compensation project would provide less value (i.e., restoration credits) than the same restoration project that is not scaled.

Once the trustees have developed the restoration alternatives, they must then evaluate them considering factors including (1) cost; (2) efficacy;

---

210. 15 C.F.R. § 990.53(a)(1).

211. *Id.* § 990.53(a)(2).

212. *Id.* § 990.53(b)(1).

213. DAMAGE ASSESSMENT & RESTORATION PROGRAM, NAT'L OCEANIC & ATMOSPHERIC ADMIN., PRIMARY RESTORATION GUIDANCE DOCUMENT FOR NATURAL RESOURCE DAMAGE ASSESSMENT UNDER THE OIL POLLUTION ACT OF 1990 1–6 (1996).

214. 15 C.F.R. § 990.53(c).

215. *Id.* § 990.53(d)(1).

(3) likelihood of success; (4) prevention of repeated injury and avoidance or minimization of collateral injury; (5) the extent to which the alternative will benefit multiple resources; and (6) the impact on public health and safety.[216] Based on the evaluation of these factors, the trustees will then select a preferred alternative. If two or more alternatives are equally preferable, the trustees must select the most cost-effective approach among them.[217]

f.   Developing Restoration Plans

Under OPA, trustees must develop a Draft Restoration Plan that includes, among other things, summary of injury assessment procedures used, description of the natural resource injuries resulting from the incident, and identification of the trustees' "tentative" preferred alternative.[218] The OPA regulations do not specify whether and how the public will be given an opportunity to review the Draft Restoration Plan before it is finalized into a Final Restoration Plan. Previous oil spill NRDAs governed by OPA included the establishment of outreach centers for community input and publication of community guides that explained cleanup and NRDA efforts.[219]

4.   Restoration Implementation

Once the Final Restoration Plan is issued, trustees are required to close the administrative record for restoration planning[220] and present a demand to the responsible parties that invites the responsible parties either to (1) implement the Final Restoration Plan "subject to trustee oversight and reimburse the trustees for their assessment and oversight costs"; or (2) "[a]dvance to the trustees a specified sum representing all trustee direct and indirect costs of assessment and restoration."[221] Should the responsible party fail to respond within 90 days of the demand or else fail to agree with the trustees regarding the scope and costs of the Final Restoration Plan, the trustees are entitled to file a judicial action for damages or seek funds from the Oil Spill Liability

---

216. *Id.* § 990.54(a).

217. *Id.* § 990.54(b).

218. *Id.* § 990.55(b). Draft Damage Assessment Plans and draft Restoration Plans are often combined in one document. *See, e.g.,* https://www.fws.gov/northeast/virginiafield/pdf/contam inants/20170317_Kinder_Morgan_Draft_DARP_for_Public_Review.pdf. This document may also be released at the same time as announcement of a settlement with the responsible parties.

219. Such measures were put in place for a spill in Chalk Point, Maryland. *See Chalk Point,* Nat'l Oceanic & Atmospheric Admin., Damage Assessment, Remediation, & Restoration, https://darrp.noaa.gov/oil-spills/chalk-point (last visited Jan. 19, 2019).

220. 15 C.F.R. § 990.61(a).

221. *Id.* § 990.62(b).

Trust Fund.[222] In practice, the order of these steps may be altered, particularly where the trustees and the responsible parties are able to negotiate and reach a settlement. In such cases, the trustees may announce a settlement and publish for comment a Damage Assessment and Restoration Plan (DARP) as well as a consent decree.

D. Aligning the CERCLA and OPA Regulations

The OPA regulations are significantly less cumbersome than the CERCLA regulations. While the OPA regulations contain general guidelines and objectives for each element of an assessment, the CERCLA regulations prescribe specific requirements.[223]

There are significant substantive differences, too. From the beginning, the focus of the OPA regulations has been restoration.[224] Under the OPA rules, restoration plans form the basis for NRD claims; trustees may present final restoration plans to responsible parties for funding, or responsible parties may implement restoration plans approved and monitored by trustees.[225] The CERCLA NRDA procedures, on the other hand, historically focused on measuring damages by quantifying the value of lost resources.

One manifestation of this difference between OPA and CERCLA was in their approaches to measuring interim losses. Under the OPA rule, responsible parties are not liable for a calculated interim loss in value of the injured resource; instead they are liable for the cost of implementing restoration actions to generate the equivalent value of the lost services.[226] The CERCLA regulations, on the other hand, historically used an approach to interim losses that calculated the interim losses, which the regulations call "compensable value,"[227] as the value of losses arising from the injury to the resource until restoration is achieved. The regulations did not explicitly authorize trustees to consider restoration actions to address interim losses until after trustees had determined the amount of damages.

---

222. *Id.* § 990.64(a).

223. *See, e.g.,* Valerie Ann Lee & P.J. Bridgen, The Natural Resource Damage Assessment Deskbook: A Legal and Technical Analysis 170 (Envtl. Law Inst. ed., 2002).

224. *See* Natural Resource Damage Assessments, 61 Fed. Reg. 440 (Jan. 5, 1996) (to be codified at 15 C.F.R. pt. 990) ("The purpose of this rule is to provide a framework for conducting sound natural resource damage assessments that achieve restoration under OPA.").

225. *See* 61 Fed. Reg. at 440; *see also* Bill Conner & Ron Gouguet, *Getting to Restoration*, 21 Envtl. F. 22, 24 (2004).

226. 61 Fed. Reg. at 442.

227. *See* 43 C.F.R. § 11.83(c).

DOI chartered a federal advisory committee in 2005 to consider, among other things, this issue of compensating for public losses pending restoration as well as other issues.[228] The committee issued its report in 2007. The report noted the "significant difference" between how OPA and CERCLA regulations treated compensation for interim losses, noting that "[r]ather than including a damages component representing the economic *value* for interim losses, the OPA Regulations seek to focus the entire claim on the cost of implementing restoration projects that will both restore injured resources *and* compensate for lost human and ecological resource services pending restoration."[229] The report said OPA's approach promoted "an early focus on feasible restoration rather than monetary damages" and could result in lower overall restoration costs.[230]

The committee's report recommended that DOI "undertake a targeted revision" of its regulations to explicitly authorize a "restoration-based approach"[231] to interim losses. The report indicated that such a revision would align the CERCLA approach with the OPA approach by emphasizing restoration rather than the monetary value of lost services and be more consistent with the restoration-based goals of NRD.[232]

In its 2008 regulatory amendments, DOI changed the CERCLA regulations in response to this aspect of the committee's report. The 2008 amendments explicitly authorized trustees to estimate compensable values for interim losses based on the cost of implementing restoration projects to restore the lost natural resource services.[233] The amended regulations provide that the economic value of lost services can be measured either "by changes in consumer surplus, economic rent, and any fees or other payments" that would otherwise have been collectable by agencies or tribes for private parties' use of natural resources (in other words, basing damages on the monetary value of lost services) or by using the restoration cost approach to measure "the cost of implementing a project or projects that restore, replace, or acquire the equivalent of natural resource services lost pending restoration to baseline."[234] DOI indicated that the amendments would promote "an earlier focus on feasible restoration

---

228. U.S. Dep't of the Interior, Natural Resource Damage Assessment and Restoration Federal Advisory Committee Final Report to the Secretary 5 (2007).

229. *Id.* at 7 (emphasis in original).

230. *Id.* at 14.

231. *Id.*

232. *See id.*

233. Natural Resource Damages for Hazardous Substances, 73 Fed. Reg. 57,259, 57,260–61 (Oct. 2, 2008) (to be codified at 43 C.F.R. pt. 11).

234. 43 C.F.R. § 11.83(c)(1).

options, which can encourage settlements by providing opportunities for designing creative and cost-effective actions to address losses."[235]

The federal advisory committee's 2007 report identified other aspects of the CERCLA NRD program where the focus on restoration could be enhanced. For example, the advisory committee's report encouraged "early and continued consideration of appropriate restoration options" and sponsorship of "workshops, research papers, and symposiums to inform guidance on explicitly linking the scale of restoration to the nature and extent of the injury."[236]

In addition, the committee recommended more extensive review of the CERCLA regulations in the long term to make them "more understandable, while maintaining consistency with sound scientific and economic principles."[237] A subcommittee report that informed the 2007 report's recommendations specifically identified revisions that could be made to the CERCLA regulations' factors for selecting restoration alternatives, as well as regulatory revisions to encourage earlier consideration of restoration options.[238]

A number of the recommended changes were intended to align the CERCLA restoration selection process with OPA's. The subcommittee noted that though "[t]he restoration planning processes under CERCLA and OPA present essentially identical procedural and substantive issues[,] . . . the CERCLA and OPA rules contain significantly different criteria for selecting among restoration alternatives."[239] For example, the subcommittee recommended that the CERCLA regulations include mandatory threshold criteria "instead of just the current system of ten unweighted discretionary criteria." The subcommittee report said OPA's threshold criteria operated as "screening criteria" allowing trustees "to eliminate plainly-inappropriate proposals early."[240] Another recommendation involved revision of the remaining selection criteria for restoration alternatives to make them more similar to the OPA criteria by including

---

235. 73 Fed. Reg. at 57,260.

236. U.S. Dep't of the Interior, Natural Resource Damage Assessment and Restoration Federal Advisory Committee Final Report to the Secretary 2 (2007).

237. *Id.* at 19.

238. U.S. Dep't of the Interior, *Subcommittee Report on Restoration Action Selection, in* Natural Resource Damage Assessment and Restoration Federal Advisory Committee Final Report to the Secretary app. A (2007).

239. *Id.* The report noted, however, that trustees appeared to have made "very little formal use" of the selection criteria, suggesting that trustees "have not viewed the factors as providing valuable guidance." *Id.*

240. *Id.*

the following factors as balancing criteria: likelihood of success of each alternative and the extent to which each alternative will prevent future injury and avoid collateral injury as a result of implementing the alternative. The subcommittee also identified specific sections of the CERCLA regulations that DOI could revise to encourage an earlier focus on restoration.

As discussed in Chapter 2, some of these recommendations are being evaluated in connection with the August 27, 2018, DOI ANPRM related to potential revision of the CERCLA NRDA regulations.

EXPERT INSIGHTS: NRDA—The Trustee's Perspective

Robert Haddad[241]

Exponent, Inc.

Public Trust Doctrine

Natural resources that exist within the public trust and the services provided by those resources are protected by the government under a long-standing common law tradition known as the Public Trust Doctrine. Under this doctrine, natural resources collectively belonging to the people are managed by the government for the benefit of all. Within the United States, this means that, for the most part, management of the natural resources in the public trust falls to the states, except where a statute puts the federal government in control. For example, while wildlife management is a state responsibility, the Endangered Species Act, the Marine Mammal Protection Act, and the Migratory Bird Treaty Act all bring certain species under federal protection. Similarly, federally recognized tribal governments also have trust authority for their people's natural resources and the services they provide based on treaty rights.

When resources in the public trust are harmed by contamination, federal, state, foreign, and tribal governments may seek compensation for injury to natural resources under certain laws. This is done in two steps: first, by assessing the injury; then, by determining how and what restoration will be required to make the public whole, including any interim losses. Damages for natural resource injury are intended to restore the natural resources to their baseline condition and to compensate the public for the lost use of those resources between the time the injury initially occurred until the resources and the services have been restored to baseline conditions.

---

241. Dr. Robert I. Haddad is the group vice president and principal scientist—environmental & earth sciences, for Exponent, Inc. Dr. Haddad was the chief, Assessment & Restoration Division, Office of Response & Restoration for the National Oceanic and Atmospheric Administration from 2007 to 2016. He holds a PhD in chemical oceanography from the University of North Carolina, Chapel Hill.

NRDA Statutory Authority

Natural Resource Damage Assessment (NRDA) is authorized by several statutes, depending on the type of contamination. These include the Comprehensive Environmental Response, Compensation, and Liability Act (CERCLA); the Clean Water Act (CWA); the Oil Pollution Act of 1990 (OPA); the National Marine Sanctuaries Act; and the Park System Resource Protection Act. In general, these statutes provide the authority for the trustees of these public resources to assess the level of natural resource injuries and then seek to restore, rehabilitate, replace, or acquire the equivalent of the injured natural resources and services.

Who Are the Trustees?

Under 42 U.S.C. § 9607(f)(2), a trustee is a federal, state, and/or tribal official who is designated to "act on behalf of the public as trustee for natural resources." OPA adds foreign trustees to this list. While the statutes identify that the trustee authority resides with either the senior executive (e.g., president, governor, tribal chairman, head of a foreign government) or the executive governing body (e.g., tribal councils), in practice, the role is usually designated downward within an organization. In the federal government, the president of the United States delegates his trust authority downward to various departments and agencies. The U.S. Department of Commerce (through the National Oceanic and Atmospheric Administration (NOAA)) and the U.S. Fish and Wildlife Service (USFWS) within the U.S. Department of the Interior (DOI) are the federal natural resource trustees (NRTs) most often involved in NRDAs. Each federal group has specific resources for which it acts as the federal trustee. However, in some cases where the natural resource injury occurs on federal land (e.g., military facilities, national parks, land managed by the Bureau of Land Management (BLM), Department of Energy (DOE) Laboratories), it is not uncommon to have federal trustees representing each of these entities (e.g., U.S. Department of Defense, U.S. National Park Service, BLM, DOE). For states, the natural resource trusteeship depends on the governor's designation. In some states, there is a single entity to which the state's trust authority is delegated (e.g., Alabama's Department of Conservation and Natural Resources); for others the trust authority is shared among multiple agencies within the state (e.g., Texas Parks and Wildlife Department, Texas General Land Office, and Texas Commission on Environmental Quality).

In most cases, the public's trust resources are co-managed by state, federal, and, sometimes, tribal governments. Because of this, the various trustees of standing usually coordinate the process of determining the extent of injury and the method(s) of restoration, including compensation amounts. They are charged with acting "on behalf of the public." The most common process is for the trustees to form a Natural Resource Trustee Council to govern the overall trustee actions and responses. As such, the council is a group of sovereign peers, which means that decisions made by the council are consensus based. Although there are challenges with the consensus-based process, it is the approach used to ensure the ultimate outcome of the NRDA process recognizes the rights of all of the sovereigns.

The Trustees' View of the NRDA World

The following paragraphs represent no official position, but rather my personal experience and my perceptions. No one individual or agency can effectively characterize how all NRTs deal with conducting a NRDA; simply because the experiences, concerns, perspectives, and skill sets of trustees are so different. At the federal level and in some states, resolving NRDA claims and moving to restoration are the trustee's primary activities. Consequently, they have substantial experience and work from the perspective of understanding the NRDA process in large and small cases, under CERCLA and under OPA, and so on. These groups are more likely to accept a degree of uncertainty in exchange for getting to the endgame. For other states and some tribes, their NRTs have much less experience conducting NRDAs or they have an experience base that is fairly narrow. Further, these NRTs may have closer ties to the natural resource injuries or they may have prior concerns or history with the responsible party(s) at the site. For these groups of trustees, uncertainty may be a concern that they feel needs to be resolved. These differences of perception, experience, and expertise can cause significant challenges within a trustee council. Yet, at the end of the day, all of these issues need to be resolved within the Trustee Council in order to achieve a consensus-based solution. Consequently, resolution of these internal challenges can sometimes add to delays in moving a case forward.

Despite the very real differences that can exist between some NRTs, each takes its trust responsibility very seriously. They are all driven to ensure that their injured natural resources are identified and that restoration is accomplished. Because of these common goals, NRTs are universally dedicated to ensuring that natural resource injuries are appropriately identified and quantified. In general, there is an understanding that the NRT's knowledge of the natural resources injuries at a site and on the services those resources provide will never be complete. And in some cases, this level of uncertainty has caused the trustees to conduct additional work to help minimize the uncertainty.

As noted earlier, the degree by which the trustees strive to minimize uncertainties in their understanding of the natural resource injury often is related to the level of the trustee's NRDA experience. This has been a large concern of many responsible parties involved with NRDA claims. Yet, the NRTs have embraced the use of tools such as Habitat Equivalency Analysis and Resource Equivalency Analysis; tools designed to highlight the importance of restoration and geared toward moving the conversation more easily toward case resolution. I find it interesting to also consider that the NRTs are driven by obtaining the appropriate types and amounts of restoration and that they really have no vested interest in prolonging cases. There are more cases in their dockets than there are NRTs to work on them, they receive no additional financial support for prolonging cases, and once they finish a case other cases are immediately assigned. It is also important to point out that such diligence by the NRTs actually benefits the responsible parties, as it provides a strong bulwark against third-party claims aimed at challenging the appropriateness of the ultimate NRD claim settlement.

In summary, most of the federal, state, and tribal trustees I have worked with over the past 25 years pride themselves on being both passionate about their trust resources and pragmatic about getting to restoration. In the end, it is the NRTs who have the responsibility to balance what might be considered a pragmatic approach to resolving an NRD claim with what is best for their trust natural resources; in doing so, they are not answerable to the responsible parties but to the public. For most NRTs, this is a sacred duty and one they take extremely seriously.

Chapter 5
NRD Assessments: Valuation Methods

The previous chapter discussed the regulatory mechanics for an NRD assessment pursuant to the CERCLA and OPA regulations. This chapter focuses on the real-world strategy of assessment, with a focus on types of compensable damages and various damages valuation techniques. While injury determination and quantification are themselves complex, technical undertakings, valuation is perhaps the most controversial piece of a NRDA because results can vary widely based on methodology. Put simply, valuing a loss or decline in natural resources is not a straightforward task. As discussed briefly in the previous chapter, both the OPA and amended CERCLA regulations strongly favor a restoration-based approach to valuation—the cost of restoring a natural resource injury is assumed by the regulations to be the value of the damage incurred. In certain circumstances the regulations allow trustees to utilize other, economics-based valuation techniques. Although the regulations have disfavored these techniques, trustees have, in practice, heavily relied on them.[1]

This chapter first discusses how to calculate the amount of compensable injury under CERCLA and OPA and the specific categories of injuries that will generally require valuation. It then sets forth in detail the possible techniques for damages quantification and their relative merits. The discussion includes the insights of three renowned natural resource economists who are experts in when and how to apply these techniques.

---

1. 42 U.S.C. § 9607(f)(1).

A. Calculation of Compensable Damages under CERCLA and OPA

Broadly, CERCLA states that the measure of NRD "shall not be limited by the sums which can be used to restore or replace such resources."[2] Specifically, the additional types of damages a trustee can recover under CERCLA include (1) damages based on injuries incurred from the onset of the release through the recovery period, less any mitigation of those injuries as a result of response actions, plus any increase of injuries that were unavoidable as a result of response actions; (2) the costs of emergency restoration efforts; (3) the reasonable and necessary costs of the NRDA; and (4) interest on the amounts recoverable.[3]

Similarly, OPA includes within the measure of NRD: (1) the cost of restoring, rehabilitating, replacing, or acquiring the equivalent of the damaged resources (primary restoration); (2) the interim loss or diminution in value of those natural resources pending restoration (compensatory restoration); and (3) the reasonable cost of assessing those damages.[4] In addition to liability for damages as just described, a responsible party is liable to the claimant for interest on its claim beginning 30 days after presentation of the claim and ending on the date on which the claim is paid.[5]

This section discusses in greater detail the concepts of primary and compensatory restoration, baseline (which is necessary to assess primary and compensatory restoration), and assessment costs.

1. Primary and Compensatory Restoration

The cost of "restoring, rehabilitating, [or] replacing" the damaged resources is referred to as primary restoration. This includes the costs of developing, selecting, and implementing necessary restoration alternatives. It may also include the cost of monitoring the resource following restoration.[6]

The interim loss or diminution in value of injured natural resources pending restoration is referred to as compensatory restoration because the intent is to compensate the public for the loss of a natural resource from the time of injury until the time of primary restoration. Compensatory restoration is generally accomplished by returning the affected natural resources to better than baseline condition, which can be accomplished by creating additional habitat

---

2. *Id.*
3. 43 C.F.R. § 11.15(a).
4. 33 U.S.C. § 2706(d).
5. *Id.* § 2713.
6. *See* Gen. Elec. Co. v. U.S. Dep't of Commerce, 128 F.3d 767, 776 (D.C. Cir. 1997).

Figure 5.1 Primary versus compensatory restoration. In this illustration, primary restoration is achieved after approximately two years; compensatory restoration is achieved after six years.

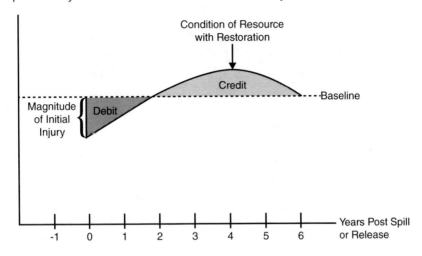

or building a facility to enhance recreational use beyond the baseline conditions, among other actions.

Primary and compensatory restoration can be thought of as "credits" designed to offset the "debit" associated with the initial injury to natural resources and the interim loss pending restoration. As illustrated in Figure 5.1, when the incident causes the condition of the natural resource to dip below baseline, a debit accumulates. When restoration causes the condition of the natural resource to exceed baseline, a credit accumulates. Primary restoration is achieved when conditions rebound to baseline, but injuries are not fully compensated until the debit (represented by the dark gray area) is equal to the credit (represented by the light gray area).

2. Establishing Baseline

To determine the level of primary and compensatory restoration necessary, trustees must determine the baseline condition of the resources. Trustees are not entitled to the restoration of resources to pristine condition; they are only entitled to the restoration of resources and services to the condition that would have existed had the incident not occurred.[7] To establish baseline, the parties

---

7. *See, e.g.*, 15 C.F.R. § 990.10 (the goal of OPA "is achieved through the return of the injured natural resources and services to baseline and compensation for interim losses"); *id.* § 990.30 ("Baseline means the condition of the natural resources and services that would have existed had the incident not occurred."); 43 C.F.R. § 11.14(e) ("*Baseline* means the condition or conditions

must consider other human and environmental forces that may have caused the observed injury, as well as how the services would have changed over time. Human forces could include other releases of hazardous substances or petroleum and other emissions or discharges (hot water, nonhazardous substances, etc.). In addition, the assessment area could have been impacted by pesticide application, urban development, acid precipitation, and global climate change, to name a few possibilities. Finally, environmental or other natural factors, including severe weather events, natural oil seeps, invasive species, and disease, may impact natural resources. Chapter 4 discusses the regulatory framework for the baseline analysis.

A robust baseline analysis must account for the underlying trajectory of the ecological services. As stated by NOAA, baseline "is the condition the resource would be in today if it had not been exposed to the release."[8] Thus, both the condition of the ecosystem prior to the release and the hypothetical condition of the ecosystem today *but for* the release must be determined. This necessitates an evaluation of ecological trends. According to NOAA, the ecological baseline could be constant (ecological services stable independent of the release), declining (ecological services in decline independent of the release), fluctuating (ecological services increasing and decreasing, such as beaches), increasing (ecological services improving or recovering independent of release), or crashing (ecological services severely harmed by storm or other event).[9] Accordingly, in order to quantify NRD, the trustee must calculate the baseline condition for each resource over both space and time.

EXPERT INSIGHT: The NRDA Baseline
Paul D. Boehm, PhD[10]
Exponent, Inc.

Overview: What Baseline Is and Is Not

The concept of the environmental "baseline" is central to all NRDAs. Regulatory language under CERCLA and OPA is quite similar: CERCLA—baseline is the "condition

---

that would have existed at the assessment area had the discharge of oil or release of the hazardous substance under investigation not occurred.").

8. NAT'L OCEANIC & ATMOSPHERIC ADMIN. DAMAGE ASSESSMENT & RESTORATION PROGRAM, JOINT ASSESSMENT TEAM MEETING: BASELINE (2003).

9. *Id.*

10. Dr. Paul Boehm is a corporate vice president and principal scientist—environmental and earth sciences with Exponent, Inc. He is a leading practitioner in NRDAs. He holds a PhD in oceanography from the University of Rhode Island.

or conditions that would have existed at the assessment area had the discharge of oil or release of the hazardous substance under investigation not occurred";[11] OPA—baseline "means the condition of the natural resources and services that would have existed had the incident not occurred."[12]

Given that determination of injuries and resultant needs for restoration focus on returning to conditions that would have existed "but for" the release(s) of hazardous substances (CERCLA) or oil (OPA), understanding that state of the environment and its natural resources is arguably the pivotal element in NRDAs. Baseline includes information on both ecological and human uses. While baseline may be thought of as those environmental (chemical, biological, physical, human use) conditions that characterized the affected environment prior to the release, in fact, proper evaluation of the baseline also, importantly, recognizes the factors that shape natural populations and human uses of natural resources that are both concurrent with and independent of the release. Such factors include physical modifications of habitats from development and natural factors; flood controls; natural erosion; climate-related changes; natural population variations and mortality; and major natural events such as hurricanes.

The NRDA baseline is literally the condition (i.e., habitat quality, resource abundance and diversity, human uses, etc.) of the resource(s) that would have existed, but for a specific release. The baseline does not refer to pristine, historical conditions devoid of any anthropogenic input. This specific misconception is especially pertinent to NRDAs in or adjacent to urban waterways, where background chemical conditions and the status of resources associated with these may have resulted from approved applications (e.g., pesticides) or non-point source releases and discharges, but have nothing to do with the specific release(s) under scrutiny in the NRDA. The baseline also may include consideration of, but is not entirely, the set of pre-release conditions, especially with regard to releases of long duration, which are historically disconnected to present natural conditions at unaffected areas.

Characterization of Baseline Conditions

The estimation of baseline is simple in concept (i.e., conditions, but for the release) but can be highly complex in actual NRDAs. In some situations, baseline can be determined in a relatively straightforward manner, for example by the use of unaffected reference areas and/or when pre-release data are available for a site. However, estimation of baseline for large, complex sites, especially those involving historical releases occurring over many decades, can be problematic and contentious. Determination of baseline services is especially difficult when many natural and anthropogenic stressors have historically influenced a resource in combination with the effects of a release being assessed in a NRDA. In all situations, estimation of baseline should involve the use of adequate data from multiple, unaffected reference areas that are appropriately

---

11. 43 C.F.R. § 11.14(e).
12. 15 C.F.R. § 990.30.

matched to the site of the NRDA with regard to the type of resources present and the natural and anthropogenic stressors affecting those resources and the services they provide. Fate and transport analyses combined with chemical forensic measurements help identify and delineate possible reference areas that are unimpacted by the release. When collecting reference-area data, the most fundamental requirement is that the reference stations should reflect, as closely as possible, the environmental conditions in the assessment area, except for the substances included in the release being assessed. Before and after sampling at locations may be part of the baseline assessment, but site-specific pre-spill information may not always be available or obtainable.

Baseline Characterization of Chemical and Other Nonbiological Conditions

Chemical and other nonbiological changes over time are part of the baseline or background conditions that need to be documented and measured in NRDA investigations. Environmental factors can also create a dynamic range of changing abiotic baseline conditions in terrestrial and aquatic environments that need to be assessed from the literature, from government databases, and from measurement programs as part of the injury assessment studies of a NRDA. Whether a release occurs in a lake or river, or in an industrialized harbor, organic compounds and heavy metals are always found that are unrelated to the release. Both CERCLA and OPA regulations recognize this fact and require that the baseline be assessed so that the addition of chemicals associated with the releases in question can be assessed properly.

The determination of the chemical background or baseline is accomplished through the sampling and analysis of reference sites that are unimpacted by the releases. This sampling includes both natural and other anthropogenic sources, as well as—in the case of sites in the midst of heavy industrialization—areas upstream or otherwise removed from the influence of the site. In the case of oil spills, sampling needs to include other petroleum sources, both natural and anthropogenic. This is especially true in areas of natural oil seeps, such as the Santa Barbara Channel and the Gulf of Mexico, and in areas with erosion of high-organic, hydrocarbon-laden shale material, such as southern coastal Alaska. There is a wealth of information in the scientific literature and in U.S. government reports on inland and coastal water that can be used to inform the determination of the chemical background at a site. Differentiating background chemicals from those contained in the release requires not only an adequate number of carefully chosen reference locations, but also the employment of techniques of chemical fingerprinting, for which there are many approaches applicable to the variety of chemicals found in urban and remote background environmental media.

Beyond the chemical background, other nonbiological features of the unimpacted baseline environment are important. Ocean currents, circulation patterns, hydrology and runoff patterns, salinity/conductivity, and/or temperature regimes are examples of factors that may change over time in aquatic environments. Weather patterns, occurrences of severe storms, droughts, and other phenomena are important aspects of the assessment of the range of baseline levels of services. Included in this category are specialized large phenomena, such as the regular occurrence of low oxygen conditions (known as hypoxia) in the coastal Gulf of Mexico from the influence of the Mississippi River and rainfall patterns contributing to terrestrial baseline conditions. Also of particular importance are large-scale storm events that can cause erosion, stream modification, and massive redistribution of sediments and associated contaminants. Data to assess baseline conditions of these abiotic factors can be collected not only from existing sources but also from measurement programs as part of the NRDA injury assessment studies.

Baseline Characterization of Biological Conditions

Baseline conditions for biological resources are frequently characterized by combining contemporary (i.e., recent) pre-release information (e.g., population trend data) with focused sampling of key biological resources at one or more reference areas that are presumed to be similar to the assessment site, except for exposure to the discharge or release. Although this fundamental requirement for reference areas is clearly identified in the CERCLA and OPA regulations and in relevant publications, NRDA cases frequently involve significant disagreements concerning the appropriateness of historical data selection and identification of reference stations used for baseline comparisons. These disagreements generally center on the degree to which the reference site is similar to the assessment site for all natural and anthropogenic factors other than the substances being assessed. As such, efforts should be made to identify the biological features (such as indicator species) that may serve as the basis for accurate and defensible comparisons.

Evaluation of the biological baseline can be similar or very different for OPA and CERCLA sites. For example, for a current oil spill, relatively recent biological studies of the impacted area or nearby areas may be available that can serve as baseline data. Even if the affected area has not been studied in the past, it may be relatively straightforward to conduct current studies of nearby unaffected areas to collect baseline data for comparative purposes. The situation for CERCLA sites can be much more complex, especially for sites where the releases being investigated may have occurred many decades ago. In such cases, there may be no comparable biological data that can be used for comparative purposes. Even if recent reference-area data are available, they may be useful only for describing current baseline conditions, which may be very different from the historical baseline. Many CERCLA sites are located in highly industrialized areas, the presence of which further complicates baseline issues because baseline must consider all other physical and chemical influences on the biological populations in addition to the release being investigated.

When identifying approaches to define the biological baseline, several overarching, constraining factors exist:

1. Baseline is a dynamic condition with multiple stressors continuously changing influences on the structure and function of biological populations.
2. Reference areas are not perfect replicas of affected areas.
3. Baseline data must be statistically adequate (e.g., a single reference station (or area) will often not be adequate to define baseline conditions).

From an optimal perspective, the use of a before-after-control-impact study design enables the most precise evaluation of any significant differences in biological conditions from reference areas. However, with the possible exception of current discharges at sites that were monitored historically, this option is not usually available. Therefore, for CERCLA assessments involving historical releases, the determination of baseline conditions is best approached using multiple lines of evidence that potentially include the use of multiple reference areas, analyses of biological responses over gradients in chemical and physical conditions, analyses of historical data and other information, and data analyses involving multivariate statistics and modeling of past or future conditions if the data are sufficiently robust to support reasonably accurate modeling.

Baseline Characterization of Human Uses

The natural environment provides various recreational and human use services, and the diminution of possible uses of natural resources by the public are compensable injuries under NRDA. As such, assessment of the human use baseline is vital.

Human uses are highly site specific but usually include some combination of non-commercial uses of the resources by the public. Recreational uses in this category may include beach visitations, boating, recreational fishing, uses of public parks, and so on. Coastal wetlands support birdwatching and hunting, and wetlands and some coastal environments also offer protection from storm events, which has great economic value. Collection of baseline data for these categories can be a large undertaking and involves historical analysis of data that are directly applicable to the affected areas in the applicable seasons. Often data on beach visitations, angler surveys, tourist information, and the possible statistical modeling of these data to assess the baseline uses over time are required for inputs to economic models. In the specific cases where potential injury to groundwater/drinking water is involved, a separate analysis of the baseline water supplies and baseline uses of those supplies is required.

3. Reasonable Assessment Costs

In addition to primary and compensatory restoration, trustees can also recover for the costs of assessing injury. Reasonable assessment costs associated with the NRD process include not only the cost of assessing the state of the natural resources post-spill or post-release but also preassessment costs such as collecting baseline data or reviewing scientific literature about the potential impact on at-risk natural resources. Under OPA, in cases where assessment costs are incurred but trustees do not pursue restoration, trustees may still be able to recover their reasonable assessment costs provided they have determined that assessment actions undertaken were premised on the likelihood of injury and need for restoration.[13] Under CERCLA, however, if it is determined that there is no injury to natural resources, as defined in the regulations, trustees may not recover assessment costs.[14]

CERCLA defines costs as reasonable when the injury determination, quantification, and damage determination phases are well-defined and coordinated.[15] For both CERCLA and OPA, reasonable assessment costs also include administrative costs and expenses, legal costs,[16] and other costs necessary to conduct assessment; monitoring and oversight costs; costs associated with public participation; and indirect costs that are necessary to conduct assessment.[17] Courts have found that allowable costs include "base costs," such as the salaries of personnel who would have been employed and working even had the spill not occurred.[18]

Regulations promulgated under OPA require that NRDAs follow certain procedures that are reasonably tailored to the incident and the utility of the information these procedures are likely to produce. For example, "[t]he additional cost of a more complex procedure must be reasonably related to the expected increase in the quantity and/or quality of relevant information provided by the more complex procedure," and "[t]he procedure must be reliable and valid for the particular incident."[19] These provisions have been interpreted to restrict somewhat the trustees' discretion in their recoverable assessment costs. One court found that this language "adequately constrains trustee discretion, giving reviewing courts the authority they need to ensure the accuracy and reasonableness of natural resource damage assessments."[20]

---

13. Natural Resource Damage Assessments, 61 Fed. Reg. 440 (Jan. 5, 1996) (to be codified at 15 C.F.R. pt. 990).

14. 43 C.F.R. § 11.15(c).

15. *Id.* § 11.14(ee).

16. Legal costs associated with assessment are distinct from attorneys' fees for litigation, which are not generally recoverable.

17. 15 C.F.R. § 990.30; 43 C.F.R. § 11.15(a)(3).

18. *See, e.g.,* United States v. Hyundai Merchant Marine Co., Ltd., 172 F.3d 1187, 1192 (9th Cir. 1999).

19. 15 C.F.R § 990.27(a).

20. Gen. Elec. Co. v. U.S. Dep't of Commerce, 128 F.3d 767, 778–79 (D.C. Cir. 1997).

Trustees and responsible parties may disagree about the reasonableness of assessment costs, but it is difficult (although not impossible) for responsible parties to prevail in such disputes. As a practical matter, trustees often will submit documentation and payment demands for assessment costs on a rolling basis. The presentation of cost demands provides an opportunity for trustees and responsible parties to engage in a dialogue—or, at a minimum, an exchange of ideas—over the scope of assessment and the appropriateness of certain procedures.

B. The Categories of Injuries Compensable under CERCLA and OPA

There are several types of injuries that may be compensable as NRD. The potential categories of injuries are discussed in the following sections.

1. Ecological Injuries

It is important to note that under the OPA regulations, "injury" is not limited to obvious impacts on organisms such as adverse effects on survival and reproduction. Instead, injuries can include adverse changes in growth, health, physiology, and biological condition. Therefore, for instance, the trustees may claim that liver inflammation experienced by waterfowl can arguably constitute injury, even in the absence of impacts on longevity or reproduction. Injuries (to organisms and nonbiological resources such as water) can also include adverse changes to behavior, community composition, ecological processes and functions, physical and chemical habitat quality or structure, and public services. In addition, an injury to natural resource services occurs if there is an adverse impact to a function "performed by a natural resource for the benefit of another natural resource and/or the public."[21]

---

21. 15 C.F.R. § 990.30 (*"Injury* means an observable or measurable adverse change in a natural resource or impairment of a natural resource service. Injury may occur directly or indirectly to a natural resource and/or service. Injury incorporates the terms 'destruction,' 'loss,' and 'loss of use' as provided in OPA. . . . *Services* (or *natural resource services*) means the functions performed by a natural resource for the benefit of another natural resource and/or the public."); 15 C.F.R. § 990.51(c) ("Trustees must determine whether an injury has occurred and, if so, identify the nature of the injury. Potential categories of injury include, but are not limited to, adverse changes in: survival, growth, and reproduction; health, physiology and biological condition; behavior; community composition; ecological processes and functions; physical and chemical habitat quality or structure; and public services.").

2. Recreational Losses

Trustees will assert damages based not only on the loss of ecological services from injuries but also based on losses experienced by the public. There are several types of these losses that may be asserted by the trustees. Recreational services impacted by injuries to natural resources are generally considered direct compensable losses by federal and state trustees. Typical recreational services evaluated include recreational fishing, hiking, hunting, and boating.

3. Nonuse/Existence Value Losses

Trustees may also claim damages for loss of "passive use" values, that is, the value individuals derive from knowing a natural resource is available now and for future generations.[22] Existence value calculations suffer from unreliability, discussed later in the "Contingent Valuation" section, but are nonetheless often pursued by trustees. Furthermore, existence value calculations may constitute double counting of the same injury. As discussed previously, the trustee is entitled to both primary restoration (returning the resource to baseline) and compensatory restoration (compensation for the time period from injury until primary restoration is achieved). In theory, if both of these are achieved, the public is then made "whole" and the calculation for existence values is arguably duplicative.

4. Other Potentially Compensable Categories of Injury

a. Public Economic Losses

Public economic services impacted by injuries to natural resources may also be asserted by the trustees as part of an NRD evaluation. Typical economic services evaluated include price increases in the marketplace, lost revenue from public resources (e.g., leases, tourism, and agriculture on public land), and commercial losses to the public (e.g., interference with navigational channels). Economic losses are often measured by comparison to actual market conditions, either in the impacted area or analogous markets. In some cases, the line between "public" economic losses and private claims is unclear. Accordingly, it is important to ensure that any economic loss asserted is carefully compared against similar losses claimed by private parties to ensure that there is no double recovery.

---

22. Ohio v. U.S. Dep't of the Interior, 880 F.2d 432, 464 (citing Frank B. Cross, *Natural Resource Damage Valuation*, 42 VAND. L. REV. 269, 285–89 (1989)) ("Option and existence values may represent 'passive' use, but they nonetheless reflect utility derived by humans from a resource, and thus, *prima facie*, ought to be included in a damage assessment.").

b. Cultural Losses

Although cultural resources are not "natural resources" under OPA or CER-CLA, trustees sometimes pursue lost use of such resources as "services" lost to the public as a result of injury to natural resources. As defined by OPA, services are "the functions performed by a natural resource for the benefit of another natural resource and/or the public."[23] NOAA guidance states that "[t]he categories of ecological and human services provided by natural resources include (but are not limited to): geo-hydrological, habitat, recreational, commercial, cultural, health, and passive uses."[24] In addition, DOI's preamble to its NRDA regulations under CERCLA characterizes the use of cultural and archaeological resources as "services":

> [A]lthough archaeological and cultural resources, as defined in other stat-utes, are not treated as "natural" resources under CERCLA, the rule does allow trustee officials to include the loss of archaeological and other cul-tural services provided by a natural resource in a natural resource damage assessment. For example, if land constituting a CERCLA-defined natural resource contains archaeological artifacts, then that land might provide the service of supporting archaeological research. If an injury to the land causes a reduction in the level of service (archaeological research) that could be per-formed, trustee officials could recover damages for the lost service.[25]

In the only case that appears to have squarely addressed the issue, *Coeur d'Alene Tribe v. ASARCO Inc.*, the court stated, in listing "injury from releases" in its section on findings of fact, "[c]ultural uses of water and soil by [the plain-tiff, an Indian tribe] are not recoverable as [NRD]."[26] Non-litigation examples involving cultural resources most often refer to cultural resources not as sepa-rate resources but as natural resources with some cultural significance. For example, one assessment where damages to cultural resources were considered referred to the "cultural importance of Panther Creek fish to certain Native American tribes."[27] In the Lower Fox River restoration plan, harm to cultural

---

23. 15 C.F.R. § 990.30.

24. Damage Assessment & Restoration Program, Nat'l Oceanic & Atmospheric Admin., Scaling Compensatory Restoration Actions Guidance Document for Natural Resource Damage Assessment Under the Oil Pollution Act of 1990 x (1997).

25. Natural Resource Damage Assessments, 59 Fed. Reg. 14,262 (Mar. 25, 1994) (to be codi-fied at 43 C.F.R. pt. 11).

26. 280 F. Supp. 2d 1094, 1107 (D. Idaho 2003).

27. Amy W. Ando et al., Natural Resource Damage Assessment: Methods and Cases, WMRC Reports 102 (2004), https://www.ideals.illinois.edu/bitstream/handle/2142/1979/RR -108.pdf?sequence=1.

resources included harm to revered animal species and to sacred locations.[28] In other cases, restoration plans analyze the *impact* of a particular restoration activity on cultural resources.[29] In one case of restoration of an historic pier, the project was undertaken not to remediate harm to the historic resource per se, but to remediate harm done to recreational uses of the river.[30] Therefore, a responsible party may have a defense against cultural resources claims on the grounds that they lie outside the scope of "natural resources" or the services they provide.

c. Aesthetic Losses

Neither the OPA nor the CERCLA regulations refer specifically to the loss of aesthetic resources or aesthetic use of natural resources. Under a broad reading, however, the regulations could arguably encompass this use, to the extent "aesthetic" value is associated with "recreation," which, although not mentioned in the regulations themselves, is referred to repeatedly in the preamble to the NOAA Final Rule. Some CERCLA cases, however, have contemplated "aesthetic value" as part of the measurement of NRD.[31] At least two sources—the New York State Department of Environmental Conservation's Enforcement

---

28. *See* U.S. Fish & Wildlife Serv. et al., Joint Restoration Plan and Environmental Assessment for the Lower Fox River and Green Bay Area 21, 24, 28 (2003), https://www.fws.gov/midwest/es/ec/nrda/foxrivernrda/documents/restorationplan/finaljune2003.pdf. The trustees did seem to consider, to a lesser extent, historic properties resulting from European settlement. The alternative ultimately proposed by the trustees sought to restore tribal cultural resources, as well as, through the acquisition of land, to preserve archaeological and historic resources. *Id.*

29. *See, e.g.*, New Bedford Harbor Trustee Council, Environmental Assessment, New Bedford Harbor Restoration—Round II, Final 17 (2001), http://www.darrp.noaa.gov/northeast/new_bedford/pdf/r2eafinl.pdf; *see also id.* at 19 (stating, that "[n]o impacts on cultural resources (archaeological or historical) or on land use patterns are expected"). The case of the *World Prodigy* oil spill is also instructive; *see also* Nat'l Oceanic & Atmospheric Admin., Final Environmental Assessment and Restoration Plan, *World Prodigy* Oil Spill Restoration Plan, Narragansett Bay, Rhode Island (1996), https://casedocuments.darrp.noaa.gov/northeast/world/wpea.html ("The Rhode Island Coastal Resources Management Program contains a policy statement to protect cultural resources within the state's coastal zone (Olsen and Seavey, 1983). Any action(s) undertaken to restore the natural resources impacted by the *World Prodigy* oil spill must comply with the historic and archaeological protection guidelines outlined by the state's approved coastal zone management plan.").

30. *See* Office of Nat. Res. Damages, N.J. Dep't of Envtl. Prot., Natural Resources Restoration Plan for Damages Associated with the *Presidente Rivera* Oil Spill of June 1989 (1996), https://www.cerc.usgs.gov/orda_docs/DocHandler.ashx?task=get&ID=409.

31. *See, e.g.*, Idaho v. Bunker Hill Co., 635 F. Supp. 665, 675 (D. Idaho 1986); Artesian Water Co. v. New Castle Cty., 659 F. Supp. 1269, 1288 n.34 (D. Del. 1987); *see also In re* Acushnet River & New Bedford Harbor Proceedings re Alleged PCB Pollution, 716 F. Supp. 676, 686.

Memorandum on NRD and an Illinois study on NRDA—refer to "aesthetic uses" as services for which trustees may recover in an NRD claim.[32]

At least one OPA restoration plan has mentioned explicit injury to aesthetic use. In describing the injury to wetlands and beach shoreline due to the Chalk Point oil spill in Maryland, the plan stated, "[a]bove-ground vegetation represents a broad range of ecological functions (or services) related to primary production, habitat structure, recreational and aesthetic value, food chain support, and fish and shellfish production."[33] Another restoration plan did not refer to aesthetic resources but did identify bird-watching as a "service."[34] Other restoration plans that include references to aesthetic resources do so in the context of describing the potential effects *restoration* activities might have on aesthetic value, rather than the harm to an aesthetic resource caused by the underlying contamination.[35]

C. Possible Techniques for Valuing Compensable Injuries

1. The Restoration Approach

Assuming an injury to natural resources and/or services is proven, the trustees must then calculate damages associated with that injury. In doing so, the trustees typically determine the type of restoration projects that are necessary to achieve primary restoration.

---

32. *See* New York Dep't of Envtl. Conservation, DEE-15 Natural Resources Damages: Enforcement Policy (1989), https://www.dec.ny.gov/regulations/25235.html; Ando, *supra* note 25, at 26–29, 37.

33. Nat'l Oceanic & Atmospheric Admin., Final Restoration Plan and Environmental Assessment for the April 7, 2000 Oil Spill at Chalk Point on the Patuxent River, Maryland 18 (2002), https://www.gc.noaa.gov/gc-rp/cp2107.pdf.

34. *See* David Chapman et al., Calculating Resource Compensation: An Application of the Service-to-Service Approach to the Blackbird Mine Hazardous Waste Site, NOAA Technical Paper 97-1 2 n.2 (1998) https://casedocuments.darrp.noaa.gov/northwest/black/pdf/blackfnl.pdf.

35. *See, e.g.,* U.S. Dep't of the Interior, et al., Restoration Plan and Environmental Assessment for the Love Canal, 102nd Street, and Forest Glen Mobile Home Subdivision Superfund Sites 28 (2005) (referring to effects of projects on aesthetic resources), https://casedocuments.darrp.noaa.gov/greatlakes/102nd/pdf/EA.pdf; *see also Tenyo Maru* Oil Spill Nat. Res. Trustees, Final Restoration Plan and Environmental Assessment for the *Tenyo Maru* Oil Spill 5-26 (2000) ("*aesthetic qualities* should not be adversely affected under the preferred alternative"), https://casedocuments.darrp.noaa.gov/northwest/tenyo/pdf/ten0008.pdf; Nat. Res. Trustees, Montrose Settlements Restoration Program Final Restoration Plan and Programmatic Environmental Impact Statement/Environmental Impact Report (2005), https://www.cerc.usgs.gov/orda_docs/DocHandler.ashx?task=get&ID=128.

A restoration-based approach compensates for NRD through a determination of the type and scale of projects needed to provide services or resources of a similar type and quality as those lost. By providing primary and compensatory restoration, any nonuse values and values associated with the loss will also be restored and the public will be fully compensated. So, for example, in the case of a contaminated river, in addition to restoring the condition and fish stock level in the river to baseline, a responsible party might also be required to pay to improve the ecological conditions in a nearby river or install new fishing access points to increase the number of future fishing trips beyond baseline. These above-baseline improvements, assuming they are properly calibrated, will compensate for the primary loss, the interim lost use, and nonuse values associated with the pollution event.

Because it sometimes is not possible or feasible to provide identical resources and/or services as those lost,[36] a restoration-based approach must allow for the replacement or acquisition of similar resources. When similar but not identical resources are used to compensate for the loss, it is important to consider the correct scale of those actions that will make the environment and public whole. So, for example, if 50 percent of the services provided by 100 acres of a forest are lost, the trustees will then calculate the cost of either restoring that forest or, if that is not possible, constructing or acquiring 50 acres of similar habitat.

2. Regulatory Preference for a Restoration-Based Approach

As discussed in Chapter 4, both the OPA and CERCLA regulations favor use of the restoration-based approach to valuation of all NRD.

The OPA regulations plainly require that the governmental trustees may proceed with an economic valuation approach only after a restoration approach has been determined to be inappropriate. Under the OPA regulations, trustees are required to first consider a resource-to-resource approach or a service-to-service approach that will provide natural resources and/or services equal in quantity to those lost. Only if they make an affirmative determination that this approach is inappropriate—presumably because an equal quantity of resources or services is not available and cannot be developed—can the trustees consider compensating the loss through a scaling approach.[37] Under a

---

36. The scarcity of restoration options is affected by the fact that the trustees have a preference for restoration of resources in the same geographic area (e.g., the same watershed) as the injured resources.

37. 15 C.F.R. § 990.53(d)(3)(i) ("Where trustees have determined that neither resource-to-resource nor service-to-service scaling is appropriate, trustees may use the valuation scaling approach.").

scaling approach, the trustees must measure the value of the loss, and identify the amount of replacement resources needed to provide the same value to the public. Damages are still measured by the cost of providing the public with the correct amount of resources and services.[38] Finally, only if the trustees also find that work to value replacement resources and/or services cannot be performed in a reasonable time frame or at a reasonable cost (a second affirmative determination), can the trustees turn to a non-restoration approach such as those discussed later in the chapter.[39]

In short, a trustee assessing damages under OPA can estimate the total value of an injured animal or an injured acre of habitat, and use that as the measure of damages *only if* the trustee finds that those resources cannot be restored or replaced with similar substitutes, *and* an alternative restoration scaling approach would be inefficient. The trustees must make each of these affirmative determinations before they can even commission a stated preference survey to measure nonuse damages.[40]

As discussed later, the approach to valuation in the CERCLA regulations has a more complex history. The initial regulations have seen various court challenges and amendments since they were first promulgated by DOI in 1986. In all versions of these rules, economic valuation techniques, such as contingent valuation (CV), are only available to measure interim losses—that is, those losses occurring during the time it takes to restore the resources and/or services lost to baseline. Unlike the OPA rules, however, some prior versions of the CERCLA rules arguably required trustees to ascertain a dollar value of interim loss damages through the use of economic tools.[41]

---

38. *Id.* ("Under the valuation scaling approach, trustees determine the amount of natural resources and/or services that must be provided to produce the same value lost to the public.").

39. *Id.* § 990.53(d)(3)(ii) ("If, in the judgment of the trustees, valuation of the lost services is practicable, but valuation of the replacement natural resources and/or services cannot be performed within a reasonable time frame or at a reasonable cost, as determined by § 990.27(a)(2) of this part, trustees may estimate the dollar value of the lost services and select the scale of the restoration action that has a cost equivalent to the lost value.").

40. These regulatory obstacles to the trustees' reliance on stated-preference methods may also apply to NRD categories beyond "nonuse" including recreational losses.

41. Note also that there is some case law regarding prior versions of the CERCLA rules that treats economic valuation of interim damages and compensation of nonuse values favorably. In *Ohio v. U.S. Dep't of the Interior*, 880 F.2d 432 (D.C. Cir. 1989), which was a challenge to the rules promulgated in 1986 and amended in 1988, the court upheld DOI's inclusion of CV as a method that could be used to estimate use and nonuse values. It also struck down DOI's rule that option and existence values be estimated in lieu of use values only when use values cannot be determined, finding instead that "[o]ption and existence values may represent 'passive' use, but they nonetheless reflect utility derived by humans from a resource, and thus, *prima facie*, ought to

Following the promulgation of the OPA rules in 1996, the lack of a focus on restoration-based approaches to valuation of interim losses under CER-CLA emerged as a concern within the NRD community, and, in December 2005, DOI convened a federal advisory committee, composed of interested stakeholders, to consider the issue.[42] A key recommendation of this advisory committee was that DOI should seek to conform the CERCLA regulations with the OPA regulations and undertake, without delay, a targeted revision to emphasize restoration over monetary damages. DOI undertook to implement this recommendation and in 2008 promulgated amendments to the rules. The new regulations, which are the version currently in effect, provide the option for a restoration-based approach to all damages, including use and nonuse interim losses. The Federal Register notice issued by DOI in connection with the revisions expresses a clear preference for this approach: "Methodologies that compare losses arising from resource injury to gains expected from restoration actions are frequently simpler and more transparent than methodologies used to measure the economic value of losses."[43]

If trustees do not adequately consider a restoration-based approach before proceeding to less reliable economic valuation methods (such as CV, discussed later), the NRD defendants will have a strong legal basis to reject not only the use of such studies in assessing damages but also claims to reimburse the trustees for the cost of implementing the studies as part of the reasonable costs of a damages assessment.[44]

3. Restoration Scaling, Habitat Equivalency Analysis (HEA), and Resource Equivalency Analysis (REA)

Calculation of restoration damages generally requires determining "the 'scale' of those actions that will make the environment and public whole"[45]—that is, the "appropriate size or spatial and temporal extent of restoration actions

---

be included in a damage assessment." *Id.* at 464 (citing Frank B. Cross, *Natural Resource Damage Valuation*, 42 Vand. L. Rev., 269, 285–89 (1989)).

42. *See also* discussion in Chapter 4, Section D.

43. Natural Resource Damages for Hazardous Substances, 73 Fed. Reg. 57,259 (Oct. 2, 2008) (to be codified at 43 C.F.R. pt. 11).

44. *See, e.g.*, Letter from Brian D. Israel, Arnold & Porter LLP, to Craig O'Connor, Special Counsel for Nat. Res., Nat'l Oceanic & Atmospheric Admin., (Feb. 8, 2012) ("Only after determining that such scaling methods are inappropriate may the Trustees turn to valuation methods. To our knowledge, the Trustees have not made any of the determinations necessary to justify their current assessment proposal. Accordingly, the regulatory conditions precedent have not been satisfied, and the Trustees are not properly following their own legal framework").

45. 15 C.F.R. § 990.53(d).

required to bring injured resources to baseline."[46] Methods for scaling restoration actions include "resource-to-resource" or "service-to-service" scaling.[47] Resource-to-resource scaling seeks to restore baseline populations of resources, that is, flora or fauna. Service-to-service scaling seeks to restore natural resources based on calculated services or functions provided by the resource and will usually focus on ecological habitats—acres of wetlands, for example. It is important to note that when both resource-to-resource and service-to-service methods are employed to determine necessary restoration, the results may be overlapping; for example, the trustees may seek to restore marsh bird populations as well as wetland acreage. Damage calculations should eliminate any such overlap, which constitutes double counting of restoration costs, because such double recovery is prohibited under both CERCLA and OPA.[48]

Regardless of the valuation method, the value of a restoration action is typically discounted for delayed provision of services. For instance, the scale of a forest restoration project that will take five years to complete may be increased to compensate for the five-year delay in implementing the restoration. NOAA generally applies a 3 percent discount rate.[49] Therefore, a five-year forest restoration project might involve the creation of 15 percent more forest acreage than necessary to restore the baseline acreage, in order to compensate for the 3 percent discount rate.

The most common technique for performing restoration scaling is referred to as a "habitat equivalency analysis" (HEA). In the following Expert Insight, natural resource economist Dr. Richard Dunford explains the HEA technique and discusses both its merits and pitfalls. The analogous approach with regard to human-use or recreational losses is referred to as "resource equivalency analysis" (REA). This technique is far less commonly used than HEA; the more common recreational loss valuation technique, travel cost model, is discussed later. A REA approach involves determining the amount of natural resources or services that must be provided to produce the same value lost to the public.[50] Although this method has some advantages, it suffers from the same potential methodological uncertainties discussed by Dr. Dunford.

---

46. Valerie Ann Lee & P.J. Bridgen, The Natural Resource Damage Assessment Deskbook: A Legal and Technical Analysis 288 (Envtl. Law Inst. ed., 2002).

47. 15 C.F.R. § 990.53(d)(2).

48. 33 U.S.C. § 2706(d)(3); 43 C.F.R. § 11.15(d).

49. Damage Assessment & Restoration Program, Nat'l Oceanic & Atmospheric Admin., Scaling Compensatory Restoration Actions Guidance Document for Natural Resource Damage Assessment Under the Oil Pollution Act of 1990 C-8 (1997).

50. 15 C.F.R. § 990.53(d)(3); 43 C.F.R. § 11.83.

Finally, this section includes a table of examples of DARPs in which NOAA has relied on HEA or REA valuation techniques (Table 5.1). Although the OPA and CERCLA regulations do require that trustees make an affirmative determination that an equal quantity of resources or services lost is not available and cannot be developed before they proceed to a scaling approach and rely on HEA or REA, Table 5.1 demonstrates that, in practice, use of these techniques is the norm, not the exception to the rule.

EXPERT INSIGHT: Habitat Equivalency Analysis

Richard W. Dunford, PhD[51]
Environmental Economics Services

Background

Habitat equivalency analysis (HEA) is a technique that NRD practitioners often use for determining the size (i.e., scale) of habitat restoration projects that will provide gains in ecological services over time (known as the credit) equal to the losses in ecological services over time (known as the debit) as a result of injuries to habitat from an oil spill or a hazardous substance release.[52] The measure of damages using HEA is the cost of implementing and monitoring the performance of appropriately scaled restoration projects.

Practitioners use HEA to estimate both debits and credits on an annual basis relative to a baseline level of ecological services. Specifically, a spill/release will reduce ecological services below baseline levels over a given geographic area from the date of the incident until the services return to their baseline level at some future point. The annual losses are converted into their present-value equivalent (i.e., debit) using the economic process of discounting. Accordingly, the units of measure for the debit are Discounted Service Acre Years (DSAYs). Similarly, the credit per acre for a restoration project is estimated on an annual basis as the gain in ecological services above the baseline level as a result of implementing the project. The annual gains per acre are converted into their present-value equivalent through discounting, with the result being measured in DSAYs per acre. The appropriate scale for the restoration project is determined by dividing the debit by the credit per acre. HEA is sometimes referred to as a "service-to-service" restoration scaling technique because the scaling is based

---

51. Dr. Richard W. Dunford is the founder and owner of Environmental Economics Services, LLC. He holds a PhD in agricultural economics from the University of Wisconsin, Madison. Dr. Dunford has participated in or led more than 40 NRDAs.

52. Resource equivalency analysis (REA) is a similar technique that focuses on scaling restoration projects for injuries to wildlife, such as birds, turtles, or fish. Most of the background, key requirements, and limitations of HEA also apply to REA.

on a comparison of service losses from an incident to service gains from restoration projects.

Key Requirements

A key HEA requirement is that the services of the injured resource and those of the restoration project must be comparable. Specifically, the restoration project must provide services of the same type, the same quality, and of comparable value to services that were lost—allowing an apples-to-apples comparison. When the lost and the replacement services are not equivalent in type and quality, HEA can produce biased results. For example, it can lead to a situation where the restoration project provides gains that are more valuable than the services that were lost from the incident. In such a situation, in the absence of a factor to account for the value difference, a HEA will result in an inappropriate scale for the restoration project.

Most natural resources provide a wide variety of ecological services. For example, wetlands may provide food for wildlife, protection for some wildlife from predators, and nesting materials for other wildlife. One of HEA's requirements is that the practitioners must select a single service or an index of multiple services (known as the service "metric") for the analysis. It is crucial that this metric reflects the overall impacts of a spill/release on ecological services, not focusing on the service most adversely or least adversely affected. Also, many HEAs rely on a "proxy" for ecological services (e.g., amount of biomass). In these applications, the proxy must be highly correlated with the main services affected by the spill/release, otherwise the proxy will not adequately reflect the resulting losses.

As noted previously, debits are estimated as the difference between the ecological services provided by the injured habitat with the spill/release relative to the baseline services of that habitat, whereas credits reflect the difference in the baseline ecological services of the habitat prior to restoration and the services of that habitat after implementing the restoration project. Consequently, it is very important to properly estimate the baseline condition of the injured and restored habitat. This can be challenging in areas where the injured habitat has undergone changes over time that are unrelated to the spill/release. For example, urban runoff and sedimentation may have reduced the ecological services provided by a river over time. The baseline services of the river need to reflect such changes. Otherwise, the debit for a spill/release into the river may include a reduction in ecological services unrelated to the spill/release.

Limitations

The underlying conceptual foundation of HEA is that the public is fully compensated for natural resource injuries when the dollar value of service gains from a restoration project equal the dollar value of the service losses resulting from the injuries. If several simplifying assumptions are met, then equating service gains with service losses will fully compensate the public.

One simplifying assumption is that the implicit value of an affected natural resource is directly proportional to the services provided by the natural resource. For example, this assumption means that the public receives 80 percent of the value of a natural resource if that natural resource is providing 80 percent of its baseline services. Usually, it is not known whether this assumption is met.

Another simplifying assumption is that the implicit value of ecological services per acre is constant in real (i.e., inflation-adjusted) terms over the duration of the assessment period. When the assessment period is long, it is unlikely that this assumption will be met. In general, if HEA's underlying assumptions are not met, then the HEA result will not accurately reflect the amount of restoration needed to compensate the public for the natural resource injury. Furthermore, violating some of HEA's underlying assumptions unambiguously leads to an overstatement of damages.

HEA is a *multiplicative process*, which means that the debit and credit per acre estimates are very sensitive to the magnitude of the inputs. Often, debit and credit inputs are uncertain, in which case professional judgment plays an important role in HEA. When debit inputs are uncertain (for example), trustees tend to advance reasonable worst-case estimates for those inputs in order to ensure that the debit for the injuries from a spill/release is not understated. However, the use of multiple reasonable worst-case input estimates usually leads to a substantially overstated debit. Similarly, the parties responsible for a spill/release do not want to excessively compensate the public, so they prefer reasonable best-case input estimates, which often leads to a substantially understated debit. It is not uncommon for initial debit estimates by trustees and responsible parties to be an order of magnitude apart.

In the 1990s, HEA was upheld in two cases for determining the appropriate compensation for physical injuries to seagrass habitat in coastal areas of Florida. However, no courts have ruled on the validity of HEA for spills/releases involving complex ecological services, complex baseline issues, and long injury/restoration time periods where HEA's underlying assumptions are unlikely to be met. Furthermore, in 2010, a state court rejected an application of REA to groundwater injuries at a site in New Jersey. Although HEA is routinely used to settle ecological damages from spills/releases, its usefulness in litigation is uncertain at best.

Conclusions

HEA is a very useful tool for scaling restoration projects in settling ecological service losses from injuries to natural resources caused by spills/releases. However, a substantial amount of professional judgment is involved in estimating HEA inputs, and restoration scaling is very sensitive to the input estimates. Furthermore, because of typical limitations on data and other information, the underlying HEA assumptions just described are rarely met, usually leading to overstated damages. Consequently, HEA's usefulness in litigation is uncertain at best.

Additional Reading

Cacela, D., J. Lipton, D. Beltman, J. Hansen, & R. Wolotira. 2005. "Associating Eco-system Service Losses with Indicators of Toxicity in Habitat Equivalency Analysis." *Environmental Management*. 35(3): 343–51.

Dunford, R.W., T.C. Ginn, & W.H. Desvousges. 2004. "The Use of Habitat Equivalency Analysis in Natural Resource Damage Assessments." *Ecological Economics*. 48(1): 49–70.

Fonseca, M.S., B.E. Julius, & W.J. Kenworthy. 2000. "Integrating Biology and Eco-nomics in Seagrass Restoration: How Much Is Enough and Why?" *Ecological Engineering*. 15: 227–37.

King, D.M. 1997. *"Comparing Ecosystem Services and Values: With Illustrations for Performing Habitat Equivalency Analysis."* Report prepared for Damage Assess-ment and Restoration Program, NOAA, U.S. Department of Commerce, Silver Spring, MD.

NOAA. 2006. *Habitat Equivalency Analysis: An Overview*. Policy and Technical Paper Series, Number 95-1. Damage Assessment and Restoration Program, NOAA, U.S. Department of Commerce.

NOAA. 1997. *Natural Resource Damage Assessment Guidance Document: Scal-ing Compensatory Restoration Actions (Oil Pollution Act of 1990)*. Damage Assessment and Restoration Program, NOAA, U.S. Department of Commerce. (December).

Thur, S.M. 2007. "Refining the Use of Habitat Equivalency Analysis." *Environmental Management*. 40: 161–70.

Zafonte, M. & S. Hampton. 2007. "Exploring the Welfare Implications of Resource Equivalency Analysis in Natural Resource Damage Assessments." *Ecological Eco-nomics*. 61: 134–45.

Table 5.1 Examples of NOAA Assessment and Restoration Plans that Relied on HEA and/or REA[53]

Year	Incident/ Contaminated Site Information	Injured Natural Resources	Restored Resources	Use of HEA/REA
1995	M/V *Miss Beholden* Grounding, March 13, 1993	Coral reef	Habitat creation and restoration (coral reef transplantation), monitoring	HEA used to determine the quantity of equivalent habitat necessary to be restored and/or created to compensate for the lost services.
1995	Wellhead Failure and Release, Dixon Bay, Louisiana, January 12–13, 1995	Marsh, water column, birds/ wildlife	Natural recovery for injured marsh vegetation	HEA used to determine an estimated amount of marsh that would need to be created as compensatory restoration for the impairment of marsh function from the time of the discharge until recovery to baseline.
1997	Florida Keys National Marine Sanctuary, Seagrass Restoration and Monitoring Plan, January 1997	Treasure salvaging activities caused damage to seagrass	Seagrass transplantation	HEA used to scale restoration.
1997	Texaco Pipeline Inc. Crude Oil Discharge, Lake Barre, Louisiana, May 16, 1997 (Damage Assessment and Restoration Plan)	Marsh, finfish and shellfish, birds, recreational shrimping and fishing (to a lesser extent due to nearby alternatives)	Natural recovery alternative chosen for primary restoration; for compensatory restoration, the trustees proposed marsh enhancement (which would also benefit birds and human use)	Trustees and Texaco cooperatively performed a field study designed to obtain data allowing use of a HEA to determine size of the marsh restoration. Input parameters for the model were jointly developed based on the field observations.

---

53. Table 5.1, focusing on the time period from 1995 to 2013, is for illustrative purposes and is not exhaustive.

Year	Incident/ Contaminated Site Information	Injured Natural Resources	Restored Resources	Use of HEA/REA
1999	Chevron Pipeline Oil Spill, Oahu, Hawaii, May 14, 1996	Air resources, surface waters, wildlife, and marine/estuarine biota	Pouhala marsh enhancement (enhance existing wetland basins, clean marsh, fence the marsh, restore marsh, exclude fish from wetland, create hydrologic link)	HEA used by PRP and trustees to evaluate injury to intertidal habitat with differing results. The trustees used a multiplier to estimate the area of habitat impacted that considered areas that may have been exposed to oil. HEA also used to scale compensatory restoration projects. For this spill, the trustees considered the area affected by the oil, estimates of initial lost ecological services, and recovery periods for each impacted habitat type as inputs into the HEA.
1999	M/V *Formosa Six* Ethylene Dichloride Discharge, Gulf of Mexico, Louisiana, April 11, 1997	Benthic species/ habitat	The trustees proposed natural recovery of injured benthic sediments and the creation of intermediate marsh for compensatory restoration.	HEA used to estimate the scale of marsh creation needed to restore, replace, or acquire resource services comparable to those lost, based on limited information available. Results suggested a minimum of one to two acres would be required to restore or replace lost benthic services.
2000	Tampa Bay Oil Spill, Tampa Bay, Florida, August 10, 1993	Mangroves, sea grasses, water column, birds, sea turtles, salt marshes, shellfish beds, bottom sediments, beach physical injury, recreation, navigation	Birds, sea turtles, sand replacement	HEA used to determine appropriate scale of restoration for mangroves and sea grasses.

Year	Incident/ Contaminated Site Information	Injured Natural Resources	Restored Resources	Use of HEA/REA
2000	Alafia River Spill, December 7, 1997, Final Damage Assessment and Restoration Plan	Freshwater wetlands; fish, crab, and shrimp; surface water; freshwater benthic invertebrates; oysters and mussels	Restoration of riverine habitat	HEA used to estimate the acres of habitat required to replace service losses resulting from injury to freshwater vegetation.
2000	Tesoro Hawaii Oil Spill, Oahu and Kauau, Hawaii, August 24, 1998, Final Restoration Plan and Environmental Assessment	Seabirds and habitat, seals, intertidal and subtidal habitat, beaches, and recreational activities	Net removal project to benefit seabirds, predator control, habitat enhancement	HEA used as a compensatory restoration scaling tool.
2001	Alcoa Point Comfort/Lavaca Bay CERCLA site, aluminum manufacturing/ processing, added to NPL list in March 1994	Benthic communities, finfish/motile shellfish, wading and shore birds, groundwater, water column	Oyster reef creation, estuarine low marsh creation/ enhancement	HEA used to scale size of restoration actions to compensate the public for potential injuries/loss of services.
2001	M/V *Westchester* Crude Oil Discharge, Lower Mississippi River, Louisiana, November 28, 2000	Finfish and shellfish, birds, freshwater river habitat, delta marsh habitat, sandflat habitat, recreational fishing and hunting	No active primary restoration; marsh creation and recreational access enhancement projects	HEA used to give the maximum likely amount of injury that could have occurred as a result of this incident.
2001	Tex Tin Superfund Site	Fish and shellfish, benthic invertebrates	Marsh creation; construction of a breakwater or wave energy barrier	HEA used to scale restoration.

Year	Incident/ Contaminated Site Information	Injured Natural Resources	Restored Resources	Use of HEA/REA
2002	M/V *Kuroshima* Oil Spill, Summer Bay, Unalaska, Alaska, November 26, 1997	Birds (e.g., bald eagle, goose, protected species), shoreline vegetation, shellfish and intertidal biota, salmonids and lake resources, recreational uses	Proposed compensatory restoration actions included predator removal to benefit seabirds, vegetation restoration; shellfish contamination testing and education on seafood safety; beach cleanup, tents for public use; community education program	The trustees and PRPs used HEA to determine how large an area of vegetation would need to be restored to compensate for the injuries resulting from the incident, including response actions.
2002	Olympic Pipe Line Gasoline Spill into Whatcom Creek, Bellingham, Washington, June 10, 1999	Aquatic biota mortalities in the creek, loss of vegetation, human use impacts, losses of passive use of recreational opportunities	Land acquisition, park enhancements, fish habitat projects, soil stabilization and revegetation, long-term monitoring and maintenance	HEA used to estimate needed size of the restoration and the adequacy of the Cemetery Creek and Salmon Park projects for injuries to fish habitat.
2002	Chalk Point Oil Spill, Patuxent River, Maryland, April 7, 2000	Wetlands, beaches, ruddy ducks, other birds, diamondback terrapins, muskrats, fish and shellfish, benthic communities, recreational services	Create tidal marsh, enhance shoreline beach, ruddy duck habitat; create oyster reef, improve recreational opportunities	HEA used to determine size of the marsh restoration to compensate for wetland losses and 376 muskrat losses resulting from the spill.

Year	Incident/ Contaminated Site Information	Injured Natural Resources	Restored Resources	Use of HEA/REA
2003 (Draft)	T/V *Posavina* Oil Spill, June 8, 2000	Marine communities, wetlands and birds, public use	Salt marsh restoration	HEA used to scale restoration of wetlands.
2003	Bailey Waste Disposal Site, Oranqe County, Texas	Tidal marsh, high marsh, ponds, ditch areas, upland areas, road areas	Estuarine marsh creation or enhancement (estuarine marsh was the most significant habitat type injured, was the only naturally occurring habitat type at the area, and the ecological services which it provides are inclusive of the services lost due to injury to other habitats)	HEA used to define the scale of restoration. The HFA method was used to estimate the scale of estuarine marsh creation needed to offset the 10 acres of assessed tidal marsh losses (at 100 percent loss of services).
2005	Equinox Oil Company Crude Oil Discharge, Lake Grande Ecaille, Louisiana, September 22, 1998	Marsh, birds, mangroves, water column, finfish, shellfish	Marsh creation (habitat and services)	Used HEA for injury assessment for benthic and marsh function. Inputs were jointly developed from observations made during response activities. Results estimated that 6.1 DSAYs of benthic habitat functioning was lost as a result of this incident. HEA also used for resource-to-resource scaling to determine restoration requirements for the benthic injury category. HEA used to determine size of marsh restoration to compensate for lost services based on the quantification of incident-related natural resource injuries.

Year	Incident/ Contaminated Site Information	Injured Natural Resources	Restored Resources	Use of HEA/REA
2005	North Pass Oil Spill, Plaquemines Parish, Louisiana, September 22, 2002	Freshwater marsh habitat (120 acres moderately oiled)	Crevasse splay marsh creation project chosen because it has a high level of service, is cost effective, and has a high likelihood of success.	HEA used to quantify interim losses of marsh habitat services and determine the size of marsh restoration.
2006	S.S. *Jacob Luckenbach* and Associated Mystery Oil Spills, July 14, 1953	Birds, a few sea otters, minimal impacts to shoreline habitats, cultural resources and water column	Restoration of breeding grounds (birds and otters)	REA used to evaluate bird restoration projects.
2006	M/V *New Carissa* Oil Spill, February 4, 1999	Birds (Western Snowy Plover, shorebirds, marbled murrelets, seabirds), lost/diminished recreation trips	Education projects, habitat restoration, predator management, recreation projects	REA used to scale snowy plover injury. Scaling done after the emergency restoration was completed to determine whether completed restoration was enough to offset the losses.
2007 (Draft)	Palmer Barge Waste Site, Port Arthur, Jefferson County, Texas, Restoration Plan and Environmental Assessment	Near-shore sediments (metals and PAH contamination), benthic organisms	Marsh creation/ enhancement, water control structures	HEA, scientific literature, and knowledge of Texas estuaries were used to determine how much credit could be realized from a restoration project.

Year	Incident/ Contaminated Site Information	Injured Natural Resources	Restored Resources	Use of HEA/REA
2008 (Draft)	Castro Cove/ Chevron Richmond Refinery	Trustees assumed overall degree of natural resource injuries and lost services were equal to degree of amphipod mortality (a type of small crustacean that inhabits bay mud) when placed in affected sediment from Castro Cove in laboratory	Restoration of 1,500 acres of diked bay lands to historical wetland state as mature tidal marsh, restoration of tidal wetlands, improved public access, and recreation areas	HEA used to calculate amount of intertidal and shallow subtidal habitat needed to compensate for lost services.
2008	Galaxy/ Spectron Site, Cecil County, Maryland	Primary injuries were to anadromous fish such as herring and alewife	Removal of a partial fish blockage and stream restoration	HEA used to calculate losses prior to remediation based on injury from contamination. The rate at which samples were found to exceed water quality criteria was incorporated into the HEA. HEA, along with scientific literature, and knowledge of the affected ecosystem were used to determine how much credit could be realized from an identified restoration project at the site.

Year	Incident/ Contaminated Site Information	Injured Natural Resources	Restored Resources	Use of HEA/REA
2009	American Transport Gasoline Spill, Beaver Butte Creek Warm Springs Reservation, Oregon, March 4, 1999	Fish (salmon) were primary injuries; other potential injuries included surface water, benthic macroinvertebrates, amphibians, riparian vegetation, cultural resources, lost fishing, ceremonial and subsistence loss	Focus on improving spawning and rearing habitat conditions in the Beaver Creek Watershed	HEA used to determine nature and amount of habitat restoration needed to compensate for the losses of juvenile Chinook salmon and steelhead. Habitat restoration was used as mechanism for compensation for anadromous fish losses. HEA designed to calculate the amount of salmon and steelhead spawning and rearing habitat restoration that would be needed to increase production of smolt/migrants to a level equal to the estimated losses.
2009	*Athos I* Oil Spill, Delaware River, Paulsboro, New Jersey, November 26, 2004	Shoreline, tributaries, aquatic resources, birds, recreational services (river trips)	Freshwater tidal wetlands restoration at John Heinz National Wildlife Refuge, creation of oyster reefs, Darby Creek dam removal and riparian habitat restoration, wetland restoration, shoreline restoration, creation of habitat for migratory geese to rest and forage	HEA developed for each affected habitat type (seawalls, sand/mud substrates, course substrate, marsh, tributaries). HEA ratios were then used to scale restoration of one habitat type to injury to another.

Year	Incident/ Contaminated Site Information	Injured Natural Resources	Restored Resources	Use of HEA/REA
2009 (Draft)	Bayou Verdine, Calcasieu Parish, Louisiana, Hazardous Substances Releases	Surface water, high trophic level organisms (fish, mammals, birds), lost use, benthic resources, sediment	Benthic resources were the focus; projects undertaken to restore benthic resources would benefit the other resources which may have had short-term impacts; marsh creation, hydrologic restoration	HEA used to estimate habitat injuries and scale restoration, specifically benthic losses.
2011	M/V *Casitas* Grounding, Hawaiian Islands, July 2, 2005	Corals	Removal of marine debris (e.g., fishing gear), a substantial source of coral injury	HEA used to scale compensatory restoration projects that address lost ecological services. Little detail on use of HEA provided in final restoration plan.
2012	*Cosco Busan* Oil Spill, November 7, 2007	Birds, shoreline habitats, eelgrass, herring, lost recreation	Creation and restoration of bird nesting habitats; grant project; restoration of shoreline habitats; human recreational use projects	REA used to quantify injury and scale restoration actions for wildlife and habitat.

Year	Incident/ Contaminated Site Information	Injured Natural Resources	Restored Resources	Use of HEA/REA
2012	M/V *Ever Reach* Oil Spill, Charleston, South Carolina, 2002	Shoreline, shorebirds, shellfish, recreational use	Saltmarsh habitat, upland islands as marsh buffer habitat	HEA used to determine on preliminary basis whether injuries to shoreline habitats were sufficiently large to justify pursuing additional studies. HEA, along with food web modeling, used to estimate the amount of saltmarsh that would compensate for bird injury.
2013	Saint Lawrence River, *United States of America, State of New York and Saint Regis Mohawk Tribe v. Alcoa Inc. and Reynolds Metals, Co.*	Sediment, fish, birds, amphibians and reptiles, mammals, recreational fishing, tribal lost use	Sediment, fish, avian, and mammals	HEA used to quantify present value of sediment, fish, birds, and some mammal losses from 1981 through the date of reasonable expected recovery and to scale restoration.

4. Travel Cost Model

To calculate damages associated with lost recreational uses, trustees may use a number of economic methodologies for estimating the dollar value associated with the loss. These methodologies collectively are referred to as travel cost models. For example, in an effort to attempt to monetize the damages to recreational anglers resulting from a Superfund site near a fishing stream, trustees will first estimate the number of fishing trips that have been or will be impacted by the site. This estimate will be based on extensive observation data (interviews, aerial over flights, historical information, etc.). Once a number of lost fishing trips is estimated, the trustees then must calculate a dollar value of damages per trip based on stated preferences (survey results) and revealed preferences (actual behavior of anglers who, for example, travel to an alternative location). Using this method and data from other sites, the trustees may calculate a loss per trip, which is then multiplied by the number of trips. This methodology is complicated and often speculative because of the uncertainty and biases associated with the various valuation techniques. For example, to the extent that the value per trip is based on survey results that do not involve real-world economic choices, it is merely hypothetical. In the following Expert Insight, Dr. Kenneth Train discusses how travel cost models work in practice.

EXPERT INSIGHT: Travel Cost Models

Kenneth Train
Department of Economics
University of California, Berkeley[54]

Often an environmental event will damage places where people go fishing, swimming, or engage in other recreational activities. Pollution in a river can reduce the fish stock, which means that anglers catch fewer fish. Tar balls from an oil spill can make beach walking less pleasant; if the oiling is heavy enough, the beaches might be closed. These losses often need to be monetized when assessing the impact of the environmental event. The situation is different from other consumer losses because there are no obvious prices associated with the recreational activities that are affected. Travel cost models provide a mechanism for valuing the losses, by recognizing that there is indeed a price associated with each recreational activity: namely, the cost of traveling for the activity.

---

54. Dr. Kenneth Train is an adjunct professor emeritus of economics at the University of California, Berkeley, and vice president of National Economic Research Associates, Inc. He holds a PhD in economics from the University of California, Berkeley.

A person who drives somewhere for recreation—to a fishing hole, or a beach for swimming or sunbathing, or a mountain trail for hiking—incurs the cost of driving there. The person values the trip sufficiently to warrant the cost of going there, or else they wouldn't have gone. This cost is the price of the trip and, like prices for standard goods, provides a measure of the value of the trip.

The cost of travel also provides information about the value that people place on specific amenities that affect their recreational enjoyment. Usually there are many places that a person can go for recreational activities, and different sites have different attractions. Some lakes offer better fishing—more fish stock—than others. Some beach sites have bathrooms and changing facilities. The extra cost of driving to a site with a particular amenity is the price of that amenity. A person who chooses to go to a more distant lake that has better fishing or to a more distant beach that has changing facilities is paying the cost of the extra travel; they value the extra fish stock or changing facilities sufficiently to spend the extra cost of driving there.

Travel cost models are statistical procedures to estimate the value of trips and the value of amenities at different locations. They are used to estimate the losses from environmental events that degrade the amenities and reduce visitation at specified sites. The models are constructed by observing where people go for recreation, and comparing those choices with the options that are available to them. A sample of households is surveyed, either once or over a period of time, to determine what recreational trips they have taken, where they went, how long the trip was, which household members went on the trip, and other information. The type of trip that is examined depends on the type of damages that are being assessed. In some cases, people are asked about the daytrips for fishing or beach-going when the damages are thought to mostly affect people close to the damaged sites. In other cases, people are asked about their multi-day trips, when the event is expected to impact people's vacations to more distant places.

For each surveyed household, the places available for the recreational activity are identified—the various locations where they could go fishing, or beaches that they could visit. The cost of travel to each location is calculated, and the amenities at each place are recorded, such as the fish stock at each available fishing site or the bathroom facilities at beach locations. The statistical analysis then compares the cost and amenities at the sites that each household actually visited with the cost and amenities of the sites that the household did not visit. This comparison provides information on the value of the trips that the household took and the value of the amenities at the sites.

Recreational losses attributed to an environmental event are calculated from these models in two ways, depending on how much information on visitation is available. In many cases, data on visitation before and after the event can be used to determine the reduction in visitation that is attributable to the event at each affected location. This reduction is called the number of "lost trips"; it is the number of trips that *would have* been taken in the absence of the event but were *not* taken because of the event. The travel cost model then provides the value of each lost trip.

In other cases, the event degrades some amenities at specified sites, such as pollution that reduces the fish stock at particular lakes, but data are not available on visitation at these sites before and after the event. In this situation, the travel cost model is used to predict the number of lost trips at each affected site. In particular, the amenities at affected sites are adjusted in the model to represent their degraded levels, such as lower fish stock at affected lakes. The model predicts the trip-making of households under these degraded amenities. Of the people who went to an affected site prior to the event, the model predicts how many of these people would go elsewhere, or not take a trip at all, when the amenities at the site are degraded. The value of these lost trips is then tabulated.

Several issues are particularly important when using a travel cost model to assess losses. First, of course, is the measurement of travel costs. Usually, travel costs include the out-of-pocket costs as well as the value of the time spent traveling. The economist who is constructing the travel cost model makes decisions on how to calculate these costs, and these decisions have an impact on the measure of loss from any event. Generally, proportionally higher travel costs translate into proportionally higher losses from any environmental degradation. The reason is clear; travel cost models consider the cost of taking a trip to be the price of the trip, and a higher price translates into greater loss when the trip is "lost." It is important, therefore, when examining the losses calculated from any travel cost model, to assess how travel costs are calculated in the model. And when comparing alternative loss calculations from different travel cost models, it is useful to identify whether the travel cost is calculated differently in the models.

Options for substitution are also important. If a site is damaged, and yet other nearby sites provide similar amenities, then the loss is not very large: people who went to the damaged site before the event can switch to other sites that provide practically as much value. But if the only other options are for people to go to much worse sites, or not take the trip at all, then the loss is greater. The economist who constructs the travel cost model makes decisions about which sites to include as options. The specification of options has an impact on the measure of losses that is calculated from the model. The issue is not simply *how many* options are included in the model, but whether close substitutes for the affected sites are included. If close substitutes actually exist but are not included in the model, then the model's measure of loss will be inaccurately high. And if options are included in the model that act as close substitutes but are not actually realistic alternatives for recreators, then the model's measure of loss will be inaccurately low.

Another issue arises when people do not go to a site because of an environmental event but the site is not actually hurt by the event. For example, after an offshore oil spill, people might cancel their vacations to places that could be affected, but then the oil ends up not reaching shore. The people who canceled their vacations because of the spill incurred a loss, which is the value of the trip that they would have taken. But the people who did not cancel their trips and went to the beaches anyway did not lose anything; the beach was not affected by the spill.

This distinction is important. Travel cost models are used to calculate the loss to two separate groups of people at each site: the people who decide not to go to a site because of the event and the people who go to the site anyway even though it was damaged by the event. The economist who is estimating losses needs to decide which components of loss to include for each potentially affected site, and these decisions can have a large impact on the resulting measure of losses. Losses for the first group arise for each site with lost trips (whether or not it was damaged), and losses for the second group arise at each damaged site (whether or not it experienced a loss in visitation). However, data are not always available to make the requisite distinctions and some assumptions will be necessary. When comparing loss estimates from different economists for the same event, it can be useful to identify which components of loss each economist included for each site.

EXPERT INSIGHT: Trip Equivalency Analysis
Doug MacNair, Ted Tomasi, George Parsons, and Heath Byrd[55]

Background

In many NRDAs, injuries to recreation are asserted, for example from closures of recreation sites, imposition of more stringent fish or game consumption advisories, or an increase in the number of tar balls on a beach from an oil spill.[56] We will focus on a closure, but the arguments apply in principle to a change in the quality of recreation sites.[57] Restoration of human use involves projects that enhance opportunities by creating new sites or improving existing ones. The issue is determining how much restoration is enough (scaling).

Suppose there is a closure of a recreation site (a beach) due to a spill. Typically, the injury would be measured as the reduction in the number of trips caused by the

---

55. Dr. Doug MacNair is a technical director at Environmental Resources Management. Dr. Ted Tomasi is a vice president and director of National Practices for Cardno, Inc. Dr. George Parsons is a professor, School of Marine Science and Policy, University of Delaware. Heath Byrd is a senior economist with Cardno, Inc.

56. Cultural use of resources by tribes is another human use which raises related issues, but we will not be explicit about applications to cultural use.

57. *See* MacNair et al. (2017).

release, multiplied by the dollar value of a trip.[58] The economic value of a recreation trip is the willingness to pay (WTP) of recreators to have the site available so they can take trips to that site on a given choice occasion, rather than go to another site or do something entirely different. The scaling task is to find restoration projects such that the increased recreation value from additional trips to the newly created site equals the injury. This is called value-to-value (VtV) scaling of the projects, since the dollar value lost is just offset by the dollar value gained.[59]

This differs from scaling of ecological restoration projects using HEA or REA, which finds restoration that augments the quantity of *services* so as to equal the injury measured as the quantity of service reductions. This service-to-service scaling avoids the measurement of economic values as WTP for ecological services, which is a highly controversial enterprise.

Although measuring WTP for recreation trips is not as controversial as for ecological services, disagreements about the appropriate economic assumptions for estimating WTP can result in significant differences in damage estimates. In addition, it is a complicated and expensive practice to gather the data and estimate statistical models used to estimate WTP. What if there was a simpler alternative that led to accurate scaling but without dollar valuation, similar to HEA and REA? There is, and we call it "trip equivalency analysis" (TEA). We next describe it in more detail and then say why it is an important advance for human use aspects of NRDA.

Trip Equivalency Analysis

TEA differs from VtV. We start with a description of VtV and then discuss how TEA is different.

The Full Economic Analysis

The standard way to estimate the value of a recreation trip is with a Travel Cost Model (TCM). Over the past two decades, most NRDAs have used a variant called the Random Utility Model (RUM). The basic principle of the RUM is that in each time period (like a day or a week) people choose (1) whether to devote time to recreation and, if so, (2) where to go. In making the choice, the person is assumed to consider the alternative sites and their attributes, including the cost of travel (hence the TCM), and to then make the best choice—the one that provides the highest "utility" (i.e., satisfaction). The person is assumed to make evaluations of the available options partly based on things known by the NRDA analyst (the cost of travel, attributes of the sites, and the person's demographics) but partly also on things not observable by

---

58. We make this a brief closure so that discounting is relevant; for longer impacts, this would be the present discounted value of the trips lost and gained.

59. Value-to-cost is often used, which equates damages (to be spent on restoration) to the dollar-denominated injury. *See* Byrd and Dunford (2017) on this approach.

the analyst. Therefore, which site provides the most utility in a time period is uncertain to the analyst—hence the name, random utility model.

The mathematics of the model shows that the loss in utility over the whole season from a closure of one site, call it J, is given by a formula involving the utility of going to J relative to that of going to any of the other sites or doing something else. The formula follows; we won't bother to explain it, but it includes the distance and quality attributes to J and all the other sites:

$$\Delta U = N \cdot \ln \{[e^{x_0 \alpha} + \sum_{-j} e^{x_j \beta}]/[e^{x_0 \alpha} + e^{x_j \beta} + \sum_{-j} e^{x_j \beta}]\}$$

To determine all the elements in this formula, one needs to (1) do a survey to get data on how many trips people took over a season, what places they chose to go to on those trips, and their demographics; and then (2) collect data on the attributes of all the sites the sample could have gone to. This is a *lot* of data and may cost several hundred thousand dollars to collect and analyze.

The dollar denominated WTP to avoid the closure of the site (the quantified injury in value-to-value scaling) is then

$$WTP = \left(\frac{1}{\beta_0}\right) \cdot \Delta U,$$

where β_0 is the increment to utility from an increment to income and is based on assumptions concerning travel costs, including vehicle operating costs and the income forgone while traveling. Dividing by this term converts utility to dollars.

To complete the scaling, one needs to apply a similar formula for the proposed newly created site to show it generates an equivalent WTP.

The Beauty of TEA

The insight from TEA is that, to a close approximation in most circumstances, the complex formula above reduces to

$$\Delta U \approx T_j,$$

which is the number of trips taken at baseline to the site that gets closed. That is a *much* easier thing to measure accurately, as it involves only counts. By implication, the number of trips taken to a particular site reflects the distance to and site attributes of all the available beach recreation opportunities as well as the option of doing something else (working, painting the shutters, bowling).

TEA additionally implies that

$$WTP \approx \left(\frac{1}{\beta_0}\right) \cdot T_j.$$

Here, we see that the "monetization" of the change in utility from the closure (measured in TEA by trips) is the same as the value of a trip. To complete restoration scaling, what is needed is to replace the lost trips, essentially "one-for-one." A restoration site needs to be able to attract visitors in the same manner as the injured one; if it has more substitutes, it needs to be closer to a population center to be as attractive, and, if it has less of one feature, it has to be more desirable in some other way. The test of all this is not in the estimation of a complex RUM but in whether people show up.

In the case of quality changes, TEA still works, but now the index of utility is the change in trips induced by the quality change, rather than trips to the site as for a closure. Again, these can be obtained from site counts and benefits transfer and do not require surveys.

Caveats

TEA holds in the context of the RUM and related models, but it may not hold if behavior is consistent with these frameworks.
- In cases where the affected site (or sites) provides the lion's share total trips to all sites, the TEA approximation is not as good, but corrections or calibrations are possible.
- While TEA still works, it is a bit more complicated when there are quality changes rather than closures, and when many sites are affected.

The Benefits of TEA

- TEA is based on counts of the number of recreators at affected sites. These are generally more accurate and less costly to conduct than survey responses based on recollections of how often one recreated and where one went.
- One doesn't need to obtain information on the attributes of all the sites (fishing piers, boat launches, beach width, water quality, etc.). One *does* need to predict how many people go to a restored site, but this may be available. In the case of a quality change, a simple reference site comparison may suffice—for example two beaches that are similar but with different access may provide the percent difference in number of trips from improved access.
- It is based on a very understandable concept—if you lose trips you need to replace them—rather than big fancy formulas that only economists really understand.

5. Contingent Valuation

Another ostensible approach for measuring damages is the contingent valuation (CV) method, which attempts to determine the intrinsic or existence value of goods and services based on the results of a questionnaire designed to collect information about the respondent's willingness to pay for the goods or services, independent of his or her use of the resource. Although the methodology continues to evolve, in the traditional CV survey, a respondent is given facts about the injuries to natural resources (e.g., the number of birds killed) and then asked how much he or she would be willing to pay to ensure that such injury does not occur again (e.g., a tax that would fund a mechanism to prevent these types of injuries). The average value response will then be multiplied by the presumed number of impacted individuals. In some cases, the trustees will multiply by the number of local residents, but for larger matters they may multiply the average value by the number of residents in the region, state, or even country. For this reason, the CV methodology will often lead to highly inflated calculations. Much has been written by economists regarding the flaws of this methodology, some of which are discussed in the Expert Insight by Daniel McFadden and Kenneth Train later in the chapter.[60]

NOAA, while acknowledging the potential for problems with the use of CV to assess passive-use values, has maintained that a well-designed study can provide reliable information. Following the passage of OPA, NOAA commissioned a panel to evaluate CV methodology, and ultimately issued a report on its findings.[61] The report recognized various problems with the methods and responses associated with CV, including inconsistency of responses with rational choice, implausible responses when multiplied (e.g., by the number of spills that actually occur each year), the lack of meaningful budget constraints in the hypothetical scenario, and difficulty in assessing the appropriate geographic scope for the survey. Nevertheless, rather than concluding that CV is fundamentally unsound, the panel set forth various guidelines for a well-designed CV study. The guidelines set forth in the report are as follows:

- **Sample type and size.** Probability sampling is essential for a survey used for damage assessment. The choice of sample-specific design and size is a difficult, technical question that requires the guidance of a professional sampling statistician.
- **Minimize nonresponses.** High nonresponse rates would make the survey results unreliable.
- **Personal interview.** The panel believed it was unlikely that reliable estimates of values could be elicited with mail surveys. Face-to-face interviews are usually preferable, although telephone interviews have some advantages in terms of cost and centralized supervision.

---

60. For a recent overview, see CONTINGENT VALUATION OF ENVIRONMENTAL GOODS: A COMPREHENSIVE CRITIQUE (Daniel McFadden, E. Morris Cox & Kenneth Train eds., 2017), https://www.e-elgar.com/shop/contingent-valuation-of-environmental-goods.

61. *See* Natural Resource Damage Assessments Under the Oil Pollution Act of 1980, 58 Fed. Reg. 4601, 4602–14, app. I (Report of the NOAA Panel on Contingent Valuation) (Jan. 15, 1993).

- **Pretesting for interviewer effects.** An important respect in which CV surveys differ from actual referenda is the presence of an interviewer (except in the case of mail surveys). It is possible that interviewers contribute to "social desirability" bias, since preserving the environment is widely viewed as something positive. In order to test this possibility, major CV studies should incorporate experiments that assess interviewer effects.
- **Reporting.** Every report of a CV study should make clear the definition of the population sampled, the sampling frame used, the sample size, the overall sample nonresponse rate and its components (e.g., refusals), and nonresponse rates for all important questions. The report should also reproduce the exact wording and sequence of the questionnaire and of other communications to respondents (e.g., advance letters). All data from the study should be archived and made available to interested parties.
- **Careful pretesting of a CV questionnaire.** Respondents in a CV survey are ordinarily presented with a good deal of new and often technical information, well beyond what is typical in most surveys. This requires very careful pilot work and pretesting, plus evidence from the final survey that respondents understood and accepted the main description and questioning reasonably well.[62]

Despite its flaws, challenges to the inclusion of CV in CERCLA and OPA regulations have been unsuccessful. In *Ohio v. U.S. Department of the Interior*,[63] industry petitioners challenged DOI's inclusion of CV in its CERCLA regulations as a method that could be used to estimate use and nonuse values.[64] The court rejected petitioners' argument that "CV methodology is inharmonious with common law damage assessment principles, and is considered less than a 'best available procedure'" as required by statute,[65] reasoning that "a motivating force behind the CERCLA natural damage provisions was Congress' dissatisfaction with the common law."[66]

---

62. *Id.* at 4608 (internal citations omitted). The report also contains more specific guidelines for value-elucidation CV surveys.

63. 880 F.2d 432, 476 (D.C. Cir. 1989).

64. *See* 43 C.F.R. § 11.83(c)(2)(vii).

65. 42 U.S.C. § 9651(c)(2)(B).

66. 880 F.2d at 476, 455 (citing S. Rep. No. 848, 96th Cong., 2d Sess. 13 (1980) ("[T]raditional tort law presents substantial barriers to recovery.") and H.R. Rep. No. 172(I), 96th Cong. 1st Sess. 17 (1979) ("Common law remedies [are] . . . inadequate to compensate victims in a fair and expeditious manner.")).

Similarly, in *General Electric Co. v. U.S. Department of Commerce*,[67] industry petitioners argued that NOAA acted arbitrarily and capriciously by not barring the use of CV altogether in its final rule under OPA, despite the NOAA panel's caution that CV studies must be conducted subject to stringent standards.[68] The court rejected this argument, observing that NOAA did not ignore the panel, but instead gave trustees discretion to use CV so long as the results were valid and reliable.[69] Finally, in *Kennecott Utah Copper Corp. v. U.S. Department of the Interior*, the D.C. Circuit rejected industry petitioners' argument that the NOAA regulations regarding methods for choosing cost-estimating and valuation methodologies left too much to the trustees' discretion.[70]

Similarly, there are examples of courts allowing CV studies to withstand motions in limine or *Daubert* challenges. For example, in *Montana v. Atlantic Richfield Co.*, Atlantic Richfield sought to exclude the CV study—a "public opinion poll . . . which asked a make-believe question, and obtained make-believe answers"—by arguing that the study was unreliable and produced arbitrary results in violation of *Daubert*. The court summarily denied Atlantic Richfield's motion.[71]

However, no court has ever relied on a CV study in assessing NRD. In a milestone NRD matter, the *Montrose* DDT litigation in California, the court excluded the CV study on a motion in limine on the grounds that the questionnaire contained unsupported factual predicates (i.e., the survey instrument asked about specific injuries that were later deemed unproven and were eventually dropped by the prosecution).[72] In *Idaho v. Southern Refrigerated Transport Inc.*, the U.S. District Court for the District of Idaho determined that the CV study put forward by the trustees as evidence of nonuse damages was unreliable because it was conducted for an independent purpose not related to the litigation and was not appropriately tailored "to determine to any degree of certainty what value should be placed on these fish based on their existence value."[73] Similarly, in the state NRD law case of *People ex rel. Department*

---

67. 128 F.3d 767 (D.C. Cir. 1997).

68. *Id.* at 773.

69. *Id.*

70. 88 F.3d 1191, 1217 (D.C. Cir. 1996).

71. *See, e.g.*, Montana v. Atl. Richfield Co., No. CV-83-317-H-PGH, 1997 U.S. Dist. LEXIS 24669, at *4 (D. Mont. Feb. 28, 1997 (decided), Mar. 3, 1997 (filed)).

72. United States v. Montrose Chem. Corp. of Cal., No. CV 90-3122-R (C.D. Cal. Apr. 17, 2000), ECF No. 1914.

73. No. 88-1279, 1991 WL 22479, at *19 (D. Idaho Jan. 24, 1991).

of *Fish & Game v. Attransco, Inc.*,[74] a jury appears to have rejected the NRD defendant's reliance on a CV study to rebut the state trustee's valuation of lost beach trips associated with the *American Trader* oil spill, an oil tanker spill in 1990 off the coast of southern California. While there is no information about the reasons behind the jury's decision, it affirmatively selected the trip value presented by the state, not the value presented by the defense based on CV surveys. These decisions indicate that it will be difficult, if not impossible, to develop a stated preference survey that accurately matches the type, location, and size of the injuries and that judges and/or juries will find reliable at trial.

Finally, it is worth noting that while trustees often commission CV studies (at great expense) they appear to disfavor reliance on these studies in their final assessment of damages. To our knowledge, NOAA, for example, has never used survey methods to measure nonuse damages under OPA.

Perhaps the most instructive example of the government's reluctance to rely on CV involved the *Deepwater Horizon* oil spill that occurred in the Gulf of Mexico in 2010. Injury from that incident was eventually assessed in a document called the *Deepwater Horizon Oil Spill: Final Programmatic Damage Assessment and Restoration Plan and Final Programmatic Environmental Impact Statement* (hereinafter *Deepwater* PDARP), prepared on behalf of multiple federal agencies as well as agencies of the states of Texas, Louisiana, Mississippi, Alabama, and Florida (the "*Deepwater* Trustees"). Initially, the *Deepwater* Trustees had commissioned multiple in-depth surveys designed to estimate the lost use and nonuse values resulting from the spill. BP Exploration & Production Inc. (BP), one of the responsible parties for the incident, challenged the *Deepwater* Trustees' decision to undertake these studies and, despite agreeing to perform a cooperative assessment and fund much of the *Deepwater* Trustees' investigation, refused to fund the nonuse surveys before the *Deepwater* Trustees had made a formal determination, as required by the OPA regulations, that in-kind restoration or scaled restoration was inappropriate. Ultimately, the damage assessment set forth in the *Deepwater* PDARP relied on none of the stated preference surveys regarding the dollar value of injured habitat and wildlife. Instead, the *Deepwater* Trustees used a restoration approach, setting forth a comprehensive restoration plan, which is discussed further later, for both use and nonuse alleged damages.

During the public comment period after the release of the draft *Deepwater* PDARP, multiple commenters asserted that the *Deepwater* PDARP was

---

74. No. 646339 (Cal. Super. Ct.).

incomplete because it failed to value ecosystem services through CV surveys. The *Deepwater* Trustees responded by stating that:

> The commenter is correct that the Trustees did not use a contingent valuation approach to value ecosystem services here, but the commenter's proposed approach is not required by law or regulations. In fact, the Oil Pollution Act regulations contain a clear preference for basing the amount of natural resource damages sought from the responsible parties on the costs of implementing a restoration plan that would repair or replace injured natural resources where practicable and compensate the public for interim losses of natural resource and ecosystem services until the ecosystem has fully recovered. That is the primary approach to damage assessment that the Trustees adopted in response to the *Deepwater Horizon* spill and the basis for the preparation of this PDARP/PEIS. . . .
>
> The Trustees performed a contingent valuation total value study for the *Deepwater Horizon* incident. However, because the Trustees concluded that natural resource injuries and ecosystem service losses in this case can be addressed by the preferred ecosystem-wide restoration alternative described in the Final PDARP/PEIS, the Trustees did not complete that study and did not rely on it.[75]

The fact that CV surveys were considered and rejected for the *Deepwater Horizon* incident is particularly significant in light of the diverse and sensitive resources that the *Deepwater* Trustees asserted had been injured. According to the *Deepwater* Trustees, the incident was "the largest offshore oil spill in the history of the United States," which "injured natural resources as diverse as deep-sea coral, fish and shellfish, productive wetland habitats, sandy beaches, birds, endangered sea turtles, and protected marine life."[76] The *Deepwater* Trustees also concluded that "[t]he oil spill prevented people from fishing, going to the beach, and enjoying their typical recreational activities along the Gulf of Mexico."[77] Given that a restoration-based approach can effectively be applied to this varied range of injuries, including resources as unique as endangered and protected species, and resources as difficult to restore as deep-sea coral, it is difficult to identify any scenario where a CV approach would be appropriate.

---

75. DEEPWATER HORIZON OIL SPILL NATURAL RESOURCE TRUSTEES, DEEPWATER HORIZON OIL SPILL: FINAL PROGRAMMATIC DAMAGE ASSESSMENT AND RESTORATION PLAN AND FINAL PROGRAMMATIC ENVIRONMENTAL IMPACT STATEMENT 8-22 (2016) [hereinafter DEEPWATER PDARP/PEIS], http://www.gulfspillrestoration.noaa.gov/restoration-planning/gulf-plan.

76. *Id.* at 1-3.

77. *Id.*

There are at least two additional policy reasons why trustee agencies should abandon CV methods and focus instead on capturing nonuse values through restoration. First, CV methods are extraordinarily expensive. The CV studies conducted in *Montrose*, *Exxon Valdez*, and *Deepwater Horizon* cost tens of millions of dollars. Given that in no case have these studies actually worked to provide a reliable damage estimate, it is hard to justify the cost.[78] In *Deepwater Horizon*—perhaps the most complicated, wide-ranging NRDA ever undertaken—the trustees spent millions of dollars on a CV study and, in the end, concluded it was not necessary or appropriate to rely on that study.

Second, CV and other survey methods rest on a flawed premise. The governmental agencies charged with assessing and restoring damages (i.e., natural resource trustees) have extensive information about the real cost of protecting and restoring natural resources, gained through their work on other NRD cases and their work to manage natural resources in national and state parks, forests, seashores, fisheries, and other public lands and waters. Agencies rely on that information and their experience to identify the actual cost of work to protect, restore, and expand these resources on a daily basis. But when they instead rely on the results of stated preference surveys in assessing damages, the trustees willingly step aside and instead rely on a randomly selected sample of the public to assign a dollar value to these resources.

The supposed rationale for relying on a public survey is that only the public can measure the value of a loss suffered by the public. But that rationale does not apply in other environmental contexts. For comparison, in the case of environmental risk from industrial activities, no one would ever think to use a survey of randomly selected members of the public to determine the levels of contaminants that present a risk to human health and the environment. Instead, we routinely rely upon scientists, economists, and other experts to make those judgments based on data and analysis. Likewise, with the valuation of damages resulting from a pollution event, the better approach for measuring such damages is for experts (not a group of randomly selected members of the public) to determine how much restoration is required to return natural resources to baseline conditions and to compensate for the interim losses. Fortunately, the NRD jurisprudence, regulations, and precedent all point to exactly that outcome.

---

78. Indeed, under the CERCLA regulations, NRDA costs are not considered reasonable, and thus are not recoverable, if "the anticipated increment of extra benefits in terms of the precision or accuracy of estimates obtained by using a more costly . . . methodology are greater than the anticipated increment of extra costs of that methodology." 43 C.F.R. § 11.14(ee).

Despite the legal and policy landscape, however, and despite extensive econometric hurdles, some economists continue to advocate for the use of CV as a viable method for capturing nonuse value.

EXPERT INSIGHT: Contingent Valuation of Environmental Goods—
A Comprehensive Critique[79]

Daniel McFadden and Kenneth Train[80]
Department of Economics
University of California, Berkeley

Contingent valuation (CV) is a procedure that attempts to estimate the value to households of public goods. While CV can be used in many contexts, we consider its use for evaluating environmental goods. The method is implemented through a survey of households. Respondents are given a detailed description of a program that will improve the environment, such as protecting wilderness areas from development or repairing coral reefs. Each respondent is asked whether they would vote in favor of or against a ballot measure to fund the project at a specified cost to each household. The cost is varied over respondents, and the share of respondents who say that they would vote in favor is tabulated for each cost level. These shares are then used to estimate the mean willingness to pay (WTP) for the program. The method is sometimes revised to ask each respondent to make choices among several different programs at different costs, instead of just one.

Inadequate Response to Cost

CV studies ask respondents whether they are willing to pay a specified dollar amount for a program or improvement that has been described to them. Different dollar

---

79. This Expert Insight is adapted from the introduction to a much longer book, also titled CONTINGENT VALUATION OF ENVIRONMENTAL GOODS: A COMPREHENSIVE CRITIQUE, edited by economists Dr. Daniel McFadden and Dr. Kenneth Train (hereinafter CONTINGENT VALUATION OF ENVIRONMENTAL GOODS). The book is a unique compilation of the numerous methodological critiques to contingent valuation of environmental goods, written by a variety of experts in the field. This excerpt provides a good summary of those various critiques, as well as its own helpful insights. NRD practitioners considering contingent valuation issues should turn to the full book, which is publicly accessible in electronic format at https://www.elgaronline.com/view /9781786434685.xml. Thank you to Dr. McFadden, Dr. Train, and Edward Elgar Publishing, Inc. for their permission to adapt and reprint the introduction. © Daniel McFadden and Kenneth Train 2017. Reproduced with permission of the Licensor through PLSclear.

80. Daniel McFadden is the E. Morris Cox Professor of Economics at the University of California, Berkeley, and the 2000 Nobel Laureate in Economics. Kenneth Train is an adjunct professor emeritus of economics at the University of California, Berkeley, and vice president of National Economic Research Associates, Inc.

amounts are asked of different respondents to obtain the variation in cost that is needed to estimate mean WTP. The question arises: How sensitive are CV estimates to the researchers' choice of cost prompts?

Burrows, Dixon, and Chan recently examined this issue for a prominent CV study conducted by NOAA on WTP for the preservation of marine species, using the original study's data.[81] The survey included several designs with cost prompts that were twice and half, respectively, the costs used in the main survey design. In these variants, one sample of respondents was presented with prompts that ranged from $5 to $50, and another sample of respondents was given prompts ranging from $20 to $200. The original study's report only presented results for the main design; it did not report how the estimates differed under the alternative sets of prompts. Burrows, Dixon, and Chan performed the relevant calculations and found that the estimated WTP was three times greater with the higher-cost prompts than with the lower prompts. That is, raising the cost prompts by a factor of four raised the estimated WTP for the program by a factor of three. This result is consistent with the view that respondents take the cost prompts as a suggestion of the amount that is reasonable to pay and adjust their concepts of their own WTP in relation to these prompts. As a result, CV is not actually estimating a true WTP, but rather is creating an estimated WTP through the researcher's choice of the cost prompts.

Parsons and Myers also recently examined the issue of cost prompts from a different perspective.[82] They review CV studies and find that the estimated WTP depends greatly on the highest cost prompt. They find that the share of "yes" votes—that is, the share of respondents who say they are willing to pay the specified cost prompt—stays relatively high no matter how large the cost prompt is. They call this the "fat tails" phenomenon. To investigate how far the fat tail extends, Parsons and Myers conducted a study about protecting the red knot, a migratory shorebird whose population has declined in recent years. In this study, they kept raising the highest cost prompt, asking new samples of respondents ever-higher prompts, and found that the yes share never approached zero. They raised the prompt as high as $10,000, and still 23 percent of the CV respondents said that, yes, they would be willing to pay $10,000. The estimated mean WTP ranged from $102 to $2,254, depending on the highest cost prompt that they used. Their study suggests that (essentially) any estimated WTP can be obtained through specification of the highest cost prompt.

---

81. *See* James Burrows et al., *Response to Cost Prompts in Stated Preference Valuation of Environmental Goods, in* CONTINGENT VALUATION OF ENVIRONMENTAL GOODS, *supra* note 79, at 1 (Daniel McFadden & Kenneth Train eds., 2017), https://www.elgaronline.com/downloadpdf/edcoll/9781786434685/9781786434685.00007.xml.

82. *See* George Parsons & Kelley Myers, *Fat Tails and Truncated Bids in Contingent Valuation: An Application to an Endangered Shorebird Species, in* CONTINGENT VALUATION OF ENVIRONMENTAL GOODS, *supra* note 79, at 17, https://www.elgaronline.com/downloadpdf/edcoll/9781786434685/9781786434685.00008.xml.

Inadequate Response to the Number of Payments

CV studies can specify the cost prompt as a one-time payment, annual payments over a period of time, or other payment schedules. The question therefore arises: Is the estimated present value willingness to pay (PV WTP), which is the relevant measure for resource allocation decisions, sensitive to the payment schedule that is specified in the CV study? The answer is yes.

Myers, Parsons, and Train recently reviewed studies that have examined this issue.[83] All of the past studies find that results differ greatly depending on how the payment schedule is specified, with the estimated PV WTP being far greater when the researcher specifies a series of periodic payments rather than a one-time, lump-sum payment. The implicit discount rate that reconciles the CV responses under different payment schedules has been found in all studies to be implausibly high. In addition to their literature review, Myers, Parsons, and Train implemented a CV study to compare one-time and annual payments. They found that the estimated PV WTP is 32 times larger when the cost prompt is specified as annual payments than when the cost prompt is specified as a one-time payment.

Inadequate Response to Scope

One important question in CV is whether CV estimates truly reflect the scope of the environmental good that is described to respondents. An early influential study (Boyle et al., 1994) found, for example, that CV estimates of WTP to protect birds were essentially the same whether respondents were told that 2,000 birds would be saved or 200,000 birds. Controversy about this issue led NOAA to convene an expert panel to provide guidelines for CV studies. The panel stated (Arrow et al., 1993, p. 38) that a CV study would be deemed unreliable if it exhibited "[i]nadequate responsiveness to the scope of the environmental insult." The panel stated that the burden of proof for demonstrating adequate response must rest with the researchers who conducted the CV study.

Recently, Desvousges, Mathews, and Train implemented an "adding-up" test on a prominent and well-funded CV survey.[84] The test examines whether the estimated WTP for each component of a multi-part program, when evaluated incrementally, sum up to the estimated WTP for the whole program—as required by the definition of WTP. They found that the test fails; the sum of the parts is estimated to be valued three times more than the whole. This finding suggests that respondents' answers to

---

83. *See* Kelley Myers et al., *Inadequate Response to Frequency of Payments in Contingent Valuation of Environmental Goods, in* CONTINGENT VALUATION OF ENVIRONMENTAL GOODS, *supra* note 79, at 43, https://www.elgaronline.com/downloadpdf/edcoll/9781786434685/9781786434685.00009.xml.

84. *See* William Desvousges et al., *An Adding-Up Test on Contingent Valuations of River and Lake Quality, in* CONTINGENT VALUATION OF ENVIRONMENTAL GOODS, *supra* note 79, at 58, https://www.elgaronline.com/downloadpdf/edcoll/9781786434685/9781786434685.00010.xml.

CV questions reflect their expression of interest in the *concept* of an improvement, rather than the scope of the actual improvement that is described to them.

In another recent analysis, Burrows, Newman, Genser, and Plewes review the CV studies that have conducted external scope tests[85] and find that more studies fail the test than pass it.[86] That is, more often than not, CV studies don't find *any* response to scope, much less an adequate response. The authors show that previous reviews that have found otherwise (i.e., that passing a scope test is more common than failing) have ignored many studies that failed, have inappropriately included internal tests, and have interpreted results as representing a pass when there is insufficient or contradictory evidence for this inference. Interestingly, the incidence of scope failures has risen over time as the quality of studies has presumably improved, which suggests that the failures cannot be attributed in general to faulty design of the studies but seem instead to be intrinsic to the CV procedure.

Difficulty Answering CV Questions

Why do CV studies evidence inadequate response to cost, the frequency of payments, and the scope of the program? In a recent analysis, McFadden reviews the history of stated preference (SP) elicitation in general and examines studies that have used these methods in various fields.[87] He identifies the features of a study, and of the good being evaluated, that affect the reliability of the method. He concludes that CV studies of environmental goods possess the very features that make SP elicitation least reliable. The main problem is that respondents are unfamiliar with making choices about environmental goods. The respondent, struggling to provide meaningful answers to CV questions, is susceptible to suggestion by the survey instrument (especially the cost prompt) and to substituting general political concerns for the specific, but unanswerable, personal valuation question.

The difficulty in answering CV questions about environmental goods seems to be evidenced neurologically. Khaw et al. (2015) measured brain activity of respondents in choice exercises for four classes of goods: snack food, market goods, daily activities, and environmental proposals. For the first three classes, activity was evidenced in the traditional valuational area of the brain, as expected. However, for the environmental

---

85. An external test uses a split-sample design, where one sample is asked about a program with a specified scope and another sample is asked about a program with a greater (or smaller) scope.

86. *See* James Burrows et al., *Do Contingent Valuation Estimates of Willingness to Pay for Non-Use Environmental Goods Pass the Scope Test with Adequacy? A Review of the Evidence from Empirical Studies in the Literature*, in CONTINGENT VALUATION OF ENVIRONMENTAL GOODS, *supra* note 79, at 82, https://www.elgaronline.com/downloadpdf/edcoll/9781786434685/9781786434685.00011.xml.

87. *See* Daniel McFadden, *Stated Preference Methods and Their Applicability to Environmental Use and Non-Use Valuations*, in CONTINGENT VALUATION OF ENVIRONMENTAL GOODS, *supra* note 79, at 153, https://www.elgaronline.com/downloadpdf/edcoll/9781786434685/9781786434685.00012.xml.

proposals, activity was not evidenced in this valuational area. Instead neurological activity appeared in a region of the brain that is associated with cognitive control and shifting decision strategies. Neural measurement is fairly new in economics, and further research is required before conclusions can be drawn. But at face value, the results are consistent with McFadden's assessment that respondents do not know how to approach the CV questions about environmental goods and are struggling for ways to approach the task.

Why is this task so difficult? At least part of the problem is thinking about a budget constraint in the context of environmental goods. A respondent can think that paying $100 to clean up a polluted lake sounds reasonable but then might start to wonder about the thousands of other lakes that need cleaning up, and realize that paying $100 for each of them is impossible. The respondent might then remember all the birds and other species that need protection, and people dying of curable diseases who could be helped with some money for medicine. The respondent faces a quandary about allocation among public goods that the CV survey ignores by asking about only one public good.[88]

Recently, Kemp, Leamer, Burrows, and Dixon examine the issue of respondents' budget awareness by asking WTP in several ways, including the traditional CV single-focus referendum and by walking the respondent explicitly through a budget allocation task for components of a much larger environmental protection program.[89] The authors found that the estimated mean WTP for a specified project is about $120 when asked in the traditional way but only $2 to $3 when the respondent budgets components of the composite good. And several findings of their study point to pervasive respondent difficulties in thinking about the costs of environmental goods in relation to one another and to other public goods.

But does a budget constraint even come into play when people answer CV questions? The fundamental assumption of CV is that respondents, in giving their response to the cost prompt, are trading off the costs of the program with the benefits. However, as explained earlier, respondents seem to have a hard time answering the CV question about WTP for environmental goods. The problem of how to think about the budget constraint in this context, and respondents' sense that the survey is an opportunity to send messages (about, say, culpability or politics) can lead the respondent to answer in ways that do not represent a trade-off of the benefits of the specified program with the cost prompt that they are offered. To examine this issue, Leamer and Lustig recently estimated a latent class model in which each class

---

88. If the respondent gets so far as to think of the "ordering" problem for public good allocations, then the respondent will also realize that the socially optimal order is not reflected in what projects CV researchers happen to do surveys about.

89. *See* Michael Kemp et al., *Some Findings from Further Exploration of the "Composite Good" Approach to Contingent Valuation, in* CONTINGENT VALUATION OF ENVIRONMENTAL GOODS, *supra* note 79, at 188, https://www.elgaronline.com/downloadpdf/edcoll/9781786434685/9781786434685.00013.xml.

represents a decision-making process that the respondent might use.[90] The authors found that fewer than 25 percent of respondents seem to be trading off benefits and costs; the other 75 percent are using decision rules that do not incorporate trade-offs and for which there is no WTP.

The Search for Appropriate Corrections

It has been suggested that CV samples can be restricted, through the use of follow-up questions, to the "core" of respondents who seem to be answering the CV question appropriately. Past studies have considered eliminating respondents who say they are unsure of their answer, or say that they think the survey is inconsequential, or say that they considered the impact of the program on jobs or other non-environmental outcomes. Each of these studies has generally looked at one issue only, determining the effect of eliminating respondents who do not adhere correctly with respect to that one issue. Myers, MacNair, Tomasi, and Schneider recently applied the procedure to all the issues in combination.[91] They use follow-up questions to address the various issues that past articles have examined only one by one. They find that, out of a sample of 1,224, only two respondents are not eliminated. That is, the "core" group of respondents that seem to be answering the CV question appropriately consists of only two people. And, interestingly, both of these people voted against the specified program.

It has also been suggested that CV estimates can perhaps be adjusted to account for hypothetical bias, that is, for the bias that arises because the data are for hypothetical programs and payments rather than real ones. The idea behind this suggestion is that, for some kinds of goods, estimates of value can be obtained in both hypothetical and actual settings, and the ratio of these estimates (called the "bias ratio") can perhaps be used to adjust CV estimates for their inherent hypothetical nature. Foster and Burrows recently examined this possibility, using 432 comparisons between paired estimates in hypothetical and real settings drawn from previous studies.[92] They find that the bias ratios vary greatly, with no ratio being "typical" or common. Using regression analysis, they find that only a small portion of the variation can be explained by attributes of the study or product. The bias ratios in past studies vary

---

90. *See* Edward Leamer & Josh Lustig, *Inferences from Stated Preference Surveys When Some Respondents Do Not Compare Costs and Benefits*, in CONTINGENT VALUATION OF ENVIRONMENTAL GOODS, *supra* note 79, at 224, https://www.elgaronline.com/downloadpdf/edcoll/9781786434685/9781786434685.00014.xml.

91. *See* Kelley Myers et al., *Assessing the Validity of Stated Preference Data Using Follow-Up Questions*, in CONTINGENT VALUATION OF ENVIRONMENTAL GOODS, *supra* note 79, at 252, https://www.elgaronline.com/downloadpdf/edcoll/9781786434685/9781786434685.00015.xml.

92. *See* Harry Foster & James Burrows, *Hypothetical Bias: A New Meta-Analysis*, in CONTINGENT VALUATION OF ENVIRONMENTAL GOODS, *supra* note 79, at 270, https://www.elgaronline.com/downloadpdf/edcoll/9781786434685/9781786434685.00016.xml.

so greatly and with so little explainable pattern that they provide no reliable guidance for adjusting CV estimates.

References

Arrow, K., R. Solow, P. Portney, E. Leamer, R. Radner, & H. Schuman (1993), *Report of the NOAA Panel on Contingent Valuation*, accessed November 25, 2016 at http://www.economia.unimib.it/DATA/moduli/7_6067/materiale/noaa%20report.pdf.

Bishop, R. and the Total Value Team (2016), "Technical Memo TM-11: Aggregate estimate of total loss value" (Revised Draft), dated January 25, 2016, to Katherine Pease.

Bishop, R., D. Chapman, B. Kanninen, J. Krosnick, B. Leeworthy, & N. Meade (2011), *Total Economics Value for Protecting and Restoring Hawaiian Coral Reef Ecosystems (Final Report)*.

Boyle, K., W. Desvousges, F. Johnson, R. Dunford, & S. Hudson (1994), "An Investigation of Part-Whole Biases in Contingent Valuation Studies," *Journal of Environmental Economics and Management*, 27(1), 64–83.

Edwards, A. & E. Gomez (2007), *Reef Restoration Concepts and Guidelines: Making Sensible Management Choices in the Face of Uncertainty*, St Lucia, Australia: Coral Reef Targeted Research & Capacity Building for Management Programme.

Khaw, M., D. Grab, M. Livermore, C. Vossler, & P. Glimcher (2015), "The Measurement of Subjective Value and Its Relation to Contingent Valuation and Environmental Public Goods," *PLOS ONE*, 10(7), e0132842, DOI:10.1371/journal.pone.0132842.

6. The Programmatic/Eco-System Level Approach (*Deepwater Horizon*)

The final valuation approach we will discuss is the approach utilized in what is the largest NRDA to date, the *Deepwater Horizon* NRDA. The *Deepwater* NRDA was completed and published following release of a proposed consent decree that included $8.1 billion in NRD funds. As discussed previously, the *Deepwater* PDARP rejected some of the more controversial economic valuation techniques, such as CV, and largely relied on a restoration-based approach. However, the *Deepwater* PDARP was novel in that it took a programmatic approach to both injury assessment and restoration valuation.

According to the *Deepwater* Trustees, "the scale of the *Deepwater Horizon* spill was unprecedented, both in terms of the area affected and the duration of the spill. Due to the enormous scope of this incident, evaluation of all potentially injured natural resources in all potentially oiled locations at all times remains cost-prohibitive and scientifically impractical."[93] Therefore, rather than conduct the specific injury assessment normally required in a DARP, the *Deepwater* Trustees evaluated representative habitats, ecosystem processes and linkages, ecological communities, specific natural resources, and human services, and extrapolated to the Gulf of Mexico ecosystem as a whole. Similarly, rather than identify or value specific restoration projects that would compensate for the exact injuries assessed, the *Deepwater* PDARP considered "programmatic alternatives, composed of Restoration Types, to restore natural resources, ecological services, and recreational use services injured or lost as a result of the *Deepwater Horizon* oil spill event."[94] The *Deepwater* PDARP identified 5 restoration goals, 13 restoration types, and 7 restoration areas across which the $8.1 billion in *Deepwater* NRD settlement funds are specifically distributed.[95]

While programmatic environmental impact statements (PEIS) are not a new tool, a programmatic DARP combined with a PEIS is novel. This approach is likely only viable in a scenario, like the *Deepwater Horizon* oil spill, where the NRD is so extensive and wide reaching that undertaking the specific inquiry contemplated by the CERCLA and OPA regulations is not viable or would result in impermissible double recovery. In this type of scenario, use of this type of programmatic approach saves time and assessment costs and may be the most effective (if not the only) way to coordinate an approach among multiple trustees in multiple jurisdictions with different political motivations. The approach's viability was also bolstered by the length of time that had passed since the incident before the plan could be developed (six years) and the magnitude of the settlement funds the *Deepwater* Trustees would have available under the plan.

But, the programmatic approach is not without critics. For example, one commenter noted that the value of NRD could not truly be estimated and that

> it is really hard to imagine that the assessment of the damages is complete or that the monetary value proposed to settle the public claims for natural resource damages is the total amount required to fully restore the public trust resources of the Gulf region, considering this restoration plan considers

---

93. Deepwater PDARP/PEIS, *supra* note 75, at 1-13.

94. *Id.* Abstract, http://www.gulfspillrestoration.noaa.gov/sites/default/files/wp-content/uploads/Front-Matter-and-Chapter-1_Introduction-and-Executive-Summary_508.pdf.

95. Deepwater PDARP/PEIS, *supra* note 75, at 1-15 to 1-20.

injuries to such a wide array of resources . . . that have yet to even be discovered were killed, injured, or impaired."[96]

In their response to this comment, the *Deepwater* Trustees were forced to acknowledge that they "were unable to address all potentially affected ecosystem services and employ all possible assessment tools" but noted that "they believe that the magnitude and ecosystem focus of the restoration plan will result in producing benefits to the full range of ecosystem services impacted by the spill."[97] Whether this reasoning would hold up against legal challenge is yet to be seen. While there were legal challenges to specific projects implemented with the *Deepwater Horizon* NRD funds, the programmatic approach itself was not challenged.

---

96. *Id*. at 8-19.
97. *Id*.

Chapter 6

Cooperative NRD Assessments: Strategy and Mechanics[1]

A. Introduction

The initial strategic decision faced by most companies in an NRD case is whether to participate with the trustees in the NRD assessment (NRDA). The decision is complex and involves numerous considerations. This chapter first discusses the elements of cooperation in the NRDA context. Next, the chapter explores the strategic advantages and disadvantages to participation in a cooperative NRDA with the government. Finally, the chapter discusses the mechanics of cooperation, including the elements of a cooperative assessment agreement.

B. What Is a Cooperative NRDA?

There is a fundamental paradox in the concept of a NRDA. On the one hand, an NRD case represents a legal claim for damages that must be prepared for litigation, similar to a tort case. Thus, in essence, the NRDA is a litigation plan including a full description of alleged injuries and calculated damages. On the other hand, there is both a regulatory and practical imperative for the plaintiff (i.e., the government trustees) to work cooperatively with the defendant (i.e., the responsible party) in the preparation of its case. From this perspective, the NRDA is often a necessary framework for settlement discussions and restoration planning.

---

1. Portions of this chapter are adapted from *Natural Resource Damages*, of the ENVIRONMENTAL LAW PRACTICE GUIDE: STATE AND FEDERAL LAW with permission. Copyright 2017 Matthew Bender & Company, Inc., a LexisNexis company. All rights reserved.

The paradox of the NRDA is baked into the regulations. As discussed elsewhere in this book, a trustee that follows the NRD regulations when conducting the assessment will benefit from a rebuttable presumption in court.[2] At the same time, however, trustees are required to invite the participation and cooperation of the potential defendants. For example, under OPA, the trustees are required to "invite the responsible parties to participate in the natural resource damage assessment."[3] Similarly, under the CERCLA regulations, the trustees must invite PRPs to participate in the NRDA.[4] Nonetheless, neither the trustees nor the PRPs are required to cooperate in the development of a NRDA.

As the NRD practice has evolved, trustees and responsible parties have increasingly sought to proceed in a cooperative manner. As DOI has stated, the department

> continues to make progress in conducting many of its damage assessment cases on a cooperative basis with responsible parties. . . . The DOI has been involved in over forty cooperative assessments across the country, where the responsible parties have elected to participate in the damage assessment process, and provide input into the selection of various injury studies and contribute funds for or reimburse the DOI's assessment and restoration planning costs.[5]

From the trustees' perspective, there are many reasons to pursue a more cooperative NRD approach. Here are a few examples of how federal and state trustees explain the benefits of a cooperative approach:

- NOAA: "Cooperative assessments encourage settlements and offer responsible parties a role in planning restoration actions without undermining the trustees' responsibilities. Collaboration generally results in lower damage assessment costs, a reduced risk of litigation, and shorter time between injury and restoration. The goals of this cooperative process are to expedite the restoration of injured natural resources, as well as to encourage innovative approaches."[6]

---

2. *See* Chapter 3, Section J.

3. 15 C.F.R. § 990.14(c)(1).

4. 43 C.F.R. § 11.32(a)(2)(iii)(A).

5. *Damage Assessment*, U.S. Dep't of the Interior Restoration Program, https://www.doi.gov/restoration/damageassessment (last visited Jan. 8, 2019).

6. *Evaluate Environmental Harm*, NOAA Damage Assessment, Remediation, & Restoration Program, https://darrp.noaa.gov/getting-restoration/assessment (last visited Jan. 8, 2019); *see also* Nat'l Oceanic & Atmospheric Admin., Cooperative Assessment Project (CAP) Framework 2 (2003) [hereinafter CAP Framework]; Office of Response and Restoration,

- Louisiana: "NRDA is often a cooperative process between the trustees and the responsible parties (RPs) to assess injuries resulting from an oil spill. State and federal NRDA regulations require the Trustees to invite RPs to participate in the assessment. Cooperation can facilitate the efficient collection and sharing of reliable data, while allowing all parties to conduct their own analysis and interpretation of that data."[7]
- Delaware: "Generally, the Trustees will attempt to engage in a cooperative assessment process with PRPs. This approach can often result in more cost-effective assessments and a reduction in the need for 'defensive' studies on both sides."[8]
- Bureau of Land Management (BLM) (at DOI): "Cooperative assessments are likely to be more cost-effective and expedient than both parties conducting separate data collection, by eliminating duplicate efforts, allowing for agreements on technical issues like the extent of injuries, and promoting earlier focus on restoration."[9]

In addition to the promise of a faster, more cost-effective resolution, the cooperative NRDA offers a much more practical benefit to the trustees—namely, funding. Since a major component of the cooperative approach is PRP funding of the damage assessment, a cooperative NRD approach provides critical funds to trustees who otherwise may not have the financial resources or budget needed to pursue a claim.[10]

Finally, as discussed previously, the trustees face several significant evidentiary obstacles when prosecuting an NRD claim, and the cooperative approach obviates the need for time-consuming, expensive, and uncertain litigation.

C. Cooperative NRDAs: Strategic Considerations

This section discusses in more detail the advantages and disadvantages of the litigation and cooperation approaches from the perspective of the PRP. This

---

Nat'l Oceanic & Atmospheric Admin, Cooperative Assessment Process (CAP) Fact Sheet (2005), www.lawseminars.com/materials/07NRDNM/Cruden2.pdf.

7. *Louisiana Deepwater Horizon Oil Spill—Natural Resource Damage Assessment*, La. Deepwater Horizon Oil Spill Nat. Res. Damage Assessment & Restoration, https://la-dwh.com/ (last visited Jan. 8, 2019).

8. *Natural Resource Damage Assessments*, Del. Dep't of Nat. Res. & Envtl. Control, http://www.dnrec.delaware.gov/dwhs/sirb/Pages/NRDA.aspx (last visited Jan. 9, 2019).

9. Bureau of Land Mgmt., U.S. Dep't of the Interior, BLM Natural Resource Damage Assessment and Restoration Handbook 65 (2008), https://www.blm.gov/sites/blm.gov/files/uploads/Media_Library_BLM_Policy_Handbook_H-1703-3.pdf.

10. *See* CAP Framework, *supra* note 6, at 2.

section also addresses the mechanics of cooperation and the logistical challenges it poses.

1. The Litigation Advantage

Because it assumes that the PRP will finance the NRDA, the cooperative approach is something akin to building one's own guillotine. However, there are principled reasons for pursuing litigation in many NRD matters. As an initial matter, it is important to point out that the PRP is under no legal obligation to cooperate with the trustee, and litigation is an entirely legitimate option. Some of the reasons why litigation may be a good strategic option are discussed in the following subsections.

a. Putting the Trustees to Their Proof

The principal reason to maintain a litigious posture when defending an NRD claim is that the trustee bears the burden of proof to show that the defendant is liable, that the injury occurred, that the injury resulted from a release or discharge by the defendant, and that the claimed damages are appropriate. Given that the financial stakes in NRD claims are often tremendous, the PRP may perceive no rational option other than to contest the claim. Obviously, as with any matter, the litigation advantage can only be evaluated in light of two major factors: first, the size of the claim and, second, the strength of the defenses. The difficulty in the cooperative approach is that it often demands a commitment (even if partial) from the PRP before that PRP is in a position to evaluate either of these factors. Fortunately, this problem can be mitigated by proceeding in an iterative manner, as discussed later in this chapter. In this way, the PRP will have an opportunity to evaluate over time whether the issues of proof justify a more defensive approach.

b. Attacking Assessment Bias

A second advantage to a defensive posture is that it allows the PRP to devote its resources toward attacking the trustee's assessment. A common observation by PRPs is that the trustee—whether in a cooperative or litigation mode—will infer the least favorable conclusion from ambiguous or inconclusive data. The following are some examples of an assessment bias that is sometimes claimed by PRPs: (1) observed injuries are too quickly attributed to the contaminants associated with the PRP, as opposed to other potential causes; (2) insufficient credit is calculated for recovering or new ecological services in an impacted area; (3) observed contaminant concentrations are extrapolated to larger areas without a sufficient basis; (4) multiple conservative assumptions and/or overly conservative assumptions are applied to address areas of uncertainty; and (5) insufficient attention is paid to understanding baseline conditions.

While these and other areas of potential bias can sometimes be addressed in the context of a cooperative approach, the PRP may feel that it cannot simultaneously cooperate with the trustee and adequately address this perceived bias. A purely defensive or litigation posture may allow the PRP to focus better on these issues. The PRP may further conclude that its interests are best served by attacking the assessment bias in the context of depositions or at trial, and that a cooperative approach will allow the trustee to make its assessment more defensible without modifying its ultimate conclusions.

c. Developing Case Law on Legal Defenses

A third advantage of litigation is that it allows the PRP to develop the decisional law. The state of NRD law is relatively immature as compared with other areas of environmental law. For example, there are few interpretations of the statutory defenses applicable to NRD matters.[11] Furthermore, there are a number of novel arguments that have not been adequately tested in the courts, including the retroactivity of NRD claims, the applicability of general CERCLA case law regarding liability to NRD actions and the burden on the government of subtracting baseline conditions. While litigation to judgment involves risk, a PRP may decide that an aggressive litigation posture is appropriate, given the stakes involved in many NRD matters and the relative paucity of circuit court decisions. This strategy may be particularly compelling for companies with multiple NRD sites across the country.

d. Postponing Liabilities

A fourth advantage to litigation for many PRPs is that it may significantly postpone the NRD liability. This consideration may be particularly salient in the NRD context, given that complex NRD litigation is notoriously slow. For example, the *Montrose* case, involving DDT contamination on the Palos Verdes shelf off the coast of California, was originally filed in June 1990. Due to a number of factors in the litigation, including the breadth and complexity of the claims asserted, the case did not go to trial until late 2000. While litigation for the purpose of obtaining delay may not appear to serve a public interest, the choice to litigate in order to obtain time is sometimes not unreasonable, given the enormity of some NRD claims. Delay also may be justified when other issues are impacting a contaminated site, such as an allocation

---

11. *See* discussion in Chapter 3.

or insurance dispute. In these situations, the PRPs may simply be unable to cooperate since there is no agreement as to which parties own the liability and to what extent.

e. Avoiding Liabilities

Finally, the non-cooperative approach may in some cases result in the avoidance of the entire NRD claim, or at least the significant minimization of the claim. A primary reason why trustees prefer the cooperative approach is that they often lack the funds to proceed with a complicated NRDA themselves. For example, the appropriated budget for the Natural Resource Damage and Assessment Program of the DOI, one of the largest federal trustees, was less than $8 million in 2018.[12] Similarly, many states report extremely modest assessment budgets or, in some cases, no appropriations whatsoever.[13] Accordingly, absent a willing PRP to conduct the assessment, the trustees will simply have to delay or postpone the NRDA, and in some cases may never conduct the assessment. Given these budget constraints, and given the lack of a legal obligation to do otherwise, a PRP may decide it is worth taking the chance that the trustee will simply be unable to conduct the assessment on its own. Further, due to the natural restorative ability of ecological systems (as well as, potentially, the progress of remediation in the same area), a delay in the NRDA may result in a significant decrease in the injury. In some cases, the damage may disappear by the time the trustee is able to assess it.

2. The Cooperation Advantage

Litigation is expensive, time-consuming, risky, and inconvenient. Furthermore, for many companies, litigation is a distraction from solving the problem at hand, namely injured natural resources. Thus, there are many reasons to consider an alternative approach. The cooperative assessment process is often the alternative. As is made clear later in the chapter, however, cooperation is not an abdication of one's own interests or objectives. Both the trustee and the PRP recognize that their respective decision to work together is for separate purposes. The objective of the trustee is to ensure that it has adequately and accurately quantified the full extent of the recoverable injury. The objective of the PRP is to ensure that it is not held responsible for damages that are not

---

12. *See* Consolidated Appropriations Act, 2018, Pub. L. No. 115-141.

13. *See* Brian D. Israel, State-by-State Guide to NRD Programs in All 50 States and Puerto Rico (Mar. 1, 2018), https://www.arnoldporter.com/-/media/files/perspectives/publications/2018/03/state-by-state-nrd-guide.pdf.

real or for which it is not liable under the law. Although these are different goals, they are not necessarily in conflict.

a. Trusting the Trusting Trustee

The first and most obvious benefit of the cooperative approach is that it provides an opportunity for the parties to work together in good faith to resolve a complex problem. In this way, mutual trust is both the prerequisite and the consequence of a successful cooperative strategy. Of course, as many commentators have noted, mutual trust and respect in a cooperative process do not mean a lack of disagreement.[14] The key, however, is that the parties demonstrate a commitment to accommodating opposing scientific, technical, and legal opinions to the greatest extent possible, consistent with their own objectives. The other benefits of a cooperative approach, as described later, cannot be achieved without mutual trust.

b. Impacting the Scope and Type of the NRDA

The NRDA is the vehicle that allows the trustee and the PRP to work together despite their competing objectives. The cooperative approach affords the PRP the opportunity to impact the damage assessment in important and legitimate ways. For example, the PRP may be able to suggest creative alternatives that achieve restoration but at less cost. As another example, particularly with regard to interim lost use calculations, the PRP will often find opportunities to assess the extent of the loss of services in a manner that will satisfy both parties. Finally, the PRP is usually both creative and assertive in modifying the assessment to account for baseline. Since the baseline calculation is required by the trustee's regulations, this effort by the PRP is not inconsistent with the trustee's objectives.

As noted earlier, one advantage to litigation is the opportunity to wage a full-fledged attack on the perceived bias found in NRDAs. To the extent the parties are working together, and to the extent the PRP is realistic and mindful of the needs of the trustee, the cooperative approach may achieve the same result.

c. Proactive Restoration

A third advantage of the cooperative approach is the enhanced ability of the PRP to propose proactive restoration measures that can be implemented sooner

---

14. *See, e.g.*, Bill Conner & Ron Gouguet, *Getting to Restoration*, 21 Envtl. F. 26 (2004) ("The parties must be able to get beyond disagreement or the process will stall and fail.").

rather than later. In some cases, the restoration efforts will be recognized by all parties as interim measures. In other cases, these efforts may be pilot studies. In yet other cases, these proactive measures may result in full restoration for at least some services. Regardless of the status, however, sensible proactive restoration efforts present a tremendous advantage to both parties. For the trustee, the resource is restored more quickly. For the PRP, rapid restoration will, in nearly all cases, lower its ultimate financial exposure, since once the PRP is able to restore the lost services, the calculation of interim lost use ceases.

d. Integration of Restoration and Remediation

Many NRD sites involve ongoing remedial investigations and cleanups under CERCLA or similar programs. Since the trustees are not entitled to double recovery, the PRP may be able to structure the cleanup in a way that also achieves restoration, thereby obtaining two objectives with the same dollar. Although this objective can often be addressed independent of the cooperative approach, to the extent that the cooperative approach provides the PRP with additional insight into the concerns of the trustee, and to the extent that the trustee is coordinating with EPA or state agencies, the cooperative approach may facilitate this result. As noted by the former Chief of the Damage Assessment Center at NOAA, "it makes more sense, saves time and money, and is consistent with the regulatory framework for trustees and response agencies to conduct simultaneous assessments and coordinate remedial and restoration planning."[15]

e. Information Sharing

In an adversarial mode, the trustees may not be required to share information with the PRP on an ongoing basis. If the matter is in active litigation, the PRP may not see the results of the trustee's investigation until they appear in an expert report. Conversely, a cooperative approach assumes the parties will be actively exchanging and sharing data and other information. While such interaction entails some risk for both parties, many PRPs would rather remain continually informed of the results of data collection. The sharing of information allows the PRP to assess its liability and evaluate its options regularly.

f. Avoiding Litigation

Of course, a critical advantage of cooperation is that it is not litigation. The trustees, as part of any cooperative agreement, will usually agree in writing not to issue notice letters or commence litigation against the PRP during the

---

15. *Id.* at 24.

effective period of the agreement. Conversely, the PRP will agree to toll any statute of limitations claims based on the period of the agreement.

g. Reducing Transaction Costs

Putting aside the risk of an adverse outcome, litigation is expensive, especially in NRD cases. This is true for two reasons. First, the cost of retaining experts and conducting ecological studies is extraordinarily high. The cost is even higher when studies are conducted for purposes of litigation. Second, if the trustees prevail, the PRP must pay its own costs plus the assessment costs of the trustees. The cooperative approach has the potential to reduce assessment costs greatly.

Additionally, the cooperative approach will sometimes facilitate the integration of data collection for multiple purposes, including the NRDA and the remedial investigation. The avoidance of duplicative data-gathering efforts represents an important opportunity to achieve efficiencies, a major incentive for many companies.[16]

3. Mechanics for Cooperation

a. Trustee Cooperative Assessment Programs

Both the CERCLA and OPA regulations require that the trustee invite the PRP to participate in the assessment process, and it is also the practice of many states.[17] Notwithstanding these provisions, the history of NRD cooperation between PRPs and trustees is mixed. Over the last several years, many federal and state trustees have aggressively sought to advance a cooperative assessment and restoration model. This new model is best exemplified by the initiatives at NOAA, including the Cooperative Assessment Project (CAP). As stated by NOAA, CAP and other similar programs are "intended to further promote cooperative damage assessments by, among other means, allowing for greater participation between natural resource trustees (Trustees) and Potentially Responsible Parties (PRPs) and encouraging the use of more streamlined and innovative approaches to settle damage assessment liability and restore natural resources."[18]

---

16. *See, e.g., id.* ("The trustees and the PRPs have the opportunity to save money through fine-tuning of investigations to satisfy both types of data needs.").

17. *See, e.g.,* 15 C.F.R. § 990.14(c)(1) (stating that the "[t]rustees *must* invite the responsible parties to participate in the natural resource damage assessment" and that the trustee should consider a binding agreement to facilitate cooperation with the PRP) (emphasis added); *see also* 43 C.F.R. § 11.32(a)(2)(iii)(A) (stating that if a PRP is known, the trustee shall "invite the participation of the potentially responsible party" in the NRDA).

18. CAP Framework, *supra* note 6, at 1.

b. Cooperative Agreements

Although a formal agreement is not absolutely necessary to proceed in a cooperative manner, both the PRPs and the trustees usually prefer such a document. As stated by NOAA, "it is strongly recommended that basic agreements and terms be somehow documented in writing to minimize future misunderstandings. This might be accomplished by a simple letter of agreement outlining the basic goals of the process or a more comprehensive project initiation agreement."[19]

The NRD cooperative agreements vary in size and scope, but often contain the following elements. In addition, a sample cooperative agreement is provided in Part D of this chapter.

- **Statements of principle.** First, many cooperative agreements include statements of principle regarding the desire of the parties to work together in good faith to assess potential injuries and damages. The NOAA draft cooperation agreement states, among other things, that the parties agree to be "open, fair and balanced to all the affected and interested Parties."[20] Although such statements may not be legally enforceable, it is very important to identify the framework of cooperation. If the PRP later feels that the trustee is not responsive to its concerns, these statements of principle are often very useful as guides for meetings between the parties. Furthermore, if necessary, the PRP can cite to these provisions if it later decides to terminate or not renew the cooperative agreement. Some principles that the parties may wish to include in their cooperative agreement are the following:
  - Trustee and PRP shall interact in good faith.
  - Trustee and PRP shall make efforts to establish a collaborative and cooperative process.
  - Trustee and PRP shall enter the process with a focus on restoration as the best method for resolving natural resource damage claims.
  - Trustee and PRP shall endeavor to identify proactive or early restoration projects.
  - Trustee and PRP shall share all data.
  - Trustee and PRP shall strive to achieve consensus decision-making.

---

19. Nat'l Oceanic & Atmospheric Admin., CAP Compendium of Additional Ideas and Example Documents (2003).

20. Nat'l Oceanic & Atmospheric Admin., CAP Project Initiation Agreement, Draft (2003).

- Trustee will maintain ultimate control over the assessment process, but trustee will meaningfully involve the PRP in the process.
- Trustee and PRP will work to resolve any disputes in a collaborative manner to the extent possible.
- Trustee and PRP will attempt to use the cooperative process to work toward a final settlement of the entire NRD claim.
- **Funding arrangements.** A major premise of the cooperative arrangement is the payment of some or all assessment costs by the PRP. The mechanics of these payments are highly variable and may include payment in advance, the establishment of an escrow account, reimbursement, or other means of payment by the PRP. In some agreements, the PRP retains the right not to fund any study or activity with which it disagrees. Obviously, such a provision will often provide an important "off ramp" for the PRP that is less drastic than termination of the cooperative process. The PRP will want to receive adequate documentation of the assessment costs incurred by the trustees. In addition, it is common that the funding provisions provide that the PRP is only obligated to pay reasonable and appropriate expenses. Finally, there should be a dispute mechanism set forth in case the PRP believes that some costs were inappropriately incurred.
- **Tolling and standstill provisions.** If the trustee is concerned that the statute of limitations may expire, the trustee will require an agreement to toll the period of the agreement. In return, the PRP may request an agreement that the trustee will not file a claim during the pendency of the cooperative assessment agreement.
- **Termination provisions.** Both parties will want the right to terminate the cooperative process at any time and for any reason. Such provisions are customary. Indeed, the ability to terminate is critical for allowing the parties to proceed with the cooperative agreement in the first place and, ironically, is extremely helpful in building mutual trust. Since each party knows that it may terminate at any time, it is more likely to take risks to build consensus. Similarly, neither party will be cavalier in responding to the concerns of the other for fear that the other could terminate the agreement.
- **Information sharing.** As discussed previously, cooperative agreements usually provide that all data and information generated as part of the agreement will be shared with each party. In addition, some agreements provide that data collected independently will be shared or may be

shared, depending on the intent of the parties. In some cases, the parties commit to notify each other if they intend to commence any study that is outside the scope of the agreement but relevant to the assessment. Of course, the parties should clearly indicate that they need not share information that is privileged or confidential.

- **Reservation of rights.** The trustee will seek to reserve its enforcement rights as well as its ultimate decision-making authority at the site. The PRP will seek to reserve all of its defenses. These reservation provisions are customary. The PRP may also seek to preserve its ability to contest the conclusions of the NRDA, notwithstanding its agreement to cooperate with the trustee.

c. Avoiding Cooperation Pitfalls

As is clear in this discussion, cooperation entails risk for both parties. In addition to negotiating a protective agreement, there are steps that the PRP should consider to ensure that it avoids some pitfalls of cooperation.

First, the PRP should actively ensure that the administrative record is complete. When assessment decisions—even if derived by consensus—do not include items that may later become relevant to the PRP's defense, the PRP or its consultant should memorialize those items. The PRP must protect itself from an argument later that its agreement to proceed with an assessment plan constituted a waiver of any other assessment needs.

Second, to the extent that the trustee is unwilling to conduct studies that the PRP believes are necessary for its defense, the PRP should be willing to proceed independently. This problem is most commonly, although not exclusively, present with regard to baseline studies. The trustee is generally focused on understanding the present injury. The PRP must ensure that any impact caused by forces other than its alleged releases are examined thoroughly.

Third, the PRP should retain independent experts. The role of these experts is to review and, if appropriate, critique assessment plans put forward by the trustees, develop alternative assessments where appropriate, and continually explore opportunities for proactive restoration. The cooperative process is not simply a funding mechanism for government scientists. For the PRP's objectives to be met, it must bring sufficient expertise to the process.

Finally, the PRP should continually evaluate its strategy. The agreement to cooperate makes sense only as long as it is working. A change in strategy may be in order based on the nature of the relationship with the trustees, the results of the assessment studies, or developments in the law.

D. Cooperative NRDA Sample Agreement

Cooperative Assessment and Funding Agreement Regarding the Assessment of Natural Resource Damages Related to the Onondaga Lake Superfund Site, New York

I. INTRODUCTION AND AUTHORITY

This Cooperative Assessment and Funding Agreement (the "Agreement") is made and entered into by and between the United States Department of the Interior ("DOI"), acting by and through the Regional Director, the United States Fish and Wildlife Service ("FWS") as Authorized Official, the Onondaga Nation ("Nation"), and the State of New York Department of Environmental Conservation ("DEC") (collectively, "Trustees"), and [Company], collectively referred to as the "Parties."

The Trustees act on behalf of natural resources belonging to, managed by, controlled by, or appertaining to each Trustee that may have been impacted by releases of hazardous substances from the Onondaga Lake Superfund Site ("Site") pursuant to Comprehensive Environmental Response, Compensation, and Liability Act ("CERCLA") Section 107(f), 42 U.S.C. § 9607(f), Executive Order 12580, the National Contingency Plan ("NCP"), 40 C.F.R. Part 300—Subpart G, and other applicable laws and regulations. The Onondaga Nation acts under this Agreement pursuant to the *Guswenta*, or the Two Row Wampum Treaty, and the 1794 Treaty of Canandaigua in its cooperative relationship with DOI, FWS, and DEC as Trustees, and with [Company].

The Trustees are authorized to conduct natural resource damage assessments and restoration activities and to sue for damages resulting from the destruction of, loss of, or injury to such natural resources by Section 107(a),(f) of CERCLA, 40 C.F.R. § 300.600 *et seq.*, and, to the extent appropriate and elected for use by the Trustees, the Natural Resource Damage Assessment Regulations at 43 C.F.R. Part 11. The Natural Resource Damage Assessment Regulations, at 43 C.F.R. § 11.32(a)(2)(iii) (A), encourage the participation of potentially responsible parties in the assessment process.

II. BACKGROUND

Preliminary investigations of natural resource damages ("NRD") related to the Site have occurred for over a decade. In September of 1994, DEC issued a Preassessment Screen Determination for the Onondaga Lake Assessment Area, followed by the issuance of an NRD Assessment Plan in November 1996. On December 28, 2006, FWS issued its Preassessment Screen Determination concerning potential natural resource damages related to the Site. Trustees continue to collect and assess data and information concerning natural resources, as defined under Section 101(16) of CERCLA, 42 U.S.C. 9601(16), that may have been impacted by releases of hazardous substances from the Site.

III. PURPOSE

The purpose of this Agreement is to provide a framework for a cooperative natural resource damage assessment ("NRDA"). This Agreement is intended to facilitate resolution of any NRD claims affiliated with, arising from, or related to releases from the Site, minimize the transaction costs associated with such claim(s), and work toward the goal of cooperatively developing and implementing a restoration plan.

The Parties agree that a cooperative assessment is desirable to:

1. Undertake cooperative NRD studies;
2. Determine the nature and extent of injuries to natural resources and/or the services provided by such resources (injury determination and quantification);
3. Conduct restoration planning and implementation (restoration); including, if and where appropriate, early restoration;
4. Facilitate payment of past and future reasonable assessment costs incurred by the Trustees;
5. Incorporate existing data in the NRDA to the extent feasible and appropriate;
6. Integrate, to the extent the Trustees determine appropriate, NRD studies and restoration activities with the remedial activities at the Site; and
7. Facilitate the resolution of any claims for natural resource damages at the Site. The Parties therefore agree as follows:

IV. FUNDING

A. Past Assessment Costs: [Company] shall reimburse the Trustees for a portion of their past assessment costs for NRDA activities undertaken by DOI, the State of New York (including assessment activities performed by DEC and the Office of the Attorney General ["OAG"]), and the Nation, including costs incurred by the Trustees in drafting and negotiating this Agreement, in the amount of $482,636.50 to DOI, $476,919 to the State of New York, and $250,000 to the Nation. Except as explicitly set forth herein, this reimbursement is not a full settlement of past costs for any of the Trustees and the Trustees' right to seek unpaid past costs are reserved in Section VIII.B. This reimbursement shall be made within ninety (90) calendar days of full execution of this Agreement.

B. Future Assessment Costs: [Company] shall fund the Trustees' reasonable and appropriate future assessment costs for "Cooperative Studies" and "General Activities" as defined below (collectively, "Funded Activities"):

1. Cooperative Studies: Once a proposed Study Plan and budget for a study are approved by the Parties pursuant to Section VI.F, such study shall become a Cooperative Study and shall include any activity (including, without limitation,

study design, peer review, contracting, original field work, and analysis of existing data) in furtherance of the Cooperative Study.

2. General Activities: General Activities shall mean activities undertaken by one or more Trustees related to this Cooperative Agreement including but not limited to, administrative activities, travel, participation in meetings with some or all of the other Parties to this Agreement, analysis of existing data, activities related to developing and implementing Cooperative Studies, evaluation of restoration projects and proposals, preparation for meetings, monitoring, oversight, legal costs, public outreach activities, and related consultant activities. General Activities shall not include· (a) such studies for which a Study Plan and budget are not approved by the Parties pursuant to Section VI.F, unless otherwise agreed to in writing by the Parties; (b) legal research specifically performed in preparation of litigation; or (c) any activities undertaken for any purpose other than for NRD assessment and restoration planning and implementation.

C. Payment of Funded Activities: [Company] shall make payments for Funded Activities as follows:

1. Cooperative Studies: Procedures and mechanisms for payments related to each Cooperative Study will be agreed upon by the Parties pursuant to the Study Plan and budget approval process in Section VI.F.

2. General Activities: For the General Activities that each of the Trustees perform, they shall submit individual reimbursement requests to [Company] with appropriate supporting documentation. The Onondaga Nation will endeavor to submit its first reimbursement request to [Company] within sixty (60) calendar days of March 31, 2009, and the Nation will submit subsequent reimbursement requests quarterly thereafter. DOI/FWS and New York State will endeavor to submit their first reimbursement requests to [Company] within sixty (60) calendar days of June 30, 2009, and they will submit subsequent requests semi-annually thereafter. [Company] shall have the right to object to any unreasonable General Activities costs, any costs incurred for activities other than General Activities, or insufficient documentation provided in the reimbursement requests. Notice of any such objection shall be provided to the Trustees in writing within twenty (20) calendar days of receipt of each reimbursement request. If any such objection is made, [Company] and the Trustees shall work to resolve the objection. If no objection is made, payment shall be made by [Company] within sixty (60) calendar days after receipt of the reimbursement request. The first reimbursement request from the Nation to [Company] will include all reasonable General Activity costs incurred by the Nation since November 1, 2008. The first reimbursement request from DOI/FWS and New York State to [Company] will include all reasonable General Activity costs incurred by DOI/FWS and New York State since August 1, 2008.

3. Appropriate Supporting Documentation: With each reimbursement request and submission of expenditures that the Trustees submit, they must include "appropriate supporting documentation" of the costs they have incurred. For purposes of this Agreement, "appropriate supporting documentation" is meant to include the following: records of labor and travel costs similar in type and extent to the documentation provided to [Company] for documentation of past assessment costs; copies of requests for proposals, contracts, and subcontracts, except to the extent that such information is privileged; payments to consultants and contractors for services rendered; and other similar documentation where appropriate. Additionally, each of the Trustees will include with its reimbursement requests a brief narrative which will describe in sufficient detail the major activities performed during the relevant time period, including the activities of consultants, if any.

D. Revision of a Cooperative Study Budget: The budget for a Cooperative Study approved by the Parties pursuant to Section VI.F. can be revised by the Parties as and if necessary.

E. Payment of Funds: The manner in which [Company] will transmit to the Trustees the payments required under this Agreement shall be in conformity with such reasonable written instructions as provided by each Trustee.

V. COOPERATIVE ASSESSMENT TEAM

The Trustees and [Company] shall meet and establish a Cooperative Assessment Team ("CAT") that will, among other NRDA related activities, identify NRDA data collection needs, which may be integrated where appropriate with any other ongoing Site-related investigations. The CAT shall recommend to the Trustees and [Company], for their approval, specific data collection and data analysis activities to be undertaken, among other NRDA related activities.

In the event that the CAT finds that certain specific facts, data or conclusions are relevant or material to the NRD assessment process and such facts, data or conclusions do not appear to the CAT to be in dispute as between the Parties, then the CAT may recommend to the Parties that they stipulate to such facts, data or conclusions. Any such stipulation shall be in writing.

Data shall be collected in a mutually agreed upon manner, by or with the oversight of the Trustees or their consultants. Data collection efforts may be coordinated with other Site-related investigations to achieve economies of time and effort. All data collected under this Agreement shall be shared in a manner that all Parties may readily access and use except that Onondaga Nation Culturally Sensitive Traditional Knowledge and Information, as defined in Section VI.D, shall not be shared. Where appropriate, QA/QC (Quality Assurance/Quality Control) procedures consistent with EPA requirements shall be used.

The CAT may also consider additional NRDA data and information needs, including identifying potential restoration opportunities that could redress potential NRD liabilities, and provide recommendations to [Company] and the Trustees.

The Parties may elect from time to time to establish additional working groups for purposes related to potential NRD claims at the Site including, but not limited to, groups to evaluate early restoration options, possible integration of NRD restoration with implementation of the remedy at the Site, and other particular aspects of the NRDA.

VI. PROCEDURES RELATED TO COOPERATIVE STUDIES

A.   Data and Associated Materials: The Parties agree that any data and/or associated material collected, pursuant to a Cooperative Study undertaken pursuant to this Agreement, shall be binding on all Parties and shall be admissible evidence in any subsequent judicial and administrative proceeding seeking damages for injury to, destruction of, or loss of natural resources but subject to objections as to relevancy, unless one or more Parties objects to the data and/or associated material in writing within ninety (90) calendar days of the receipt of the final report containing such data and/or associated material and provided further that the written objection identifies the specific data and/or associated material that is the subject of the objection and states the grounds for the objection. For purposes of this Section, "associated material" refers to the study design, data collection activities and methodologies, and QA/QC procedures. Any data and/or associated material subject to an objection under this Section that cannot be resolved, shall be recollected and/or re-analyzed as a Funded Activity, if it is determined by the Parties that such recollection and/or re-analysis will address the grounds for the objection.

B.   Interpretation and Analysis: The Parties will endeavor in good faith to reach agreement on the interpretation of data and/or associated material. If the Parties agree (in whole or in part) as to the interpretation, analysis and conclusions of a Cooperative Study, they shall enter into a stipulation with respect to the agreed-upon findings, and such stipulation shall be binding. With the exception of any such stipulations, the Parties each reserve its right at any time to produce its own independent interpretation and analysis of any Cooperative Study or any data collected pursuant to such activity.

C.   Participation: The Parties agree that a representative from each Party may be present during all data collection and laboratory work for any Cooperative Study, but only to the extent that the Trustees reasonably determine such participation will not interfere with study activities. The Party responsible for implementing any Cooperative Study shall provide at least ten (10) calendar days notice to the other Parties prior to any data collection or laboratory work. Notwithstanding the preceding, in the case of data collection from human respondents (*e.g.* the use of surveys, interviews, etc.), the presence of all Parties and the sharing of complete data may impede the collection of accurate, complete and candid responses. In such cases, and to the extent necessary to promote the accuracy, volume, and candor of responses, the Parties shall agree on procedures for the collection and sharing of such data, which procedures may include, for example, the use of neutral interviewers, the aggregation of aggregate data prior to dissemination to protect the confidentiality of individual responses, or require the absence of any Party during data collection activities, etc.

D. Onondaga Nation Culturally Sensitive Traditional Knowledge and Information: The Onondaga Nation possesses special traditional knowledge and information concerning tangible and intangible cultural resources, spiritual interests, activities and beliefs. As set forth herein, the Onondaga Nation seeks, and the Parties agree, to provide special protection to certain categories of Onondaga Nation traditional knowledge and information. Specifically, any information or data that reveals the following shall be deemed "Onondaga Nation Culturally Sensitive Traditional Knowledge and Information" or, alternatively, "Sensitive Information":

- Locations of spiritual or ceremonial activities, if such locations have been maintained as confidential by the Nation;
- Descriptions of spiritual or ceremonial activities, if such descriptions have been maintained as confidential by the Nation; or
- Roles, names or other identification or descriptions of Nation citizens who perform spiritual or ceremonial activities, if such information has been maintained as confidential by the Nation.

Sensitive Information is held collectively by the Onondaga Nation and its citizens and is held in trust by the Nation or by special medicine societies within the Nation for the benefit of the Nation and is protected by Onondaga and Haudenosaunee Law and custom. The United Nations Declaration on the Rights of Indigenous Peoples, Articles 11, 12, and 31 recognizes the rights of indigenous peoples to protect such Sensitive Information.

The Parties understand the importance in maintaining Sensitive Information as secret and in preventing its exploitation. However, it is also understood that Sensitive Information may be incidentally gathered by the Nation, its citizens, employees, contractors, or agents during activities performed under this Agreement. The Parties agree that any such Sensitive Information is not relevant for the purposes of this Agreement.

The Parties also understand the need for transparent data collection in Cooperative Studies under this Agreement. Thus, for the purposes of protecting Sensitive Information and allowing for transparency of all relevant data, the Nation shall redact any Sensitive Information, prior to allowing the Parties to review any information or data collected pursuant to this Agreement.

Except as provided above, information or data collected by the Nation, its citizens, employees, contractors, or agents pursuant to this Agreement will be accessible to the Parties for viewing at a suitable location within Onondaga Nation Territory.

The Parties may not remove information or data from Onondaga Nation Territory, unless the Onondaga Nation and the Party requesting the information or data agree otherwise.

E. Data Availability and Retention: Except as provided in Section VI.D, any data collected or records generated in the course of implementation of any Coopera-tive Study shall be available to all Parties upon request in both paper and electronic format. All samples and data taken or collected in the course of any Cooperative Study shall be retained, unless otherwise agreed to in writing by the Parties.

F. Study Plan: For any proposed study pursuant to this Agreement, the CAT shall jointly develop a proposed Study Plan which shall include without limitation the following components, where applicable: (1) purpose and need of the study; (2) study design and methods; (3) designation of a principal investigator(s); (4) analytical pro cedures to be conducted; (5) quality assurance and quality control plan; (6) work product expected; (7) anticipated duration; (8) confidentiality agreement for cultural assessment, and (9) budget, which will include assessment and administrative costs, and the procedures and mechanisms necessary for payment to those entities respon-sible for providing goods and services in furtherance of the study. Upon approval of the Parties, the proposed Study Plan shall become the Final Study Plan and shall be a Cooperative Study pursuant to this Agreement.

G. Prior Studies: In order to ensure a cost effective NRDA process, the Parties agree to incorporate data collected in existing studies or studies undertaken pursu-ant to Onondaga Lake Site remedial activities to the extent feasible, appropriate and necessary for the purposes of the NRDA.

VII. PUBLIC INVOLVEMENT AND CONFIDENTIALITY

A. Public Participation: The Parties recognize and agree that public participa-tion during the injury assessment and restoration planning process is both desirable and necessary. The Parties further recognize that the Trustees are required by law to give public notice and to solicit public review and comment during certain phases of the injury assessment and restoration planning process. The Trustees will undertake public outreach and will provide public notice and solicit public review and comment on the documents the Trustees deem appropriate. Costs associated with public out-reach constitute reasonable assessment costs and shall be reimbursed as a General Activity pursuant to this Agreement, Section IV.B.2.

B. Confidentiality: The Parties agree that oral communications between the Trustees and [Company] leading up to and pursuant to this Agreement shall be treated by the Parties as "Settlement Confidential" and shall be deemed in furtherance of settlement negotiations pursuant to Federal Rule of Evidence 408. Furthermore, any written communication which is marked "Settlement Confidential" by the Party(ies) generating such written communication shall be treated by the Parties as confiden-tial and shall be deemed in furtherance of settlement negotiations pursuant to Fed-eral Rule of Evidence 408. No Party shall publicly disclose or discuss any "Settlement

Confidential" statements, materials or positions of another Party unless agreed to in writing by such other Party. However, the Parties understand that certain documents marked "Settlement Confidential" shall be disclosed to the public if such disclosure is required under federal and/or state freedom of information laws, by a judge or a court, or pursuant to a formal determination by a federal or state agency under its rules, regulations, and requirements implementing such freedom of information laws. The Parties agree that any proposed Study Plan which the Trustees determine requires public review and comment, any Final Study Plan, as well as any data collected pursuant to this Agreement, shall not be a "Settlement Confidential" communication.

    C. Internal Communications: Notwithstanding Section VII.B, the Parties recognize that each other Party, including their respective attorneys may, from time to time, need to share confidential information with other members of their respective organization, including contractors, provided however that all such communications must be done in a manner reasonably calculated to prevent disclosure of such information beyond the organization. In no event shall confidential information be disclosed to individuals who are not members (or contractors) of the Party's organization without the prior written consent of all other Parties.

    D. Public Statements: Except as set forth in Section VII.A and this Section, the Parties agree that they will not make public representations about the legal or factual positions of another Party to this Agreement unless agreed to in writing by such Party. Subject to the provisions of Section VII.B and the proceeding sentence, the Parties agree that a Party may publicly describe the general terms of this Agreement. The Parties further agree that this Agreement itself, once executed, shall not be confidential.

    E. Information Requests: Any Party who receives a request for documents pursuant to federal or state freedom of information requests, or who is served with a subpoena or discovery request for any document or statement which the Parties have agreed should be treated as confidential, shall provide timely notice to the other Parties so as to allow them, if they choose, to assert a privilege or statutory exception seeking to prevent the release of such document or statement.

VIII. GENERAL PROVISIONS

    A. Cooperative Principles: All Parties agree to be guided by the principles set forth in the proposed Cooperative Assessment Approach and Framework, attached hereto and incorporated herein as Exhibit A. These Cooperative Principles are general guidelines to inform the Parties' conduct in the cooperative spirit of this Agreement and are not enforceable in any judicial or administrative proceeding.

    All Parties understand and agree that the Trustees retain final responsibility for, and authority over, the development and implementation of this NRDA, including but not limited to the assessment plan, data collection, and other studies undertaken to implement the NRDA plan. Nothing in this Agreement limits, restricts or derogates any rights or authority that each Trustee may have under law.

B. Reservations of Rights and Claims: Except as provided in Section VI of this Agreement, nothing in this Agreement is intended to be nor should it be construed as an admission or concession, including an admission of liability or any fact, or waiver of any claim, right or defense of liability by any Party to this Agreement, nor shall this Agreement be cited or relied upon directly or indirectly to advance or support any claim asserted, motion to intervene, or other action taken by any of the Parties in regard to any other action or proceeding. [Company] specifically reserves its right to raise all legal defenses to any future NRD claim, including but not limited to, its possible defenses that injuries, if any, have been or will be restored through remedial activities at the Site and that the Trustees lack standing to assert an NRD claim.

Except as explicitly set forth herein, [Company] is not released from any liability under this Agreement, including but not limited to claims for injury, loss or destruction of natural resources or their services, claims for restoration, rehabilitation, replacement, or acquisition of the equivalent of natural resources or lost services of those resources including all reasonable costs of the assessment including administrative, monitoring, oversight and legal costs except for those costs that have actually been paid under this Agreement.

By way of example and without limitation, [Company] is not released for the following past assessment costs: 1) the reasonable assessment costs incurred by the Onondaga Nation from May 1, 2005 until August 31, 2007, which are not being reimbursed under this Agreement; 2) the reasonable assessment costs incurred by the State of New York for the preparation of a recreational impact assessment (including both consultant costs and internal costs incurred preparing, overseeing or otherwise conducting the recreational impact assessment) ("NYS Retained Past Cost Claim"), which are not being reimbursed under this Agreement; and 3) the assessment costs incurred by DOI/FWS prior to August 1, 2008, totaling $85,171.13 ("DOI/FWS Retained Past Cost Claim"), which are not being reimbursed under this Agreement.

Notwithstanding any other provision of this Agreement, the payment of $250,000 by [Company] to the Onondaga Nation for assessment costs incurred by the Onondaga Nation from September 1, 2007 through October 31, 2008, as provided in Section IV.A, shall release [Company] from liability for any other claims that the Onondaga Nation may have for costs incurred during that period of time.

Additionally, notwithstanding any other provision of this Agreement, the payment of $476,919 by [Company] to the State of New York for past assessment costs as provided in Section IV.A, shall release [Company] from liability for any other claims that the State of New York may have for assessment costs incurred by the State of New York prior to August 1, 2008 with the exception of the NYS Retained Past Cost Claim. Additionally, notwithstanding any other provision of this Agreement, the payment of $482,636.50 by [Company] to DOI for past assessment costs as provided in Section IV.A, shall release [Company] from liability for any other claims the DOI and FWS may have for assessment costs incurred by the DOI and/or FWS prior to August 1, 2008 with the exception of the DOI/FWS Retained Past Cost Claim.

In the event that [Company] objects to reimburse the Trustees for any costs submitted under Section IV.C.2, and the "resolution" of such objection does not provide for full payment of such costs, then [Company] is not released from liability for those unpaid costs.

Except as set forth in the preceding with respect to specific releases for past costs, nothing in this Agreement is intended to be nor should it be construed as a limitation on the Trustees' (or the entities comprising them) authority to pursue any claims or causes of action against [Company] for damages or otherwise, provided, however, that any payments of Trustee costs and the funding of any Trustee activities by [Company] shall be credited against future claims for such assessment costs and damages.

The Parties expressly reserve the right to perform independent NRDA studies. Any data resulting from such independent studies performed by a Party during the term of this Agreement shall be shared with the other Parties, except as provided under Section VI.D. The Trustees reserve their right to seek reimbursement of costs arising from or related to these independent studies to the extent permitted under law. Each Party reserves its full rights to conduct studies, as appropriate, in the event that this Agreement is terminated. For purposes of this Agreement, "independent studies" refers to biological, chemical, physiological, geophysical or any other injury determination or quantification studies that involve data collection. Nothing herein shall be interpreted to require any Party to provide any other Party any material that is protected by any applicable privilege including, without limitation, attorney work product, attorney client communications and joint defense/prosecution privileges.

This Agreement shall be binding on the heirs, successors in interest, representatives and assignees of the Parties.

C.   Effective Date, Term, & Termination: The effective date of this Agreement shall be the date of the last signature.

This Agreement can be executed in one or more counterparts, each of which will be considered an original document.

This Agreement may not be amended except by written agreement of all Parties.

Either [Company] or the Trustees may withdraw from this Agreement upon giving thirty (30) calendar days written notice to all other Parties or as otherwise provided for herein.

Withdrawal by [Company] shall terminate this Agreement, in which event [Company] shall remain obligated pursuant to this Agreement to reimburse otherwise compensable Trustee costs or expenses, including General Activities, incurred prior to [Company]'s termination of this Agreement.

In the event that any Trustee withdraws from this Agreement, the other Trustees shall have the right to either continue work under this Agreement or terminate it. No further payments shall be made to any Trustee withdrawing from this Agreement except for payments for costs or expenses incurred pursuant to this Agreement prior to said Trustee's termination.

This Agreement will terminate automatically upon the termination of the Memorandum of Agreement by and between the Trustees or upon completion of all agreed work to be performed under this Agreement, whichever occurs first, unless extended by the mutual written agreement of all of the Parties.

Termination of this Agreement by the withdrawal of a Party, by expiration or otherwise, shall not terminate the rights and obligations of Sections IV.B.1 (Cooperative Studies), VI.A (Data and Associated Materials), VI.B (Interpretation and Analysis), VI.D (Sensitive Information), VI.E (Data Availability and Retention), VII.A (Public Participation), VII.B (Confidentiality), VII.C (Internal Communications), VII.E (Information Requests), and VIII.B (Reservation of Rights and Claims), which provisions shall be deemed to continue in force and binding effect.

D. Notices: Any general information or notices required to be given in writing under this Agreement shall be deemed to have been sufficiently given if delivered either personally or overnight delivery service, fax, or e-mail (if followed by letter) to each of the addresses set forth below, or to such other address for either Party as may be designated by written notice.

For [Company]:

For the Trustees:

E. Dispute Resolution: The Parties shall endeavor in good faith to make decisions by consensus.

In the absence of consensus, the Parties shall attempt in good faith, for a period not to exceed sixty (60) calendar days after receipt of written notice that briefly identifies the subject on which there is no consensus, to reach consensus through consultation among the Parties' representatives, who are currently designated as:

For [Company]:

For the Trustees:

In the event consensus is not reached by the representatives pursuant to the provisions above, the Parties shall attempt in good faith for a period not to exceed sixty (60) calendar days to reach consensus through consultation among the following management representatives.

For [Company]:

For the Trustees:

If necessary, the Parties may establish other mechanisms by which disputes may be resolved.

In the event consensus cannot be reached by the representatives, the Parties shall terminate this Agreement as provided in Section VIII.C above.

F. Applicable Law: This Agreement shall be governed in all respects, including validity, interpretation, and effect, by the laws of the State of New York, without giving effect to the principles of conflicts of laws of such state.

G. Execution & Authority: This Agreement and any modifications or addenda hereto may be executed in several counterparts by the Parties and when so executed shall be considered fully executed to the same extent as if the Parties had signed the original document. Facsimile execution is authorized.

The person executing this Agreement on behalf of each Party represents and warrants that he or she has full power and authority to do so on behalf of such Party.

[Signature pages follow]

Chapter 7

NRD Litigation: Strategy, Procedures, and Preparation

A. Introduction

The overarching objective when faced with a valid NRD claim is to achieve a reasonable, cost-effective resolution, consistent with the legal framework, while minimizing transaction costs to the greatest degree possible. Often—especially in large cases with significant exposure and/or aggressive trustee claimants—the critical path toward a reasonable resolution is the preparation of a robust defense. Paradoxically, the best way to settle an NRD case is often to litigate that case. Stated differently, to achieve success, one must prepare for failure.

This chapter addresses several key aspects of developing and implementing a strategy for litigating an NRD case. As with any litigation, there are two critical elements to success: namely, developing a compelling narrative and ensuring the admissibility of evidence to support that narrative. In addition, an NRD defendant must understand the special procedural issues associated with NRD claims, such as the rebuttable presumption, ripeness, the right to a jury, and standing, among others. In many NRD cases, these procedural issues are as important as substantive defenses and will be fundamental ingredients to any litigation strategy. Chapter 3 discusses these defenses. Finally, an NRD defendant must also understand the mechanics of defending a scientifically complex claim, with dozens (sometimes hundreds) of environmental and economic experts.

This chapter first reviews, at a high level, key considerations when developing an NRD litigation plan. Second, we discuss several "lessons learned" from ten of the largest NRD cases ever litigated, including lessons related to procedural and evidentiary issues. Finally, we provide a more detailed discussion of the "top ten" cases, including a review of key pre-trial motions.

B. Developing a Litigation Plan

Every NRD case is unique, and the development of a litigation narrative will depend, of course, on the specific facts of the case and the claims being asserted by the trustees. Nonetheless, a key element of any litigation strategy is a systematic effort to determine key trial themes that are compelling, supportable, and succinct. In large NRD cases, one of the greatest challenges is to synthesize massive quantities of environmental data covering numerous resource categories into one consistent, persuasive "story" that accurately describes the environmental event, its impact on natural resources, and actions taken to accelerate the process of restoring injured resources.

The trustees frequently rely on similar litigation themes, emphasizing some elements of their case while de-emphasizing others. For example, regardless of the type of NRD matter, the trustees will focus heavily on exposure to pollutants, either hazardous substances or oil. In a large oil spill, the trustees will simply point to the facts of the incident such as the quantity of oil and the size of the affected habitat. In most NRD cases, the trustees will focus on the geographic and temporal extent of the releases of hazardous substances. In developing an "exposure" theme, the trustees will rely on their best evidence, including pictures of oiled animals or habitat, high concentrations of contaminants, and plume maps. With regard to injury, it is common for the trustees to focus on impacts to individual organisms, rather than populations. This is because it is relatively easier to prove that an individual animal was harmed, and significantly harder to show that a local population suffered any adverse impact. Similarly, the trustees often focus on impacts to resources themselves and not the impacts on the services provided by those resources. With regard to damages, the trustees will frequently emphasize the unique nature of the impacted resources and the perceived difficulty of restoring those resources. In cases where it may be impossible to identify, much less quantify, an injury, the trustees may emphasize future uncertainty associated with the ongoing exposure to a pollutant.

Faced with trustee assertions with which it disagrees, a defendant must develop a counter-narrative that is both accurate and compelling. And the defendant's litigation themes must be simple. Of course, as stated previously, the development of defense themes is case-specific, but several are frequently relevant. For example, in many cases, the NRD defendant should point to data and evidence showing that the damages are far more limited in scope and degree than asserted by the trustees. As part of this narrative, a defendant is often able to leverage site-specific field data showing healthy or recovering populations or habitats.

As a second example, defendants should be unafraid to attack the trustees' science where warranted. If the matter has proceeded to full-blown litigation, the defendant likely has a good-faith basis for arguing that the trustees' calculation of damages is overstated or speculative. At the end of the day, the trustees bear the burden of proof, including to show causation, and it is entirely appropriate for the defendant to develop a litigation plan to demonstrate where the trustees have failed. Furthermore, while the trustees have a rebuttable presumption in favor of their damages determinations, they can only take advantage of the presumption if they adhere to the regulations governing the NRDA process, including the requirement that their assessments be "reliable and valid for the particular incident."[1] A key trial strategy would be to unmask all of the trustees' assessment methodologies and conclusions that fail to live up to this standard.

Third, the defendant should present a positive story of cleanup and recovery. The trier-of-fact, whether judge or jury, will want to know that the underlying matter has been or is being addressed appropriately. In some cases, the defendant may want to include its own cost-effective restoration plan to counter the plan put forward by the government. By putting forward and proving a narrative of positive recovery, cleanup, and restoration, a defendant will be able to show that the trustee's case is more about punishment than restoration, and therefore is not an appropriate recovery under the NRD laws.

Fourth, in many NRD cases, it is absolutely critical to develop a litigation plan that includes a robust presentation of baseline conditions. Simply stated, the NRD defendant is rarely responsible for all environmental problems identified by the trustees. There are numerous stressors on the health of the ecosystem, from urbanization to other spills to land use decisions, some of which are caused by the same governmental entities asserting the NRD claim. Neither OPA nor CERCLA obligates a defendant to mitigate these or the multiple other stressors that continue to negatively impact the environment. Rather, both statutes provide that the defendant must restore injured resources only to "baseline" conditions, that is, the condition that would have existed had the

---

1. *See* 15 C.F.R. § 990.27(a)(3); Gen. Elec. Co. v. U.S. Dep't of Commerce, 128 F.3d 767, 772 (D.C. Cir. 1997).

release not occurred.[2] During an NRD trial, it is critical to accurately establish baseline conditions, as they provide the benchmark for the defendant's restoration obligations.

These are just a few examples of possible litigation themes that may be appropriate. In most large NRD cases, the defendant will need to develop a specific litigation plan for each resource category, from aquatic organisms to zooplankton, literally from "a" to "z." In developing a comprehensive litigation plan, the defendant should focus on the specific issues applicable to each resource category, but also on the larger narrative and how each piece will fit into an actual trial presentation.

C. NRD Trials—Key Lessons

As with all areas of environmental law, most NRD cases settle long before trial. Nonetheless, there have been several cases that have either been tried in court or progressed substantially toward trial. This section provides some of the key "lessons learned" from ten important NRD trials or near trials, including issues related to managing evidence and experts. The following section provides an in-depth discussion of each of the ten matters.

The ten NRD cases evaluated are outlined in Table 7.1.

1. Lesson One—NRD Trials Are Marathons Not Sprints

NRD litigation is long, drawn out, and complicated. For the largest of NRD claims, discovery is likely a multi-year endeavor, and trial could last for multiple months. For example, just the first phase of the *Coeur d'Alene* River Basin trial, which addressed only liability and general categories of injury and is discussed in detail later in the chapter, required 78 days in court.[3] Had the *Coeur d'Alene* case not settled before the damages phase of trial, it would have been much longer. Even where the sums of money at stake are relatively small, NRD cases can consume significant time and resources. For example, in one of the only examples of a damages valuation trial, the *Little Salmon River* case, NRD claims that resulted in only a $45,000 judgment involved 12 days of trial.[4]

Because of the complexity of NRD claims, courts regularly segment both discovery and adjudication of issues. Common approaches to segmentation

---

2. *See, e.g.,* 15 C.F.R. § 990.30.
3. Coeur d'Alene Tribe v. ASARCO Inc., 280 F. Supp. 2d 1094, 1101 (D. Idaho 2003).
4. *See* Idaho v. S. Refrig. Transp. Inc., No. 88-1279, 1991 WL 22479 (D. Idaho Jan. 24, 1991).

Table 7.1 Ten Important NRD Trials

	Case	Court	NRD Statute	Length of Trial	Jury	Outcome	Final Value
1	Coeur d'Alene (1991–2011)	D. Idaho	CERCLA	78 days	No	Settled mid-trial	>$342.8 M
2	Upper Clark Fork (1983–2008)	D. Mont.	CERCLA	51 days	No	Settled mid-trial	~$215 M
3	Little Salmon (1988–1991)	D. Idaho	CERCLA	12 days	No	Court verdict	$45 K
4	Montrose (1990–2001)	C.D. Cal.	CERCLA	5 days	No	Settled mid-trial	$140.2 M
5	Highland Bayou (2008–2009)	S.D. Tex.	OPA	6 days	Yes	Jury verdict	$0
6	Bayway/ Bayonne (2004–2014)	NJ Super. Ct.	State Law	8 months	No	Settled post-trial	$225 M
7	American Trader (1991–1997)	Cal. Super. Ct.	State Law	34 days	Yes	Jury verdict	$18.1 M
8	St. Croix S. Shore (2005–2014)	D.V.I.	CERCLA	NA	Yes	Settled pre-trial	~$130 M
9	South Valley NM (1999–2007)	D.N.M.	CERCLA	NA	Yes	Dismissed pre-trial	$0
10	Ohio River (2003–2006)	S.D. Ohio	CERCLA	NA	Yes	Settled pre-trial	$3.35 M

include bifurcation into liability and damages phases (e.g., *Coeur d'Alene*[5]), or multiphasing based on resource categories (e.g., *Upper Clark Fork*[6]). Another reason courts may choose to phase a trial is that portions of an NRD claim may become ripe at different times. So, for example, whether a responsible party is liable for NRD may be an issue that is ripe well before the natural resource injuries resulting from the responsible party's actions are clear. For example, in the *Upper Clark Fork* case, adjudication of damages was delayed for areas of the river basin where the EPA had not yet selected the remedial measures because what remedial measures were chosen could diminish the values of impacts for which the defendant was liable.

2. Lesson Two—The Trustees Have to Prove Their Case

In Chapter 3, we discuss the legal issues associated with the rebuttable pre-sumption, NRD causation standard, and record review. One way to look at all three of these issues is that they represent (individually and collectively) a significant dilution of the burden of proof for the trustees. Indeed, if a trustee were able to convince a court that it was entitled to a rebuttable presumption, that it has sufficiently demonstrated a low causation standard, and that the defendants were precluded from presenting contrary evidence outside of the administrative record, the trustees would enjoy a huge litigation advantage.

Fortunately, it is clear that judges are reluctant to relieve trustees of their ultimate burden of proof, nor are they willing to fully strip defendants of their ability to defend themselves. For example, in two cases discussed in this chap-ter, *Coeur d'Alene* and *Upper Clark Fork*, the trustees argued that because a NRDA is a formal agency determination, courts should review only the record that formed the basis of the assessment determination under the arbitrary and capricious standard set forth in the APA. In both cases, the district court rejected this argument, finding that a court should review NRDA determina-tions de novo because the idea of record review is contrary to the CERCLA statutory scheme and would interfere with NRD defendants' right to a jury trial.[7] The federal district court for the District of Idaho in the *Coeur d'Alene* case also held that trustees are not "agencies" within the meaning of the APA,

---

5. *See* United States v. ASARCO Inc., No. 3:96-cv-00122 (D. Idaho Mar. 31, 1999), ECF No. 566.

6. Montana v. Atl. Richfield Co., No. 6:83-cv-00317 (D. Mont. Jan. 21, 1997), ECF No. 832.

7. Montana v. Atl. Richfield Co., No. CV-83-317-HLN-PGN, 1997 U.S. Dist. LEXIS 24671, at *24–26 (D. Mont. Feb. 28, 1997 (decided), Mar. 3, 1997 (filed)); Coeur d'Alene Tribe v. ASARCO Inc., No. 3:96-cv-00122, 1998 WL 1799392 (D. Idaho Mar. 31, 1998).

and said record review would deprive NRD defendants subject to expensive damages assessments of their due process rights under the U.S. Constitution.[8]

Notwithstanding this jurisprudence, if there remains a risk that a particular matter will be limited to review of the trustees' administrative record, the NRD defendant will need to evaluate whether or not to supplement the record and, if so, as to which issues. There are many methods for supplementing the NRD administrative record, from submitting letters to the trustees to publishing scientific articles in peer reviewed journals that are then submitted to the trustees. The method and timing for ensuring the record is complete will differ depending on many factors. Strategic and practical considerations associated with protecting the administrative record are discussed in more detail in Chapter 10.

3. Lesson Three—Experts: Critical to NRD Trials and Rarely Excluded

In all ten of the cases discussed in this chapter, experts were a critical component of both trustees' and defendants' cases. A broad range of experts have testified in NRD trials, including historians, ecologists, biologists, toxicologists, chemists, statisticians, economists, and more.

There are several important points related to the treatment of experts in our ten examples. First, it is important to note that where the fact finder at trial will be a judge rather than a jury, courts rarely rule on expert admissibility issues prior to trial. Therefore, the majority of the expert-related rulings issued in the NRD context occurred in cases where a jury trial was scheduled. Even where the fact finder is a jury, however, the reliability bar for expert opinions is relatively low—courts have often allowed scientists whose primary research focus is quite limited to testify to broader categories of opinions, or to opinions that are in categories substantially similar to their own focus. Where experts are excluded, it is often not due to a lack of qualifications or reliability, but rather because the legal questions at issue have been narrowed, rendering portions of their opinions not relevant. Of particular note for understanding expert issues in the NRD context are the cases of *South Valley, New Mexico* and *St. Croix South Shore*, both of which included extensive pre-trial expert rulings, and are discussed later in the chapter.

One critical factor in the expert equation is whether the trustees have completed a damages assessment. Particularly in the early CERCLA cases discussed here, where the trustees brought litigation prior to completing a NRDA in order to avoid their NRD claims becoming time-barred, the individuals

---

8. *Coeur d'Alene*, 1998 WL 1799392, at *4.

who contributed to the NRDA were the same individuals who were designated as testifying experts. In at least one case, the *Upper Clark Fork* case, the NRDA reports issued during the regulatory process were the exact same documents disclosed as expert reports. In the *Bayway and Bayonne* case, a New Jersey state court case, the trustees sought to have the fees paid to their litigation experts reimbursed as regulatory assessment costs. Although a New Jersey appellate court denied the pre-trial award of such fees, it suggested that the litigation expert fees were theoretically recoverable as NRDA costs so long as they were reasonable (i.e., not duplicative of assessment work already completed). Of course, if a court were ever to grant the trustees' motion for record review, expert testimony would necessarily be aligned with the content of the NRDA decision record.

Finally, from the perspective of the defendant, the retention of qualified experts is a critical component of preparing for litigation. Indeed, experts (including ecologists, biologists, economists, toxicologists, chemists, statisticians, etc.) should be retained throughout the assessment process, long before litigation begins. The right expert can help ensure that assessment plans are developed and implemented in line with valid scientific principles and accepted field and laboratory protocols; identify potential strategic concerns associated with gaps or biases in the available data; locate and review literature and/or unpublished data that may inform factual determinations such as baseline populations or impacts of contamination on survival and reproduction; evaluate the scientific validity of the trustees' data interpretation; and, eventually, provide expert testimony. Where appropriate, retained experts may also prepare scholarly articles for publication in peer-reviewed journals in order to help to support an assessment based on sound science.

EXPERT INSIGHT: NRD Expert Search
Jason Miller[9]
Ramboll Environ, Inc.

In many NRD cases, the necessary scientific experts, both testifying and consulting, can be identified based on the prior experience of clients, counsel, or other previously identified experts. For larger or more complex cases, however, a more detailed expert

---

9. Jason Miller is a principal with Ramboll Environ. He specializes in management and analysis of environmental data. Mr. Miller holds an MS in nuclear engineering from the University of Tennessee.

search process may be necessary. In those cases, counsel may find themselves needing a targeted expertise (e.g., an individual with experience in the baseline conditions or life cycle of a particular species with limited range) or a broader bench of expert support (e.g., to cover the variety of habitats, species, and economic uses under consideration). There are several steps that can be taken to pursue a more extensive expert search, and to preliminarily vet potential candidates.

In many instances, it is beneficial to start a search with the relevant departments at local and regional colleges or universities. Curriculum vitae and research interests are commonly posted on department websites, and these can be a rich source of information. Local university staff are more likely to be familiar with local species and habitats, local baseline conditions, and preexisting stressors. Their local connections may also make them attractive testifying experts or scientific advocates. Even if staff at the local universities are not available or interested in supporting a project, their personal networks may be sources for other candidates.

Advancing beyond local universities, professional societies often serve as sources for scientific experts. In particular, organizations such as the National Academy of Sciences, where membership is achieved by election, are rich sources of scientific experts. These organizations routinely publish consensus studies, and the authors of relevant studies may be expert candidates themselves or may be able to identify other candidates, if they are unavailable to support a project. The leaders and members of committees in other professional societies, such as the Society of Environmental Toxicology and Chemistry, are readily identifiable and may also be expert candidates or sources of other candidates.

Peer-reviewed scientific literature may be the richest vein of information on potential scientific experts, though the volume of information available can make expert identification a challenge. A search of scientific papers on nearly any subject is likely to turn up thousands of results. While Internet search tools have markedly increased the accessibility of the corpus of published scientific literature, careful search strategies are necessary to winnow the wheat from the chaff. In some instances, it may be possible to define search terms and a search strategy based on prior experience, but in many instances a scientific background and experience in literature searches may be necessary to develop a productive search strategy that can quickly identify potential experts. Such search strategies commonly begin with the creation of a list of search phrases, with appropriate wild cards and exclusion terms. The search term list is intended to target relevant articles while removing superfluous articles. Lists may be developed either with a bias toward including false positives or toward excluding potentially interesting articles, depending on the scope and type of the project. Once search term lists are developed, a variety of Internet search tools may be used to query literature databases. Although general search tools, such as Google Scholar, can be effective for identifying individual articles, they include a number of questionable sources and do not allow for more sophisticated search approaches. As a result, their utility for expert identification is limited.

Specialized literature search tools such as Elsevier's Scopus and Clarivate Analytics' Web of Science enable more elaborate search strategies that are more appropriate for expert identification. These search engines are supported by substantial metadata concerning individual scientific journals, authors, and institutions. As a result, these search engines allow searches to targeted journals and specific articles with the highest impact score. Articles with higher impact scores, for example, have been cited at a higher rate than other publications, suggesting that the article is considered by other scientific practitioners to be of greater value. Similarly, journals with higher impact scores more commonly publish highly cited articles. Focusing searches on journals with higher impact scores will tend to improve the richness of search results, while simultaneously removing journals that are not actually peer-reviewed from your search results. Sorting article search results by impact or citation score offers a quick way to focus a search on the most cited relevant articles.

The authors of frequently cited, relevant articles are obvious scientific expert candidates. However, several other search filters are recommended at this stage to narrow the field and eliminate false leads. Using Scopus, Web of Science, and related tools, it is possible to further research the authors of identified articles. These tools allow for a deeper dive into an individual's publication history. Typically, elements of such a search could include a review of publication dates, an analysis of whether the author's primary areas of interest have changed over time, and a review of the author's overall publication rate. Collectively, these data points help to indicate whether an author is in the early, middle, or late portion of his or her career and whether he or she is still focused on the area of interest to the case. These searches can also identify retractions or other publications that may be of concern.

Relevant articles may provide lists of potential experts beyond the author list. The reference lists of relevant articles often contain an abundance of other relevant articles. Tools such as Scopus and Web of Science allow quick review of these references, and the authors of cited works may also be of interest as potential scientific experts.

The collective use of scientific literature searches, professional society searches, and local university searches is likely to generate a long list of potential experts. Once these initial identification steps are complete, preliminary vetting of potential expert candidates can be conducted using some of the same web and literature search tools to narrow the candidate list before interviews begin. This should help to minimize low-quality interviews and discussions with candidates who would be clearly disqualified based on their past experience.

For example, review of detailed publication history information from tools such as Scopus and Web of Science can be used to screen candidates who are no longer specializing in the area of interest or who might be considered to be over- or under-specialized for a particular case. As noted previously, these searches will also identify articles that have been retracted or that are the source of significant scientific controversy. Of course, these searches will also identify any prior work the candidates have published on the matter at hand. Review of funding source descriptions in articles may identify preexisting relationships that represent a conflict of interest in a particular case, and these searches can be buttressed by targeted searches for funding decisions by organizations (e.g., industry-funded research grant programs, university grants, private research programs, government programs such as the National Institutes of Health or National Science Foundation) that could be a perceived source of bias, depending on the particulars of the case.

Scopus, Web of Science, and similar tools will also reveal opinion pieces authored by potential expert candidates and published in scientific journals. These opinion pieces are often valuable, even if not directly relevant to the case, because they provide some sense of the author's tone when discussing more subjective issues. This can be particularly valuable for candidates who do not have a substantial history as testifying experts. Similarly, it is possible to search for conference poster and presentation abstracts, and, in some cases, transcripts of talks at scientific conferences, which are less edited and more dynamic than scientific publications and may provide a clearer view of how a candidate will react in a trial situation.

Of course, once such searches of scientific source materials are complete, it is necessary to search legal data sources, including, for example, PACER and LexisNexis, to identify prior expert testimony and exclusions under evidentiary standards such as *Daubert* and state equivalents, but these searches are more similar to those that would be conducted for any expert witness.

The value of scientific data sources to expert identification and preliminary vetting should not be overlooked. By designing a targeted search of such materials, using tools developed to search scientific data sources, and interpreting the findings through a knowledgeable lens, it is possible to develop a rich list of potential expert candidates. Such a search is more likely to identify highly credentialed scientists with specific knowledge of the NRD area of interest, regardless of their history with expert testimony, than more traditional searches that rely primarily on legal data sources. In addition, the rise of richly featured, targeted scientific search systems has reduced the complexity of such searches and the time required to conduct them, so that these searches can be valuable contributors to cases where existing relationships have proven insufficient to identify the needed experts.

4. Lesson Four—Scientific Evidence Is Different in NRD Cases

Courts in NRD cases have to grapple with several types of scientific evidence. For example, many cases involve the trustees' regulatory assessment of NRD. Assuming record review is not sought or has been denied, the existence of such documents raises several questions including whether or not the reports themselves are admissible evidence and the extent to which experts can rely on them. Only one case, *Coeur d'Alene*, addressed these questions in detail. In that case, the court denied the wholesale admission of the trustees' assessment report, but permitted experts to rely on portions thereof and permitted defendants to cross-examine the experts on the data contained therein.[10]

A second type of scientific evidence in NRD cases is data, often voluminous and diverse. Courts have generally allowed broad discovery of scientific databases (see *Coeur d'Alene*); however, at least one court, in the *St. Croix South Shore* case, has applied the work-product doctrine to scientific data collected in anticipation of litigation. Scientific data is generally admissible, although courts have been reluctant to issue wholesale authenticity, relevance, or admissibility rulings with regard to voluminous collections of any type of evidence, including databases. Most data have been admitted as part of expert testimony. Data issues underlie many of the expert-related holdings in all of the cases described in this chapter, but are discussed most thoroughly in the *Coeur d'Alene* case.

A third type of evidence is the damages valuations. Of particular interest, and controversy, are CV surveys used to assign a nonuse existence value to NRD claims.[11] Use of CV surveys as evidence of nonuse existence values is discussed in *Upper Clark Fork*, *Little Salmon*, and *Montrose*. In *Upper Clark Fork*, the court allowed the admission of a CV survey. In *Little Salmon*, the court heard evidence regarding a CV survey, but rejected the reliability of the study in its post-trial order. In *Montrose*, the court granted defendants' motion to exclude the trustees' CV survey. Interestingly, another use of CV surveys has been as evidence relied on by defendants to rebut allegedly overstated or unsupported damages estimates.[12] The use of, and holding related to, CV surveys is discussed in greater detail in the summary of each of the following cases.

In sum, while most scientific data have been held to be both discoverable and admissible, there have been exceptions, and courts are reluctant to issue blanket holdings even with regard to voluminous data sets. Further, there are several categories of evidence, such as surveys, where courts are appropriately reluctant to allow the admission of such evidence. Finally, where the defendant has decided to collect environmental data independently of the trustees, they must ensure that all data collection efforts are appropriate. For example, sampling methods must be consistent with generally accepted scientific

---

10. United States v. ASARCO Inc., No. 3:96-cv-00122-EJL (D. Idaho Jan. 10, 2001), ECF No. 1002.

11. *See also* Brian D. Israel et al., *Legal Obstacles for Contingent Valuation Methods in Environmental Litigation, in* CONTINGENT VALUATION OF ENVIRONMENTAL GOODS 292 (Daniel McFadden & Kenneth Train eds., 2017).

12. See *American Trader* and *St. Croix South Shore*, later in the chapter.

methodologies; data sets must be sufficiently robust to ensure statistical significance and representativeness; and laboratory results must be reliable and verifiable.

EXPERT INSIGHT: Uniform Data Quality Ecotoxicity Assessment
Dallas Wait and Tim Verslyck[13]
Gradient

The underpinnings to any successful NRD investigation are that data produced to support the study are reliable, defensible, and fit for purpose. Over the past few decades, quality assurance (QA) and quality control (QC) systems have been established for chemistry measurements that, when crafted and implemented properly, should result in usable data.[14] There are many aspects to a robust QA/QC program that must be considered.[15] Most important is to establish a complete understanding of the data quality objectives (DQOs) of the study prior to the investigation; this will support the development of an appropriate and adequate QA/QC program.[16] Once DQOs are established, basic QA/QC tenets to be considered include accuracy, precision, representativeness, comparability, and completeness in meeting the data acquisition goals. Comparability involves the consistency in the acquisition and analysis of samples necessary for comparing results, as well as the methodology for assessing the quality, usability, and interpretation of the data.

One key issue in considering comparability is data verification and validation. Data verification is the process of evaluating the completeness, correctness, and conformance of a specific data set against method requirements, whereas data validation is an analyte- and sample-specific process that extends the evaluation of data beyond method compliance to determine the analytical quality of a specific data set.[17] Federal and state agencies provide a plethora of guidance and requirements on how to validate environmental chemistry measurements that may be used for NRD investigations. These directives provide guideposts to scientists about a level of uniformity they can assume about the quality of data they intend to use for decision making.

---

13. Dr. A. Dallas Wait is a principal with Gradient. He holds a PhD in organic chemistry from the University of Rhode Island. Dr. Tim Verslycke is a principal with Gradient. He holds a PhD in bio-engineering and allied biological sciences from Ghent University (Belgium).

14. A.D. Wait, C. Ramsey, & J. Maney, *The Measurement Process, in* INTRODUCTION TO ENVIRONMENTAL FORENSICS, 3d ed. 65–97 (B.L. Murphy & R.D. Morrison, eds., 2015).

15. T.A. Verslycke & A.D. Wait, *Data Quality in Natural Resource and Environmental Damage Litigation,* 31(4) NATURAL RESOURCES & ENVIRONMENT 15–19 (2017).

16. A.D. Wait, *Challenges in Producing Defensible Environmental Chemistry Measurements for Litigation,* 14 ENVTL. CLAIMS J. 415–54 (2002).

17. EPA, GUIDANCE ON ENVIRONMENTAL DATA VERIFICATION AND DATA VALIDATION, EPA/240/R-02/004, EPA QA/G-8, at 95 (2002).

NRDA relies not just on analytical chemistry data but also on non-chemistry data, such as ecotoxicity test data. No similar regulatory guideposts exist for qualifying the quality and usability of ecotoxicity data. Qualifying ecotoxicity test data is further complicated by the fact that it involves a wide variety of test methods and includes chemical, physical, biological, and toxicological data. Since ecotoxicity data are a key focus for most NRD investigations, comparative analysis of ecotoxicity data using differing approaches can confound data interpretation and in turn jeopardize NRD decisions.

Ecotoxicity data may be generated using a wide variety of methods that range from short-term acute tests with simple endpoints (such as mortality) to long-term chronic, full life cycle, or multigenerational tests with complex endpoints (such as growth, reproduction, biochemistry, and pathology). Many ecotoxicity test methods have gone through formal method development (e.g., EPA[18] and Organisation for Economic Co-operation and Development (OECD)[19] ecotoxicity test guidelines) and have been used to support environmental decision making for decades. Further, ecotoxicity data can be generated following good laboratory practice (GLP) regulations published by EPA,[20] the U.S. Food and Drug Administration (FDA),[21] and/or OECD,[22] which specify (1) use of a written protocol for each study; (2) the methods for collecting, recording, reporting, and storing data; and (3) the inclusion of a quality assurance review of reports. Despite the existence of regulatory test methods and GLP guidance, much of the ecotoxicity data relied on during NRD investigations may not have been generated under GLP and may be using novel methods that have not been demonstrated beyond their original development. As a result, ecotoxicity data users conducting NRD investigations are faced with the daunting task of evaluating the reliability and usability of potentially widely varying ecotoxicity data sets.

To address this issue, research groups have been developing more specific guidance for evaluating ecotoxicity test data. For example, Klimisch scores[23] are used to evaluate the reliability of ecotoxicity data in many regulatory programs by assigning data into one of four reliability categories: reliable without restriction (Category 1), reliable with restriction (Category 2), not reliable (Category 3), and not assignable (Category 4). Typically, Category 1 studies or data are those conducted following

18. EPA, *Test Guidelines for Pesticides and Toxic Substances* (2017), www.epa.gov/test-guidelines-pesticides-and-toxic-substances.

19. OECD, *OECD Series on Principles of Good Laboratory Practice (GLP) and Compliance Monitoring* (2017), http://www.oecd.org/chemicalsafety/testing/oecdseriesonprinciplesofgoodlaboratorypracticeglpandcompliancemonitoring.htm.

20. EPA, *Good Laboratory Practice Standards* (1997), 40 C.F.R. 160; EPA, *Good Laboratory Practice Standards* (2011), 40 C.F.R. 792.

21. FDA, *Good Laboratory Practice for Nonclinical Laboratory Studies*, 21 C.F.R. 58.

22. OECD, *supra* note 19.

23. H.J. Klimisch, M. Andreae, U. Tillmann, *A Systematic Approach for Evaluating the Quality of Experimental Toxicological and Ecotoxicological Data*, 25(1) REGULATORY TOXICOLOGY & PHARMACOLOGY 1–5 (1997).

a standard guideline under GLP conditions, although any study may be placed into this category if it is described sufficiently and carried out according to a scientifically acceptable standard. If some criteria of a standard test method are not met (Category 2), a qualified reviewer may still find the data to be valid for its intended use. Often, Category 1 and 2 studies or data are found to be of sufficient quality to support decision making, whereas Category 3 and 4 studies are generally considered supporting evidence or not relevant. More recently, a new method called "Criteria for Reporting and Evaluating Ecotoxicity Data (CRED)"[24] was developed to provide further detail and guidance and ensure greater consistency in the evaluation of ecotoxicity data. The CRED method is currently being piloted and tested in several regulatory programs in the European Union. While availability of these methods and associated "reliability flags" has helped ecotoxicity data users, it has not replaced the need for an independent data quality assessment to ensure that any prior data reliability assessments are relevant to the specific purposes of the data.

A further complicating factor is the substantial flexibility allowed within regulatory test guidelines. For example, the same ecotoxicity test method typically can be conducted in many different ways: using a variety of different animal or plant species; using nominal or analytically verified test concentrations; using different variations of artificial or natural test media (e.g., artificially created sediment versus sediment collected from a "clean" site); using different test conditions (e.g., temperature, light); and using sediment, water, or food-based exposure. Ecotoxicity data users need to account for these procedural differences when comparing and selecting the best possible data.

It is clear that there are significant data quality challenges that are unique to ecotoxicity data and that need to be carefully considered in the context of NRD claims. When ecological damage investigations rely on ecotoxicity data, the data must be representative and of a known quality and integrity to ensure scientifically sound decisions that can be defended. Ultimately, the goal is for the data to be admissible in court. Evidence will more likely be admitted when a reliable, relevant, and defensible method is implemented correctly by a trained operator and all relevant data are maintained.

5. Lesson Five—The Jury Curveball

The legal jurisprudence surrounding the right to a jury in an NRD matter is discussed in Chapter 3. And while most cases described in this chapter did not involve a jury, courts that have ruled on this question have held that

---

24. M. Ågerstrand, A. Kuster, J. Bachmann, M. Breitholtz, I. Ebert, B. Rechenberg, C. Ruden, *Reporting and Evaluation Criteria as Means towards a Transparent Use of Ecotoxicity Data for Environmental Risk Assessment of Pharmaceuticals*, 159(10) ENVTL. POLLUTION 2487–92 (2011), doi 10.1016/j.envpol.2011.06.023.

such a right does exist under the U.S. Constitution for NRD claims, at least in part. The court explicitly addressed this question in *Coeur d'Alene, Upper Clark Fork,* and *Highland Bayou.* Additionally, jury trials were set to occur in the *Ohio River* and *St. Croix South Shore* cases before these cases settled on the eve of trial. Still, only one federal NRD jury trial, in the *Highland Bayou* case, has actually occurred. In that case, the trial focused on liability issues, and the jury's dispositive verdict finding defendants not liable meant that it never reached the NRD questions. Thus, the best example of an NRD jury trial comes from the California state court case relating to the *American Trader* spill. That trial focused on lost recreational use claims resulting from a pre-OPA oil spill off the coast of Orange County, California. While little is known about the dynamics of this jury's deliberation, it is clear that the verdict largely favored the trustees' positions, but that jury members did perform some novel calculations in arriving at the final NRD liability value imposed on the defendant.

D. NRD Trials—An Overview of Ten Cases

In this section, we provide an in-depth discussion of ten major NRD cases that either proceeded to trial or were substantially far along the path towards trial. In each case, we provide the following: (1) the name of the case and court; (2) a summary of the facts, claims asserted, and outcome; (3) key pre-trial and trial motions; and (4) a discussion of major evidentiary and legal issues presented in the case.

1. Coeur d'Alene River Basin (D. Idaho 1991–2011)

Coeur d'Alene Tribe v. ASARCO Inc., No. 3:91-cv-00342-EJL; *United States v. ASARCO Inc.,* No. 3:96-cv-00122-EJL

a. Summary

The *Coeur d'Alene* trial was a 78-day, 100-witness bench trial in 2001 that addressed NRD liability under CERCLA for decades of mining activity in the Coeur d'Alene River Basin (the Basin) in Idaho. The trial related to the first of two phases of the litigation and addressed liability, causation, and general categories of natural resource injuries resulting from the mining activities. The second phase of the trial, which was to relate to the specific dollar value of NRD, never occurred, as one of the two remaining defendants, ASARCO, entered a bankruptcy settlement covering all its nationwide CERCLA liabilities, and the second, Hecla, settled.

b. The Facts

The Bunker Hill site in the Basin was historically one of the largest mining sites in the world. In all, according to the state of Idaho, more than 100 million tons of mining waste were deposited in the area's river system and more than 15,000 acres of wildlife habitat contained sediments/soils that were alleged to be acutely toxic to waterfowl. The state of Idaho reported that due to the contamination, about 20 miles of streams were unable to sustain a reproducing fish population, and about ten miles of tributaries had virtually no aquatic life at all.

In 1987, the state of Idaho settled some of its NRD claims for $4.5 million. In 1991, the Coeur d'Alene Tribe filed suit against ASARCO, Hecla, and several other companies, and in 1996, the federal government filed against the same defendants seeking recovery of costs and NRD under CERCLA, CWA, and the Resource Conservation and Recovery Act (RCRA).[25] These cases were subsequently consolidated.

Although the court initially indicated that liability and damages should be addressed at the same time, trial for the case was bifurcated into two phases because no final remedial plan for the Basin had been issued.[26] The first phase was to address liability, causation, and general damages; the second phase was to address the specific dollar value of damages.

While some defendants settled shortly after the liability phase of trial began, two defendants, ASARCO and Hecla, continued for the entire length of the Phase 1 trial, which was conducted over 78 days in 2001. In Phase 1 alone (which covered liability, causation, and general damages), approximately 100 witnesses were called, 8,695 exhibits were admitted into the record, and 16,000 pages of trial transcript were generated.[27] In its 2003 order ruling on this phase of the trial, the court determined that ASARCO and Hecla were liable under CERCLA and the CWA for a majority (combined 53 percent, based on their contributions to historical releases of mining tailings) of the damage to natural resources in the Basin.[28] The NRD findings related to the Phase 1 trial are discussed in more detail later.

In 2005, defendant ASARCO filed for bankruptcy and the matter was stayed as to all parties.[29] ASARCO subsequently entered into a global settle-

---

25. Coeur d'Alene Tribe v. ASARCO Inc., No. CV 91-0342-N-EJL (D. Idaho); United States v. ASARCO Inc., No. 3:96-cv-00122 (D. Idaho Mar. 22, 1996).

26. United States v. ASARCO Inc., No. 3:96-cv-00122 (D. Idaho Mar. 31, 1999), ECF No. 566.

27. Coeur d'Alene Tribe v. ASARCO Inc., 280 F. Supp. 2d 1094, 1101 (D. Idaho 2003).

28. *Id.* at 1105, 1135.

29. *See* United States v. Hecla Ltd. (*Hecla*), No. 3:96-cv-00122-EJL, slip op. at 2 (D. Idaho Sept. 8, 2011), ECF No. 1614 (setting forth case's procedural history).

ment of all its CERCLA claims nationwide, including the Coeur d'Alene Basin claim. The bankruptcy settlement, approved in 2007, allocated $79.4 million to restore natural resources in the Basin. After the claims against ASARCO were dismissed, the remaining parties (Hecla and the trustees) requested, and the court agreed, that the case remain stayed so that they could continue their settlement negotiations. After months of negotiation under supervision of a mediator, the parties lodged a detailed consent decree with the court in 2011, pursuant to which Hecla agreed to pay $263.4 million for both cleanup and restoration of the Basin.[30]

Restoration projects funded by the pre-2007 settlements are currently being implemented in the Basin. Restoration planning for the rest of the funds, including those from the ASARCO and Hecla settlements, is still underway.

c. Outcome

In its post-trial order relating to the liability phase, the court stated that "[d]efendants are correct when they argue there has been an exaggerated over-statement by the Federal Government and the Tribe of the conditions that exist and the source of the alleged injury to natural resources."[31] For example, the court found that "there was no evidence supporting injury to any . . . species of wildlife [other than birds, fish, and benthic organisms]," that there was "no credible evidence shown to establish any injury to the people living in Northern Idaho resulting from the consumption of fish and birds from the Basin," and that "[c]ultural uses of water and soil by Tribe are not compensable."[32] The court did, however, make some general findings of fact regarding natural resource injuries that did occur, including that injury to some species of birds, some fish, benthic organisms, and vegetation occurred; that levels of certain hazardous substances were elevated in various areas of the ecosystem; and that lead levels in children in the Basin were elevated.

d. Scheduling and Timing

i. Bifurcation

The tribe and the United States moved to trifurcate the trial into three phases, beginning with a liability determination and postponing any damages determination until the Basin risk investigation, feasibility study, and record of decision (ROD) were complete. Defendants objected to trifurcation and sought to

---

30. *See Hecla*, slip op. at 13.
31. *Coeur d'Alene*, 280 F. Supp. 2d at 1101.
32. *Id.* at 1107.

have liability and damages addressed at one time. The court determined that "in this particular case the determination of liability, causation and damages cannot be separated," but acknowledged that actual NRD might be reduced after the EPA completed remedial actions in the Basin.[33]

ii. Ripeness/Justiciability

Defendants argued that the claims for NRD were not ripe because the remedial investigation, feasibility study, and ROD for the site had not yet been completed at the time of suit. The court disagreed, stating that "[i]njury evidence has been presented by the Plaintiffs and based on this Court's bifurcation of the trial, the dollar amount of damages will not be addressed until the second phase of the trial."[34] In other words, the court found that adjudication of general NRD liability is ripe for review as soon as injury has been established, even where a remediation is not complete and a dollar value of damages cannot yet be ascertained. The court refused, however, to undertake the damages phase of litigation until a ROD was issued.

e. Discovery Issues

i. Access to Large Databases

The Coeur d'Alene Tribe, rather than the United States, maintained the NRDA GIS database used in the trustees' NRDA. ASARCO moved for the court to order that the tribe provide it with a copy of this database, arguing that it provided critical support to the trustees' NRDA. The tribe moved for a protective order, arguing that the database was tribe property and that ASARCO was entitled only to public access to the database through the tribe's office. The court sided with ASARCO and found that "the database is part of the administrative record relied upon by the trustees in completing their assessment as required by the statute and regulations for a natural resource damages action. Accordingly, the database should be provided to ASARCO."[35] However, the court did not require that the trustees provide the software necessary to read the database and found that any technical assistance requested from the trustees to understand and work with the database would be at ASARCO's expense.[36]

---

33. *See* United States v. ASARCO Inc., No. 3:96-cv-00122-EJL, slip op. at 2 (D. Idaho Mar. 31, 1999), ECF No. 566.

34. *Coeur d'Alene*, 280 F. Supp. 2d at 1109.

35. United States v. ASARCO Inc., No. CV 96-0122-N-EJL, CV 91-342-N-EJL, 1998 WL 1799392, at *6 (D. Mont. Mar. 31, 1998).

36. *Id.*

ii. Interrogatory Responses

In some of their interrogatory responses, rather than providing narrative responses, the plaintiffs directed defendants to large portions of the initial disclosures (which largely consisted of documents in the administrative record). The court disagreed with this approach, directing the plaintiffs to supplement their earlier responses with greater specificity in narrative form because "the subject matter of many of the interrogatories is extremely relevant so that all parties can more completely understand the complex and multiple claims of the Trustees," and "the Plaintiffs are in a far better position to summarize information."[37]

iii. Attorneys' Fees

The United States conceded that it was not entitled to recover attorneys' fees related to its NRD claims, but did seek to recover $19.6 million in attorneys' fees associated with its cost recovery claims. Defendant Hecla sought to compel the United States to provide testimony and documents regarding this amount so it could determine whether the United States was fairly allocating fees to the response cost claims rather than to the NRD claims. The court granted the motion, compelling the United States to provide information and a witness on the amount of NRD costs incurred, stating that "[t]he amount of NRD litigation fees and costs that have been incurred may lead to admissible evidence to defend whether the attorneys' fees and costs being claimed as response costs by DOJ for approximately $19.6 million are 'reasonable.'"[38]

f. Record Review

The United States and the tribe sought to limit the NRD proceeding to record review. The trustees' motion for record review was denied for several reasons, including that record review would be at odds with the rebuttable presumption in CERCLA, and that defendants' right to a jury trial for NRD claims would be deprived by record review.[39] As previously discussed, in response to plaintiffs' argument that the APA required record review of the trustees' damages assessment, the court found that "the Trustees are not 'agencies' within the meaning of the APA; the assessment is not final 'agency action' as defined by [the APA], and it is the duty of the trustee in a natural resources damages action, not

---

37. *Id.* at *7.
38. United States v. ASARCO Inc., No. 3:96-cv-00122-EJL, slip op. at 7 (Mar. 31, 2005), ECF No. 1460.
39. *ASARCO Inc.*, 1998 WL 1799392, at *2–4.

the Defendant, to seek judicial review of the trustee's assessment."[40] Lastly, the court found that record review for NRD actions would violate defendants' due process rights. It stated that "[t]he Plaintiffs, as Trustees, seek millions of dollars in damages from the defendants. To interpret CERCLA to prohibit the defendants from effectively challenging the assessment of injury and the causation of damages as well as the ability to assert certain defenses, is too restrictive and potentially leaves too much power in the hands of the trustees."[41]

g. Evidentiary Issues

i. Trustees' Injury Assessment Report

The United States moved for the court to admit the trustees' injury assessment report (the Report) as a public records exception to the hearsay rule. Defendants objected, arguing, among other things, that admission of the Report would deny the court the opportunity to hear live testimony, that the Report was prepared in anticipation of litigation rather than pursuant to CERCLA, and that the Report had improper findings on "ultimate facts" in this case. The court agreed with the United States that the Report fell under the public records exception to the hearsay rule.[42] However, the court allowed admission of the Report only under certain conditions: the trustees were required to call specific experts relating to each alleged area of injury, and to the extent these experts relied on the Report in their opinions, the defendants would be allowed to expose any flaws via cross-examination; the Report alone would be considered insufficient to establish injury or causation.[43] The court stated that "[i]n sum, the Court is admitting the Report, but is reserving its ruling on the trustworthiness of the data contained in the Report."[44] After the United States relied on the Report at trial, ASARCO again moved to exclude the Report as untrustworthy and irrelevant or, in the alternative, to strike certain portions of the Report which were not testified to as required by the earlier order. The court granted in part and denied in part ASARCO's motion. The court found that the question of trustworthiness and relevance had previously been established by the earlier order, but agreed that portions of the Report either were not relevant or had not been

---

40. *Id.* at *4.
41. *Id.*
42. United States v. ASARCO Inc., No. 3:96-cv-00122-EJL, slip op. at 2 (D. Idaho Jan. 10, 2001), ECF No. 1002.
43. *Id.* at 3.
44. *Id.*

testified to in sufficient detail to support admission of the entire Report in connection with the liability phase of the trial.[45]

ii. Data

The United States and the tribe sought to have the court enter an order finding that the extensive scientific data exhibits they intended to introduce were authentic and admissible. The court declined to grant such an order, finding that while these exhibits were voluminous and likely authentic, it could not issue an authenticity and admissibility ruling for any exhibits it had not yet reviewed.[46] It was "up to the parties to determine (outside the time set for testimony) which exhibits can be stipulated to for admission for each witness," and "if any party has an authenticity issue regarding an exhibit this needs to be brought to the Court's attention prior to the witness who will be using the exhibit testifying and outside the time set for the Court to take testimony."[47]

h. Use of Experts

Experts were heavily relied upon in the 78-day liability trial, and their expertise was far-reaching, including Superfund cost documentation, land use planning, history of technology, mineral process engineering, management of natural resources, geochemistry and fate and transport, ecology, fisheries, limnology, environmental toxicology, aquatic toxicology, wildlife pathology, veterinary sciences, effects of metals on birds, anthropology, soil sciences, fish habitat, eagle and raptor biology, and benthic macroinvertebrate communities.

Various substantive motions to strike and motions in limine were filed regarding the testimony of experts. Almost all were denied or rendered moot. One successful motion in limine related to an expert presented by the United States as an expert in the history of mining technology. His expert report included opinions on historical records of where alleged hazardous waste had come to be located. ASARCO moved to exclude the expert's testimony on the movement of mining tailings, arguing that he did not have the relevant expertise to testify to such facts. The court allowed the expert to testify, stating that "the historical background of mining in the Basin will be beneficial to the Court in order to aid the Court in understanding what type of mining was

---

45. United States v. ASARCO Inc., No. 3:96-cv-00122-EJL, slip op. at 3 (D. Idaho July 2, 2001), ECF No. 1178.

46. United States v. ASARCO Inc., No. 3:96-cv-00122-EJL (D. Idaho Jan. 10, 2001), ECF No. 1002.

47. *Id.* at 4.

done and how methods of mining changed over time."[48] The court agreed, however, that the expert was not "qualified to testify as to movement of mining tailings in a watershed or as to specific hazardous substance releases and the alleged causation of injury to natural resources."[49]

i. Burden of Proof and the Rebuttable Presumption

In the same order denying plaintiffs' motion for record review, the court found that if plaintiffs are entitled to the benefit of the rebuttable presumption, it "applies to the assessment of damages by the Trustees and not just the damages demand allocations."[50] In other words, according to the court, the rebuttable presumption extends not only to the trustees' valuation assigned to the damage that did occur but also to the trustees' assessment of what injuries resulted from a responsible parties' actions.

However, the rebuttable presumption was not discussed in the court's post-trial liability phase order, presumably because its application relates to the valuation of NRD (which was not at issue in the Phase 1 trial).

In determining which general NRD injuries had been shown at the Phase 1 trial, the court held plaintiff trustees to a "preponderance of the evidence" standard, finding, for example, that "even though scientific evidence exists showing Canadian geese and wood ducks have died due to lead poisoning, the Court finds the limited deaths are countered by the increase in the overall populations of such birds."[51] "When the total population for such birds is considered, the Court concludes that the releases by the Defendants are not harming the Canadian geese and wood ducks at a level to justify liability being imposed on Defendants for damages to natural resources."[52]

j. Treatment of Causation

In the midst of trial, the court issued an order setting forth the causation standard to be applied to the plaintiffs' NRD claims.[53] It specifically rejected application of the causation standard set forth in the *Montrose* case, discussed

---

48. United States v. ASARCO Inc., No. 3:96-cv-00122-EJL, slip op. at 3 (D. Idaho Jan. 22, 2001), ECF No. 1029.

49. *Id.* at 4.

50. United States v. ASARCO Inc., No. CV 96-0122-N-EJL, 1998 WL 1799392, at *3 (D. Idaho Mar. 31, 1998).

51. Coeur d'Alene Tribe v. ASARCO Inc., 280 F. Supp. 2d 1094, 1123 (D. Idaho 2003).

52. *Id.*

53. Coeur d'Alene Tribe v. ASARCO Inc., No. CV91-0342NEJL, CV96-0122NEJL, 2001 WL 34139603 (D. Idaho Mar. 30, 2001).

later in the chapter,[54] which utilized a "sole or substantially contributing cause" standard. Instead, it found that in a case such as this, where waste from multiple defendants was commingled, the correct causation standard is a contributing factor test, defined as "more than a de minimis amount—to an extent that at least some of the injury would have occurred if only the Defendant's amount of release had occurred."[55] At trial, therefore, the trustees had the burden of proving that ASARCO's waste was a "contributing factor" to injury to natural resources.[56] The court did acknowledge that "[i]n cases where releases have *not* been commingled, the burden would be to show that such release was the sole or proximate cause to the injury to the natural resources."[57]

k. Issues Related to Multiple Trustees

At trial, defendants argued that plaintiffs' NRD claims failed because plaintiffs lacked trusteeship over the resources in question. Specifically, they argued that the United States and the tribe lacked actual stewardship over the resources because, for example, the United States had delegated much of its authority to regulate the resources to the state of Idaho. In its 2003 Post-Trial Liability Order, the court held that the determination of trusteeship is a question of both fact and law. It noted that "in many instances, co-trustees are the norm and not the exception," but it rejected the United States' argument that "mere statutory authority is sufficient to establish trusteeship over a natural resource."[58] The court held that to avoid double recovery (which is expressly prohibited under CERCLA), a trustee could recover only the percentage of damages that accorded with its actual stewardship over a particular resource.[59] It then deferred determination of trusteeship over certain resources until the second phase of the trial when evidence could be presented on stewardship percentages.[60]

In 2005, however, the court reversed the 2003 holding with regard to the treatment of co-trusteeship, explaining that its initial "reliance on traditional tort concepts in allocating trusteeship was misplaced and that this type of case is distinguishable from other tort actions" because "the recovery, if any, is not for the benefit of a given party, but goes to the trustee as the fiduciary

---

54. *See* Chapter 7, Section D.4.
55. *Coeur d'Alene*, 2001 WL 34139603, at *5.
56. *See Coeur d'Alene*, 280 F. Supp. 2d at 1124.
57. *Coeur d'Alene*, 2001 WL 34139603, at *5 (emphasis in original).
58. *Coeur d'Alene*, 280 F. Supp. 2d at 1115.
59. *Id.* at 1116.
60. *Id.* at 1117.

to accomplish the stated goals."[61] In the end, the court held that "a co-trustee acting individually or collectively with the other co-trustees may go after the responsible party or parties for the full amount of the damage, less any amount that has already been paid as a result of a settlement to another trustee by a responsible party."[62]

2. Upper Clark Fork River Basin (D. Mont. 1983–2008)
Montana v. Atlantic Richfield Co., No. 6:83-cv-00317-SEH

a. Summary
The *Montana v. Atlantic Richfield Co.* case related to injuries to natural resources allegedly caused by decades of mining in the Upper Clark Fork River Basin. Almost 15 years after a complaint was filed, a partial bench trial occurred over 51 days in 1997 and 1998. This trial addressed liability for, and injury to, aquatic, terrestrial, and groundwater resources. A trial never proceeded regarding the two final planned segments of the case, relating to damages and counterclaims, as the parties reached a number of partial settlement agreements, finally culminating in the 2008 settlement of all remaining NRD claims. The final total value Atlantic Richfield Company (ARCO) paid was approximately $215 million to resolve its NRD liability, an amount equal to about 30 percent of the value Montana claimed at the start of trial.

b. The Facts
In 1983, the state of Montana filed suit under CERCLA against ARCO for NRD to the Upper Clark Fork River Basin. Montana alleged that decades of mining and smelting in the area had caused harm to natural resources in the river basin and deprived Montanans of their use of these resources.

The litigation was initially stayed, upon request of the parties, from 1983 until 1989 while EPA finalized its remedial investigation and feasibility studies regarding the four Upper Clark Fork River Basin NPL sites.[63] The stay was removed on ARCO's motion on December 5, 1989. After multi-year

---

61. United States v. ASARCO Inc., 471 F. Supp. 2d 1063, 1068 (D. Idaho 2005).

62. *Id.*

63. *See* Montana v. Atl. Richfield Co., 266 F. Supp. 2d 1238, 1239–40 (D. Mont. 2003) (setting forth case's procedural history). The 1986 amendments to CERCLA prohibit an NRD suit prior to selection of a remedial action at a site. *See* 42 U.S.C. § 9613(g)(1)(B). However, it is important to note that because this suit was filed prior to 1986, that provision of CERCLA was inapplicable to these NRD claims. *See id.* ("The limitation in the preceding sentence on commencing an action . . . before selection of the remedial action does not apply to actions filed on or before October 17, 1986.").

discovery, another stay to facilitate settlement negotiations, and several years of pre-trial motions practice, the trial was subdivided into five segments, discussed in more detail in the following subsections. The first three phases of trial proceeded over a total of 51 trial days in 1997 and 1998. During and after these phases, the parties engaged in extensive court-supervised settlement negotiations resulting in two consent decrees approved by the court in 1999. However, the consent decrees represented only partial settlement of Montana's NRD claims, and only addressed the claims relating to certain areas of the river basin, namely the three OUs for which a ROD had not been issued by EPA. As discussed further later in the chapter, one of the 1999 consent decrees also resolved all of the NRD claims of the Confederated Salish and Kootenai Tribes and all of the United States' NRD claims except for certain specific parcels of land owned by the United States along the Clark Fork River.

After entry of the consent decrees in 1999, the court developed a case management plan that contemplated that the court would first make a determination from the existing record on liability, causation, and injury for the remaining claims. A trial on the damages portion of the claims would follow if ARCO was held liable for the injuries.[64]

Soon thereafter, the presiding judge passed away, and the parties agreed, by stipulation, that it would be appropriate for the new presiding judge, upon review of the existing record, to make a de novo determination with regard to ARCO's liability. In 2003, the court held that Montana's remaining NRD claims relating to upland areas around the Anaconda Smelter were not compensable because the injuries to the environment occurred prior to 1980, the year CERCLA was enacted.[65] A stay was entered to allow for further settlement negotiations, and eventually, in 2008, the parties settled all remaining NRD claims.[66]

c. Outcome

Entering trial, Montana's NRD claim totaled $764 million, $342 million of which was restoration cost damages, $410 million of which was compensable value damages, and $12 million of which was assessment and legal costs.

---

64. *Atl. Richfield Co.*, 266 F. Supp. 2d at 1240; *see also* Montana v. Atl. Richfield Co., No. 6:83-cv-00317 (D. Mont. Apr. 20, 2000), ECF No. 1218.

65. *Atl. Richfield Co.*, 266 F. Supp. 2d at 1244–45.

66. Consent Decree for the Clark Fork River Operable Unit and for Remaining State of Montana Clark Fork Basin Natural Resource Damage Claims, Montana v. Atl. Richfield Co., No. 6:83-cv-00317 (D. Mont. Aug. 21, 2008), ECF No. 1380.

Ultimately, in the various settlement agreements just discussed, ARCO paid the state approximately $215 million to settle its NRD claims.

d. Scheduling and Timing

In January 1997, the court issued a pre-trial order segmenting the trial into five phases: (1) aquatic resources, (2) terrestrial resources, (3) groundwater resources, (4) damages, and (5) ARCO's counterclaims.[67] Per this order, the first three segments (aquatic, terrestrial, and groundwater resources) were each to be further divided into two sub-segments—the first related to liability and the second related to causation and injury.

Leading up to trial, Montana filed 13 motions for partial summary judgment by which it sought a determination on the issue of liability and the dismissal of 45 of ARCO's 49 affirmative defenses. ARCO filed five motions for partial summary judgment seeking judgment in its favor on nearly all of Montana's claims. Ruling from the bench, the court determined it would not decide any summary judgment motions prior to the presentation of evidence at trial.

A trial was held with regard to the first three segments. These segments proceeded as follows:

- Segment 1: Aquatic Resources—32 days
  - Liability subsegment lasted ten days (Mar. 3, 1997 to Mar. 20, 1997) and included over ten witnesses.
  - Injury/causation subsegment lasted 22 days (Apr. 4, 1997 to June 4, 1997) and included approximately 30 witnesses.
- Segment 2: Terrestrial Resources—12 days (Nov. 3, 1997 to Nov. 19, 1997), almost 20 witnesses.
- Segment 3: Groundwater Resources—7 days (Jan. 12, 1998 to Jan. 22, 1998), more than ten witnesses.

Issues litigated at trial were wide-ranging. For example, contested issues in the aquatic resources phase of the trial included, among other things, corporate successorship issues and which facilities' releases ARCO was liable for; the definition of a relevant baseline for the Upper Clark Fork River Basin; geographic scope of mining impacts; severity of impact to surface water, sediment, fish, and aquatic insects; causation of population impacts to fish; adequacy of the state's injury quantification; the state's compliance with the NRD

---

67. Montana v. Atl. Richfield Co., No. 6:83-cv-00317 (D. Mont. Jan. 21, 1997), ECF No. 832.

regulations (and entitlement to CERCLA's rebuttable presumption); and the availability of affirmative defenses.

Before the fourth and fifth segments could proceed, in November 1998, the parties lodged two consent decrees, partially resolving the state's and the United States' NRD claims and all of the tribes' NRD claims. These consent decrees were approved by the court in 1999. The remaining unsettled claims related to NRD in three locations: Anaconda Smelter uplands, the Butte Priority Soils OU, and the Clark Fork River OU. These claims were stayed pending issuance of a ROD relating to those sites.

After a ROD for the three remaining sites, the Anaconda Regional Waste, and the Water and Soils OU was issued and settlement negotiations failed, the court subdivided resolution of the upland area claims into multiple phases.[68] The first phase was planned to address (1) liability, causation, and injury for all three upland areas (i.e., Mt. Haggin, Smelter Hill, and Stucky Ridge); (2) damages for the Mt. Haggin area only; and (3) ARCO's counterclaims with respect to the Mt. Haggin area only. The second phase was planned to address damages and counterclaims with regard to the Smelter Hill and Stucky Ridge areas. Because facts at issue in the first phase had already been tried, and in order to determine whether a trial for this phase would be necessary, the court ordered the parties to first submit proposed findings of fact regarding these issues based on testimony and exhibits offered in the preexisting trial record. The new second phase of litigation was delayed pending EPA's approval of a remedial action plan/final design report for the Smelter Hill and Stucky Ridge areas.

After the judge assigned to the case died before ruling on the liability, causation, and injury issues, the parties agreed that the new judge should determine whether ARCO was liable for restoration costs at the upland areas based on de novo assessment and consideration of the existing record.[69] In May 2003, the court issued its order granting ARCO summary judgment and dismissing the state's upland area NRD claims on the grounds that the injuries to those areas occurred wholly before the enactment of CERCLA.[70] Eventually, and without further trial proceedings, the parties settled the remaining claims, and in 2008, a final consent decree was lodged with the court.[71]

---

68. Montana v. Atl. Richfield Co., No. 6:83-cv-00317 (D. Mont. Apr. 20, 2000), ECF No. 1218.

69. *See* Montana v. Atl. Richfield Co., 266 F. Supp. 2d 1238, 1240 (D. Mont. 2003).

70. *See id.* at 1244–45.

71. Consent Decree, *supra* note 66.

e. Use of Experts

i. Types of Experts

Whereas liability witnesses included both fact and expert witnesses, witnesses in the injury portions of trial consisted almost entirely of experts, including benthic ecologists, environmental toxicologists, NRDA/ecological risk assessment experts, and many fisheries experts.

ii. Timing of Disclosure

Montana's Report of the Natural Resource Damages Assessment, consisting of some 40 separate reports, was issued in 1995. These reports also served as Montana's expert witness disclosures in the NRD litigation.

iii. Exclusionary Rule

Prior to the commencement of trial, Montana moved to exclude witnesses so they could not hear the testimony of other witnesses. Over ARCO's objection, the court granted Montana's request to invoke the exclusionary rule.[72]

f. Issues Relating to Contingent Valuation

To determine nonuse values, Montana conducted a CV survey, sending questionnaires and making telephone calls to 1,500 randomly selected households in Montana, 933 of which participated. The survey asked participants to place a value on cleaning up the Basin. The resulting report, published in January 1995, is available at https://archive.org/details/contingentvaluat00schurich.

During discovery, a dispute arose as to whether ARCO should be allowed to discover the identity of Montana's CV survey respondents in order to depose them. It does not appear that the court ever ruled on these motions, and depositions of survey participants did not appear to play any role at trial. ARCO also filed a motion to exclude evidence of Montana's CV survey and all related testimony from trial. In an order issued on the eve of trial, the court denied ARCO's motion to exclude testimony related to the CV survey and provided no analysis explaining its decision.[73]

g. Record Review

In 1996, Montana filed a motion requesting judicial review of its NRD claims limited to the administrative record under an arbitrary and capricious

---

72. *See* Montana v. Atl. Richfield Co., No. 6:83-cv-00317 (D. Mont. Mar. 3, 1997), ECF No. 861.

73. *Id.*

standard. On the first day of trial in 1997, the court issued an opinion denying that motion. The court held that it is "appropriate to review the State's natural resource damage claims *de novo* for two reasons."[74]

First, the court held that CERCLA's statutory scheme supports a de novo determination of damages. Specifically, it held that "[t]he rebuttable presumption provision in CERCLA cannot be reconciled with a record review, because a rebuttable presumption and a record review are premised upon divergent rules of evidence," and record review would render the rebuttable presumption provision superfluous.[75] Furthermore, the court held that Congress's 1986 amendments to CERCLA, which included an amendment to explicitly require record review in the response costs context but did not include such an amendment to the NRD provisions, indicated an intent to preserve de novo review in the NRD context.

Second, the court held that a defendant has a constitutional right to a jury trial in an NRD action, and that a record review, under an arbitrary and capricious standard, interferes with that right. It stated that "[b]ecause a record review infringes upon the jury's role as the ultimate and independent fact finder, it necessarily violates the Seventh Amendment."[76]

On these two bases, the court denied Montana's motion and proceeded with a de novo trial.

h. Issues Related to Multiple Trustees

Based on a claim of trusteeship as a result of certain off-reservation treaty rights, in 1994, the tribes sought permission to intervene in the case. Because it feared that tribal intervention would delay or prejudice the adjudication of the rights asserted by the original parties and questioned certain tribal claims that overlapped with its own, Montana opposed the tribes' request for intervention as of right and argued that if the tribes were permissively allowed to intervene, they should be excluded from participating in the liability phase of trial. ARCO at first supported the tribes' motion to intervene in the hopes that a consolidated action would help avoid duplicative and/or conflicting claims and the possibility of double recovery. However, after the tribes failed to promptly assess their NRD claims, ARCO eventually opposed the tribes' intervention.

---

74. Montana v. Atl. Richfield Co., No. CV-83-317-HLN-PGH, 1997 U.S. Dist. LEXIS 24671, at *23–24 (D. Mont. Feb. 28, 1997 (decided); Mar. 3, 1997 (filed)).

75. *Id.* at *24–25.

76. *Id.* at *36.

Ultimately, the court granted the tribes' limited permissive intervention, allowing them to attend trial, but not allowing them to participate in the presentation of the evidence. The court further provided that upon conclusion of the presentation of evidence in each of the first three resource segments of trial, the tribes would be allowed to identify, via motion, "any natural resource damage claims they have against ARCO, which are separate and distinct from the natural resource damage claims advanced by the State."[77] If the tribes were successful in convincing the court that they possessed unique claims, the court would permit them to conduct discovery and present evidence on such claims in a separate proceeding. The tribes did move for a trial regarding their aquatic resources damages claims and concurrently filed a complaint.

The claims of the tribes were settled in one of the two 1998 consent decrees, before the court ruled on the tribes' motion. Pursuant to the consent decree, ARCO agreed to pay $18.3 million to the tribes in full settlement of the tribes' NRD claims. In the same 1999 consent decree, ARCO agreed to pay the United States $1.7 million in settlement of all of the United States' NRD claims, excluding claims relating to the Grant Kohrs Ranch National Historic Site and 15 parcels of BLM land within the riparian zone of the Clark Fork River. The United States' reserved NRD claims were ultimately settled in a 2008 consent decree for an additional payment of $3.35 million.[78]

i. Burden of Proof and the Rebuttable Presumption

In its order denying record review, the court addressed in dicta the reach of the CERCLA rebuttable presumption. In holding that the idea of record review was at odds with the existence of CERCLA rebuttable presumption, it stated that "a rebuttable presumption does not alter the burden of proof, which always remains with the plaintiff." Further, the court stated that

> [t]he rebuttable presumption, which carries sufficient weight to constitute a *prima facia* case, merely operates to shift the burden of production to the opposing party to rebut the presumption, by offering evidence which would support a finding that the presumed fact does not exist. Once the presumption is rebutted, the presumption disappears from the case. Accordingly, the rebuttable presumption provision in CERCLA contemplates that the burden of proof in a natural resource damage action shall always remain with the plaintiff.[79]

---

77. Montana v. Atl. Richfield Co., No. 6:83-cv-00317, slip op. at 6 (D. Mont. Jan. 21, 1997), ECF No. 833.

78. Consent Decree, *supra* note 66, ¶ 20.

79. *Atl. Richfield Co.*, 1997 U.S. Dist. LEXIS 24671, at *25 (citations omitted).

3. Little Salmon River Fungicide Spill (D. Idaho 1988–1991)
Idaho v. Southern Refrigerated Transport, Inc., No. 1:88-cv-01279-MHW

a. Summary
The *Southern Refrigerated Transport* trial related to a 1987 spill of fungicide on the banks of the Little Salmon River that all parties agreed resulted in impacts to the fish populations of the river. After a 12-day bench trial, the court, relying on various pieces of evidence from both parties, essentially conducted its own NRDA to determine the total value of NRD liability resulting from the spill.

b. The Facts
On December 19, 1987, a tractor trailer containing over 60 drums of Vitavax 200, an agricultural fungicide, overturned on the banks of the Little Salmon River near New Meadows, Idaho. An estimated 375 gallons of Vitavax 200 were unsalvageable—an estimated 110 to 250 gallons of which reached the river, with the remainder absorbed by soil along the river bank.

Plaintiff, the state of Idaho, brought claims seeking response costs, NRDA costs, civil penalties, and NRD under CERCLA, the Idaho Hazardous Materials/Hazardous Waste Transportation Act, the Idaho Environmental Protection and Health Act, and Idaho common law. The court granted Idaho's motion for summary judgment on the question of liability prior to trial.[80] At trial, the parties agreed that a variety of fish species were affected by the spill, and the litigation focused on the level of impact to a single species—the steelhead. Idaho alleged that the fungicide spill killed 90 to 100 percent of fish in the Little Salmon River. Trial focused on the extent of, and valuation of, this injury.

c. Outcome
After a 12-day trial, the court made detailed factual findings regarding the extent of injury—determining both the pre-spill baseline number of steelhead in the river and the exact number of fish killed by the spill. Table 7.2 summarizes the court's ultimate findings.[81]

---

80. *See* Idaho v. S. Refrig. Transp. Inc., No. 88-1279, 1991 WL 22479, at *1 (D. Idaho Jan. 24, 1991) (noting that court held two defendants strictly liable under CERCLA as owners/operators of a facility).

81. *See* S. Refrig. Transp., 1991 WL 22479, at *17–23.

Table 7.2 The Court's Findings

	Trustee Position	Court Holding
Total Fish Prior to the Spill	336,510	304,807
Total Fish Present After the Spill	62,335	72,786
Total Fish Killed by the Spill	274,175	43,835
Total Commercial Value of Fish Killed	$169,029	$31,702
Total Recreational Value Lost	$48,426	$7,672
Total Existence Value Lost	$28,645	$0
Total Assessment Value	$9,266.48	$6,079.37
Total NRD Judgment	$255,375.48	$45,453.37

d. Evidentiary Issues

i. Injury Assessment Techniques

Baseline: Critical to the court's findings was an analysis of the baseline number of fish in the river. The government's experts relied on pre-spill snorkeling surveys conducted in areas they contended were representative of the 24 miles of river impacted by the spill, but admitted that a larger sample would have provided more accurate results. Defendants argued that these surveys were not sufficiently representative to measure pre-spill populations. The court sided with the state, finding that the snorkel surveys were sufficient to establish baseline because they were the best and only information available to answer the baseline question, and were sufficient to rise above the level of speculation and conjecture. It stated that "[t]he snorkel surveys provide the best information available, and, in fact, the only information that can be produced on this issue. The court further finds that these scientific studies, not prepared with any view towards litigation, rise above the level of speculation and conjecture."[82]

Toxicity: There were no chemistry samples taken in the Little Salmon River following the spill. Idaho relied on admittedly nonrepresentative toxicity test results and incomplete post-spill electrofishing surveys to determine that a 90 to 100 percent fish kill occurred. Defendants relied on computer models to show that chemical concentrations would have rapidly diluted. The court ultimately relied on the fate modeling of the defendants, combined with the

---

82. *Id.* at *12.

toxicity test results of the government, to determine that Idaho had not met its burden of proof in claiming that a high fish kill rate occurred. Critical to the court's conclusion were the facts that only 342 dead fish were collected after the spill and that the Little Salmon River experienced a record fish run in 1990. The court stated that "[i]t seems only logical that if 274,000 fish were killed, more than 342 would have been seen and/or collected following the spill."[83] To determine the actual post-spill number of fish, the court again relied on snorkel studies.

ii. Calculation of Value Lost

Idaho asserted damages for three types of uses of the killed fish: commercial, recreational, and existence (or nonuse).

Commercial Use Value: The court found that Idaho met its burden of proof with regard to its claim for commercial use damages, which were measured as the market price or exchange value of the resource.

Recreational Use Value: The court also found that Idaho met its burden of proof with regard to the recreational value of each individual fish killed, determined based on a "travel cost method" study performed by various federal agencies and the University of Idaho for the purpose of resource management, which looked at people's actual expenditures associated with recreationally catching a single fish. However, the court found Idaho had not met its burden of proof with regard to its claim for value lost due to fishing season closures. The court agreed that such a claim could theoretically exist, but held that

> [f]rom the evidence presented, an inference could be drawn that perhaps some fishing trips were canceled when the season was closed. However, an equally plausible inference is that steelhead fishermen, being a particularly determined lot who fish in all types of weather conditions, merely traveled a few more miles to fish at an equally comparable location.[84]

Existence Value: Idaho attempted to prove nonuse values through reliance on a CV survey. The court recognized that nonuse values may theoretically be recoverable, but found that "the study is not persuasive and it would be conjecture and speculation to allow damages based on this study. Idaho must prove its damages with reasonable certainty and this study does not do

---

83. *Id.* at *16.
84. *Id.* at *21.

so."[85] Key to this finding was the fact that the survey targeted the existence value of fish in the entire river basin and did not specifically explore the existence value of the fewer fish at issue in the litigation.

e. Use of Experts

Experts were used extensively to proffer NRD-related testimony. It does not appear that *Daubert* motions played a substantial factor.

f. Burden of Proof and the Rebuttable Presumption

The post-trial ruling does not discuss the rebuttable presumption. The court stated that, "Idaho has the burden of proving its damages by a preponderance of the evidence and it is well-established that damages cannot be based on speculation or conjecture."[86] This could be a result of the fact that DOI's CERCLA NRDA regulations, which a trustee must follow to gain the benefit of the rebuttable presumption, were still very new at the time this action was initiated in the fall of 1988, and the plaintiff was a state, not a federal, trustee.

g. Treatment of Causation

The court appears to have applied a "but for" causation standard, stating, for example, that "[b]ut for [the truck driver's] negligence, the truck would not have overturned, the Vitavax 200 would not have been released into the Little Salmon River, and fish would not have been killed."[87]

4. Montrose Chemical/Palos Verdes Shelf (C.D. Cal. 1990–2001)

United States v. Montrose Chemical Corporation of California, No. 2:90-cv-03122-R

a. Summary

The *Montrose* CERCLA NRD case involved DDT and PCB contamination in sediments on the Palos Verdes shelf off the coast of California. The case was originally filed by the United States and the state of California in June 1990 but did not go to trial until late 2000. Over the course of the litigation, the case produced numerous important rulings on NRD matters. Defendants ultimately settled for a total of $140.2 million.

---

85. *Id.* at *19.
86. *Id.* at *12.
87. *Id.* at *9.

b. The Facts

This case concerned DDT and PCB contamination on the Palos Verdes shelf off the coast of Los Angeles. According to the government's complaint, from 1947 to 1982, the Montrose Chemical facility discharged 5.5 million pounds of DDT through the Los Angeles County sewer system, through ocean dumping, surface runoff, and aerial deposition from manufacturing operations. Also, according to the complaint, companies operating an electrical transmission equipment repair plant and a paper manufacturing plant discharged PCBs into the sewer system. Trustees alleged that the PCB and DDT contamination was present on the ocean floor in sediment deposits from 5 centimeters to greater than 60 centimeters thick. The trustees included NOAA, USFWS, the U.S. National Park Service, the California Department of Fish and Game, the California Department of Parks and Recreation, and the California State Lands Commission.

In 1990, the United States and the state of California filed a claim alleging that nine separate corporate defendants released DDT and PCBs into the affected areas. The complaint alleged injury to birds, fish, and marine mammals as a result of DDT and PCB contamination. Plaintiffs added additional defendant corporations and sanitation companies from several California municipalities as third-party defendants. According to the government, the contamination affected the San Pedro Channel, the Palos Verde Shelf, the Los Angeles–Long Beach Harbors, and the area surrounding Santa Catalina Island and the Channel Islands.

Defendants responded that plaintiffs exaggerated the extent of contamination and that populations and ecosystems alleged to have been harmed were comparable to those in other areas or, to the extent they had been injured, had largely recovered.

At the time of the suit, plaintiffs had not conducted a NRDA, but they were concerned about the running of the statute of limitations.[88] The trustees finalized a damage assessment case management plan in January 1992. Thus, the assessment process was on a parallel track with the litigation.

On March 19, 1991, the matter was referred to a special master for discovery and pre-trial motions. The court dismissed the complaint with leave to

---

88. In 1995, the district court dismissed NRD claims on the grounds that the statute of limitations had run, citing 42 U.S.C. § 9613(g)(1), which requires the trustees to bring suit within the later of three years after discovery of the loss or promulgation of final DOI regulations. The Ninth Circuit reversed, finding that the district court set the date of promulgation of DOI regulations about seven months too early. California v. Montrose Chem. Corp. of Cal., 104 F.3d 1507 (9th Cir. 1997); *see also* Chapter 3, Section A.1.a.

amend in March 1991 (see discussion of causation ruling later in the chapter). An amended complaint was filed in August 1991. A long period of discovery and motions practice followed, punctuated by a two-year stay of discovery after the district court dismissed the NRD claims on statute of limitations grounds, and the plaintiffs appealed.

The trustees announced settlements with local government entities (LGEs) and the paper manufacturing defendants in 1993. The corporate defendants appealed the settlement with LGEs, and the Ninth Circuit overturned the LGE settlement because the trustees did not advance a public estimate of the total restoration costs.[89]

Plaintiffs asked for reassignment based on alleged bias of the original trial judge. The Ninth Circuit declined to reassign, but the case was transferred to a new judge on November 10, 1999.

The new judge established a final discovery and trial schedule in February 2000. On October 2, 2000, the court granted partial summary judgment on the issue of injury to birds from DDT, based on evidence that peregrine falcons on the Channel Islands had thin egg shells and bald eagles there were unable to reproduce absent human intervention.[90] On the fifth day of trial, a settlement was announced and further proceedings were delayed. A final settlement was approved in March 2001.

c. Outcome

On the fifth day of trial in October 2000, the parties announced that they had reached settlement. By 2001, the NRD defendants had all agreed to a final settlement, totaling $140.2 million. The total amount recovered for environmental restoration in this area was $137.5 million. A restoration plan was finalized in 2005, and restoration is still ongoing. Restoration projects include artificial reefs to provide new habitat for fish and a program to reintroduce bald eagles and peregrine falcons to Santa Catalina and the other Channel Islands.

d. Scheduling and Timing

i. Sufficiency of Facts Alleged in an NRD Complaint

The court initially dismissed plaintiffs' NRD claim, holding that "[t]he allegations in the first claim for relief fail adequately to apprise the Court and

---

89. United States v. Montrose Chem. Corp. of Cal., 50 F.3d 741 (9th Cir. 1995).

90. United States v. Montrose Chem. Corp. of Cal., No. 2:90-cv-03122 (C.D. Cal. Oct. 3, 2000), ECF No. 2518.

defendants of the nature of, and basis for, the claim."[91] The court ordered plaintiffs to file an amended complaint to cure these defects and specifically required that the amended complaint allege the following:

> (1) WHAT natural resources have been injured; *i.e.,* plaintiffs shall identify each alleged injury to natural resources for which plaintiffs seek to recover natural resource damages, and shall identify the specific natural resource injured (*e.g.,* the particular species of fish, bird, mammal or other natural resource in issue); (2) the specific locations WHERE each such injury has occurred and where the releases of hazardous substances alleged to be the sole or substantially contributing cause of each such injury occurred; . . . (3) WHEN each such injury occurred and the releases occurred; and (4) WHICH defendant's release(s) of WHAT hazardous substance was the sole or substantially contributing cause of each such injury, and by what pathway exposure to the hazardous substance occurred.[92]

ii. Request for Reassignment

In its appeal of several district court orders, the plaintiff trustees also requested that, on remand, the Ninth Circuit reassign the case to a different district court judge. Their basis for this request was several comments made by the district court judge assigned to the case at a March 22, 1995, hearing, including references to environmental scientists as "pointy heads" and "so-called experts" and general displeasure with the government, and the U.S. Department of Justice in particular. The Ninth Circuit agreed that "these comments are not as restrained as we would wish them to be," but denied the request, stating that "there is no indication in the March 22, 1995 transcript that the judge was ruling against the government based upon his often expressed opinions concerning environmental science or the government."[93]

e. Use of Experts

Like other NRD trials, this trial relied heavily on experts. The trustees initially produced 28 expert reports and designated 84 expert witnesses, and submitted 12 supplemental reports.[94] The trustees withdrew all but 35 experts by August

---

91. United States v. Montrose Chem. Corp. of Cal., No. CV 90-3122 AAH (JRX), 1991 WL 183147, at *1 (C.D. Cal. Mar. 29, 1991).

92. *Id.*

93. *Montrose*, 104 F.3d at 1521.

94. *See* Montrose Natural Resource Damage Assessment and Litigation Timeline, https://www.gc.noaa.gov/gc-rp/mon-E-F.pdf.

1997. Depositions began in March 1995 and continued until April 2000. Pursuant to orders from the new judge assigned to the case in November 1999, final expert designations were submitted in April 2000. Defendants ultimately designated 27 experts.

Pursuant to a local rule allowing admission of expert affidavits into evidence in non-jury trials, the court granted the government's request to limit direct testimony of experts to a written narrative statement.[95] The parties could conduct live testimony for highlighting particular portions, but the side calling the witness was limited to either 20 minutes for fact witnesses or 40 minutes for expert witnesses.[96]

The court ruled on a number of motions to exclude witnesses and testimony on various grounds, but did so without explanation or analysis. The most significant ruling was the court's exclusion of the trustees' CV study, discussed in greater detail later. The court also excluded 13 trustee experts for alleged misconduct involving omission of relevant data from final reports. In response to a defense motion for sanctions for the misconduct, the court precluded the government from substituting any experts for the ones stricken, precluded the government from recovering costs associated with the stricken reports, and encouraged defendants to bring motions seeking recovery of their costs associated with the reports.[97]

f.   Discovery Issues

Plaintiffs sought to preclude discovery related to withdrawn experts. The special master agreed but the district court reversed, finding that, "Defendants may conduct discovery reasonably calculated, among other things, to obtain evidence to substantiate their allegations of misconduct by Plaintiffs or their experts, including deposing all persons designated by Plaintiffs as experts, including withdrawn experts."[98]

In 1997, EPA initiated administrative procedures to conduct an engineering evaluation and cost analysis for the offshore contamination. Plaintiffs moved to restrict discovery regarding EPA's actions. The special master agreed but the court reversed:

---

95. United States v. Montrose Chem. Corp. of Cal., No. 2:90-cv-03122-R (C.D. Cal. June 27, 2000), ECF No. 2031.

96. *Id.*

97. United States v. Montrose Chem. Corp. of Cal., No. 2:90-cv-03122 (C.D. Cal. Aug. 1, 2000), ECF No. 2085.

98. United States v. Montrose Chem. Corp. of Cal., 980 F. Supp. 1112, 1113 (C.D. Cal. 1997).

The Court does not need to determine at this time what the scope of judicial review of any action yet to be taken by EPA would be. Defendants are entitled, among other things, to conduct discovery reasonably calculated to obtain evidence which the Court may use to supplement any administrative record compiled or to be compiled by the EPA.[99]

g. Burden of Proof and the Rebuttable Presumption

i. Rebuttable Presumption

In a motion filed in 1993, Westinghouse sought to preclude DOI from relying on the rebuttable presumption. Westinghouse argued that plaintiffs had violated 43 C.F.R. § 11.31(a)(4)[100] by not sharing data with the defendants. Plaintiffs argued that the court-mandated procedures for sharing information during litigation satisfied the regulatory requirements. Westinghouse also argued that plaintiffs had illegitimately delayed announcing whether they would rely on the rebuttable presumption. Plaintiffs argued that the motion was premature because they had not yet decided whether to rely on the presumption and had not yet submitted a formal Report of Assessment to the court, which would be required under the regulations.

The district court denied Westinghouse's motion, noting that "Plaintiffs persuade the Court that the Master's Order Re: Discovery Coordination provides for full compliance with any requirements of the DOI regulation."[101] The court did, however, express its discomfort with potential delay of the government's decision to take advantage of the rebuttable presumption, stating that "this Court agrees with Westinghouse that Plaintiffs should not be allowed, at the eve of trial, to spring on the Defendants Plaintiffs' decision to avail themselves of the presumption on the eve of trial."[102] Ultimately, plaintiffs did not seek to avail themselves of the presumption.

ii. Per Se Injury

A major component of the trustee's claim relied on a per se injury under CERCLA. The United States and California argued that since there were concentrations of DDT in the water column above the Palos Verdes shelf that exceeded the EPA water quality criterion of one part per billion, the surface

---

99. *Id.*

100. That section provided: "The Assessment Plan shall contain procedures and schedules for sharing data, split samples, and results of analyses, when requested, with any identified potentially responsible parties and other natural resource trustees."

101. United States v. Montrose Chem. Corp. of Cal., 835 F. Supp. 534, 541 (C.D. Cal. 1993).

102. *Id.* at 540–41.

water was injured as a matter of law.[103] For per se injury, assuming that the parties agree on the integrity of the data, the trustees can establish injury by comparing environmental data to regulatory criteria.

h. Treatment of Causation

The court held in 1991 that trustees "must show that a defendant's release of a hazardous substance was the sole or substantially contributing cause of each alleged injury to natural resources."[104] This test is now referred to as the "sole or substantially contributing cause" standard.[105] Although the court's order cited no authority and resulted from an un-noticed and un-briefed oral motion, at least one other federal court has, in dicta, validated this approach for situations where releases were not commingled.[106]

i. Issues Relating to Contingent Valuation

The trustees conducted CV surveys[107] to calculate lost nonuse value for affected resources. The studies themselves cost eight to ten million dollars, or up to a third of the total NRDA costs of $30 million. As part of the surveys, the researchers made presentations to the survey respondents and represented that bald eagles, peregrine falcons, white croaker, and kelp bass had reproductive problems in the affected area. The presentations also included statements about the time period for natural recovery and the shorter time period for recovery if certain remedies were implemented. The study found losses of between $305 million and $575 million. To obtain that figure, the researchers determined that respondents in the survey would be willing to pay, on average, $29.52 in one survey, and $55.58 in the other, to implement the remedy. They then multiplied that amount by the number of households in California (10.3 million).

---

103. Memorandum of Contentions of Law and Fact of Plaintiffs United States and State of California at 19, United States v. Montrose Chem. Corp. of Cal., No. CV 90-3122-R (C.D. Cal. Aug. 7, 2000), ECF No. 2109.

104. United States v. Montrose Chem. Corp., No. CV 90-3122 AAH (JRX), 1991 WL 183147, at *1 (C.D. Cal. Mar. 29, 1991).

105. *See* discussion in Chapter 3, Section H.1.

106. *See* Coeur d'Alene Tribe v. ASARCO Inc., No. 3:96-cv-00122-EJL, slip op. at 11 (D. Idaho Mar. 30, 2001), ECF No. 1101 ("In cases where releases have *not* been commingled, the burden would be to show that such release was the sole or proximate cause to the injury to the natural resources.").

107. *See* NAT. RES. DAMAGE ASSESSMENT, INC., PROSPECTIVE INTERIM LOST USE VALUE DUE TO DDT AND PCB CONTAMINATION IN THE SOUTHERN CALIFORNIA BIGHT, Vol. I (1994), https://pprg.stanford.edu/wp-content/uploads/1994-Montrose-Report.pdf.

Defendants conducted extensive discovery on the surveys, including depositions of the NOAA researchers who provided information to the economists who conducted the surveys. The defendants found that the assumed injuries were not accurately stated in the survey questions, among other problems. For example, in deposition testimony, NOAA scientists contradicted assertions made in the survey about reproductive problems experienced by white croaker in the area. The court granted the defendants' motion to exclude the trustees' CV studies.[108]

j. Issues Related to Multiple Trustees

Defendant Westinghouse argued that the Submerged Lands Act (SLA)[109] precluded federal trustees from asserting damages to resources within the state's three-mile ocean boundary. Section 1311 of the SLA gives states ownership of the submerged lands and the natural resources within the waters included in the state's maritime borders (usually three miles from shore). The special master rejected these arguments and dismissed Westinghouse's underlying motion, both on procedural and substantive grounds. The district court judge upheld the dismissal on procedural grounds only and did not reach the substantive issue.[110]

5. Highland Bayou Oil Spill (S.D. Tex. 2008–2009)

United States v. Viking Resources, No. 4:08-cv-01291

a. Summary

The Highland Bayou oil spill litigation involved a six-day jury trial in 2009 related to liability arising from an oil spill in Galveston County, Texas. At trial, the United States sought to recover NRDA costs the USCG's National Pollution Funds Center (NPFC) had negotiated and paid to the state of Texas for its assessment of damage resulting from the spill. Ultimately, the jury found that the defendant was not liable for the spill under OPA and never reached a determination regarding the NRDA costs the United States sought to recover.

b. The Facts

On December 18, 2004, an oil spill originated from an old tank battery near Hitchcock, Galveston County, Texas. The oil flowed into a wetland

---

108. United States v. Montrose Chem. Corp. of Cal., No. CV 90-3122-R (C.D. Cal. Apr. 17, 2000), ECF No. 1914.

109. 43 U.S.C. §§ 1301–1356b.

110. United States v. Montrose Chem. Corp. of Cal., 835 F. Supp. 534 (C.D. Cal. 1993), *rev'd on other grounds*, 104 F.3d 1507 (9th Cir. 1997).

immediately adjacent to Highland Bayou. The USCG, NOAA, and EPA conducted removal operations, which were complete by January 13, 2005, and involved the collection of 225 barrels of oil from the land, water, and wetlands.

In November 2006, the Texas General Land Office (TGLO) submitted a claim to the NPFC for past and future NRDA costs arising from the Highland Bayou spill. The NPFC ultimately determined that $271,179 of the requested assessment costs were reasonable and compensable—$6,111 related to past NRDA costs, $230,495 related to future NRDA costs, and $34,574 for "unforeseen" future NRDA costs. TGLO accepted this offer, and the NPFC and TGLO entered a settlement agreement to that effect.

In 2008, the United States filed suit against Viking Resources and Roger Chambers, the owner of Viking, to recover the $271,179 in NRDA costs, along with almost $400,000 in response costs related to the spill. Viking Resources was the last known lessee and operator of the land where the old tank battery was located. However, Viking and Chambers contended throughout the case and at trial that Viking was not an "owner" of the tank battery itself and that neither Viking nor Chambers was a liable party under OPA. In a February 2009 pre-trial order, the court denied cross-motions for summary judgment on the question of liability, and held that in order to demonstrate liability, the United States would have to show that Viking and Chambers owned or operated the tank battery itself, not just the underlying land.[111]

c. Outcome

After a six-day jury trial, the jury found that the government had not met its burden of proof in showing that Viking and/or Chambers owned the old tank battery itself.[112] As a result of this finding, the jury never reached the question of what response or NRDA costs were recoverable under OPA.

d. Scheduling and Timing

i. Right to Jury Trial

The United States filed a motion to strike defendants' jury demand, arguing that defendants were not entitled to a jury trial in this case. In a February 11, 2009 order, the court found that the Seventh Amendment to the U.S. Constitution did not provide a right to a jury trial for the United States' cost recovery claims, but that it did provide such a right with regard to factual issues

---

111. United States v. Viking Res., Inc., 607 F. Supp. 2d 808, 818 (S.D. Tex. 2009).

112. Verdict Form, United States v. Viking Res., Inc., No. 4:08-cv-01291 (S.D. Tex. July 21, 2009), ECF No. 108.

surrounding the question of liability under OPA and at least one component of the United States' NRD claim.[113] The court concluded that "judicial efficiency would be best promoted by ordering that the entire case be tried to a jury," but that for those issues that were equitable in nature, and therefore not triable of right by jury, the jury's verdict would be only advisory.[114]

ii. Bifurcation of Trial

Defendants filed an unopposed motion to separate the trials for determination on liability and damages. The court denied the motion.[115] It found that because both factual issues related to liability and the NRD claims contained issues that triggered a right to a jury trial, bifurcation would require two jury trials, and two jury trials would not be expedient or promote judicial economy.

e. Evidentiary Issues

i. Basis for Recovery of NPFC Costs

As a basis for summary judgment on the $271,179.82 in NRDA costs sought by the United States, the United States cited the declaration of Kristina Williams, an employee of the NRD Claims Division of the NPFC. Williams averred that the NPFC and the NRD trustees had entered a settlement agreement forming the basis for the asserted NRDA costs value.[116] Chambers and Viking argued, among other things, that Williams' affidavit was an improper basis for summary judgment because it failed to provide the underlying data, or even the underlying settlement agreement, upon which her averments were based. In its February 11, 2009, order, the court agreed and denied the United States' motion for summary judgment on the NRD claims.[117]

f. Use of Experts

The only NRD witness on either plaintiffs' or defendants' trial witness lists was the chief of the NPFC's NRD Claims Division. He testified for the defense.

g. Burden of Proof and the Rebuttable Presumption

The question of whether the United States was entitled to the benefit of a rebuttable presumption was never briefed.

---

113. *Viking Res., Inc.*, 607 F. Supp. 2d at 829–33.

114. *Id.* at 832.

115. *Id.* at 833.

116. Declaration of Kristina Williams, United States v. Viking Res., Inc., No. 4:08-cv-01291 (S.D. Tex. Nov. 17, 2008), ECF No. 23-3.

117. *Viking Res., Inc.*, 607 F. Supp. 2d at 825.

The court's jury instruction adopted a preponderance of the evidence standard for all the United States' claims, including the NRD claims. The Jury Verdict Form asked the following question with regard to NRD:

> Does the Jury unanimously find by a preponderance of the evidence that the U.S. Coast Guard, to include actions taken by the Texas General Land Office, incurred natural resource damages caused by the Highlands Bayou oil spill?[118]

It then included a blank space for the jury to insert its own judgment with regard to the value of NRD costs the United States had incurred. Because it made a dispositive ruling with regard to liability, the jury never reached these questions.

h. Treatment of Causation

NRD causation was not an issue in this litigation, presumably because the only NRD costs plaintiffs sought were assessment costs.

The United States' briefing argued that the defendants were strictly liable for the entire value of NRDA costs deemed reasonable by the NPFC. As discussed earlier, however, the court found that the United States proffered insufficient evidence supporting a finding of summary judgment with regard to this value.[119] Although the value paid by the NPFC appears to have been the only potential value on the table at trial, the court's jury instructions gave the jury the option of determining on its own the exact value of NRDA costs recoverable.

6. Bayway and Bayonne (N.J. Super. Ct., Union Co. 2004–2014)

New Jersey Department of Environmental Protection v. Exxon Mobil Corp., No. UNN-L-3026-04

a. Summary

New Jersey Department of Environmental Protection v. Exxon Mobil Corp. was an NRD case brought by the state of New Jersey under the New Jersey Spill Act related to oil contamination caused by decades of operating petroleum refineries and petrochemical plants in New Jersey. After years of litigation, including two interlocutory appeals and entry of summary judgment finding Exxon Mobil (Exxon) strictly liable for NRD, an eight-month trial to address

---

118. Verdict Form, *supra* note 112, at 9.
119. *Viking Res., Inc.*, 607 F. Supp. 2d at 825.

valuation of damages occurred in 2014. The state of New Jersey originally sought $10.1 billion in NRD ($2.6 billion in primary restoration, $6.3 billion in compensatory restoration, and $1.2 billion in NRDA costs). After trial, but before the court could rule, the parties settled all the claims for a total of $225 million. Environmental groups challenged the amount, but the superior court nonetheless approved the settlement. This decision was affirmed on appeal.[120]

b. The Facts

Starting in the early twentieth century, Exxon operated petroleum refineries and petrochemical plants in Linden, New Jersey (the "Bayway Refinery Site") and Bayonne, New Jersey (the "Bayonne Terminals Site"). In 2004, the New Jersey Department of Environmental Protection (NJDEP) and the New Jersey Spill Compensation Fund (the NJ Fund) filed two separate actions, one in New Jersey Superior Court in Union County alleging claims against Exxon related to the Bayway Refinery Site (the Bayway Matter), and one in New Jersey Superior Court in Hudson County alleging claims against Exxon and AGC Chemicals America related to the Bayonne Terminals Site (the Bayonne Matter). The two cases were consolidated in 2005.

With respect to both sites, the complaints alleged that Exxon's petroleum refining and petrochemical operations caused injury to groundwater, surface water, and ecological resources in violation of New Jersey's Spill Compensation and Control Act (NJ Spill Act). The state sought $8.9 billion in NRD, including compensation for the restoration of over 570 acres of on-site wetlands as well as the creation of over 33,000 acres of new wetlands and forests. In addition to the NRD claims, plaintiffs alleged common law nuisance and trespass claims and sought reimbursements of the state's response costs as well as declaratory and injunctive relief.

Prior to trial, numerous motions were ruled upon, and there were two interlocutory appeals. One of these interlocutory appeals related to the state's ability to recover for loss of use damages. As discussed in more detail later in the chapter, the trial court found that the NJ Spill Act did not provide this relief, but the appellate court disagreed. Summary judgment was entered against Exxon, finding it liable for NRD, including loss of use damages, under the NJ Spill Act. Liability for NRD under common law was also addressed at the summary judgment stage—Exxon was found liable under public nuisance, trespass, and strict liability theories, but plaintiffs' claim for unjust enrichment

---

120. N.J. Dep't of Envtl. Prot. v. Exxon Mobil Corp., 453 N.J. Super. 272 (App. Div. 2018).

was dismissed. The case involved a variety of other motions, including discovery motions, expert challenges, and evidentiary motions.

After a decade of litigation, an eight-month bench trial was held. Before the court could issue a post-trial ruling, however, the parties settled the claims with Exxon agreeing to pay the state $225 million in NRD. The consent decree received significant criticism during the notice and comment period and was challenged in court by environmental groups. The superior court nonetheless affirmed the settlement and was affirmed on appeal.

c. Outcome

At trial, NJDEP sought to recover $10.1 billion in NRD ($2.6 billion in primary restoration, $6.3 billion in compensatory restoration, and $1.2 billion in NRDA costs). Exxon argued for an award of no damages, asserting that the state had not met its burden of proof. However, Exxon also proposed several alternative awards, the first for nominal damages, and the second for damages of $3 million (a number arrived upon by Exxon's experts' HEA and presented as an alternative to the state's HEA). The final post-trial NRD settlement value was $225 million.

The state of New Jersey hired outside special counsel, Allan Kanner & Associates, P.C., to prosecute the case on a contingency fee basis. In accordance with that arrangement, after expenses were reimbursed, outside special counsel was paid 20 percent of the total verdict amount.

d. Collateral Challenges

During the notice and comment period with regard to the $225 million settlement, NJDEP received over 16,000 comments, primarily objections. Several objectioners, most notable a state senator from the relevant area and several environmental groups, also sought intervention in the litigation to oppose entry of the settlement. The superior court denied their intervention into the proceeding, holding that in order to intervene as of right, the movants must demonstrate standing, and they could not do so because, among other reasons, they were not trustees entitled to bring an NRD action.[121] However, the superior court suggested, instead, that the movants apply for amicus status and delayed oral argument on the approval of the consent judgment in order to allow them to fully participate as amici.

---

121. N.J. Dep't of Envtl. Prot. v. Exxon Mobil Corp., No. UNN-L-3026-04, slip op. at 32 (N.J. Super. Ct. Law Div. July 13, 2015).

The amici made several arguments contesting the settlement, all centered around the contention that the amount of the settlement, $225 million for NRD at the Bayway and Bayonne sites as well as 16 other sites throughout New Jersey, was "suspiciously low" and represented an abrupt change in course given the NJDEP's assessment of $8.9 billion in NRD that included only the Bayway and Bayonne sites.

The superior court subsequently approved the consent judgment. In the 81-page order discussing its approval, the court noted that its task in approving a consent decree is "'quite limited' [but] not without teeth."[122] The court found the settlement was procedurally fair because "the negotiations [were] between two highly sophisticated parties with sharply conflicting interests [that] were full of adversarial vigor."[123] It then discussed in detail the potential litigation risks for NJDEP had it not settled and NJDEP's analysis in entering the settlement, noting that the

> average per-acre NRD recovery was $83,770. Had the State recovered this amount per-acre for Bayway/Bayonne, Exxon's payment for these sites would have only been approximately $159 million. As $220 million of the total $225 million from the Proposed Consent Judgment is for the Bayway/Bayonne recovery, this means the State beat its historical average by $61 million.[124]

The state senator and the environmental groups filed for appeal, arguing that they were improperly denied the right to fully intervene in the consent decree fairness proceeding and that, independent of their right to intervene in that proceeding, that they had a right to appeal the entry of the consent decree. The appellate court agreed with the superior court that, because they had no right to recover NRD, the state senator and the environmental groups did not have a right to fully intervene in the fairness proceeding, but agreed with the environmental groups that they nonetheless had a right to appeal entry of the consent decree.[125] The appellate court stated that "we have not necessarily preconditioned the right to appeal upon participation in the prior proceeding," and concluded that an individual, like the state senator, lacks standing to appeal an NRD consent decree, but that the environmental groups, because they broadly represent citizens' interests throughout the

---

122. N.J. Dep't of Envtl. Prot. v. Exxon Mobil Corp., 453 N.J. Super. 588, 618 (Law Div. 2015).

123. *Id.* at 623.

124. *Id.* at 635.

125. N.J. Dep't of Envtl. Prot. v. Exxon Mobil Corp., 181 A.3d 257, 274–75 (N.J. Super. Ct. App. Div. 2018).

states, did have standing to appeal.[126] Nonetheless, the appellate court upheld the superior court's entry of the settlement, finding no abuse of discretion.[127] The New Jersey Supreme Court declined to review the case, ending 14 years of litigation.[128]

e. Summary Judgment

i. Geographic Scope of Claims

Exxon filed a number of motions for summary judgment attempting to limit the geographic extent of the claims by arguing that certain areas covered by the claims were not held in the public trust and thus were not subject to NRD claims under the NJ Spill Act or the common law. For example, Exxon argued that private property above the mean high tide mark and wetlands in private ownership were not part of the public trust. The court denied these motions.[129]

ii. Availability of NRD under the NJ Spill Act

NJDEP moved for partial summary judgment seeking a determination that Exxon was strictly liable for all cleanup, removal, and NRD costs under the NJ Spill Act. Exxon cross-moved for summary judgment on the ground that the NJ Spill Act does not provide for liability for loss of use of natural resources. The trial court held that Exxon was strictly liable under the NJ Spill Act for NRD, including restoration, but dismissed NJDEP's statutory claims for loss of use damages.[130] The appellate court reversed this determination, finding that, under the NJ Spill Act, the NJDEP was able to recover compensation for the loss of use of natural resources.[131]

iii. Common Law Claims

In 2008, the court entered summary judgment against defendants holding that Exxon's behavior constituted an abnormally dangerous activity and that Exxon was liable for common law public nuisance, but held that NJDEP was not allowed to recover loss of use damages pursuant to these common law

---

126. *Id.* at 273–74.

127. *Id.* at 278.

128. N.J. Dep't of Envtl. Prot. v. Exxon Mobil Corp., 185 A.3d 876 (N.J. 2018).

129. N.J. Dep't of Envtl. Prot. v. Exxon Mobil Corp., No. UNN-L-3026-04, 2009 WL 2494754 (N.J. Super. Ct. Law Div. July 24, 2009).

130. N.J. Dep't of Envtl. Prot. v. Exxon Mobil Corp., No. UNN-L-3026-04, 2006 WL 1477161 (N.J. Super. Ct. Law Div. May 26, 2006).

131. N.J. Dep't of Envtl. Prot. v. Exxon Mobil Corp., 923 A.2d 345, 359 (N.J. Super. Ct. App. Div. 2007).

claims. The court also went on to deny NJDEP's common law trespass claim because the state was not in the exclusive possession of the land in question. It also denied NJDEP's claim for unjust enrichment, holding that because the NJ Spill Act provides NJDEP with an adequate remedy at law, no claim for unjust enrichment was available.[132]

f. Scheduling and Timing

i. Removal and Remand

Prior to consolidation of the Bayway and Bayonne matters, Exxon removed the Bayonne action to the U.S. District Court for the District of New Jersey alleging federal question jurisdiction existed because the federal government owned the property in question and that Exxon Mobil acted at the direction of the federal government when contaminating the natural resources of New Jersey. The District of New Jersey court ultimately rejected these arguments, finding that Exxon had failed to demonstrate that the federal government exercised the "requisite amount of control" in ordering the production of substances that were ultimately disposed of at the Bayonne site.[133] The case was remanded to New Jersey Superior Court in March 2005.[134]

ii. Motion for a More Definite Statement

Following remand and consolidation, Exxon moved for a more definite statement, arguing that the complaints stated "almost nothing" regarding what natural resources were allegedly injured, or the nature or location of these resources; rather, Exxon claimed, the complaints described only the general importance of those resources to the state. Exxon further argued that plaintiffs' definition of "hazardous substances" was too broad. Plaintiffs opposed the motion, arguing that their claims had been sufficiently pled—including specific block and lot numbers for each parcel of property alleged to be contaminated—and that Exxon was "well aware of the location and nature" of the alleged injury given that it was obligated under a 1991 consent decree to "delineate the nature and extent of natural resource injury caused by its activities." The court ultimately sided with the state and denied Exxon's motion for a more definite statement.

---

132. N.J. Dep't of Envtl. Prot. v. Exxon Mobil Corp., No. UNN-L-3026-04, 2008 WL 4177038 (N.J. Super. Ct. Law Div. Aug. 29, 2008).

133. N.J. Dep't of Envtl. Prot. v. Exxon Mobil Corp., 381 F. Supp. 2d 398, 404–05 (D.N.J. 2005).

134. *Id.*

iii. Bifurcation

In 2006, the court memorialized an agreement between the parties to bifurcate the case. Plaintiffs had asserted both "surface water claims" and "property claims."[135] The court stayed the surface water claims and allowed the property claims to proceed first.

iv. Joinder of Third Parties

The bifurcation of trial was originally intended to "streamline third party litigation" regarding the NRD liability and required Exxon to join any third party with respect to the property claims within 90 days of the issuance of that order. Exxon moved for an order excusing it from this obligation, arguing that it had identified more than 20 third parties and that joinder thereof would significantly complicate the case. It further argued that if plaintiffs were ultimately unsuccessful in imposing liability on Exxon, all efforts devoted to third-party practice would "be for naught," and that the ultimate value of damages awarded would inform Exxon's decision as to which and how many third parties were worth pursuing. Plaintiffs opposed this motion, arguing that without joinder of these third parties now, Exxon's assertion that others are responsible "would go unchecked by those parties," and "[i]f any portion of the claims raised in this matter are determined not to be governed by joint and several liability . . . the addition of alleged contributors is essential." The court sided with the plaintiffs and required Exxon to name and join all third-party defendants "known at this time." Exxon did file third-party claims against two parties, but these claims were eventually dismissed without prejudice in 2007.[136]

g. Discovery Issues

i. Deliberative Process Privilege Applied to NRDA Documents

Exxon moved to compel the production of over 600 NJDEP documents relating to the Office of Natural Resource Restoration's calculation of NRD and Exxon's argument that the actual policies of the NJDEP regarding the assessment of NRD differed from those set forth in official directives. Specifically, Exxon argued that NJDEP was requiring more than was generally required

---

135. N.J. Dep't of Envtl. Prot. v. Exxon Mobil Corp., No. UNN-L-3026-04 (N.J. Super. Ct. Law Div. Jan. 11, 2006) (case management order bifurcating adjudication of claims).

136. Stipulation of Dismissal Without Prejudice and Without Costs as to the Third Party Complaint, Counterclaim and All Crossclaims, N.J. Dep't of Envtl. Prot. v. Exxon Mobil Corp., No. UNN-L-3026-04 (N.J. Super. Ct. Law Div. Apr. 24, 2007).

in NRD cases—it was requiring restoration to pristine 1870 condition rather than restoration to pre-release baseline conditions (all that NJDEP typically required). Exxon also moved to compel the depositions of several high-ranking NJDEP employees including, among others, Lisa Jackson, who had been NJDEP commissioner at the relevant time but who had since been appointed EPA administrator, and two former assistant commissioners, who it contended could testify to NJDEP's actual policies. The discovery master judge reviewed 50 percent of the requested documents in camera and recommended that this motion be denied based on the deliberative process privilege. Exxon opposed this recommendation. The trial court sided with the discovery master and denied the motion, finding that NJDEP had met its burden of establishing that the deliberative process privilege applied and that Exxon had failed to raise a substantial and compelling need to pierce it. The court did, however, grant Exxon's motion to compel depositions of former NJDEP officials, including Lisa Jackson, finding that these depositions could conceivably yield testimony that could aid Exxon's contentions that the directives in this matter were inconsistent with NJDEP NRD policies.[137]

h. Evidentiary Issues

i. Relevant Documents Obtained Post-Discovery

Discovery in this matter was closed in 2008. At trial, Exxon sought to use approximately 500 post-2008 documents, arguing that they were relevant evidence relating to the practicality of restoration and changed circumstances at the sites. The court rejected the wholesale admission of post-2008 documents, finding that admission would result in undue prejudice to the state and that Exxon had ample opportunity to make application to amend their discovery submissions well before the commencement of trial and chose not to without adequate justification. The court did, however, reserve the possibility that certain post-2008 documents or testimony that were relevant and the admission of which would not unduly prejudice the state could be admitted.[138]

ii. Evidence of Other NRD Sites and Settlements

At trial, NJDEP sought to bar Exxon from introducing evidence of other NRD settlements and other sites regulated by the state. Exxon argued this

---

137. N.J. Dep't of Envtl. Prot. v. Exxon Mobil Corp., No. UNN-L-3026-04 (N.J. Super. Ct. Law Div. May 21, 2013).

138. N.J. Dep't of Envtl. Prot. v. Exxon Mobil Corp., No. UNN-L-3026-04 (N.J. Super. Ct. Law Div. Feb. 10, 2014).

evidence was relevant to support its argument that NJDEP's claims against Exxon were contrary to DEP policy. The court sided with the state, holding that because liability had already been established and the extent of restoration was all that was at issue, "[c]omparison of other sites and settlements would be inapposite and ineffective" and stating that "[p]arties often take varying positions in settlements and different factors are taken into account depending on the case."[139] The court did, however, permit testimony regarding the sites referred to in the state's case-in-chief.

i. Use of Experts

i. Reliability

Motions regarding the reliability of experts' methodologies were reserved until the end of trial because "[a] bench trial provides such an opportunity without any concern for prejudice."[140]

ii. Payment of Expert Fees as NRDA Costs

During the discovery phase, NJDEP moved for an order compelling Exxon to pay the invoices of five experts who, as part of the litigation, had prepared reports regarding the NRDA at the sites. NJDEP argued that these litigation expert invoices were compensable NRDA costs. In support of its motion, NJDEP submitted certifications of the director of NJDEP's Office of Natural Resource Restoration. Exxon opposed this motion and, in response, filed several expert reports that opined that the NJDEP expert reports in question were unreliable and invalid. The trial court denied the state's motion for payment of these fees, finding that there was a genuine issue of material fact as to whether the expert reports in question would constitute duplicative NRDA expenditures. NJDEP appealed, and the appellate court affirmed the trial court's denial of this motion, finding that there was a significant factual dispute as to the reasonableness of the costs that could not be adjudicated at the summary judgment stage. The appellate court did, however, disagree with Exxon's emphasis on the fact that these reports were prepared in litigation rather than as part of an administrative process. It stated that "[t]he trial judge made clear, and we agree, that DEP's entitlement to reimbursement does not turn on whether DEP ultimately 'wins' the litigation, but rather in successfully

---

139. N.J. Dep't of Envtl. Prot. v. Exxon Mobil Corp., No. UNN-L-3026-04 (N.J. Super. Ct. Law Div. June 10, 2014).

140. N.J. Dep't of Envtl. Prot. v. Exxon Mobil Corp., No. UNN-L-3026-04 (N.J. Super. Ct. Law Div. May 8, 2014) (concerning plaintiff's motion to exclude opinions of defendant's expert).

proving to the trier of fact that the experts' analysis was 'appropriate, reasonable' and able to 'stand up to scrutiny.'"[141] In other words, the appellate court left open the possibility that litigation expert invoices, if reasonable, could constitute compensable NRDA costs.

iii. Experts Relying on Other Experts

In one deposition, an expert for the state testified that he relied on the expert data and opinion of an individual who had been removed from the state's list of testifying experts. The testifying expert incorporated the data of the expert who had been removed from the state's list into a model he developed specifically for this litigation and testified in his deposition that he lacked the expertise to give an opinion on these inputs himself. Exxon sought to compel the deposition of the expert removed from the list or, in the alternative, an order barring the expert trial testimony of the removed expert. The court granted Exxon's motion to compel the deposition, but avoided the question of whether experts may rely on other non-testifying experts. Rather, it found that NJDEP waived any right to protect the expert from deposition by leading Exxon to believe that the expert was a testifying expert until five days prior to his scheduled deposition.

iv. Rebuttal of HEA Methodology

In support of a motion to exclude an expert opinion of a state witness who relied on HEA methodology, Exxon offered the testimony of an economist who had not been disclosed as a testifying expert and who had not been deposed. The economist asserted that the expert opinions of the state's expert resulting from application of the HEA methodology were not sufficiently reliable. The court permitted the economist to testify, but only if he was deposed, and his testimony was to be limited to demonstrating that the HEA methodology is generally not accepted or reliable (issues relating to admissibility). He was not permitted to testify regarding the state's expert's credibility, and was prohibited, therefore, from testifying to the state's expert's application of the methodology. The court provided Exxon with several cautions in choosing whether to proceed with calling the economist as a witness, stating, for example,

> I note that [the economist] carefully concludes that [the State's witness's] methodology is not accepted by 'economists' as opposed to experts in

---

141. N.J. Dep't of Envtl. Prot. v. Exxon Mobil Corp., Nos. L-3026-04, L-1650-05, 2011 WL 2304026, at *8 (N.J. Super. Ct. App. Div. 2011).

natural resource damage assessments or ecologists, which is what [the State's witness] purports to be. I will reserve commenting on this point until I rule on the R. 104 motion to bar [the State's witness's] testimony at the end of this case.

7. *American Trader* Spill (Cal. Super. Ct., Orange County 1991–1997)
People of the State of California v. Attransco, Inc., Case No. 64-63-39

a. Summary
The *American Trader* spill trial was a 34-day jury trial in California state court that focused on lost recreational use damages.[142] The jury returned a verdict in favor of the trustees, awarding over $12 million for lost recreational use resulting primarily from beach closures in Orange County, California, following the *American Trader* oil spill in 1990.

b. The Facts
On February 7, 1990, an oil tanker, the *American Trader*, ran over its anchor while mooring 1.3 miles off Huntington Beach, Orange County, California. As a result, according to the state of California, the tanker spilled approximately 400,000 gallons of crude oil, fouled approximately 15 miles of beach, and killed more than 1,000 birds. Beaches were closed for approximately five weeks following the spill.

In 1991, the state of California brought suit under the state clean water code which prohibits discharge of oil into state waters. The suit sought NRD from several companies: BP America, Inc. (which owned the oil and chartered the tanker), Golden West Refining (the refinery that operated the offshore terminal), and Attransco Inc. (which owned the vessel). The state alleged that approximately $20 million in damages resulted from the spill.

Several settlements were reached—a $3.89 million settlement with BP America for ecological damage and response costs, and a $3 million settlement with the petroleum industry fund to be applied to cleanup costs and damages. In 1996, a settlement totaling $4.15 million was reached with Golden West Refining Co. The sole remaining claims after these settlements were economic damage and civil penalty claims against Attransco.

---

142. *See generally* David J. Chapman & W. Michael Hanemann, *Environmental Damages in Court: The American Trader Case*, *in* THE LAW AND ECONOMICS OF THE ENVIRONMENT 319 (Anthony Heyes ed., 2000) (providing an in-depth description and analysis of the *American Trader* case and trial).

In 1997, a 34-day jury trial ensued. At trial, California presented losses to six recreational activities: (1) general beach use, (2) surfing, (3) private boating, (4) party/charter boat fishing, (5) whale watching, and (6) excursions to Catalina Island off the coast of Los Angeles. The economic portion of the trial focused largely on concepts such as consumer surplus, the quality of the estimates of the number of beach trips lost as a result of the spill, and the value that should be applied to these trips.

c. Outcome

At trial, California sought to recover $14.5 million in economic loss, and $7.9 million in fines for damage to aquatic life. After two-and-a-half days of deliberation, during which jury members requested a calculator, the jury returned a verdict requiring that Attransco pay $18.1 million in damages and fines, $12.7 million of which was for lost recreational use of beaches and harbors.

Also of note were the fines sought by the state, which included a component to compensate for loss of microorganisms, such as plankton. According to one summary of the verdict, "the fine marks the first time that a California jury has put a dollar figure on the loss of microorganisms—such as plankton—that anchor the marine food chain."[143]

d. Issues Relating to Contingent Valuation

Surveys of actual consumer behavior were relied on heavily at trial, but neither side relied on CV surveys as affirmative evidence. Defendants, however, did rely on a CV survey in rebutting plaintiffs' estimated beach recreation estimates. In arguing that plaintiffs' estimates were too high, defendants cited a CV question that asked:

> Suppose the agency that manages this site started charging a *daily* admission fee of $X *per person*. The money from the admission fee will be used to maintain the site in the present condition, but there would be *no* improvements. Would you continue to use this site?[144]

The daily admission fee for each survey participant was one of ten randomly assigned amounts between $1 and $75. Most of those who responded said "no." It appears that the jury did not give great weight to this information, as its assigned daily beach trip value—$13.19—was based on a different

---

143. Scott Martelle & Deborah Schoch, *Oil Company Owes $18.1 Million for Spill, Jury Decides*, L.A. Times, Dec. 9, 1997, http://articles.latimes.com/1997/dec/09/news/mn-62164.

144. Chapman & Hanemann, *supra* note 142, at 325 (providing quotation from the survey).

survey relied on by plaintiffs. It is unclear, however, whether lack of reliability associated with the CV survey factored into the jury's judgment.

8. St. Croix South Shore (D.V.I. 2005–2014)

Commissioner Department of Planning & Natural Resources v. Century Alumina Company, No. 1:05-cv-00062-HB

a. Summary

The St. Croix South Shore litigation was a suit brought under CERCLA and territory law seeking to recover NRD associated with the contamination from a coastal industrial area in the USVI that included an alumina refinery and an oil refinery. Plaintiffs' claims were substantially narrowed in partial summary judgment orders, including an order holding that many of its CERCLA claims were time-barred. All claims settled just weeks before a multi-week jury trial was set to begin and after the court had ruled on several summary judgment motions as well as all expert and evidentiary motions. With more than ten expert-related orders issued, this case represents the most extensive set of NRD-related expert rulings by any court in an NRD case.

b. The Facts

In 2005, plaintiffs—commissioner of the USVI Department of Planning and Natural Resources (DPNR) and the government of the USVI (the Territory)—filed a multi-count suit, including CERCLA, common law, and USVI Oil Spill Prevention and Pollution Control Act claims, to recover NRD and cleanup costs from entities who at various times owned portions of the South Coast Industrial Area on the island of St. Croix. The area included both an alumina refinery and an oil refinery. The defendants included eight companies: Century Aluminum Company (Century), Virgin Islands Alumina Corporation (VIALCO), St. Croix Alumina, LLC (SCA), Lockheed Martin Corporation (Lockheed), Alcoa World Alumina, LLC (Alcoa), St. Croix Renaissance Group LLP (SCRG), HOVENSA, LLC (HOVENSA), and Hess Oil Virgin Islands Corporation (Hess).

From 2010 to 2014, the court issued a number of summary judgment rulings, substantially narrowing plaintiffs' claims, including a 2010 order in which it held that many of plaintiffs' CERCLA claims were barred by CERCLA's statute of limitations, and a 2011 order in which the court dismissed the claims against Century, finding that Century had already established that it was not liable in a prior related litigation. In 2012, three alumina company defendants, SCA, Alcoa, and SCRG, entered into a settlement with the Territory, agreeing to perform and/or finance a series of remedial activities and dispensing of claims raised against them. Over objections from all the non-settling defendants, the court approved the consent decree.[145]

A jury trial was set to begin on June 24, 2014, to adjudicate the claims against the remaining oil refinery defendants and Lockheed. By the time the parties filed pre-trial memoranda and proposed jury charges, plaintiffs had agreed not to pursue any CERCLA claims and were therefore seeking only damages under USVI Territory law.

Just weeks before trial was set to begin, the Territory and the remaining defendants settled all remaining claims.[146]

c. Outcome

USVI's damages expert conducted two types of valuations of the claim: a total economic value (TEV) analysis that aggregated the value of various functions provided by the resources, or, in the alternative, a REA. In his expert report, the TEV calculation was $129.6 million, and the alternative REA calculation was $40.7 million. For the claims that remained at the time of pre-trial briefing, plaintiffs' TEV calculation was $91.5 million, and plaintiffs' alternative REA calculation was $26.9 million. In addition to the TEV or REA value, in their pre-trial memorandum, plaintiffs sought an additional $27.2 million to execute a project to remediate harmful nutrient loadings in the Alucroix Channel.

While not all aspects of the settlements involved monetary compensation, the estimated value of all settlements entered with all defendants was between $125 million and $145 million.

d. Summary Judgment Orders

i. Statute of Limitations

As discussed in greater detail later, multiple claims were dismissed on summary judgment as barred under CERCLA's three-year statute of limitations.[147]

---

145. Comm'r of the Dep't of Planning & Nat. Res. v. Century Alumina Co., No. 05-0062, 2012 WL 446086 (D.V.I. Feb. 13, 2012).

146. *See* Agreement and Consent Decree Regarding the Former Alumina Refinery Property, Anguilla Estate, St. Croix, U.S. Virgin Islands, Comm'r of the Dep't of Planning & Nat. Res. v. Century Alumina Co., No. 05-0062 (D.V.I. July 21, 2014), ECF No. 1541 (Lockheed Martin consent decree); Joint Stipulation of Dismissal, Comm'r of the Dep't of Planning & Nat. Res. v. Century Alumina Co., No. 05-0062 (D.V.I. July 9, 2014), ECF No. 1538 (joint stipulation of dismissal for defendant VIALCO); Joint Stipulation of Dismissal, Comm'r of the Dep't of Planning & Nat. Res. v. Century Alumina Co., No. 05-0062 (D.V.I. June 5, 2014), ECF No. 1530 (joint stipulation of dismissal for defendants Hess and HOVENSA).

147. Comm'r of the Dep't of Planning & Nat. Res. v. Century Alumina Co., No. 05-0062, 2010 WL 2772695 (D.V.I. July 13, 2010).

ii. Liability of Past Owners under CERCLA

In the order addressing the CERCLA statute of limitations, certain CERCLA claims against multiple defendants were, without full briefing, dismissed on summary judgment because the court held that these defendants "did not own or operate the [relevant facility] at the time of the [relevant] release and are not the current owners or operators."[148] Plaintiffs filed for reconsideration, arguing that the ruling was outside the scope of the limited statute of limitations summary judgment motion before the court at the time. The court agreed that it erroneously decided the issue without full briefing and vacated the summary judgment order on this point.[149]

iii. Liability for Damage to Privately Held Resources

On summary judgment, the court dismissed the trustees' claims to recover for damages to land held as private property, holding that plaintiffs were not trustees of such land.[150] With regard to groundwater, however, the court held that private ownership of groundwater rights does not entitle a party to pollute that water and denied a defendant's motion for summary judgment regarding CERCLA NRD claims related to pollution of groundwater underlying private property.[151]

iv. Preclusive Effect of Related Environmental Actions

Defendant Century had been a defendant in a prior cost recovery action related to one of the same facilities at issue in this case. In the cost recovery action, the court held that the Territory had adduced no evidence that Century was liable under CERCLA for either its own actions or that of its subsidiary, VIALCO. The court in this matter held that the ruling with regard to Century's liability in the cost recovery action had preclusive effect on Century's liability in this NRD action and dismissed the relevant claims.[152]

v. Abnormally Dangerous Activity

The Territory's claims included an allegation that defendants were strictly liable under common law for damage to natural resources because operation of

---

148. *Id.* at *12.

149. Comm'r of the Dep't of Planning & Nat. Res. v. Century Alumina Co., No. 05-0062, 2010 WL 3310726 (D.V.I. Aug. 20, 2010).

150. Comm'r of the Dep't of Planning & Nat. Res. v. Century Alumina Co., No. 05-62, 2011 WL 882547 (D.V.I. Mar. 11, 2011).

151. Comm'r of the Dep't of Planning & Nat. Res. v. Century Alumina Co., No. 05-62, 2012 WL 1901297 (D.V.I. May 24, 2012).

152. Comm'r of the Dep't of Planning & Nat. Res. v. Century Alumina Co., No. 05-62, 2011 WL 6010009 (D.V.I. Nov. 30, 2011).

the refineries constituted an abnormally dangerous activity. These claims were dismissed on summary judgment because the court found that, "[w]hile we do not minimize the dangerous attributes of a refinery and its storage facilities, they do not outweigh the substantial benefit and value the refinery and its storage facilities brought to the community of the Virgin Islands."[153]

e. Scheduling and Timing

i. Statute of Limitations

Defendants moved for summary judgment alleging that plaintiffs' claims were barred by CERCLA's three-year statute of limitations. They argued that this three-year period was triggered by constructive knowledge of the NRD, while plaintiffs asserted that only actual knowledge could trigger the tolling of the claim. The court held that constructive knowledge was all that is required, stating that "[t]he Trustee's claim accrues when he discovered or *should have discovered* any loss to natural resources and its connection to the release in question."[154] In connection with this holding, the court dismissed any trustee claim where uncontroverted evidence showed that the trustee agency had pre-2002 constructive knowledge that the release in question caused NRD. For several of the trustees' claims, the court held there were genuine issues of material fact as to whether the trustees had pre-2002 constructive knowledge that the alleged NRD existed, and summary judgment with regard to those claims was denied. However, by the time the final settlement was entered on the eve of trial, the Territory had abandoned all CERCLA claims.

f. Discovery Issues

i. Attorney Work-Product Privilege Applied to Scientific Data

After litigation was initiated, defendants Hess and HOVENSA hired two marine biologist consultants to perform dives into the allegedly contaminated waters adjacent to their oil refinery. The only item defendants produced in discovery related to these dives was correspondence indicating that the dives had been performed; defendants did not designate the consultants as testifying experts. In discovery negotiations, defendants refused to produce any documents related to the work the consultant divers performed, claiming these

---

153. Comm'r of the Dep't of Planning & Nat. Res. v. Century Alumina Co., No. 05-62, 2014 WL 184445 (D.V.I. Jan. 16, 2014).

154. Comm'r of the Dep't of Planning & Nat. Res. v. Century Alumina Co., No. 05-0062, 2010 WL 2772695, at *6 (D.V.I. July 13, 2010) (emphasis added); *see also* Chapter 3, Section A.1.a (discussing application of statute of limitations defense in this case).

were protected by the work-product doctrine. Plaintiffs filed a motion to compel seeking the scientific data and/or recorded observations associated with the work, arguing that the constantly changing conditions inherent in the marine environments at issue make every test and observation unique and impossible to reproduce.

The court denied the motion, finding that "[t]he data and observations at issue, while unique, do not relate to a moment in time critical to the litigation," and did not, therefore, warrant departure from the general rule that facts and opinions held by a non-testifying expert retained in anticipation of litigation are not discoverable.[155] Notably, the court distinguished this case, where the alleged environmental damage was not traceable to a single event, from oil spills, implying that data collected in connection with a single event, where an individual moment in time would be more critical to understanding impacts, might be subject to a motion to compel.

g. Use of Experts

Because this case was to proceed as a jury trial, the court ruled on all expert motions ahead of trial, issuing over ten separate orders under *Daubert v. Merrell Dow Pharmaceuticals, Inc.*[156]

i. Sample Design Reliability

Defendants sought to exclude a seagrass survey performed by the plaintiffs' marine benthic ecologist, arguing that his sample size was too small and locations were improperly selected. The court rejected this challenge, finding that "[a]ny deficiencies in . . . sample size or the locations of his stations may be addressed on cross-examination but do not cause his observations to be unreliable under *Daubert*."[157]

ii. Conclusory Causation Determinations

- The court excluded the marine benthic ecologist's conclusions with regard to the cause of injury to seagrasses, finding that he insufficiently

---

155. Comm'r of the Dep't of Planning & Nat. Res. v. Century Alumina Co., 279 F.R.D. 317, 319 (D.V.I. 2012).

156. 509 U.S. 579 (1993).

157. *See* Comm'r of the Dep't of Planning & Nat. Res. v. Century Alumina Co., No. 05-62, slip op. at 7 (D.V.I. Dec. 18, 2012), ECF No. 1309; *see also* Comm'r of the Dep't of Planning & Nat. Res. v. Century Alumina Co., No. 05-62, 2013 WL 4534742 (D.V.I. Aug. 26, 2013) (making a similar finding with regard to samples analyzed by defendants' expert chemical oceanographer, Dr. Paul Boehm).

explained why he concluded that contaminants, and not any other causes, caused the damage to seagrass.[158] The court stated that the expert's "report was conclusory and did not mention any alternative causes that he considered."[159] Important to the court's decision was the fact that the expert report did not provide any chemical concentrations or comparisons to controls to support his conclusions. As a result of this failure, the court held that the expert was allowed to testify as to his observations of the seagrass, but not as to his causation conclusions.

- The defendant Lockheed's aquatic ecologist filed an expert report in response to the plaintiffs' marine benthic ecologist's report. Among other things, plaintiffs sought to exclude the defense expert's opinion regarding the alleged effects of inadequate sewage operations on the resources in question. In support of this opinion, the defense expert relied on data from DPNR showing that there were sewage problems throughout St. Croix. The court held that the defense expert could testify as to the existence of the sewage problems, but that she could not state that sewage contamination caused the harmful conditions observed in the relevant channel.[160] Important to this decision was the fact that "[t]here is a clear difference between data supporting the fact that sewage problems exist and data supporting the fact that the sewage problems caused the [harmful conditions]."[161] In her deposition, the defense expert admitted that she did not know whether the DPNR data showed that these sewage problems caused the harmful conditions at issue.

iii. Reliability of Control Comparisons

Defendants also took issue with a comparison to a control site included in the plaintiffs' marine benthic ecologist's report, arguing that the control site was not adequately representative to produce a reliable comparison. The court held that defendants' criticisms of the ecologist's control site were best addressed on cross-examination and were not a basis to exclude the testimony.[162]

---

158. *See* Comm'r of the Dep't of Planning & Nat. Res. v. Century Alumina Co., No. 05-62 (D.V.I. Dec. 18, 2012), ECF No. 1309.

159. *Id.* at 8.

160. Comm'r of the Dep't of Planning & Nat. Res. v. Century Alumina Co., No. 05-62 (D.V.I. Aug. 15, 2013), ECF No. 1389.

161. *Id.* at 8.

162. Comm'r of the Dep't of Planning & Nat. Res. v. Century Alumina Co., No. 05-62, slip op. at 10 (D.V.I. Dec. 18, 2012), ECF No. 1309.

iv. Experts Relying on Qualitative Information

In his deposition, plaintiffs' groundwater hydrologist admitted that he incorporated non-quantitative, qualitative considerations into his estimate of the extent of the plume of contamination in the groundwater. Defendants moved to exclude these opinions, arguing that they were not based on scientific principles or an accepted methodology used by experts in the field. The court denied the motion, finding that the hydrologist's methodology was similar to that used in other studies of groundwater contamination and that "defendants, of course, are welcome to bring out at trial that these differences in . . . methodology make [the hydrologist's] opinions not credible."[163]

v. Measure of Damages

Plaintiffs' damages expert computed two different values for the damages associated with contamination of groundwater on St. Croix.

The first methodology used was a REA that computed the costs of buying land to protect areas of the aquifer from contamination and diminished recharge. This analysis resulted in a valuation of $40.7 million. Defendants argued that this type of REA analysis is typically used to value injuries to individual wildlife species and was inapplicable to analyses of economic damages for groundwater contamination. The court disagreed, holding that application of a REA to groundwater loss was sufficiently reliable under *Daubert*, and that defendants could cross-examine the plaintiffs' damages expert on the credibility of the assumptions made in completing his REA.[164]

The second methodology used was a TEV approach that involved two components. First, the damages expert calculated a "wasteful use" value that measured the value of the loss to the current generation from the wasteful use of the water. Second, he calculated the "benefit transfer of existence values," which measured how much money residents of St. Croix would theoretically pay to ensure that uncontaminated groundwater is available for future generations. This was measured through valuing similar resources at different locations. The damages expert's entire TEV calculation resulted in a value of $129.6 million. Defendants argued, among other things, that the second component of this analysis—the "benefit transfer existence values"— was unreliable because the expert did not conduct a poll of the attitudes of

---

163. Comm'r of the Dep't of Planning & Nat. Res. v. Century Alumina Co., No. 05-62, slip op. at 8 (D.V.I. Mar. 26, 2013), ECF No. 1352.

164. Comm'r of the Dep't of Planning & Nat. Res. v. Century Alumina Co., No. 05-62, slip op. at 5–6 (D.V.I. Mar. 26, 2013), ECF No. 1356.

people on St. Croix but instead used an existing "meta-analysis equation." The defendants contended that the meta-analysis equation had too high of an error rate and had been critiqued as unreliable. The court rejected all these challenges and found that the TEV approach was sufficiently reliable to allow the expert to testify to this opinion.[165]

vi. Toxicity

Plaintiffs' toxicologist performed laboratory bioassays using samples collected from multiple locations around the alumina refinery site to determine the lowest level of toxicity at which effects on the test species were always present. These values were used as site-specific effects thresholds. Defendants' primary argument in moving to exclude the toxicologist's opinions was that his methodology was unreliable because he took samples from a few of the most impacted areas of the site while ignoring the less impacted areas. The court rejected this criticism, pointing out that the toxicologist's goal was not to characterize the entire site, but rather to determine whether a lack of vegetation was attributable to the contaminants and, if so, what contaminants contributed to the toxicity.[166]

vii. Experts Relying on Other Experts

Many testifying experts relied on conclusions of other testifying experts. The court held that when relying on the opinion of other experts, an expert must "'assess the validity of the opinions of the other experts . . . relied upon' rather than 'unblinking[ly] rel[y] on those experts' opinion.'"[167] So, for example, the court permitted plaintiffs' groundwater injury expert to testify regarding groundwater damages numbers that were calculated by a different expert where she testified that she considered the other expert's methods and independently determined that they were appropriate.[168] The court did not, however, allow her to testify as to property values used to calculate restoration credit where she did not independently analyze those property values.[169]

---

165. *Id.* at 10–12.

166. Comm'r of the Dep't of Planning & Nat. Res. v. Century Alumina Co., No. 05-62 (D.V.I. June 28, 2013), ECF No. 1379.

167. Comm'r of the Dep't of Planning & Nat. Res. v. Century Alumina Co., No. 05-62, slip op. at 12 (D.V.I. Feb. 28, 2013), ECF No. 1345.

168. *Id.*

169. *Id.* at 13.

viii. Expert Declarations Filed in Support of Opposition to *Daubert* Motion

In response to *Daubert* motions, plaintiffs in multiple instances attached to their opposition briefs declarations of the experts whose opinions were challenged. Although such declarations were submitted after the close of expert discovery, the court allowed the declarations where they clarified opinions set forth in the expert's report and discussed a topic on which the expert was deposed.[170]

ix. Scope of Responsive Expert Reports

The court rejected plaintiffs' argument that responsive expert opinions that went beyond the content of the report to which they were responding should be excluded.[171] It stated that "plaintiffs have not cited any cases that stand for the proposition that a responsive expert report must directly mirror the expert report to which it is responding, and we see no reason why it should do so."[172]

9. South Valley Site, New Mexico (D.N.M. 1999–2007)

New Mexico v. General Electric Co., No. 6:99-cv-01118-BSJ, 99-cv-1254 BSJ (consolidated)

a. Summary

In 1999, the state of New Mexico and the state of New Mexico *ex rel.* Patricia A. Madrid (the newly confirmed attorney general of the state of New Mexico) filed both state and federal actions seeking to recover lost use damages related to groundwater contamination that was the subject of multiple EPA- and New Mexico-led remedial actions near Albuquerque, New Mexico. After 48 months of preparations for a jury trial, some 24 days' worth of in-court pre-trial conferences, including evidentiary and expert hearings, the court ultimately dismissed the action, finding that all of the state's claims were preempted, displaced, and/or barred as a result of the comprehensive remedial

---

170. *See, e.g.,* Comm'r of the Dep't of Planning & Nat. Res. v. Century Alumina Co., No. 05-62, slip op. at 13 (D.V.I. Mar. 26, 2013), ECF No. 1366 ("Dr. Hennet does not change any of his opinions in the declaration or provide any new opinions. . . . This is sufficient under the circumstances to avoid surprise or prejudice.").

171. Comm'r of the Dep't of Planning & Nat. Res. v. Century Alumina Co., No. 05-62 (D.V.I. Mar. 26, 2013), ECF No. 1389.

172. *Id.* at 7.

activities underway to address the contamination. The case has been cited as an example of how not to pursue a claim for NRD.[173]

b. The Facts

Albuquerque's South Valley area was the site of a variety of manufacturing operations, including a welding plant, U.S. Atomic Energy Commission nuclear weapon component parts manufacturing, both private and U.S. Air Force aircraft engine parts manufacturing, a petroleum pipeline and several bulk petroleum distribution facilities, and an industrial chemical distribution facility. An aquifer on which the city of Albuquerque relied for drinking water underlay the area. In the early 1980s, the site was listed on the NPL pursuant to CERCLA, and EPA initiated remedial activities. In 1988, EPA issued a ROD, with which the state of New Mexico concurred. The ROD required General Electric to perform the selected remedy and treat the contaminated groundwater. The state of New Mexico also entered into several Hydrocarbon Remediation Agreements with the petroleum facility operators, requiring remediation of petroleum contamination that was exempt under CERCLA's hydrocarbon exclusion provision. New Mexico's designated trustee had pursued certain steps toward conducting a NRDA for the site, including entering tolling agreements with several of the responsible parties and seeking NRDA funding from the state legislature, but had not completed an assessment.

In 1999, while groundwater remediation activities were still ongoing pursuant to the EPA ROD—and without either a completed NRDA or the support of the designated state trustee—the state of New Mexico and the attorney general of the state of New Mexico filed a complaint in federal court alleging claims under CERCLA against a variety of private corporations and federal agencies and seeking to recover loss-of-use damages for contamination of the groundwater underlying the South Valley Site. On the same day, the attorney general filed a complaint in state court seeking loss-of-use damages under state law for contamination of the groundwater underlying the South Valley Site from the same defendants (excluding the federal agencies).

Defendants in the state case filed notices of removal, and after the state withdrew its motion for remand, the CERCLA and state law claims were eventually consolidated. For several years, the CERCLA claims and the state law claims proceeded on separate tracks, in separate pleadings, with separate

---

173. *See, e.g.*, Patrick E. Tolan, Jr., *Natural Resource Damages under CERCLA: Failures, Lessons Learned, and Alternatives*, 38 N.M. L. Rev. 409, 410 (2008) ("Others can learn important lessons from New Mexico's failures in this case, so they are not condemned to repeat them.").

motions to dismiss before the same federal judge. By mid-2001, "it was apparent [that this separate tracks process] had grown cumbersome and confusing for both court and counsel," and the court granted plaintiffs' leave to file a single amended complaint.[174]

At the start of the pre-trial conference, in fall 2002, the state sought to recover $4 billion. However, in the first week of pre-trial conference, the state's claimed value was significantly reduced by, in the words of the court, "paring out" speculative and legally deficient claims.[175] On November 20, 2002, based on a stipulation by counsel for all parties, the court entered an order dismissing plaintiffs' CERCLA claims and all federal defendants.[176] Plaintiffs then filed a renewed motion for remand. The court denied this motion, holding that even though only state law claims remained pending, these claims were inescapably defined in terms of CERCLA and, as a result, presented federal questions.[177] Also important to the court's denial of remand was the fact that "until very recently [the state of New Mexico] was vigorously pursuing *all* of its claims in *this* forum," including through "extensive discovery, voluminous document production, numerous depositions, [and] intense expert witness and pretrial preparations."[178]

Thereafter, plaintiffs continued to seek damages under state law, and defendants continued to seek dismissal through a variety of summary judgment motions. On April 6, 2004, the court issued a partial summary judgment ruling that substantially limited the scope of plaintiffs' state law claims and the available damages.[179] All that remained after the April 6 order were claims for damages to groundwater that were outside the reach of the EPA CERCLA remedy and the state of New Mexico's hydrocarbon remediation activities. Damages, if any, were to be limited to groundwater in which contaminant levels exceeded the federal drinking water quality standards, and were to be measured based on restoration value, rather than fair market replacement value.

Finally, in an order on June 19, 2004, the court dismissed all claims, finding that plaintiffs "failed to raise a genuine issue of material fact on the

---

174. New Mexico v. Gen. Elec. Co., 335 F. Supp. 2d 1157, 1166 (D.N.M. 2003) [hereinafter *Gen. Elec. Co. I*].

175. *Id.* at 1169.

176. New Mexico v. Gen. Elec. Co., 6:99-cv-01118 (D.N.M. Nov. 20, 2002), ECF No. 909.

177. *Gen. Elec. Co. I*, 335 F. Supp. 2d at 1177–78.

178. *Id.* at 1180–81.

179. New Mexico v. Gen. Elec. Co., 335 F. Supp. 2d 1185 (D.N.M. 2004) [hereinafter *Gen. Elec. Co. II*].

essential elements of injury and damages."[180] Plaintiffs had failed to establish the presence of any contamination that was beyond the reach of the EPA- and state-led remedial actions that were ongoing in the basin.

Plaintiffs appealed the district court's dismissal of the action, and, in 2006, the Tenth Circuit affirmed the district court's entry of summary judgment, but on slightly different grounds. It found that CERCLA preempted state law claims to recover unrestricted NRD funds if those funds would also be recoverable under CERCLA's NRD provisions.[181] As a matter of law, therefore, all of plaintiffs' claims were preempted.

Although the court ultimately found that there were no triable issues at stake in this litigation, it took 48 months of preparations for a jury trial, some 24 days of in-court pretrial conferences, including evidentiary and expert hearings, and many rulings of the court to get to that holding. As a result of this substantial pre-trial practice, the *New Mexico* litigation provides some helpful insights for NRD practitioners, many of which are discussed next.

Perhaps the most useful lesson from the case comes from the behind-the-scenes politics surrounding the action. The action was brought by an attorney general who lacked the support of the head of the agency designated as the state of New Mexico's natural resource trustee, and the trustee was named in the action as an involuntary plaintiff. Eventually, after the New Mexico Supreme Court affirmed the attorney general's authority to represent the state,[182] and the federal district court noted that "it appears to me all the necessary parties, including the trustee, are here," the trustee agreed to cooperate with the attorney general's lawyers.[183] However, the trustee had not conducted a NRDA in accordance with the DOI regulations and therefore was not entitled to the benefit of the rebuttable presumption. And, indeed, lack of cooperation with the state and federal regulatory agencies, along with deficiencies in the plaintiffs' approach to valuing damages, ultimately prevented recovery.

---

180. New Mexico v. Gen. Elec. Co., 322 F. Supp. 2d 1237, 1271 (D.N.M. 2004) [hereinafter *Gen. Elec. Co. IV*].

181. *See* New Mexico v. Gen. Elec. Co., 467 F.3d 1223, 1250 (10th Cir. 2006) [hereinafter *Gen. Elec. Co. V*] ("Accepting the State's argument might place [Defendants] in the unenviable position of being held liable for monetary damages because they are complying with an EPA-ordered remedy which [Defendants] have no power to alter without prior EPA approval.").

182. *See id.* at 1236 n.21.

183. The politics surrounding the claim are discussed in greater detail in Tolan, Jr., *supra* note 173, at 409, 410, 428.

c. Outcome

The state initially sought to recover $4 billion in NRD. As mentioned earlier, in the first week of pre-trial conference, that value was significantly reduced through "paring out" speculative and legally deficient claims.[184] All claims were eventually dismissed before trial, but the court made several instructive holdings along the way.

i. Claims for Loss of Use of the Aquifer Itself

In addition to their claims for loss of use of the groundwater, plaintiffs also claimed that the aquifer itself (i.e., the soil and minerals) had independent economic value that had also been lost. The court held that

> [a]bsent proof of some possessory ownership interest in *land* at the South Valley Site—title to the surface or subsurface estate, a reservation of minerals, or the like—the State has no legally cognizable interest in the aquifer beneath the South Valley Site. Plaintiffs thus have no legal footing for their damages claim based upon injury to the aquifer itself.[185]

ii. Conflict Preemption and CERCLA's Bar to Challenging a Remedy

After plaintiffs agreed to withdraw their CERCLA claims, defendants asserted that plaintiffs' state law claims should be dismissed because they constituted an impermissible challenge to the still ongoing EPA-ordered remediation of the site, barred by CERCLA section 113(h), which provides that no federal court "shall have jurisdiction . . . to review any challenges to . . . [a] remedial action" under CERCLA, and the claims were preempted by federal law under the doctrine of conflict preemption.[186]

The district court agreed with defendants that

> [i]mposing onerous damages liability upon [defendants] because the remedy ordered by the EPA . . . will somehow prove inadequate would punish the defendants for the *EPA's* selection of remedy, and likely would "stand as an obstacle to the objectives of CERCLA, whose purpose is to effect the expeditious and permanent cleanup of hazardous waste sites, and to allow the EPA the flexibility needed to address site-specific problems."[187]

---

184. *Gen. Elec. Co. I*, 335 F. Supp. 2d at 1169.
185. *Gen. Elec. Co. II*, 335 F. Supp. 2d at 1205.
186. 43 U.S.C. § 9613(h).
187. *Gen. Elec. Co. II*, 335 F. Supp. 2d at 1227 (internal citations omitted).

However, the court held that "[p]laintiffs have carefully pleaded their remaining state law claims, marking the periphery of the CERCLA remedy as their boundary, and thus avoiding the risk of an impermissible double recovery as well as potential conflict preemption by CERCLA should a state law remedy somehow frustrate CERCLA's remedial objectives."[188] To the extent plaintiffs could prove actual damages "beyond the intended scope of the existing CERCLA remediation," they could recover.[189] Several months later, the court ruled that because the reach of the EPA remedy was still flexible to address new areas of contamination, plaintiffs had not raised a triable issue of fact.[190] On appeal, the Tenth Circuit affirmed the dismissal and was even more emphatic in finding that CERCLA rendered New Mexico's state law claims unavailable.[191]

d. Evidentiary Issues

i. Choice of Water Quality Standard to Apply

In determining whether groundwater services had been lost, the court applied state law. Because the primary loss of use asserted was loss of use of drinking water, defendants argued that this question could be determined through application of the federal drinking water quality standards, which had been adopted by the state through regulation. Incidentally, most of the groundwater in question met this standard. New Mexico, on the other hand, argued that the lower levels of the contamination still deprived it "of the opportunity to make contaminant-free water," and advocated for application of water quality standards set forth in regulations promulgated under the New Mexico Water Quality Act (the state corollary to the federal CWA that seeks to protect water quality through a system of discharge permits), which were more stringent than the federal drinking water quality standards.[192]

The court held that the drinking water quality standards advocated for by defendants, rather than the standards promulgated under the New Mexico Water Quality Act, were the standards the New Mexico legislature intended to govern the use and supply of drinking water. Therefore, "groundwater that meets those same standards has not been lost to use as drinking water."[193] It further held that while damages could theoretically result from less contami-

---

188. *Id.* at 1261.
189. *Id.*
190. *Gen. Elec. Co. IV,* 322 F. Supp. 2d at 1261.
191. *Gen. Elec. Co. V,* 467 F.3d at 1247.
192. *Gen. Elec. Co. II,* 335 F. Supp. 2d at 1212.
193. *Id.* at 1210.

nation, "[n]o expert witness has testified as to the economic value of water that may prove to be drinkable, but still not pristine."[194]

ii. Measurement of Damages

Plaintiffs sought to recover the market value for the groundwater, which, according to the court, was the correct measure for damages only if the loss of groundwater in question was permanent.[195] The court rejected the state's assumption that the losses in question were necessarily permanent, admonishing it for ignoring the ongoing remediation at the site, and stating that the state of New Mexico should not be permitted "to abandon the groundwater beneath the South Valley Site in favor of a lucrative damages award to be extracted from defendants—all of whom, the Court notes, continue to conduct remediation activities at South Valley that have been expressly approved or required by the State of New Mexico."[196] The court held that "[w]here use of the injured resource may be restored, the cost of restoration proves to be the most logically compelling measure of damages resulting from the injury, at least where that cost bears some reasonable relationship to the economic value of the restored resource use."[197] The court also held that plaintiffs could not recover lost use damages for uses that were merely speculative or conjectural.[198]

e. Use of Experts

On December 9–12, 2003, and January 7–8, 2004, the court held evidentiary hearings examining the admissibility of the parties' proffered expert testimony on the issues of injury and damages. On May 7, 2004, after the court had substantially limited plaintiffs' state law claims and the types of damages available, it issued a ruling with regard to all expert issues.

i. Relevance

Significant portions of the plaintiffs' expert opinions had been rendered not relevant by the court's prior rulings and were excluded. For example, because the court has ruled that damages, if any, would be measured based on restoration value, rather than market value, plaintiffs' damages experts' opinions, which discussed only the market value of the resources, were excluded.[199]

---

194. *Id.* at 1211.
195. *Id.* at 1221–22.
196. *Id.* at 1221.
197. *Id.*
198. *Id.* at 1254.
199. New Mexico v. Gen. Elec. Co., 335 F. Supp. 2d 1266 (D.N.M. 2004) [hereinafter *Gen. Elec. Co. III*].

Because plaintiffs' damages experts' opinions were excluded, so too were those opinions of defendants' damages experts that were responsive to the plaintiffs' damages experts' opinions.

ii. Reliability of Kriging

Plaintiffs' expert performed groundwater analyses and computer-assisted modeling (relying on the statistical tool called "kriging") to estimate the extent and transport of contaminant plumes in the aquifer. Defendants filed a motion to exclude these opinions, arguing that the expert's groundwater flow and contaminant transport modeling "'does not reflect reality,' and involve[s] the 'use of flawed software' with a starting point 'based on incomplete data and unreliable kriging.'"[200] Specifically, defendants alleged that actual data showed that "vast areas within [the expert's] predicted plume are either entirely uncontaminated or have chemicals at concentrations below the maximum contaminant levels for drinking water."[201] The court emphasized that kriging results in estimates that are "inescapably uncertain," and that other geostatistical methods could be employed to perform the same task with varying results.[202] However, it found that in a civil action "we are concerned with facts proven by a preponderance of the evidence," and "[t]he geostatistical language of probability meshes with the legal language of preponderance, and an analysis expressed in one may assist in resolving an issue expressed in the other."[203]

The court refused to find that the plaintiffs' expert's "rough estimate" was unreliable, holding instead that "[d]efendants' criticisms of [the expert's] methods of analysis . . . go to the weight and credibility that the trier of fact should afford [the expert's] opinions."[204] Important to this holding was that defendants' criticisms of the expert's approach were themselves dependent on statistical probabilities and estimation techniques.[205] The court did, however, exclude the plaintiffs' expert's opinions on different grounds. It ruled that the expert's plume estimate was developed relying on facts and assumptions that were no longer relevant to the trier-of-fact in light of the court's various summary judgment rulings limiting the reach of plaintiffs' state law claims. To the extent the testimony was not relevant, the expert's opinions were excluded.

---

200. *Id.* at 1281.
201. *Id.*
202. *Id.* at 1282.
203. *Id.* at 1283.
204. *Id.* at 1284.
205. *Id.*

Because the testimony was excluded, so too were some portions of the opinions of various responsive and rebuttal experts.[206]

f. Burden of Proof and the Rebuttable Presumption

As discussed earlier, the trustee was a reluctant participant in the case, and no NRDA was conducted prior to the lawsuit. As a result, plaintiffs were not entitled to the benefit of the CERCLA rebuttable presumption.[207] The burden of proof applied was the "preponderance of the evidence" standard.[208]

g. Treatment of Causation

The court held that plaintiffs could not recover lost use damages for uses that are merely speculative or conjectural.[209]

Part of the reason the court excluded the testimony of plaintiffs' ground-water plume modeling expert was that the expert's estimates of the contaminant plume included contamination caused by non-parties.[210]

10. Elkem Metals/Ohio River (S.D. Ohio 2003–2006)
United States v. Elkem Metals, No. 2:03-cv-00528

a. Summary

This litigation proceeded through discovery and pre-trial motions but settled on the eve of trial. The case arose from wastewater discharges of hazardous substances in 1999 and 2000 into the Ohio River. The United States, Ohio, and West Virginia sued for civil penalties under the CWA and for NRD under CERCLA. The parties settled NRD liability for $2.5 million. There are no substantive rulings in the case, but plaintiffs' proposed jury charges are of some interest.

b. The Facts

In June and October 1999, there were fish kills in the Ohio River near defendant's manufacturing facility in Marietta, Ohio, which produced ferroalloys and electrolytic chromium. Defendants had been adding a chemical called

---

206. *See id.* at 1299, 1301, 1306.

207. *See Gen. Elec. Co. V*, 467 F.3d at 1235, 1242 & n.28.

208. *See Gen. Elec. Co. III*, 335 F. Supp. 2d at 1283 ("[i]n the context of this civil action, we are concerned with facts proven by a preponderance of the evidence").

209. *Gen. Elec. Co. II*, 335 F. Supp. 2d at 1254.

210. *Gen. Elec. Co. III*, 335 F. Supp. 2d at 1285–86.

Amersep MP-3R to its wastewater to treat elevated hexavalent chromium levels. The government alleged that this chemical increased the concentration of several hazardous compounds in the facility's discharges, including thiram and various metal compounds. Affected resources included fish, native mussels, and gastropods (snails) in the river and the Ohio River Islands National Wildlife Refuge. Investigations included histopathology studies of specimens collected from the fish kill and observations of mussel beds in the area. The United States and co-trustees Ohio and West Virginia brought the complaint for National Pollutant Discharge Elimination System (NPDES) permit violations and CERCLA NRD against both the former owner of the facility (Elkem Metals) and the then-current owner (Eramet Marietta).

c. Outcome

Claims were settled on the eve of jury trial for $3.25 million. A civil penalty of $750,000 was for CWA claims, $2,040,000 was for NRD, and $460,000 was for NRDA costs ($32,500 to the state of Ohio and $427,500 to the United States).

d. Scheduling and Timing

The complaint was filed on June 10, 2003. At defendant's unopposed request, the trial was bifurcated into a liability phase and a damages phase. The court set a discovery and deposition schedule. Defendants filed a motion for summary judgment on the NRD claim, arguing that they were entitled to the "federally permitted release" defense under 42 U.S.C. § 9607(j) because Amersep MP-3R was added as part of the companies' compliance with its NPDES permit levels for hexavalent chromium. The United States disputed the applicability of the defense. The case settled before the court ruled on any substantive motions.

e. Use of Experts

Defendants announced a list of 23 witnesses expected to be called at trial and 17 may-call witnesses. Defendants' list included three government fact witnesses (from EPA, the U.S. Geological Survey, and USFWS) on their initial will-call list. Plaintiffs announced 7 witnesses expected to be called and 13 may-call witnesses. Four of plaintiffs' witnesses were slated to testify on the effects of the discharges. Various motions to exclude testimony were filed, but the court never ruled on these motions.

f. Burden of Proof and the Rebuttable Presumption

The United States' proposed jury instructions were fairly straightforward with respect to burden of proof issues on liability questions and applied the preponderance of the evidence standard. The rebuttable presumption was not addressed in any of the filings. It is unclear whether the trustees would have sought the benefit of the presumption in the second phase of the trial on damages if that phase had proceeded.

g. Treatment of Causation

Citing *Coeur d'Alene* and *In re Acushnet River*, the plaintiffs' proposed jury instructions explained the causation issue as follows:

> A release of a hazardous substance is a cause of an injury or damage if it played any part, no matter how small, in bringing about the injury or damage. Therefore, even if the release of a hazardous substance operated in combination with the acts of another, or in combination with some other cause, the release of [sic] was a cause of the injury or damage if it played any part, no matter how small, in bringing about the injury or damage.[211]

The plaintiffs also proposed that once the jury concluded that the defendants were liable for NRD, they must conclude that the release of hazardous substances was a "contributing factor" to the death of fish, mussels, and snails observed at particular times and places.[212] Defendants objected to the plaintiffs' proposed jury instruction, including because it "misstates CERCLA's requirements regarding proof of natural resource injuries, including Plaintiffs' burden of proof on causation."[213]

Defendants proposed the alternative instruction regarding causation:

> Plaintiffs must prove by a preponderance of the evidence that the release of the hazardous substance was the sole or proximate cause of the injury. An injury is proximately caused by an act whenever it appears from the evidence that the act played a substantial part in bringing about or actually causing

---

211. Parties' Proposed Preliminary and Final Jury Instructions at 57, United States v. Elkem Metals Co., No. 2:03cv528 (S.D. Ohio Sept. 14, 2005), 2005 WL 2872312.

212. *Id.* at 64.

213. Defendants' Joint Objections to Plaintiffs' Proposed Preliminary and Final Jury Instructions at 11, United States v. Elkem Metals Co., No. C2-03-528 (S.D. Ohio Sept. 21, 2005), 2005 WL 2872665.

the injury or damage, and that the injury or damage was either a direct result or a reasonably probable consequence of the act.[214]

Plaintiffs objected on the basis that "[t]his boilerplate from ordinary tort cases is inapplicable to natural resource damage cases under CERCLA. The appropriate standard is whether defendants' releases were a contributing factor to the injury."[215]

The case settled prior to the court ruling on appropriate jury instructions, and the question of the applicable causation standard was not resolved.

h. Issues Related to Multiple Trustees

Defendants disputed plaintiffs' right to assert a joint claim for NRD given the statutory limitations on the jurisdiction of each plaintiff. Again, the court did not rule on the underlying motions before settlement.

---

214. Proposed Preliminary and Final Jury Instructions at 71, *Elkem Metals Co.*, No. 2:03cv528, 2005 WL 2872312.

215. Plaintiffs' Objections to Defendants' Joint Proposed Case-Specific Jury Instructions at 23, United States v. Elkem Metals Co., No. 2:03cv528 (S.D. Ohio Sept. 14, 2005), 2005 WL 2872676.

Chapter 8

NRD Restoration:
A Strategic Perspective

A. Introduction

Based on our experience, good restoration projects often resolve hard NRD cases. This is true because a collection of popular and important restoration projects can often allow the parties to gloss over differences related to the injury assessment or damages calculation. Moreover, a restoration focus as part of the NRDA process has many other potential benefits, including obviating the need for much of the damages quantification effort and helping the parties step out of the normal prosecutorial versus defense dynamic.

Although most companies recognize the value of focusing on restoration as part of a settlement strategy or cooperative NRD assessment (NRDA), many companies often overlook the importance of restoration for litigation planning. This is a critical strategic mistake because determining the appropriate type and extent of restoration is just as important as the quantification of injury and calculation of damages. For example, imagine that a particular injury was agreed on (say, the parties agree that an oil spill caused the loss of 1,000 birds), the NRD exposure could range from x to 10x, or more, depending on competing assumptions related to restoration needs for those 1,000 birds. In other words, injury is only half of the equation, and a litigation strategy that ignores the second half is like going into a fight with one arm tied behind your back.

This chapter explores the contours of a restoration strategy, including the importance of restoration for settling hard NRD cases; the interplay between restoration planning and litigation planning; the advantages, disadvantages, and mechanics of early restoration; and the challenges and opportunities presented by involving third parties (including environmental organizations) in restoration planning.

B. The Elements of Restoration

The purpose of the NRD legal scheme is to restore damaged natural resources and services. The NRD regime is not about punishment or public health; there are other legal mechanisms to achieve those objectives.

The principal NRD regulations are clear on this point. For oil spills, the NOAA regulations state that the purpose of an NRD claim is "to promote expeditious and cost-effective restoration of natural resources and services injured as a result of an incident."[1] For hazardous substance claims brought under CERCLA, the DOI regulations establish the requirements for "evaluation of the need for, and the means of securing, restoration of public natural resources"[2] following the release of hazardous substances into the environment.

As currently defined in the NOAA regulations, restoration is "any action . . . to restore, rehabilitate, replace, or acquire the equivalent of injured natural resources and services."[3] Restoration, per the regulations, includes two types: primary and compensatory. Primary restoration is the action needed to return natural resources to their baseline condition, that is, the condition that they would be in at the time of the assessment had the release not occurred.[4] Compensatory restoration is the action needed to compensate the public for the interim loss of the natural resources from the time of the date of the injury until primary restoration is achieved.[5]

C. Good Restoration Projects Settle Hard Cases

Good restoration projects will often help settle difficult NRD cases even where the parties cannot agree on the nature and extent of the injury or the appropriate calculation of damages. A worthwhile NRD project will often enjoy significant support within trustee agencies as well as the public. Once the parties

---

1. 15 C.F.R. § 990.10.
2. Natural Resource Damages for Hazardous Substances, 73 Fed. Reg. 57,259, 57,259 (Oct. 2, 2008) (to be codified at 43 C.F.R. pt. 11).
3. 15 C.F.R. § 990.30.
4. *Id.*; *see* Chapter 5, Section A.2. (discussion of baseline).
5. 15 C.F.R. § 990.30; *see* Chapter 5 (discussion of quantification of interim losses).

shift their mindset from a "damages case" to a "restoration project"—or suite of projects—the entire tenor of NRD negotiations can change for the better.

Furthermore, if an appealing restoration opportunity is fleeting (for example, if there is a pending development or sale of property), then the trustees are often significantly more flexible in their valuation of restoration credit, thereby allowing the parties to overcome seemingly intractable differences. In a large CERCLA case settled by one of the authors, the federal and state trustees were so enamored with an ephemeral restoration opportunity involving significant land acquisition near a national park that the trustees were willing to provide *three* times the credit calculated by the PRP for the project. Obviously, providing triple credit for a great restoration project can go a long way to resolving any disagreement over injury.

There are unlimited opportunities for restoration projects—from boat launches to restore lost fishing, to habitat creation to restore ecological damages. One particularly appealing type of restoration project is conservation of property that would otherwise be available for development. As in the preceding example, depending on the quality of the property and the pressure to develop it, the trustees are frequently quite generous in valuing such projects. Furthermore, companies may own property that they do not need and for which they have few immediate prospects for development. In those cases, it is sometimes possible to provide a "win-win" scenario whereby the trustees get something that they value very highly, while the company is able to utilize an asset that has little or no immediate monetary value. For this reason, conveying a conservation easement or providing title to the government or an NGO is frequently a highly effective way to help resolve complex NRD matters.

When using restoration projects to resolve NRD cases, there is a related but separate question about who should implement the project—the trustees or the liable party. In many cases, companies prefer to identify the project and then use the anticipated cost of that project as a basis for cashing out. In other cases, companies prefer to implement projects themselves.

Both strategies have advantages and disadvantages. Here is a brief strategic discussion of the pros and cons of each approach. The specific mechanics of including restoration projects in consent decrees is discussed in Chapter 9.

There are at least four reasons why a company may prefer to cash out of its NRD liability and allow the trustees (or their contractors) to conduct the restoration projects themselves.

- First, a cash-out settlement provides immediate certainty for the company and full resolution of the NRD matter. Except for issues surrounding reopeners (discussed later), the company can pay its NRD money and walk away from the matter.

- Second, the construction of NRD projects often includes uncertainties related to land acquisition, permitting, access agreements, technical feasibility, construction delays, and so on. Many companies would prefer to structure a settlement so that the trustees assume these responsibilities and risks.

- Third, restoration projects usually include performance criteria. While the definition and scope of performance criteria are subject to negotiation—as are the consequences of failing to meet those criteria—a company responsible for implementing a project must expect that the project will be subject to some degree of monitoring and that the company will be required to provide some assurance to the trustees that the project will meet the negotiated performance criteria. A settlement where the trustees conduct the project usually avoids this risk for the company.

- Fourth, there are some instances where the government is much better positioned to implement the project in a cost-effective manner. An example of this may be a project that is to take place in a federal wilderness area or state park. In some cases, it may not even be legally possible or feasible for the company to implement the project. In other cases—say, if the project includes an extension of work already being done by the government—the marginal cost for the trustees may be modest compared to the cost for a company.

For all of these reasons and others, companies often prefer to identify cost-effective restoration projects, negotiate a fair dollar amount to implement those projects, and then seek a cash-out resolution of the trustees' NRD claim. Conversely, there are at least four reasons why companies may prefer to implement projects themselves, depending on the nature of the projects and the goals of the company.

- First, many companies are able to implement projects more efficiently and cost-effectively than the government. At many sites, companies are already mobilized for purposes of conducting cleanup operations or other activities, and the marginal increase in cost to implement an NRD restoration project is far less for the company than the government.

- Second, many companies wish to see agreed-upon projects implemented properly and quickly. In some cases, companies have long-standing relationships with community groups, including environmental NGOs.

Companies may prefer to retain "ownership" of the project as part of their ongoing relationship with the community. Moreover, based on complicated intra-trustee dynamics or past negative experiences with the relevant agencies, a company may feel that it is better equipped to undertake a project in a timely manner.

- Third, in a cash-out setting, the government will often insist on a premium to account for risk and uncertainty, and in some cases that premium may be unreasonable or unnecessary. For example, if the government demands a cash-out that is double the estimated cost of a project, and the company is confident in its ability to implement the project successfully at or near the estimated cost, then it often is preferable for the company to do the project, even if there is some small risk of cost overruns or performance difficulties.

- Fourth, while the trustees will oversee implementation of the NRD projects, the cost of overseeing companies is far less than the internal costs of overseeing contractors, indirect surcharges, and other internal trustee costs.

For these reasons and others, companies often prefer to undertake NRD projects themselves. Of course, the best strategy for a company will depend heavily on the specific factors relevant in each particular case.

D. Restoration and Litigation Planning

Unfortunately, many companies mistakenly assume that restoration planning is a settlement strategy, unrelated to litigation. Restoration, however, is not only about *resolving* cases; it is also about *defending* them. Indeed, understanding restoration options is a critical aspect of litigation planning. This is because a company's NRD exposure is a function of the extent of the injury multiplied by the cost to restore that injury. Stated simply, the trustees may demand a shiny new convertible Mustang when a safe but used Smart Car would do the trick.

Here's a slightly more complicated formula to make the point:

$$\text{Damages} = (I \times PR) + (IL \times CR) + AC + TC$$

I = Injury
PR = Cost to achieve primary restoration (returning resources to baseline)
IL = Interim losses (injury from occurrence of event until primary restoration is achieved)

CR = Cost to achieve compensatory restoration (additional projects to compensate for interim losses)

AC = Assessment costs (trustees' reasonable NRDA costs)

TC = Transaction costs (experts, litigation, etc.)

The key point is that, putting aside assessment costs and transaction costs, restoration *costs* (as opposed to the extent of injury) are half of the equation when determining NRD exposure. In some cases, the significance of restoration costs can represent more than half of the NRD exposure since restoration costs are themselves a function of three independent variables: restoration selection (which projects are desired), restoration scaling (how much benefit will be achieved by the projects and therefore the amount of restoration needed to fully restore the injury), and costs to implement and monitor the projects taking into account uncertainty and risk.

Accordingly, companies should develop a litigation defense that includes a cost-effective, tailored, and provable restoration plan. As part of defense planning, companies will need to prove that their restoration plan is technically and legally feasible. Second, companies will need to demonstrate and quantify—usually through expert testimony and data—the ecological or recreational benefits that will be achieved by their selected projects. Finally, companies will also need to show that their restoration plan is more cost-effective than the trustees'.

Companies defending their own restoration plans should bear in mind the following reasons why their plans may be more cost-effective than the trustees' plan:

First, the trustees frequently develop separate restoration options to address separate injury categories. For example, the trustees may seek one type of project to restore injured benthic habitat while also seeking another type of project to restore lost fish populations. In so doing, the trustees are failing to credit the fishery gains associated with the benthic habitat project. While somewhat disguised, this frequent error is a form of double recovery prohibited by the NRD statutes.[6] To the extent the trustees are obtaining a fisheries

---

6. *See, e.g.*, 33 U.S.C. 2706(d)(3) ("No double recovery"). It is worth noting that the trustees are supposed to account for all benefits associated with projects. *See, e.g.*, 15 C.F.R. § 990.54 (stating that the trustees, when evaluating restoration alternatives, should consider "the extent to which each alternative benefits more than one natural resource and/or service."). That said, trustees sometimes fail to take a comprehensive look at such secondary and tertiary benefits. Moreover, the trustees may fail to consider the interplay between the multiple benefits achieved by certain projects and the legal obligation to select cost-effective restoration. A company should actively seek out projects that provide multiple types of benefits as a way to identify the most cost-effective restoration strategy.

benefit twice (once directly through the fisheries project and once indirectly through the benthic habitat project), the trustees will have recovered twice for the same injury.

This double recovery problem can exist across all injury types: habitats and species, multiple species, ecological and recreational, and so on. The key point is that a restoration plan must account for all NRD benefits associated with that project, not just the benefits that are the project's principal focus. In litigation, a company should identify and quantify all benefits associated with restoration projects to ensure there is no prohibited double recovery.

Second, in developing their restoration plan, trustees will often overcompensate the public by overstating the uncertainty associated with projects, particularly over time. Although the trustees are permitted to consider uncertainty associated with benefits over time,[7] companies should test whether the trustees' assumptions are reasonable and valid. Given that benefits creditable against the NRD debit will accrue over the lifetime of a project, any overstatement of uncertainty can have a material impact on the overall cost of the restoration plan.

There are numerous other ways in which restoration plans can overcompensate the public. For example, the plans may overstate legal obstacles for less expensive projects, may inappropriately cater to public preferences for costly restoration projects, may understate projects' benefits, or may overstate projects' implementation costs. The main point is that defendants in NRD litigation must be prepared to defend against unreasonable restoration plans.

To rebut a proposal for an unnecessarily costly restoration plan, a company preparing for litigation should develop its own restoration plan that is well designed and cost-effective. In most cases, the company's restoration litigation strategy must be scaled to the injury the company has delineated, not the injury the trustees' allege. And there may be resource categories alleged by the trustees where the company believes its injury defense is so strong that no restoration plan is warranted. However, as with many types of litigation, it is often prudent to be prepared to mount a multipronged defense, including arguments in the alternative. That is, there may be circumstances where a company should defend itself in the alternative in accordance with the following logic:

- As we have demonstrated, this resource was not injured in any material way.

---

7. 15 C.F.R. § 990.53(d)(4) ("Discounting and uncertainty").

- However, to the extent the court finds that the resource was injured, the trustees' restoration plan is unreasonable and inconsistent with the NRD regulations.
- Accordingly, while no restoration is required (because there is no compensable injury), if the court finds otherwise, there is a better restoration option that is far superior to the trustees' and significantly more cost-effective.

E. Early Restoration

Early restoration refers to undertaking restoration prior to the completion of the NRDA and involves a company's agreement to perform or pay for an early restoration project that the trustees have selected and approved, in exchange for an "NRD credit." In some cases, this NRD credit is quantified up-front (i.e., as part of the agreement to undertake the early restoration), and in some cases the quantification is put off for the future. In the latter case, the trustees will agree that the project is entitled to NRD credit.

NRD credit is like an installment payment on a debt. Each credit is used to reduce the total amount of NRD that the company will owe at the conclusion of the case. Because trustees will seek compensation for interim losses and since early restoration can shorten the time between the date of injury and the date of primary restoration (i.e., return to baseline), early restoration can also serve to reduce a company's overall liability.

Early restoration also has the potential to create a foundation for an earlier settlement of claims or issues. Successful early restoration negotiations will tend to improve relationships and build trust. If negotiations fail, they may at least give the parties some insight into the other's thinking, which could be helpful for litigation planning or efforts to find common ground at a later date.

While early restoration has potential benefits for all stakeholders, the current NRD regulations do not specifically allow for early restoration. Some commentators have even argued that the regulations require the trustees to assess all damages resulting from an incident before pursuing restoration for any portion thereof. Accordingly, many have argued that DOI and NOAA should modify their regulations to provide an optional program that allows trustees and PRPs to enter agreements to assess and restore known or readily ascertainable injuries before the full assessment is complete.

Early restoration was used to commence restoration of a variety of wildlife, habitat, and recreational resources in the *Deepwater Horizon* case, and that experience provides valuable insight into how to implement such a program. In April 2011, less than a year after the *Deepwater Horizon* incident, BP voluntarily agreed to provide up to $1 billion toward early restoration projects, under the terms of a "framework agreement," as a preliminary step toward the restoration of injured natural resources and services resulting from the incident.[8] This framework agreement provided an opportunity to make progress toward the restoration of resources that were obviously or visibly injured, including oiled birds, beaches, and other shoreline habitats, while the trustees continued with more complex aspects of the assessment and restoration planning activities.

There were four critical aspects of the *Deepwater Horizon* framework agreement. For each early restoration project: (1) all parties had to agree to the project details, including the cost and schedule; (2) all parties had to agree on the amount or value of the resources that would be generated by the project, which became the "NRD credit"; (3) all parties had to sign an early restoration project stipulation, which was an agreement among the parties regarding the project scope, schedule, cost, NRD credit, and other details regarding which parties would implement the work; and (4) the trustees published early restoration proposals for public review and comment, giving the public an opportunity for input on each proposed early restoration project, including the NRD credits it would provide, before the parties agreed to fund and implement that project. When the public comment process was complete, if the parties decided to enter a stipulation to implement a particular early restoration project, the signed stipulation became a binding agreement that provided the PRP with NRD credits to partially settle a portion of the trustees' NRD claims. All of these criteria can easily be applied and scaled to an NRD site of any size or complexity.

To create incentives for PRPs to participate in a voluntary early restoration program, perhaps the most critical element for success is assurance that fair credit will be provided for each early restoration project that they fund or perform. The parties should quantify the resources that will be created or the benefits that will be provided by the early restoration project. These benefits need to be defined in a way that can later be applied in the final damages assessment. Because each early restoration project agreement is a partial settlement, the benefits that each project is expected to create (the NRD credits)

---

8. Framework for Early Restoration Addressing Injuries Resulting from the Deepwater Horizon Oil Spill (2011), https://www.gulfspillrestoration.noaa.gov/sites/default/files/wp-content/uploads/2011/05/framework-for-early-restoration-04212011.pdf.

will eventually be subtracted from the total damages that the trustees would otherwise claim. In a simple case, the early restoration project benefits, and the final damage assessment, would use the same measure of damages.

In the *Deepwater Horizon* case, the parties experimented with different ways to calculate the project benefits, beginning with common measures like DSAYs, and similar measures for wildlife (for example, discounted bird years or discounted sea turtle hatchlings). Over time, to address disputes about the extent of injury, the parties developed contingent forms of credit that would apply first to a particular injury, to the extent it existed. If the credits were not needed for that purpose (because the assessment concluded injury was less than anticipated for that resource), the credits would instead apply to a related injury. For example, in the case of projects to create oyster beds, the project stipulation set forth that if the final alleged oyster injury was less than the value of the credits provided by the project, the credits could instead be applied to restore assessed injury to other benthic species in same area.

In cases where the parties are interested in early restoration, and are willing to negotiate credits, it can still be difficult for trustees and PRP companies to assess the benefits of early restoration when the magnitude of the assessment is unknown. Early restoration asks both trustees and PRPs to settle a portion of the NRD liability without knowing what exact portion they are resolving. For this reason, early restoration credits must be carefully defined in early restoration stipulations, and trustees must give PRPs sufficient information about the methods they plan to use to assess final damages. This is the only way to provide all parties with assurance that the credits generated through early restoration will be applied to the damage assessment the trustees are preparing, and will provide real value to the settling parties.

F. Restoration Banking

One recent advance in the NRD field has been the advent of alternative means to provide restoration credit against an NRD debit incurred as a result of a release or incident. Restoration or credit banking refers to the idea that restoration credits are a commodity for which there is a market that players (including beyond trustees and PRPs) could invest in separate and apart from the associated NRDA process. There are several potential models for restoration banking that differ depending on when and by whom the restoration is performed and what constraints are imposed. For example, restoration banking could refer to outside organizations funding restoration projects developed by the trustees to create credits that could then be purchased by PRPs to settle liability. It could also refer to a concept similar to mitigation banking—that is, the performance of restoration in advance of a release or incident that can then be credited against liability incurred as a result of the release or incident. While there may be several potentially workable approaches, two are worth particular focus:

1. At mega-sites with multiple OUs, both remediation and NRD sometimes proceed in a stepwise fashion. NRD at one OU might warrant restoration well before NRD is assessable at another. But, because the OUs are often geographically connected and part of the same ecosystem, it may be far more efficient to approach restoration holistically. In order to avoid waiting for remediation of all OUs and assessment of all NRD before any restoration is implemented, PRPs and trustees should together consider whether to restore resources in one OU above and beyond baseline and "bank" the excess credits to apply to forthcoming NRD claims at nearby OUs.

2. State and local governments and environmental organizations will often, at or near a site where a release occurs, have already developed environmental conservation or restoration projects designed to address historical and anticipated future losses to natural resources and habitats. Many such projects around the country lack sufficient funding. Where a public-interest organization or government entity has already designed a project that would replace or restore some or all of the resources for which a PRP is liable, and the public has had an opportunity to comment on and approve the project(s), PRPs should be permitted to help fund these desirable projects, and "bank" credit against their NRD liabilities in return.

One example of this type of arrangement is a three-party settlement entered at the Lower Duwamish Waterway site in Washington State. The site trustees, the city of Seattle (a PRP), and a private third-party restoration company entered the agreement, pursuant to which the third party will carry out restoration projects to generate credits. The environmental credits will then be purchased by the city of Seattle and other PRPs to be applied against or used in settlement of their NRD liability. There are a few critical constraints under this agreement: (1) the third party must obtain agreement from the trustees before implementing any project that will generate credits; (2) certain proximity requirements for project eligibility; and (3) the trustees retain authority to define the number of credits a project garners (including reducing the number should a project be unsatisfactorily completed).[9]

Restoration banking is a promising development that has potential to get to restoration faster and decrease assessment and other transaction costs. However, proper calibration and careful consideration of the utility of credits generated is key. Advance credit generation and banking procedures would need to be developed further to address the potential risks and benefits to all parties. In the following Expert Insight, Dr. Mark Laska discusses the elements of restoration banking.

EXPERT INSIGHT: The Future of NRD Habitat Restoration Is "Banking"
Mark S. Laska, PhD[10]

Great Ecology

One of the greatest challenges in NRD cases centers on implementing habitat restoration projects that offset environmental injuries. There are dozens of NRD cases evaluating injury, but relatively few habitat projects have been completed as part of a settlement. Here I discuss whether NRD liability can be resolved through purchasing "NRD offset credits" from an independent source—an NRD "bank"—rather than developing new projects at the end of a settlement process, or paying dollars into a state or federal NRD fund. As readers of this book have learned, only a small percentage of NRD cases reach litigation and almost all cases take many years—and sometimes decades—to reach settlement. NRD banking is a way to "speed" restoration and follows the tried and true model of compensatory wetland mitigation banking.

Once an NRD settlement is reached, there is generally either a transfer of money from a responsible party or the implementation of a project. In theory, trustees use these funds to conduct restoration projects, or the responsible parties conduct their own restoration projects to offset liability. Although responsible parties can produce successful restoration projects, this is not usually a responsible party's core business—and the regulatory process can slow down these projects.

I suggest these entities instead turn the assessment, planning, design, and construction of these restoration projects over to professional restoration bankers to

---

9. For further discussion of this example and the topic of restoration banking, see Rachel Jacobsen et al., *Natural Resource Damages for the Entrepreneurial Practitioner: Innovations in NRD Assessment and Restoration*, SUPERFUND & NAT. RES. DAMAGES LITIG. COMM. NEWSL. (ABA Sec. of Env't, Energy, & Res., Chicago, IL), Jan. 2018, at 5, https://www.americanbar.org /content/dam/aba/publications/nr_newsletters/snrdl/201801_snrdl.pdf.

10. Dr. Mark Laska is the founder and president of Great Ecology. He holds a PhD in ecology and evolution from Rutgers University.

conduct the restoration project and assume liability for its success—or better still, make use of NRD banks.

Using mitigation or NRD banking professionals increases the likelihood of a successful project because these professionals integrate engineering, design, and ecology into the projects. More importantly, the professionals remain fiscally responsible for ensuring the ecological integrity and success of these projects. If the habitat doesn't work, the NRD banker doesn't get paid or the investor doesn't get the return on the investment.

What Is Mitigation (or Habitat Restoration) Banking?

Mitigation is the preservation, enhancement, restoration, or creation of wetlands, estuaries, or aquatic habitats; streams, riparian areas, vernal pools, or tidal systems; forests, grasslands, or other upland habitats; or specialized habitat areas that supported special status species. In the United States, mitigation occurs under many regulatory systems (local, state, and federal) and is intended to offset anticipated and planned adverse impacts to nearby, similar ecosystems, such as impacts resulting from real estate or infrastructure development or to offset unplanned impacts resulting from accidents, disasters, or other unanticipated events. These impacts are also thought of as "debits" (as in an accounting system). Mitigation banking occurs when "credits" are produced from restoration projects in advance of the impacts to offset the debits, usually to satisfy regulatory or permitting compliance requirements.

In short, it is a system of credits and debits that helps ensure that lost ecological function caused by development is compensated by the restoration, preservation, or creation of wetlands, streams, and upland habitat areas elsewhere. I will return to this concept later.

What Is Ecological Habitat Restoration and How Is It Measured?

Ecological habitat restoration is a complex process that requires an understanding of the biotic and abiotic resources in an ecosystem. Ecological restoration aims to return a landscape to its pre-disturbance state. This may include the following physical/engineered actions:

- Contouring the land
- Revegetation with native species to encourage forage, breeding, nesting, and/or residency by fish or wildlife species
- Invasive species removal
- Stream channel or bank stabilization
- Removing contaminants
- Dam removal
- Floodplain reconnection
- Adding substrate
- Other activities that should increase ecosystem services and overall functionality

The goal of restoration projects is to create "ecological uplift," which is an improvement in one or more ecosystem services at a project site and is the net measure of the "credit." This uplift is measured against the baseline, or when the baseline is not known because impacts occurred before a functional assessment took place, through use of a tool called Functional Assessments (FAs). Historically, the U.S. Army Corps of Engineers calculated credits by land size (the acre being the fundamental metric), but that model is gradually shifting across the country now.

FAs, of which there are many models used throughout the United States, are now the preferred way to measure the ecosystem services provided by a particular landscape. For planned projects under NEPA, CWA, and other laws, ecosystem function is assessed before the anticipated impacts occur. The baseline determined from this assessment can then be used to calculate the acreage or functional loss from the project. We are then able to develop a mitigation plan to offset the known impacts to wetlands or other target resources.

Since NRD impacts are unplanned, we are usually uncertain about pre-disturbance functionality or the extent of ecosystem services provided by these systems before the impact. To estimate the loss of ecosystem services, ecologists use a particular kind of FA models called HEA models. HEA allows ecologists to scale the lost services and functionality to a habitat restoration project to provide the appropriate replacement measures, and includes a time factor to capture the loss of ecosystem services between the time of disturbance and the replacement of habitat.

Traditionally HEA was used exclusively in NRD, but now many federal natural resource regulatory agencies have decided HEA is an appropriate metric to use for planned projects. In a case related to Agrium (now Nutrien), BLM wanted to use a HEA model to calculate damages to wildlife as a result of planned mine operations in southeastern Idaho that were permitted under NEPA. At the time, there was no formal way to use HEA for a planned project, so we had to establish one. Great Ecology represented Agrium, and we worked with Arcadis, the regulators' consultant, to develop a methodology for implementing a HEA model for that project, which is now part of the public record. The methodology is now being applied to other projects demonstrating that HEA can evolve from being used exclusively for NRD cases to help determine appropriate mitigation and restoration for planned projects.

Why Does Mitigation Banking Work?

Habitat restoration projects are regulated under a variety of laws on the local, state, and federal levels.

So what, more specifically, is mitigation banking? As stated earlier, traditionally mitigation banking refers to habitat preservation, enhancement, restoration, or creation of a wetland, stream, or other aquatic resource (conservation banks do this for threatened or endangered species). The mitigation is completed in advance by a third party, with the intent of generating mitigation credits for sale. Before the sale of credits can take place, regulators must approve credits for the project, which the third party can then sell to an entity in need of credits to offset planned impacts. Without approval from regulators, no credits can be sold. As part of this process, the mitigation banker carries insurance and produces evidence that they can keep the project going in perpetuity. To ensure a market for the credits, a mitigation bank typically tries to provide resources that projects or other events in a particular region are likely to affect.

For entities planning a project that would have wetland impacts, purchasing credits from a mitigation bank can dramatically decrease your permitting time. This is because the project developers have essentially taken a wildcard out of their wetland application. (It takes a very long time to permit a wetland restoration project and is much faster to simply buy credits from an established bank.)

But for this to work, the third "independent" party (or their investors) needs to be willing to invest capital into the bank and go through that long restoration permitting process—in anticipation of development projects in the area. This is a speculative approach to building a bank. Sometimes banks are built in response to known projects likely to occur.

Investors in these banks need to see that there is a viable habitat restoration project worth investing in, and that the mitigation banking professional can manage the risk. To help a banker determine if this is the appropriate project—and by extension, if it is appropriate to approach investors with the opportunity—it is helpful to consider:

- Environmental practicality
  - Can the project be built on the site?
  - What are the key resources being impacted in the region?
  - Is it feasible to get enough uplift to generate credits?
- Economic viability
  - Will investors get a return on investment?
  - Does the market/demand exist?
  - Who are the credit buyers, and what is their timeline for credit purchase?
- Regulatory climate
  - Will this project likely be permitted?

Since getting a mitigation bank permitted can take a long time, it is critical that a prospective mitigation banker have a good idea of the site ecology, anticipated market, and regulatory climate before the banker buys land and starts the restoration process. It is very difficult, for instance, to create a wetland at a location that does not have soils with hydric factors or to begin a profitable mitigation bank in a market that is already saturated with projects.

The four vital ingredients for the success of the mitigation banking concept in the United States are:

1. A confluence of strong and consistent regulations applied to projects no matter their size;
2. A strong consulting and legal system that promotes compliance with the regulations;
3. A private sector interested, willing, and able to invest capital into mitigation banks; and
4. A stakeholder or NGO community that will put pressure on developers, regulators, and bankers.

Today there are more than 1,500 active wetland and habitat banks, and more than 3,000 have been created in the United States. While some banks went out of business (we did not know what we were doing in those early days), many of the 3,000 banks that were created have sold out of credits and are now being maintained in perpetuity.

The first mitigation bank transaction took place in 1982 (Goose Creek in Chesapeake, Virginia), and now mitigation banking is a $2 billion market annually in the United States. In other words, there is a track record of more than 35 years in the successful permitting, regulating, building, and running of banks, and in selling credits. In addition, there is an inventory of thousands of credits that have not been sold. Hold onto this fact—it becomes important to the conversation about NRD banking.

Part of why mitigation banking works for those who need credits is because the bulk of risk falls on the mitigation banker since they build the bank in advance of credit sales. Through the transaction by which the bank sells the credits to a permittee, liability for compensating for losses to ecological resources is transferred to the mitigation bank. Once an entity purchases credits, it is freed of liability.

Regulators drive entities seeking credits toward mitigation banks, a result of the federal 2008 compensatory mitigation rule, the preamble for which states that

> [s]ince a mitigation bank must have an approved mitigation plan and other assurances in place before any of its credits can be used to offset permitted impacts, this rule establishes a preference for the use of mitigation bank credits, which reduces some of the risks and uncertainties associated with compensatory mitigation.[11]

This rule emphasizes a watershed approach to ecological mitigation and reduces the number of different permits that must be obtained because it deprioritizes the need for a separate permit held by each entity whose development projects cause disturbance to target resources.

Additionally, President Barack Obama's November 2015 Presidential Memorandum on *Mitigating Impacts on Natural Resources from Development and Encouraging*

---

11. Compensatory Mitigation for Losses of Aquatic Resources, 73 Fed. Reg. 19,594, 19,594 (Apr. 10, 2008) (to be codified at 33 C.F.R. pts. 325, 332; 40 C.F.R. pt. 230).

Related Private Investment was a game-changer.[12] It encouraged private investment to achieve conservation and restoration goals. The policies and directives included:

- A focus on advance ecological compensation through mitigation, where the environmental benefits are achieved before the harmful impacts to resources occur;
- Encouragement of private investment in restoration and public-private partnerships; and
- Directives to five federal agencies and to federal natural resource trustees to develop mitigation banking rules, practices, guidelines, and policies.

From a broad ecological restoration perspective, the 2008 rule and the 2015 memorandum prioritize mitigation banking as a preferred alternative for ecological compensation for damages to the environment. Although President Donald Trump rescinded the 2015 memorandum in 2017,[13] the industry still clearly recognizes the potential of banks to speed up the regulatory process.

Natural Resource Damage Banks—An Idea Whose Time Has Arrived

Of the roughly 1,500 mitigation banks that exist, a few are NRD banks. In addition, Louisiana has codified an NRD banking program for its coastal area. There are two NRD banks in the area of the Portland Harbor Superfund site (specifically set up for NRD transactions in the past two years). There also are two older NRD banks in Seattle, Washington, and there was an attempt at establishing an NRD groundwater bank in New Jersey a decade ago (which did not advance). The Louisiana state program will provide the state's natural resource trustees with a streamlined alternative for seeking NRD that allows them to move forward efficiently after oil spill events along the Louisiana coast. The credits created through this program will only be used to satisfy Oil Spill Act or the Louisiana Oil Spill Prevention and Response Act and will only be used in coastal areas.

There are mitigation bankers excited at the prospect of participating in Louisiana's program, which will allow them to be among those contacted to satisfy future NRD liability from oil spills along the Louisiana stretch of the Gulf Coast. Some of this excitement should be tempered since the success of NRD banking depends on future disturbance to ecosystems. However, the Louisiana program provides another opportunity for investment and a market for those willing to take the risk.

And while there *is* risk—as there is with any mitigation banking project—for some it may be worth it. Looking back, it is possible to see how NRD banking could be used to limit impacts that result from delays in permitting.

This is where the inventory of thousands of unsold wetlands mitigation credits should be considered again. Some of these surplus credits exist in coastal areas, and

---

12. 80 Fed. Reg. 68,743 (Nov. 6, 2015).
13. Exec. Order No. 13,783, 82 Fed. Reg. 16,093 (Mar. 31, 2017).

were developed by mitigation bankers in anticipation of impacts that fall under the regulatory umbrella of the CWA. Unfortunately, as indicated in numerous conversations with regulators but not clearly codified anywhere specifically, there has been resistance to using those credits for NRD impacts because they were set aside for a different program. Currently, there is not a way to retroactively convert these various CWA credits to NRD offset credits.

I believe that some of these surplus credits could eventually be converted to NRD offset credits. The responsible party would likely still be liable for emergency response and cleaning up the oil spill or other disturbance, but the NRD credits could constitute a portion of the restoration plan to address impacts determined by the injury assessment and HEA modeling.

The Future of NRD Restoration Is Banking

The future of NRD restoration is banking—or it can be, at least. NRD banking could be combined with standard mitigation banking, and CWA mitigation credits could be retroactively converted to NRD offset credits. Indeed, in the future, there is no reason not to include HEA calculations in traditionally regulated compensatory mitigation banks. In this situation, investment in NRD banking is not likely to be any riskier than investment in standard mitigation banking. If NRD banks must be established exclusively for NRD purposes, however, then these properties become a riskier investment because there is no way to know where the next NRD liability need will occur. Restoration banks providing credits exclusively for NRD could prove more difficult to get permitted, and would be less likely to attract savvy investors. However, we take the optimistic view that Louisiana's program and the existing NRD bank case studies in the Pacific Northwest can lead to more NRD banking in the years to come.

Chapter 9

NRD Settlements

A. Introduction

Although NRD cases may be litigated for some time, most NRD cases will eventually settle. This chapter provides an overview of natural resource damage settlement strategies and focuses on key areas that practitioners must consider in determining whether, when, and how to settle. This chapter also provides key insights related to the negotiation of an NRD consent decree or settlement document. Finally, this chapter will review several major NRD settlements and lessons learned from those settlements. A catalogue of over 400 NRD settlements, including type of NRD case, settlement amount, and other key information, is provided in the Appendix.

The first strategic issue for any NRD settlement relates to finality. In most NRD settlements, companies seek a resolution to assure their management that they have finally and completely resolved their risk of NRD liability. In many cases, that objective is in tension with that of the trustees, who are concerned with making sure that they have an opportunity to reopen the settlement in case new information comes to light after a consent decree is entered. The issue of finality touches on multiple consent decree provisions, including the scope of the release, the breadth of any reopener, the definition of a site, and even the definition of natural resource damages. This chapter discusses all of these topics.

A second key strategic consideration is the performance of restoration projects. As discussed earlier, in many cases, companies want to conduct work themselves, while in other cases they are seeking to cash out and resolve their liability without further involvement in the site. A company's objectives for involvement in the restoration project will dictate its preferences related to a number of subsidiary issues, including establishing performance criteria, ensuring that projects are conducted appropriately by the trustees (if the company wishes to cash out), assuring money is spent locally, and providing for oversight costs. This chapter addresses the landscape of settlements and strategies regarding implementation of restoration projects.

A third key consideration is settlement timing. This chapter covers strategies related to timing, including issues related to the robustness of the NRD assessment, the interaction of multiple trustees, and the relationship between NRD and remedial actions.

Finally, a number of other important issues may need to be resolved as part of any NRD settlement, including the timing of payment, approaches to public notice and comment, and covenants required by the defendant. This chapter also discusses these issues.

B. Background on NRD Settlements

1. Settlement Process

Of the over 400 NRD cases that we have identified through 2018 that have been resolved, all but a handful settled without trial or partial trial. As academic commentators have noted, much information about settlements is kept confidential, so aside from practitioner experience, the primary public sources of information are consent decrees themselves, along with a handful of illuminating academic and professional analyses.[1]

One key step in the settlement process is often a presentation by the trustees of their initial conclusions from the damages assessment along with a settlement demand. Responsible parties will typically respond with a counteroffer. For large and complex sites, it may take years of assessment before the trustees make this kind of presentation to the responsible parties, and it may take years from that point until the parties reach an agreement. As with many other types of cases, parties will often engage in multiple rounds of offer and counteroffer before reaching an agreement in principle. After the agreement in principle, it can also take some time before the parties work out the details of a formal agreement. Parties may resolve liability in whole or in part, for example by settling for specific types of damages.

---

1. *See, e.g.*, Karen Bradshaw, *Settling for Natural Resource Damages*, 40 HARV. ENVTL. L. REV. 211, 224 (2016) ("Due to a variety of recordkeeping issues, there is little publicly available information about natural resource damages settlements. The economic and ecological importance of settlements is underestimated and unreported, offering few incentives to explore further. There is no centralized record of settlements. Trustees keep settlements confidential.") (footnotes omitted).

NRD settlements can be memorialized as administrative orders on consent that are approved internally by the trustees, or as formal consent decrees that are approved by a court. Administrative orders are generally used for smaller or less complicated sites. The main difference between these two forms is that administrative orders are issued by an agency, but consent decrees must be submitted to a court and are subject to judicial proceedings on the fairness of the settlement and court approval.

We have located 411 administrative orders and consent decrees through December 2018. The payment amounts listed in an administrative order obviously do not represent the full cost of the matter to the responsible party, since that amount (like the amount noted in consent decrees) does not include government assessment costs previously paid by the responsible party, any assessment costs incurred by the responsible party directly, or any transaction costs incurred by the responsible party, such as attorneys' fees or internal costs of staffing an NRD matter. However, many of the cases that settle under administrative orders are relatively small, so we would expect these additional costs to the responsible party to be relatively small as well.

2. Data on Settlement Values

A recent overview of NRD settlement values by Professor Karen Bradshaw used public sources, Freedom of Information Act requests, and follow-up discussions with federal trustees to compile extensive information on settlement values as reported by the agencies themselves. Professor Bradshaw concludes that between 1989 and April 2016, U.S. trustees have settled "at least $10.4 billion in natural resource damages claims" and that "$8.1 billion of the $10.4 billion come from the *Deepwater Horizon* settlement."[2] Professor Bradshaw also notes that 273 CERCLA claims were settled for slightly less than $1.2 billion dollars in total, 86 OPA claims were settled for about $8.24 billion dollars (including $8.1 billion for *Deepwater Horizon*), 30 claims under the CWA were settled for about $950 million (including $900 million for the *Exxon Valdez*), 76 claims under the National Marine Sanctuaries Act were settled for $24 million, and 259 cases under the Park System Resource Protection Act were settled for $21 million.[3]

As Professor Bradshaw notes, these data provide a valuable overall view of certain aspects of NRD liability and are fruitful material for high-level discussions about the underlying statutory frameworks. The data also have several limitations. First, the data from the agencies appear to be nominal dollar

2. *Id.* at 232.
3. *Id.* at 235–38.

values.[4] This likely distorts the analysis somewhat by undervaluing earlier settlement relative to later ones. Second, while trustees reported the dollar value of settlements, they did not report these amounts relative to their valuation of the damages. Thus, it is unclear how much of a "discount" (if any) the trustees accepted to settle the case, just as the responsible parties' valuations of the damages are unknown. Third, these amounts do not include settlements with state trustees.[5] Finally, these amounts are a partial accounting of the settlement value to responsible parties, because they only report what the federal trustees agreed to settle for; they do not include any amounts that responsible parties spent themselves on assessment or restoration projects that were not specifically monetized in the eyes of the federal government. Responsible parties also incur assessment costs for work conducted by their consultants and employees, but these costs are not accounted for in consent decrees or in any other federal tally of settlement values. And when a responsible party implements a restoration project as part of a settlement, the cost to the responsible party is not memorialized in a consent decree or public document.[6]

There are other ways to evaluate the value of NRD settlements, but they also have their limitations. For example, one could calculate the NRD settlement value per gallon of oil spilled under OPA. Including the *Exxon Valdez* matter (before OPA), but excluding *Deepwater Horizon*, the average of the 25 OPA NRD settlements where the cost of restoration is known is $33.5 million. By analyzing the gallons spilled and settlement amounts in past spills, it is also possible to determine the average cost paid by responsible parties per gallon spilled. Based on values drawn from the 25 settlements, responsible parties paid on average $56.29 in NRD per gallon spilled. If assessment costs are included in the NRD total, responsible parties paid on average $66.79 per gallon spilled. It is important to note that these calculations rely on several assumptions: (1) the calculation values were drawn only from the settlements summarized below; (2) the calculations include only spills where the costs and gallons spilled were enumerated and where there was no unenumerated restoration;[7] (3) where the total gallons spilled was stated in the settlement documents as a range, the average of the values was used; (4) where assessment

---

4. *Id.* at 235.

5. *Id.* at 233.

6. Occasionally, trustees may issue public statements regarding the estimated value of responsible party-implemented projects, but the relationship between those statements and the actual cost of such projects when they are finally implemented is unclear and would be difficult to study in a public, comprehensive manner.

7. Unenumerated restoration includes instances in which the responsible party agreed to implement restoration projects in whole or in part.

costs were uncertain, the NRD costs alone or the largest possible assessment value was used; (5) the calculation includes the *Exxon Valdez* settlement values, which was the only pre-OPA settlement included; (6) and the spills with the two highest and the two lowest NRD costs per gallon were discarded from the calculation as outliers.

C. Key Issue 1: Finality

1. Basic Considerations

In general, a key reason why companies settle all types of legal claims is that they want finality; they want to move beyond the dispute and put it behind them. This is true in NRD cases as well, where companies want to manage their risk of future liabilities, and where individuals involved in negotiating NRD matters want to be able to assure management that they have dealt effectively with this liability. However, there are a number of complicating factors. As we have seen, the science of NRD is constantly evolving, as new analytical techniques allow scientists to collect more detailed information about the environment, new computing techniques allow for ever more sophisticated models, and shifts in research direction (such as the turn to gene sequencing) facilitate new or more detailed understanding of particular environmental systems and processes. Many NRD cases involve contaminants that were released many decades ago, or contamination about which there are significant data gaps regarding extent and effects. Although in some small or discrete NRD cases all parties may agree that they have resolved all outstanding technical questions, scientific certainty is generally elusive. Thus, if a precondition of NRD settlements were resolution of all scientific or technical uncertainty, few cases would ever settle. Trustees often would prefer to resolve known issues and leave open the possibility of additional recovery later. This creates a tension that needs to be resolved in settlement negotiations.

The heart of any settlement agreement for NRD is an exchange; defendants make certain payments for damages and costs, or agree to implement restoration projects, and in exchange, the trustees covenant not to sue defendant companies to recover NRD. Parties typically face issues of finality in three major areas related to this basic bargain: (1) the scope of the release, including the conditions under which the trustees can reopen the settlement and seek additional damages based on new information or unknown conditions; (2) the definition of the site or geographic area applicable to the settlement (including specific carve outs); and (3) the definition of NRD itself. This section discusses each of these three issues in turn.

2. Scope of the Release and Reopener

Trustees include covenants not to sue for NRD, but these covenants are typically subject to a number of reservations. Parties tend to focus a lot of attention on these reservations in the negotiation process. The most basic reservations specify the other kinds of actions that trustees and federal and state governments are not precluded from bringing, such as claims for response costs, criminal actions, actions to recover for damages resulting from future releases of oil or hazardous substances, or actions to enforce the consent decree itself. Typically these kinds of limitations are uncontroversial because they merely confirm the parties' understandings that they are settling NRD claims and *not* other types of claims, or that they are settling only NRD claims that have been assessed.

More controversial—and more heavily contested in settlement negotiations—are reservations that would allow the trustees to reopen the settlement and seek NRD from the same defendants for conditions that are currently unknown. These so-called reopener clauses allow the government in specified circumstances to seek additional damages in the future. From the trustees' perspective, such reopeners are a method of attempting to ensure that the public can be made whole for damages that have not yet been discovered. However, from the perspective of settling companies, such clauses are incompatible with finality and expose the company to unpredictable future claims.

Even though trustees like reopeners for unknown conditions, many settlements do not have them. About half of the major settlements under OPA do not contain a reopener. See Table 9.1.

In the OPA context, the *Deepwater Horizon* NRD settlement illustrates one possible alternative to a reopener. In that settlement, the trustees specifically covenanted not to sue the defendants for "past, present, or future Natural Resource Damages, whether known or unknown, including assessment costs, resulting from the *Deepwater Horizon* Incident."[8] However, the settlement also required the defendants to make payments of up to $700 million for the trustees to use for two purposes: (1) to address injuries to natural resources "unknown to the Trustees as of July 2, 2015, including for any associated Natural Resource Damage assessment and planning activities," and (2) "to adapt, enhance, supplement, or replace restoration projects or approaches initially

---

8. Consent Decree Among Defendant BP Exploration & Production Inc. ("BPXP"), the United States of America, and the States of Alabama, Florida, Louisiana, Mississippi, and Texas ¶ 60, *In re* Oil Spill by the Oil Rig "Deepwater Horizon" in the Gulf of Mexico, on April 20, 2010, No. MDL 2179 (E.D. La. Apr. 4, 2016) [hereinafter *Deepwater Horizon* Consent Decree], ECF No. 15.

Table 9.1 OPA Settlements—No Reopener

Name	Year	Name	Year
Exxon Mobil Pipeline (Yellowstone River)	2016	*Westchester* [M/V]	2003
Cosco Busan	2012	*Kuroshima* [M/V]	2002
Polar Texas [T/V]/Polar Tankers/ Dalco Passage	2010	Platform Irene	2002
Puget Sound Energy	2009	Tesoro Hawaii Oil Spill	2001
Barge Foss 248-P2 (Foss Maritime)	2008	*Julie N.* Oil Spill	2000
Kure [M/V]	2008	North Cape Oil Spill	2000
American Transport, Inc./Beaver Butte Creek	2006	Chevron Refinery/Waiau Marsh and Pearl Harbor	1999
Anitra [T/V]	2004	*Command* [M/T]	1999
Olympic Pipe Line Company/ Whatcom Creek	2004	Colonial Pipeline Company	1998
Pilot Petroleum Corp. Tanker Truck Accident	2003	Tampa Bay Oil Spill	1998
Star Evviva [M/V]	2003	ARCO Pipeline Crude Oil Spill, Santa Clara	1996
		Avila Beach (Unocal)	1996

selected by the Trustees."[9] Specifically, between 2026 and 2032, the trustees have the option of requesting that the defendants pay accrued interest on unpaid NRD payment amounts.[10] In addition, the defendants must make a one-time payment of $232 million on the sixteenth anniversary of the effective date.[11]

CERCLA settlements often include a reservation of rights for future unknown conditions. This is partly because a 1989 court decision regarding the Acushnet River/New Bedford Harbor site expressed concern about the absence of a reopener provision in an NRD consent decree related to historical contamination.[12] As the court in *Acushnet River* noted, CERCLA section

---

9. *Id.* ¶ 21.

10. *Id.* ¶ 21a.

11. *Id.* ¶ 21b.

12. *In re* Acushnet River & New Bedford Harbor: Proceedings re Alleged Pollution, 712 F. Supp. 1019 (D. Mass. 1989).

122(f)(6) prohibits settlements related to environmental cleanups unless there is a reopener for unknown future conditions.[13] The court noted that this section of CERCLA explicitly only refers to environmental remediation, not damages to natural resources.[14] However, the court stated that it was "troubled" by the absence of a reopener for future unknown conditions related to NRD. Faced with statutory silence on the issue, the court reasoned that Congress had never considered the issue squarely, because NRD are typically "residual" claims that are evaluated and pursued after remedial action.[15] The court then found that even though Congress did not speak on this precise issue, the same kinds of congressional concerns that led it to require unknown conditions reopeners for remedial actions should also apply to reopeners for NRD. Part of the reason why CERCLA settlements are more likely to require unknown condition reopeners than OPA settlements is that there is no analogous provision in OPA to CERCLA's section 122(f)(6), and no analogous decision in the OPA context to *Acushnet River.*

Of course, it is possible that the court in *Acushnet River* got it wrong as a matter of statutory interpretation. For example, it is not entirely clear that NRD should be strictly viewed as a "residual" claim. Remedial actions can sometimes take years or decades to complete, but that does not mean that trustees and responsible parties cannot understand to some degree of certainty the scope of NRD. For example, this could be the case if remedial actions are expected to continue for many years (say, for dredging in a river system), but known NRD are largely in the past. Remedial actions also may have several phases, cover different types of resources, and pertain to different geographic areas at a site. Waiting for all of these remedial actions to be completed before giving companies a release without a reopener can be a recipe for endless delay. In addition, by the time NRD cases reach the settlement stage, the trustees (and the responsible parties) have developed sophisticated understanding of the

---

13. 42 U.S.C. § 9622(f)(6)(A) ("(6) Additional condition for future liability: (A) Except for the portion of the remedial action which is subject to a covenant not to sue under paragraph (2) or under subsection (g) (relating to de minimis settlements), a covenant not to sue a person concerning future liability to the United States shall include an exception to the covenant that allows the President to sue such person concerning future liability resulting from the release or threatened release that is the subject of the covenant where such liability arises out of conditions which are unknown at the time the President certifies under paragraph (3) that remedial action has been completed at the facility concerned.").

14. *In re Acushnet River*, 712 F. Supp. at 1034–35.

15. *Id.* at 1035 ("[C]ustomarily, natural resource damages settlements follow or are contemporaneous with cleanup settlements. This is so because, customarily, natural resource damages are viewed as the difference between the natural resource in its pristine condition and the natural resource after the cleanup, together with the lost use value and the costs of assessment.").

damages as well as the effects of current and future remedial actions. Nonetheless, the reasoning of *Acushnet River* tends to inform trustee approaches to CERCLA settlements.

As with OPA settlements, some CERCLA NRD reopeners are very broad, allowing trustees to re-sue if "conditions at the site previously unknown to the Trustees are discovered" or "new information is received by the Trustees that indicates that there is injury of a type unknown to the Trustees at the time of entry of this Consent Decree." That said, not all CERCLA NRD settlements include such broad NRD reopeners and some include no reopener at all. Prominent examples of CERCLA settlements without unknown conditions reopeners are the following:

- *CBS Westinghouse, Indiana* (2009).[16] A revised consent decree in 2009 was the last of a series of agreements related to PCB contamination at plant and six sites in Bloomington, Indiana. This final consent decree was for final remediation work at three sites and NRD at all six and any other sites. Total cleanup costs totaled over $250 million. The consent decree also included a $1.88 million payment as a complete settlement of all NRD liability, of which $1.5 million was for restoration and the rest for assessment costs. The consent decree also includes a broad covenant not to sue for NRD that "shall not be subject to any reservation of rights by the United States or any other Party to reassert such claims against CBS on any new information or previously unknown or unforeseen conditions."[17]

- *Calhoun Park, South Carolina* (2011).[18] This settlement concerned response costs and NRD liability at a site of a former manufactured gas plant, steam plant, sawmill, wood treatment plant, and shipyard. Industrial operations at the site were linked to soil, sediment, and groundwater contamination, including at Fort Sumter National Monument (which is U.S. National Park Service land). South Carolina Electric & Gas settled for $3.4 million in past response costs, $200,000 in Park System Resource Protection Act damages, $150,000 for an oyster reef project and assessment costs, and a conservation easement on 16.6

---

16. Entry on the U.S.' Motion to Enter the Agreed Amendment to the Consent Decree Providing for Remedial Actions at Neal's Landfill, Lemon Lane Landfill and Bennett's Dump, United States v. CBS Corp., No. 1:81-cv-448-RLY-KPK (S.D. Ind. July 23, 2009), ECF No. 57.

17. *Id.* at 33.

18. Consent Decree, United States v. S.C. Elec. & Gas Co., No. 2:11-cv-1110-CWH (D.S.C. Aug. 10, 2011) [hereinafter Calhoun Park Consent Decree], ECF No. 9.

acres of nearby land. Federal and state trustees provided a covenant not to sue and no reopener for unknown conditions.

- *Centredale Manor, Rhode Island* (2006).[19] This is the site of a former mill, chemical plant, and drum reconditioning facility in North Providence that now has apartment buildings. There is active remediation work at the site. In 2014, EPA issued a Unilaterial Order to Emhart Industries and Black & Decker, and projected remediation costs were over $100 million. In 2006, United States and Rhode Island entered into a settlement with then current owners of Section 8 housing at the site. Under the settlement, the current owners made payments of $3.76 million for response costs and NRD at site. The NRD portion of the settlement was $136,900. The settlement included a covenant not to sue for NRD, subject to reservation only for off-site NRD.

There are also many examples where the reopeners in CERCLA consent decrees are limited to very specific conditions:

- *Montrose DDT, California* (2001).[20] This NRD case against industrial DDT defendants settled for $30 million after the commencement of trial. The consent decree includes a reopener that excludes "an increase [in damages] solely in the Trustees' assessment of the magnitude of the injury, destruction or loss to natural resources."[21] The reopener also excludes "a determination by the Trustees that a previously identified . . . injury was caused by any DDT Defendant's release of a hazardous substance."[22] Finally, the reopener excludes "any [NRD] arising from any re-exposure or resuspension" of the DDT- or PCB-contaminated sediments.[23]
- *Palmerton Zinc, Pennsylvania* (2009).[24] The site is the location of an historic zinc smelter including portions of the Appalachian Trail. State

---

19. Consent Decree, United States v. Centerdale Manor Associates, No. 1:05-cv-00195-ML-DLM (D.R.I. Nov. 7, 2006), ECF No. 64.

20. Partial Consent Decree with Montrose Chemical Corp. of California, Aventis Cropscience USA, Inc., Chris-Craft Industries, Inc., and Atkemix Thirty Seven, Inc. (Relating to Offshore Matters and Department of Justice Costs), United States v. Montrose Chem. Corp. of Cal., No. CV 90-3122-R (C.D. Cal. Mar. 15, 2001).

21. *Id.* ¶ 9(B).

22. *Id.*

23. *Id.*

24. Amendment to Consent Decree Relating to Natural Resource Damages, United States v. Horsehead Industries, Inc., No. 3:98-cv-00654 (M.D. Pa. Oct. 27, 2009) [hereinafter Palmerton Zinc Consent Decree], ECF No. 247.

and federal trustees settled NRD liabilities with a responsible party for cash and property transfer. The settlement included a reopener for unknown conditions/new information. However, unknown conditions/ new information was defined to *exclude* any NRD from any airborne release of *any* hazardous substance from the zinc smelting operations prior to the consent decree.[25] Also *excluded* was any NRD arising from the re-exposure, resuspension, or migration by natural causes of hazardous substances known to be present in the sediments at the site.[26]

- *Onondaga Lake, New York* (2018).[27] This site covers Onondaga Lake near Syracuse, New York. State, federal, and tribal trustees settled NRD liabilities with two responsible parties for cash and a series of restoration projects. Like Palmerton Zinc, this consent decree includes a reopener for unknown conditions/new information. Unknown conditions/new information was defined to exclude NRD resulting from the release, prior to the consent decree, of hazardous substances at the site from former operations of the settling defendants.[28]

There are a number of recent consent decrees that incorporate and build on *Palmerton Zinc*'s exclusion from the reopener of NRD resulting from *resuspension or migration* of hazardous substances known to be at the site. For example, a 2017 consent decree with three PRPs addressed NRD at the St. Louis River/Interlake/Duluth Tar State Superfund Site. The site is located in Duluth, Minnesota, on the St. Louis River and includes areas of soil and sediment where cleanup activities have been undertaken for the past several decades. The NRD consent decree includes a reopener for unknown conditions/new information but excludes any NRD from (1) an increase "solely in the Trustees' assessment of the magnitude" of injury to natural resources, and (2) injury to natural resources "arising from the re-exposure, re-suspension, or migration of hazardous substances known to be present at the Site by natural causes or causes other than the Settling Defendants."[29]

---

25. *Id.* ¶ 42(a).

26. *Id.* ¶ 46.

27. Consent Decree, United States v. Honeywell International Inc., No. 5:17-cv-01364-FJS-DEP (N.D.N.Y. Mar. 14, 2018) [hereinafter Onondaga Consent Decree], ECF No. 5.

28. *Id.* ¶¶ 74, 77.

29. Consent Decree ¶ 18, United States v. XIK, LLC, No. 0:17-cv-02368 (D. Minn. June 29, 2017) [hereinafter SLRIDT Consent Decree], ECF No. 2-1. *See also* Consent Decree with Tecumseh Products Co. ¶ 23, United States v. Tecumseh Prods. Co., No. 2:17-cv-1728 (E.D. Wis. Apr. 19, 2018) [hereinafter Tecumseh Consent Decree], ECF No. 21.

Consent decrees that include a reopener typically specify that the provision is triggered by information that the trustees obtain after the date of lodging that indicate that there are NRD at the site of a type unknown to the trustees as of the date of lodging.[30] This provision implies a question about what precisely constitutes knowledge of the trustees for purposes of the limitation. Over the course of the NRDA process, trustees typically amass a substantial amount of information regarding the site, contaminants that have been detected there, natural resources, and recreational uses at the site. Consent decrees may include simple provisions that include such information in the scope of the reopener, by specifying, for example, that "conditions and information known to the Trustees on the Date of Lodging shall include the conditions and information set forth in any sampling data and any other data or information in the possession and control of the Trustees at any time prior to the Date of Lodging and any evaluation by the United States, the States, or the Tribes of such data or information as of the Date of Lodging."[31] Parties may also include language that further specifies that knowledge of the trustees includes information provided by the defendants to the trustees prior to the date of lodging,[32] information developed by trustees' independent consultants prior to the date of lodging,[33] or all information from surveys or other studies performed at the site by the government, regardless of whether the information was conducted for purposes of the NRDA.[34]

3. Definition of Site and Relationship to Covered Natural Resources and Scope of Release

Consent decrees often define the site and the covered NRD according to (1) specific geographic locations of the injury, (2) specific locations where the releases occurred, and/or (3) the location of certain contaminants and their associated effects. Consent decrees may also combine all of these concepts and may implement these concepts across several sections of the consent decree, including the definitions of "site," definitions of "natural resource damages,"

---

30. *See, e.g.*, SLRIDT Consent Decree, *supra* note 29, ¶ 17(b).

31. *Id.* ¶ 18.

32. *See* Palmerton Zinc Consent Decree, *supra* note 24, ¶ 46.

33. *Id.*

34. Onondaga Consent Decree, *supra* note 27, ¶ 77 ("For purposes of this Paragraph, the conditions and information known to the Trustees on the date of lodging of this Consent Decree shall include the conditions and information set forth in any sampling data and other data and information in the possession or control of the United States or the State at any time prior to the date of lodging of this Consent Decree; and/or all analyses, diagrams, maps, reports, and surveys performed at the Lake Bottom Subsite by or on behalf of the United States or the State.").

the covenants not to sue, and the limitations on the covenants. Choices among these definitions and provisions can have different effects on the achievement of finality at a given site depending on the specific facts, including the nature of the releases and the location of the contamination at issue.

A consent decree that focuses on specific locations of the injury may be appropriate, and may provide sufficient finality, where contaminants are located in a discrete, fairly well-identified area. Consent decrees that take this kind of approach may also include a reference to the locations as defined in the remediation context. For example, in the Calhoun Park consent decree, which concerned NRD at a site of a former manufactured gas plant, steam plant, sawmill, wood treatment plant, and shipyard, the site is defined as "the Calhoun Park Area Site, located in Charleston, South Carolina, as defined in EPA's Records of Decision for the Calhoun Park Area Site."[35] The consent decree resolves liability for damages to natural resources at the site "as a result of the release of hazardous substances."[36] The Sheboygan River and Harbor Superfund Site NRD settlement takes the same basic approach.[37] The effect of these provisions is to resolve liability for damages at the site, but to leave open the possibility of recovery for NRD that arise outside of the boundaries of the site.

Some consent decrees focus on a defined geographic area in a slightly different way: by defining the covered natural resources or NRD with reference to releases at a specific geographic area. For example, the Ottawa River consent decree defines covered natural resource damages to include injury to natural resources resulting from releases into or migration of contaminants into the Ottawa River Assessment Area.[38] The Ottawa River Assessment Area is then defined geographically to mean "(1) all waters, sediments, shorelines, connected wetlands, and natural resources of the Ottawa River primarily located in Lucas County, Ohio, from River Mile 8.8 to River Mile 0.0, at the mouth of the Ottawa River, and (2) Sibley Creek."[39] In this approach, the consent decree is silent as to the origin of the hazardous substances but

---

35. Calhoun Park Consent Decree, *supra* note 18, at 4.

36. *Id.* at 3.

37. *See* Tecumseh Consent Decree, *supra* note 29, ¶ 3(s) ("Natural Resource Damages" are defined in part as "damages . . . for injury to, destruction of, loss of, loss of use of, or impairment of Natural Resources at the Site as a result of a release of hazardous substances."); *id.* ¶ 3(bb) ("Site" is defined as the Superfund Site from the remediation context.); *id.* ¶ 18 (The plaintiffs covenant not to sue the defendant for "Natural Resource Damages relating to the Site.").

38. Consent Decree Regarding Ottawa River Assessment Area Natural Resource Damages ¶ 4(n), United States v. Aerojet Rocketdyne Holdings, Inc., No. 3:16-cv-2022 (N.D. Ohio Feb. 21, 2017) [hereinafter Ottawa River Consent Decree].

39. *Id.* ¶ 4(s).

focuses on the area that the trustees studied in order to determine the extent of any injury.[40] A consent decree at the Calcasieu Estuary Superfund Site takes a similar approach by including a government covenant not to sue for "Natural Resource Damages," defined as injury, destruction, loss of, or loss of use of natural resources "resulting from past disposals or discharges of hazardous substances that resulted in the release of hazardous substances at or from the Site, the response actions previously conducted at the Site, and the response actions to be implemented under the Consent Decree for Removal Action and Recovery of Response Costs filed contemporaneously herewith."[41] The "site," in turn, is defined as the "aerial extent of contamination" within areas encompassing several specific bayous, waterbodies, and a section of the Calcasieu River, all depicted on a map included in the consent decree.[42]

The distinction between focusing on the location of the injury and the location of the releases can seem like a fairly arcane one. However, both natural resources (like migratory birds) and contamination can move. Thus, a focus on injuries at a specific location leaves open the possibility that injuries that arise outside of the defined area, but result from releases in or from the area, may not be covered by the consent decree. Additional provisions can be added to address these kinds of situations. For example, the Ottawa River consent decree addresses migration of contamination by excluding from the reopener "liability arising from further migration of previously released hazardous substances present in the environment of the Ottawa River Assessment Area as of the Lodging Date."[43]

Some consent decrees take a different approach and focus on the location of the releases of hazardous substances. For example, a consent decree with Boeing for the Lower Duwamish River focuses on the location of the releases.[44] The consent decree concerns injuries in the Lower Duwamish River and Elliott Bay, a large area that includes a heavily industrialized waterway. The consent decree defines "Covered Natural Resource Damages" to include injury to

---

40. In this consent decree, the covenant not to sue covers NRD "located within" the assessment area. *Id.* ¶ 58.

41. Consent Decree for Natural Resource Damages ¶¶ 3 (definition of "Natural Resource Damages", 38 (covenant not to sue), United States v. ConocoPhillips Co. (W.D. La. 2:10-cv-01556-PM-KK), ECF No. 6.

42. *Id.* ¶ 3 (definitions of "Site" and "Calcasieu Estuary Superfund Site"). The Calcasieu Estuary settlement specifically excludes from the covenant NRD resulting from offsite disposal of hazardous substances from the site. *See id.* ¶ 39(c)(iv).

43. Ottawa River Consent Decree, *supra* note 38, ¶ 62(c).

44. *See* Consent Decree, United States v. Boeing Co., No. 2:10-cv-00758-RSM (W.D. Wash. Dec. 14, 2010), ECF No. 8.

natural resources "resulting from releases of hazardous substances or discharges of oil to the Lower Duwamish Waterway and/or Elliott Bay" *from* seven specific locations defined by 29 tax parcels.[45] This consent decree specifically excludes releases into the Lower Duwamish Waterway and/or Elliott Bay if the releases did not originate from the specific tax parcels. The Onondaga Lake NRD settlement takes a similar approach by defining "Natural Resource Damages" as damages to natural resources from releases of oil or hazardous substances at or from the site.[46] This approach focuses on the location of the releases, not the specific location of the resulting injuries, and reflects the responsible party's interest in obtaining finality with respect to damages resulting from releases to the waterways from specific facilities or areas.

A final approach is to focus on the location of the contaminants at issue, regardless of where those contaminants are currently located. For example, the 2017 DuPont Waynesboro NRD consent decree concerned NRD associated by the trustees with mercury releases from an acetate fiber plant operated by DuPont on the South River in Waynesboro, Virginia.[47] In exchange for a $42 million payment and implementation of a fish hatchery project, the trustees covenanted not to sue DuPont for "Natural Resource Damages at the Site,"[48] with "these are defined terms in the agreement Natural Resource Damages" defined as damages for injury to natural resources at the site from mercury from the Waynesboro facility,[49] and "Site" defined as "the Waynesboro Facility and any area in which mercury released from that Facility may be found."[50] In other words, this consent decree resolved all of DuPont's liability for NRD resulting from mercury from the Waynesboro facility, regardless of where in the environment that mercury ended up.

Depending on the circumstance of the particular case, it may make sense to combine some or all of these concepts (location of the injuries, location of the releases, location of the contamination). For example, the Palmerton Zinc settlement includes a covenant not to sue for NRD (1) resulting from releases from multiple OUs at the site, (2) resulting from airborne releases from two specific former facilities at the site, and (3) related to injuries that occurred at two specific former facility properties.[51]

---

45. *Id.* ¶ 4(c).
46. *See* Onondaga Consent Decree, *supra* note 27, ¶ 5(O).
47. *See* Consent Decree, United States v. E.I. du Pont de Nemours & Co., No. 5:16-cv-00082 (W.D. Va. Dec. 15, 2016) [hereinafter Waynesboro Consent Decree], ECF No. 42.
48. *Id.* ¶ 49.
49. *Id.* ¶ 6(i).
50. *Id.* ¶ 6(p).
51. *See* Palmerton Zinc Consent Decree, *supra* note 24, ¶ 42(a).

4. Definition of NRD

Consent decrees can define NRD in different ways. A fairly typical way of describing NRD includes references to basic statutory or regulatory provisions. For example, the NRD settlement for the 68th Street Dump site in Baltimore County, Maryland, defines "Natural Resource Damages" as:

> (i) the costs of assessing such injury, destruction, or loss or impairment arising from or relating to such a release; (ii) the costs of restoration, rehabilitation, or replacement of injured or lost Natural Resources or of acquisition of equivalent resources; (iii) the costs of planning such restoration activities; (iv) compensation for injury, destruction, loss, impairment, diminution in value, or loss of use of Natural Resources; and (v) each of the categories of recoverable damages described in 43 C.F.R. § 11.15 and applicable state and tribal law.[52]

It is typical for the definition of NRD to include assessment, restoration, and restoration planning costs along with compensation for injury, destruction, loss, impairment, diminution in value, and loss of use of natural resources. Some consent decree provisions are more expansive regarding applicable law. For example, the Ottawa River NRD consent decree defines natural resource damages in part as:

> any damages recoverable by the United States or the State, as Trustees or *parens patriae* on behalf of the public, under Section 107(a)(4) of CERCLA, 42 U.S.C. § 9607(a)(4), Section 311(f)(4) or (f)(5) of the Clean Water Act, 33 U.S.C. § 1321(f)(4) or (f)(5), or state law.[53]

Other variations include specific references to state statutory provisions as well as common law claims.[54]

---

52. Consent Decree ¶ 4, United States v. AAI Corp., No. 1:17-cv-02909-RDB (D. Md. Nov. 29, 2017) [hereinafter 68th Street Dump Consent Decree], ECF No. 8.

53. Ottawa River Consent Decree, *supra* note 38, ¶ 4(n).

54. *See, e.g.*, Consent Decree ¶ 5(J), United States v. Chevron U.S.A. Inc., No. 1:05-cv-00021-MAC (E.D. Tex.) ("'Natural Resource Damages' means the damages for injury to, destruction of, or loss of natural resources, including the reasonable cost of assessing such injury, destruction, or loss that result from the release of hazardous substances and/or the discharge of hazardous substances and/or oil at the Site, including due to response actions. 'Natural Resource Damages' includes, but is not limited to, natural resource damages recoverable under CERCLA Section 107(a)(C), 42 U.S.C. § 9607(a)(C); CWA Section 311(f), 33 U.S.C. § 1321(f)(4); OPA Section 1002(b)(2)(A), 33 U.S.C. § 2702(b)(2)(A); and OSPRA, Tex. Nat. Res. Code Ann., §§ 40.107(c)(7)(F) and 40.203(b), and common law claims that have been subsumed by those statutes.").

The *Deepwater Horizon* NRD consent decree provides another example of an expansive definition of NRD in response to particular circumstances.[55] In that consent decree, NRD is defined broadly to include references to applicable law at the federal, state, and local level, as well as compensation for injury related to response actions.[56]

For responsible parties, the key consideration in the definition of NRD is to make sure to obtain the broadest possible definition. Given overlapping jurisdictions, multiple statutory authorities for NRD, and some potential overlap between different kinds of claims related to environmental damage (statute, common law), obtaining a broad definition of NRD is important for companies that wish to obtain finality.

D. Key Issue 2: Cash or Projects

1. Basic Considerations

NRD settlements commonly include a mix of obligations for the responsible parties. The most common obligation is the payment of cash to the trustees.

---

55. *See Deepwater Horizon* Consent Decree, *supra* note 8, ¶ 9(ee) ("'Natural Resource Damages' means any costs or damages recoverable by the United States or any of the Gulf States (including the Trustees) as trustees or *parens patriae* on behalf of the public under Section 1002(b)(2)(A) of OPA, 33 U.S.C. § 2702(b)(2)(A), the Park System Resource Protection Act, 54 U.S.C. § 100722 and the former 16 U.S.C. § 19jj-1 (repealed Dec. 19, 2014), the National Marine Sanctuaries Act, 16 U.S.C. § 1443, Section 311(f)(4) and (5) of the CWA, 33 U.S.C. §§ 1321(f)(4) and (5), Section 107(a)(4)(C) of CERCLA, 42 U.S.C. § 9607(a)(4)(C), any other federal law, state law, common law, or any federal, state, or local regulation, rule, guidance or ordinance, as compensation to the public for injury to, destruction of, loss of, or loss of use of Natural Resources, including any natural resource services they provide, resulting from a release or threat of release of oil or a hazardous substance or any removal or response action (including any diversion of freshwater).").

56. Another example of a broad definition of NRD is the Onondaga settlement. *See* Onondaga Consent Decree, *supra* note 27, ¶ 5(O) ("'Natural Resource Damages' shall mean any damages recoverable by the United States or the State pursuant to Sections 107(a)(4)(C) and 107(f) of CERCLA, 42 U.S.C. §§ 9607(a)(4)(C) and 9607(f), and/or any other federal law, state law, local law, common law, or regulation for injury to, destruction of, loss of, loss of use of, or impairment of natural resources, including any services such natural resources provide, resulting from a release of oil, Solvay Waste, or hazardous substances at or from the Site. Natural Resource Damages include, without limitation: (i) the costs of assessing injury to, destruction of, loss of, loss of use of, or impairment of natural resources and the resulting damage; (ii) the costs of restoration, rehabilitation, or replacement of injured or lost natural resources and the services they provide, or of acquisition of equivalent resources; (iii) the costs of planning such restoration activities; (iv) compensation for injury, destruction, loss, impairment, diminution in value, or loss of use of natural resources or natural resource services; and (v) each of the categories of recoverable damages described in 43 C.F.R. § 11.15 and applicable state law.").

However, in about one-third of settled cases, responsible parties also agree to implement specific restoration projects subject to reporting and oversight by the trustees. In some cases, responsible parties have already partially or fully implemented restoration projects, and the consent decree memorializes responsible party effort. As discussed earlier, there are many reasons why responsible parties and trustees agree to specific mixes of cash and projects. Some of the factors that companies may consider in weighing cash versus projects are the following:[57]

The relative cost of trustee-implemented projects may be higher than company-implemented projects. In the CERCLA remediation context, it is common for responsible parties to prefer voluntary cleanup to government-implemented remedies because the costs of government-implemented remedies may be higher. In the NRD context, the situation may be similar for companies. Some companies may already have experience in implementing engineering projects and may believe that they can do so more efficiently than government entities. Private parties may have the ability to be more nimble in their contracting than government parties, and their incremental overhead costs may be lower. If companies can implement restoration projects more efficiently than the government, then the relative restoration value of a responsible party-implemented project may be higher and resolve a relatively greater proportion of asserted NRD liability.

Ongoing involvement has advantages and disadvantages. Cash payments can allow a company to resolve liability with minimal future involvement at the site. For many companies and in many situations, such a resolution is attractive, particularly for small cases where the NRD liability is not subject to much dispute and the company has limited resources. For larger cases, or cases where the relationship between the company and the community is more complex, a simple cash payment may present certain risks. A company may be interested in promoting good will in a community by taking a more active role in a restoration project, for example. In addition, a company may be reluctant to cede complete control over a restoration project to government entities, where the company has a concern that project failure will reflect poorly on the company. The long time horizons in NRD projects may make such circumstances difficult to predict. However, companies and government parties may have long-standing experience with each other and may draw from these

---

57. For a more detailed discussion of the advantages and disadvantages of companies implementing restoration projects, see discussion in Chapter 8, Section C.

experiences in assessing the relative value of ongoing involvement in NRD restoration.

Cash may not ultimately produce projects. Companies considering cash over projects should consider that cash paid in settlements does not always produce projects. A recent academic study found that DOI had $600 million in unspent NRD settlement funds in 2016.[58] Some of that money will be spent on projects, but, realistically speaking, some may not, at least in the short to medium term. Companies may have a variety of reasons to be interested in associating themselves with specific projects rather than payment of money to the trustees. For example, it is probably difficult for a company to generate good will in a community for money paid to the government where no tangible benefit in the community results. Companies may have a genuine interest (rooted in a corporate ethos, internal sustainability goals, or in longstanding relationships within the community) in seeing tangible fruits from money it allocates to NRD.

2. Performance Criteria

One issue that highlights the significance of the choice between cash and projects is trustee requirements that projects implemented by settling parties meet performance criteria. Parties that pay cash to trustees to resolve NRD liability do not need to worry about performance criteria (or any other criteria for success of a project), but parties that choose to implement projects as part of a consent decree may be required to meet performance criteria.

Performance criteria are specified goals that a restoration project must meet; they often include metrics (e.g., percent cover for a plant species in a marsh) and specific time periods within which the metrics must be met. Responsible parties need to understand that performance criteria become enforceable obligations when they are incorporated into a consent decree.

From the perspective of trustees, performance criteria assist the trustees in evaluating whether a restoration project is providing the expected benefits.[59]

---

58. *See* Bradshaw, *supra* note 1, at 215.

59. *See, e.g.,* Ass'n. of State & Territorial Solid Waste Mgmt. Officials, Accomplishing Restoration: A Reference Guide for Restoring Natural Resources Under the Comprehensive Environmental Restoration, Compensation, and Liability Act, Oil Pollution Act and Federal and State Laws 10 (2006), https://www.fws.gov/mountain-prairie/nrda/useful_documents/ASTSWMO_Restoration.pdf ("Generally, establishment of performance criteria is necessary to measure whether a restoration project provides the anticipated resource benefits. Performance criteria will vary depending on the nature of the project and the resource benefits to be achieved. Once performance criteria are selected, a plan should be

NOAA regulations specify that, among other things, a trustee draft restoration plan "should include . . . a description of monitoring for documented restoration effectiveness, including performance criteria that will be used to determine the success of restoration or need for interim corrective action."[60] The preamble for the final OPA regulations states:

> Performance criteria include structural, functional, temporal, and/or other demonstrable goals that the trustees should determine with respect to all restoration actions. For example, an agreement to create new intertidal marsh habitat as compensation for a marsh injured by oil could be described by performance criteria including the number of acres to be created, location, elevation of new habitat, species to be planted and details for planting such as density, and time frame in which identifiable stages of the project should be completed.[61]

The preamble also explains:

> When developing the Draft Restoration Plan, trustees must clearly define plan objectives that specify the desired outcome to be accomplished, and the performance criteria by which successful restoration will be judged. Trustees must, at a minimum, determine what criteria will constitute success such that responsible parties are relieved of responsibility for further restoration actions or necessitate corrective actions in order to comply with the terms of a restoration or settlement agreement.[62]

---

developed to monitor the project with respect to these performance criteria. Monitoring also can help with adaptive management of a project to make adjustments based upon lessons learned during implementation. The duration of monitoring should be commensurate with the time it takes to show that the anticipated levels of benefits are likely to be attained and maintained. Provisions for adequate funding for monitoring and management of restoration projects are essential for project success.").

60. *See* 15 C.F.R. § 990.55(b)(1)(vii). A subcommittee of DOI's NRDA federal advisory committee (discussed at Chapter 4, Section D) recommended that DOI

> should develop practical and cost-effective procedures for oversight and management of restoration actions, to include reasonable and flexible monitoring protocols, performance criteria, thresholds for corrective actions and timelines for given types of restoration actions. These guidelines could be readily incorporated on a case-specific basis into requirements associated with funding of third party implemented restoration actions or into settlement documents of potentially responsible party implemented restoration.

See U.S. DEP'T OF THE INTERIOR, NATURAL RESOURCE DAMAGE ASSESSMENT AND RESTORATION FEDERAL ADVISORY COMMITTEE FINAL REPORT TO THE SECRETARY 20 (2007).

61. *See* Natural Resource Damage Assessments, 61 Fed. Reg. 440, 445 (Jan. 5, 1996) (to be codified at 15 C.F.R. pt. 990).

62. *Id.*

From the trustee perspective, then, performance criteria are an important tool for ensuring that restoration projects are successful.

However, from the responsible party's perspective (including the interest in finality), the trustee approach has certain risks. Performance standards can add obligations that are difficult to foresee in advance, and responsible parties may be concerned that the standards are used as a stalking horse for project elements that trustees would like to see implemented but that go beyond what is necessary to resolve NRD liability.[63]

For example, for a habitat restoration project, hypothetical performance criteria that require a particular population of an animal species to be established in an area within five years would expose the responsible party to the risk that other factors outside of the company's control (such as a natural disaster, or an unanticipated influx of predators) could impede the establishment of that population. If a responsible party does not meet the performance criteria, the consent decree usually specifies that they are in violation of the consent decree and subject to all the enforcement mechanisms (including stipulated monetary penalties for noncompliance). Parties negotiating performance criteria must scrutinize them carefully to ensure that they can actually be met.

Performance criteria vary in their degree of specificity.[64] For example, in a 2012 consent decree settling NRD claims related to a 2002 oil spill in Cooper River and Charleston Harbor, South Carolina, Evergreen International agreed to perform a marsh restoration project.[65] The consent decree mentions performance criteria but does not define the term.[66] A monitoring plan attached to

---

63. In addition, the preamble text indicates that performance criteria are necessary to determine whether "responsible parties are relieved of responsibility for further restoration actions or necessitate corrective actions in order to comply with the terms of a restoration or settlement agreement." *Id.* However, this reasoning is somewhat circular where compliance with performance criteria itself is required under the settlement agreement. The basic underlying question with respect to performance measures is not what is required for the responsible parties to satisfy their obligations, but how to account for the risk that a restoration project does not meet its objectives.

64. An analogous idea to performance criteria is a future payment to be made if certain conditions are not met. For example, in the Hooker Landfill consent decree, the responsible parties agreed to fund a state-implemented habitat creation project seeded with wild celery, and agreed to pay up to $20,000 for corrective actions if planting did not succeed within six years of project completion. *See* Consent Decree Between the United States of America, the State of New York and Occidental Chemical Corp. and Olin Corp. ¶ 97(a), United States v. Occidental Chem. Corp., No. 79-987 (W.D.N.Y. July 19, 1999).

65. *See* Consent Decree, United States v. Evergreen Int'l, S.A., No. 2:12-cv-02532-RMG (D.S.C. Oct. 24, 2012), ECF No. 11.

66. *See, e.g., id.* ¶ 6(b).

and incorporated into the consent decree specifies certain "success criteria," including (1) "[h]ydrologic restoration will result in a semi-diurnal inundation/wetting of the restoration site during average high tides and allow for sufficient drainage during average low tides," and (2) "[t]he percent of vegetative cover, bare ground, and stem counts within the restoration site will not vary significantly from the reference site."[67]

Performance criteria can be much more detailed. For example, the Lavaca Bay NRD settlement includes an implementation plan for a marsh restoration project, including performance criteria of specific vegetative cover, a requirement that the "[p]rimary channels must be open and free-flowing, without substantial sediment buildup or evidence of closure," minimum water depths in primary channels and flow requirements in secondary channels, and "approximately 45 acres of emergent marsh must be present based on aerial photo review."[68] An oyster reef implementation plan likewise includes performance criteria characterizing appropriate surface elevation of the reef, total acreage, and "[e]vidence of sessile mollusk colonization on the constructed reef within 30 months post-construction."[69]

In the Onondaga Lake consent decree, the parties utilized scopes of work to set forth specific performance criteria for a wide variety of projects including both ecological enhancement projects and recreational use projects. For example, several projects require the PRP to enhance onshore habitat by conserving habitat, enhancing wetlands, and creating vernal pools. The scopes of work specify that the invasive wetland grass *Phragmites* shall not exceed 20 percent areal coverage, native species shall constitute at least 40 percent areal coverage, and at least 20 native wetland species shall be present.[70] The scopes of work also specify areal coverage limits for invasive species within the vernal pools.[71] While the PRP is required to meet certain performance criteria, this obligation is also limited in duration. For example, the performance criteria for *Phragmites* coverage in the onshore enhancement projects described here must be met within five years. If the criteria are not met within five years, the PRP must coordinate with the trustees on additional measures to meet the criteria.

---

67. *Id.* at 63–64 (court numbering).

68. *See* Consent Decree for Natural Resource Damages at Exh. 3 pp. 5–6, United States v. Alcoa Inc., No. V-04-119 (S.D. Tex. Dec. 10, 2004), http://www.gc.noaa.gov/gc-cd/cd-lav3.pdf.

69. *See id.* at Exh. 4 p. 4, http://www.gc.noaa.gov/gc-cd/cd-lav4.pdf.

70. *See Maple Bay Onshore Habitat Enhancement Project, in* Onondaga Consent Decree, *supra* note 27, app. C at 4–6; *Northwest Shoreline Onshore Enhancement Project, in* Onondaga Consent Decree, *supra* note 27, app. C at 7–8.

71. *See id.*

As the NOAA regulations discussed earlier indicate, consent decrees may also provide for contingency measures that apply when performance standards are not met. As with the performance standards themselves, parties seeking to resolve NRD liability must evaluate proposed contingency measures carefully to ensure that they are both clear and realistic.

3. Local Spending and Trustee Use of Funds

Companies deciding whether to use cash or projects to resolve NRD liability should consider whether it matters to them whether funds are spent locally. As Professor Bradshaw's research emphasizes, while all NRD monies must be used to restore or replace lost resources, trustees may take years to spend these funds and may opt to undertake restoration projects from the site of the injury.[72] This may be unsatisfying to some companies, particularly where settlement values are large and companies have a significant presence in a particular community. Companies may have an interest in seeing that money spent sooner and in ways that benefit local communities in tangible ways. One way to ensure that NRD funds are spent locally is for companies to perform the projects themselves, which allows the companies to have control over choice of contracting partners. As noted earlier, companies may have developed significant expertise in implementing projects in a particular area and may believe that they can implement restoration projects more cost effectively.

If a company decides that it would rather pay money than perform projects, there are other approaches that companies can take to ensure tangible and near-term local benefits. For example, companies can agree to fund trustee performance of specific restoration projects. Some consent decrees leave a significant amount of leeway to the trustees to choose restoration projects. For example, in a 2002 consent decree related to pipeline ruptures that led to oil discharge in the San Jacinto River, Equilon Pipeline and Colonial Pipeline agreed to pay $250,000 to the trustees.[73] The consent decree specifies that the "Trustees shall use $220,000 to construct estuarine and freshwater marsh habitat."[74] The consent decree does not specify any other details about the habitat restoration project such as location or timelines for completion.

---

72. *See, e.g.*, Bradshaw, *supra* note 1, at 215 (noting that in 2016, DOI had over $600 million in unspent funds from NRD settlements).

73. *See* Consent Decree Addressing Natural Resource Damages, United States v. Equilon Pipeline Co., No. H 01-3171 (S.D. Tex. Mar. 13, 2002). Note: this settlement was only a partial settlement of NRD liability.

74. *Id.* ¶ 38.

Other consent decrees, however, identify specific projects for the trustees to fund or implement. For example, as part of a 2006 settlement related to NRD from historic production facilities in New Castle County, Delaware, DuPont agreed to fund trustee wetland restoration projects at a particular property as outlined in the DARP.[75] Under the consent decree, DuPont paid $742,653 to the trustees for the project, an amount that was "expected" to cover the costs.[76] The consent decree also requires the trustees to notify DuPont if "unanticipated conditions require actions outside the DARP to assure the success of the Restoration Projects" and to give DuPont an opportunity to comment on or object to trustee plans, although the trustees have the authority to make the "final decision" on the activities in the notice.[77] DOI also is required to give DuPont regular written accounting of how the monies are spent.[78]

4. Oversight Costs

Companies that are considering whether to provide cash or implement projects also need to account for trustee oversight costs. In the NRD context, it is common to negotiate a lump sum payment that will allow a company to satisfy trustee future oversight costs in full. Future oversight costs can also be structured as a not-to-exceed amount.[79]

E. Key Issue 3: Settlement Timing

As complex as the decisions *whether* and *how* to settle an NRD case are, so are the issues related to *when* to settle an NRD case. The strategic considerations related to the timing of settlement negotiations depend on several variables, including internal company considerations, the interest of the trustees, the availability of funds, the status of the site cleanup, and the status of the NRD assessment. Several of these issues are discussed next.

1. The Status of the NRD Assessment and Possibilities for Using Simplified Assessments

A key issue impacting the timing of settlement discussions is the status of the NRD assessment, particularly at large sites. When a company is faced with NRD settlement discussions, it often will conduct its own evaluation of the

---

75. *See* Consent Decree, United States v. E.I. du Pont de Nemours & Co., No. 1:06-cv-00612-JJF-MPT (D. Del. 2006), ECF No. 3.

76. *See id.* ¶ 23.

77. *Id.* ¶ 24.

78. *Id.* ¶ 25.

79. *See, e.g.,* 68th Street Dump Consent Decree, *supra* note 52, ¶ 58.

site-specific environmental data, along with a review of similar cases, legal defenses, and other factors. Frequently, a company will conduct a scenario-planning exercise to determine possible "best case" and "worst case" outcomes as well as competing litigation positions and risks. As a practical matter, the availability of sufficient information to conduct this analysis in a meaningful and robust manner will often impact the ability for PRPs to engage in settlement discussions.

Moreover, the NRD assessment process itself is cumbersome, lengthy, and expensive, thereby making timely settlement discussions more difficult. In one current case that the authors are working on, a principal PRP and the government trustees signed a cooperative assessment agreement in 2003. Despite good faith efforts on all sides, numerous settlement proposals by the parties, and progress on several technical aspects of the assessment, a final resolution is nowhere in sight. After 15 years of a cooperative process, the company's liability is not resolved, assessment and other transaction costs continue to increase, and restoration is not occurring.

The process and timing for settlements is further aggravated by the significant uncertainty surrounding the science of NRD. This uncertainty arises from the inherent complexity of natural systems as well as human interactions with those systems (such as recreational fishing practices and associated regulations). In addition, the scientific techniques for NRD assessments have become more complex over time, which means (theoretically) that more information can be integrated into the assessment.

All of these problems raise the question whether there is a more efficient and timely way to resolve NRD cases, or at least commence settlement negotiations. In fact, when CERCLA was enacted, Congress was clear that a large portion of NRD assessments should be completed under "standard procedures for simplified assessments requiring minimal field observation."[80] The current DOI regulations purport to implement this congressional mandate through so-called Type A assessments.[81] The Type A assessment procedures, however, are only available for minor, short-duration releases in coastal, marine, and Great Lakes environments and are rarely used. Instead, almost all assessments proceed under the time-consuming, expensive Type B regulations that account for many of the inefficiencies of the current NRD program. This failure to make broader use of standardized procedures is inefficient and arguably inconsistent with the statute.

---

80. 42 U.S.C. § 9651(c)(2).
81. 43 C.F.R. pt. 11, subpt. D.

Fortunately, NRD practitioners now have years of experience and advances to help expedite NRD settlements in appropriate cases. Over the last two decades, NRD scientists and economists have embraced equivalency models as a tool for approximating damages. At a high level, these models involve calculating baseline and the percentage of service loss, and identifying the amount of equivalent resources or services required to compensate for the loss. For habitat losses, this model is called a HEA; for specific animals and discrete resources, a REA; and, for recreational trips, a TEA.[82] In essence, these tools allow practitioners to quickly estimate the value of damaged habitat, resources, or recreational activities by comparing the damaged resource or service to the cost of replacing that resource or service, discounted over time, and accounting for various uncertainties. These models are easy to use and allow for rapid assessments, even at larger and more complex sites than the ones we are proposing to address in the Type A process. Furthermore, because these models are focused on restoration (in lieu of monetary valuation), they are well-suited for achieving restoration faster.

Accordingly, one possible way to expedite settlement timing is to establish a voluntary program that allows parties to agree to conduct a simplified assessment and select one or more restoration projects on an expedited basis.[83] Once an NRD case is initiated, the trustees could quickly, in the preassessment phase, determine whether an expedited assessment using simplified equivalency models is feasible. If so—and if the PRPs concur—these simplified, expedited procedures could provide the parties with an early potential "on ramp" into a program to quickly assess injury and identify potential restoration projects that could become the basis for an early settlement of NRD claims. Finally, negotiation with PRPs could be time-limited (with the option to mutually agree to extend), and if no mutual agreement regarding procedures and results is reached during the time limit, the assessment could pivot back to the more traditional Type B procedures.

---

82. The concept of a TEA has been advanced by two highly regarded NRD economists, Doug MacNair and Ted Tomasi, among others, and has been used at several NRD sites; for more detailed discussion of these concepts, see Chapter 5.

83. These concepts were originally set forth in Brian D. Israel and Lauren Daniel, *Standardizing NRD Assessments: A Win-Win for Regulators, Responsible Parties, the Public, and the Law*, 49 ABA TRENDS (2018), https://www.americanbar.org/groups/environment_energy_resources/publications/trends/2017-2018/july-august-2018/standardizing_nrd_assessments/.

2. Pre-ROD Settlements

A second strategic issue related to settlement timing involves CERCLA sites where cleanup decisions have not yet been made.

NRD is often conceived of as a residual damage after any remedy required under CERCLA is complete. This concept is rooted in the statute, which ties both the ripeness of NRD claims and the statute of limitations to the remedy.[84] Under CERCLA section 113(g), many claims for NRD may not be brought until after selection of the remedial action under CERCLA, and CERCLA gives the trustees three years to commence an NRD suit for many claims after completion of the remedial action. The basic concept behind the linkage of remedial action and NRD is simple: removal and remediation may also restore natural resources and theoretically could eliminate damages entirely.[85]

It would be simple if NRD always proceeded after the remedy, and in many cases this makes sense for all the parties involved. However, increasingly, both trustees and PRPs prefer to engage in NRD settlement discussions prior to the site cleanup. There are many reasons for this, including the desire to resolve NRD sooner, achieve restoration faster, and, in some cases, incorporate restoration in the remedial process. As noted by the former chief of the Damage Assessment Center at NOAA, "It makes more sense, saves time and money, and is consistent with the regulatory framework for trustees and response agencies to conduct simultaneous assessments and coordinate remedial and restoration planning."[86]

However, there are many complications in such an approach. Given the residual nature of NRD, trustees may be reluctant to settle NRD claims before the final remedy selection out of a fear that the PRP may ultimately fail to implement the remedy. PRPs, on the other hand, may be reluctant to allow the settlement be fully effective only after final remedy selection because that arrangement gives too much leverage to EPA as the party requiring the

---

84. See discussion in Chapter 3, Sections A and B.

85. *See Natural Resource Damages: A Primer*, U.S. ENVTL. PROT. AGENCY, https://www.epa.gov/superfund/natural-resource-damages-primer (last visited Jan. 18, 2019) ("The assessment of Natural Resource Damages (NRD) takes place following cleanup because cleanups sometimes also effectively restore habitat."). *See also In re* Acushnet River & New Bedford Harbor: Proceedings re Alleged PCB Pollution, 712 F. Supp. 1019, 1035 (D. Mass. 1989) ("[C]ustomarily, natural resource damages are viewed as the difference between the natural resource in its pristine condition and the natural resource after the cleanup, together with the lost use value and the costs of assessment. . . . [and] are thus not generally settled prior to a cleanup settlement.").

86. Bill Conner & Ron Gouguet, *Getting to Restoration*, ENVTL. F., May/June 2004, at 18, 24.

remedy. There are ways to structure settlements to address such problems, but they require careful thought. Here are three examples of how parties have resolved NRD cases in advance of cleanup decisions.

In 2012, DOI and the state of Arizona settled with the owner of the Morenci Mine complex in southeastern Arizona for NRD related to historical open-pit copper mining operations. The trustees asserted that hazardous substances including metals and sulfuric acid had migrated from the site and had damaged a variety of natural resources, and that tailings ponds had injured migratory birds. The parties settled the trustees' NRD claims for a payment of $6.8 million before any RI/FS was issued for the site. As part of the agreement, the trustees covenanted not to sue the owners for NRD at the site, subject to (among other things) a reservation where:

> after completion of remedial investigation and feasibility study for the Site . . . or a corrective action . . . (i) Defendants fail to perform timely any CERCLA or [state law-based] response action or corrective action selected or approved for the Site by the United States or the State; and (ii) such failure to perform or its untimely performance contributes to an injury to, destruction of, or loss of Natural Resources materially greater than or materially different from that assessed by the Trustees in this action.[87]

In other words, the parties agreed to settle NRD claims except where the government orders a cleanup, the owners fail to perform the cleanup, and that failure causes additional natural resource damages.

In the *Palmerton Zinc* case, the parties reached an agreement with a similar structure as to timing of the effectiveness of the trustees' covenant not to sue for NRD, with some additional features. Federal and state trustees asserted claims against a group of responsible parties associated with an historic zinc smelter in Palmerton, Pennsylvania. Trustees alleged that the operations had caused contamination of nearby areas through aerial deposition and that metals had migrated from a residue pile into a shallow groundwater aquifer. The parties agreed in 2003 to implement an EPA-selected remedy for portions of the site, but the parties had not yet agreed to the remedy for the final portion (OU4), which included site-wide ecological risk, surface and groundwater, and certain other areas where EPA alleged that there was risk of further erosion. Defendants submitted a draft RI/FS work plan for OU4, but EPA was still reviewing the draft in 2009.

---

87. Consent Decree ¶ 15(a), United States v. Freeport-McMoRan Corp., No. 4:12-cv-00307-CKJ-HCE (D. Ariz. June 29, 2012).

To facilitate settlement before the final remedy for OU4 was selected, the parties agreed to the following provisions in a 2009 consent decree:

- Trustees covenanted not to sue for NRD at the site except for releases to groundwater or surface water (OU4 Releases) that occurred before two years after EPA's eventual selection in the ROD of the remedial action for OU4;
- Trustees further covenanted not to sue for the remainder of NRD (related to releases to groundwater or surface water after two years after EPA's selection of the OU4 remedy) if at least one defendant agreed in a consent decree to implement the remedy for OU4 and had successfully done so;
- If no parties entered into a consent decree, the covenant regarding OU4 releases was null and void as to such releases occurring after the date of the NRD consent decree.[88]

These provisions illustrate one way to address the timing issues related to settlement before selection of a final remedy so that both sides have an incentive to implement the remedy, and neither side bears all the risk in case of failure to do so.

In the Blackbird Mine NRD settlement (1995), the trustees and defendants addressed the relationship of remedy and NRD by embedding certain remedy concepts into the NRD consent decree itself. In this case, metals (including copper) were discharged into watershed as a result of decades of mining operations. State and federal government settled NRD with companies for $4.7 million in assessment costs, $1 million in oversight costs, and implementation of a watershed restoration project valued at around $60 million. The trustees covenanted not to file a civil action for items addressed in the consent decree. The consent decree included a "commitment" by the defendants (1) to perform the response actions and the final remedial action to be issued in the ROD, (2) to maintain water quality targets related to fish health in affected creeks, and (3) to conduct a removal action and bank stabilization project.[89] The consent decree also included a reopener provision that allows the trustees to bring a suit for NRD if (1) the companies did not implement the remedy to be issued in the ROD, or (2) if water quality levels in affected creeks were not "capable of sustaining salmonids through all life stages" by January 1, 2005.[90]

---

88. Palmerton Zinc Consent Decree, *supra* note 24, ¶ 42(b).
89. Consent Decree ¶ 5, State of Idaho v. M.A. Hanna Co., No. 83-4179 (R) (D. Idaho Sept. 1, 1995).
90. *Id.* ¶ 71.

F. Timing of Payment

Many NRD settlement agreements require defendants to pay funds to government entities. Trustees ordinarily have an incentive to receive money sooner rather than later, both because of the time value of money and because an earlier payment reduces uncertainty. For most settlements, defendants make single, lump-sum payments. Where settlement values are large, lump-sum payments could exceed a company's ability to pay in the short term.

The *Deepwater Horizon* settlement is one example where the parties found a creative way to structure a future payment stream that allowed the defendant to make payments over a period of many years, while providing corporate guarantees that reduced the risk to government parties that the settling entity could become insolvent and fail to pay in the future.

On April 4, 2016, the Eastern District of Louisiana approved a consent decree for multidistrict litigation that resolved the United States' CWA penalty claim against BP Exploration and Production (BPXP), along with all NRD claims of the United States and the five Gulf States, as well as certain other federal and state claims. The *Deepwater Horizon* NRD settlement was the largest NRD settlement to date. The consent decree required BPXP to pay $8.1 billion over 15 years for NRD (which included the $1 billion previously committed for early restoration, discussed in Chapter 8), up to $700 million for adaptive management and to address natural resource conditions that are presently unknown, and $350 million for NRDA costs incurred by the trustees.

The consent decree addressed these issues by stretching the NRD payments (excluding the $1 billion early restoration payment) over 15 years, according to a specific schedule that began with the effective date of the agreement (see Table 9.2).[91]

A similar schedule addressed trustee NRDA costs of $350 million.[92]

The consent decree provided that interest on the unpaid balance accrued as of the effective date and was compounded annually.[93] This interest was to be used to fund a portion of a payment for "unknown conditions and adaptive management" that trustees may demand starting in 2026.[94] (As discussed in more detail earlier, this payment takes the place of a reopener for unforeseen conditions.)

---

91. *Deepwater Horizon* Consent Decree, *supra* note 8, ¶ 16.
92. *Id.* ¶ 22.
93. *Id.* ¶ 27.
94. *Id.* ¶ 21.

Table 9.2: Payment Schedule for $7.1 Billion Payment
for Natural Resource Damages

Payment Date	Assumed Year	Amount
Anniversary of the Effective Date	2017	$489,655,172
Anniversary of the Effective Date	2018	$244,827,586
Anniversary of the Effective Date	2019	$489,655,172
Anniversary of the Effective Date	2020	$489,655,172
Anniversary of the Effective Date	2021	$489,655,172
Anniversary of the Effective Date	2022	$489,655,172
Anniversary of the Effective Date	2023	$489,655,172
Anniversary of the Effective Date	2024	$489,655,172
Anniversary of the Effective Date	2025	$489,655,172
Anniversary of the Effective Date	2026	$489,655,172
Anniversary of the Effective Date	2027	$489,655,172
Anniversary of the Effective Date	2028	$489,655,172
Anniversary of the Effective Date	2029	$489,655,172
Anniversary of the Effective Date	2030	$489,655,172
Anniversary of the Effective Date	2031	$489,655,178
Total		$7,100,000,000

NRD payments of this magnitude present an administrative challenge for the trustees, and an extended payment schedule can be advantageous.[95] Selecting and planning the restoration projects from these funds will take an extended period of time, so the payment schedule will prevent funds from going unused for long periods of time. Since interest begins to accrue immediately, there is less benefit to the trustees to having the funds in hand than if interest had been left unaddressed. And extending the payment over many years will give the trustees time to develop "appropriate systems for management of such large amounts of funding, including financial accountability systems."[96]

---

95. *See* Memorandum in Support of Unopposed Motion by the United States for Entry of Consent Decree with BP at 20–21, *In re* Oil Spill by the Oil Rig "Deepwater Horizon" in the Gulf of Mexico, on April 20, 2010, No. MDL 2179 (E.D. La. Mar. 22, 2016), ECF No. 16022-1.
   96. *See id.* at 26.

G. Defendant Covenants

Defendants commonly covenant not to sue or to take civil or administrative action against the trustees, and agreements alternate between general and specific language to describe the waived claims. For example, in more general agreements, defendants covenant not to sue for "any and all civil claims that arise from, or are based on," the spill at issue. In more specific agreements, defendants covenanted not to sue for "claim[s] . . . under OPA, the CWA, or any other federal or state law or regulation."[97] Depending on the spill, defendants also covenant not to assert claims for reimbursement from the Oil Spill Liability Trust Fund, for removal costs, or for other costs associated with restoration.[98] Defendants covenants often extend to "[p]laintiffs, their employees, agents, experts or contractors," or other related parties.[99]

Less frequent than the basic covenants are defendant certifications that to the best of their "knowledge and belief," they had "fully and accurately disclosed to the [trustees] all information requested by the Trustees which [was] currently in the possession of [defendant's] officers, employees, contractors, and agents which relate[d] in any way" to the incident.[100] These certifications appear more frequently in settlement agreements than in consent decrees. Defendants also sometimes agree not to assert any defense or claim in the future based on the contention that claims were or should have been brought in the instant case.[101]

H. Final Steps: Lodging, Court Approval, and Entry

Once the parties have concluded negotiations and agreed to the terms of a settlement in an NRD case, there are a series of practical steps that must be taken to ensure that the settlement gets across the finish line. All of the parties

---

97. *See, e.g.*, Consent Decree ¶ 38, United States v. Countrymark Coop., L.L.P., No. 1:09-cv-01018-SEB-TAB at 26–27 (S.D. Ind. Nov. 2, 2009) [hereinafter Countrymark Consent Decree], ECF No. 6.

98. *See, e.g.*, Consent Decree ¶ 20, United States v. Foss Maritime Co., No. 2:08-cv-01364-MJP (W.D. Wash. Nov. 3, 2008); Consent Decree ¶ 43, United States v. Marine Oil Trader 3, Ltd., No. 03-2030 (E.D. La. Sept. 16, 2003), ECF No. 4.

99. *See, e.g.*, Countrymark Consent Decree, *supra* note 97, ¶ 38; Consent Decree ¶ 45, United States v. EW Holding Corp., No. CA 00-332T (D.R.I. Oct. 6, 2000).

100. *See, e.g.*, U.S. Dep't of Interior et al., High Island Spill Agreement for High Island Oil Spill, September 5, 1991 5 (1992); North Pass Settlement Agreement 8 (2006).

101. *See, e.g.*, Consent Decree ¶ 15, United States v. F/V North Wind, Inc., No. 1:06-cv-00272-DAE-BMK (D. Haw. Feb. 17, 2009), ECF No. 32; Consent Decree ¶ 19, United States v. Tesoro Haw. Corp., No. CV01-00560 SOM LEK (D. Haw. Oct. 17, 2001).

must of course sign the consent decree before it is final.[102] Once that is accomplished, the trustees will lodge the decree in court, along with a complaint asserting the legal claims that the consent decree resolves. Usually the trustees will lodge the consent decree with the district court that is closest to the assessment area. Although they are not required to do so, as a courtesy, the government will typically alert the responsible parties that they are filing the decree and the complaint shortly before the documents are filed.

The proposed consent decree is subject to a period of public comment.[103] In recent years, trustees have been releasing the restoration plan at the same time the consent decree is lodged and have sought public comment concurrently for both the consent decree and the restoration plan. In some cases, particularly where the settlement is high profile, third parties may seek to go beyond merely submitting public comments and attempt to intervene in the judicial proceedings to challenge the entry of the consent decree. Given the deference that reviewing courts show after a consent decree is entered, it is difficult for third parties to intervene to challenge entry.[104]

As with other settlements, the court where the consent decree is lodged may schedule a so-called fairness hearing to determine if the consent decree should be entered. Courts reviewing a consent decree will ask whether it is "fair, adequate, and reasonable" as well as consistent with the goals of the statute.[105] The standard that courts apply is deferential. For example, one federal court noted that presumption in favor of settlement "is particularly strong where a consent decree has been negotiated by the Department of Justice on

---

102. Practitioners also need to be aware that internal government approval for settlements, particularly at the federal level, can take time. This process involves the preparation of an internal briefing memorandum, obtaining approvals at appropriate levels given the amounts at issue, and review according to U.S. Department of Justice policies. This review and approval process does not involve private parties. The U.S. Department of Justice typically insists that the federal trustees be the last parties to sign a consent decree. This can mean that, when multiple parties are involved, the final stages of approval can take additional time, since the approval mechanics for tribal, state, and federal trustees proceed along different schedules.

103. *See, e.g.,* 42 U.S.C. § 6973(d).

104. *See, e.g.,* N.J. Dep't of Envtl. Prot. v. Exxon Mobil Corp., 453 N.J. Super. 272, 278 (App. Div. 2018) (finding that intervenors had standing under state law to challenge entry of Bayonne and Bayway NRD consent decree, but that judge had not erred in approving consent decree after "presid[ing] over an extended trial and the post-trial proceedings").

105. *See, e.g.,* Cotton v. Hinton, 559 F.2d 1326, 1330 (5th Cir. 1977); United States v. Browning-Ferris Indus. Chem. Servs., Inc., 704 F. Supp. 1355, 1356 (M.D. La. 1988); *In re* Methyl Tertiary Butyl Ether ("MTBE") Prods. Liab. Litig., 33 F. Supp. 3d 259, 265 (S.D.N.Y. 2014) (Under CERCLA, "[a] court should approve a consent decree if it is fair, reasonable, and consistent with CERCLA's goals.") (citation omitted).

behalf of a federal administrative agency like EPA which enjoys substantial expertise in the environmental field."[106]

Courts usually approve NRD consent decrees, but there are some exceptions.[107] In the *Montrose* case discussed in more detail in Chapter 7, the Ninth Circuit Court of Appeals rejected a proposed NRD settlement between the federal and state trustees and a group of PRPs consisting of local governmental entities when corporate codefendants objected.[108] A court-appointed special master had supervised the settlement negotiations. The trustees created and disclosed to the special master alone an overall monetary framework for early settlement of the entire litigation, including specific allocations among the defense groups, based on the trustees' estimates of potential damages and individual liability, and taking into account the costs and risks of litigation. The special master recommended approval of the consent decree to the district court in a report. The report did not disclose the total damages that the trustees had estimated for the entire site but rather stated that the proposed settlement had a reasonable relationship to this total.[109] The district court approved

---

106. *See* United States v. Akzo Coatings of Am., Inc., 949 F.2d 1409, 1436 (6th Cir. 1991). *See also* United States v. Hooker Chems. & Plastics Corp., 540 F. Supp. 1067, 1080 (W.D.N.Y. 1982), *aff'd*, 749 F.2d 968 (2d Cir. 1984); U.S. Sec. & Exch. Comm'n v. Citigroup Glob. Mkts., Inc., 752 F.3d 285, 293 (2d Cir. 2014) (noting a "strong federal policy favoring the approval and enforcement of consent decrees") (citation omitted).

107. In *United States v. Great American Financial Resources*, for example, a court rejected a proposed CERCLA cost recovery consent decree in part because the decree reserved the right of the United States to seek costs arising from "liability for damages for injury to, destruction of, or loss of natural resources, and for the costs of any natural resource damage assessments." No. 6:10-cv-01783-MSS-KRS, slip op. at 6 (M.D. Fla. Sept. 12, 2011), ECF No. 11. According to the court, "[t]his provision is not bounded in scope or time, and any environmental degradation, however minor, could trigger liability for 'injury to, destruction of, or loss of natural resources,' regardless of whether the parties had agreed to resolve such claims through the consent decree. When the United States reserves its rights to pursue claims against the Defendant in such sweeping terms, and the Defendant waives the right to interpose *res judicata* and related defenses, it is not clear what degree of finality, if any, the consent decree confers upon the Defendant." *Id.* at 6–7. This lack of finality was unfair, according to the court, and would make it difficult to administer CERCLA section 113(f)(2)'s contribution protection for a person "who has resolved its liability to the United States." *Id.* at 8 (emphasis omitted). The government argued on reconsideration that the reservation for NRD was necessary because EPA was authorized to seek such claims here, and the United States had not alleged such claims (on behalf of the natural resource trustees) against the defendant. U.S.' Memorandum in Support of Its Motion for Reconsideration of the Court's Order Denying Entry of the Proposed Consent Decree at 17-8, United States v. Great Am. Fin. Res., Inc., No. 6:10-cv-01783-MSS-KRS (M.D. Fl. Oct. 18, 2011), ECF No. 15. The court granted the motion for reconsideration and approved the consent decree. *See* United States v. Great Am. Fin. Res., Inc., No. 6:10-cv-01783-MSS-KRS (M.D. Fla. Oct. 31, 2011), ECF No. 17.

108. *See* United States v. Montrose Chem. Co. of Cal., 50 F.3d 741, 746 (9th Cir. 1995).

109. *Id.* at 745.

the decree, but the Ninth Circuit reversed, finding that "the district court could not adequately evaluate the fairness and reasonableness of the proposed consent decree without having before it at least an estimate of the projected total natural resource damages at issue in this case."[110]

Even given the strong presumption in favor of approval of settlements, courts sometimes seek additional information. For example, the 2017 DuPont Waynesboro consent decree resolved NRD claims by the United States and the state of Virginia relating to mercury contamination that the trustees alleged resulted from historical releases from a DuPont manufacturing plant on the South River near Waynesboro in northwest Virginia.[111] The trustees alleged that mercury contamination affected local wildlife, especially mussels, fish, amphibians and songbirds, and affected recreational fishing due to fish consumption advisories that the state first imposed in the 1970s. The settlement required DuPont to pay $42 million in cash to the trustees for restoration projects and to fund a fish restocking effort downstream from Waynesboro in Front Royal.

Several parties filed comments on the consent decree with the court. Many of the comments were critical of the trustees' decision to reject a proposed trout restocking project in Waynesboro as a restoration alternative; several commenters also complained about the relative brevity of a trustee-organized public hearing on the consent decree and restoration plan.[112]

The court ordered a public hearing on the fairness of the decree and invited the public to participate.[113] The court specifically asked the parties to provide

> an overview addressing the principal provisions of the proposed consent decree and the major issues addressed in the various public comments, including: the amount of the settlement; the expenditure of monies on mussel restoration; the impact of the settlement on the Waynesboro area; the expenditure of monies on the Front Royal Fish Hatchery for smallmouth

---

110. *Id.* at 743.

111. *See* Waynesboro Consent Decree, *supra* note 47.

112. *See, e.g.,* Letter from Thomas R. Benzing, United States v. E.I. du Pont de Nemours & Co., No. 5:16-cv-00082-MFU (W.D. Va. Jan. 24, 2017), ECF No. 3; Letter from William G. Buchanan, United States v. E.I. du Pont de Nemours & Co., No. 5:16-cv-00082-MFU (W.D. Va. Jan. 31, 2017), ECF No. 6. The Waynesboro City Manager submitted a letter in support of the settlement, on behalf of the city council; *see* Letter from Michael G. Hamp II, City Manager, City Council of the City of Waynesboro, United States v. E.I. du Pont de Nemours & Co., No. 5:16-cv-00082-MFU (W.D. Va. Mar. 2, 2017), ECF No. 12.

113. United States v. E.I. du Pont de Nemours & Co., No. 5:16-cv-00082-MFU, slip op. at 4 (W.D. Va. July 28, 2017), ECF No. 40.

bass and other species (muskellunge and walleye) propagation versus a trout grow-out facility in Waynesboro.[114]

The public court hearing included testimony in support of the consent decree from the USFWS case manager (on injury assessment, quantification, and restoration planning), a DuPont remediation director (on remediation and on bank stabilization efforts), the vice mayor of Waynesboro (on the benefits of local projects contemplated by the settlement), the deputy director of Virginia's Department of Game and Wildlife (on the fish hatchery project), and Virginia's director of Natural Resources (on the state's decision to support the settlement).[115] The court also conducted its own fact finding by visiting a site where NRD studies were conducted, a riverbank remediation project near the facility, and the site of a recreational fishing enhancement project.[116] Finally, after the public hearing, the court asked the parties to provide a supplemental briefing on the adequacy of the amount of the settlement, specifically "the range of expected costs calculated by the Trustees for completing the restoration necessary to fully compensate for natural resource damages."[117]

The court ultimately concluded without much difficulty that the consent decree was fair, adequate, and reasonable. In a lengthy opinion approving the consent decree, the court detailed the public comments both for and against entry of the decree, along with the results of the court's own fact-finding efforts. The court noted multiple times that the consent decree and the restoration plan were grounded in a substantial amount of scientific study.[118] The court also evaluated in detail the public objections to the exclusion of trout-related projects from the restoration plan, as well as the trustee responses; these issues animated much of the critical comments that the trustees received

---

114. United States v. E.I. du Pont de Nemours & Co., No. 5:16-cv-00082-MFU, slip op. at 2 (W.D. Va. May 5, 2017), ECF No. 19.

115. United States v. E.I. du Pont de Nemours & Co., No. 5:16-cv-00082-MFU, slip op. at 5–14 (W.D. Va. July 28, 2017), ECF No. 40.

116. *See id.* at 5.

117. United States v. E.I. du Pont de Nemours & Co., No. 5:16-cv-00082-MFU, slip op. at 2 (W.D. Va. July 10, 2017), ECF No. 35. The court cited the Ninth Circuit decision in *Montrose* in support for this request. *Id.*

118. *See, e.g.,* United States v. E.I. du Pont de Nemours & Co., No. 5:16-cv-00082-MFU, slip op. at 26 (W.D. Va. July 28, 2017) (consent decree was "backed up by a decade of scientific study with significant stakeholder involvement along the way"); 26–27 (parties arrived at the $42 million figure "following an eighteen month period of negotiation based on substantial scientific research"); 28 (damages were "extensively studied" and consent decree "is grounded in the results of those many years of scientific study").

from the public and that the court heard during its own hearing.[119] As to the settlement amount, the court noted that the amount of monetary damages "is the subject of reasonable debate," and the outcome of a lengthy trial, with "dueling teams of scientific and economic experts as to the appropriate methodology and measure of natural resource damages," would be uncertain.[120] Litigation would be "costly, diverting monies from restoration," and "would take years to play out, further delaying restoration efforts."[121] Given the well-developed scientific basis for the payment amount, and the uncertainty of the alternative of having the parties resort to litigation, the court concluded that the settlement amount was fair, adequate, and reasonable.

The Waynesboro case is important for practitioners because it illustrates several important issues in the final stages of a settlement. First, even where there is a deferential standard for approval of consent decrees, the proponents of consent decrees should never take anything for granted. An NRD consent decree is usually the result of a long period of scientific study and hard fought negotiations between parties with good factual and legal arguments on their side. The judge who must approve the consent decree has not been a part of any of those negotiations, and he or she has an independent duty to evaluate whether the consent decree is in the public interest.

Second, parties should be aware of the potential for organized opposition to a consent decree. As a practical matter, the bulk of the burden for defending a consent decree against such opponents falls to the trustees because the trustees (not the defendants) have the obligation to respond to public comments adequately. However, it may be necessary for the parties to coordinate to some degree, particularly if the court seeks additional information from the parties. In the Waynesboro case, the trustees took the lead defending the consent decree at the public hearing, but there was also testimony from DuPont in an area where the company likely had the most significant expertise, namely,

---

119. *See id.* at 33 (noting that the "principal criticism voiced by opponents of the Consent Decree" was the exclusion of restoration projects focused on trout restocking). The trustees addressed the issue of trout in the responses to comments and in the final restoration plan, in part by noting that trout were not subject to mercury advisories in the South River and thus were not an affected resource (either ecologically or recreationally).

120. *Id.* at 31.

121. *Id.* at 32. In addition, DuPont had a significant legal defense that caused additional uncertainty regarding whether there would be any recovery: a 1984 release with the state of Virginia "which had the potential of eviscerating Virginia's claim for any natural resource damages." *Id.*

background information on the history of remedial efforts at the site.[122] And the parties submitted a joint memorandum on the final issue that the court wanted to understand, following *Montrose*: the reasonableness of the final settlement amount, given each party's separate evaluation of the case.[123]

I. Conclusion

For practitioners, settlement strategy and consent decree negotiations are key components of NRD. In some ways, this is no different from other areas of the law. However, there are certain inherent tensions and complexities in NRD practice that make settlements especially challenging, including the scope of the release and reopener, and the timing of settlement discussions.

---

122. *Id.* at 6.

123. *See* Joint Supplemental Memorandum in Support of Motion to Enter, United States v. E.I. du Pont de Nemours & Co., No. 5:16-cv-00082-MFU (W.D. Va. July 24, 2017), ECF No. 39.

Chapter 10

Complex Situations and Novel Approaches

A. Resources with Multiple Trustees/ Overlapping Trusteeship

Most NRD actions will involve trustees from at least the federal government and the government of the state in which the incident occurred. Each of these governments may have designated more than one agency as trustees over the affected resources. For example, in the case of injuries to navigable rivers, both DOI's USFWS and the U.S. Department of Commerce are likely designated as federal trustees. Where tribal resources are impacted, or the impacts extend beyond the jurisdictional boundaries of the state in which the incident occurred, even more governments, each with potentially multiple trustee agencies, may have claims. In the *Deepwater Horizon* NRD matter, for example, BP faced claims alleged by the federal government, at least five state governments, and several foreign nations, most of which had designated multiple trustee agencies. This section addresses the legal effect of multiple entities exercising trusteeship over an injured resource and discusses some of the practical challenges faced in administering damages assessments and negotiating claims when multiple trustees are at the table.

1. Who Has Trusteeship over What Resources?

OPA and CERCLA provide only general definitions of the categories of resources within a given entity's trusteeship. Pursuant to OPA, the U.S. government has trusteeship over "natural resources belonging to, managed by, controlled by, or appertaining to the United States," any state has trusteeship over "natural resources belonging to, managed by, controlled by, or appertaining to such State," and any Indian tribe has trusteeship over "natural resources belonging to, managed by, controlled by, or appertaining to such Indian tribe."[1] Similarly, CERCLA restricts trusteeship of the states to "natural resources within the State or belonging to, managed by, controlled by, or appertaining to such State," and trusteeship of Indian tribes to "natural resources belonging to, managed by, controlled by, or appertaining to such tribe, or held in trust for the benefit of such tribe, or belonging to a member of such tribe if such resources are subject to a trust restriction on alienation."[2]

The federal regulations designating trustees clarify these definitions to some extent. Generally, federal agencies are designated as trustees over the natural resources, including the supporting ecosystem, within their control.[3] For example, the Secretary of the Interior "shall act as trustee for natural resources managed or controlled by the DOI,"[4] and the Secretary of Commerce "shall act as trustee for natural resources . . . managed or controlled by other federal agencies and that are found in, under, or using waters navigable by deep draft vessels, tidally influenced waters, or waters of the contiguous zone, the exclusive economic zone, and the outer continental shelf."[5]

The regulations also set forth broad categories of resources, injury to which is recoverable, without regard to whether or not the federal government and/or state and/or tribes might have co-trusteeship.[6] For example, a loggerhead sea turtle is managed under the federal Endangered Species Act and is therefore under the trusteeship of the United States. However, if it nests on a beach in Alabama for parts of its life, it may also be under the trusteeship of Alabama. Similarly, a species of fish may migrate throughout its lifetime

---

1. 33 U.S.C. § 2706(a)(1)–(3). Importantly, "natural resources" are defined under OPA as including "land, fish, wildlife, biota, air, water, ground water, drinking water supplies, and other such resources *belonging to, managed by, held in trust by, appertaining to, or otherwise controlled by the United States (including the resources of the exclusive economic zone), any State or local government or Indian Tribe, or any foreign government.*" *Id.* § 2701(20) (emphasis added). This definition seems to imply that recovery is not available for damage to privately held natural resources. Courts have indicated that trustees are not limited to bringing claims for damage to government-owned resources, but have held that they may not bring claims for damage to all property within a state; "damage to private property—absent any government involvement, management or control—is not covered by the natural resource damage provisions of the statute." Ohio v. U.S. Dep't of the Interior, 880 F.2d 432, 460 (D.C. Cir. 1989).

2. 42 U.S.C. § 9607(f)(1).

3. 40 C.F.R. § 300.600.

4. *Id.* § 300.600(b)(2).

5. *Id.* § 300.600(b)(1).

6. *See, e.g.*, 40 C.F.R. § 300.605 ("State trustees shall act on behalf of the public as trustees for natural resources, including their supporting ecosystems, *within the boundary of a state* or belonging to, managed by, controlled by, or appertaining to such state.") (emphasis added).

between the waters of various states, and each of those states, along with the federal government, arguably is a co-trustee of that resource. Another species of fish may spawn in state waters but spend most of its adult life in exclusively federals waters. If so, the federal government explicitly exercises trusteeship over all life stages of the species, while the state may share in that trusteeship only for the period during which the species is spawning.

Determining the stewardship of any particular natural resource is a mixed question of fact and law.[7] In some cases—impacts to sediments in U.S. waters outside any state's jurisdiction, for example—determining who exercises trusteeship is easy. But in cases where resources extend beyond jurisdictional boundaries, and especially in cases where migratory species are at issue, determination of trusteeship will require careful legal analysis combined with sound scientific input.

2. Legal Impact of Co-Trusteeship

Because both OPA and CERCLA explicitly prohibit double recovery, the effect of co-trusteeship on ultimate NRD liability is limited.[8] A trustee is not entitled to recover for damages already paid to another trustee, and trustees are precluded from recovering for the same damages under both CERCLA and OPA. Co-trusteeship may nonetheless have substantial impacts on NRD strategy.

Both CERCLA and OPA are silent as to how co-trusteeship operates. Some commentators, noting that both statutes provide that "[t]he President, *or* the authorized representative of any State, shall act on behalf of the public as trustee of such natural resources,"[9] argue that "[t]he fact that trusteeship is established in the disjunctive—either the President *or* a state trustee—suggests that Congress did not intend broad co-trusteeship by state and federal governments of the same natural resources."[10] However, the legislative history of OPA suggests that Congress contemplated co-trusteeship, and that the express prohibition on double recovery accounts for this possibility.[11]

As discussed next, courts have addressed the issue of co-trusteeship in inconsistent ways.

---

7. *Cf.* Coeur d'Alene Tribe v. ASARCO Inc., 280 F. Supp. 2d 1094, 1115 (D. Idaho 2003).

8. 33 U.S.C. § 2706(d)(3).

9. 42 U.S.C. § 9607(f) (emphasis added); *see also* 33 U.S.C. § 2706(b)(1).

10. 1 James T. O'Reilly, Superfund & Brownfields Cleanup § 14:10 (2018).

11. H.R. Rep. 101-241, 34 (1989) ("Because more than one of the trustees could exercise jurisdiction over a particular natural resource, the bill provides that there shall be no double recovery for natural resource damages.").

a. The Conflicting *Coeur d'Alene* Holdings

Co-trusteeship was addressed in detail by the U.S. District Court for the District of Idaho in the *Coeur d'Alene* case, a CERCLA case that sought recovery for NRD to the Coeur d'Alene River Basin caused by decades of mining activity. The *Coeur d'Alene* court was itself so conflicted on the issue of co-trusteeship that it sua sponte reversed portions of its initial holding with regard to this issue. Nonetheless, the holdings are instructive. The United States, the state of Idaho, and the Coeur d'Alene Tribe (the Tribe) claimed trusteeship over resources in the Coeur d'Alene Basin. The state and the PRPs settled, but the claims of the United States and the Tribe were litigated in a 78-day, 8,695-exhibit NRD trial.

The defendants argued that the NRD claims failed because the plaintiffs lacked trusteeship over the resources in question. Specifically, the defendants argued that the United States and the Tribe lacked *actual* stewardship over the resources—because the United States, for example, had delegated much of its authority to the state of Idaho.

In its initial ruling, *Coeur d'Alene I*,[12] the court held that the determination of trusteeship is a question of both fact and law. It noted that "in many instances, co-trustees are the norm and not the exception," but it rejected the United States' argument that the "mere statutory authority is sufficient to establish trusteeship over a natural resource."[13] The court held that to avoid double recovery, a trustee could recover only the percentage of damages that accorded with its actual stewardship over a particular resource. It then deferred determination of trusteeship over certain resources until the second phase of the trial, when evidence could be presented on stewardship percentages.

In *Coeur d'Alene II*,[14] the court sua sponte reversed much of its initial holding, explaining that "its reliance on traditional tort concepts in allocating trusteeship was misplaced and that this type of case is distinguishable from other tort actions" because "the recovery, if any, is not for the benefit of a given party, but goes to the trustee as the fiduciary to accomplish the stated goals."[15] Notably, it held that "a co-trustee acting individually or collectively with the other co-trustees may go after the responsible party or parties for the full amount of the damage, less any amount that has already been paid as a

---

12. Coeur d'Alene Tribe v. ASARCO Inc., 280 F. Supp. 2d 1094 (D. Idaho 2003) [hereinafter *Coeur d'Alene I*].

13. *Id.* at 1115.

14. United States v. ASARCO Inc., 471 F. Supp. 2d 1063 (D. Idaho 2005) [hereinafter *Coeur d'Alene II*].

15. *Id.* at 1068.

result of a settlement to another trustee by a responsible party."[16] Under *Coeur d'Alene II*, any disagreement between the co-trustees as to how to apportion the damages "would have to be resolved by successive litigation between the trustees, but it could in no way affect the liability of the responsible party."[17]

b. The *Tyson Foods* and *Quapaw Tribe* Cases

Two subsequent cases illustrate the potential implications of a *Coeur d'Alene I*-type approach. In the 2010 *Tyson Foods* case, the U.S. District Court for the Northern District of Oklahoma explicitly relied on the reasoning in *Coeur d'Alene I*, ignoring the fact that the holding had been overturned.[18] In *Tyson Foods*, the state of Oklahoma and the Cherokee Nation (the Nation) were co-trustees over the Illinois River Watershed contaminated by poultry waste. The state sued Tyson Foods in 2005 and, after substantial pre-trial practice, trial was set for September 2009.

In July 2009, citing *Coeur d'Alene I*, the court held that the Nation was an indispensable party under Rule 19 of the Federal Rules of Civil Procedure.[19] Specifically, the court found that proceeding in the Nation's absence would impair the Nation's ability to protect its interests and create risk to defendants of multiple or inconsistent obligations given (1) the state's and the Nation's disparate views regarding ownership of the natural resources at issue;[20] (2) that the Nation could assert similar claims against defendants in subsequent litigation; and (3) that to avoid double recovery or unjust enrichment of one trustee at the expense of another, the court must award damages in the percentage of stewardship, a percentage it could not determine in the Nation's absence.[21] The court also held, however, that joinder of the Nation was not feasible because of tribal immunity. Because joinder of the Nation was necessary but not feasible, the court granted defendants' motion to dismiss claims for monetary damages pursuant to Rule 19 for failure to join a necessary party.[22]

---

16. *Id.*

17. *Id.*

18. Oklahoma v. Tyson Foods, Inc., 258 F.R.D. 472 (N.D. Okla. 2009).

19. *Id.* at 480 (reasoning that "the only feasible way to compensate the co-trustees and avoid a double recovery or unjust enrichment to one trustee at the expense of another is to award damages in the ratio or percentage of actual management and control that is exercised by each of the various co-trustees").

20. The court noted that the state "resisted for over two years the defendants' efforts to clarify what specific lands and resources the State claims to own." *Id.* at 483.

21. *Id.* at 479–80.

22. *Id.* at 484 (finding that the state's monetary claims "should not, in equity and good conscience, be allowed to proceed among the existing parties"). The Nation's September 2009 motion to intervene on the eve of trial was dismissed as untimely. *See* Oklahoma ex rel. Edmondson v. Tyson Foods, Inc., 619 F.3d 1223 (10th Cir. 2010) (affirming denial of untimely motion).

The subsequent *Quapaw Tribe* case clarified the potential reach of *Tyson Foods*.[23] There, the Quapaw Tribe (the Tribe) performed its own calculation of the value of its NRD associated with the Tar Creek Superfund Site in Oklahoma. It originally sought recovery under CERCLA for damages to a broad category of resources including aquatic life, waterways, and migratory wildlife, none of which existed exclusively within tribal lands. The defendants filed a motion to dismiss, citing the *Tyson Foods* case, arguing that joinder of the state as a co-trustee over many of these resources was both unnecessary and infeasible due to sovereign immunity considerations. In an effort to avoid the co-trusteeship issues, the Tribe then narrowed its claims to seek NRD only for terrestrial plant life on tribal lands. The court denied the motion to dismiss, finding that "[u]nlike *Tyson Foods*, the natural resources at issue are located solely on Tribal lands and do not fall within the regulatory authority of the State."[24]

Tyson Foods and *Quapaw Tribe* indicate that if a *Coeur d'Alene I*-type approach were followed in other litigation with multiple trustees, any NRD proceeding involving natural resources under potential shared stewardship might require that all co-trustees of those natural resources be joined as necessary parties.

3. Coordination between Overlapping Trustees

The federal regulations designating trustees recognize that dividing a resource between multiple trustees may be a difficult task and therefore recommend that "[w]here there are multiple trustees, because of coexisting or contiguous natural resources or concurrent jurisdictions, they should coordinate and cooperate in carrying out these responsibilities."[25] Cooperation is not, however, a legal mandate.

Overlapping trustees do often elect to coordinate their efforts, forming TWGs. TWGs are generally organized by reference to natural resource categories, which may be based on habitat (e.g., shoreline) or animal species (e.g., fish or turtles). Each TWG will typically contain a representative from each trustee, but a single trustee agency (or a single individual within an agency) will generally be appointed to serve as the head of each TWG. Where the assessment is proceeding cooperatively, responsible parties may also be represented in the TWGs.

---

23. Quapaw Tribe of Okla. v. Blue Tee Corp., No. 03-CV-0846-CVE-PJC, 2010 WL 3368701 (N.D. Okla. Aug. 20, 2010).
    24. *Id.*
    25. 40 C.F.R. § 300.615.

4. Effect of Settlement with a Single Trustee

Under *Coeur d'Alene II*, any settlement with a single trustee should apply against the final injury to resources assessed to be within the trusteeship of that trustee, regardless of whether or not there are co-trustees over a portion of those resources. However, a settlement with a single trustee regarding resources held in co-trusteeship would not necessarily preclude a subsequent suit by a different co-trustee for the same resources.[26] The non-settling co-trustee may claim, for example, that the damage to the resource is greater than the value assigned to it in the settlement. Therefore, the *Coeur d'Alene II* approach would eliminate the primary settlement incentive of finality. The *Coeur d'Alene II* holding notes that "[t]here is some incentive to settle, however, because it still saves substantial fees and costs in litigation of this nature and the sums paid are deducted from the total amount allowed for damages."[27]

Under *Coeur d'Alene I*, there also is risk associated with settling with a single co-trustee unless, for example, all the co-trustees first enter a settlement apportioning among themselves the resources held in co-trusteeship. Until a responsible party knows what percentage of each resource is held by each co-trustee, it will be difficult to evaluate adequately a settlement with a single trustee. Because the settlement would not bind other trustees, there is risk that a defendant could settle with one co-trustee for an amount premised upon a higher percentage of stewardship over the resource than the percentage ultimately adjudicated by the court. Similarly, there is risk that a settlement is premised on exclusive trusteeship of a natural resource over which another trustee later claims co-trusteeship. Given the uncertainty surrounding the co-trustee issues, defendants need to proceed cautiously in considering carve-out settlements with individual trustees.

B. Third-Party Practice and Resolving Contribution Claims

As with cleanup costs, multiple parties are frequently responsible for damages to natural resources. For cleanup costs, CERCLA and OPA make clear that responsible parties, with a few limited exceptions, are jointly and severally liable for cleanup costs. They also make clear that in light of this joint

---

26. *See Coeur d'Alene II*, 471 F. Supp. 2d at 1068 ("[A] co-trustee acting individually or collectively with the other co-trustees may go after the responsible party or parties for the full amount of the damage, *less any amount that has already been paid as a result of a settlement to another trustee by a responsible party*.") (emphasis added).

27. *Id.*

and several liability, parties that pay more than their fair share of cleanup costs may recover from other responsible parties. CERCLA's NRD provisions lack an explicit authorization of joint and several liability,[28] but trustees have argued that NRD liability is joint and several.[29] Where trustees seek to impose joint and several NRD liability on responsible parties, the existence of a right of contribution is critical.

1. The Legal Basis for NRD Contribution Actions—CERCLA

CERCLA sets forth two alternative statutory claims under which private parties are entitled to recover costs incurred at a contaminated site from other responsible parties:

- First, section 107(a), 42 U.S.C. § 9607(a), creates a cause of action permitting a party to recover response costs from other responsible parties: "[the various categories of CERCLA responsible parties] shall be liable for . . . any . . . necessary costs of response incurred by any other person consistent with the national contingency plan."
- Second, under section 113(f)(1), 42 U.S.C. § 9613(f)(1), a person may seek contribution from another responsible party, provided that such action is brought during or after a civil action brought under section 106 or 107: "[a]ny person may seek contribution from any other person who is liable or potentially liable under section 9607(a) of this title, during or following any civil action under section 9606."

The first of these claims, a section 107 cost recovery claim, is not available to recover NRD costs for two reasons. First, a section 107 claim applies to "the necessary costs of response incurred," which is broadly defined, but does not incorporate NRD.[30] Second, courts have held that a section 107 NRD claim would amount to a responsible party stepping into the shoes of the trustees, something they lack standing to do pursuant to the terms of CERCLA.[31]

---

28. *See* 42 U.S.C. §§ 9607(a)(4)(C), 9607(f).

29. *See, e.g.,* United States v. ASARCO Inc., No. CV 96-0122-N-EJL, CV 91-342-N-EJL, 1999 WL 33313132, at *1 (D. Idaho Sept. 30, 1999) ("The United States contends . . . [that] the Defendants are jointly and severally liable for the injury to natural resources that has occurred and continues to occur since the enactment of CERCLA.").

30. *See* 42 U.S.C. § 9601(25) (defining "response" to include "remove, removal, remedy, and remedial action," but not including damages).

31. *See* NCR Corp. v. George A. Whiting Paper Co., 768 F.3d 682, 709 (7th Cir. 2014), *reh'g denied* (Nov. 5, 2014) ("Private parties lack standing to bring natural resource damages claims under section 107; such actions can be initiated only by the federal government or a state or tribal government for lands in that government's possession or control, or held in public trust.") (citing 42 U.S.C. § 9607(f)(1); Nat'l Ass'n of Mfrs. v. U.S. Dep't of the Interior, 134 F.3d 1095, 1113

A section 113 contribution claim is therefore the only potential avenue for private parties to recover NRD from other responsible parties.[32] This fact has important consequences that distinguish a party's ability to recover response costs from its ability to recover NRD costs. First, in the absence of a trustee action for NRD, PRPs may not be able to make contribution claims for NRD against other PRPs under section 113.[33] NRD costs expended in a purely voluntary context may not be recoverable by private PRPs. Second, parties involved in contribution claims for NRD will only have the ability to recover the costs of NRD if they have paid more than their equitable shares, and will not benefit from joint and several liability.[34] This lowers the incentive for responsible parties to enter NRD settlements pursuant to which they assume more than their equitable share of NRD costs, particularly where there are orphan shares and/or many other PRPs from which the party will subsequently need to recover.

2. The Legal Basis for NRD Contribution Actions—OPA

OPA broadly provides that a "person may bring a civil action for contribution against any other person who is liable or potentially liable under this Act or another law."[35] Liability under OPA includes NRD, so presumably, and given the precedent with regard to the similar CERCLA contribution provision, this right to seek contribution includes a right to seek contribution for NRD. Courts have held that a contribution claim is available under OPA regardless of the plaintiff's fault; plaintiffs may recover when costs or damages incurred exceed their proportionate share.[36]

OPA does contain a requirement that "all claims for removal costs or damages shall be presented first to the responsible party or guarantor of the source."[37] A claimant may not file an action in court until either (1) "each person to whom the claim is presented denies all liability for the claim" or

---

(D.C. Cir. 1998) ("It is true that CERCLA does not permit private parties to seek recovery for damages to natural resources held in trust by the federal, state or tribal governments.")).

32. *See, e.g.*, Appleton Papers Inc. v. George A. Whiting Paper Co., No. 08-C-16, 2011 WL 4585343, at *3 (E.D. Wis. Sept. 30, 2011).

33. *See* Champion Labs., Inc. v. Metex Corp., No. 02-5284 (WHW), 2008 WL 1808309, at *5 (D.N.J. Apr. 21, 2008) ("For Champion to properly assert a contribution action under section 113(f)(1), it must first have been sued under section 106 or section 107 of CERCLA." (citing Cooper Indus., Inc. v. Aviall Servs., Inc., 543 U.S. 157, 168 (2004))).

34. 42 U.S.C. § 9613(f)(1).

35. 33 U.S.C. § 2709.

36. *See, e.g.*, *In re* Settoon Towing, L.L.C., 859 F.3d 340 (5th Cir. 2017); Chevron Pipe Line Co. v. Pacificorp, No. 2:12-CV-287-TC, 2017 WL 3382065, at *5 (D. Utah Aug. 4, 2017).

37. 33 U.S.C. § 2713(a).

(2) "the claim is not settled by any person by payment within 90 days after the date upon which (A) the claim was presented, or (B) advertising was begun pursuant to section 2714(b) of this title, whichever is later."[38] Courts have suggested that the presentment requirement applies to any claim brought under OPA, including a claim brought by a private plaintiff.[39] And several district courts have held that the presentment requirement extends to contribution claims.[40] However, in 2017, the Fifth Circuit allowed a contribution claim to proceed despite failure to meet the OPA presentment requirements.[41] Nevertheless, given the relatively simple and minimally burdensome presentment process, satisfaction of the presentment requirements is still recommended prior to filing OPA contribution claims in most circumstances.

3. NRD Contribution Litigation

The Seventh Circuit has held in *NCR Corp. v. George A. Whiting Paper Co.* that in order to state a contribution claim for NRD, a PRP is not required to present evidence that the target of its contribution claim is directly liable for the NRD, as would be required in an NRD claim brought by trustees under section 107.[42] It is enough that the PRP bringing the contribution claim is liable for the NRD and the third-party defendant is a PRP for some form of CERCLA damages. (Whether the third-party plaintiff ultimately recovers depends on whether the court determines it is "equitably entitled to contribution" under CERCLA section 113.) PRPs at a given site should thus be on notice that it may be easier for PRPs who have been held liable for NRD to seek contribution from other PRPs.

Second, since claims for NRD are barred when both the damages and relevant release of hazardous substances occurred prior to CERCLA's December 11, 1980, enactment,[43] the Seventh Circuit held that it is essentially impossible for an NRD contribution action to involve pre-1980 NRD. This is because a trustee must initiate a section 107 suit, and trustees are barred from bringing actions for pre-1980 costs.[44]

Other issues particular to NRD arose in *NCR Corp.* at the district court level. The district court held that contribution is available for overpayments

---

38. *Id.* § 2713(c).
39. Boca Ciega Hotel, Inc. v. Bouchard Transp. Co., 51 F.3d 235, 238 (11th Cir. 1995).
40. *See* Keller Transp., Inc. v. Wagner Enters., LLC, 873 F. Supp. 2d 1342, 1354 (D. Mont. 2012); Gabarick v. Laurin Maritime (Am.) Inc., 623 F. Supp. 2d 741, 750–51 (E.D. La. 2009).
41. *In re Settoon Towing*, 859 F.3d at 345.
42. *See* 768 F.3d 682, 710 (7th Cir. 2014), *reh'g denied* (Nov. 5, 2014).
43. 42 U.S.C. § 9607(f)(1).
44. *NCR Corp.*, 768 F.3d at 710. *See generally* discussion in Chapter 3, Section C.

of NRD to cover assessment costs—even when the results of the investigation were never used—as long as the assessment costs resulted from a bona fide effort to assess damages.[45] The district court also held that for costs to be counted toward the amount of NRD paid, they had to be properly documented as assessment-related.[46]

In addition to *NCR Corp.*, several other cases discuss circumstances in which PRPs may bring contribution actions for NRD. A few provide insight on when declaratory judgment actions may be brought for future contribution for NRD. In general, a PRP with a section 107 case pending against it may bring a declaratory judgment action for contribution. In *Sensient Colors, Inc. v. Kohnstamm*, a case involving a contaminated property in Camden, New Jersey, the court upheld a third-party plaintiff's claim for a declaratory judgment for NRD and response costs.[47] Additionally, the Third Circuit has noted that, before a party has been held liable for NRD, a declaratory judgment—rather than monetary relief—is the proper remedy for future NRD.[48]

Correspondingly, courts have held that when no action under section 107 is pending against it, a PRP may not state a claim for declaratory relief for future response costs and NRD. In *Reichhold, Inc. v. U.S. Metals Refining Co.*, the court dismissed Reichhold's declaratory relief claim for contribution, since no case was pending against Reichhold for those costs. Although the state had threatened that it would bring a suit for recovery of NRD against Reichhold, the court held that this threat of NRD action was not sufficiently "inevitable or immediate" to justify the declaratory judgment action for contribution.[49]

Some NRD contribution actions involve claims against the government. One such case was *United States v. Montrose Chemical Corp. of California*, in which Montrose filed a claim for contribution against the United States and the state of California.[50] Federal and state trustees had previously brought a section 107 claim against Montrose for cleanup costs and NRD related to the contam-

---

45. Appleton Papers Inc. v. George A. Whiting Paper Co., No. 08-C-16, 2012 WL 2704920, at *13 (E.D. Wis. July 3, 2012), *aff'd sub nom.* NCR Corp. v. George A. Whiting Paper Co., 768 F.3d 682 (7th Cir. 2014).

46. *Appleton Papers*, 2012 WL 2704920, at *15.

47. 548 F. Supp. 2d 681, 686, 690 (D. Minn. 2008).

48. F.P. Woll & Co. v. Fifth & Mitchell St. Corp., 326 F. App'x 658, 661 n.4 (3d Cir. 2009) ("[A]bsent an agency determination that Woll destroyed natural resources, these damages were too speculative to support monetary relief."). The NRD claim in *F.P. Woll & Co.* was brought under Pennsylvania's state law CERCLA analogy, which is discussed further later in this chapter.

49. No. 03-453(DRD), 2007 WL 2363168, at *4 (D.N.J. Aug. 14, 2007), *op. clarified*, 522 F. Supp. 2d 724 (D.N.J. 2007). The clarified opinion did not alter the dismissal of Reichhold's claim for declaratory judgment for contribution.

50. 788 F. Supp. 1485 (C.D. Cal. 1992).

ination of the San Pedro Channel Areas, Los Angeles–Long Beach Harbors, Santa Catalina Island, and Channel Islands. The court held that the federal government had waived sovereign immunity when it filed a claim against Montrose, and found that Montrose had properly alleged that the entities were owners, operators, transporters, and arrangers within the area in question.[51]

State law-based NRD claims potentially could also give rise to contribution actions. Some states have CERCLA-like statutes with NRD provisions, and some state NRD enforcement programs are fairly robust.[52] A state NRD claim was brought, for example, in *F.P. Woll & Co. v. Fifth & Mitchell Street Corp.*[53] And in *Mathes v. Vulcan Materials Co.*, a dry cleaning company that had been liable for NRD in a consent judgment with the U.S. Virgin Islands Commissioner of Natural Resources brought contribution claims for NRD against chemical manufacturing companies under territorial law, not CERCLA, although the court ultimately found that it did not have subject matter jurisdiction to hear the case.[54]

C. Insurance Issues

EXPERT INSIGHT: A General Overview of Insurance Coverage for NRD Claims

Ira M. Gottlieb and Cynthia S. Betz[55]

Introduction

There are a variety of lines of insurance that may provide for defense costs and indemnity against losses arising from NRD claims.[56] The following discussion gener-

---

51. *Id.* at 1490, 1496–97; *see also* Ford Motor Co. v. United States, 56 Fed. Cl. 85 (2003), *rev'd*, 378 F.3d 1314 (Fed. Cir. 2004) (noting that Ford had filed a contribution claim against the United States).

52. *See* Brian D. Israel, State-by-State Guide to NRD Programs in All 50 States and Puerto Rico (Mar. 14, 2019), https://www.arnoldporter.com/-/media/files/perspectives/publica tions/2018/03/state-by-state-nrd-guide.pdf.

53. 326 F. App'x 658, 661 n.4 (3d Cir. 2009).

54. No. 2006-229, 2009 WL 2614710, at *9 (D.V.I. Aug. 21, 2009).

55. Ira M. Gottlieb is a partner with McCarter & English, LLP, and the practice group leader of the firm's Environment & Energy Practice Group. Cynthia S. Betz is a senior associate in McCarter & English's Insurance Coverage and Environment & Energy Practice Groups. Both Mr. Gottlieb and Ms. Betz devote a substantial amount of their practice to NRD and environmental matters, including insurance coverage counseling and litigation concerning such claims.

56. For example, such lines of insurance might include Pollution Legal Liability (PLL) policies, or related products such as Pollution and Remediation Legal Liability policies. In some

ally focuses on Commercial General Liability (CGL) insurance. Despite the extensive exclusionary language found in many types of modern-day insurance policies carving out coverage for pollution-related liabilities, insurance recovery for NRD may still be found under older CGL polices.[57] This form of insurance—especially policies written prior to 1986—remains an important asset and possible source of recovery for long-tail environmental losses,[58] including for NRD.

Basics of CGL Coverage

Very generally speaking, CGL policies are often written on an "occurrence" basis, meaning they will respond when an "occurrence," "accident," or damage for which the policyholder seeks coverage happens during the policy period.[59] Under pre-1986 CGL policies, the actual suit or demand for damages can follow many years after the policies were issued, but the policy will nonetheless respond because the "occurrence" happened in that particular policy year.

---

circumstances, Directors and Officers, or Errors and Omissions, insurance policies may be applicable to NRD claims, as may other lines of insurance coverage, depending on the facts presented by a particular claim. In other instances, specialized insurance, specifically written or tailored for certain risks (e.g., through manuscript insurance or special endorsements), might afford insurance coverage. Some of these types of policies (e.g., PLL) are written on a "claims-made" basis, making their reach more time restrictive despite their intention to cover pollution losses.

57. In general, CGL insurance policies became widely available in or around the late 1940s and continue to be offered in varied forms by insurers through the present. *See generally* NEW APPLEMAN ON INSURANCE LAW LIBRARY EDITION § 16.02 (2017). Although the standard form of such policies changed over time, it frequently provided coverage for losses for accidents and occurrences that were neither expected nor intended, resulting in property damages and bodily injuries to third parties. While beyond the scope of the present discussion, starting in the late 1960s, and continuing until approximately 1986, CGL insurance began to undergo revisions that affected coverage with respect to certain circumstances relating to whether occurrences and losses were sudden and accidental or otherwise unintended. With respect to occurrences and losses related to pollution, these insurance policy revisions culminated in the so-called absolute pollution exclusion. *Id.*

58. As two commentators recently explained, "the term 'long-tail harm' describes indivisible harm, whether bodily injury or property damage, that is attributable to continuous or repeated exposure over time to the same or similar substances or conditions or that has a long latency period." *See* Kyle D. Logue & Tom Baker, *Allocation in Long-Tail Harm Claims Covered by Occurrence-Based Policies*, THE ALI ADVISER (Apr. 4, 2017), http://www.thealiadviser.org/liability -insurance/allocation-long-tail-harm-claims-covered-occurrence-based-policies/. Long-tail liabilities, such as NRD, are often set in motion by events that continue to cause unknown losses for many years before they are realized. Such damages may sometimes be considered inchoate until fully recognized.

59. Liability for and knowledge of occurrence-based losses may take place many years after the occurrences that gave rise to damages are set in motion. *See supra* note 56 concerning the important distinction between "claims made" and "occurrence"-based insurance policies. While beyond the scope of this discussion, this is a critical distinction that materially affects which insurance policies may be applicable to losses and damages (e.g., those in existence at the time of occurrence versus those in effect at the time the losses or damages become known) and when an insured must report and notify its insurers of claims.

CGL insurance may cover a vast range of third-party liabilities, and—importantly for NRD claims—this insurance covers property damage to third-party property, which may include resources held in public trust, arising out of an insured's historical ownership of facilities, past operations, or other conduct that may have unintentionally caused NRD. A search for older CGL coverage will often uncover policies spanning many years, including primary and excess or umbrella levels in various amounts (e.g., limits of liability). How such insurance coverage is triggered, summed up, and/or allocated among potentially applicable years for any one claim or set of occurrences presents complicated insurance coverage issues that can dramatically affect the amount of insurance available for defense and indemnification of losses.[60]

Most CGL policies are a standard form (typically an Insurance Services Office (ISO) form), preprinted and modified only by the endorsements attached to it. The most relevant part of a CGL policy for environmental liabilities is often referred to as "Coverage A," which is the portion that usually states:

> The company [insurer] will pay on behalf of the insured all sums which the insured shall become legally obligated to pay as damages because of
>
> > A. bodily injury, or
> > B. property damage
>
> to which this insurance applies, caused by an occurrence, and the company shall have the right and duty to defend any suit against the insured seeking damages on account of such bodily injury or property damage . . . .[61]

Therefore, absent applicable exclusions,[62] the insurer's obligation to "pay . . . all sums" (otherwise known as the duty to indemnify) and defend against "suits" (otherwise known as the duty to defend) for environmental liabilities will be triggered where there has been (1) property damage, (2) caused by an "occurrence," (3) resulting in damages for which the policyholder is alleged liable. The interpretation of these

---

60. Even a survey of those issues is beyond the scope of this discussion. For a general discussion of some of the issues, see 15 COUCH ON INS. § 220 at 25–26 (citing cases and discussing trigger theories); NEW APPLEMAN ON INSURANCE LAW LIBRARY EDITION § 22.03 (2017) (discussing commonly adopted means of allocation).

61. *See* ISO Form GL 00 02 01 73, *General Liability Insurance Policy—Comprehensive* (1973), *reprinted in* MILLER'S STANDARD INSURANCE POLICIES ANNOTATED (7th ed.).

62. The most notable exclusion in the context of environmental liabilities is the so-called absolute pollution exclusion, which will likely be found in CGL policies issued after 1985. Prior to the early 1970s, CGL policies often covered pollution-related claims, but beginning in the early to mid 1970s, insurers increasingly added more restrictive language to obviate coverage for environmental liabilities, making the search for historical coverage all the more important when faced with an NRD claim. *See* NEW APPLEMAN ON INSURANCE LAW LIBRARY EDITION § 18.03 (2017) (discussion of pollution exclusion).

key phrases has been—and continues to be—the source of many insurance coverage disputes.[63]

Over the course of many years, enforcement and contribution actions have focused primarily on liability for cleanup of environmentally impaired sites. Thus, there are relatively few published decisions in which courts have squarely addressed the issue of insurance coverage for NRD. However, the numerous cases addressing insurance coverage for response and remediation costs provide guidance and insight on how to analyze some insurance coverage issues that might arise with respect to NRD claims.

Are Natural Resource Damages "Property Damage"?

Courts across the United States have routinely determined that CERCLA-imposed response costs are "damages," as such term is used in common CGL policies.[64] The reasoning of these courts makes it abundantly clear that losses resulting from natural resource injuries are also covered "damages." Indeed, in some cases addressing whether CERCLA-imposed cleanup costs are "damages" within the meaning of CGL policies, insurers argued that, because CERCLA expressly distinguishes between response costs and NRD, response costs should not be considered "damages" for purposes of insurance coverage. In so contending, insurers have tacitly accepted the proposition that NRD are covered under CGL policies. Moreover, even the few courts that have held that response costs are not recoverable "damages" under CGL policies have recognized that coverage is afforded under such policies for NRD.[65]

"Occurrence" Coverage and CERCLA's "Wholly Before" 1980 Provision

Although forms vary to some degree, CGL policies frequently define the term "occurrence" broadly to mean "an accident, including continuing or repeated exposure to

---

63. *See, e.g.,* Armstrong World Indus., Inc. v. Aetna Cas. & Sur. Co., 45 Cal. App. 4th 1, 39, 52 Cal. Rptr. 2d 690, 699 (1996) ("A recurring problem in interpreting standard CGL policies that provide coverage for injuries 'caused by an occurrence' is determining what has come to be called the 'trigger of coverage'—that is, the operative event which activates the insurer's defense and indemnity obligations."); *see also* New Appleman on Insurance Law Library Edition § 18.02 (2017) (citing cases).

64. *See, e.g.,* Cent. Ill. Light Co. v. Home Ins. Co., 821 N.E.2d 206 (Ill. 2004) (holding remediation costs that the insured incurred were costs that the insured was "legally obligated to pay"); AIU Ins. Co. v. Super. Ct., 51 Cal. 3d 807 (1990) (holding insurance policies afforded coverage for remediation expenses, whether such costs were incurred to satisfy a liability under CERCLA to reimburse a government agency or were incurred directly by FMC in order to comply with a CERCLA "injunction"); Hazen Paper Co. v. U.S. Fid. & Guar. Co., 407 Mass. 689 (1990) (holding remediation expenses incurred by an insured to address releases of hazardous substances into the environment are "damages," as such term was used in the CGL policies); *see also* New Appleman on Insurance Law Library Edition § 18.02 [8][b] (2017).

65. *See, e.g.,* Aetna Cas. & Sur. Co. v. Gen. Dynamics Corp., 783 F. Supp. 1199 (E.D. Mo. 1991); Cont'l Ins. Cos. v. Ne. Pharm. & Chem. Co., 842 F.2d 977 (8th Cir. 1988).

conditions which results in bodily injury or property damage during the policy period neither expected nor intended from the standpoint of the insured."[66]

The common definition of "occurrence" also makes clear that, in order to establish that a policy in a given year has been triggered, an insured generally need only prove that injury or damage, and not the accident, event, happening, or exposure, occurred in such year.[67] Where property damage occurs in a particular year, including damage resulting from the progression or migration of contamination, courts have held that the policy in force in such year is triggered, even if the accident, event, happening, or exposure that first gave rise to the contamination may have occurred in an earlier year or years.[68]

Because CGL policies issued after 1985 are likely to have the so-called absolute pollution exclusion, older policies, which address long-tail harms and inchoate damages, may be more pertinent to NRD claims. This may present a seeming inconsistency between standard insurance coverage principles related to continuing occurrences and the "wholly before" language of CERCLA section 107(f)(1).

CERCLA mandates that "[t]here shall be no recovery under the authority of subparagraph (c) of subsection (a) where such [natural resource] damages and the release of a hazardous substance from which such damages resulted have occurred wholly before December 11, 1980."[69]

---

66. ISO Form GL 00 00 01 73, *reprinted in* Miller's Standard Insurance Policies Annotated (7th ed.).

67. Although beyond the scope of this general overview, we note that important issues may be raised with respect to whether NRD claims involve the "continuous trigger" theory to insurance allocation, or some other insurance trigger theories that have been adopted by some courts. *See, e.g.,* Owens-Illinois, Inc. v. United Ins. Co., 138 N.J. 437 (1994); Montrose Chem. Corp. of Cal. v. Admiral Ins. Co., 913 P.2d 878 (Cal. 1995), *as modified on denial of reh'g* (Aug. 31, 1995). These trigger theories will affect the amount of insurance that may be available for NRD and which insurers may be responsible for covering losses. Another important issue that may arise relates to the long-standing insurance coverage issue of "number of occurrences." *See, e.g.,* Stonewall Ins. Co. v. E.I. du Pont de Nemours & Co., 996 A.2d 1245 (Del. 2010); Dutton-Lainson Co. v. Cont'l Ins. Co., 778 N.W. 2d 433 (Neb. 2010); Nicor, Inc. v. Assoc.'d Elec. & Gas Ins. Servs., Ltd., 860 N.E.2d 280 (Ill. 2006). For example, does an NRD claim arise from the same occurrence(s) as those that require remedial action, or are there separate occurrences giving rise to NRD insurance claims; are alleged injuries to different resource services separate occurrences; that is, are these multiple occurrences? These questions have important implications because, subject to the terms of the applicable policies in play, the answers may have a substantial impact on the amount of insurance coverage that may be available for NRD claims.

68. *See, e.g.,* Cont'l Cas. Co. v. Plantation Pipe Line Co., 902 So. 2d 36, 39 (Ala. 2004) (holding policies from 1969 to 1972 should respond to pay cleanup costs, settlement expenses, and prejudgment interest for contamination caused by 1972 leak of petroleum products from insured's underground pipeline, which was not discovered until 1999); City of San Bernardino v. Pac. Indem. Co., 56 Cal. App. 4th 666, (1997) (holding insurer from 1947 to 1973 was obligated to defend 1986 lawsuit by owners of neighboring property alleging environmental contamination caused by county landfill).

69. 42 U.S.C. § 9607(f)(1).

Courts that have considered this provision for purposes of CERCLA liability have reached different conclusions regarding whether injury and damages occur at or about the same time, or whether damages instead begin to accrue when trustees first incur expenses for assessing damages.[70]

NRD is a continuous injury that—for insurance coverage purposes—often results in damages both before and after 1980. Thus, in the context of insurance coverage, those damages are neither wholly before nor wholly after 1980. In an effort to avoid coverage for a claim on a policy that pre-dates 1980, an insurer might attempt to invoke this CERCLA provision, arguing that pre-1980 releases are not covered. But to do so would conflate a debatable underlying NRD liability defense under CERCLA with separate and distinct insurance policy (contractual) obligations to provide coverage for occurrences that happen during an insurance policy period (and then continue thereafter through periods beyond its policy dates, including subsequent to 1980).[71]

In *Aetna Casualty & Surety Co. v. Pintlar Corp.*[72]—one of the few published cases to address insurance coverage for NRD—the Ninth Circuit found that the distinctions between releases, injuries, and damages that occur in the context of the CERCLA statutory liability defense, and how those terms apply with respect to an insurer's separate contractual obligation to provide coverage for property damage (i.e., NRD), are meaningful and do not permit an insurer to avoid coverage for NRD. Moreover, the Ninth Circuit held that "coverage is not limited to 'damages' occurring during the policy period; it also includes 'damages' occurring after the period, as long as those 'damages' are caused by an 'occurrence', that is, a release which results in injury

---

70. *See In re* Acushnet River & New Bedford Harbor Proceedings re Alleged PCB Pollution, 716 F. Supp. 676, 681–83 (D. Mass. 1989) (noting that damages amount to monetary quantification of injury and occur when expenses are incurred due to the injury); Idaho v. Bunker Hill Co., 635 F. Supp. 665, 675 (D. Idaho 1986) (noting that to the extent release occurred prior to enactment, but the resultant damage occurred post-enactment, recovery is not barred). *But see* Montana v. Atl. Richfield Co., 266 F. Supp. 2d 1238, 1242–44 (D. Mont. 2003) (finding that damages accrue when the injury to resources occurs regardless of when damages are assessed or quantified). *See also* discussion in Chapter 3, Section C.

71. In connection with a similar argument, the court in *In re Acushnet River*, 716 F. Supp. at 683, held that "'damages'—*i.e.,* monetary quantification of the injury done to the natural resources—'occur' as a general rule when the property owner . . . incurs expenses due to the injury to natural resources." Based on that arguably erroneous premise, the court reasoned that the "damages" at issue occurred wholly after 1980, regardless of the fact that the releases and injuries occurred before 1980 and continued after 1980. Nonetheless, in response to an insurer's effort to latch onto the underlying "wholly before" liability defense to avoid coverage claims, the court declined to extend its holding to insurance claims. The court stated that "[w]hat the term 'occurrence' may mean in the context of the contractual understanding between an alleged polluter and its insurer may be something else altogether—a point on which this court presently expresses no opinion." *Id.* at 683 n.9. Indeed, the principles applying to a continuous NRD injury and occurrence would dictate a materially different outcome.

72. 948 F.2d 1507 (9th Cir. 1991).

during the policy period."[73] This is true even if the damages continue or the natural resource trustees assess damages after 1980.

Conclusion

NRD insurance claims raise numerous issues. Courts have explored some of these issues in the context of insurance for response action claims, while other separate questions may give rise to nuances that are endemic to NRD losses. As NRD claims arise, perhaps in the aftermath of response actions, insurance policyholders and insurers may confront these issues with increasing frequency. This may require additional analysis and adaptation of existing insurance coverage principles to NRD claims. While the groundwork has been laid for the resolution of such claims, it is still uncertain how courts may view the peculiarities of NRD insurance claims.

D. Historic and Cultural Resources

1. Recovery for Injury to Historic and Cultural Resources[74]

Although cultural resources are not "natural resources" under CERCLA or OPA,[75] the question arises whether trustees may recover for the lost use of such resources as "services" lost to the public as a result of injury to natural resources.[76] As defined in the regulations, the term "services" does not itself refer to historic or cultural resources. The DOI regulations define services as "the physical and biological functions performed by the resource *including the human uses of those functions*. These services are the result of the physical, chemical, or biological quality of the resource."[77] The OPA regulations define services as "the functions performed by a natural resource for the benefit of another natural resource and/or the public."[78]

The DOI regulations do not define "human uses." Nor do they explain further what nexus must exist between the natural resource and the human

---

73. *Id.* at 1516.

74. This section is adapted from *Natural Resource Damages*, of the Environmental Law Practice Guide: State and Federal Law with permission. Copyright 2017 Matthew Bender & Company, Inc., a LexisNexis company. All rights reserved.

75. *See* 43 C.F.R. § 11.14(z); 15 C.F.R. § 990.30.

76. The scope of recoverable damages is based on the services lost as a result of an injury. As the DOI regulations state: "The measure of damages is the cost of (i) restoration or rehabilitation of the injured natural resources to a condition where they can provide the level of services available at baseline, or (ii) the replacement and/or acquisition of equivalent natural resources capable of providing such services." 43 C.F.R. § 11.80(b).

77. *Id.* § 11.14(nn) (emphasis added).

78. 15 C.F.R. § 990.30.

use. The examples of "services" listed in the regulations, however, suggest a close nexus: "services include provision of habitat, food and other needs of biological resources, recreation, other products or services used by humans, flood control, ground water recharge, waste assimilation, and other such functions that may be provided by natural resources."[79] Thus, the rule on its face would seem not to include historic or cultural resources as "services."

At the same time, the DOI's preamble to its NRDA regulations directly termed the use of cultural and archaeological resources "services":

> [A]lthough archaeological and cultural resources, as defined in other statutes, are not treated as "natural" resources under CERCLA, the rule does allow trustee officials to include the loss of archaeological and other cultural services provided by a natural resource in a natural resource damage assessment. For example, if land constituting a CERCLA-defined natural resource contains archaeological artifacts, then that land might provide the service of supporting archaeological research. If an injury to the land causes a reduction in the level of service (archaeological research) that could be performed, trustee officials could recover damages for the lost service. Further clarification is beyond the scope of this rulemaking.[80]

In *Kennecott Utah Copper Corp. v. U.S. Department of the Interior*, industry petitioners challenged this aspect of the regulations, arguing that DOI had exceeded its authority in authorizing the recovery of injury to archaeological and cultural resources.[81] Petitioners argued that such resources were outside the purview of CERCLA: first, because state tort law already provided a private remedy for injury to cultural and archaeological resources,[82] and CERCLA precluded double recovery; second, because taken to its logical conclusion, DOI's reasoning that a natural resource that contained artifacts "might provide the service of supporting archaeological research" could apply to just about any human activity. As described by the opinion, the petitioners argued that DOI's reasoning "[knew] no bounds; since virtually all human activities are supported in some form by land and other natural resources, the rule would expose defendants to liability for harms that lie well beyond the stated reach of the CERCLA."[83]

---

79. 43 C.F.R. § 11.71(e).

80. Natural Resource Damage Assessments, 59 Fed. Reg. 14,262, 14,269 (Mar. 25, 1994) (to be codified at 43 C.F.R. pt. 11).

81. 88 F.3d 1191, 1222–23 (D.C. Cir. 1996).

82. The court cited to *In re* Exxon-Valdez Litigation, No. 3AN-89-2533C1 (Alaska Sept. 24, 1994), for this proposition.

83. *Kennecott*, 88 F.3d at 1222–23.

The court did not reach the merits of the challenge, finding instead that the issue was not ripe for review. Specifically, the court found that petitioners had failed to demonstrate that the 1994 preamble had "a direct and immediate rather than a distant and speculative impact upon them." According to the court:

> [the preamble] indicated only that a trustee could recover damages for an injury to land that reduces archaeological research. . . . [I]t does not represent an interpretation of an identified statutory provision, nor a clarification of an otherwise binding regulation. The guidance offered is hypothetical and non-specific; it is not crafted as a concrete rule that can be applied under identified circumstances. Instead, Interior has merely advised that recovery could be available for injury to non-natural resources, and illustrated one type of injury that would qualify.[84]

The court thus chose to wait for a more concrete case, in which a trustee invoked the preamble in an attempt to affect the outcome of a real dispute, before ruling on the issue whether the preamble properly included cultural and archaeological resources within a NRDA.

When DOI revised its regulations to address other issues in response to *Kennecott*, the agency assuaged a commenter's concern that the revisions would hinder trustees' ability to recover the value of lost cultural natural resource services. DOI said the revisions did not alter treatment of such losses, and that "[c]ultural, religious, and ceremonial losses that rise from the destruction of or injury to natural resources continue to be cognizable under the revisions."[85]

In the only other case that appears to have addressed the issue, however, a district court stated, in listing "injury from releases" in its section on findings of fact: "Cultural uses of water and soil by [the] Tribe are not recoverable as natural resource damages."[86] One commentator has agreed with this perspective, opining that CERCLA and OPA do not contemplate recovery of NRD related to losses to cultural resources.[87] The commentator noted that other NRD statutes—the National Marine Sanctuaries Act and the Park System Resource Protection Act—specifically provide for recovery for injuries to cultural or non-living resources. The commentator also argued that the legislative

---

84. *Id.* at 1223.

85. Natural Resource Damages for Hazardous Substances, 73 Fed. Reg. 57,259, 57264 (Oct. 2, 2008) (to be codified at 43 C.F.R. pt. 11).

86. Coeur d'Alene Tribe v. ASARCO Inc., 280 F. Supp. 2d 1094, 1107 (D. Idaho 2003).

87. *See* Sarah Peterman, *CERCLA's Unrecoverable Natural Resource Damages: Injuries to Cultural Resources and Services*, 38 ECOL. L. CURRENTS 17 (2011).

history for CERCLA did not suggest that Congress intended for injuries to cultural resources to fall within the scope of NRD.[88]

But other commentators have suggested that losses to cultural resources may be recoverable.[89] One study pointed to Washington State's procedure for assessing compensation for oil spills, which based its compensation schedule for unquantifiable damages in part on the sensitivity of the affected area, which depends partly on the "importance of the area for recreational, aesthetic or archaeological use."[90]

In practice, losses related to cultural resources have been addressed in assessments. Examples of assessments involving cultural resources most often refer to cultural resources not as separate resources, such as artifacts, but as natural resources with some cultural significance. Restoration plans also often acknowledge lost cultural resources without directly compensating for them. For example, one assessment where damages to cultural resources were considered referred to the "cultural importance of Panther Creek fish to certain Native American tribes."[91] In the Lower Fox River restoration plan, harm to cultural resources included harm to revered animal species and to sacred locations.[92] In one case of restoration of an historic pier, the project was undertaken not to remediate harm to the historic resource per se, but to remediate harm done to recreational uses of the river.[93]

---

88. *Id.* at 22. The commentator wrote that "DOI's attempt to create an exception allowing for recovery of cultural resource damages when couched as lost cultural services provided by an injured natural resource splits too fine a hair. It is unpersuasive and confusing." *Id.* at 23.

89. *See* Amy W. Ando et al., Natural Resource Damage Assessment: Methods & Cases, WMRC Reports 71 (2004), https://www.ideals.illinois.edu/bitstream/handle/2142/1979/RR-108.pdf?sequence=1 (listing cultural resources as resources for which damages have been sought, alongside surface water, wetlands, air, fish, and wildlife); Valerie Ann Lee & P.J. Bridgen, The Natural Resource Damage Assessment Deskbook: A Legal and Technical Analysis 287 fig. 13-1 (Envtl. Law Inst. ed., 2002) (listing "historical resource uses" as human uses that would constitute a service lost to the public); *see also* Connie Sue Manos Martin, *Spiritual and Cultural Resources as a Component of Tribal Natural Resource Damages Claims*, 20 Pub. Land & Res. L. Rev. 1 (1999).

90. Ando et al., *supra* note 89, at 29.

91. *Id.* at 102.

92. *See* U.S. Fish & Wildlife Serv. et al. Joint Restoration Plan and Environmental Assessment for the Lower Fox River and Green Bay Area 21, 24, 28 (2003), https://www.fws.gov/midwest/es/ec/nrda/foxrivernrda/documents/restorationplan/finaljune2003.pdf. The trustees did seem to consider, to a lesser extent, historic properties resulting from European settlement. The alternative ultimately proposed by the trustees sought to restore tribal cultural resources, as well as, through the acquisition of land, to preserve archaeological and historic resources. *Id.*

93. *See* Office of Nat. Res. Damages, N.J. Dep't of Envtl. Prot., Natural Resources Restoration Plan for Damages Associated with the *Presidente Rivera* Oil Spill of June 1989 (1996), https://www.cerc.usgs.gov/orda_docs/DocHandler.ashx?task=get&ID=409.

One of the most significant restoration plans undertaken related to asserted cultural resources occurred at the Onondaga Lake site in upstate New York. The six Nations of the Haudenosaunee, and in particular the Onondaga Nation, consider Onondaga Lake to be "'an intrinsic part of [the Onondaga Nation's] existence,' once providing water, food, and medicinal plants as well as a place to fish, hunt, play, swim, and learn."[94] Although the Nation does not own any property on or adjacent to the lake, and the Nation ultimately withdrew from the cooperative damages assessment, the federal and state trustees included the Onondaga Nation in its assessment and restoration planning for many years out of respect for the cultural significance of the resource. Moreover, the final restoration plan included "several projects [that] attempt to reconnect the residents of Onondaga County, including the Onondaga Nation, and the City of Syracuse to the lake."[95] The trustees also left open the possibility that as-yet-unallocated funds could be used for cultural projects: "Reconnecting the public to Onondaga Lake is a priority for the Trustees, and it will continue to be an important factor in the selection of future projects in and around the lake."[96]

2. Consideration of Historic and Cultural Resources in Restoration Planning

In performing the NEPA review required for restoration planning, restoration plans are required to analyze the impact of a particular restoration activity on cultural resources. The NEPA regulations require agencies to consider "[u]nique characteristics of the geographic area such as proximity to historic or cultural resources"[97] and "[t]he degree to which the action may adversely affect districts, sites, highways, structures, or objects listed in or eligible for listing in the National Register of Historic Places."[98] The NEPA regulations also require that, "[t]o the fullest extent possible, agencies shall prepare draft environmental impact statements concurrently with and integrated with environmental impact analyses and related surveys and studies required by . . . the National Historic Preservation Act."[99]

---

94. Indus. Econ., Inc., Onondaga Lake Natural Resource Damage Assessment Restoration Plan and Environmental Assessment 20 (2017), https://www.fws.gov/northeast/nyfo/ec/files/onondaga/Onondaga%20RP%20EA%20and%20Appendices%208-11-2017_reduced%20(2).pdf.

95. *Id.* at E-6.

96. *Id.*

97. 40 C.F.R. § 1508.27(b)(3).

98. *Id.* § 1508.27(b)(8).

99. *Id.* § 1502.25(a).

Section 106 of the National Historic Preservation Act (NHPA) requires an agency with direct or indirect jurisdiction over a federal or federally assisted undertaking, prior to the approval or execution of that undertaking, to "take into account the effect of the undertaking on any historic property."[100] The NHPA regulations detail the "section 106 process," which involves identifying any potentially affected historic properties, assessing the impact of federal action on those properties, and resolving any adverse effects through consultation with the national Advisory Council on Historic Preservation and other parties.[101]

In practice, historic and cultural preservation impacts are often given cursory treatment in restoration plans and their accompanying environmental assessments or environmental impact statements. This is presumably because, for political and other reasons, trustees are unlikely to give serious consideration to projects that would materially impact important historic or cultural resources. In the Onondaga Lake Final Restoration Plan and Environmental Assessment, for example, the trustees stated that

> [c]ultural and historic resources and land use could experience indirect, long-term, minor adverse impacts resulting from habitat restoration. The land use in the floodplain, including any potential culturally sensitive areas, would change as the water resources in the floodplain changed (*e.g.*, as a result of wetland restoration). Because land use would stabilize in the floodplain over time, the impact is expected to be minor.[102]

Further examples of how restoration plans have addressed projects' impacts on historic and cultural resources are included in the footnote.[103]

---

100. 54 U.S.C. § 306108 (formerly 16 U.S.C. § 470f).

101. 36 C.F.R. pt. 800.

102. Indus. Econ., Inc., *supra* note 94, at 61.

103. *See, e.g.*, New Bedford Harbor Trustee Council, Environmental Assessment, New Bedford Harbor Restoration Round II, Final 17 (2001), https://www.gc.noaa.gov/gc-rp/nbh-fnl.pdf; *see also id.* at 19 (stating that "[n]o impacts on cultural resources (archaeological or historical) or on land use patterns are expected"). The case of the *World Prodigy* oil spill is also instructive. *See* Nat'l Oceanic & Atmospheric Admin., Final Environmental Assessment and Restoration Plan, *World Prodigy* Oil Spill Restoration Plan, Narragansett Bay, Rhode Island 1996, https://casedocuments.darrp.noaa.gov/northeast/world/wpea.html ("The Rhode Island Coastal Resources Management Program contains a policy statement to protect cultural resources within the state's coastal zone (Olsen and Seavey, 1983). Any action(s) undertaken to restore the natural resources impacted by the *World Prodigy* oil spill must comply with the historic and archaeological protection guidelines outlined by the state's approved coastal zone management plan.").

E. Climate Change

EXPERT INSIGHT: Climate Change and NRD

Michael B. Gerrard[104]

Columbia Law School

Arnold & Porter

Climate change is one of the most pressing environmental issues of the day, and probably for many years to come. As discussed here, it appears unlikely that there will be successful suits brought against greenhouse gas emitters based on NRD theories. However, climate change is very relevant to many NRD sites and cases—both because of its pertinence to evaluating baselines, and its importance in planning restoration projects and projecting future benefits from those projects.

Climate change may also increase the number and severity of spills and other incidents that damage natural resources in the first place. For example, melting ice caps will lead to more shipping in the Arctic, and therefore more spills there; melting permafrost may rupture pipes; extreme storms may flood tank farms and other industrial facilities; landfills and capped sites may become inundated; wildfires may damage all manner of facilities.

NRD Claims Based on Climate Change

There is little question that many natural environments are severely affected by climate change, and that much climate change results from human activities, especially greenhouse gas emissions from the combustion of fossil fuels in power plants, vehicles, and other energy users. However, attempts to bring NRD actions against greenhouse gas emitters, or the coal, oil, and gas companies that supply the fuel, would face great obstacles.

First, and almost certainly fatal, is the provision in CERCLA that NRD actions may be brought only for the release of "hazardous substances" within the meaning of the statute.[105] None of the greenhouse gases fall within this definition. The NRD provisions of OPA apply only to the discharge of oil into or upon the navigable waters or adjoining shorelines.[106]

Second, climate change results from the cumulative emissions of billions of emitters over the course of more than a century. No emitter is responsible for more than

---

104. Michael B. Gerrard is the Andrew Sabin Professor of Professional Practice at Columbia Law School and senior counsel at Arnold & Porter Kaye Scholer LLP. He holds a JD from New York University School of Law.

105. 42 U.S.C. § 9607(a).

106. 33 U.S.C. § 2702(a).

a tiny fraction of these cumulative emissions. If the emissions are attributed to the fossil fuel companies that extracted the fuel, several large companies each account for several percentage points of the total global emissions. No judicial decision has found liability on this basis, and two cases asserting such liability under the federal common law of nuisance were dismissed.[107] Beginning in July 2017, a number of municipalities in California and New York City filed cases asserting such liability under state common law.[108]

One academic article has argued that NRD for greenhouse gas emissions should be available under the public trust doctrine, an old common law doctrine.[109] This issue has never been adjudicated.

Changing Baselines

In NRDAs, the baseline is the condition of the ecological services "but for" the release of oil or hazardous substances. NOAA's regulations define baseline as "the condition of the natural resources and services that would have existed had the incident not occurred."[110] DOI's regulations define baseline as the "condition or conditions that would have existed at the assessment area had the discharge of oil or release of the hazardous substance under investigation not occurred."[111] These regulations go on to specify that in selecting the baseline data, "both natural processes and those that are the result of human activities" should be taken into account,[112] and the baseline data "should include the normal range of physical, chemical, or biological conditions for the assessment area or injured resource," and that "[c]auses of extreme or unusual value in baseline data should be identified and described."[113]

107. *See* Native Vill. of Kivalina v. ExxonMobil Corp., 696 F.3d 849 (9th Cir. 2012), *cert. denied*, 569 U.S. 1000 (2013); Comer v. Murphy Oil USA, Inc., 2007 WL 6942285 (S.D. Miss. Aug. 30, 2007). *Comer* had a complicated appellate history, and eventually the case was refiled, but the Fifth Circuit ruled in 2013 that the new action was barred by res judicata. *See* 718 F.3d 460 (5th Cir. 2013).

108. *See* Cty. of San Mateo v. Chevron Corp., No. 17CIV03222 (Cal. Super. Ct. July 17, 2017); Cty. of Marin v. Chevron Corp., No. CIV1702586 (Cal. Super. Ct. July 17, 2017); City of Imperial Beach v. Chevron Corp., C17-01227 (Cal. Super. Ct. July 17, 2017); People of State of California v. BP p.l.c., No. CGC-17-561370 (Cal. Super. Ct. Sept. 19, 2017) (filed by San Francisco); People of State of California v. BP p.l.c., No. RG17875889 (Cal. Super. Ct. Sept. 19, 2017) (filed by Oakland); Cty. of Santa Cruz v. Chevron Corp., No. 17CV03242 (Cal. Super. Ct. Dec. 20, 2017); City of Santa Cruz v. Chevron Corp., No. 17CV03243 (Cal. Super. Ct. Dec. 20, 2017); City of New York v. BP p.l.c., No. 1:18-cv-00182 (S.D.N.Y. Jan. 9, 2018); City of Richmond v. Chevron Corp., No. C18-00055 (Cal. Super. Ct. Jan. 22, 2018).

109. Mary Christina Wood & Dan Galpern, *Atmospheric Recovery Litigation: Making the Fossil Fuel Industry Pay to Restore a Viable Climate System*, 45 ENVTL. L. 259 (2015).

110. 15 C.F.R. § 990.30.

111. 43 C.F.R. § 11.14(e).

112. *Id.* § 11.72(b)(1).

113. *Id.* § 11.72(b)(2).

In many geographic locations, climate change has the potential to change numerous aspects of the physical environment that forms the baseline of future conditions absent the subject spill or other incident. Sea level (and the associated effect on the extent of coastal wetlands) may be the most obvious example. Others include:

- Saltwater intrusion
- Ocean temperature
- Ocean chemistry
- Coastal erosion and sediment transport
- Rainfall frequency and intensity
- Temperature range
- Stream flows and temperature
- Glacial melt
- Soil moisture
- Snow pack
- Wildfire frequency and intensity
- Species abundance, range, migration pathways
- Invasive species

Considering these factors creates several difficulties:

First, the baseline is not fixed. The sea level may be x today, x + 10 inches in ten years, x + 20 inches in 20 years, and so forth. *Second*, a broad range of future estimates may be available, depending on such factors as assumed future levels of global greenhouse gas emissions, and the behavior of the Antarctic and Greenland ice sheets.

The application of these two factors is illustrated in the official estimates of future sea level rise issued by the New York State Department of Environmental Conservation in 2017 based on a number of scientific studies.[114] Four time intervals are given—2020s, 2050s, 2080s, and 2100. For each of these time intervals, five projections are given: low, low-medium, medium, high-medium, and high. For the year 2100, for example, the low projection is 15 inches; medium, 36 inches; and high, 75 inches.

For purposes of planning infrastructure that is expected to have a long life span, it may make sense to use the high estimate, since it would be most unfortunate to build an airport runway, for example, assuming the medium value of 36 inches of sea level rise if it turns out that the high estimate of 75 inches is more accurate, and the runway is often submerged. On the other hand, for purposes of assessing money damages in an NRD process, the medium value may be more appropriate.

Another difficulty is that future impacts may vary considerably from one location to another that is not very far away. The New York numbers just presented are actually just for the New York City/lower Hudson River region. The Department of Environmental Conservation also issued projections for the mid-Hudson region (north

---

114. 6 N.Y.C.R.R. pt. 490.

of New York City) and the Long Island region (east). The variations are no more than four inches, but these differences do exist.

A great deal of data and many projections are available for the New York City region. That is not the case for all locations. In some parts of the United States, projections may only be available on a statewide basis, if that. The National Climate Assessment of the United States Global Change Research Program may be the most authoritative source for national-level and regional-level climate projections, but numerous other sources are available, some of them very geographically specific.[115]

Planning Restoration Projects and Predicting Benefits from Projects

Many of the climate factors listed earlier are also relevant to the selection, planning, implementation, and monitoring of remedies and restoration projects. A project to restore a coastal wetland that has been impaired by an oil spill, for example, should take into account the future hydrological conditions in the location. An assessment of the expected use of this restored wetland by wildlife should likewise consider how wildlife abundance at the location will be affected by climate change.

All of this greatly complicates the needed analysis. It is difficult enough to predict wildlife use of a restored habitat years from now, without having to consider how wildlife abundance will be affected then by climate-related factors, such as changed rainfall patterns and temperatures, and availability of the food on which the wildlife rely. Scientific techniques for making these assessments are being developed, but they have not yet become approved methodologies for use in NRD decision making.

However, the EPA Superfund program has devoted considerable attention to the effects of climate change on CERCLA remedies. One outcome was a fact sheet on consideration of climate change in contaminated sediment remedies. The EPA fact sheet identified ways in which a sediment remedy system may be particularly vulnerable to climate-related factors:

- Potential scour of a sediment cap or underlying sediment due to an increase in surface water flow velocity and/or turbulence associated with intense storms or sustained freeze conditions
- A significant increase in urban or agricultural runoff entering the sediment containment/treatment zone due to increased intensity, frequency, and/or duration of storms

---

115. The various sources are compiled in Jessica Wentz, Assessing the Impacts of Climate Change on the Built Environment under NEPA and State EIA Laws: A Survey of Current Practices and Recommendations for Model Protocols (Sabin Ctr. for Climate Change Law, Columbia Law Sch., 2015), http://columbiaclimatelaw.com/files/2016/06/Wentz-2015-08-Climate-Change-Impact-on-Built-Environment-.pdf; and Jessica Wentz, Considering the Effects of Climate Change on Natural Resources in Environmental Review and Planning Documents: Guidelines for Agencies and Practitioners (Sabin Ctr. for Climate Change Law, Columbia Law Sch., 2016), http://columbiaclimatelaw.com/files/2017/01/Wentz-2016-09-Considering-the-Effects-of-Climate-Change-on-Natural-Resources.pdf.

- Entrance of additional waste or debris from upland or upstream sources due to flooding, intense wind, or landslide
- Increased discharge of groundwater to the associated water body due to increased intensity, frequency, and/or duration of storms
- Increased turbidity of water in a treatment zone due to high wind in shallow surface water or arrival of floodwater or increased discharge
- Unexpected desiccation in the containment/treatment zone due to low precipitation

The document then listed a variety of adaptation measures that could be employed to prepare for temperature, precipitation, wind, sea level rise, and wildfires, broken down among underwater components; upland components; and remedy construction, operation, and maintenance.

EPA has prepared similar fact sheets for adaptation to climate change with groundwater remediation systems,[116] and landfills and containment as elements of site remediation.[117]

One study supported by grants from EPA and the Department of Agriculture contained several findings and recommendations beyond those just addressed. These included:

- Consideration will be required of controversial decisions in response to, or in anticipation of, climate change, such as off-site restoration efforts, or on-site restoration of functionally equivalent resources.
- There should be a focus on managing the stressors that could be exacerbated by climate change, such as pollution and habitat loss.
- Increased temperatures can affect the chemical behavior of certain contaminants, such as mercury, and the biological behavior of microbes.
- If climate change generally accelerates the decline in services associated with exposure to hazardous substances, then initiation of cleanup and the restoration process must also be accelerated; otherwise the injury (and associated restoration costs) may be greater.
- Use restoration projects as opportunities to mitigate climate-related impacts, such as by enhancing the sequestration of carbon; adding refugia or migration corridors; creating or enhancing riparian habitat to mitigate thermal stress in aquatic systems; and restoring coastal salt marshes, which can reduce erosion of shorelines, attenuate wave action, and limit flooding of coastal communities.

---

116. Office of Superfund Remediation & Tech. Innovation, U.S. Envtl. Prot. Agency, EPA 542-F-13-004, Climate Change Technical Fact Sheet: Groundwater Remediation Systems (2013), https://semspub.epa.gov/work/HQ/175851.pdf.

117. Office of Superfund Remediation & Tech. Innovation, U.S. Envtl. Prot. Agency, EPA 542-F-14-001, Climate Change Adaptation Technical Fact Sheet: Landfills and Containment as an Element of Site Remediation (2014), https://semspub.epa.gov/work /HQ/175853.pdf; see also Office of Solid Waste & Emergency Response, U.S. Envtl. Prot. Agency, Adaptation of Superfund Remediation to Climate Change (2012).

This last suggestion is of particular note. The day may come when compensation of some sort is provided for those who take actions to absorb carbon dioxide or take other actions that help in addressing the climate change problem. A price on carbon is the most obvious example of such a policy. The political climate in the United States as this is written is not hospitable to such measures, but as with many things related to the physical climate, the future is difficult to predict.

F. Protecting the Administrative Record

Pursuant to both the CERCLA and OPA regulations, the trustees are required to create and maintain an administrative record to support their final damages assessment. As discussed earlier, trustee agencies have argued that the statutes require judges to limit their review to the administrative record, employing an arbitrary and capricious standard.[118] And although courts who have addressed this issue have rejected the agencies' argument, PRPs would be wise to ensure that the trustees' final administrative record is complete and includes critical data and analysis to support their technical arguments. Using the OPA regulations as the principal framework, this section explains the process, mechanics, and strategy related to protecting the administrative record.

In the *preassessment phase*, the trustees prepare a Notification of Incident, Determination of Jurisdiction, and a Determination to Conduct Restoration Planning. Trustees also prepare and send to the responsible party an NOI.[119] Under OPA regulations, a public administrative record must be established in the preassessment phase, and regulations indicate that it should be established

---

118. *See* Montana v. Atl. Richfield Co. [hereinafter *ARCO*], No. 6:83-cv-00317-SEH (D. Mont. Mar. 3, 1997); United States v. ASARCO Inc., No. CV 96-0122-N-EJL, CV 91-342-N-EJL, 1998 WL 1799392 (D. Idaho Mar. 31, 1998). As the court in *ARCO* explained:

Under an administrative record review, the court would review the administrative record created by the [government] under the traditional administrative model embodied in the Administrative Procedure Act, 5 U.S.C. §§ 701-706, giving substantial deference to the [government's] selection of appropriate restoration alternatives and determination of recoverable damages.

[The defendant] could challenge the [government's] selection of restoration alternatives and determination of damages based only on the information compiled in the administrative record. The [government's] determination of damages would be set aside only if it was found to be arbitrary and capricious.

ARCO, slip op. at 8 n.11.

119. For the *Deepwater Horizon* NOI, see Discharge of Oil from Deepwater Horizon/Macondo Well, Gulf of Mexico; Intent to Conduct Restoration Planning, 75 Fed. Reg. 60,800 (Oct. 1, 2010).

concurrently with the NOI.[120] Under both CERCLA and OPA regulations, the trustees must support their decisions with an administrative record in order to be entitled to the rebuttable presumption.[121] Under CERCLA, no regulatory provisions specifically require the trustees to make the administrative record publicly available. Under CERCLA, the administrative record must be "complete" and must include a "Report of Assessment" if the trustees desire to claim the benefit of the rebuttable presumption, but otherwise the trustees determine on a case-by-case basis whether to prepare a formal administrative record and what it should contain.[122]

The *restoration planning* phase includes the bulk of the work in any significant NRDA. The first stage is injury assessment, when trustees develop assessment plans and assess the injury to particular resources. The regulations specifically encourage cooperation with the responsible party at this stage. At a minimum, the regulations specify that the responsible party should have an opportunity to comment on the documents that "significantly affect the nature and extent of the assessment."[123] Responsible parties often provide detailed comments on injury assessment plans and document responsible

---

120. *See* 15 C.F.R. § 990.45(a) ("If trustees decide to proceed with restoration planning, *they must open a publicly available administrative record* to document the basis for their decisions pertaining to restoration. The administrative record *should be opened concurrently* with the publication of the Notice of Intent to Conduct Restoration Planning.") (emphasis added). Unlike OPA regulations, CERCLA regulations do not specifically require that the administrative record should be public, and they do provide an indication of when the administrative record should be opened. *See* Bureau of Land Mgmt., U.S. Dep't of the Interior, BLM Natural Resource Damage Assessment and Restoration Handbook 28 (2008) [hereinafter BLM Handbook] ("The NRDAR guidance under CERCLA does not specify when to open an AR. Under CERCLA, the decision to assemble the AR should be made with input from the Solicitor and may depend on when the trustee council releases NRDAR documents to the public and the PRPs. The Coordinator should consider opening an AR when the trustees determine to conduct a formal NRDAR.").

121. 43 C.F.R. § 11.91(c) ("When performed by a Federal or State official in accordance with this part, the natural resource damage assessment and the resulting Damage Determination supported by a complete administrative record of the assessment including the Report of Assessment as described in § 11.90 of this part shall have the force and effect of a rebuttable presumption on behalf of any Federal or State claimant in any judicial or adjudicatory administrative proceeding under CERCLA, or section 311 of the CWA.").

122. BLM guidance outlines some of the strategic factors that the trustees take into account when deciding whether and how to prepare an administrative record. BLM Handbook, *supra* note 120, at 28. In cooperative assessments, parties may memorialize their understanding of the administrative record in their MOU. A common term in such MOUs provides that parties will include in the administrative record interpretations of the data on which the parties fail to agree. *See, e.g.*, Memorandum of Agreement Regarding Natural Resource Damage Assessment, Restoration and Other Natural Resource Trustee Activities Arising from the PEPCO Chalk Point Oil Spill 10–11 (2000).

123. 15 C.F.R. § 990.14(c)(4).

party concerns regarding scope and method in these plans.[124] Trustees often prepare and circulate to the responsible party injury assessment reports on specific resources. In cooperative assessments, injury assessment documents may be authored by TWGs set up early in the process that typically have representatives from the trustees and the responsible party. Responsible parties often provide specific comments on these injury assessment documents for inclusion in the administrative record. In some cases, trustees also provide specific responses to responsible party comments on the injury assessment reports. Injury assessment reports may be circulated to the responsible parties before their public release. Because trustees often do not make material changes to their assessment between the drafting of assessment reports and the publication of the draft restoration plan, responsible party comments on the injury assessment reports often form the basis of the responsible party's public comments on the restoration plan itself.

In the second major stage of restoration planning, called restoration selection, trustees must select and evaluate restoration alternatives. The regulations then require the trustees to develop and submit for public comment a draft and a final restoration plan. These plans are designed to tie all of the phases of the NRDA together; they should explain (1) the assessment methods, (2) the results of the assessment, (3) the goals and objectives of restoration, (4) the restoration alternatives and how those alternatives were developed, (5) the trustees' preferred alternatives, (6) the nature of responsible party participation (past and future), and (7) procedures for ensuring restoration success.[125]

1. Publication of Draft DARP

Arguably most relevant for the settlement context is the trustees' draft restoration plan, usually called formally a draft Damage Assessment and Restoration Plan/Environmental Assessment (DARP/EA or DARP), which is usually completed around the time that the settlement is announced. The "Environmental Assessment" (EA) portion of the title refers to a section of the document devoted to fulfillment of trustee obligations under NEPA. NRDA regulations specifically require the trustees to adhere to NEPA.[126] Under NEPA, federal agencies are required to consider and disclose the environmental impacts of

---

124. OPA regulations also allow the responsible parties to propose alternate assessment techniques at this stage if they agree to certain restrictions, such as not challenging the results of the assessments if the trustees agree to employ them. 15 C.F.R. § 990.14(c)(6).

125. *Id.* § 990.55.

126. *Id.* § 990.23.

major federal actions.[127] NEPA requires federal agencies to prepare an EIS that discusses the significant environmental impacts of a proposed project and reasonable alternatives to avoid or minimize those impacts. An agency can also determine that an EIS is not necessary, but that determination must be documented in an EA.

Over time, NOAA has developed a standardized outline for draft DARPs, such that the main elements remain the same and some language (such as the standard descriptions of trustee and public input) has become boilerplate. In addition to satisfying the seven basic criteria specified in 15 C.F.R. § 990.55 and described earlier, the draft DARP also generally includes an index to the administrative record or other information on its location and how the public can access it.

A public comment period on the draft DARP follows. OPA regulations specify minimum comment periods, but no maximum ones.[128] If the draft DARP also includes an EA, the comment period "must be consistent with the federal trustee agency's NEPA requirements, but should generally be no less than thirty (30) calendar days."[129] If the DARP is also accompanied by an EIS, however, the document "must be made available for public review for a minimum of forty-five (45) calendar days."[130] On occasion, as is also common with other administrative proceedings, trustees have sometimes extended or reopened comment periods.

2. Publication of Final DARP and Written Demand

After the close of the comment period, the trustees publish a final DARP. This document should include responses to comments on the draft and an indication of how the final document was revised in response to the comments.[131]

---

127. 42 U.S.C. §§ 4321–4370m-12.

128. 15 C.F.R. § 990.55(c) ("The nature of public review and comment on the Draft and Final Restoration Plans will depend on the nature of the incident and any applicable federal trustee NEPA requirements, as described in §§ 990.14(d) and 990.23 of this part." Section 990.14(d) gives the trustees wide latitude in determining when to allow public involvement, so long as they do so after restoration plans have been developed: "Trustees must provide opportunities for public involvement after the trustees' decision to develop restoration plans or issuance of any notices to that effect, as provided in § 990.55 of this part. Trustees may also provide opportunities for public involvement at any time prior to this decision if such involvement may enhance trustees' decision-making or avoid delays in restoration."). Section 990.23 specifies that NEPA applies and explains how NEPA obligations can be fulfilled in the specific NRDA context.

129. 15 C.F.R. § 990.23(c)(1)(ii)(D).

130. 15 C.F.R. § 990.23(c)(2)(ii)(C). A final DARP/EIS must also be published in the *Federal Register* 30 days before the trustees make a final decision on restoration actions. *Id.* § 990.23(c)(2)(ii)(E).

131. *Id.* § 990.55(d).

After finalization of the DARP, trustees send a written demand to the responsible party.[132] The demand includes (among other things) an index to the administrative record.[133]

3. Closing the Administrative Record

The trustees also formally close the administrative record at this stage. The regulations require that the administrative record should be closed within a "reasonable time" after the trustees complete restoration planning.[134] OPA guidance indicates that the administrative record should remain available for public review until final settlement or completion of litigation of damages on the final restoration plan.[135] After the record is closed, the regulations also limit the kinds of materials that the agency may subsequently add to the record. Material may be added to the record only if it is from a party that had no notice of the draft DARP, is not duplicative of information already in the record, and "raise[s] significant issues" regarding the final restoration plan.[136]

If any parties, including the responsible party, become plaintiffs to challenge the EA portion of the DARP/EA (as opposed to the substance of the assessment and restoration planning), they could seek to add additional material to the record under limited circumstances. Case law under NEPA establishes that the reviewing court has limited authority to determine that evidence outside the administrative record is necessary on the question of whether or not an agency acted within the scope of its authority.[137] Plaintiffs in NEPA cases could seek to supplement the administrative record with additional studies and documents, depositions by experts, and other exhibits not included in the administrative record. Courts may also invoke the practice of judicial notice to supplement the record with additional scientific propositions.[138] The

---

132. *Id.* § 990.62.

133. *Id.* § 990.62(e)(4).

134. *Id.* § 990.61.

135. Damage Assessment & Restoration Program, Nat'l Oceanic & Atmospheric Admin., Preassessment Phase Guidance Document for Natural Resource Damage Assessment Under the Oil Pollution Act of 1990 app. I, at I-6 (1996).

136. 15 C.F.R. § 990.61(a).

137. Citizens to Pres. Overton Park, Inc. v. Volpe, 401 U.S. 402, 420–21 (1971) ("[S]ince the bare record may not disclose the factors that were considered or the [agency]'s construction of the evidence it may be necessary for the District Court to require some explanation in order to determine if the [agency] acted within the scope of [its] authority and if the [agency]'s action was justifiable under the applicable standard.... If the District Court decides that additional explanation is necessary, that court should consider which method will prove the most expeditious so that full review may be had as soon as possible.").

138. *See* Fed. R. Evid. 201.

practice of taking judicial notice is when a court accepts "for purposes of convenience and without requiring a party's proof, . . . well-known and indisputable fact[s]."[139] Outside of these and similar special circumstances that could arise in litigation, a responsible party that wishes to ensure material is placed in the administrative record and is considered by a reviewing court in the context of a challenge to the agency's action should ensure that the material is included in the record before it is closed by the trustees.

4. Restoration Implementation Phase

In this phase, the trustees take specific steps to conduct the restoration outlined in the restoration plan. A new administrative record is opened for this phase. In some cases, particularly for smaller NRDAs that are less complicated, responsible parties have settled their liability by this stage, so their involvement in the administrative record for this phase is minimal.

5. Two Examples of Public Comment Processes

Some examples of how the public comment process has worked may help illustrate some of the options available to responsible parties and other parties throughout the process. In this section, we discuss two examples where responsible parties and others provided technical comments throughout the assessment process and provided specific documents for the administrative record as well.

a. M/V *Kure*

On November 5, 1997, a fuel tank ruptured when the M/V *Kure* collided with a loading dock in Humboldt Bay, causing approximately 4,500 gallons of bunker fuel oil to spill into Humboldt Bay in Samoa, northern California. Affected resources included birds (3,950 estimated killed), salt marsh, mudflats, and various recreational resources. Trustees and the responsible party conducted a cooperative NRDA for the spill. After protracted settlement negotiations, the responsible party settled its liabilities for $4.82 million in a consent decree signed by the U.S. Department of Justice in March 2008. The responsible party submitted no comments on the draft DARP.

Trustees included the California Department of Fish and Game, the California State Lands Commission, and USFWS. The trustees opened a single 45-day comment period on the draft DARP, which was submitted on

---

139. *Judicial Notice*, BLACK'S LAW DICTIONARY (9th ed. 2009).

September 14, 2007. The comment period was not extended. Written public comments on the DARP were sparse (the final DARP includes three brief submissions, two from interested individuals and one minor comment from BLM).[140] The four-page formal trustee response to comments was organized around 15 questions largely derived from oral comments at public meetings and covering such issues as "why did this case take so long," how the trustees made baseline determinations, and the allocation of money to specific projects.[141] The final DARP was released in July 2008.

The responsible party's submissions to the administrative record in this case primarily documented technical disagreements with the trustees during the assessment phase. Some of the communication came from the responsible party's attorneys, who either drafted cover letters and forwarded documents prepared by technical consultants or provided comments in the body of the letter itself. Responsible party consultants also submitted comments directly as part of the cooperative process. The responsible party provided early documentation of its disagreement with a proposed study plan on the marbled murrelet, a bird that USFWS classified at threatened.

The responsible party's disputes with the trustees over the NRDA in this spill concerned the number of birds killed. These disputes were documented in technical comments sent to the trustees and transmitted by the responsible party's attorneys. The responsible party did not submit separate written comments on the draft DARP for the administrative record, perhaps because agreement had already been reached with the trustees in substance. However, the consent decree also is notable because it records the disagreement between the responsible party and the trustees on the bird injury.[142]

---

140. CAL. DEP'T OF FISH & GAME ET AL., KURE/HUMBOLDT BAY OIL SPILL FINAL DAMAGE ASSESSMENT AND RESTORATION PLAN/ENVIRONMENTAL ASSESSMENT app. N (2008).

141. *Id.* at app. M.

142. Consent Decree at 4, United States v. Kure Shipping S.A., No. 3:08-cv-01328-JSW (N.D. Cal. Mar. 7, 2008), ECF. No. 16 ("After the Spill, the USFWS and the CDFG, as Trustees for Natural Resources, (hereinafter, the 'Trustees') and the Settling Defendants entered into a Cooperative Natural Resource Damage Assessment, pursuant to which the Trustees and the Settling Defendants conducted a number of assessment activities. These activities included gathering and analyzing data and other information that they used to attempt to determine and quantify the resource injuries. They estimated that the Spill oiled approximately 6,200 acres of mudflats, salt marsh, and other habitats, and resulted in approximately 800 days of lost recreation. *In a separate analysis, the Trustees determined that the Spill killed approximately 4,000 birds, including 130 Marbled Murrelets. The Settling Defendants dispute these numbers and contend that far fewer birds were killed.*" (emphasis added)).

b. M/T *Athos I* Spill

On November 26, 2004, while delivering cargo to the Paulsboro marine terminal on the Delaware River, the M/T *Athos I* struck submerged objects and spilled roughly 265,000 gallons of crude oil. The spill moved up-river with the advancing tide. Resources affected included marshes, sandy beaches, tidal flats, aquatic organisms, birds and wildlife, and recreational use. Frescati Shipping Company, Ltd. (Frescati) and Tsakos Shipping & Trading S.A. (Tsakos), the owner and manager of the vessel, were identified as responsible parties and entered into a cooperative NRD process with the trustees, which included NOAA, USFWS, and the states of Pennsylvania, New Jersey, and Delaware. Frescati and Tsakos spent over $180 million in response to the incident but were entitled to limit their liability under OPA to $45,474,000. Consultants for Frescati and Tsakos were involved in the assessment process early on and commented extensively on draft injury assessment documents.

According to public comments submitted by Frescati and Tsakos on the draft DARP, the cooperative process broke down after August 2006, when Frescati and Tsakos obtained a favorable determination on the OPA limitation. Litigation over the spill continued as the United States sought reimbursement for response costs from CITGO entities, which were partial subrogees to U.S. claims against Frescati.[143] A bench trial began in early 2015 before Judge Slomsky in the U.S. District Court for the Eastern District of Pennsylvania on the question of who was responsible for ensuring that the Delaware River was free of the obstruction that caused the spill and whether the response costs were reasonable.

NOAA's request for public comment on the draft DARP was dated December 19, 2008, and published in the Federal Register on January 6, 2009. Comments were due by February 20, 2009. The comment period was not extended. On February 13, 2009, the *Athos I* trustees gave a presentation to Delaware Riverkeeper that provided an overview of the assessment and restoration process in this case.[144] The principal comments were from environmental NGOs, local planning districts, and other interested corporate parties such as CITGO Petroleum and the International Tanker Owners Pollution Federation Limited. The American Bird Conservancy praised some of the wetland restoration

---

143. CITGO Asphalt Refining Company, CITGO Petroleum Corporation, and CITGO East Coast Oil Corporation contracted for the shipment and operated the terminal where it was to be unloaded. *See In re* Petition of Frescati Shipping Co., 886 F.3d 291 (3d Cir. 2018).

144. Athos Trustees, *Athos I* Oil Spill Presentation (2009), https://casedocuments .darrp.noaa.gov/northeast/athos/pdf/Athos_Feb_13_presentation_Final.pdf.

projects for the potential effects on birds, but criticized the oyster reef projects for not directly benefitting affected bird species and expressed a preference for horseshoe crab projects that were considered by the trustees but ultimately rejected. In 11 pages of detailed comments, Delaware Riverkeeper echoed the American Bird Conservancy's concerns about particular projects, suggested to the trustees that public involvement in the assessment was necessary so that the public could see how the responsible party "swayed the findings and outcomes," and criticized certain human-use projects as either exacerbating boat traffic congestion or being outside of the impact area. CITGO criticized the draft DARP primarily for (1) using modeling to determine bird losses and lost recreational trips where actual data on recovery are available and (2) selecting restoration projects that were actually previously identified public infrastructure projects. A consultant for the company submitted detailed technical criticisms of the draft DARP on its own behalf. The main concerns raised by the consultant were the use of sheen data to indicate shoreline oiling, a critique of the service accounting related to marsh creation for bird species, and the use of production forgone for bird injury.

The DARP was finalized in September 2009, and the amount for restoration projects was revised upward to $26.47 million. In September 2010, the USCG's NPFC awarded the trustees $30.44 million for NRD injury and assessment costs, including $26.41 million for restoration projects. The responsible parties did not pay for restoration because they reached their limits of liability under OPA during extensive response operations.

Three administrative record filings consist of comments on draft trustee assessment documents that were apparently circulated to the relevant trustee working groups, which included representatives of the responsible party. The criticisms of the trustee approaches in these comments on the assessment documents formed the technical basis for the comment document submitted on behalf of Frescati and Tsakos during the formal comment period on the draft DARP.

Significant areas of disagreement identified in the responsible party submissions include criticism of trustee assumptions about provenance of polycyclic aromatic hydrocarbons detected in sediments, use of production forgone and rejection of density dependence in estimating bird injury, and apparent flaws in lost recreational use survey instruments. The trustees did not adjust the final DARP in any substantive way after responsible party comments.

The responsible parties commented early with detailed technical disagreements on injury assessment for key resources. These critiques formed the basis for the responsible parties' ultimate comments on the DARP during the public comment period. The ability to submit early comments was enhanced by the availability of the trustee assessment reports and the cooperative posture of the early part of the case. Despite the cooperative posture, however, the responsible parties documented significant, early technical disagreements with trustee injury assessment techniques. The trustees largely ignored the responsible parties' comments. The responsible parties' stake in the ultimate outcome was also probably diminished because the responsible parties successfully invoked OPA limitation.

6. Strategic Considerations Regarding Administrative Record Submissions

Based on these cases and others, here are a few observations relevant to strategic thinking regarding submissions to the administrative record.

- *Public comments on the draft DARP do not appear to be an effective means to influence the shape of the final DARP or the ultimate restoration outcome.* We identified no instance in which responsible party comments significantly altered either the assessment or the selection of restoration proposals. There are several probable reasons for this. Most critical public comments by the responsible party build on sustained efforts by the responsible party to shape the scope of the assessment and the interpretation of results. If the comments do not bear fruit early in the assessment process, there is probably little reason to believe that they will bear fruit later in the assessment process. By the time a draft DARP is submitted, the positions of the trustees and the responsible party with respect to contentious issues are usually fairly clear to both sides.

- *Accordingly, the creation of the administrative record should be viewed as an opportunity primarily to shape the views of the reviewing court (or to affect future discussions over reopeners, if applicable) rather than the views of the trustees.* In the case of litigation, courts are likely to be reluctant to conduct record review, particularly in cases where the trustees seek to take advantage of regulatory provisions giving them a rebuttable presumption if they follow the regulations. However, if a subsequent judicial proceeding turns out to be a record review and not a full-blown trial, the responsible party needs to have its critical data and facts already part of the administrative record in the case. In addition, some consent decrees contain reopener provisions that may be triggered by new information about injury. As discussed earlier, what counts as "new information" can sometimes be defined with reference to information in the administrative record. Even where a consent decree does not contain such a reference, where there is a reopener, responsible parties have an interest in ensuring that the administrative record is as expansive as possible to limit later claims that information is "new."

- *Litigation over the shape and content of the NRD administrative record appears to be nonexistent.* Theoretically, responsible parties could raise a specific legal claim that the trustees did not fulfill their obligations with respect to maintaining an administrative record under OPA NRDA regulations or guidance. Although NEPA litigation is relatively common, we have identified no instance in which a party sued to prevent implementation of a final DARP for NEPA violations.[145]

- *In the process of DARP commenting, responsible parties tend to use the same consultants who have been involved in response and assessment.* Administrative record comments tend to be authored by outside lawyers, corporate officials (including in-house counsel), and technical consultants who have already been responsible party representatives in the assessment process. As in other public comment contexts, responsible parties do not always identify the consultants who author the comments. Parties who employ new consultants specifically to comment publicly on the DARP should not expect to maintain work-product privilege. In cases where administrative record comments and litigation have overlapping schedules, the responsible party may consider that there are some advantages of having expert reports circulated to the trustees as part of the litigation in accordance with judicial orders rather than as part of the public comment process.

- *Responsible party comments in the administrative record tend to focus on rebuttal rather than affirmative points.* Responsible parties use the administrative record to memorialize disagreements with the trustees on critical issues that have already been raised in the assessment process, rather than submitting the results of their own full-blown assessment.

---

145. An NGO sued the trustees for NEPA violations related to a Phase III early restoration project in the *Deepwater Horizon* matter. Gulf Restoration Network v. Sally Jewell, No. 1:15-cv-00191-CG-C (S.D. Ala.).

Chapter 11
The European NRD Regime

Outside of the United States, one of the most developed NRD programs is the Environmental Liability Directive (ELD), the European Union's (EU's) NRD regime. This chapter first gives an overview of the structure of the ELD and then compares the ELD to OPA and CERCLA NRD programs in the United States. The chapter then describes some of the challenges the ELD has faced as it has been transcribed into the laws of the EU member states. The final section of the chapter describes some aspects of the ELD's implementation over the past ten years.

A. The Environmental Liability Directive

European Union Directive 2004/35/EC, or the ELD, was passed on April 21, 2004, with the goal of creating a unified European legal framework for NRD.[1] The ELD is based around "polluter pays principle," meaning that it has the goal of making polluters fully internalize the damage they cause to the environment.[2] The ELD was created in the European Parliament and Council, and is being implemented by EU member states and transposed into their own laws.

1. Regulatory Structure

As an EU directive, the ELD must be "transposed" into the laws of each of the EU member states. Although the ELD itself does not have direct binding

---

1. Council Directive 2004/35, Environmental Liability with Regard to the Prevention and Remedying of Environmental Damage, 2004 O.J. (L 143) 56 [hereinafter ELD].
   2. *Id.* ¶ 2.

effect on polluters, it has binding legal effect on member states of the EU, which must create laws that implement the ELD.[3]

The ELD requires each member state to designate a "competent authority" to administer ELD in the nation.[4] The competent authority has authority to order polluters to remediate environmental damage or to conduct its own remediation and seek reimbursement from polluters.[5] The competent authority has power to specify how a polluter will remediate a site, guided by the principles set forth in Annex II of the ELD.[6] The competent authority is also the body that a citizen or NGO may petition to ask to take action on environmental damage.[7]

2. Scope of Liability

Liability under the ELD applies to "operators" conducting "occupational activities" that result in "environmental damage."[8] Occupational activities are defined to encompass "any activity carried out in the course of an economic activity, a business or an undertaking."[9] This definition does not include purely private or recreational activities.[10] The ELD defines operator as one who "operates or controls" the occupational activity, although this definition has been expanded by many member states in their transposition of the ELD.[11]

Liability under the ELD applies only to damage to natural resources, or "environmental damage" as the directive labels it.[12] There are three categories of environmental damage:

- **Damage to protected species and natural habitats.** Damage in this category requires "significant adverse effects" to species and habitats defined in two other EU directives: Birds Directive 79/409/EEC and the Habitats Directive 92/43/EEC.[13]

---

3. *See, e.g.*, Case C 32/18, Commission of the European Communities v. Republic of France, 2009 (holding France liable for failing to transpose the ELD by the required date).

4. ELD, *supra* note 1, art. 11, ¶ 1.

5. *Id.* art. 6, ¶ 2.

6. *Id.*

7. *Id.* art. 12.

8. *Id.* art. 3, ¶ 1.

9. *Id.* art. 2, ¶ 7.

10. Stevens & Bolton LLP, *Study on Analysis of Integrating the ELD into 11 National Legal Frameworks, Final Report,* at 59 (Dec. 16, 2013) [hereinafter *Legal Integration Study*], http://ec.europa.eu/environment/legal/liability/pdf/Final%20report%20-%20ELD.pdf.

11. ELD, *supra* note 1, art. 2, ¶ 6.

12. *Id.* ¶ 1.

13. *Id.* ¶ 1(a).

- **Water damage.** Damage in this category requires "significant adverse effects" to waters. Waters included in this category are defined in the Water Framework Directive 2000/60/EC.[14]
- **Land damage.** Damage in this category differs from both water and species in that the "adverse effect[]" protected against is an adverse effect to human health. Any contamination of land that creates a risk to human health is environmental damage under this category.[15]

Notably, there is a threshold requirement for environmental damage—an adverse effect must be "significant" before liability is triggered.[16] All three categories of damage include this significance threshold, although land damage differs because its significance threshold refers to risk to human health rather than damage to the environment. As discussed later in this chapter, this significance threshold has been a troublesome provision in both the transposition and implementation of the ELD. In transposition, member states have interpreted "significant" inconsistently, leading to an uneven standard of what constitutes environmental damage across the EU.[17] For implementation, the significance threshold requirement has served as a barrier to bringing cases, especially in member states which have interpreted "significant" to essentially mean "severe" harm.[18]

3. Exceptions

The ELD is specifically intended to cover environmental damage, which did not give rise to liability in many nations prior to the ELD.[19] The ELD is therefore somewhat of a gap-filling law, compelling a more complete internalization by polluters of the costs of the environmental damages their activities cause.[20] Due to its gap-filling function, the ELD generally does not give rise to liability for pollution-related harms that are already covered by other laws.[21]

---

14. *Id.* ¶ 1(b).

15. *Id.* ¶ 1(c).

16. *See id.* ¶ 1.

17. *Legal Integration Study*, *supra* note 10, at 12.

18. BIO Intelligence Serv., *Implementation Challenges and Obstacles of the Environmental Liability Directive (ELD), Final Report*, at 12 (May 16, 2013) [hereinafter *Implementation Study*], http://ec.europa.eu/environment/archives/liability/eld/eldimplement/pdf/ELD%20implementation_Final%20report.pdf.

19. ELD, *supra* note 1, ¶ 11.

20. *Id.* ¶ 3.

21. European Comm'n, *Environmental Liability Directive: A Short Overview*, at 5 (Mar. 28, 2006), http://ec.europa.eu/environment/legal/liability/pdf/Summary%20ELD.pdf.

Broadly, there are several areas where the ELD's jurisdiction is limited by the presence of other regulation.

- **Civil liability.** The ELD does not cover liability for personal or private property injuries caused by pollution. Liability for such injuries should be pursued through the normal civil law of the member nation.[22]
- **Diffuse pollutants.** The ELD does not cover diffuse pollution such as greenhouse gases or nitrates.[23] These forms of pollutions are already regulated under other EU laws that have been considered more effective at dealing with them.[24] Additionally, it is very difficult to attribute environmental damage from a diffuse pollutant to any individual operator.[25] However, there is an exception to this rule that provides that a diffuse pollutant can give rise to ELD liability when there is a "causal link between the damage and the activities of individual operators."[26]
- **International conventions.** The ELD does not apply to specific forms of pollution that are governed by international conventions for marine oils spills and nuclear waste.[27] The rationale is that because these forms of pollution implicate international issues, they are best governed by international treaties that bind parties outside of the EU as well.[28]

There are also some more general exceptions to the applicability of the ELD based on traditional force majeure concepts. They include:

- **War.** The directive does not cover damage caused by "an act of armed conflict, hostilities, civil war or insurrection."[29]
- **National defense.** "This Directive shall not apply to activities the main purpose of which is to serve national defence [sic] or international security."[30]
- **Natural disasters.** Natural disasters create exemptions in two ways. First, damage of an "irresistible character" caused by natural disasters is

---

22. *Id.* at 1; ELD, *supra* note 1, ¶ 11.

23. ELD, *supra* note 1, art. 4, ¶ 5; *Questions and Answers Environmental Liability Directive*, at Question 5, EUROPEAN COMM'N (Apr. 27, 2007) [hereinafter *Q&A*], http://europa.eu/rapid/press-release_MEMO-07-157_en.htm?locale=en.

24. *Q&A, supra* note 23, Question 5.

25. ELD, *supra* note 1, ¶ 13.

26. *Id.* art. 4, ¶ 5.

27. *Id.* ¶ 4 (nuclear); *id.* ¶ 2 (oil spills).

28. *Q&A, supra* note 23, Question 6.

29. ELD, *supra* note 1, art. 4, ¶ 1(a).

30. *Id.* ¶ 6.

not subject to liability.[31] Second, activities for which "the sole purpose . . . is to protect from natural disasters" do not give rise to liability under the ELD even if they create environmental damage.[32]

Finally, there are two exceptions where the operator may still be required to remediate or prevent damage, but is not responsible for the costs. Instead, the member state should take measures to enable the operator to recover costs of cleanup.[33] These exceptions are:

- **Proven causation by third party.** This exception applies when environmental damage "was caused by a third party and occurred despite the fact that appropriate safety measures were in place." This is not a full exemption from liability, so the operator must still remediate or prevent the damage, although they may not be financially liable.[34] The member states must create a way to reimburse the operator or devise other means to relieve the operator of the cost.[35]
- **Damage resulted from compliance with specific government order.** This exception applies to damage that "resulted from compliance with a compulsory order or instruction" from a government authority. As with the third-party exception, the operator would still have to remediate the damage but would not be financially liable.[36]

4. Potentially Liable Parties

The ELD has two separate liability regimes: (1) a strict liability regime for operators conducting high-risk activities, and (2) a negligence regime for other occupational activities. The strict liability regime applies to classes of activities specified in Annex III of the directive.[37] The operators that conduct these activities are usually organizations with the highest risk of causing environmental damage, such as companies with large industrial installations; waste management companies; agricultural companies; and entities that produce, store, use, and release toxic chemicals.[38] Such operators face strict liability for environmental damage in any of the three categories caused by their Annex III occupational activities.

---

31. *Id.* ¶ 1(b).
32. *Id.* ¶ 6.
33. *Id.* art. 8, ¶ 3.
34. *Id.* ¶ 3(a).
35. *Id.* ¶ 3.
36. *Id.* ¶ 3(b).
37. *Id.* art. 3, ¶ 1(a).
38. *See id.* Annex III.

There are two optional defenses to financial liability that can apply to operators in the strict liability regime. Member states can exempt Annex III operators from bearing the cost of remediation only if they are not at fault or negligent *and* meet one of two exemptions:

- **Permit defense.** Under this defense, operators may be shielded from liability for environmental damage caused by an "emission or event" expressly authorized by the government.[39]
- **State-of-the-art defense.** Under this defense, parties that employ state-of-the-art equipment to prevent pollution harming the environment will not be held liable if that equipment fails to prevent all pollution and some environmental damage occurs.[40]

The second liability regime applies to any category of occupational activity not listed in Annex III. For parties conducting non-Annex III activities, the directive limits liability to damage only where the operator was at fault or was negligent. Under this regime, there is only liability for negligent species or habitat damage, not for negligent water or land damage.[41]

5. Triggers of Liability

There are three ways in which liability may be triggered. First, the competent authority designated by the member state may discover the environmental damage on its own. When this occurs, the competent authority may either conduct the remediation or prevention efforts itself and seek reimbursement from the operator, or it may require the operator to conduct the cleanup in the first instance.[42] There is some disagreement among member states as to whether there is a duty or right of the competent authority to order remediation of environmental damage, although the majority of member states interpret the language of the ELD to mean there is a duty.[43]

Second, the operator has a duty to report environmental damage when it causes it. This duty requires operators to notify the competent authority of the damage and to take immediate action to limit the damage.[44] Again, the

---

39. *Id.* art. 8, ¶ 4(a).

40. *Id.* ¶ 4(b).

41. *Id.* ¶ 1(b).

42. *See id.* art. 5, ¶ 3 (ability to prevent or order prevention), art. 6, ¶ 2 (ability to remediate or order remediation), art. 8, ¶ 2 (right of competent authority to seek compensation).

43. *Legal Integration Study*, *supra* note 10, at 89–90.

44. ELD, *supra* note 1, art. 6, ¶ 1.

remediation may either be conducted by the competent authority or by the operator.

Third, an interested party such as an NGO or citizen may petition the competent authority to take action against an operator.[45] If an NGO or citizen has a "sufficient interest" or "impairment of a right," they may petition the competent authority to take action on some environmental damage or potential environmental damage.[46] If the competent authority rejects taking action on the petition, the petitioner may appeal to a court to force the competent authority to act.[47] If the petitioner's claim of environmental damage under the ELD is meritorious, then the court may order the competent authority to take action.[48]

6. Prevention and Remediation of Environmental Damage

A polluter may either be found liable for imminent potential environmental damage or actual environmental damage. For potential damage, a polluter has a duty to inform the competent authority of the threat.[49] A polluter also has a duty to take immediate action to prevent the environmental damage from occurring.[50] If a polluter fails to take action to prevent the damage, the competent authority may step in and prevent the threat, and later seek reimbursement.[51] If an imminent threat exists, a competent authority may also require the polluter to provide additional information.[52] The duty for preventing environmental damage is relatively simple: identify potential damage, inform the competent authority, and take action that prevents that potential environmental damage from becoming actual environmental damage.

Remediation of actual environmental damage is a more complicated process because there is greater uncertainty involved in determining actual environmental damage and its remediation. The underlying principle is that whatever has been adversely impacted by environmental damage must be restored to its baseline condition.[53] Another key principle is that the remediation cost should not be disproportionate to either the environmental damage

---

45. *See id.* art. 12.
46. *Id.* art. 12, ¶ 1.
47. *Id.* art. 13.
48. *Id.*
49. *Id.* art. 5, ¶ 2.
50. *Id.* ¶ 1.
51. *Id.* ¶ 3.
52. *Id.* ¶ 3(a).
53. *Id.* Annex II(1.1.1).

or the benefit it confers.[54] Disproportionate is not defined in the ELD, but it has been interpreted under EU principles to include any instance where the cost of remediation is greater than either the environmental harm it remedies or the benefit it confers.[55]

Remediation requirements vary depending on the type of environmental damage. Annex II of the ELD sets forth the basic framework for selecting remediation measures. For land damage, there is a clear requirement that land must be restored to a state where it no longer poses a risk to human health.[56] For water, species, and natural habitat damage, there is only the guidance that the area must be returned to its baseline condition.[57]

There are three categories of remediation described in Annex II of the ELD. The first and simplest category is primary remediation. Primary remediation is the direct cleanup of the adversely impacted area itself, with the goal of returning it to its baseline state.[58]

However, it may not always be possible or cost-effective to achieve a full recovery working only on the affected area. The second form of remediation, complementary remediation, allows for additional remediation outside of the affected area to ensure a return to a level of natural resources and services similar to the baseline.[59] Complementary remediation is ideally conducted in areas adjacent to or otherwise geographically linked to the primary site, although that is not required.[60]

The third type of remediation is compensatory remediation. Even when a site is fully returned to its baseline state, there is still harm from the site existing in a degraded state during the interim period between harm and the completion of remediation. Compensatory remediation accounts for such harm.[61] Like complementary remediation, compensatory remediation may be conducted in a different area than the one adversely affected.[62]

---

54. *Id.* Annex II(1.3.3(b)).

55. European Comm'n, *Environmental Liability Directive: Protecting Europe's Natural Resources*, at 18 (2013) [hereinafter *ELD Brochure*], http://ec.europa.eu/environment/legal/liability/pdf/eld_brochure/ELD%20brochure.pdf.

56. ELD, *supra* note 1, Annex II(2).

57. *Id.* Annex II(1).

58. *Id.* Annex II(1(a)).

59. *Id.* Annex II(1.1.2).

60. *Id.*

61. *Id.* Annex II(1.1.3).

62. *Id.*

The following example illustrates the three remediation types.[63] Suppose a stretch of stream that once supported 100 fish had its entire fish population wiped out by a chemical impound dam bursting upstream. Primary remediation at the site (decontamination of stream bottom, introduction of new fish) could only restore 80 fish to an area that once supported 100. Complementary remediation would then be done to improve an adjacent stream to increase its fish population by 20, restoring the baseline of 100 fish. Suppose that primary and complementary remediation restored 50 fish right at the end of year one and all 100 fish at the end of year two. The harm of this degraded period is the loss of 150 fish-years (100 the first year, 50 the second). Compensatory remediation would need to be done to restore the 150 fish-years lost in another location.

This illustration is also an example of the preferred equivalency method for calculating and conducting remediation. The equivalency method identifies resources that are "'sufficiently similar' to the damaged resources and services and quantifies the amount to be remediated (credit) to be equal to the loss due to damage (debit)."[64] Remediation projects aim to replace an equivalent amount of whatever resources were destroyed by the pollution. There are three types of equivalency that may be employed:

- **Resource-to-resource.** Metrics to be restored are environmental resources such as fish or units of clean water.[65]
- **Service-to-service or habitat equivalency analysis.** Metrics to be restored are expressed in terms of area of similar habitat (acres of wetland) or ecosystem services (percentage of service impaired).[66]
- **Value-to-value or value-to-cost.** The metric is monetary. Parties must calculate the monetary value of the environmental damage and balance it with remediation benefits of equal value. Where the value of the remediation benefits cannot be calculated, the cost of the restoration effort may be used to balance out the environmental harm instead. This method is not preferred and should be used only when other equivalency methods cannot be reliably applied.[67]

---

63. Adapted from *ELD Brochure, supra* note 55, at 19.
64. *Id.* at 16.
65. *Id.*
66. *Id.*
67. *Id.*

B. Differences between the ELD and U.S. Federal NRD Law

In general, the EU NRD regime under the ELD and the U.S. NRD regime under CERCLA or OPA are similar. They have the same function of attaching liability to the harm that pollution can cause to natural resources not owned by any individual. Both the EU and the U.S. regimes aim to achieve the same general goal: restoration of damaged resources at the polluter's cost.

However, there are differences in the details of the two regimes. Some differences stem from the different functions and authority of the legislative body that created each regime. The European Council governs independent nations, and directives such as the ELD necessarily give flexibility and discretion to the sovereign nations that they bind. Other differences may simply be a result of slight differences in each regime's purpose and scope. The following discussion highlights some of the differences between the EU and U.S. regimes, focusing on the most apparent differences that may affect how the regimes function.

1. Regulatory Structure

The structure of the governmental entities that implement the NRD programs differs slightly between the U.S. and the EU regimes. Under CERCLA, EPA is limited to a notification and coordination role, whereas natural resource trustees such as state and local governments and certain federal officials conduct the actual cleanup and seek compensation from polluters.[68] Under OPA, EPA or USCG may initiate cleanup to control a spill, but the ultimate NRD liability is still owed to trustees.[69]

By contrast, the competent authorities under the ELD may play all roles involved in environmental liability. In some member states, the EPA–equivalent environmental agency holds all of the authority for NRD and no trustee-equivalent entity exists.[70] Liability is owed to the national environmental agency, which also has the ability to investigate and order remediation of damage.[71] Other member states have structured their regulatory system more like the U.S. regime by designating both large national agencies and smaller local governing bodies as competent authorities.[72] In those

---

68. 42 U.S.C. §§ 9607(f)(1), 9622(j)(1).

69. 33 U.S.C. § 1321(c) (EPA's duty to initiate cleanup). *See also* 33 U.S.C. § 2706(a) (liability owed to trustees).

70. *Legal Integration Study*, *supra* note 10, at 41–46.

71. *See* ELD, *supra* note 1, art. 11.

72. *Legal Integration Study*, *supra* note 10, at 41–46.

member states, the competent authorities play a more similar role to trustees in the U.S. system.

2. Interim Damages Calculations

There is a slight difference between CERCLA and the ELD in how interim damages are calculated. Under the ELD, the preference is for equivalency calculations based on the cost of restoring natural resources.[73] Liability for interim degradation is calculated in terms of the cost to restore the resources lost, with a preference against calculating in terms of compensation for value lost. Under CERCLA, the preference historically was for the opposite.[74] The CERCLA regulations required that calculation of interim damages be based on the value lost in the interim period, not on the cost of restoring or replacing those resources.[75] In 2008, however, the CERCLA regulations were amended to authorize measurement of interim damages using a restoration cost approach.[76] Under OPA, interim damages have always been calculated using a restoration costs approach.[77]

3. Threshold Requirement

One of the key differences between the U.S. and EU regimes is that the ELD has a threshold requirement that NRD have a "significant adverse affect[]" on the environment.[78] Under CERCLA and OPA, there is no such threshold, and liability applies when there are "damages for injury to, destruction of, or loss of natural resources."[79] Although there is the requirement under CERCLA and OPA that an injury be a "measurable adverse change,"[80] "measurable" is certainly an easier bar to meet than "significant." Reports on implementation thus far have found that this threshold requirement has had an impact on the effectiveness of the ELD.[81] The threshold has served as an impediment to bringing claims under the ELD.

---

73. *ELD Brochure, supra* note 55, at 16.

74. Tony Penn, Nat'l Oceanic & Atmospheric Admin., A Summary of the Natural Resource Damage Assessment Regulations under the United States Oil Pollution Act (2015), http://ec.europa.eu/environment/legal/liability/pdf/tp_enveco.pdf.

75. *Id.*; 43 C.F.R. § 11.83(c)(1).

76. Natural Resource Damages for Hazardous Substances, 73 Fed. Reg. 57,259, 57,260 (Oct. 2, 2008) (to be codified at 43 C.F.R. pt. 11).

77. *See* Penn, *supra* note 74.

78. ELD, *supra* note 1, art. 2, ¶ 1.

79. 42 U.S.C. § 9607(a)(4)(C); *see also* 33 U.S.C. § 2702(b)(2).

80. 43 C.F.R. § 11.14(v); 15 C.F.R. § 990.30.

81. *Implementation Study, supra* note 18, at 12–13.

4. Citizen Suits

The ELD has a clear role for third parties such as citizens and NGOs. These third parties can petition—and eventually sue if their petition is denied—competent authorities that fail to remediate environmental damage.[82] While similar citizen suits exist under CERCLA, they are not applicable in the natural resources context.[83] Private citizens cannot sue polluters directly, and suits against a trustee are likely to be ineffective because the trustee has only an authorization, but not a nondiscretionary obligation, to remedy NRD.[84] Under OPA, citizens have a right (not frequently utilized) similar to that provided in the ELD where they may sue trustees for failing to carry out their nondiscretionary duties under OPA.[85]

5. Interaction with Other Laws

One issue unique to the ELD is its interaction with existing national laws. Prior to the enactment of the ELD, some EU member states already had laws addressing NRD. The ELD sought to fill the gaps and ensure that all member states enacted similar laws, but it explicitly allowed member states to apply their own more stringent laws so long as the requirements of the ELD were met.[86] As a result, nations such as France have continued to apply their own existing laws and have virtually ignored the ELD provisions that were transposed into their laws.[87]

CERCLA and OPA, on the other hand, apply uniformly across states based on regulations promulgated by federal agencies. States have their own NRD laws, but they do not displace or replace the federal programs. As a result, there is likely to be a much more even application of U.S. NRD laws compared to the ELD's application.

The ELD's explicit calls in some contexts for member states to apply their own legal concepts increases the likelihood of its disparate application. For instance, concepts such as standard of liability, level of causation, and

---

82. ELD, *supra* note 1, art. 12.

83. *See* Barry Breen, *Citizen Suits for Natural Resource Damages: Closing a Gap in Federal Environmental Law*, 24 WAKE FOREST L. REV. 851 (1989).

84. *See* Michael Gordon & Sal M. Anderton, *Protecting the Passaic: A Call to Citizen Action*, 29 SETON HALL L. REV. 76, 84–85 (1998).

85. 33 U.S.C. § 2706(g).

86. *See* ELD, *supra* note 1, art. 16.

87. BIO Intelligence Serv., *Study on Implementation Challenges and Obstacles of the Environmental Liability Directive (ELD), Background Document for the Workshop*, at 910 (Jan. 16, 2013), http://ec.europa.eu/environment/archives/liability/eld/eldimplement/pdf/Workshop%20on%20ELD%20implementation.pdf.

secondary liability are governed by purely national law.[88] Other areas of the ELD were explicitly left up to the member states to define. Member states create their own definitions for the meaning of "operator," identify the parties able to petition competent authorities, and define mechanisms for dividing liability among multiple parties.[89] These varying definitions and concepts result in uneven application of the ELD across member states. Again, the U.S. regime does not have these issues. Everyone uses the same definitions under CERCLA and OPA, no matter the state in which the damage occurs. In addition, NRD claims under CERCLA and OPA are litigated in a single court system, further reducing the likelihood of uneven application across states.

6. Uniformity of Assessment Process

The U.S. regulations for the assessment process are also more uniform. The United States has regulations promulgated by DOI (for CERCLA) and NOAA (for OPA) that describe in detail the process for assessing and valuing environmental damage.

There are no analogous regulations under the ELD. Annex II describes generally the requirements of remediation, but only offers a broad overview and is not intended as specific guidance. There are some training materials available through the EU, but the task of providing guidelines for quantifying damage is primarily given to the member states, producing uneven results. Some member states have provided detailed guidance, while others have provided nothing.[90] In workshops and discussions following the adoption of the ELD, the lack of guidance and other tools to support implementation has been one of the frequently voiced challenges to pursuing ELD cases.[91]

7. Split Liability Regimes

One clear difference between the U.S. and EU regimes is that the ELD contains two separate liability regimes while U.S. regulations have the same liability regime for all actors. The ELD designates certain operators in Annex III to face strict liability for environmental damage caused by certain high-risk occupational activities.[92] CERCLA and OPA are both strict liability statutes and resemble the first liability scheme of ELD in that respect. However, the ELD also contains a second liability scheme that has no analog in the U.S. regime.

---

88. *Legal Integration Study, supra* note 10, at 12.
89. *Id.* at 11.
90. *Implementation Study, supra* note 18, at 29.
91. *Id.* at 16.
92. ELD, *supra* note 1, art. 3, ¶ 1.

When an activity not designated in Annex III causes environmental damage, operators are not held liable unless they are proven negligent or at fault.

In practice, this negligence liability scheme has been difficult to implement. Few ELD cases have been pursued under this regime because it is often hard to prove negligence.[93] While there exists a clear difference on paper, there may not actually be much of a practical difference between EU and U.S. NRD liability schemes. Both will hold the most common polluters strictly liable for damage to natural resources in the majority of cases brought.

8. Liable Parties

CERCLA has a more expansive scope than the ELD for who may be liable for NRD. CERCLA holds four categories of parties liable for damages: current owners or operators, past owners or operators who were the owners or operators at the time of the disposal of a hazardous substance, arrangers, and transporters.[94] The ELD, on the other hand, only makes current owners or operators liable and does not mention the other three categories. However, the ELD also permits member states to alter the definition of "operators," and many have changed the definition to include a broader scope of actors. Estonia, for example, has a very broad definition of operator that might conceivably include some of the other categories of parties covered by CERCLA.[95]

9. Retroactivity

CERCLA is also broader with respect to the time frame of liability covered. CERCLA is famously (or infamously) retroactive, attaching liability to parties for pollution that occurred decades in the past. The ELD is explicitly not retroactive and does not cover any damage that occurred before the planned final transposition date of April 30, 2007.[96] The ELD does not even cover damage that occurred after that date if the damage "derive[d] from a specific activity that took place and finished before said date."[97] Additionally, the ELD does not cover any damage that occurred more than 30 years before the bringing

---

93. *Report from the Commission to the Council, the European Parliament, the European Economic and Social Committee and the Committee of the Regions, Under Article 14(2) of Directive 2004/35/CE on the Environmental Liability with Regard to the Prevention and Remedying of Environmental Damage*, at 3, COM (2010) 581 final (Dec. 10, 2010) [hereinafter *2010 Report*], https://eur-lex.europa.eu/legal-content/EN/TXT/PDF/?uri=CELEX:52010DC0581&from=EN.

94. 42 U.S.C § 9607(a).

95. *Legal Integration Study*, *supra* note 10, at 59.

96. ELD, *supra* note 1, art. 17.

97. *Id.*

of the suit.[98] The ELD does, however, apply to environmental damage that occurred after April 30, 2007, but was caused by a facility authorized and put into operation before that date.[99]

10. Exceptions

The ELD and CERCLA have some similar exceptions. They both have an exception allowing for certain specifically permitted activity to escape liability for environmental damage. Under CERCLA, no NRD liability can be imposed if a facility was operating within the terms of its permit and if an EIS (or equivalent analysis) specifically contemplated the "irreversible and irretrievable commitment" of natural resources at issue.[100] ELD is similar in its language, allowing the exception to apply when the activity is "expressly authorised by, and fully in accordance with" an applicable permit.[101] Additionally, they both have exceptions for force majeure events, such as natural disasters or war.[102]

The ELD, however, has additional exceptions not analogous to anything in CERCLA or OPA. For example, it allows member nations to exempt parties that used state-of-the-art equipment.[103] Additionally, the biggest "exception" might be the rule that any polluter not engaged in an occupational activity listed in Annex III is not liable so long as it is not negligent. Parties in the United States have no opportunity to argue they were not negligent in causing NRD.

CERCLA also has exceptions not found anywhere in the ELD. For example, the "innocent landowner defense" allows purchasers of contaminated land to be exempt from liability if they did their due diligence, were unaware of the contamination, and comply with other requirements.[104] Under CERCLA, such landowners would otherwise be liable as owners. However, it is not clear that such an exemption is needed under the ELD. A later purchaser of land might not be considered an "operator" under the ELD and would have no need for an exception.

---

98. *Id.*

99. *See* Case C-529/15, Folk, ECLI:EU:C:2017:419. The court also said that the ELD precludes national laws that exclude damage from being considered "environmental damage" under the ELD merely because the national law authorized the damage.

100. 42 U.S.C. § 9607(f).

101. ELD, *supra* note 1, art. 8, ¶ 4(a).

102. 42 U.S.C. § 9607(b); ELD, *supra* note 1, art. 4, ¶¶ 1, 6.

103. ELD, *supra* note 1, art. 8, ¶ 4(b).

104. 42 U.S.C § 9601(35)(a).

11. Liability Limits

In line with its polluter-pays principle, the ELD provides no limits on the amount of liability that can attach to environmental damage. However, member states do have the authority to cap remediation efforts in cases where remediation efforts have already eliminated the risk to human health or when the benefit of further remediation would be disproportionate to its cost.[105] In the U.S. regime, both OPA and CERCLA have caps on damages.[106] However, both OPA and CERCLA provide for circumstances where liability is not capped (e.g., where the polluter's acts are grossly negligent or in violation of federal safety regulations).[107]

The ELD's rationale for not having a cap is that setting a cap either too high or too low could have negative consequences. If the ELD cap were set too low, polluters would escape liability for environmental damage that they caused and the polluter-pays principle would be undermined. If the cap were set too high, the worry is that it would force polluters to buy insurance up to the full limit of the cap, even though they were unlikely to face liability to that amount.[108] This would create higher insurance costs and increase the costs of the ELD for businesses.

C. Issues in the Transposition of the ELD

As an EU directive, the ELD was transposed into the national laws of each of the EU member states. This process led to variations in environmental liability regimes in each nation, particularly because the ELD explicitly let some standards be governed by national law and made other provisions optional for member states. In 2017, the European Parliament noted that many member states had transposed the ELD "in a patchy and superficial way."[109] This section focuses on the transposed national laws that have incorporated the ELD and discusses the variations that have emerged in the ELD's transposition.

---

105. ELD, *supra* note 1, Annex II(1.3.3).

106. 42 U.S.C. § 9607(c); 33 U.S.C § 2704.

107. *See* 33 U.S.C. § 2704(c); 42 U.S.C. § 9607(c)(2).

108. *Q&A*, *supra* note 23, Question 16.

109. European Parliament Resolution of 26 October 2017 on the Application of Directive 2004/35/EC of the European Parliament and of the Council of 21 April 2004 on Environmental Liability with Regard to the Prevention and Remedying of Environmental Damage (the 'ELD') (2016/2251(INI)), 2018/C 346/24, 2018 O.J. C 346/184 [hereinafter 2017 Resolution], https://eur-lex.europa.eu/legal-content/EN/TXT/PDF/?uri=CELEX:52017IP0414&from=GA.

1. Procedural Variation

Studies conducted on the transposition of the ELD have divided variation in transposition into procedural and substantive categories. Some of the procedural differences are a result of the transposition process itself. For example, there is no rule governing whether a directive should be transposed as stand-alone legislation or integrated into existing legislation, so member states took different courses.[110] Other procedural differences are specific to the ELD. The ELD did not specify whether to designate only one competent authority, so states have varied in whether they designate one competent authority or multiple competent authorities.[111] The following are some of the major procedural variations:

- **Differences in administrative and judicial systems.** Although all states designate a competent authority, that authority has different powers and operates through different processes depending on the judicial system of the member state. In states with administrative courts, for example, it is procedurally simpler for a competent authority to enforce orders related to the ELD.[112] In courts without a separate administrative system, it may be more cumbersome to bring the case through the normal judicial system.

- **Integration into existing laws.** Some member states chose to integrate the ELD into existing environmental laws, whereas others just enacted the ELD as its own new environmental law. One study found that those member states that transposed the ELD as a stand-alone law were likely to ignore that new law and continue to use their existing, less stringent environmental laws.[113]

- **Designation of one or more than one competent authority.** Member states varied widely in the number of competent authorities they designated. Some designated only one, whereas others designated hundreds. The majority designated multiple competent authorities instead of just one. Those with multiple competent authorities divided responsibility based on geography, government hierarchical level, or subject matter.[114]

---

110. *Implementation Study, supra* note 18, at 8.
111. *Legal Integration Study, supra* note 10, at 41.
112. *Id.* at 34.
113. *Implementation Study, supra* note 18, at 8.
114. *Legal Integration Study, supra* note 10, at 41.

- **Publication of guidelines.** Some of the member states published guidance and training materials on the implementation of their national laws, although most did not.[115] The development of such guidance appeared to have an impact on implementation. Implementation studies found that lack of specific guidance was one of the main struggles that officials faced in implementing the ELD.[116]

2. Substantive Variation

Many substantive variations arose across member states' laws transposing the ELD. This chapter focuses on three factors that seemed to compel the substantive variety. First, several ELD provisions were completely optional. Second, some ELD provisions called for application of existing national law concepts, which of course already varied between nations. Third, member states interpreted ambiguous language in the ELD differently.

a. Optional Provisions

The ELD expressly made adoption of certain provisions optional for member states. The inevitable result was that some nations adopted certain provisions while others did not, creating uneven environmental damage liability rules across member states. The optional provisions included:

- **Optional defenses.** Both the permit defense and state-of-the-art defense for Annex III activities were optional under the ELD. These defenses allowed operators to escape financial liability if they could show both that they were not negligent and that they were operating under a permit or using state-of-the-art control equipment. There was no consensus among member states on whether to adopt these optional defenses. Twelve member states fully incorporated both defenses, while six member states incorporated the defenses partially or in a modified form. Five member states incorporated one of the defenses, and seven member states incorporated neither defense.[117] Despite the patchy implementation, business stakeholders consider these defenses

---

115. *Id.* at 47.

116. *Implementation Study, supra* note 18, at 9.

117. *Commission Staff Working Document, REFIT Evaluation of the Environmental Liability Directive,* at 50, SWD (2016) 121 final (Apr. 14, 2016) [hereinafter *REFIT Evaluation*], https://eur-lex.europa.eu/legal-content/EN/TXT/PDF/?uri=CELEX:52016SC0121&from=EN; *see also 2010 Report, supra* note 93, at 4 (reporting that less than half of member states use both defenses, less than half use neither defense, and less than half only use one of them).

"politically indispensable."[118] A 2016 report described concerns that the two defenses undermined the ELD's strict liability standard and removed incentives for operators to take steps to minimize risk, but concluded that elimination of the defenses would not be a viable option.[119] In 2017, however, the European Parliament called for elimination of the defenses.[120]

- **Mandatory financial security.** The ELD leaves it to member states to determine if they want to require operators engaging in Annex III activities and other risky operations to have insurance or some sort of other financial protection. Financial guarantees may be necessary to prevent the government from being stuck with cleanup costs if a polluter is unable to pay. The ELD does not impose an obligation on member states to remediate damage themselves, so if a polluter is insolvent, a member state may just decide not to do the cleanup at all.[121] In 2010, eight countries had some sort of financial security requirement in place.[122] Several other nations were considering a requirement of financial security.[123] In 2017, the European Parliament called for introduction of mandatory financial security in all member states.[124]

- **Biodiversity expansion.** Species and habitats covered by the ELD are specified in Birds Directive 79/409 and the Habitats Directive 92/43. However, the ELD permits member states to include other species and habitats, drawing from their own national lists of protected species and habitats. Fourteen member states chose to expand protected habitats and species based on national or regional protection schemes.[125]

b. Provisions Interacting with National Law

Differences in transposition also arose as a result of the ELD's interaction with national law. Some definitions and legal concepts were left to national law to

---

118. *REFIT Evaluation*, *supra* note 117, at 50.

119. *Id.* at 51.

120. *See* 2017 Resolution, *supra* note 109.

121. *Q&A*, *supra* note 23, Question 17.

122. *2010 Report*, *supra* note 93, at 4.

123. *Legal Integration Study*, *supra* note 10, at 57. Not much had changed by the time of the next report. *See REFIT Evaluation*, *supra* note 117, at 10, 19 (reporting that one-third of member states established mandatory financial security or were working on it, while two-thirds relied on voluntary measures).

124. *See* 2017 Resolution, *supra* note 109.

125. *2010 Report*, *supra* note 93, at 3–4; *see also REFIT Evaluation*, *supra* note 117, at 53 (half of the member states have extended scope for biodiversity protection).

define. Others are fundamental legal concepts, such as the level of causation that will necessarily vary between the different legal systems of member states.

- **Operator definition.** The ELD definition for operator requires that a party "operates or controls" the occupational activity in order to be considered its potentially liable operator.[126] The ELD allows national legislation to include other parties. Some member states have used considerably broader definitions of operator. For example, Estonia's definition essentially finds that anyone who causes pollution is an operator, even if the pollution is not caused by an economic "occupational activity" as is normally required by the ELD.[127]

- **Multiple party liability.** The ELD explicitly claims not to address how to resolve liability among multiple liable parties.[128] Therefore, it was entirely up to each individual member state to create their own rules to govern the issue. The majority of member states have decided to make all liable parties jointly and severally liable.[129] A small minority of nations employ modified forms of proportionate liability.[130]

- **Scope of interested parties.** The ELD allows interested parties, such as citizens and NGOs, to petition competent authorities to act on environmental damage. The ELD left it up to member states to interpret what the necessary "sufficient interest" is to be able to petition the competent authority.[131] Some nations, such as Portugal, have a very broad definition, in part because their constitution already specified that every citizen has a right to petition a government agency.[132] Other nations, such as Poland, require that a petitioning organization be registered with the relevant official body and have its official purpose as protecting the environment.[133]

- **Standard of liability.** Operators conducting non-Annex III activities may be found liable for causing the environmental damage only if they are "at fault or negligent."[134] Some nations have interpreted this negligence

---

126. ELD, *supra* note 1, art. 2, ¶ 6.
127. *Legal Integration Study*, *supra* note 10, at 59.
128. ELD, *supra* note 1, art. 9.
129. *2010 Report*, *supra* note 93, at 4; *Legal Integration Study*, *supra* note 10, at 63–64.
130. *Legal Integration Study*, *supra* note 10, at 63–64.
131. *Id.* at 64.
132. *Id.* at 65–66.
133. *Id.* at 65.
134. ELD, *supra* note 1, art. 3, ¶ 1(b).

standard to be more akin to gross negligence, while others have passed national legislation that finds liability for simple negligence.[135]

- **Level of causation.** Environmental damage must be "caused by" an operator's activities in order to be covered by the ELD.[136] Nations have different concepts of the level of causation necessary, which affects the stringency of the ELD in each nation. Some establish a low threshold level for proof of causation by providing for a rebuttable presumption of causation that the operator must disprove.[137] Laws of other nations provide that it must be more probable than not that the operator caused the damage.[138] Other nations are stricter, requiring more than just a balance of probabilities in favor of causation.[139]

c. Ambiguous Language

Further substantive variation in the ELD is due to differing interpretations of ambiguous language. Like any law, the ELD has provisions that are subject to more than one reasonable interpretation. The different interpretations adopted by different member states have led to variation in the stringency and applicability of environmental damage liability.

- **Defenses to cost vs. defenses to liability.** There are four defenses under the ELD where the operator is required to prevent or remediate the damage, but may be excused from financial liability.[140] Most nations have interpreted these as defenses to cost only. A minority, however, has interpreted these as defenses to liability, meaning that a polluter could use one of these defenses to escape cleanup responsibility as well as financial liability.[141]
- **Power versus duty of competent authority.** There is disagreement among member states as to whether a competent authority has a duty or a right to require an operator to remediate or prevent environmental damage covered by the ELD. This is somewhat surprising because the language does not appear to be ambiguous. The ELD states that "[t]he

---

135. *Legal Integration Study, supra* note 10, at 82.

136. ELD, *supra* note 1, art. 3, ¶ 1(b).

137. *Legal Integration Study, supra* note 10, at 83.

138. *Id.*

139. *Id.*

140. ELD, *supra* note 1, art. 8, ¶¶ 3–4. These include the permit defense, state-of-the art defense, third-party defense, and government order defense.

141. *Legal Integration Study, supra* note 10, at 88–89.

competent authority shall require that the preventive [remedial] measures are taken by the operator."[142] Still, a small minority of nations find only a right to force an operator to remediate, and a slightly greater number find only a right to force an operator to prevent environmental damage.[143]

- **Significant adverse effect threshold.** The ELD attaches liability to pollution only when it has a "significant adverse effect" on natural resources. The significance threshold's "significant" language is ambiguous and has been interpreted to mean different things. In the biodiversity context, some have interpreted significant to essentially mean "severe," which has caused the threshold to be a difficult one to overcome.[144] Other states find the threshold is not that high, interpreting the guidance in Annex I to mean that there is significant biodiversity damage anytime there is pollution that will negatively impact the conservation status of a species.[145] In a resolution adopted in 2017, the European Parliament called attention to the varying interpretations and applications of the significance threshold and called the variations "one of the main barriers to an effective and uniform application of the ELD."[146] The resolution called for a clarification of the significance threshold to standardize the application of the ELD across member states.

D. Implementation of the ELD

Member states were required to transpose the ELD into law by April 30, 2007,[147] but there were delays and the transposition was not completed in all nations until 2010.[148] This section draws on several reports that have examined the implementation of the ELD[149] and on reports submitted by member states.[150]

---

142. ELD, *supra* note 1, art. 5, ¶ 4 (preventive), art. 6, ¶ 3 (remedial).

143. *Legal Integration Study, supra* note 10, at 89–90.

144. *Implementation Study, supra* note 18, at 12.

145. *Id.*

146. 2017 Resolution, *supra* note 109, at C 346/186.

147. ELD, *supra* note 1, art. 19, ¶ 1.

148. *Legal Integration Study, supra* note 10, at 32–33.

149. *See Legal Integration Study, supra* note 10; *Implementation Study, supra* note 18; *2010 Report, supra* note 93.

150. For links to the member state reports, see *Environmental Liability*, EUROPEAN COMM'N, http://ec.europa.eu/environment/legal/liability/ (last visited Jan. 17, 2019).

1. Trends in Enforcement

The Commission issued its first report on the ELD in 2010. At the time of the 2010 report, there was not a robust data set from which to draw conclusions about the implementation of the law. Nevertheless, the report did include some information about trends in implementation. Most of the cases involved damage to water and land, and few cases related to damage to habitat or species.[151] Almost all cases were strict liability for Annex III activities with almost no cases involving negligence claims for non-Annex III activities.[152] Finally, most cases involved only primary remediation and not complementary or compensatory remediation.[153] These trends could indicate that member states were pursuing only the easier cases under the ELD. There do not appear to be many cases pursuing trickier environmental damage claims involving negligent polluters, more complicated remediation plans, or hard-to-measure damage against species or habitats.

In the reports submitted by member states after the Commission's 2010 report, the only clear trend appeared to be that nations varied widely in their application of the ELD. The second Commission report, issued in 2016, indicated that eleven nations had reported no cases involving the ELD, while two countries—Hungary and Poland—accounted for more than 86 percent of all cases.[154] Poland also accounted for 44 of the 60 cases in which judicial review was sought. Other differences involved the type of damages arising from an incident. Poland, for example, reported a large majority of land cases while Germany reported only a small proportion. Additionally, Poland listed only one type of damage for each incident, while the United Kingdom and Germany often reported multiple types of damage arising from the same incident.

2. Factors Driving Variable Application

Both legal and non-legal factors have contributed to the variable implementation of the ELD in the European Union. Legally, the most important factor is the ELD's relationship with national law. Those countries that have analogous

---

151. *2010 Report, supra* note 93, at 5.

152. *Id.*

153. *Id.*

154. *Report from the Commission to the Council and the European Parliament Under Article 18(2) of Directive 2004/35/EC on Environmental Liability with Regard to the Prevention and Remedying of Environmental Damage*, at 3, COM (2016) 204 final (Apr. 4, 2016) [hereinafter *2016 Report*], https://eur-lex.europa.eu/legal-content/EN/TXT/PDF/?uri=CELEX:52016DC0204&from=EN.

provisions to the transposed ELD provisions are likely to continue to use the national provisions and not to rely on the ELD.[155] There is, however, a lack of data on ELD incidents and comparable incidents that have been addressed under national laws,[156] but a low number of ELD cases in a given country does not necessarily mean that the ELD is not achieving its polluter-pays purpose. Often, the countries not using the ELD are ones that already had stringent environmental damage laws in place.[157] Nations such as Poland that lacked a developed environmental damage scheme before the ELD appear to be the ones that are using it the most.[158]

Other legal factors include whether the member state interpreted the ELD to contain an obligation of a competent authority to order a cleanup, or just a right to do so. Those that have an obligation are more likely to pursue cases under the ELD.[159] The interpretation and transposition of certain ELD provisions, such as the "significant damage" threshold, also drove the variation in implementation.[160] In addition, nations with laws providing broader access for NGOs to petition competent authorities are better able to implement the ELD.[161]

In addition to these legal factors, application of the ELD is also driven by factors related to the capacity of the member state government and other entities within a nation. Governments that track and publish public information on environmental incidents are better able to bring ELD cases to remedy them.[162] Reporting and notification systems for environmental incidents also may lead to increased application of the ELD,[163] as may opportunities for interested parties to submit comments and engage with the competent authorities.[164] The capacity of NGOs in a nation may affect the number of ELD cases brought, as more active and able NGOs will be able to petition the competent authorities more effectively.[165] Finally, the knowledge and capacity of the operators themselves, including awareness of the ELD, can affect the number of ELD cases brought.[166] Where operators are sophisticated and seek

---

155. *See id.* at 9; *Implementation Study, supra* note 18, at 8.
156. *See 2016 Report, supra* note 154, at 9.
157. *Legal Integration Study, supra* note 10, at 6.
158. *Id.*
159. *Id.*; *2016 Report, supra* note 154, at 9.
160. *2016 Report, supra* note 154, at 9.
161. *Legal Integration Study, supra* note 10, at 6.
162. *Id.*; *2016 Report, supra* note 154, at 3.
163. *Legal Integration Study, supra* note 10, at 6.
164. *2016 Report, supra* note 154, at 3.
165. *Id.*
166. *Id.*

to avoid environmental liability through effective pollution control, there will simply be fewer potential cases that arise.

3. Implementation Challenges

There are some factors that limit the effective implementation of the ELD across all member states. These factors may be loosely grouped into both legal and capacity factors. In the legal category, the significance threshold serves as a hurdle to bringing ELD cases. The threshold may deter competent authorities from bringing cases, especially when the damage is relatively minor and primarily affects biodiversity or habitat.[167] Similarly, proving negligence can be a barrier to successfully pursuing ELD liability for operators engaged in activities outside of Annex III.[168] Additionally, the scope of Annex III is not always conducive to effectively prosecuting environmental damage.[169] In the French *Coussouls de Crau* case, for example, it was not possible to find an oil pipeline operator liable under ELD law because oil pipelines were not covered under Annex III.[170] As a result, France was forced to prosecute the case under its existing environmental laws instead of its transposed ELD provisions.[171]

Outside of legal barriers, some of the biggest challenges in implementing the ELD are simply lack of experience, expertise, institutional capacity, and resources. In some cases, the competent authorities themselves lack experience with and knowledge of the ELD and also lack data and expertise for determining damages.[172] Other entities involved in implementation of the ELD also lack expertise. For example, parts of the insurance sector in some countries may not have been familiar with pricing the risk of environmental liability.[173] In addition, there were initially some challenges with calculating environmental damages in the way that the ELD demands. Even with experienced consultants, it could still be difficult to calculate damages because of a lack of baseline data.[174] These are all issues that will get easier with time, but that have presented challenges to the implementation of the ELD.

---

167. *Implementation Study, supra* note 18, at 12.

168. *Id.* at 15.

169. *Id.*

170. *See* BIO Intelligence Serv., *Implementation Challenges and Obstacles of the Environmental Liability Directive, Annex—Part B,* at 17–24 (May 16, 2013), http://ec.europa.eu/environment /archives/liability/eld/eldimplement/pdf/ELD%20implementation_Annex%20Part%20B.pdf.

171. *Id.*

172. *Implementation Study, supra* note 18, at 15–16.

173. *Id.* at 16.

174. *Id.* at 15.

4. Potential Actions to Address Implementation Challenges

As this chapter was being prepared, the tenth anniversary of the deadline for the ELD's implementation in member states was passing, and the EU was beginning to formulate potential measures to address the challenges encountered as member states transposed the ELD and began implementing it. In 2017, the European Commission developed a Multi-Annual ELD Work Programme (MAWP) to improve implementation of the ELD.[175] The MAWP indicated that a 2016 evaluation of the ELD's implementation had found that "the ELD is working, but to a much lower extent compared to original expectations and with a great variation between Member States." The MAWP proposed that the European Commission and member states work together on actions in three "working areas" from 2017 to 2020 to increase use of the ELD:

1. Improving the evidence base for evaluation of the ELD, including by developing an EU-wide comprehensive database/information system on environmental liability cases that involve application of the ELD as well as application of national laws.[176]

2. Developing tools and other measures for a more even and increased implementation of the ELD. Work in this area was intended to focus on measures such as development of guidance and interpretive notices, training programs, and "helpdesks" for practitioners to provide information, assistance, and assessment support, as well as complementary measures at the national level. The MAWP described the preparation of a "common understanding document" that would clarify key definitions and concepts in the ELD.[177]

3. Ensuring sufficient availability and demand for financial security to cover ELD liabilities. The MAWP indicated that the supply of financial security products was "largely sufficient," but indicated that demand was "significantly lagging."[178] Particular problems encountered by member states included large losses due to major accidents, with operators lacking sufficient financial cover to remedy the environmental damage on their own; losses where operators could not be identified; and operators that either have insufficient financial capacity or manage to

---

175. *See Commission Multi-Annual ELD Work Programme (MAWP) for the Period 2017–2020: "Making the Environmental Liability Directive More Fit for Purpose"* (Feb. 28, 2017), http://ec.europa.eu/environment/legal/liability/pdf/MAWP_2017_2020.pdf.

176. *Id.* at 8–10.

177. *Id.* at 10–12.

178. *Id.* at 12.

escape their liabilities.[179] The primary activity planned in this work area was further study, including review of the strengths and weaknesses of available financial security instruments for ELD liabilities.[180]

In October 2017, the European Parliament issued a resolution calling for a number of changes to the ELD.[181] The resolution indicated the Parliament's view that the ELD had not resulted "in a level playing field" and that implementation was "currently totally disparate in both legal and practical terms, with great variability in the amount of cases between Member States."[182] The resolution expressed the opinion "that additional efforts are required to enable regulatory standardisation to take place across the EU."[183] Some of the actions for which the European Parliament advocated were the same as actions set forth in the MAWP. However, many of the actions called for in the resolution would alter the regulatory scheme more significantly, including by revisiting the definition of "environmental damage" and clarifying the concept of "significance threshold."[184] Other changes called for in the 2017 resolution included introducing mandatory financial security, adopting a regime for secondary liability of successors of liable parties, removing the options for granting the permit and state-of-the-art defenses, extending strict liability to non-Annex III activities, and ensuring the application of the ELD to "environmental damage caused by any occupational activity and to ensure strict producer liability."[185]

---

179. *Id.* at 13.
180. *Id.* at 14.
181. *See* 2017 Resolution, *supra* note 109.
182. *Id.* ¶ 4.
183. *Id.*
184. *Id.* ¶¶ 24, 25.
185. *Id.* ¶¶ 29, 32, 34, 36, 37.

Appendix

Name	State	Web Site Link(s)	Consent Decree/ Settlement Docs Link(s)
102nd Street Landfill (Hooker, NY)	NY	http://www.cerc.usgs.gov/orda_docs/CaseDetails?ID=134 https://casedocuments.darrp.noaa.gov/greatlakes/102nd/admin.html	http://www.cerc.usgs.gov/orda_docs/DocHandler.ashx?task=get&ID=694
68th Street Dump	MD	https://darrp.noaa.gov/hazardous-waste/68th-street	https://casedocuments.darrp.noaa.gov/northeast/68_street_dump/pdf/68th_Street_Dump_Superfund_Site_Settlement_Consent_Decree_Nov_2017.pdf
Adak Petroleum	AK	http://www.cerc.usgs.gov/orda_docs/CaseDetails?ID=1052 https://casedocuments.darrp.noaa.gov/northwest/adak/admin.html	http://www.cerc.usgs.gov/orda_docs/DocHandler.ashx?task=get&ID=1131 https://casedocuments.darrp.noaa.gov/northwest/adak/pdf/denver_448957_v_1_adak_entered_cd.pdf
Alcoa (Point Comfort)/Lavaca Bay NPL Site	TX	https://www.cerc.usgs.gov/orda_docs/CaseDetails?ID=932	https://www.cerc.usgs.gov/orda_docs/DocHandler.ashx?task=get&ID=484
Alcoa Davenport Works NPL Site	IA	https://www.cerc.usgs.gov/orda_docs/CaseDetails?ID=81	https://www.cerc.usgs.gov/orda_docs/DocHandler.ashx?task=get&ID=244
Alcoa/Reynolds Metals Site	OR	http://www.cerc.usgs.gov/orda_docs/CaseDetails?ID=154	http://www.cerc.usgs.gov/orda_docs/DocHandler.ashx?task=get&ID=391
Alec Owen Maitland [M/V]	FL		http://www.gc.noaa.gov/gc-cd/alec.pdf
American Chemical Service Inc. NPL Site (Turkey Creek)	IN	http://www.cerc.usgs.gov/orda_docs/CaseDetails?ID=64	http://www.cerc.usgs.gov/orda_docs/DocHandler.ashx?task=get&ID=669
American Trader [T/V] Crude Oil Spill	CA	http://www.cerc.usgs.gov/orda_docs/CaseDetails?ID=959 https://www.wildlife.ca.gov/OSPR/NRDA/american-trader https://casedocuments.darrp.noaa.gov/southwest/amtrader/admin.html	https://www.cerc.usgs.gov/orda_docs/DocHandler.ashx?task=get&ID=100 https://casedocuments.darrp.noaa.gov/southwest/amtrader/pdf/at-cd1.pdf

Date	Federal Statute(s)	NRD Assessment Costs (Past)	NRD Assessment Costs (Future)	NRD Restoration Payments	PRP/RP Implemented NRD Projects (Cost Projection if Provided)
7/19/1999	CERCLA	$50,605.95		$655,258.61	No
11/28/2017	CERCLA	$240,000.00	$250,000.00	$712,170.00	Yes [not specified]
9/5/2013	OPA	$277,027.08	Included, but not quantified		Yes [not specified]
2/27/2005	CERCLA	$785,196.46	$195,000.00	$350,000.00	Yes [not specified]
12/11/2008	CERCLA	$39,137.00		$159,098.00	No
9/10/2008	CERCLA	$21,120.00			Yes [not specified]
12/19/1991	Not specified			$1,450,000.00	No
7/12/2000	CERCLA	$30,000.00		$300,000.00	No
3/5/1997	CWA, TAPAA			$3,894,246.00	No

Name	State	Web Site Link(s)	Consent Decree/ Settlement Docs Link(s)
American Transport, Inc./ Beaver Creek Oil Spill	OR	http://www.cerc.usgs.gov/orda_docs/CaseDetails?ID=905 https://darrp.noaa.gov/oil-spills/beaver-creek	http://www.cerc.usgs.gov/orda_docs/DocHandler.ashx?task=get&ID=393 http://www.gc.noaa.gov/gc-cd/Beaver_Creek_CD.pdf https://casedocuments.darrp.noaa.gov/northwest/beavercreek/pdf/Beaver_Creek_CD.pdf
Amoco Pipeline Company/High Island Spill	TX	http://www.cerc.usgs.gov/orda_docs/CaseDetails?ID=181	Draft: http://www.cerc.usgs.gov/orda_docs/DocHandler.ashx?task=get&ID=1214 Final: http://www.gc.noaa.gov/gc-cd/high-sa.pdf
Androw	FL		http://www.gc.noaa.gov/gc-cd/cd-androw.pdf
Anitra [T/V] Crude Oil Spill	NJ	http://www.cerc.usgs.gov/orda_docs/CaseDetails?ID=952	http://www.cerc.usgs.gov/orda_docs/DocHandler.ashx?task=get&ID=343
Anniston PCB NPL – Caliber Site	AL	http://www.cerc.usgs.gov/orda_docs/CaseDetails?ID=249 http://www.fws.gov/daphne/Contaminants/index-AnnistonNRDA.html	
Applied Environmental Sciences (AES) NPL Site/Shore Realty	NY	http://www.cerc.usgs.gov/orda_docs/CaseDetails?ID=135 https://darrp.noaa.gov/hazardous-waste/applied-environmental-services	http://www.cerc.usgs.gov/orda_docs/DocHandler.ashx?task=get&ID=786
ARCO Pipe Line Co. Crude Oil Spill, Santa Clara	CA	http://www.cerc.usgs.gov/orda_docs/CaseDetails?ID=939 https://www.wildlife.ca.gov/OSPR/NRDA/ARCO-Santa-Clara-River	http://www.cerc.usgs.gov/orda_docs/DocHandler.ashx?task=get&ID=652 https://www.fws.gov/ventura/docs/ec/scriver-restoration/Part%2008%20-%20Consent%20Decree.pdf
Army Creek Landfill NPL Site	DE	http://www.cerc.usgs.gov/orda_docs/CaseDetails?ID=43	http://www.cerc.usgs.gov/orda_docs/DocHandler.ashx?task=get&ID=664

Date	Federal Statute(s)	NRD Assessment Costs (Past)	NRD Assessment Costs (Future)	NRD Restoration Payments	PRP/RP Implemented NRD Projects (Cost Projection if Provided)
5/16/2006	OPA			$315,222.50	No
10/19/1992	Likely OPA	$32,218.00			Yes [$343,961.00]
1/10/2008	NMSA			$5,000.00	No
11/23/2004	OPA	$237,800.95		$1,262,199.05	No
	CERCLA				
6/18/1992	CERCLA	$14,000.00		$110,000.00	Yes [$50,000.00]
12/27/1996	OPA	$277,557.09		$7,350,000.00	No
Undated	CERCLA			$800,000.00	No

Name	State	Web Site Link(s)	Consent Decree/ Settlement Docs Link(s)
ASARCO Ray Mine and Hayden Smelter Sites	AZ	http://www.cerc.usgs.gov/ orda_docs/CaseDetails?ID=1046	http://www.cerc.usgs.gov/ orda_docs/DocHandler. ashx?task=get&ID=29 http://www.doi.gov/ restoration/library/casedocs/ upload/AZ_Ray_Mine_Hayden_ Smelter_SA_09.pdf
Asbestos Dump NPL Site (Millington)	NJ	http://www.cerc.usgs.gov/ orda_docs/CaseDetails?ID=124	Various (see below):
Asbestos Dump NPL Site (Millington) – 1st Settlement	NJ		1st Settlement: http://www.cerc.usgs.gov/ orda_docs/DocHandler. ashx?task=get&ID=793
Asbestos Dump NPL Site (Millington) – 2nd Settlement	NJ		2nd Settlement: http://www.cerc.usgs.gov/ orda_docs/DocHandler. ashx?task=get&ID=794
Ashland Lakefront NPL Site	WI	http://www.cerc.usgs.gov/ orda_docs/CaseDetails?ID=245	On file with authors
Ashtabula River and Harbor	OH	http://www.cerc.usgs.gov/orda_ docs/CaseDetails?ID=145 http://www.fws.gov/midwest/es/ec/ nrda/AshtabulaRiverNRDA/	Various (see below):
Ashtabula River and Harbor – Fields Brook	OH		Information obtained from Restoration Plan: https://www.cerc.usgs.gov/ orda_docs/DocHandler. ashx?task=get&ID=818
Ashtabula River and Harbor – Cabot Corp. et al.	OH		Cabot Corp et al.: http://www.cerc.usgs.gov/ orda_docs/DocHandler. ashx?task=get&ID=698
AT&SF (Albuquerque) NPL Site	NM	http://www.cerc.usgs.gov/ orda_docs/CaseDetails?ID=131	http://www.cerc.usgs.gov/ orda_docs/DocHandler. ashx?task=get&ID=691
AT&SF (Clovis) NPL Site	NM	http://www.cerc.usgs.gov/ orda_docs/CaseDetails?ID=132	http://www.cerc.usgs.gov/ orda_docs/DocHandler. ashx?task=get&ID=1207
Athos I [M/T] Crude Oil Spill	NJ	http://www.cerc.usgs.gov/orda_ docs/CaseDetails?ID=976 https://darrp.noaa.gov/oil-spills/ mt-athos-i https://casedocuments.darrp.noaa. gov/northeast/athos/admin.html	Claim Determination: http://www.cerc.usgs.gov/ orda_docs/DocHandler. ashx?task=get&ID=171 Acceptance: http://www.cerc.usgs.gov/ orda_docs/DocHandler. ashx?task=get&ID=172

Date	Federal Statute(s)	NRD Assessment Costs (Past)	NRD Assessment Costs (Future)	NRD Restoration Payments	PRP/RP Implemented NRD Projects (Cost Projection if Provided)
3/30/2009	CERCLA			$4,000,000.00	Yes [not specified]
	CERCLA				
7/15/1992	CERCLA				
10/1/1992	CERCLA			$3,500,000.00	No
11/2/2012	CERCLA				Yes [not specified]
	CERCLA, CWA				
1999	CERCLA, CWA			$850,000.00	No
7/12/2012	CERCLA, CWA	$1,947,277.82		$595,758.82	Yes [$1,454,711.00]
1/27/2005	CERCLA	$38,807.40		$1,051,192.60	No
1/14/2004	CERCLA	$30,000.00		$459,000.00	No
10/8/2010	OPA	$2,939,560.35		$27,495,751.00	No

Name	State	Web Site Link(s)	Consent Decree/ Settlement Docs Link(s)
Atlas Shipping/ Oaxaca [M/V]/ Contship Houston	FL		http://www.gc.noaa.gov/gc-cd/ atl-cd1.pdf
Avila Beach/Unocal Pipeline Crude Oil Spill	CA	http://www.cerc.usgs.gov/ orda_docs/CaseDetails?ID=942	http://www.cerc.usgs.gov/ orda_docs/DocHandler. ashx?task=get&ID=134 http://www.gc.noaa.gov/gc-cd/ union-a.pdf http://www.gc.noaa.gov/gc-cd/ union-b.pdf
Avtex Fibers, Inc. NPL Site	VA		Trustees entered into an MOA on 2/16/2010: https://www.cerc.usgs.gov/ orda_docs/DocHandler. ashx?task=get&ID=612
Bailey Waste Disposal NPL Site	TX	https://www.cerc.usgs.gov/orda_ docs/CaseDetails.aspx?ID=183	http://www.cerc.usgs.gov/ orda_docs/DocHandler. ashx?task=get&ID=474
Barge Apex Houston Crude Oil Spill (Central CA)	CA	http://www.cerc.usgs.gov/orda_ docs/CaseDetails?ID=963 https://casedocuments.darrp.noaa. gov/southwest/apex/admin.html	http://www.cerc.usgs.gov/ orda_docs/DocHandler. ashx?task=get&ID=33 http://www.gc.noaa.gov/gc-cd/ hous-cd.pdf https://casedocuments.darrp. noaa.gov/southwest/apex/pdf/ hous-cd.PDF
Barge Foss 248-P2 (Foss Maritime)	WA	http://www.cerc.usgs.gov/ orda_docs/CaseDetails?ID=973	http://www.cerc.usgs.gov/ orda_docs/DocHandler. ashx?task=get&ID=555
Barge Morris J. Berman [T/B]	PR	http://www.cerc.usgs.gov/orda_ docs/CaseDetails?ID=912 https://darrp.noaa.gov/oil-spills/ barge-berman	Settlement Agreement: http://www.cerc.usgs.gov/ orda_docs/DocHandler. ashx?task=get&ID=796 The Settlement Agreement did not specify the total amount to be allocated to NRD; therefore, the information here was obtained from the Restoration Plan (https:// casedocuments.darrp.noaa. gov/southeast/berman/pdf/ FinalRPEAReport.pdf)

Date	Federal Statute(s)	NRD Assessment Costs (Past)	NRD Assessment Costs (Future)	NRD Restoration Payments	PRP/RP Implemented NRD Projects (Cost Projection if Provided)
8/3/1999	NMSA	$115,866.39		$1,400,000.00	Yes [not specified]
3/22/1996	OPA			$1,200,000.00	No
9/5/2000	CERCLA	$82,934.14		$522,065.85	No
8/31/1994	CWA, NMSA	$692,070.00		$5,416,430.00	No
11/3/2008	OPA	$43,615.00	$73,000.00	$265,281.00	No
12/29/2000	OPA			$9,765,617.00	No

Name	State	Web Site Link(s)	Consent Decree/ Settlement Docs Link(s)
Barge Nestucca Bunker Fuel Oil Spill	WA	https://www.cerc.usgs.gov/orda_docs/CaseDetails.aspx?ID=961	Information obtained from Restoration Plan: https://www.cerc.usgs.gov/orda_docs/DocHandler.ashx?task=get&ID=521
Barge RTC 380 [T/B]	CT	http://www.cerc.usgs.gov/orda_docs/CaseDetails?ID=136	http://www.cerc.usgs.gov/orda_docs/DocHandler.ashx?task=get&ID=356
Barges Apex 3417 and 3503 [M/T Shinoussa, Houston Ship Channel, Galveston Bay]	TX	http://www.cerc.usgs.gov/orda_docs/CaseDetails?ID=182	http://www.cerc.usgs.gov/orda_docs/DocHandler.ashx?task=get&ID=472
Batavia Landfill NPL Site	NY	http://www.cerc.usgs.gov/orda_docs/CaseDetails?ID=137	http://www.cerc.usgs.gov/orda_docs/DocHandler.ashx?task=get&ID=695
Bean Stuyvesant [M/V] Fuel Oil Spill	CA	http://www.cerc.usgs.gov/orda_docs/CaseDetails?ID=948	http://www.cerc.usgs.gov/orda_docs/DocHandler.ashx?task=get&ID=76 http://www.gc.noaa.gov/gc-cd/stuy-cd.pdf
Bennington Municipal Sanitary Landfill NPL Site	VT	http://www.cerc.usgs.gov/orda_docs/CaseDetails?ID=199	http://www.cerc.usgs.gov/orda_docs/DocHandler.ashx?task=get&ID=713
Berge Banker [M/V] – Skaubay [M/V] Collision	TX	http://www.cerc.usgs.gov/orda_docs/CaseDetails?ID=994	http://www.cerc.usgs.gov/orda_docs/DocHandler.ashx?task=get&ID=710
Bermuda Islander [M/V]	DE	http://www.cerc.usgs.gov/orda_docs/CaseDetails?ID=1037	http://www.doi.gov/restoration/library/casedocs/upload/DE_Bermuda_Islander_SA_08.pdf
Berry's Creek Watershed	NJ	https://darrp.noaa.gov/hazardous-waste/berrys-creek-watershed	Third Joint Notice to Successor Liquidation Trust: http://www.cerc.usgs.gov/orda_docs/DocHandler.ashx?ID=335
Big River Mine Tailings – St. Joe Minerals Corp./ Southeast Missouri Lead Mining District	MO	https://www.fws.gov/Midwest/es/ec/nrda/SEMONRDA/index.html	ASARCO: http://www.cerc.usgs.gov/orda_docs/DocHandler.ashx?ID=1410
Blackbird Mine	ID	https://casedocuments.darrp.noaa.gov/northwest/black/admin.html	Various (see below):
Blackbird Mine – Consent Decree	ID		https://casedocuments.darrp.noaa.gov/northwest/black/pdf/Consent_Decree.pdf

Date	Federal Statute(s)	NRD Assessment Costs (Past)	NRD Assessment Costs (Future)	NRD Restoration Payments	PRP/RP Implemented NRD Projects (Cost Projection if Provided)
1991	CWA			$500,000.00	No
11/22/1994	OPA	$30,971.95		$200,000.00	No
10/26/1994	CWA			$1,700,000.00	No
9/29/2000	CERCLA	$51,000.00			No
9/29/2006	OPA	$877,000.00		$6,711,060.00	No
8/18/1997	CERCLA	$16,600.00			No
12/30/1999	OPA, PSRPA	$132,092.00		$1,568,077.00	Yes [not specified]
12/23/2008	OPA	$63,644.59		$206,355.41	No
4/2/2009	CERCLA				
3/3/2008	CERCLA	$233,000.00		$36,017,000.00	No
	CERCLA, CWA				
4/25/1995	CERCLA, CWA	$4,700,000.00	$1,000,000.00	$2,500,000.00	Yes [contingent]

Name	State	Web Site Link(s)	Consent Decree/ Settlement Docs Link(s)
Blackbird Mine – Amendment to Consent Decree	ID		Amendment to Consent Decree: https://casedocuments.darrp. noaa.gov/northwest/black/pdf/ bbm-cdam.PDF Order Approving Amendment: https://casedocuments.darrp. noaa.gov/northwest/black/pdf/ bbm-ords.PDF
Blackburn and Union Privileges NPL Site	MA	http://www.cerc.usgs.gov/orda_ docs/CaseDetails?ID=1051 https://www.mass.gov/ service-details/natural -resource-damages-program -groundwater-settlements-massdep	http://www.cerc.usgs.gov/ orda_docs/DocHandler. ashx?ID=681 https://www.mass.gov/files/ documents/2017/08/28/ ENV_ENFORCEMENT- %232116274-v1-Blackburn_-_ NRD_CD_as_entered.PDF
Blacksburg Country Club	VA	http://www.cerc.usgs.gov/ orda_docs/CaseDetails?ID=1039	http://www.cerc.usgs.gov/ orda_docs/DocHandler. ashx?ID=717
Bow Mariner [T/V] Fuel Oil and Ethanol Spill	VA	http://www.cerc.usgs.gov/ orda_docs/CaseDetails?ID=970	
Breton Sound (Hess Spill)	LA		On file with authors
Brio Refining Inc. and Dixie Oil Processors Inc. NPL Sites	TX	http://www.cerc.usgs.gov/ orda_docs/CaseDetails?ID=184	http://www.cerc.usgs.gov/ orda_docs/DocHandler. ashx?ID=476
Buffalo River/Lake Erie	NY	https://www.fws.gov/northeast/ nyfo/ec/buffalo.htm	
Buick Mine and Mill/Buick Smelter	MO	https://www.fws.gov/midwest/ InsideR3/May15Story13.htm	https://www.cerc.usgs.gov/ orda_docs/DocHandler. ashx?task=get&ID=1404
Burgess Brothers Landfill NPL Site	VT	http://www.cerc.usgs.gov/ orda_docs/CaseDetails?ID=200	http://www.cerc.usgs.gov/ orda_docs/DocHandler. ashx?ID=714
Burlington Northern Railroad Company/Nemadji River	WI	http://www.cerc.usgs.gov/ orda_docs/CaseDetails?ID=1027	
Buzzards Bay/ Bouchard B-120 [T/B] Grounding Fuel Oil Spill	MA	http://www.cerc.usgs.gov/orda_ docs/CaseDetails?ID=966 https://darrp.noaa.gov/oil-spills/ bouchard-barge-120	Various (see below):

Date	Federal Statute(s)	NRD Assessment Costs (Past)	NRD Assessment Costs (Future)	NRD Restoration Payments	PRP/RP Implemented NRD Projects (Cost Projection if Provided)
10/19/1995	CERCLA, CWA	$4,700,000.00	$1,000,000.00	$2,500,000.00	Yes [$1,000,000.00 – contingent]
12/12/2011	CERCLA	$94,169.56		$1,000,000.00	No
4/25/2012	CERCLA	$18,964.34			Yes [$51,011.00]
11/9/2018	OPA	$93,394.88		$8,630,000.00	No
2005	CERCLA	$277,940.86	$61,455.00		No
	CERCLA, OPA, CWA				
11/5/2014	CERCLA, CWA	$254,677.00		$7,030,000.00	No
7/2/1999	CERCLA	$374,143.51	$100,000.00		No
	CERCLA				
	OPA				

Name	State	Web Site Link(s)	Consent Decree/ Settlement Docs Link(s)
Buzzards Bay/ Bouchard B-120 [T/B] Grounding Fuel Oil Spill – Settlement Agreement	MA		Settlement Agreement: http://www.cerc.usgs.gov/ orda_docs/DocHandler. ashx?ID=292
Buzzards Bay/ Bouchard B-120 [T/B] Grounding Fuel Oil Spill – Consent Decree (2011)	MA		Consent Decree: http://www.cerc.usgs.gov/ orda_docs/DocHandler. ashx?ID=293 http://www.gc.noaa.gov/ gc-cd/051911-cb-bouchard.pdf
Buzzards Bay/ Bouchard B-120 [T/B] Grounding Fuel Oil Spill – Consent Decree (2018)	MA		Consent Decree (2018): https://www.cerc.usgs.gov/ orda_docs/DocHandler. ashx?task=get&ID=2958
C&R Battery Company, Inc. NPL Site	VA	http://www.cerc.usgs.gov/ orda_docs/CaseDetails?ID=913	http://www.cerc.usgs.gov/ orda_docs/DocHandler. ashx?ID=1060 Information obtained from Restoration Plan: https://www.fws.gov/ northeast/virginiafield/pdf/ contaminants/Final%20 Restoration%20Plan%20 C&R_2009.pdf
Calcasieu Estuary/ Bayou D'Inde	LA	https://darrp.noaa.gov/ hazardous-waste/bayou-dinde	
Calcasieu Estuary Bayou Verdine/ Calcasieu Estuary NPL Site	LA	https://casedocuments.darrp.noaa. gov/southeast/bayou_verdine/ admin.html	https://casedocuments. darrp.noaa.gov/southeast/ bayou_verdine/pdf/2_%20 ENV_ENFORCEMENT-calcasieu_FINALSIGNED_NRD_ Concent%20Decree.pdf http://www.cerc.usgs.gov/ orda_docs/DocHandler. ashx?ID=260
Calhoun Park	SC		http://www.gc.noaa.gov/gc-cd /081011-calhoun_park-cd.pdf
Cannelton Industries	MI	https://casedocuments.darrp.noaa. gov/greatlakes/cannelton/admin. html	

Date	Federal Statute(s)	NRD Assessment Costs (Past)	NRD Assessment Costs (Future)	NRD Restoration Payments	PRP/RP Implemented NRD Projects (Cost Projection if Provided)
3/25/2004	OPA				
5/17/2011	OPA	$1,573,530.12		$6,076,393.00	No
1/24/2018	OPA			$13,300,000.00	No
9/26/1994	CERCLA			$63,523.00	No
	CERCLA				
4/20/2011	CERCLA	$1,199,640.09	$750,000.00		Yes [not specified]
8/10/2011	CERCLA	$29,471.12		$470,528.88	No
	CERCLA				

Name	State	Web Site Link(s)	Consent Decree/ Settlement Docs Link(s)
Cantara Loop/ Southern Pacific Railroad Train Derailment, Sacramento River	CA	http://www.cerc.usgs.gov/ orda_docs/CaseDetails?ID=946	Various (see below):
Cantara Loop/ Southern Pacific Railroad Train Derailment, Sacramento River – Amvac/American Vanguard	CA		Amvac/American Vanguard: http://www.cerc.usgs.gov/ orda_docs/DocHandler. ashx?ID=657
Cantara Loop/ Southern Pacific Railroad Train Derailment, Sacramento River – Settling Defendants	CA		Settling Defendants: On file with authors. But also see: Final Report on the Recovery of the Upper Sacramento River: https://www.cerc.usgs.gov/ orda_docs/DocHandler. ashx?task=get&ID=54 and Trustees Memorandum of Agreement: https://www.cerc.usgs.gov/ orda_docs/DocHandler. ashx?task=get&ID=578
Cape Flattery [M/V]	HI	http://www.cerc.usgs.gov/orda_ docs/CaseDetails?ID=1032 https://casedocuments.darrp.noaa. gov/southwest/capeflattery/admin. html	https://www.cerc.usgs.gov/ orda_docs/DocHandler. ashx?task=get&ID=1065 http://www.gc.noaa.gov/ gc-cd/031913_cape_flattery_ cd.pdf
Cape Mohican [SS]/San Francisco Drydock Bunker Fuel Oil Spill	CA	http://www.cerc.usgs.gov/orda_ docs/CaseDetails?ID=921 https://casedocuments.darrp.noaa. gov/southwest/cape/admin.html https://www.wildlife.ca.gov/OSPR/ NRDA/Cape-Mohican	http://www.cerc.usgs.gov/ orda_docs/DocHandler. ashx?ID=67 https://casedocuments.darrp. noaa.gov/southwest/cape/pdf/ capemoh.pdf http://www.gc.noaa.gov/gc-cd/ capemoh.pdf

Date	Federal Statute(s)	NRD Assessment Costs (Past)	NRD Assessment Costs (Future)	NRD Restoration Payments	PRP/RP Implemented NRD Projects (Cost Projection if Provided)
	CERCLA				
3/11/1994	CERCLA			$2,000,000.00	No
3/13/1994	CERCLA			$3,500,000.00	No
3/27/2013	OPA	$1,618,820.00		$5,881,180.00	No
9/15/1998	OPA, NMSA	$233,324.86		$4,263,832.47	No

Name	State	Web Site Link(s)	Consent Decree/ Settlement Docs Link(s)
Carver Scrap Salvage Yard Site	MO	http://www.cerc.usgs.gov/ orda_docs/CaseDetails?ID=263	Information obtained from FWS website: https://www.fws.gov/midwest/ es/ec/nrda/MoTriState/Spring fieldPlateauFSJan2012.html
Casitas [F/V] (North Wind, Inc.)	HI	http://www.cerc.usgs.gov/orda_ docs/CaseDetails?ID=1030 https://casedocuments.darrp.noaa. gov/southwest/casitas/admin.html	http://www.cerc.usgs.gov/ orda_docs/DocHandler. ashx?ID=193 https://casedocuments.darrp. noaa.gov/southwest/casitas/ pdf/Casitas%20Final%20 Signed%20CD.pdf http://www.gc.noaa.gov/ gc-cd/912_r_North_Wind_ cd_final.pdf
CBS Westinghouse PCB NPL Sites/ Bloomington PCB Sites	IN	http://www.cerc.usgs.gov/ orda_docs/CaseDetails?ID=902	http://www.cerc.usgs.gov/ orda_docs/DocHandler. ashx?ID=215
Centredale Manor	RI	http://www.cerc.usgs.gov/ orda_docs/CaseDetails?ID=171	Various (see below):
Centredale Manor – Brook Village	RI		Brook Village: http://www.cerc.usgs.gov/ orda_docs/DocHandler. ashx?ID=448
Centredale Manor – Centerdale	RI		Centerdale: http://www.cerc.usgs.gov/ orda_docs/DocHandler. ashx?ID=447
Century Aluminum [USVI]	VI	Commissioner of the Department of Planning and Natural Resources v. Century Alumina Co. LLC et al., case number 1:05-cv-00062, in the U.S. District Court for the District of the Virgin Islands	
Certus, Incorporated	VA	http://www.cerc.usgs.gov/ orda_docs/CaseDetails?ID=987	http://www.cerc.usgs.gov/ orda_docs/DocHandler. ashx?ID=718
Chalk Point/ PEPCO Power Plant Pipeline Fuel Oil Spill	MD	http://www.cerc.usgs.gov/orda_ docs/CaseDetails?ID=1000 https://darrp.noaa.gov/oil-spills/ chalk-point	http://www.cerc.usgs.gov/ orda_docs/DocHandler. ashx?ID=288 http://www.gc.noaa.gov/gc-cd/ chalkpoint-cd.pdf
Charles George Reclamation Trust Landfill Site	MA	http://www.cerc.usgs.gov/ orda_docs/CaseDetails?ID=106	http://www.cerc.usgs.gov/ orda_docs/DocHandler. ashx?ID=682

Date	Federal Statute(s)	NRD Assessment Costs (Past)	NRD Assessment Costs (Future)	NRD Restoration Payments	PRP/RP Implemented NRD Projects (Cost Projection if Provided)
2/1/1995	CERCLA			$3,000.00	No
2/13/2009	OPA	$124,039.35		$2,857,626.48	No
7/23/2009	CERCLA			$1,881,000.00	No
	CERCLA				
1/19/2005	CERCLA	$68,450.00			No
1/19/2005	CERCLA	$68,450.00			No
4/7/2003	CERCLA, CWA	$574,534.56		$3,707,432.84	No
12/31/2002	OPA	$313,225.14		$2,710,498.00	No
8/21/1992	CERCLA			$1,378,350.00	No

Name	State	Web Site Link(s)	Consent Decree/ Settlement Docs Link(s)
Chemical Leaman Tank Lines NPL Site	NJ	http://www.cerc.usgs.gov/ orda_docs/CaseDetails?ID=126	http://www.cerc.usgs.gov/ orda_docs/DocHandler. ashx?ID=619 (Memorandum of Agreement)
Chevron Perth Amboy Facility, NJ	NJ	https://casedocuments.darrp.noaa. gov/northeast/chevron/admin.html	
Chevron Questa Mine NPL Site (Molycorp Site)	NM	https://www.cerc.usgs.gov/ orda_docs/CaseDetails?ID=1087	https://www.cerc.usgs.gov/ orda_docs/DocHandler. ashx?task=get&ID=1501
Chevron Refinery/ Waiau Marsh and Pearl Harbor	HI	http://www.cerc.usgs.gov/orda_ docs/CaseDetails?ID=916 https://casedocuments.darrp.noaa. gov/southwest/chevron/admin.html	http://www.cerc.usgs.gov/ orda_docs/DocHandler. ashx?ID=190 https://casedocuments.darrp. noaa.gov/southwest/chevron/ pdf/chev-cd.PDF http://www.gc.noaa.gov/gc-cd/ chev-cd.pdf
Chevron Refinery/ Castro Cove	CA	http://www.cerc.usgs.gov/orda_ docs/CaseDetails?ID=1035 https://casedocuments.darrp.noaa. gov/southwest/castro/admin.html https://www.wildlife.ca.gov/OSPR/ NRDA/Chevron-Castro-Cove	http://www.cerc.usgs.gov/ orda_docs/DocHandler. ashx?ID=13 https://casedocuments.darrp. noaa.gov/southwest/castro/ pdf/SANFRAN-94480-v1- Chevron_-_Signed_Entered_ Consent_Decree.pdf http://www.gc.noaa.gov/gc-cd/ Castro-Cove_CD.pdf
Chevron USA Production Company/Dixon Bay	LA	http://www.cerc.usgs.gov/ orda_docs/CaseDetails?ID=90	Restoration Cooperative Agreement: http://www.cerc.usgs.gov/ orda_docs/DocHandler. ashx?ID=262 http://www.gc.noaa.gov/gc-cd/ dixon.pdf
Chevron/Former Gulf Oil Refinery Port Arthur Waste Site	TX	http://www.cerc.usgs.gov/orda_ docs/CaseDetails?ID=943 https://darrp.noaa. gov/hazardous-waste/ chevron-refinery-port-arthur	http://www.cerc.usgs.gov/ orda_docs/DocHandler. ashx?ID=477 https://casedocuments.darrp. noaa.gov/southeast/chevron_ port_arthur/pdf/703332-v1- chevron_cd_pdf_508.pdf

Date	Federal Statute(s)	NRD Assessment Costs (Past)	NRD Assessment Costs (Future)	NRD Restoration Payments	PRP/RP Implemented NRD Projects (Cost Projection if Provided)
3/16/2001	CERCLA			$4,152,261.00	No
	OPA				
9/30/2015	State Law				
9/13/1999	OPA, PSRPA	$963,898.42		$1,550,000.00	Yes [not specified]
3/18/2010	CERCLA			$2,850,000.00	No
2/15/1996	OPA	$53,439.13	$11,875.30		Yes [not specified]
1/18/2005	CERCLA, OPA, CWA	$212,669.97			Yes [not specified]

Name	State	Web Site Link(s)	Consent Decree/ Settlement Docs Link(s)
Chevron – Hampden, Maine	ME		https://www.justice.gov/sites/ default/files/enrd/pages/ attachments/2016/05/19/ chevron_filed.pdf
Ciba-Geigy Corp. NPL Site (McIntosh Plant) [Tombigbee River – US v. BASF]	AL	http://www.cerc.usgs.gov/orda_ docs/CaseDetails?ID=870 https://casedocuments.darrp.noaa. gov/southeast/ciba/admin.html	http://www.cerc.usgs.gov/ orda_docs/DocHandler. ashx?ID=1155 https://casedocuments.darrp. noaa.gov/southeast/ciba/pdf/ Ciba-ConsentDecree.pdf
Cibro Savannah Oil Spill	NY		http://www.gc.noaa.gov/gc-cd/ cibro-a.pdf http://www.gc.noaa.gov/gc-cd/ cibro-b.pdf
Citgo Refinery, Calcasieu River	LA	https://darrp.noaa.gov/oil-spills/ citgo-refinery-calcasieu-river	
Cleveland Mill NPL Site	NM	http://www.cerc.usgs.gov/ orda_docs/CaseDetails?ID=133	http://www.cerc.usgs.gov/ orda_docs/DocHandler. ashx?ID=1210
Coakley Landfill NPL Site	NH	http://www.cerc.usgs.gov/ orda_docs/CaseDetails?ID=930	http://www.cerc.usgs.gov/ orda_docs/DocHandler. ashx?ID=687
Coeur d'Alene – Hecla Mining, Bunker Hill Mining	ID	http://www.cerc.usgs.gov/orda_ docs/CaseDetails?ID=898 http://www2.epa.gov/enforcement/ case-summary-hecla-mining- company-settlement-bunker-hill- mining-and-metallurgical	Various (see below):
Coeur d'Alene – Hecla Mining, Bunker Hill Mining – Sunshine Mining	ID		Sunshine Mining: https://www.cerc.usgs.gov/ orda_docs/DocHandler. ashx?task=get&ID=1276
Coeur d'Alene – Hecla Mining, Bunker Hill Mining – ASARCO (amended)	ID		ASARCO (amended): https://www.cerc.usgs.gov/ orda_docs/DocHandler. ashx?task=get&ID=1275

Date	Federal Statute(s)	NRD Assessment Costs (Past)	NRD Assessment Costs (Future)	NRD Restoration Payments	PRP/RP Implemented NRD Projects (Cost Projection if Provided)
5/18/2016	OPA	$42,862.00		$880,000.00	No
10/2/2013	CERCLA, CWA	$1,300,000.00		$3,700,000.00	No
1/7/1999	CERCLA, CWA	$196,060.00		$328,940.00	No
	OPA				
1/19/1995	CERCLA	$35,000.00		$165,000.00	No
6/22/1995	CERCLA			$155,473.00	No
	CERCLA				
1/22/2001	CERCLA, CWA			Sunshine Mining is to provide warrants to purchase common stock with an equity value of $33,000,000; net smelter return payments may be allocated for NRD payments, but total NRD value is not specified	No
6/5/2009	CERCLA			$67,500,000 (claims in bankruptcy)	No

Name	State	Web Site Link(s)	Consent Decree/ Settlement Docs Link(s)
Coeur d'Alene – Hecla Mining, Bunker Hill Mining – Mascot Mines	ID		Mascot Mines: https://www.cerc.usgs.gov/ orda_docs/DocHandler. ashx?task=get&ID=201
Coeur d'Alene – Hecla Mining, Bunker Hill Mining – United Resource	ID		United Resource: https://www.cerc.usgs.gov/ orda_docs/DocHandler. ashx?task=get&ID=202
Coeur d'Alene – Hecla Mining, Bunker Hill Mining – Zanetti Brothers	ID		Zanetti Brothers: https://www.cerc.usgs.gov/ orda_docs/DocHandler. ashx?task=get&ID=203
Coeur d'Alene – Hecla Mining, Bunker Hill Mining – Douglas Mining	ID		Douglas Mining: https://www.cerc.usgs.gov/ orda_docs/DocHandler. ashx?task=get&ID=199
Coeur d'Alene – Hecla Mining, Bunker Hill Mining – Atlantic Richfield	ID		Atlantic Richfield: https://www.cerc.usgs.gov/ orda_docs/DocHandler. ashx?task=get&ID=198
Coeur d'Alene – Hecla Mining, Bunker Hill Mining – Lookout Mountain Mining	ID		Lookout Mountain Mining: https://www.cerc.usgs.gov/ orda_docs/DocHandler. ashx?task=get&ID=1277
Coeur d'Alene – Hecla Mining, Bunker Hill Mining – Hecla Ltd.	ID		Hecla Ltd.: https://www.cerc.usgs.gov/ orda_docs/DocHandler. ashx?task=get&ID=667 http://www.epa.gov/ enforcement/consent-decree -hecla-mining-company -settlement-bunker-hill-idaho
Coeur d'Alene – Hecla Mining, Bunker Hill Mining – Alice Consolidated	ID		Alice Consolidated: https://www.cerc.usgs.gov/ orda_docs/DocHandler. ashx?task=get&ID=666
Cokers Landfill NPL site, Leipsic River	DE	http://www.cerc.usgs.gov/ orda_docs/CaseDetails?ID=44	http://www.cerc.usgs.gov/ orda_docs/DocHandler. ashx?ID=665
Cold Spring Harbor Barge	NJ	https://casedocuments.darrp.noaa. gov/northeast/coldspring/admin. html	

Date	Federal Statute(s)	NRD Assessment Costs (Past)	NRD Assessment Costs (Future)	NRD Restoration Payments	PRP/RP Implemented NRD Projects (Cost Projection if Provided)
4/12/2010	CERCLA			$2,900.00	No
4/12/2010	CERCLA			$200.00	No
9/23/2010	CERCLA			$37,500.00	No
12/22/2010	CERCLA			$4,000.00	No
1/13/2011	CERCLA			$1,687,500.00	No
3/22/2011	CERCLA			For 50 years, Lookout Mountain Mining is to pay 2% of its net smelter returns, but the NRD value is not specified	No
9/8/2011	CERCLA			$59,720,000.00	No
1/19/2012	CERCLA			$1,802,125.00	No
4/8/1992	CERCLA			$80,000.00	No
	OPA				

Name	State	Web Site Link(s)	Consent Decree/ Settlement Docs Link(s)
Colonial Pipeline Company	VA	http://www.cerc.usgs.gov/ orda_docs/CaseDetails?ID=206	http://www.cerc.usgs.gov/ orda_docs/DocHandler. ashx?ID=719
Command [T/V]	CA	http://www.cerc.usgs.gov/orda_ docs/CaseDetails?ID=945 https://casedocuments.darrp.noaa. gov/southwest/command/admin. html https://www.wildlife.ca.gov/OSPR/ NRDA/command	http://www.cerc.usgs.gov/ orda_docs/DocHandler. ashx?ID=108 https://casedocuments. darrp.noaa.gov/southwest/ command/pdf/pearlcd0.pdf
Commencement Bay	WA	https://www.cerc.usgs.gov/orda_ docs/CaseDetails?ID=954 https://casedocuments.darrp.noaa. gov/northwest/cbay/admin.html	Various (see below): Also, List of CDs with Various PRPs Can Be Found At: https://www.doi.gov/ restoration/library/casedocs/ WA_Commencement_Bay
Commencement Bay – St. Paul Waterway Sediments – Simpson Tacoma Kraft	WA		Simpson/Champion, and WDNR: https://casedocuments.darrp. noaa.gov/northwest/cbay/pdf/ Simpson_Champion.pdf
Commencement Bay – Sitcum Waterway – Port of Tacoma	WA		Port of Tacoma: https://casedocuments.darrp. noaa.gov/northwest/cbay/pdf/ Port_of_Tacoma.pdf
Commencement Bay – St. Paul Waterway Sediments – Simpson Tacoma Kraft – Amendment 1	WA		Simpson/Champion, and WDNR (Amended): https://casedocuments.darrp. noaa.gov/northwest/cbay/pdf/ Simpson_Baywide.pdf
Commencement Bay – State of Washington	WA		WDNR/State of Washington: https://casedocuments.darrp. noaa.gov/northwest/cbay/pdf/ WADNR.pdf
Commencement Bay – City of Tacoma	WA		City of Tacoma: https://casedocuments.darrp. noaa.gov/northwest/cbay/pdf/ city_tacoma.pdf
Commencement Bay – Ace Tank	WA		Ace Tank: https://casedocuments.darrp. noaa.gov/northwest/cbay/pdf/ acetank.pdf

Date	Federal Statute(s)	NRD Assessment Costs (Past)	NRD Assessment Costs (Future)	NRD Restoration Payments	PRP/RP Implemented NRD Projects (Cost Projection if Provided)
1/27/1998	OPA	$282,279.14	$73,295.00	$253,314.00	Yes [not specified]
3/21/2000	OPA, CWA, NMSA	$42,758.00		$4,007,242.00	No
12/13/1991	CERCLA, FWPCA	$100,000.00	$75,000.00	$500,000.00	No
10/8/1993	CERCLA	$335,000.00		$12,000,000.00	Yes [not specified]
11/30/1995	CERCLA	$75,000.00			Yes [$1,000,000.00]
5/28/1997	CERCLA				Yes [not specified]
12/30/1997	CERCLA	$227,000.00	$500,000.00	$500,000.00	Yes [$3,689,929.00]
4/13/1998	CERCLA			$65,000.00	No

Name	State	Web Site Link(s)	Consent Decree/ Settlement Docs Link(s)
Commencement Bay – Kaiser Aluminum Bankruptcy	WA		Kaiser Aluminum: https://www.cerc.usgs.gov/ orda_docs/DocHandler. ashx?task=get&ID=528
Commencement Bay – Murray Pacific	WA		Murray Pacific: https://www.cerc.usgs.gov/ orda_docs/DocHandler. ashx?task=get&ID=721
Commencement Bay – Ryder System	WA		Ryder Systems: https://www.cerc.usgs.gov/ orda_docs/DocHandler. ashx?task=get&ID=724
Commencement Bay – AOL Express	WA		AOL Express, Inc.: https://casedocuments.darrp. noaa.gov/northwest/cbay/pdf/ AOL.pdf
Commencement Bay – Streich Brothers	WA		Streich Bros.: https://casedocuments.darrp. noaa.gov/northwest/cbay/pdf/ Streich.pdf
Commencement Bay – Glacier Northwest	WA		Glacier Northwest: https://www.cerc.usgs.gov/ orda_docs/DocHandler. ashx?task=get&ID=527
Commencement Bay – United States (Settling Federal Agencies)	WA		United States: https://www.cerc.usgs.gov/ orda_docs/DocHandler. ashx?task=get&ID=725
Commencement Bay – BHP Hawaii	WA		BHP Hawaii: https://www.cerc.usgs.gov/ orda_docs/DocHandler. ashx?task=get&ID=525
Commencement Bay – Weyerhaeuser	WA		Weyerhaeuser: https://www.cerc.usgs.gov/ orda_docs/DocHandler. ashx?task=get&ID=1272
Commencement Bay – General Metals	WA		General Metals: https://www.cerc.usgs.gov/ orda_docs/DocHandler. ashx?task=get&ID=526
Commencement Bay – Petroleum Reclaiming Service	WA		Petroleum Reclaiming: https://www.cerc.usgs.gov/ orda_docs/DocHandler. ashx?task=get&ID=723
Commencement Bay – Occidental Chemical	WA		Occidental Chemical: https://www.cerc.usgs.gov/ orda_docs/DocHandler. ashx?task=get&ID=722

Date	Federal Statute(s)	NRD Assessment Costs (Past)	NRD Assessment Costs (Future)	NRD Restoration Payments	PRP/RP Implemented NRD Projects (Cost Projection if Provided)
8/21/2003	CERCLA			$5,500,000 (claim in bankruptcy)	No
12/9/2005	CERCLA, OPA, CWA	$30,160.20		$271,839.80	No
5/12/2006	CERCLA, OPA, CWA	$3,686.61		$22,152.00	Yes [not specified]
6/16/2006	CERCLA, OPA, CWA	$1,793,888.46	$150,000.00		Yes [not specified]
7/20/2007	CERCLA, OPA, CWA	$20,189.15		$181,948.00	No
8/8/2007	CERCLA, OPA, CWA	$20,804.24		$187,512.00	No
12/12/2007	CERCLA			$13,526,760.33	No
6/13/2008	CERCLA, OPA, CWA	$5,169.33		$46,592.00	No
6/13/2008	CERCLA, OPA, CWA	$47,411.99		$728,884.00	No
7/11/2008	CERCLA, OPA, CWA	$479,559.38	$50,000.00		Yes [not specified]
6/5/2009	CERCLA, OPA, CWA	$111,608.94		$638,391.06	No
8/18/2009	CERCLA, OPA, CWA	$1,550,000.00	$50,000.00		Yes [not specified]

Name	State	Web Site Link(s)	Consent Decree/ Settlement Docs Link(s)
Commencement Bay – Foss Maritime	WA		Foss Maritime: https://www.cerc.usgs.gov/ orda_docs/DocHandler. ashx?task=get&ID=529
Conoco Incorporated [ethylene dichloride spill, Clooney Island Loop, Calcasieu River]	LA	http://www.cerc.usgs.gov/ orda_docs/CaseDetails?ID=91	http://www.cerc.usgs.gov/ orda_docs/DocHandler. ashx?ID=1204 http://www.gc.noaa.gov/gc-cd/ conoco-a.pdf
Conoco-Phillips Bayway, NJ	NJ	https://casedocuments.darrp.noaa. gov/northeast/conoco/admin.html	
Cornell-Dubilier Electronics, Inc. NPL Site	NJ	http://www.cerc.usgs.gov/orda_ docs/CaseDetails?ID=244 https://casedocuments.darrp.noaa. gov/northeast/cornell/admin.html	https://www.cerc.usgs.gov/ orda_docs/DocHandler. ashx?task=get&ID=2505
Cortese Landfill NPL Site	NY	http://www.cerc.usgs.gov/ orda_docs/CaseDetails?ID=138	http://www.cerc.usgs.gov/ orda_docs/DocHandler. ashx?ID=696
Cosco Busan [M/V]	CA	http://www.cerc.usgs.gov/orda_ docs/CaseDetails?ID=1059 https://casedocuments.darrp.noaa. gov/southwest/cosco/admin.html	http://www.cerc.usgs.gov/ orda_docs/DocHandler. ashx?ID=654 http://www.gc.noaa.gov/ gc-cd/Cosco_Busan_Consent_ DecreeFinal.pdf
Countrymark Cooperative LLP	IN	http://www.cerc.usgs.gov/ orda_docs/CaseDetails?ID=1025	http://www.cerc.usgs.gov/ orda_docs/DocHandler. ashx?ID=216
Cyprus Tohono Mine Site	AZ	http://www.cerc.usgs.gov/ orda_docs/CaseDetails?ID=958	http://www.cerc.usgs.gov/ orda_docs/DocHandler. ashx?ID=31
Deepwater Horizon	LA	https://www.cerc.usgs.gov/orda_ docs/CaseDetails?ID=1053 http://www.gulfspillrestoration. noaa.gov/ https://www.justice.gov/enrd/ deepwater-horizon	https://www.justice.gov/enrd/ file/838066/download
Denver Radium NPL Site Operable Unit 8/Shattuck Chemical Co. Site	CO	http://www.cerc.usgs.gov/ orda_docs/CaseDetails?ID=33	http://www.cerc.usgs.gov/ orda_docs/DocHandler. ashx?ID=661
Diamond Alkali NPL Site	NJ	https://casedocuments.darrp.noaa. gov/northeast/passaic/admin.html	Various (see below):

Date	Federal Statute(s)	NRD Assessment Costs (Past)	NRD Assessment Costs (Future)	NRD Restoration Payments	PRP/RP Implemented NRD Projects (Cost Projection if Provided)
5/23/2011	CERCLA, OPA, CWA	$700,000.00	$300,000.00	$7,802,081.29	No
12/18/1996	CWA	$40,964.34	$10,213.50		Yes [not specified]
	OPA				
2/24/2015	CERCLA			$22,000.00	No
1/19/1996	CERCLA			$84,850.00	No
1/27/2012	OPA, NMSA	$6,903,960.61		$32,443,033.00	No
11/2/2009	OPA	$22,800.12			Yes [not specified]
7/17/2009	CERCLA			$825,000.00	No
4/4/2016	OPA, PSRPA, NMSA, CWA	$350,000,000.00		$7,800,000,000.00	No
8/26/2002	CERCLA			$1,500,000.00	No
	CERCLA				

Name	State	Web Site Link(s)	Consent Decree/ Settlement Docs Link(s)
Diamond Alkali NPL Site – Consent Decree	NJ		Consent Decree (General Motors): https://www.cerc.usgs.gov/ orda_docs/DocHandler. ashx?task=get&ID=1194
Diamond Alkali NPL Site – Settlement Agreemenet	NJ		Settlement Agreement: https://www.cerc.usgs.gov/ orda_docs/DocHandler. ashx?task=get&ID=338
DL6236X	FL		http://www.gc.noaa.gov/ gc-cd/121509-DL6236X_ settlement.pdf
Double Eagle Refinery Company NPL Site	OK	http://www.cerc.usgs.gov/ orda_docs/CaseDetails?ID=935	Various (see below):
Double Eagle Refinery Company NPL Site – 3M	OK		3M: https://www.cerc.usgs.gov/ orda_docs/DocHandler. ashx?task=get&ID=699
Double Eagle Refinery Company NPL Site – BNSF	OK		BNSF: https://www.cerc.usgs.gov/ orda_docs/DocHandler. ashx?task=get&ID=700
Double Eagle Refinery Company NPL Site – Third Parties	OK		Third Parties: https://www.cerc.usgs.gov/ orda_docs/DocHandler. ashx?task=get&ID=386
Double Eagle Refinery Company NPL Site – Albert Investments	OK		Albert Investments: https://www.cerc.usgs.gov/ orda_docs/DocHandler. ashx?task=get&ID=387
Douglass Road Landfill NPL Site	IN	http://www.cerc.usgs.gov/ orda_docs/CaseDetails?ID=67	Various (see below):
Douglass Road Landfill NPL Site – Bankruptcy Settlement Agreement	IN		Information obtained from Restoration Plan: https://www.cerc.usgs.gov/ orda_docs/DocHandler. ashx?task=get&ID=589
Douglass Road Landfill NPL Site – Consent Decree	IN		Information obtained from Restoration Plan: https://www.cerc.usgs.gov/ orda_docs/DocHandler. ashx?task=get&ID=589
Dover Chemical NPL site	OH		
Dreifort	FL		http://www.gc.noaa.gov/ gc-cd/061709-dreifort.pdf

Date	Federal Statute(s)	NRD Assessment Costs (Past)	NRD Assessment Costs (Future)	NRD Restoration Payments	PRP/RP Implemented NRD Projects (Cost Projection if Provided)
3/30/2011	CERCLA	$44,721 (claim in bankruptcy)			No
5/20/2008	CERCLA	$420,000.00			No
12/15/2009	NMSA			$48,000.00	No
	CERCLA				
2/21/2007	CERCLA	$140.00		$2,360.00	No
1/30/2009	CERCLA	$840.00		$14,160.00	No
12/6/2010	CERCLA	$11,793.00		$438,207.00	No
12/6/2010	CERCLA	$18,785.09		$316,681.93	No
	CERCLA				
1992	CERCLA			$144,000.00	No
1993	CERCLA			$19,035.00	No
	CERCLA				
6/17/2009	NMSA				Yes [$2,400,000.00]

Name	State	Web Site Link(s)	Consent Decree/ Settlement Docs Link(s)
DuPont (Newport Pigment Plant Landfill) NPL Site	DE	http://www.cerc.usgs.gov/orda_docs/CaseDetails?ID=928 https://casedocuments.darrp.noaa.gov/northeast/dupont/admin.html	http://www.cerc.usgs.gov/orda_docs/DocHandler.ashx?task=get&ID=164 http://www.gc.noaa.gov/gc-cd/092806-Dupont%20CD.pdf
DuPont Waynesboro South River/South Fork	VA	https://www.cerc.usgs.gov/orda_docs/CaseDetails?ID=231 https://www.fws.gov/northeast/virginiafield/environmentalcontaminants/dupont_waynesboro.html http://www.deq.virginia.gov/Programs/Water/WaterQualityInformation TMDLs/WaterQuality Monitoring/FishTissue Monitoring/Shenandoah Mercury/NaturalRresources DamageAssessment.aspx	Consent Decree: https://www.fws.gov/northeast/virginiafield/pdf/contaminants/dupont_waynesboro/20170728_ENV_ENF_2675793_v1_DuPont_S_River_Entered_Consent_Decree.PDF#2675793_v1_DuPont_S_River_Entered_Consent_Decree.PDF Memorandum Opinion Approving Consent Decree: https://www.fws.gov/northeast/virginiafield/pdf/contaminants/dupont_waynesboro/20170728_ENV_ENF2675792_v1_DuPont_Order_Entering_Consent_Decree.PDF#2675792_v1_DuPont_Order_Entering_Consent_Decree.PDF
Eagle Picher Creta Copper Operation Site	OK	https://www.cerc.usgs.gov/orda_docs/CaseDetails?ID=290	http://www.cerc.usgs.gov/orda_docs/DocHandler.ashx?task=get&ID=1167
East Walker River/ Advanced Fuel Filtration Systems Inc. Tanker Truck Fuel Oil Spill	CA	http://www.cerc.usgs.gov/orda_docs/CaseDetails?ID=953	http://www.cerc.usgs.gov/orda_docs/DocHandler.ashx?task=get&ID=60 http://www.doi.gov/restoration/library/casedocs/upload/CA_East_Walker_River_SA_04.pdf
Eastern Kansas Smelters Sites	KS	http://www.fws.gov/mountain-prairie/nrda/EastKS_Smelter/Estrn_KSSmltr-KS.htm	Various (see below):
Eastern Kansas Smelters Sites – National Zinc	KS		National Zinc: http://www.cerc.usgs.gov/orda_docs/DocHandler.ashx?task=get&ID=252

Date	Federal Statute(s)	NRD Assessment Costs (Past)	NRD Assessment Costs (Future)	NRD Restoration Payments	PRP/RP Implemented NRD Projects (Cost Projection if Provided)
8/11/2006	CERCLA	$296,552.51		$750,653.00	Yes [$50,000.00]
7/28/2017	CERCLA CWA	$214,083.22		$42,069,916.78	Yes [$10,000,000.00]
11/13/2012	CERCLA	$46,770.24		$1,753,229.76	No
1/7/2004	OPA	$68,000.00		$350,000.00	No
	CERCLA				
11/26/2007	CERCLA	$20,000.00		$475,750.00	No

Name	State	Web Site Link(s)	Consent Decree/ Settlement Docs Link(s)
Eastern Kansas Smelters Sites – Girard Zinc Works	KS		Girard Zinc Works: http://www.cerc.usgs.gov/ orda_docs/DocHandler. ashx?task=get&ID=251
Eastern Kansas Smelters Sites – Blue Tee	KS		Blue Tee: http://www.cerc.usgs.gov/ orda_docs/DocHandler. ashx?task=get&ID=253
Easy Going	FL		http://www.gc.noaa.gov/ gc-cd/092809-easygoing_sa.pdf
Eden North Carolina Coal Ash Spill [Dan River]	NC	https://www.cerc.usgs.gov/orda_ docs/CaseDetails?ID=984 https://deq.nc.gov/news/hot-topics/ coal-ash-nc/dan-river-coal-ash-spill	
Elliott Bay/Lower Duwamish River	WA	https://casedocuments.darrp.noaa. gov/northwest/elliott/admin.html https://darrp.noaa. gov/hazardous-waste/ lower-duwamish-river	Various (see below):
Elliott Bay/Lower Duwamish River – City of Seattle	WA		City of Seattle: https://casedocuments.darrp. noaa.gov/northwest/elliott/ pdf/eb-cd.pdf
Elliott Bay/Lower Duwamish River – City of Seattle, Amended	WA		City of Seattle, Amended: https://casedocuments.darrp. noaa.gov/northwest/elliott/ pdf/eb-cd3.pdf https://casedocuments.darrp. noaa.gov/northwest/elliott/ pdf/eb-cd4.pdf
Elliott Bay/Lower Duwamish River – Boeing	WA		https://casedocuments. darrp.noaa.gov/northwest/ lowerduwamishriver/pdf/ Order_Entering_Boeing_NRD_ CD_for_Duwamish_Waterway. pdf
Elpis [M/V]	FL		http://www.gc.noaa.gov/gc-cd/ elpis-cd.pdf
Enbridge Energy Pipeline (Blackwater Creek)	MN	http://www.cerc.usgs.gov/ orda_docs/CaseDetails?ID=1019	http://www.cerc.usgs.gov/ orda_docs/DocHandler. ashx?task=get&ID=319

Date	Federal Statute(s)	NRD Assessment Costs (Past)	NRD Assessment Costs (Future)	NRD Restoration Payments	PRP/RP Implemented NRD Projects (Cost Projection if Provided)
3/7/2008	CERCLA	$10,145.00		$123,255.00	No
3/8/2011	CERCLA	$106,257.27		$74,041.00	Yes [$50,000.00]
9/28/2009	NMSA			Community service	No
	CERCLA				
	CERCLA				
12/23/1991	CERCLA	$125,000.00		$2,500,000.00	Yes [$2,500,000.00]
10/13/1999	CERCLA	$125,000.00		$2,500,000.00	Yes [$2,500,000.00]
12/14/2010	CERCLA, OPA	$1,943,184.86			Yes [$360,000.00]
8/14/1991	MPRS			$2,075,000.00	No
1/13/2009	OPA	$16,300.00			Yes [not specified]

Name	State	Web Site Link(s)	Consent Decree/ Settlement Docs Link(s)
Enbridge Pipeline Release (Kalamazoo River)	MI	http://www.cerc.usgs.gov/orda_docs/CaseDetails?ID=1054 https://www.fws.gov/midwest/es/ec/nrda/MichiganEnbridge/ https://darrp.noaa.gov/oil-spills/enbridge-pipeline-release	https://www.fws.gov/midwest/es/ec/nrda/MichiganEnbridge/pdf/EnvEnforcement2561057v1EnbridgeDKT_NRD_Decree.pdf http://www.cerc.usgs.gov/orda_docs/DocHandler.ashx?task=get&ID=1523
Equilon Pipeline (Colonial) (San Jacinto Spill)	TX		http://www.gc.noaa.gov/gc-cd/cd-equil.pdf
Equinox Oil Company – Well Blowout	LA	http://www.cerc.usgs.gov/orda_docs/CaseDetails?ID=951	http://www.cerc.usgs.gov/orda_docs/DocHandler.ashx?task=get&ID=269 http://www.gc.noaa.gov/gc-cd/010506-767575-v1-Equinox.pdf
Ever Reach [M/V]	SC	http://www.cerc.usgs.gov/orda_docs/CaseDetails?ID=1021 https://www.darrp.noaa.gov/oil-spills/cooper-river-mv-everreach	http://www.cerc.usgs.gov/orda_docs/DocHandler.ashx?task=get&ID=708
Explorer Pipeline	TX	http://www.cerc.usgs.gov/orda_docs/CaseDetails?ID=1016	http://www.cerc.usgs.gov/orda_docs/DocHandler.ashx?task=get&ID=709
Exxon Bayway Refinery Pipeline Heating Oil Spill	NJ	http://www.cerc.usgs.gov/orda_docs/CaseDetails?ID=938 https://darrp.noaa.gov/oil-spills/exxon-bayway	http://www.cerc.usgs.gov/orda_docs/DocHandler.ashx?task=get&ID=1549 http://www.gc.noaa.gov/gc-cd/exx2.pdf
Exxon Pipeline Company (Chiltipin Creek)	TX	http://www.cerc.usgs.gov/orda_docs/CaseDetails?ID=187	http://www.cerc.usgs.gov/orda_docs/DocHandler.ashx?task=get&ID=798
Exxon Valdez [T/V] Crude Oil Spill	AK	http://www.cerc.usgs.gov/orda_docs/CaseDetails?ID=983 http://www.evostc.state.ak.us/	Various (see below):
Exxon Valdez [T/V] Crude Oil Spill – State of Alaska	AK		State of Alaska: http://www.cerc.usgs.gov/orda_docs/DocHandler.ashx?task=get&ID=5
Exxon Valdez [T/V] Crude Oil Spill – Exxon Corp.	AK		Exxon Corp.: http://www.cerc.usgs.gov/orda_docs/DocHandler.ashx?task=get&ID=1066

Date	Federal Statute(s)	NRD Assessment Costs (Past)	NRD Assessment Costs (Future)	NRD Restoration Payments	PRP/RP Implemented NRD Projects (Cost Projection if Provided)
12/3/2015	OPA	$1,634,952.00	$561,874.00	$1,703,174.00	Yes [not specified]
3/13/2002	OPA			$250,000.00	Yes [$746,000.00]
1/5/2006	OPA	$295,850.00		$904,150.00	No
10/24/2012	OPA	$820,685.27	Included but not quantified	$121,000.00	Yes [not specified]
2/2/2009	OPA, CWA	$16,292.03		$193,503.50	No
6/14/1991	CERCLA			$9,550,000.00	Yes [not specified]
4/15/1994	OPA	$73,372.57		$131,500.00	No
	CWA				
8/28/1991	CWA				No
10/8/1991	CWA			$900,000,000.00	No

Name	State	Web Site Link(s)	Consent Decree/ Settlement Docs Link(s)
Farmland Industries Pipeline Oil Spill	OK	http://www.cerc.usgs.gov/ orda_docs/CaseDetails?ID=955	Bankruptcy Settlement: https://www.cerc.usgs.gov/ orda_docs/DocHandler. ashx?task=get&ID=1474
Fenton Creek Dump Site/Chrysler Dump Site	MO	http://www.cerc.usgs.gov/ orda_docs/CaseDetails?ID=929	http://www.cerc.usgs.gov/ orda_docs/DocHandler. ashx?task=get&ID=322
Fernald/Fernald Environmental Management Project	OH	http://www.cerc.usgs.gov/ orda_docs/CaseDetails?ID=235	http://www.cerc.usgs.gov/ orda_docs/DocHandler. ashx?task=get&ID=692
Fish Creek #2 Diesel Spill (9/15/93)/ NORCO, Inc.	IN	http://www.cerc.usgs.gov/ orda_docs/CaseDetails?ID=1001	http://www.cerc.usgs.gov/ orda_docs/DocHandler. ashx?task=get&ID=672
Fisher-Calo Chemical NPL Site, Travis Ditch, Kingsbury Creek	IN	https://www.cerc.usgs.gov/ orda_docs/CaseDetails?ID=69	http://www.cerc.usgs.gov/ orda_docs/DocHandler. ashx?task=get&ID=790
Flat Creek/Iron Mountain Mine NPL Site (Montana)	MT	https://www.cerc.usgs.gov/ orda_docs/CaseDetails?ID=1069	http://www.cerc.usgs.gov/ orda_docs/DocHandler. ashx?task=get&ID=1196
Forest Glen Mobile Home Subdivision NPL Site	NY	http://www.cerc.usgs.gov/orda_ docs/CaseDetails?ID=139 https://casedocuments.darrp.noaa. gov/greatlakes/forestglen/admin. html	Information obtained from Final Restoration Plan: https://casedocuments.darrp. noaa.gov/greatlakes/forest glen/pdf/FinalLoveCanal102 ForestGlenRestorationPlan 7-05.pdf
Former Coal Tar Processing Facility Site (Island End River, MA)	MA	https://darrp.noaa.gov/hazardous -waste/island-end-river https://casedocuments.darrp.noaa. gov/northeast/island/admin.html	Various (see below):
Former Coal Tar Processing Facility Site (Island End River, MA) – Honeywell	MA		Honeywell: http://www.gc.noaa.gov/gc-cd/ fctpf-honeywell_sa.pdf https://casedocuments.darrp. noaa.gov/northeast/island/pdf/ FCTPF_Honeywell_Settlement_ Agreement.pdf
Former Coal Tar Processing Facility Site (Island End River, MA) – National Grid	MA		National Grid: http://www.gc.noaa.gov/gc-cd/ fctpf-national_grid_sa.pdf https://casedocuments.darrp. noaa.gov/northeast/island/ pdf/FCTPF_National_Grid_ Settlement_Agreement.pdf

Date	Federal Statute(s)	NRD Assessment Costs (Past)	NRD Assessment Costs (Future)	NRD Restoration Payments	PRP/RP Implemented NRD Projects (Cost Projection if Provided)
2/1/2005	OPA			$80,000.00	No
1/21/1999	CERCLA	$2,419.00		$49,707.00	Yes [not specified]
11/11/2008	CERCLA	$200,000.00		$13,750,000.00	Yes [not specified]
10/2/1996	OPA	$289,884.00		$2,507,500.00	No
5/9/1996	CERCLA			$1,800.00	No
3/13/2009	CERCLA			$36,000.00	No
2001	CERCLA	$20,370.00	$13,350.00	$411,280.00	No
	CERCLA				
12/23/2008	CERCLA			$100,000.00	No
12/23/2008	CERCLA			$100,000.00	No

Name	State	Web Site Link(s)	Consent Decree/ Settlement Docs Link(s)
Former Coal Tar Processing Facility Site (Island End River, MA) – Beazer East	MA		Beazer East: http://www.gc.noaa.gov/gc-cd/fctpf-beazer_east_sa.pdf https://casedocuments.darrp.noaa.gov/northeast/island/pdf/FCTPF_Beazer_East_Settlement_Agreement.pdf
Former Indian Refinery Site	IL	http://www.cerc.usgs.gov/orda_docs/CaseDetails?ID=226 https://www.dnr.illinois.gov/programs/NRDA/Pages/ERBSHA.aspx	https://www.dnr.illinois.gov/programs/NRDA/Documents/LawrencevilleNRD-ConsentDecree.pdf
Formosa Six [M/V]	LA		http://www.gc.noaa.gov/gc-cd/form-sa.pdf
Fort Lauderdale Mystery Oil Spill	FL		No responsible party was located.
Fort Wayne Reduction Dump Site	IN	http://www.cerc.usgs.gov/orda_docs/CaseDetails?ID=70	http://www.cerc.usgs.gov/orda_docs/DocHandler.ashx?task=get&ID=670
Fortuna Reefer [M/V]	PR	https://casedocuments.darrp.noaa.gov/southeast/fortuna/admin.html	http://www.gc.noaa.gov/gc-cd/fort-cd.pdf https://casedocuments.darrp.noaa.gov/southeast/fortuna/pdf/fort-cd.pdf
Fox River/Green Bay NPL Site	WI	https://www.fws.gov/midwest/es/ec/nrda/foxrivernrda/index.html https://www.cerc.usgs.gov/orda_docs/CaseDetails?ID=899	Various (see below):
Fox River/Green Bay NPL Site – Fort James	WI		Fort James: http://www.cerc.usgs.gov/orda_docs/DocHandler.ashx?task=get&ID=568
Fox River/Green Bay NPL Site – Whiting Paper	WI		Whiting Paper: http://www.cerc.usgs.gov/orda_docs/DocHandler.ashx?task=get&ID=1279
Fox River/Green Bay NPL Site – De minimis	WI		De minimis: http://www.cerc.usgs.gov/orda_docs/DocHandler.ashx?task=get&ID=569
Fox River/Green Bay NPL Site – NCR Corp.	WI		NCR Corp.: http://www.cerc.usgs.gov/orda_docs/DocHandler.ashx?task=get&ID=1154

Date	Federal Statute(s)	NRD Assessment Costs (Past)	NRD Assessment Costs (Future)	NRD Restoration Payments	PRP/RP Implemented NRD Projects (Cost Projection if Provided)
12/23/2008	CERCLA			$100,000.00	No
12/29/2010	CERCLA, CWA	$250,000.00		$1,727,000.00	Yes [not specified]
5/11/1999	CERCLA, CWA	$25,000.00		$65,000.00	No
4/3/2000	CERCLA	$90,000.00	$8,000.00		Yes [not specified]
9/11/1997	OPA			$1,250,000.00	No
	CERCLA				
5/21/2002	CERCLA	$1,550,000.00		$4,600,000.00	Yes [$3,900,000.00]
9/23/2009	CERCLA			$35,700.00	No
12/16/2009	CERCLA			$446,590.90	No
6/26/2013	CERCLA			$4,350,000.00	No

Name	State	Web Site Link(s)	Consent Decree/ Settlement Docs Link(s)
Fox River/Green Bay NPL Site – NewPage	WI		NewPage: http://www.cerc.usgs.gov/ orda_docs/DocHandler. ashx?task=get&ID=1331
Fox River/Green Bay NPL Site – Kimberly-Clark	WI		Kimberly-Clark: https://www.justice.gov/enrd/ ConsentDecrees/Kimberly_ Clark_Consent_Decree.pdf
Fox River/Green Bay NPL Site – Cashout Settling Defendants & State	WI		Cashout Settling Defendants & State: On file with authors
Fox River/Green Bay NPL Site – P.H. Glatfelter Co. & Georgia-Pacific	WI		P.H. Glatfelter Co. & Georgia-Pacific: On file with authors
Freeport – McMoRan – Chino, Tyrone, & Cobre Mines	NM	https://onrt.env.nm.gov/ chino-cobre-and-tyrone-mines/	https://onrt.env.nm.gov/ wp-content/uploads/FMI -NMConsentDecreesignedby Judge021111.pdf
French Gulch	CO	https://www.cerc.usgs.gov/orda_ docs/CaseDetails?ID=34 http://www.fws.gov/mountain-prairie/NRDA/frenchgulch/index. html	http://www.cerc.usgs.gov/ orda_docs/DocHandler. ashx?task=get&ID=139 http://www.doi.gov/ restoration/library/casedocs/ upload/CO_French_Gulch_ CD_05.pdf
French Limited NPL Site	TX	https://www.cerc.usgs.gov/ orda_docs/CaseDetails?ID=188	http://www.cerc.usgs.gov/ orda_docs/DocHandler. ashx?task=get&ID=481
Galaxy Spectron NPL site	MD	https://www.cerc.usgs.gov/ orda_docs/CaseDetails?ID=103	http://www.cerc.usgs.gov/ orda_docs/DocHandler. ashx?task=get&ID=680
GB Biosciences Corp. Site/Greens Bayou	TX	https://www.cerc.usgs.gov/ orda_docs/CaseDetails?ID=967	http://www.cerc.usgs.gov/ orda_docs/DocHandler. ashx?task=get&ID=877

Date	Federal Statute(s)	NRD Assessment Costs (Past)	NRD Assessment Costs (Future)	NRD Restoration Payments	PRP/RP Implemented NRD Projects (Cost Projection if Provided)
12/15/2014	CERCLA			$206,653.00	No
12/15/2014	CERCLA			$225,000.00	No
2/6/2015	CERCLA	$4,650,000.00		$41,025,000.00	No
1/3/2019	CERCLA			$500,000.00	No
2/11/2011	CERCLA, CWA	$205,691.78		$12,794,308.22	No
5/16/2005	CERCLA			$200,000.00	No
3/10/1993	CERCLA	$35,732.10	$30,000 for maintenace of marsh project; also, future costs included in CD but not quantified	$30,000.00	Yes [not specified]
3/16/2007	CERCLA	$61,700.00		$445,600.00	No
4/3/2013	CERCLA	$44,072.19	Included but not quantified		Yes [not specified]

Name	State	Web Site Link(s)	Consent Decree/ Settlement Docs Link(s)
GE Housatonic River/RCRA Site	CT, MA	CT: https://www.cerc.usgs.gov/orda_docs/CaseDetails?ID=1100 MA: https://www.cerc.usgs.gov/orda_docs/CaseDetails?ID=915 https://darrp.noaa.gov/hazardous-waste/housatonic-river http://www.ma-housatonicrestoration.org/ http://www.ct.gov/deep/cwp/view.asp?a=2723&Q=517810&deepNav_GID=1641, http://www.fws.gov/newengland/Contaminants-NRDAR-restoration_projects-HousatonicRiver.htm	http://www.cerc.usgs.gov/orda_docs/DocHandler.ashx?task=get&ID=1518 http://www.cerc.usgs.gov/orda_docs/DocHandler.ashx?task=get&ID=662
Genesis Crude Oil Spill	MS	https://www.cerc.usgs.gov/orda_docs/CaseDetails?ID=927	http://www.cerc.usgs.gov/orda_docs/DocHandler.ashx?task=get&ID=686
Genmar Progress [M/T]	PR	https://www.cerc.usgs.gov/orda_docs/CaseDetails?ID=1041	Various (see below):
Genmar Progress [M/T] – Settlement Agreement	PR		Settlement Agreement: http://www.cerc.usgs.gov/orda_docs/DocHandler.ashx?task=get&ID=797
Genmar Progress [M/T] – Consent Decree	PR		Consent Decree: On file with authors
Getty Petroleum Marketing Inc. Site	MA	https://www.mass.gov/service-details/natural-resource-damages-program-groundwater-settlements-massdep	Per Mass website: In 2015, MassDEP received $41,065 in NRD for several Getty Petroleum Marketing, Inc. sites. These funds were part of a bankruptcy settlement.
Golden Lady	FL		http://www.gc.noaa.gov/gc-cd/lady.pdf

Date	Federal Statute(s)	NRD Assessment Costs (Past)	NRD Assessment Costs (Future)	NRD Restoration Payments	PRP/RP Implemented NRD Projects (Cost Projection if Provided)
10/5/1999	CERCLA			$15,735,000.00	Yes [Not fully specified, but at least $4,000,000 for one part]
7/27/2004	OPA	$35,439.13	$49,217.73	$25,480.71	Yes [not specified]
	OPA				
10/8/2010	OPA	$662,345.39			No
	OPA	$83,090.00		$2,666,910.00	No
2015	Not specified			$41,065.00	No
6/1/1998	NMSA	$27,258.55		$26,372.00	No

Name	State	Web Site Link(s)	Consent Decree/ Settlement Docs Link(s)
Goodrich Petroleum W-6 Facility Oil Barge Removal	LA	https://www.cerc.usgs.gov/ orda_docs/CaseDetails?ID=1050	Per Restoration Plan (https://www.cerc.usgs.gov/ orda_docs/DocHandler. ashx?task=get&ID=1174): As a result of the grounding, natural resources and services were injured or potentially injured. DOI/ FWS has determined that restoration of resources is appropriate as a result of the incident. The settlement and release agreement required Goodrich to pay $225,000 in damages to DOI/FWS in order to compensate the public for natural resource injuries pursuant to OPA.
Grand Calumet River/Indiana Harbor Canal	IN	https://www.cerc.usgs.gov/orda_ docs/CaseDetails?ID=71 https://www.fws.gov/midwest/es/ ec/nrda/GrandCalumetRiver/index. html	Various (see below):
Grand Calumet River/Indiana Harbor Canal – Settlement Agreement (LTV Steel Bankruptcy)	IN		Settlement Agreement (LTV Steel Bankruptcy): http://www.cerc.usgs.gov/ orda_docs/DocHandler. ashx?task=get&ID=226
Grand Calumet River/Indiana Harbor Canal – Consent Decree (ARCO)	IN		Consent Decree (ARCO): http://www.cerc.usgs.gov/ orda_docs/DocHandler. ashx?task=get&ID=227
Great Lakes Asphalt Site	IN	https://www.cerc.usgs.gov/ orda_docs/CaseDetails?ID=72	http://www.cerc.usgs.gov/ orda_docs/DocHandler. ashx?task=get&ID=1064
Great Lakes Dredge & Dock Co.	FL		Various (see below):
Great Lake Dredge & Dock Co. – Coastal Marine Towing (FL)	FL		Coastal Marine Towing (FL): unable to find publicly available

Date	Federal Statute(s)	NRD Assessment Costs (Past)	NRD Assessment Costs (Future)	NRD Restoration Payments	PRP/RP Implemented NRD Projects (Cost Projection if Provided)
2009	OPA			$225,000.00	No
	CERCLA, CWA				
7/1/2003	CERCLA, CWA			Not specified in Settlement Agreement, but according to USFWS website (https:// www.fws.gov /midwest/es/ec /nrda/Grand CalumetRiver /index.html), $4,000,000.00	No
1/31/2005	CERCLA	$2,700,000.00		$53,653,000.00	Yes [not specifed]
5/25/1994	CERCLA			$40,000.00	No
	NMSA				
4/2/1999	NMSA			$17,519.84	No

Name	State	Web Site Link(s)	Consent Decree/ Settlement Docs Link(s)
Great Lakes Dredge & Dock Co. – Coastal Marine Towing (NOAA)	FL		Coastal Marine Towing (NOAA): http://www.gc.noaa.gov/gc-cd/ gl-cmt-cd.pdf
Great Lakes Dredge & Dock Co. – Great Lakes Dredge & Dock Company	FL		Great Lakes Dredge & Dock Co.: http://www.gc.noaa.gov/gc-cd/ cd-gl02.pdf
Green Canyon Block 248 (Shell Offshore Inc.)	LA	https://darrp.noaa.gov/oil-spills/ shell-green-canyon-248	https://pub-data.diver.orr. noaa.gov/admin-record/6103/ Consent%20Decree%20 Entered%208.27.18.pdf
Greenhill Petroleum Corp.	LA	https://www.cerc.usgs.gov/ orda_docs/CaseDetails?ID=92	On file with authors
Guadalupe Oil Field (Unocal)	CA	https://www.cerc.usgs.gov/orda_ docs/CaseDetails?ID=940 https://www.wildlife.ca.gov/OSPR/ NRDA/Guadalupe-Oil-Field	Various (see below):
Guadalupe Oil Field (Unocal) – Settlement Agreement & Judgment	CA		Settlement Agreement and Judgment: http://www.waterboards. ca.gov/rwqcb3/water_issues /programs/gap/docs/guad _settlement_agreement.pdf
Guadalupe Oil Field (Unocal) – Memorandum of Agreement	CA		Memorandum of Agreement: http://www.cerc.usgs.gov/ orda_docs/DocHandler. ashx?task=get&ID=62
Gulf State Utilities/ North Ryan Street Utilities Yard NPL site	LA	https://www.cerc.usgs.gov/ orda_docs/CaseDetails?ID=93	http://www.cerc.usgs.gov/ orda_docs/DocHandler. ashx?task=get&ID=266
H. O. Bouchard, Inc./Sanborn Pond	ME	https://www.cerc.usgs.gov/ orda_docs/CaseDetails?ID=1009	http://www.cerc.usgs.gov/ orda_docs/DocHandler. ashx?task=get&ID=278
Hackensack River Study Area	NJ	https://casedocuments.darrp.noaa. gov/northeast/hackensack/admin. html	
Halby Chemical	DE		
Hanford Nuclear Reservation NPL Sites	WA	https://www.cerc.usgs.gov/orda_ docs/CaseDetails?ID=845 http://www.hanfordnrda.org/	

Date	Federal Statute(s)	NRD Assessment Costs (Past)	NRD Assessment Costs (Future)	NRD Restoration Payments	PRP/RP Implemented NRD Projects (Cost Projection if Provided)
9/1/1999	NMSA			$618,484.86	No
12/3/2002	NMSA			$969,000.00	No
8/27/2018	OPA	$246,169.54		$3,625,000.00	No
1/17/1994	Likely OPA (not specified in CD)	$118,091.67	$28,024.48		Yes [not specifed]
	State Law				
7/20/1998	State Law			$9,200,000.00	No
10/28/1998	State Law				
10/12/2009	CERCLA	$6,658.33		$90,000.00	No
9/26/2007	OPA			$125,000.00	No
	CERCLA				
	CERCLA				
	CERCLA				

Name	State	Web Site Link(s)	Consent Decree/ Settlement Docs Link(s)
Hardage-Criner NPL Site	OK	https://www.cerc.usgs.gov/ orda_docs/CaseDetails?ID=151	Settlement with City of Okmulgee on file with authors.
Hayton Mill Pond Site	WI	https://www.cerc.usgs.gov/ orda_docs/CaseDetails?ID=241	
Hi View Terrace NPL Site	NY	https://www.cerc.usgs.gov/ orda_docs/CaseDetails?ID=990	http://www.cerc.usgs.gov/ orda_docs/DocHandler. ashx?task=get&ID=693
Holyoke Coal Tar Deposits Site	MA	https://www.cerc.usgs.gov/ orda_docs/CaseDetails?ID=293	http://www.cerc.usgs.gov/ orda_docs/DocHandler. ashx?task=get&ID=1181
Howard/White Unit No. 2 Oil Spill	TN	https://www.cerc.usgs.gov/ orda_docs/CaseDetails?ID=956	http://www.cerc.usgs.gov/ orda_docs/DocHandler. ashx?task=get&ID=463
Hudson River (GE)	NY	https://www.cerc.usgs.gov/orda_ docs/CaseDetails?ID=937 https://www.fws.gov/northeast/ ecologicalservices/hudson.html https://darrp.noaa.gov/hazardous -waste/hudson-river http://www.dec.ny.gov/lands/25609. html	
I. Jones Recycling, Inc. Site	IN	https://www.cerc.usgs.gov/ orda_docs/CaseDetails?ID=73	
I. Jones Recycling, Inc. Site – Administrative Order on Consent – Cost Recovery Settlement	IN		Administrative Order on Consent – Cost Recovery Settlement: http://www.cerc.usgs.gov/ orda_docs/DocHandler. ashx?task=get&ID=1063
I. Jones Recycling, Inc. Site – Settlement information from Restoration Plan	IN		Settlement information from Restoration Plan: https://www.cerc.usgs.gov/ orda_docs/DocHandler. ashx?task=get&ID=235
Indian River Power Plant	DE	https://www.cerc.usgs.gov/ orda_docs/CaseDetails?ID=964	No Consent Decree, but RP conducted restoration project to compensate for lost natural resources. See 2009 Fact Sheet: https://www.cerc.usgs.gov/ orda_docs/DocHandler. ashx?task=get&ID=166

Date	Federal Statute(s)	NRD Assessment Costs (Past)	NRD Assessment Costs (Future)	NRD Restoration Payments	PRP/RP Implemented NRD Projects (Cost Projection if Provided)
4/14/2006	CERCLA			$430,000.00	No
	CERCLA				
9/29/1995	CERCLA			$25,000.00	No
11/5/2004	CERCLA	$155,000.00		$345,000.00	No
10/28/2009	OPA			$770,836.85	No
	CERCLA				
	CERCLA				
4/17/1991	CERCLA				
1991	CERCLA			$31,308.93	No
	OPA				Yes [not specifed]

Name	State	Web Site Link(s)	Consent Decree/ Settlement Docs Link(s)
Industri-Plex NPL Site OU-2 & 3 [Bayer Cropscience & Pharmacia]	MA	https://www.cerc.usgs.gov/ orda_docs/CaseDetails?ID=242	http://www.cerc.usgs.gov/ orda_docs/DocHandler. ashx?task=get&ID=827 http://www.gc.noaa.gov/ gc-cd/Bayer-cd_011713.pdf
International Petroleum Corporation Oil Spill	DE	https://www.cerc.usgs.gov/ orda_docs/CaseDetails?ID=1038	http://www.cerc.usgs.gov/ orda_docs/DocHandler. ashx?task=get&ID=167 http://www.doi.gov/ restoration/library/casedocs/ upload/DE_Intl_Petroleum_ CD_09.pdf
Iron Mountain Mine NPL Site (Boulder Creek, CA)	CA	https://www.cerc.usgs.gov/ orda_docs/CaseDetails?ID=17	http://www.cerc.usgs.gov/ orda_docs/DocHandler. ashx?task=get&ID=63
Irving Oil, Chelsea Creek	MA	https://casedocuments.darrp.noaa. gov/northeast/irving/admin.html	
Jack's Creek Sitkin Smelting and Refining, Inc. NPL Site	PA	https://www.cerc.usgs.gov/ orda_docs/CaseDetails?ID=926	Various (see below):
Jack's Creek Sitkin Smelting and Refining, Inc. NPL Site – De Minimis Settlement (1994)	PA		De Minimis Settlement/AOC: http://www.cerc.usgs.gov/ orda_docs/DocHandler. ashx?task=get&ID=1062
Jack's Creek Sitkin Smelting and Refining, Inc. NPL Site – De Minimis Settlement (1995)	PA		De Minimis Settlement/AOC: http://www.cerc.usgs.gov/ orda_docs/DocHandler. ashx?task=get&ID=1061
Jacob Luckenbach Oil Spill [SS]	CA	https://www.cerc.usgs.gov/orda_ docs/CaseDetails?ID=962 https://www.wildlife.ca.gov/OSPR/ NRDA/Jacob-Luckenbach	Multiple Claim Determinations (see below):
Jacob Luckenbach Oil Spill [SS] – 1st Partial Claim	CA		1st Partial Claim Determination: http://www.cerc.usgs.gov/ orda_docs/DocHandler. ashx?task=get&ID=94
Jacob Luckenbach Oil Spill [SS] – 2nd Partial Claim	CA		2nd Partial Claim Determination: http://www.cerc.usgs.gov/ orda_docs/DocHandler. ashx?task=get&ID=95

Date	Federal Statute(s)	NRD Assessment Costs (Past)	NRD Assessment Costs (Future)	NRD Restoration Payments	PRP/RP Implemented NRD Projects (Cost Projection if Provided)
1/11/2013	CERCLA	$437,873.00		$3,812,127.00	No
3/4/2009	State Law	$58,212.07		$194,011.00	No
12/8/2000	CERCLA	$2,000,000.00		$9,000,000.00	No
	OPA				
	CERCLA				
12/12/1994	CERCLA			$2,245,000.00	No
5/25/1995	CERCLA			$2,633.02	No
	OPA				
9/29/2008	OPA	$621,309.00	$462,568.00	$2,769,215.00	No
1/4/2010	OPA	$82,352.08	$686,615.00	$16,211,492.00	No

Name	State	Web Site Link(s)	Consent Decree/ Settlement Docs Link(s)
Jacob Luckenbach Oil Spill [SS] – 3rd Partial Claim	CA		3rd Partial Claim Determination: http://www.cerc.usgs.gov/ orda_docs/DocHandler. ashx?task=get&ID=96
Jacquelyn L. [M/V]	FL		http://www.gc.noaa.gov/gc-cd/ jacq-cd.pdf
Jahre Spray/Coastal Eagle Point	PA/NJ		http://www.gc.noaa.gov/gc-cd/ jahre-sa.pdf
Julie N [M/T] Oil Spill	ME	https://www.cerc.usgs.gov/ orda_docs/CaseDetails?ID=901	http://www.cerc.usgs.gov/ orda_docs/DocHandler. ashx?task=get&ID=280 http://www.gc.noaa.gov/gc-cd/ julien-cd.pdf
Kalamazoo River NPL Site	MI	http://www.fws.gov/midwest/es/ec/ nrda/KalamazooRiver/index.html	
Kalamazoo River NPL Site – Plainwell Bankruptcy	MI		Plainwell Bankruptcy: http://www.michigan.gov/ documents/deq/deq-rrd -ce-fy05BankPlainwell Paper_238457_7.pdf http://www.doi.gov/ restoration/library/casedocs/ upload/MI_Kalamazoo_River_ Plainwel_SA_03.pdf
Kalamazoo River NPL Site – Lyondell Bankruptcy	MI		Lyondell Bankruptcy: http://elr.info/sites/default/ files/doj-consent-decrees/r _lyondell_chemical_company _settlement_agreementfinal .pdf See FWS website for allocation.
Keesler AFB	MS		
Kennecott Utah Copper Site	UT	https://www.cerc.usgs.gov/ orda_docs/CaseDetails?ID=196	https://www.cerc.usgs.gov/ orda_docs/DocHandler. ashx?task=get&ID=494
Kentucky [M/T] – Paulsboro NJ Oil Spill	NJ	https://www.cerc.usgs.gov/ orda_docs/CaseDetails?ID=162	http://www.cerc.usgs.gov/ orda_docs/DocHandler. ashx?task=get&ID=407

Date	Federal Statute(s)	NRD Assessment Costs (Past)	NRD Assessment Costs (Future)	NRD Restoration Payments	PRP/RP Implemented NRD Projects (Cost Projection if Provided)
7/6/2010	OPA		$141,341.00	$2,406,000.00	No
8/14/1997	Likely OPA (not specified in CD)			$257,500.00	No
10/31/1996	OPA	$37,416.15		$117,000.00	No
5/2/2000	OPA	$487,588.88		$1,000,000.00	No
	CERCLA				
5/18/2005	CERCLA	$16,640.00		$883,360.00	No
3/30/2010	CERCLA			$2,000,000.00	No
2/14/2008	CERCLA	$113,800.00	$52,000.00		Yes [$175,000.00]
11/17/1995	OPA	$20,870.63		$34,500.00	No

Name	State	Web Site Link(s)	Consent Decree/ Settlement Docs Link(s)
Kerr-McGee Chemical Corp. NPL Site	NC	https://www.cerc.usgs.gov/ orda_docs/CaseDetails?ID=272	Tronox Bankruptcy Settlement: http://www.cerc.usgs.gov/ orda_docs/DocHandler. ashx?task=get&ID=1230 Order Approving Tronox Bankruptcy Settlement: http://www.cerc.usgs.gov/ orda_docs/DocHandler. ashx?task=get&ID=1231
Keystone Sanitation Landfill NPL Site	PA	https://www.cerc.usgs.gov/ orda_docs/CaseDetails?ID=161	Various (see below):
Keystone Sanitation Landfill NPL Site – Original Generator Defendants	PA		Original Generator Defendants: http://www.cerc.usgs.gov/ orda_docs/DocHandler. ashx?task=get&ID=703
Keystone Sanitation Landfill NPL Site – Third and Fourth Parties	PA		Third and Fourth Parties: http://www.cerc.usgs.gov/ orda_docs/DocHandler. ashx?task=get&ID=704
Keystone Sanitation Landfill NPL Site – Keystone Sanitation Co.	PA		Keystone Sanitation Co.: http://www.cerc.usgs.gov/ orda_docs/DocHandler. ashx?task=get&ID=702
Kinder Morgan Sodium Hydroxide Spill	NJ	https://casedocuments.darrp.noaa. gov/northeast/kinder/admin.html	
Kinder Morgan Pipeline Diesel Spill / Suisun Marsh	CA	https://www.cerc.usgs.gov/ orda_docs/CaseDetails?ID=972	Various (see below):
Kinder Morgan Pipeline Diesel Spill/Suisun Marsh – Original Consent Decree	CA		Original Consent Decree: https://www.cerc.usgs.gov/ orda_docs/DocHandler. ashx?task=get&ID=64 http://www.doi.gov/ restoration/library/casedocs/ upload/CA_Kinder_Morgan_ Suisun_MarshCD_07.pdf

Date	Federal Statute(s)	NRD Assessment Costs (Past)	NRD Assessment Costs (Future)	NRD Restoration Payments	PRP/RP Implemented NRD Projects (Cost Projection if Provided)
1/26/2011	CERCLA			$915,836.00	No
	CERCLA				
9/10/1999	CERCLA			$155,000.00	No
9/10/1999	CERCLA			$80,000.76	No
5/31/2001	CERCLA			$155,000.00	No
	OPA				
	OPA				
5/21/2007	OPA	$156,583.00	Included but not quantified	$1,171,099.00	No

Name	State	Web Site Link(s)	Consent Decree/ Settlement Docs Link(s)
Kinder Morgan Pipeline Diesel Spill / Suisun Marsh – Amended Consent Decree	CA		Amended Consent Decree: https://www.cerc.usgs.gov/ orda_docs/DocHandler. ashx?task=get&ID=65 http://www.doi.gov/ restoration/library/casedocs/ upload/CA_Kinder_Morgan_ Suisun_Marsh_Amended_ CD.pdf
Koch Pipeline Company [Gum Hollow Creek]	TX	https://www.cerc.usgs.gov/ orda_docs/CaseDetails?ID=1003	http://www.cerc.usgs.gov/ orda_docs/DocHandler. ashx?task=get&ID=482
Koch Pipeline Co. Storage Tank Crude Oil Spill [Marcelinas Creek]	TX	https://www.cerc.usgs.gov/ orda_docs/CaseDetails?ID=1089	http://www.cerc.usgs.gov/ orda_docs/DocHandler. ashx?task=get&ID=1483
Koppers Company, Inc. (Charleston Plant) NPL Site	SC	https://darrp.noaa.gov/ hazardous-waste/koppers-co-inc	Link to Proposed CD: https://www.justice.gov/enrd/ consent-decree/file/1112396/ download
Koppers Company Inc. (Texarkana Plant) NPL Site	TX	https://www.cerc.usgs.gov/ orda_docs/CaseDetails?ID=190	http://www.cerc.usgs.gov/ orda_docs/DocHandler. ashx?task=get&ID=483
Krejci Dump NPL Site	OH	https://www.cerc.usgs.gov/ orda_docs/CaseDetails?ID=146	Various (see below):
Krejci Dump NPL Site – Partial Consent Decree	OH		Partial: http://www.cerc.usgs.gov/ orda_docs/DocHandler. ashx?task=get&ID=375
Krejci Dump NPL Site – Supplement	OH		Supplement: http://www.cerc.usgs.gov/ orda_docs/DocHandler. ashx?task=get&ID=376
Kummer Sanitary Landfill Site	MN	https://www.cerc.usgs.gov/ orda_docs/CaseDetails?ID=116	http://www.cerc.usgs.gov/ orda_docs/DocHandler. ashx?task=get&ID=685
Kure [M/V] Fuel Oil Spill [Humboldt Bay]	CA	https://www.cerc.usgs.gov/orda_ docs/CaseDetails?ID=947 https://www.wildlife.ca.gov/OSPR/ NRDA/Kure	http://www.cerc.usgs.gov/ orda_docs/DocHandler. ashx?task=get&ID=74 http://www.doi.gov/ restoration/library/casedocs/ upload/CA_MV_Kure_CD_08. pdf

Date	Federal Statute(s)	NRD Assessment Costs (Past)	NRD Assessment Costs (Future)	NRD Restoration Payments	PRP/RP Implemented NRD Projects (Cost Projection if Provided)
7/27/2007	OPA	$156,583.00	Included but not quantified	$1,171,099.00	No
11/12/2008	OPA, CWA	$136,668.01	Included but not quantified		Yes [not specified]
9/30/2015	OPA	$153,641.36		$616,358.58	No
1/7/2019	CERCLA, CWA	$1,000,000.00		$790,000.00	Yes [not specified]
9/25/2008	CERCLA		Included but not quantified		Yes [not specified]
	CERCLA				
8/1/2005	CERCLA	$30,000.00			No
10/23/2008	CERCLA			$440,100.00	No
Undated	CERCLA			$22,000.00	No
5/7/2008	OPA	$1,093,092.00		$3,660,159.00	Yes [$352,933.00]

Name	State	Web Site Link(s)	Consent Decree/ Settlement Docs Link(s)
Kuroshima [M/V] Oil Spill	AK	https://www.cerc.usgs.gov/orda_ docs/CaseDetails?ID=989 https://casedocuments.darrp.noaa. gov/northwest/kuro/admin.html	http://www.cerc.usgs.gov/ orda_docs/DocHandler. ashx?task=get&ID=2 https://casedocuments.darrp. noaa.gov/northwest/kuro/pdf/ kuro-cd.pdf
Lake Barre (Equilon Pipeline/Texaco Pipeline)	LA	https://www.cerc.usgs.gov/orda_ docs/CaseDetails?ID=993 http://www.gc.noaa.gov/natural-office1.html#Lake1	http://www.cerc.usgs.gov/ orda_docs/DocHandler. ashx?task=get&ID=267
Lake Roosevelt/ Upper Columbia River	WA	https://fortress.wa.gov/ecy/gsp/ Sitepage.aspx?csid=12125	
Lakeland Disposal Service, Inc. NPL Site [Sloan Ditch and Sloan Creek]	IN	https://www.cerc.usgs.gov/ orda_docs/CaseDetails?ID=74	http://www.cerc.usgs.gov/ orda_docs/DocHandler. ashx?task=get&ID=236 http://www.doi.gov/ restoration/library/casedocs/ upload/IN_Lakeland_Disposal_ CD_07.pdf
Landfill and Resource Recovery, Inc. NPL Site	RI	https://www.cerc.usgs.gov/ orda_docs/CaseDetails?ID=172	http://www.cerc.usgs.gov/ orda_docs/DocHandler. ashx?task=get&ID=784
LCP Chemicals NPL Site (Georgia)	GA	https://darrp.noaa.gov/ hazardous-waste/lcp-chemical	
Legacy/Atochem Site [Arkema]	TX	https://www.cerc.usgs.gov/ orda_docs/CaseDetails?ID=1045	http://www.cerc.usgs.gov/ orda_docs/DocHandler. ashx?task=get&ID=1130
Lehigh Portland Cement Co. Site	IA	https://www.cerc.usgs.gov/ orda_docs/CaseDetails?ID=82	http://www.cerc.usgs.gov/ orda_docs/DocHandler. ashx?task=get&ID=791
Liberty Industrial Finishing NPL Site	NY	https://www.cerc.usgs.gov/orda_ docs/CaseDetails?ID=141 https://darrp.noaa. gov/hazardous-waste/ liberty-industrial-finishing	http://www.cerc.usgs.gov/ orda_docs/DocHandler. ashx?task=get&ID=362 https://casedocuments.darrp. noaa.gov/northeast/liberty/ pdf/CJ_FNL_FILED.pdf
LNG Carrier Matthew Grounding	PR	https://darrp.noaa. gov/ship-groundings/ lng-carrier-matthew	https://casedocuments.darrp. noaa.gov/southeast/matthew/ pdf/Matthew_2681404-v1 -Consent_Decree_signed-by-J -Gelpi_1_1.pdf

Date	Federal Statute(s)	NRD Assessment Costs (Past)	NRD Assessment Costs (Future)	NRD Restoration Payments	PRP/RP Implemented NRD Projects (Cost Projection if Provided)
5/22/2002	OPA	$560,151.25	Included but not quantified	$653,017.00	No
11/15/1999	OPA	$468,158.38	Included but not quantified	$40,000.00	Yes [not specified]
	CERCLA				
8/8/2007	CERCLA	$50,000.00		$200,000.00	No
1/28/1997	CERCLA			$200,000.00	Yes [$525,000.00]
	CERCLA				
8/27/2013	CERCLA	$283,053.38		$1,116,946.62	No
2/19/2001	CERCLA			$35,000.00	No
7/18/2006	CERCLA	$54,000.00	$77,500.00		Yes [not specified]
6/1/2017	OPA	$192,000.00		$1,718,000.00	No

Name	State	Web Site Link(s)	Consent Decree/ Settlement Docs Link(s)
Lone Mountain Processing, Inc. Coal Slurry Spill	VA	https://www.cerc.usgs.gov/ orda_docs/CaseDetails?ID=914	http://www.cerc.usgs.gov/ orda_docs/DocHandler. ashx?task=get&ID=720
Lordship Point Site	CT	https://darrp.noaa.gov/ hazardous-waste/lordship-point	https://casedocuments. darrp.noaa.gov/northeast/ lordship-point/pdf/USA%20 v%20Sporting%20Goods%20 Prop%20Inc%20-%20 PACER%20stamped%20CD.pdf
Los Alamos National Laboratory	NM	https://www.cerc.usgs.gov/ orda_docs/CaseDetails?ID=285	
Love Canal NPL site	NY	https://www.cerc.usgs.gov/ orda_docs/CaseDetails?ID=142	http://www.cerc.usgs.gov/ orda_docs/DocHandler. ashx?task=get&ID=697
Lower Passaic River and Greater Newark Bay/ Diamond Alkali	NJ	https://darrp.noaa.gov/hazardous-waste/lower-passaic-river-and-greater-newark-bay	
Macalloy Corporation NPL site	SC	https://www.cerc.usgs.gov/ orda_docs/CaseDetails?ID=1029	http://www.cerc.usgs.gov/ orda_docs/DocHandler. ashx?task=get&ID=461
Magellan Midstream Partners	KS	https://www.cerc.usgs.gov/ orda_docs/CaseDetails?ID=1033	http://www.cerc.usgs.gov/ orda_docs/DocHandler. ashx?task=get&ID=255
Malone Service Company NPL Site	TX	https://www.cerc.usgs.gov/ orda_docs/CaseDetails?ID=237	http://www.cerc.usgs.gov/ orda_docs/DocHandler. ashx?task=get&ID=711
Mar Vida	FL		http://www.gc.noaa.gov/ gc-cd/082409-mar_vida_sa.pdf
Marathon Oil Company Indianapolis Refinery	IN	https://www.cerc.usgs.gov/ orda_docs/CaseDetails?ID=999	http://www.cerc.usgs.gov/ orda_docs/DocHandler. ashx?task=get&ID=671
Marathon Pipe Line LLC	IL	https://www.cerc.usgs.gov/ orda_docs/CaseDetails?ID=1049	http://www.cerc.usgs.gov/ orda_docs/DocHandler. ashx?task=get&ID=668
Margara [T/V]	PR	https://darrp.noaa.gov/ ship-groundings/tv-margara	
Maritime Logistics	CA		http://www.gc.noaa.gov/gc-cd/ maritime_logistics_cd.pdf

Date	Federal Statute(s)	NRD Assessment Costs (Past)	NRD Assessment Costs (Future)	NRD Restoration Payments	PRP/RP Implemented NRD Projects (Cost Projection if Provided)
3/5/2001	CERCLA			$2,450,000.00	No
4/23/2004	CERCLA	$31,773.31		$218,226.29	Yes [not specified]
	CERCLA				
3/19/1996	CERCLA			$375,000.00	No
	CERCLA				
10/31/2006	CERCLA	$50,000.00		$350,000.00	No
12/10/2008	CERCLA, CWA	$11,975.00		$440,560.00	Yes [$360,000]
9/24/2012	CERCLA			$3,109,000.00	No
8/24/2009	NMSA			Community service	No
3/26/1996	CWA, OPA	$31,250.00		$273,380.00	No
2/15/2012	OPA	$90,629.03			Yes [not specified]
	OPA				
10/11/2007	NMSA, OPA, CERCLA			$392,936.00	No

Name	State	Web Site Link(s)	Consent Decree/ Settlement Docs Link(s)
Massachusetts Military Reservation NPL Site/Textron	MA	https://www.cerc.usgs.gov/ orda_docs/CaseDetails?ID=107	http://www.cerc.usgs.gov/ orda_docs/DocHandler. ashx?task=get&ID=300 https://www.mass.gov/ service-details/natural- resource-damages-program- groundwater-settlements- massdep
Mattiace Petrochemical Company Site (Glen Cove Creek)	NY	https://www.cerc.usgs.gov/orda_ docs/CaseDetails?ID=143 https://darrp.noaa. gov/hazardous-waste/ mattiace-petrochemical	http://www.cerc.usgs.gov/ orda_docs/DocHandler. ashx?task=get&ID=366 https://casedocuments.darrp. noaa.gov/northeast/mattiace/ pdf/CD_fnl.pdf
McGrath Lake/ Berry Petroleum Crude Oil Spill	CA	https://www.wildlife.ca.gov/OSPR/ NRDA/McGrath	http://www.cerc.usgs.gov/ orda_docs/DocHandler. ashx?task=get&ID=653
Metal Bank	PA	https://darrp.noaa.gov/ hazardous-waste/metal-bank	
Mid-America Tanning Company Site	IA	https://www.cerc.usgs.gov/ orda_docs/CaseDetails?ID=83	http://www.cerc.usgs.gov/ orda_docs/DocHandler. ashx?task=get&ID=676
Midvale Slag NPL Site	UT	https://www.cerc.usgs.gov/ orda_docs/CaseDetails?ID=197	Information obtained from Fact Sheet: https://www.cerc.usgs.gov/ orda_docs/DocHandler. ashx?task=get&ID=495
Milltown Reservoir/ Clark Fork River NPL Site	MT	https://dojmt.gov/lands/	Various (see below):
Milltown Reservoir/Clark Fork River NPL Site – Streamside Tailings OU	MT		Streamside Tailings OU: https://media.dojmt.gov/ wp-content/uploads/2011/06/ settlementagreement02.pdf
Milltown Reservoir/ Clark Fork River NPL Site – State CD 1	MT		State CD I: https://media.dojmt.gov/ wp-content/uploads/1999- State-v-ARCO-CD-CV-83-317-H- PGH.pdf

Date	Federal Statute(s)	NRD Assessment Costs (Past)	NRD Assessment Costs (Future)	NRD Restoration Payments	PRP/RP Implemented NRD Projects (Cost Projection if Provided)
2/21/2008	CERCLA	$125,000.00		$1,175,000.00	No
6/1/2003	CERCLA			$200,000.00	No
10/22/1996	OPA			$1,315,000.00	No
	CERCLA				
2/10/1998	CERCLA			$100,000.00	No
1991	CERCLA			$2,300,000.00	No
	CERCLA				
4/19/1999	CERCLA			$20,000,000.00	Yes [$11,600,000.00]
4/19/1999	CERCLA	$15,000,000.00	$80,000,000.00	$118,000,000.00	Yes [$2,000,000.00]

Name	State	Web Site Link(s)	Consent Decree/ Settlement Docs Link(s)
Milltown Reservoir/ Clark Fork River NPL Site – Milltown Site	MT		Milltown Site: http://cfrtac.org/images/pdf/ august2005/milltown_cd.pdf
Milltown Reservoir/ Clark Fork River NPL Site – State CD 2	MT		State CD II: https://media.dojmt.gov/ wp-content/uploads/2011/06/ consentdecree2008.pdf
Milltown Reservoir/ Clark Fork River NPL Site – ASARCO Bankruptcy	MT		ASARCO Bankruptcy: https://dojmt.gov/wp-content/ uploads/2011/06/20080425settl ement.pdf
Milltown Reservoir/ Clark Fork River NPL Site – Clark Fork OU	MT		Clark Fork OU: https://media.dojmt.gov/ wp-content/uploads/2008- Clark-Fork-CD-CV-83-317-H- SEH.pdf
Miss Beholden [M/V]	FL	https://www.gc.noaa.gov/natural-office1.html	
Missouri Dioxin Sites	MO	https://www.cerc.usgs.gov/ orda_docs/CaseDetails?ID=119	http://www.cerc.usgs.gov/ orda_docs/DocHandler. ashx?task=get&ID=324
Mobil Mining & Minerals Company	TX	https://www.cerc.usgs.gov/ orda_docs/CaseDetails?ID=1008	http://www.cerc.usgs.gov/ orda_docs/DocHandler. ashx?task=get&ID=489
Montrose/Palos Verdes Shelf NPL Site	CA	https://www.cerc.usgs.gov/orda_ docs/CaseDetails?ID=23 https://darrp.noaa.gov/hazardous-waste/montrose http://www.montroserestoration. noaa.gov/	Various (see below):
Montrose/Palos Verdes Shelf NPL Site – Local Government Entities	CA		Local Government Entities: http://www.gc.noaa.gov/gc-cd/ mon3122d.pdf http://www.gc.noaa.gov/gc-cd/ mon3122e.pdf http://www.gc.noaa.gov/gc-cd/ mon3122f.pdf http://www.gc.noaa.gov/gc-cd/ mon3122g.pdf

Date	Federal Statute(s)	NRD Assessment Costs (Past)	NRD Assessment Costs (Future)	NRD Restoration Payments	PRP/RP Implemented NRD Projects (Cost Projection if Provided)
2/8/2005	CERCLA				Yes [$3,900,000.00]
2008	CERCLA				
2008	CERCLA			$8,500,000.00	No
8/21/2008	CERCLA	$4,500,000.00		$71,350,000.00	Yes [not specified]
	NMSA				
1990	CERCLA			$200,000.00	No
6/12/1996	CERCLA	$130,101.57	Included but not specified	$100,000.00	Yes [not specified]
	CERCLA				
8/19/1999	CERCLA			$23,700,000.00	No

Name	State	Web Site Link(s)	Consent Decree/ Settlement Docs Link(s)
Montrose/Palos Verdes Shelf NPL Site – CBS	CA		CBS: http://www.gc.noaa.gov/gc-cd/mon3122h.pdf http://www.gc.noaa.gov/gc-cd/mon3122i.pdf http://www.gc.noaa.gov/gc-cd/mon3122j.pdf
Montrose/Palos Verdes Shelf NPL Site – Potlach Corp. and Simpson	CA		Potlach Corp. and Simpson: http://www.gc.noaa.gov/gc-cd/mon3122k.pdf http://www.gc.noaa.gov/gc-cd/mon3122l.pdf http://www.gc.noaa.gov/gc-cd/mon3122m.pdf
Montrose/Palos Verdes Shelf NPL Site – Aventis Cropscience, Chris-Craft, and Atkemix	CA		Aventis Cropscience, Chris-Craft, and Atkemix: http://www.gc.noaa.gov/gc-cd/mon3122a.pdf http://www.gc.noaa.gov/gc-cd/mon3122b.pdf http://www.gc.noaa.gov/gc-cd/mon3122c.pdf
Mosaic Riverview Phosphogypsum Stack Discharge	FL	https://www.cerc.usgs.gov/orda_docs/CaseDetails.aspx?ID=1055 https://darrp.noaa.gov/hazardous-waste/mosaic	On file with authors
Mosquito Bay	LA	https://www.cerc.usgs.gov/orda_docs/CaseDetails?ID=1014	
Motiva Enterprises LLC, Port Arthur Refinery Site	TX	https://www.cerc.usgs.gov/orda_docs/CaseDetails?ID=1017	http://www.cerc.usgs.gov/orda_docs/DocHandler.ashx?task=get&ID=491
Mulberry Phosphates Inc. (Alafia River Spill)	FL	https://www.cerc.usgs.gov/orda_docs/CaseDetails?ID=986 https://darrp.noaa.gov/hazardous-waste/mulberry	http://www.cerc.usgs.gov/orda_docs/DocHandler.ashx?task=get&ID=179
Nahant Marsh NPL Site	IA	https://www.cerc.usgs.gov/orda_docs/CaseDetails?ID=84	http://www.cerc.usgs.gov/orda_docs/DocHandler.ashx?task=get&ID=677

Date	Federal Statute(s)	NRD Assessment Costs (Past)	NRD Assessment Costs (Future)	NRD Restoration Payments	PRP/RP Implemented NRD Projects (Cost Projection if Provided)
8/19/1999	CERCLA			$2,250,000.00	No
8/19/1999	CERCLA			$8,000,000.00	No
3/15/2001	CERCLA			$30,000,000.00	No
3/22/2013	CERCLA, CWA	$140,726.98	Included but not quantified		Yes [not specified]
	OPA				
2/15/2008	CERCLA, CWA	$83,786.52		$1,116,213.48	No
7/31/2002	CERCLA	$1,020,328.00		$3,656,119.00	No
12/23/1999	CERCLA			$5,000.00	No

Name	State	Web Site Link(s)	Consent Decree/ Settlement Docs Link(s)
Nautilis Motor Tanker [M/T]	NY/NJ		http://www.gc.noaa.gov/gc-cd/nautilis.pdf
Nease Chemical NPL Site	OH		https://www.cerc.usgs.gov/orda_docs/DocHandler.ashx?task=get&ID=2450
New Almaden Mine/New Almaden Quicksilver	CA	https://www.cerc.usgs.gov/orda_docs/CaseDetails?ID=24	Various (see below):
New Almaden Mine/New Almaden Quicksilver – Newson, Inc.	CA		Newson, Inc.: http://www.cerc.usgs.gov/orda_docs/DocHandler.ashx?task=get&ID=89 http://www.doi.gov/restoration/library/casedocs/upload/CA_New_Almaden_Mines_CD_Newson_05.pdf
New Almaden Mine/New Almaden Quicksilver – Sunoco	CA		Sunoco: http://www.cerc.usgs.gov/orda_docs/DocHandler.ashx?task=get&ID=90 http://www.doi.gov/restoration/library/casedocs/upload/CA_New_Almaden_Mines_CD_Sunoco_05.pdf
New Bedford Harbor	MA	https://www.cerc.usgs.gov/orda_docs/CaseDetails?ID=108 https://darrp.noaa.gov/hazardous-waste/new-bedford-harbor	Various (see below):
New Bedford Harbor – AVX Corp.	MA		AVX Corp.: http://www.cerc.usgs.gov/orda_docs/DocHandler.ashx?task=get&ID=304 https://casedocuments.darrp.noaa.gov/northeast/new_bedford/pdf/nb-cd1.pdf http://www.gc.noaa.gov/gc-cd/nb-cd1.pdf

Date	Federal Statute(s)	NRD Assessment Costs (Past)	NRD Assessment Costs (Future)	NRD Restoration Payments	PRP/RP Implemented NRD Projects (Cost Projection if Provided)
4/4/1994	CERCLA	$700,000.00		$3,300,000.00	No
12/22/2016	CERCLA, CWA	$195,000.00	Included but not specified		Yes [$366,000.00]
	CERCLA				
11/16/2005	CERCLA			$475,000.00	No
11/16/2005	CERCLA			$85,000.00	Yes [not specified]
	CERCLA				
2/3/1991	CERCLA			$7,000,000.00	No

Name	State	Web Site Link(s)	Consent Decree/ Settlement Docs Link(s)
New Bedford Harbor – Aerovox, Inc.	MA		Aerovox, Inc./Belleville Industries, Inc.: http://www.cerc.usgs.gov/ orda_docs/DocHandler. ashx?task=get&ID=303 http://www.gc.noaa.gov/gc-cd/ nb-cd2.pdf
New Bedford Harbor – National Wildlife Federation	MA		National Wildlife Federation: https://casedocuments.darrp. noaa.gov/northeast/new_ bedford/pdf/nb-cd3.pdf http://www.gc.noaa.gov/gc-cd/ nb-cd3.pdf
New Bedford Harbor – Federal Pacific Electric/ Cornell Dubilier Electronics, Inc.	MA		Federal Pacific Electric Co./ Cornell Dubilier Electronics, Inc.: http://www.cerc.usgs.gov/ orda_docs/DocHandler. ashx?task=get&ID=305
New Carissa [M/V]	OR	https://www.cerc.usgs.gov/ orda_docs/CaseDetails?ID=992	Various (see below):
New Carissa [M/V] – Consent Decree & Judgment	OR		Consent Decree & Judgment: http://www.cerc.usgs.gov/ orda_docs/DocHandler. ashx?task=get&ID=396
New Carissa [M/V] – NPFC Claim Determination	OR		NPFC Claim Determination: http://www.cerc.usgs.gov/ orda_docs/DocHandler. ashx?task=get&ID=397
Newton County Wells NPL Site/FAG Bearings	MO	https://www.cerc.usgs.gov/ orda_docs/CaseDetails?ID=1028	http://www.cerc.usgs.gov/ orda_docs/DocHandler. ashx?task=get&ID=828
Newtown Creek	NY	https://darrp.noaa.gov/ hazardous-waste/newtown-creek	https://www.gc.noaa. gov/gc-cd/Newtown-Creek-Getty-Notice-of-Lodging&Settlement-Agreement-10212014.pdf
Ninth Avenue Dump, Midco I, and Midco II Sites (Bankruptcies)	IN	https://www.cerc.usgs.gov/ orda_docs/CaseDetails?ID=76	Information obtained from Fact Sheet: https://www.cerc.usgs.gov/ orda_docs/DocHandler. ashx?task=get&ID=239

Date	Federal Statute(s)	NRD Assessment Costs (Past)	NRD Assessment Costs (Future)	NRD Restoration Payments	PRP/RP Implemented NRD Projects (Cost Projection if Provided)
7/17/1991	CERCLA	$566,000.00		$2,584,000.00	No
6/5/1992	CERCLA				
11/24/1992	CERCLA	$329,807.75		$19,670,192.25	No
	OPA				
6/7/2004	OPA			$4,000,000.00	No
1/24/2007	OPA			$25,598,063.00	No
6/29/2007	CERCLA	$6,739.00		$130,724.00	No
12/17/2014	CERCLA	$16,590.91		$1,138,609.09	No
	CERCLA			$200,000.00	Yes [not specified]

Name	State	Web Site Link(s)	Consent Decree/ Settlement Docs Link(s)
North Bronson Industrial Area Site	MI	https://www.cerc.usgs.gov/ orda_docs/CaseDetails?ID=113	http://www.cerc.usgs.gov/ orda_docs/DocHandler. ashx?task=get&ID=684
North Cape [T/B] Heating Oil Spill	RI	https://www.cerc.usgs.gov/orda_ docs/CaseDetails?ID=920 https://darrp.noaa.gov/oil-spills/ north-cape	http://www.cerc.usgs.gov/ orda_docs/DocHandler. ashx?task=get&ID=432 https://casedocuments.darrp. noaa.gov/northeast/north_ cape/pdf/nccondec.pdf http://www.gc.noaa.gov/gc-cd/ nccondec.pdf
North Pass Crude Oil Spill (Ocean Energy/Devon)	LA	https://www.cerc.usgs.gov/ orda_docs/CaseDetails?ID=1020	http://www.cerc.usgs.gov/ orda_docs/DocHandler. ashx?task=get&ID=274
North Shore Restoration Area/ Lake Apopka Bird Kill	FL	https://www.cerc.usgs.gov/ orda_docs/CaseDetails?ID=1013	http://www.cerc.usgs.gov/ orda_docs/DocHandler. ashx?task=get&ID=789
Northside Sanitary Landfill NPL Site/ Envirochem NPL Sites	IN	https://www.cerc.usgs.gov/ orda_docs/CaseDetails?ID=988	From Superfund: Status of Selected Federal Natural Resource Damage Settlements (Letter Report, 11/20/96, GAO/ RCED-97-10): In three 1990 and 1991 consent decrees, the PRPs agreed to pay DOI's Fish and Wildlife Service (FWS) $55,000 to settle natural resource damage claims at the Envirochem facility and the Northside Sanitary Landfill. In 1992 and 1994, EPA issued administrative orders on consent to settle the federal government's claim for natural resource damages at the Great Lakes Asphalt facility. Under the administrative orders, the PRPs agreed to pay FWS a total of $29,800. FWS also received $930 for a bankruptcy claim against a PRP at the Great Lakes Asphalt facility.

Date	Federal Statute(s)	NRD Assessment Costs (Past)	NRD Assessment Costs (Future)	NRD Restoration Payments	PRP/RP Implemented NRD Projects (Cost Projection if Provided)
6/30/1999	CERCLA			$104,740.45	Offered as an option in lieu of part of damages payment
10/6/2000	OPA	$4,323,414.80		$8,000,000.00	No
5/3/2006	OPA	$96,570.33		$21,370.00	No
10/8/2003	CERCLA	$26,868.11	$30,000.00	$25,226.00	Yes [$80,000,000.00]
	CERCLA			$85,730.00	No

Name	State	Web Site Link(s)	Consent Decree/ Settlement Docs Link(s)
Nyanza Chemical Waste Dump NPL site	MA	https://www.cerc.usgs.gov/orda_docs/CaseDetails?ID=262 http://www.mass.gov/eea/agencies/massdep/cleanup/nrd/nyanza-chemical-waste-dump-superfund-site-nrd-settlement.html	https://www.mass.gov/files/documents/2017/08/29/Nyanza_Consent_Decree_0.pdf
Ohio River Fish & Mussel Kill/Elkem Metals Company, L.P.	OH	https://www.cerc.usgs.gov/orda_docs/CaseDetails?ID=1007	http://www.cerc.usgs.gov/orda_docs/DocHandler.ashx?task=get&ID=377
Okmulgee Sewage Discharge	OK	https://www.cerc.usgs.gov/orda_docs/CaseDetails?ID=974	http://www.cerc.usgs.gov/orda_docs/DocHandler.ashx?task=get&ID=383
Old Southington Landfill NPL Site	CT	https://www.cerc.usgs.gov/orda_docs/CaseDetails?ID=39	http://www.cerc.usgs.gov/orda_docs/DocHandler.ashx?task=get&ID=155
Olympic Pipe Line Co./Whatcom Creek	WA	https://www.cerc.usgs.gov/orda_docs/CaseDetails?ID=1012 https://darrp.noaa.gov/oil-spills/whatcom-creek	https://www.cerc.usgs.gov/orda_docs/DocHandler.ashx?task=get&ID=557 https://darrp.noaa.gov/sites/default/files/case-documents/whatcd2.pdf
Omaha Lead Smelter NPL Site	NE	https://www.cerc.usgs.gov/orda_docs/CaseDetails?ID=1057	https://www.cerc.usgs.gov/orda_docs/DocHandler.ashx?task=get&ID=327
Onondaga Lake NPL Site	NY	https://www.cerc.usgs.gov/orda_docs/CaseDetails?ID=224 https://www.fws.gov/northeast/nyfo/ec/onondaga.htm	https://www.cerc.usgs.gov/orda_docs/DocHandler.ashx?task=get&ID=2980
Ottawa River/ Maumee Bay	OH	https://www.fws.gov/midwest/es/ec/nrda/Ottawa/index.html	http://epa.ohio.gov/portals/30/remedial/docs/dffo/Ottawa%20River%20NRD%20-%20ORG%20Consent%20Decree_022117.PDF
Outboard Marine Corp. NPL Site/ Waukegan Harbor	IL	https://www.cerc.usgs.gov/orda_docs/CaseDetails?ID=58	https://www.cerc.usgs.gov/orda_docs/DocHandler.ashx?task=get&ID=206
Pago Pago Harbor (American Samoa)/ Nine Abandoned Fishing Vessels	AS	https://www.cerc.usgs.gov/orda_docs/CaseDetails?ID=996	
Palmer Barge Waste Site	TX		https://www.gc.noaa.gov/gc-cd/palmer-sa020907.pdf

Date	Federal Statute(s)	NRD Assessment Costs (Past)	NRD Assessment Costs (Future)	NRD Restoration Payments	PRP/RP Implemented NRD Projects (Cost Projection if Provided)
6/22/1998	CERCLA			$923,077.00	No
4/19/2006	CERCLA	$460,000.00		$2,040,000.00	No
4/14/2006	CWA, CERCLA			$430,000.00	No
11/23/2009	CERCLA	$13,455.85		$3,781,504.38	No
11/12/2004	OPA			$7,088,000.00	Yes [not specified]
8/9/2011	CERCLA			$100,000.00	No
3/14/2018	CERCLA	$916,934.00		$8,586,172.00	Yes [not specified]
2/21/2017	CERCLA	$1,521,269.79		$435,726.69	Yes [$400,000.00]
9/16/2008	CERCLA			$147,747.00	No
	OPA				
DRAFT 4/13/2007	CERCLA, CWA		Included but not quantified	No monetary payment required; work not given a value	Yes [not specified]

Name	State	Web Site Link(s)	Consent Decree/ Settlement Docs Link(s)
Palmerton Zinc NPL Site	PA	https://www.cerc.usgs.gov/ orda_docs/CaseDetails?ID=164	https://www.cerc.usgs.gov/ orda_docs/DocHandler. ashx?task=get&ID=412
Paoli Rail Yard NPL site	PA	https://www.cerc.usgs.gov/ orda_docs/CaseDetails?ID=165	https://www.cerc.usgs.gov/ orda_docs/DocHandler. ashx?task=get&ID=705
Phelps Dodge Industrial Mining Complex	AZ NM	https://www.cerc.usgs.gov/ orda_docs/CaseDetails?ID=1024	Various (see below):
Phelps Dodge Industrial Mining Complex	AZ NM		Consent Decree (New Mexico): https://www.cerc.usgs.gov/ orda_docs/DocHandler. ashx?task=get&ID=1193
Phelps Dodge Industrial Mining Complex	AZ NM		Consent Decree (Arizona): https://www.cerc.usgs.gov/ orda_docs/DocHandler. ashx?task=get&ID=1176
Picillo Farm NPL Site	RI	https://www.cerc.usgs.gov/ orda_docs/CaseDetails?ID=174	https://www.cerc.usgs.gov/ orda_docs/DocHandler. ashx?task=get&ID=707
Pilot Petroleum Corp./Pilot Spill	AZ	https://www.cerc.usgs.gov/ orda_docs/CaseDetails?ID=1010	https://www.cerc.usgs.gov/ orda_docs/DocHandler. ashx?task=get&ID=651
Platform Irene Oil Pipeline Crude Oil Spill	CA	https://www.cerc.usgs.gov/ orda_docs/CaseDetails?ID=950	https://www.cerc.usgs.gov/ orda_docs/DocHandler. ashx?task=get&ID=655
Polar Texas [T/V]/ Polar Tankers, Inc./ Dalco Passage	WA	https://www.cerc.usgs.gov/ orda_docs/CaseDetails?ID=218	https://www.cerc.usgs.gov/ orda_docs/DocHandler. ashx?task=get&ID=563
Pools Prairie Site/ Newton County Wells	MO	https://www.cerc.usgs.gov/ orda_docs/CaseDetails?ID=1002	
Port Gardner Bay	WA	https://darrp.noaa.gov/ hazardous-waste/port-gardner	https://casedocuments. darrp.noaa.gov/northwest/ port_gardner/pdf/ Consent_Decree%20Final_ Entered_Signed_Port%20 Gardner_04-05-2018.PDF
Port of Portland T6	OR	https://www.cerc.usgs.gov/ orda_docs/CaseDetails?ID=1022	Information obtained from Monitoring Report: https://www.cerc.usgs.gov/ orda_docs/DocHandler. ashx?task=get&ID=734
Port Stewart [T/V] Grounding	PR	https://darrp.noaa.gov/ ship-groundings/tv-port-stewart	On file with authors

Date	Federal Statute(s)	NRD Assessment Costs (Past)	NRD Assessment Costs (Future)	NRD Restoration Payments	PRP/RP Implemented NRD Projects (Cost Projection if Provided)
10/27/2009	CERCLA, CWA, PSRPA	$2,500,000.00		$9,875,000.00	Yes [$8,720,000.00]
4/20/1999	CERCLA			$850,000.00	No
	CERCLA				
2/21/2012	CERCLA	$2,482,590.33		$5,500,000.00	Yes [not specified]
6/28/2012	CERCLA	$940,622.50		$6,701,861.30	No
10/8/1997	CERCLA			$52,160.00	No
12/30/2003	OPA			$145,000.00	No
7/23/2002	OPA			$2,397,000.00	No
5/21/2010	OPA	$100,700.00		$487,300.00	No
	CERCLA				
1/26/2018	CWA, OPA	$344,253.00	$35,000.00	$3,946,633.00	No
	OPA			$45,740.00	No
7/31/2017	OPA	$138,000.00		$412,000.00	No

Name	State	Web Site Link(s)	Consent Decree/ Settlement Docs Link(s)
Portland Harbor NPL Site/Lower Willamette River	OR	http://www.fws.gov/oregonfwo/ Contaminants/PortlandHarbor/ https://darrp.noaa.gov/ hazardous-waste/portland-harbor	Various (see below):
Portland Harbor NPL Site/Lower Willamette River – Smurfit-Stone (Bankruptcy)	OR		Settlement Agreement (Smurfit-Stone Bankruptcy): https://www.cerc.usgs.gov/ orda_docs/DocHandler. ashx?task=get&ID=402
Portland Harbor NPL Site/Lower Willamette River – Linnton Plywood	OR		Consent Decree (Linnton Plywood): https://www.cerc.usgs.gov/ orda_docs/DocHandler. ashx?task=get&ID=1450
Portland Harbor NPL Site/Lower Willamette River	OR		Confidential Settlement Agreement and Release – Liberty Mutual: https://pub-data.diver. orr.noaa.gov/portland-harbor/19000101_ LinntonSettAgr_2297.pdf
Posavina [T/V] Fuel Oil Spill	MA	https://www.cerc.usgs.gov/ orda_docs/CaseDetails?ID=957	https://www.cerc.usgs.gov/ orda_docs/DocHandler. ashx?task=get&ID=792
Presidente Riveria [M/V]	PA	https://www.cerc.usgs.gov/ orda_docs/CaseDetails?ID=163	https://www.cerc.usgs.gov/ orda_docs/DocHandler. ashx?task=get&ID=408
PSC Resources NPL Site	MA	https://www.cerc.usgs.gov/ orda_docs/CaseDetails?ID=109	https://www.cerc.usgs.gov/ orda_docs/DocHandler. ashx?task=get&ID=683
Publicker Industries NPL Site	PA	https://www.cerc.usgs.gov/ orda_docs/CaseDetails?ID=919	https://www.cerc.usgs.gov/ orda_docs/DocHandler. ashx?task=get&ID=795
Puget Sound Energy Oil Spill	WA	https://www.cerc.usgs.gov/ orda_docs/CaseDetails?ID=1044	https://www.cerc.usgs.gov/ orda_docs/DocHandler. ashx?task=get&ID=560
R. Lavin and Sons, Inc.	IL	https://www.cerc.usgs.gov/ orda_docs/CaseDetails?ID=59	https://www.cerc.usgs.gov/ orda_docs/DocHandler. ashx?task=get&ID=207
Refugio Beach Oil Spill	CA	https://darrp.noaa.gov/oil-spills/ refugio-beach-oil-spill	
Rio Algom Mining LLC-Quivira Mine	NM	https://www.cerc.usgs.gov/ orda_docs/CaseDetails?ID=1056	
Rio Tinto Mine	NV	https://www.cerc.usgs.gov/ orda_docs/CaseDetails?ID=243	https://www.cerc.usgs.gov/ orda_docs/DocHandler. ashx?task=get&ID=876

Date	Federal Statute(s)	NRD Assessment Costs (Past)	NRD Assessment Costs (Future)	NRD Restoration Payments	PRP/RP Implemented NRD Projects (Cost Projection if Provided)
	CERCLA				
1/6/2011	CERCLA			$3,000,000.00	No
6/24/2015	CERCLA			$162,500 plus the Net Proceeds of the Sale of Defendant's Property	No
6/20/2016	CERCLA			Indeterminable how much of $3,500,000 payment was provided for NRD	No
3/1/2004	OPA	$48,615.00		$100,000.00	No
9/24/1993	CERCLA, CWA			$2,650,000.00	No
Undated	CERCLA			$153,720.00	No
10/13/1989	CERCLA			$40,000.00	No
2/12/2009	OPA	$49,614.47		$512,856.59	No
10/24/2006	CERCLA	$21,616.10		Included but indeterminable	No
	CERCLA				
	CERCLA				
5/20/2013	CERCLA			$859,527.81	No

Name	State	Web Site Link(s)	Consent Decree/ Settlement Docs Link(s)
Rocky Mountain Arsenal NPL Site	CO	https://www.cerc.usgs.gov/ orda_docs/CaseDetails?ID=998	https://www.cerc.usgs.gov/ orda_docs/DocHandler. ashx?task=get&ID=141
Rose Atoll/Jin Shiang Fa [F/V] Diesel and Lube Oil Spill	AS	https://www.cerc.usgs.gov/ orda_docs/CaseDetails?ID=917	Claim Determination: https://www.cerc.usgs.gov/ orda_docs/DocHandler. ashx?task=get&ID=8 http://www.doi.gov/ restoration/library/casedocs/ upload/AS_Rose_Atoll_CD_ 03.pdf
Rose Hill NPL Site	RI	https://casedocuments.darrp.noaa. gov/northeast/rosehill/admin.html	https://casedocuments.darrp. noaa.gov/northeast/rosehill/ pdf/Rose_Hill_CD.pdf
Rouge River Mystery Oil Spill	MI	https://www.cerc.usgs.gov/ orda_docs/CaseDetails?ID=1026	Assessment Claim (costs redacted): https://www.cerc.usgs.gov/ orda_docs/DocHandler. ashx?task=get&ID=1068
Saegertown Industrial Area NPL site	PA	https://www.cerc.usgs.gov/ orda_docs/CaseDetails?ID=167	https://www.cerc.usgs.gov/ orda_docs/DocHandler. ashx?task=get&ID=706
Saginaw River and Bay	MI	https://www.cerc.usgs.gov/orda_ docs/CaseDetails?ID=114 http://www.fws.gov/midwest/es/ec/ nrda/SaginawNRDA/index.html	https://www.cerc.usgs.gov/ orda_docs/DocHandler. ashx?task=get&ID=787 https://www.fws.gov/midwest/ es/ec/nrda/SaginawNRDA/ documents/ConsentJudgment SaginawGM_PCB_NRDA TrusteeMOU.pdf
Salt Fork/Saline Branch	IL	https://www.cerc.usgs.gov/ orda_docs/CaseDetails?ID=1023	https://www.cerc.usgs.gov/ orda_docs/DocHandler. ashx?task=get&ID=208
Saltville Waste Disposal Ponds NPL site	VA		
Salvors, Inc.	FL		http://www.gc.noaa.gov/gc-cd/ sal-cd.pdf
Sangamo Electric Dump/Crab Orchard NWR	IL	https://www.cerc.usgs.gov/ orda_docs/CaseDetails?ID=1004	See Restoration Plan for details on settlement: https://www.cerc.usgs.gov/ orda_docs/DocHandler. ashx?task=get&ID=211

Date	Federal Statute(s)	NRD Assessment Costs (Past)	NRD Assessment Costs (Future)	NRD Restoration Payments	PRP/RP Implemented NRD Projects (Cost Projection if Provided)
2/27/2009	CERCLA			$7,400,000.00	No
7/7/2003	OPA			$1,452,917.49	No
12/19/2002	CERCLA	$8,000.00		$117,000.00	Yes [$715,000.00]
11/2/2005	OPA			Not disclosed on Assessment Claim (redacted)	No
11/9/1994	CERCLA			$94,510.00	No
6/4/1999	CERCLA	$1,770,000.00		$14,734,974.74	Yes [$11,037,850.85]
2/7/2008	CWA	$41,000.00		$450,000.00	No
	CERCLA				
7/30/1997	MPRSA	$237,663.00		$351,648.00	No
1991	CERCLA			$2,500,000.00	No

Name	State	Web Site Link(s)	Consent Decree/ Settlement Docs Link(s)
Sangamo-Weston, Inc./TwelveMile Creek/Lake Hartwell PCB NPL Site	SC	https://www.cerc.usgs.gov/ orda_docs/CaseDetails?ID=176	https://www.cerc.usgs.gov/ orda_docs/DocHandler. ashx?task=get&ID=456
Santa Clara [M/V]	SC	https://casedocuments.darrp.noaa. gov/northeast/santa_clara/admin. html	Stipulation of Compromise Settlement (U.S. v. M/V Santa Clara, C.A. No. 2:92-0389-18)
Selendang Ayu Oil Spill [M/V]	AK	https://www.cerc.usgs.gov/orda_ docs/CaseDetails?ID=1031 http://www.fws.gov/alaska/fisheries/ contaminants/spill/sa_index.htm	
Sheboygan River and Harbor NPL Site	WI	https://www.cerc.usgs.gov/orda_ docs/CaseDetails?ID=259 https://darrp.noaa.gov/hazardous-waste/sheboygan-river-and-harbor-site http://www.fws.gov/midwest/es/ec/ nrda/SheboyganHarbor/index.html	Various (see below):
Sheboygan River and Harbor NPL Site – Tecumseh Products Co.	WI		Tecumseh Products Co.: https://www.cerc.usgs.gov/ orda_docs/DocHandler. ashx?task=get&ID=4008 https://casedocuments. darrp.noaa.gov/greatlakes/ sheboygan/pdf/Sheboygan_ final_signed_Consent_Decree_ Tecumseh_2018.pdf
Sheboygan River and Harbor NPL Site – Thomas Industries	WI		Thomas Industries: https://www.cerc.usgs.gov/ orda_docs/DocHandler. ashx?task=get&ID=4005 https://casedocuments. darrp.noaa.gov/greatlakes/ sheboygan/pdf/Sheboygan_ final_signed_Consent_Decree_ Thomas_2018.pdf

Date	Federal Statute(s)	NRD Assessment Costs (Past)	NRD Assessment Costs (Future)	NRD Restoration Payments	PRP/RP Implemented NRD Projects (Cost Projection if Provided)
1/9/2006	CERCLA	$537,501.00	RP to pay, but not quantified in CD	$11,960,000.00	Yes [not specifed]
2/7/1994					
	OPA				
	CERCLA				
4/19/2018	CERCLA	$695,000.00		$3,111,250.00	No
4/19/2018	CERCLA			$550,000.00	No

Name	State	Web Site Link(s)	Consent Decree/ Settlement Docs Link(s)
Sheboygan River and Harbor NPL Site – Wisconsin Public Service Corp.	WI		Wisconsin Public Service Corp.: https://www.cerc.usgs.gov/ orda_docs/DocHandler. ashx?task=get&ID=4006 https://casedocuments. darrp.noaa.gov/greatlakes/ sheboygan/pdf/Sheboygan_ final_signed_Consent_Decree_ WPSC_2018.pdf
Shell Oil Co. Refinery/Shell Martinez	CA	https://www.cerc.usgs.gov/orda_ docs/CaseDetails?ID=26 https://www.wildlife.ca.gov/OSPR/ NRDA/shell-martinez	See Shell Oil Spill Litigation Settlement Trustee Committee Final Report: https://nrm.dfg.ca.gov/ FileHandler.ashx?DocumentID =17366&inline=true
Sinclair Refinery NPL Site	NY	https://www.fws.gov/northeast/ nyfo/ec/nrda.htm	https://www.fws.gov/ northeast/nyfo/ec/files/ Final_settlement-sinclair_ agreement_2-28-17.PDF
Solvents Recovery Service of New England, Inc. NPL Site	CT	https://www.cerc.usgs.gov/ orda_docs/CaseDetails?ID=918	Various (see below):
Solvents Recovery Service of New England, Inc. NPL Site – De Minimis Settlement	CT		De Minimis Settlement: https://www.cerc.usgs.gov/ orda_docs/DocHandler. ashx?task=get&ID=157 http://www.doi.gov/ restoration/library/casedocs/ upload/CT_Solvents_Recovery_ de_minimus_SA_08.pdf
Solvents Recovery Service of New England, Inc. NPL Site – M. Swift & Sons, Inc.	CT		M. Swift & Sons, Inc.: https://www.cerc.usgs.gov/ orda_docs/DocHandler. ashx?task=get&ID=156 http://www.doi.gov/ restoration/library/casedocs/ upload/CT_Solvents_ Recovery_M-_Swift_Sons_ CD_08.pdf
South Municipal Wellfield NPL Site	NH	https://www.cerc.usgs.gov/ orda_docs/CaseDetails?ID=931	https://www.cerc.usgs.gov/ orda_docs/DocHandler. ashx?task=get&ID=688
Southern Lakes Trap and Skeet Club NPL Site	WI	https://www.cerc.usgs.gov/ orda_docs/CaseDetails?ID=222	https://www.cerc.usgs.gov/ orda_docs/DocHandler. ashx?task=get&ID=574

Date	Federal Statute(s)	NRD Assessment Costs (Past)	NRD Assessment Costs (Future)	NRD Restoration Payments	PRP/RP Implemented NRD Projects (Cost Projection if Provided)
4/19/2018	CERCLA			$166,750.00	No
4/1/1990	OPA				
2/28/2017	CERCLA, OPA, CWA	$10,500.00		$264,500.00	No
	CERCLA				
8/12/2008	CERCLA			$2,825,000.00	No
9/30/2008	CERCLA			$2,775.00	No
7/17/1997	CERCLA			$93,000.00	No
11/25/1998	CERCLA			$75,000.00	No

Name	State	Web Site Link(s)	Consent Decree/ Settlement Docs Link(s)
Southern Ohio Coal Company Meigs Mine No. 31	OH	https://www.cerc.usgs.gov/ orda_docs/CaseDetails?ID=148	https://www.cerc.usgs.gov/ orda_docs/DocHandler. ashx?task=get&ID=785
Springfield Plateau	MO	http://www.fws.gov/midwest/ es/ec/nrda/motristate/ SpringfieldPlateauFSJan2012.html (includes settlement history)	
St. Lawrence River (Alcoa and Reynolds Sites/ Massena)	NY	https://www.cerc.usgs.gov/orda_ docs/CaseDetails?ID=936 https://darrp.noaa.gov/hazardous-waste/st-lawrence-river https://www.fws.gov/northeast/ nyfo/ec/stlaw.htm	Various (see below):
St. Lawrence River (Alcoa and Reynolds Sites) – General Motors	NY		General Motors: https://www.cerc.usgs.gov/ orda_docs/DocHandler. ashx?task=get&ID=1278
St. Lawrence River (Alcoa and Reynolds Sites) – Alcoa/Reynolds	NY		Alcoa/Reynolds: https://www.cerc.usgs.gov/ orda_docs/DocHandler. ashx?task=get&ID=884
St. Louis River/ Interlake/ Duluth Tar NPL (SLRIDT) Site	MN	https://www.cerc.usgs.gov/orda_ docs/CaseDetails?ID=997 https://darrp.noaa. gov/hazardous-waste/ st-louis-riverinterlakeduluth-tar	Proposed Consent Decree: https://www.justice.gov/ sites/default/files/pages/ attachments/2017/06/29/ env_enforcement-2669816-v1-lodged_consent_decree.pdf
St. Regis Paper Company NPL site	MN	https://www.cerc.usgs.gov/ orda_docs/CaseDetails?ID=995	
Standard Metals Corp. Sites (7 mines) [Colorado]	CO	https://www.cerc.usgs.gov/ orda_docs/CaseDetails?ID=1043	https://www.cerc.usgs.gov/ orda_docs/DocHandler. ashx?task=get&ID=144
Standard Metals Corporation, Inc. (Antler Mine) [Arizona]	AZ	https://www.cerc.usgs.gov/ orda_docs/CaseDetails?ID=1042	https://www.cerc.usgs.gov/ orda_docs/DocHandler. ashx?task=get&ID=56 http://www.doi.gov/ restoration/library/casedocs/ upload/AZ_Standard_Metals_ CD_09.pdf
Star Evviva [M/S]	SC	https://www.cerc.usgs.gov/ orda_docs/CaseDetails?ID=1005	On file with authors

Date	Federal Statute(s)	NRD Assessment Costs (Past)	NRD Assessment Costs (Future)	NRD Restoration Payments	PRP/RP Implemented NRD Projects (Cost Projection if Provided)
1995	CWA, CERCLA	$240,200.00		$100,000.00	Yes [$1,900,000.00]
	CERCLA				
	CERCLA				
3/31/2011	CERCLA			$9,500,000 (claims in bankruptcy)	No
7/17/2013	CERCLA	$933,950.00		$16,698,081.00	Yes [$1,784,000.00]
6/29/2017	CERCLA	$183,201.00		$8,016,799.00	No
	CERCLA				
2/2/2009	CERCLA			It is unclear in the settlement how much was provided to cover NRD	No
2/2/2009	CERCLA			It is unclear in the settlement how much was provided to cover NRD	No
9/12/2003	CWA, OPA	$124,054.00		$1,875,946.00	No

Name	State	Web Site Link(s)	Consent Decree/ Settlement Docs Link(s)
Stuyvesant [M/V]/ Humboldt Oil Spill	CA	https://www.cerc.usgs.gov/orda_docs/CaseDetails?ID=948 https://www.wildlife.ca.gov/OSPR/NRDA/Stuyvesant-Humboldt	https://www.cerc.usgs.gov/orda_docs/DocHandler.ashx?task=get&ID=76 http://www.doi.gov/restoration/library/casedocs/upload/CA_Stuyvesant_CD_06.pdf
Summitville Mine/ Friedland	CO	https://www.fws.gov/mountain-prairie/nrda/summitvillecolo/summitville.htm	Information obtained from FWS website: https://www.fws.gov/mountain-prairie/nrda/summitvillecolo/summitville.htm
Sunoco Inc. Pipeline Crude Oil Spill/John Heinz National Wildlife Refuge	PA	https://www.cerc.usgs.gov/orda_docs/CaseDetails?ID=922	https://www.cerc.usgs.gov/orda_docs/DocHandler.ashx?task=get&ID=423
Superior Block and Supply Company	CT	https://www.cerc.usgs.gov/orda_docs/CaseDetails?ID=41	https://www.cerc.usgs.gov/orda_docs/DocHandler.ashx?task=get&ID=158
Sutton Brook Disposal Area NPL Site	MS	https://www.cerc.usgs.gov/orda_docs/CaseDetails.aspx?ID=110 https://www.mass.gov/service-details/natural-resource-damages-program-groundwater-settlements-massdep	https://www.cerc.usgs.gov/orda_docs/DocHandler.ashx?task=get&ID=309 https://www.mass.gov/files/documents/2017/08/28/MA_Sutton_Brook_Disposal_Area_CD_2010.pdf
Tampa Bay Oil Spill	FL	https://www.cerc.usgs.gov/orda_docs/CaseDetails?ID=906	https://www.cerc.usgs.gov/orda_docs/DocHandler.ashx?task=get&ID=185
Tank Barge DBL 152	TX	https://darrp.noaa.gov/oil-spills/tank-barge-dbl-152	NOAA will be submitting a NPFC claim as the RP dropped out of the NRDA process
Tansitor Electronics, Inc. NPL Site	VT	https://www.cerc.usgs.gov/orda_docs/CaseDetails?ID=971	https://www.cerc.usgs.gov/orda_docs/DocHandler.ashx?task=get&ID=716
Tenyo Maru [F/V] Fuel Oil, Diesel and Lube Oil Spill	WA	https://www.cerc.usgs.gov/orda_docs/CaseDetails?ID=908	https://www.cerc.usgs.gov/orda_docs/DocHandler.ashx?task=get&ID=550
Tesoro Hawaii Oil Spill	HI	https://www.cerc.usgs.gov/orda_docs/CaseDetails?ID=911	https://www.cerc.usgs.gov/orda_docs/DocHandler.ashx?task=get&ID=196

Date	Federal Statute(s)	NRD Assessment Costs (Past)	NRD Assessment Costs (Future)	NRD Restoration Payments	PRP/RP Implemented NRD Projects (Cost Projection if Provided)
9/29/2006	CWA, OPA	$877,000.00		$6,711,020.00	No
2000	CERCLA			$5,000,000.00	No
2005	OPA			$865,000.00	Yes [not specified]
11/27/1996	OPA	$10,815.16		$40,357.81	No
11/9/2010	CERCLA	$932,022.35		$1,542,977.65	No
4/16/1998	OPA	$1,266,180.00			Yes [$4,520,196.00]
1/11/1999	CERCLA			$21,000.00	No
12/23/1994	OPA			$8,500,000.00	No
10/17/2001	CWA, OPA	$110,000.00		$510,000.00	Yes [$55,000]

Name	State	Web Site Link(s)	Consent Decree/ Settlement Docs Link(s)
Texaco Exploration and Production, Inc. Well No. 118 Crude Oil Spill	LA	https://www.cerc.usgs.gov/ orda_docs/CaseDetails?ID=1061	https://www.cerc.usgs.gov/ orda_docs/DocHandler. ashx?task=get&ID=276
Texaco Refinery Oil Spils (Fidalgo Bay]	WA	https://www.cerc.usgs.gov/ orda_docs/CaseDetails?ID=968	On file with authors (1998 EPA Consent LEXIS 73)
Texas City Y Oil Spill/Kirby Barge	TX	https://www.cerc.usgs.gov/ orda_docs/CaseDetails?ID=1071	Various (see below):
Texas City Y Oil Spill/Kirby Barge – Advanced Funding Agreement	TX		Advanced Funding Agreement: https://www.cerc.usgs.gov/ orda_docs/DocHandler. ashx?task=get&ID=1267
Texas City Y Oil Spill/Kirby Barge – Memorandum of Agreement	TX		Memorandum of Agreement: https://www.cerc.usgs.gov/ orda_docs/DocHandler. ashx?task=get&ID=1554
Texmo Oil Company	AZ	https://www.cerc.usgs.gov/ orda_docs/CaseDetails?ID=981	https://www.cerc.usgs.gov/ orda_docs/DocHandler. ashx?task=get&ID=57 http://www.doi.gov/ restoration/library/casedocs/ upload/AZ_Texmo_CD_07.pdf
Tex-Tin Corp. NPL Site	TX	https://www.cerc.usgs.gov/orda_ docs/CaseDetails?ID=925 https://darrp.noaa. gov/hazardous-waste/ tex-tin-corporation	Information obtained from DOI webpage: https://www.cerc.usgs.gov/ orda_docs/CaseDetails?ID=925
Thatcher Trucking Co. Tanker Truck Hydrochloric Acid Spill	OR	https://www.cerc.usgs.gov/ orda_docs/CaseDetails?ID=979	https://www.cerc.usgs.gov/ orda_docs/DocHandler. ashx?task=get&ID=701
Thermo Fluids Oil Spill	OR	https://www.cerc.usgs.gov/ orda_docs/CaseDetails?ID=980	
Third Site (Finley Creek and Eagle Creek)	IN	https://www.cerc.usgs.gov/ orda_docs/CaseDetails?ID=78	Information obtained from Restoration Plan: https://www.cerc.usgs.gov/ orda_docs/DocHandler. ashx?task=get&ID=242
Tittabawassee River	MI	https://www.fws.gov/midwest/es/ ec/nrda/TittabawasseeRiverNRDA/ index.html	

Date	Federal Statute(s)	NRD Assessment Costs (Past)	NRD Assessment Costs (Future)	NRD Restoration Payments	PRP/RP Implemented NRD Projects (Cost Projection if Provided)
12/19/1991	Likely OPA (not specified in Agreement)	$21,489.00			Yes [not specified]
7/8/1998	OPA			$500,000.00	No
	OPA, CWA, PSRPA				
4/10/2014	OPA, CWA, PSRPA				
11/12/2014	OPA, CWA, PSRPA				
9/12/2007	OPA			$1,217,382.91	No
8/1/2000	CERCLA			$3,200,850.00	Yes [not specified]
9/25/1992	CERCLA			$275,000.00	No
	CERCLA OPA				
11/4/1999	CERCLA			$39,986.00	No
	CERCLA				

Name	State	Web Site Link(s)	Consent Decree/ Settlement Docs Link(s)
Tomales Bay Oyster Co.	CA		Proposed Consent Decree: https://www.justice.gov/sites/ default/files/enrd/pages/ attachments/2017/01/19/tboc_ consent_decree_as_filed.pdf
Tri-State Mining District-Cherokee County	KS	https://www.fws.gov/ mountain-prairie/contaminants/ cherokeeCountyKansas.php	Various (see below):
Tri-State Mining District-Cherokee County – In re ASARCO Bankruptcy Settlement Agreement	KS		ASARCO Bankruptcy Settlement Agreement: On file with authors
Tri-State Mining District-Cherokee County – DuPont	KS		DuPont: https://www.doi.gov/ restoration/news/ upload/KS_Cherokee- County-Waco-Subsite_ CD-DuPont_06-06-2012.pdf
Tri-State Mining District-Cherokee County – Peabody Bankruptcy Settlement Agreement	KS		Peabody Bankruptcy Settlement Agreement: https://www.justice.gov/ sites/default/files/pages/ attachments/2017/07/20/ env_enforcement-2672503-v1- lodged_settlement.pdf
Tronox LLC Site	TX	https://www.cerc.usgs.gov/ orda_docs/CaseDetails?ID=1064	Various (see below):
Tronox LLC Site – Bankruptcy Consent Decree and Settlement Agreement	TX		Tronox Bankruptcy Settlement: https://www.cerc.usgs.gov/ orda_docs/DocHandler. ashx?task=get&ID=1398
Tronox LLC Site – Litigation Trust Agreement	TX		Litigation Trust Agreement: http://www.gc.noaa.gov/gc-cd/ tronox-021411-lit_trust_agree. pdf
Tronox LLC Site – Multistate Environmental Trust Agreement	TX		Multistate Environmental Trust Agreement: http://www.gc.noaa.gov/gc-cd/ tronox-021411-multistate_ trust_agree.pdf
Tronox LLC Site – Cimarron Environmental Trust Agreement	TX		Cimarron Environmental Trust Agreement: http://www.gc.noaa.gov/gc-cd/ tronox-021411-cimarron_ envtl_resp.pdf

Date	Federal Statute(s)	NRD Assessment Costs (Past)	NRD Assessment Costs (Future)	NRD Restoration Payments	PRP/RP Implemented NRD Projects (Cost Projection if Provided)
3/16/2017	System Unit Resource Protection Act			$280,000.00	No
	CWA, CERCLA				
10/26/2007	CERCLA	$2,000,000.00		$65,000,000 (claims in bankruptcy)	No
6/6/2012	CWA, CERCLA	$70,887.00		$181,852.00	No
7/14/2017	CERCLA			$2,418,826.77	No
	CERCLA				
1/26/2011	CERCLA			$484,115 (claims in bankruptcy)	No
2/14/2011	CERCLA				
2/14/2011	CERCLA				
2/14/2011	CERCLA				

Name	State	Web Site Link(s)	Consent Decree/ Settlement Docs Link(s)
Tronox LLC Site – Nevada Environmental Trust Agreement	TX		Nevada Environmental Trust Agreement: http://www.gc.noaa.gov/gc-cd/ tronox-021411-nevada_envtl_ resp.pdf
Tronox LLC Site – Savannah Environmental Trust	TX		Savannah Environmental Trust Agreement: http://www.gc.noaa.gov/gc-cd/ tronox-021411-savannah_ envtl_resp.pdf
Tronox LLC Site – West Chicago Environmental Trust	TX		West Chicago Environmental Trust Agreement: http://www.gc.noaa.gov/gc-cd/ tronox-02144-west_chicago_ envtl_resp.pdf
Tulalip Landfill NPL Site	WA	https://www.cerc.usgs.gov/ orda_docs/CaseDetails?ID=804	Various (see below):
Tulalip Landfill NPL Site – De Minimis Parties (Ace Galvanizing et al.)	WA		De Minimis Parties (Ace Galvanizing et al.): http://www.gc.noaa.gov/gc-cd/ tul-cd1.pdf
Tulalip Landfill NPL Site – De Minimis Parties (Boeing Co. et al.)	WA		De Minimis Parties (Boeing Co. et al.): http://www.gc.noaa.gov/gc-cd/ tul-cd2.pdf
Tulalip Landfill NPL Site – Goodwill Industries	WA		Goodwill Industries: http://www.gc.noaa.gov/gc-cd/ tul-cd5.pdf
Tulalip Landfill NPL Site – Manson Construction & Engineering Co.	WA		Manson Construction & Engineering Co.: http://www.gc.noaa.gov/gc-cd/ tul-cd3.pdf
Tulalip Landfill NPL Site – R.W. Rhine, Inc.	WA		R.W. Rhine, Inc.: http://www.gc.noaa.gov/gc-cd/ tul-cd4.pdf
Tulalip Landfill NPL Site – Ace Tank Co. et al.	WA		De Minimis Parties (Ace Tank Co. et al): http://www.gc.noaa.gov/gc-cd/ tul-cd6.pdf
Tulalip Landfill NPL Site – Associated Grocers/Fog-Tite, Inc.	WA		Associated Grocers/Fog-Tite, Inc.: https://www.cerc.usgs.gov/ orda_docs/DocHandler. ashx?task=get&ID=562
Tulalip Landfill NPL Site – BFI Waste Systems	WA		BFI Waste Systems: http://www.gc.noaa.gov/gc-cd/ cd-tul-bfi.pdf

Date	Federal Statute(s)	NRD Assessment Costs (Past)	NRD Assessment Costs (Future)	NRD Restoration Payments	PRP/RP Implemented NRD Projects (Cost Projection if Provided)
2/14/2011	CERCLA				
2/14/2011	CERCLA				
2/14/2011	CERCLA				
	CERCLA				
8/15/1997	CERCLA				
12/22/1997	CERCLA			$166,568.00	No
1/20/1998	CERCLA			$19,102.00	No
1/20/1998	CERCLA			$897,105.00	No
1/20/1998	CERCLA			$26,734.00	No
10/19/1998	CERCLA			$917,108.00	No
4/3/2000	CERCLA			$43,153.00	No
5/20/2002	CERCLA			$37,981.00	No

Name	State	Web Site Link(s)	Consent Decree/ Settlement Docs Link(s)
Tulalip Landfill NPL Site – Quemetco, Inc.	WA		Quemetco, Inc.: http://www.gc.noaa.gov/gc-cd/cd-tul-que.pdf
Tulalip Landfill NPL Site – University of Washington	WA		University of Washington: http://www.gc.noaa.gov/gc-cd/cd-tul-uw.pdf
Tulalip Landfill NPL Site – Seattle Disposal	WA		Seattle Disposal: http://www.gc.noaa.gov/gc-cd/tul-1126.pdf
Tulalip Landfill NPL Site	WA		Waste Management: http://www.gc.noaa.gov/gc-cd/tul-cd983.pdf
U.S. DOE Oak Ridge Reservation NPL Site/Lower Watts Bar Reservoir	TN	https://www.cerc.usgs.gov/orda_docs/CaseDetails?ID=975	https://www.cerc.usgs.gov/orda_docs/DocHandler.ashx?task=get&ID=468
United Heckathorn NPL Site (Lauritzen Channel, Parr Channel, Richmond Harbor, San Francisco Bay)	CA	https://www.cerc.usgs.gov/orda_docs/CaseDetails?ID=960	Various (see below):
United Heckathorn NPL Site (Lauritzen Channel, Parr Channel, Richmond Harbor, San Francisco Bay) – Levin Group	CA		Levin Group: https://www.cerc.usgs.gov/orda_docs/DocHandler.ashx?task=get&ID=657
United Heckathorn NPL Site (Lauritzen Channel, Parr Channel, Richmond Harbor, San Francisco Bay) – Miscellaneous Defendants	CA		Miscellandous Defendants: https://www.cerc.usgs.gov/orda_docs/DocHandler.ashx?task=get&ID=659
United Heckathorn NPL Site (Lauritzen Channel, Parr Channel, Richmond Harbor, San Francisco Bay) – Montrose Group	CA		Montrose Group: https://www.cerc.usgs.gov/orda_docs/DocHandler.ashx?task=get&ID=658

Date	Federal Statute(s)	NRD Assessment Costs (Past)	NRD Assessment Costs (Future)	NRD Restoration Payments	PRP/RP Implemented NRD Projects (Cost Projection if Provided)
5/20/2002	CERCLA			$39,839.00	No
5/20/2002	CERCLA			$39,139.00	No
6/3/2002	CERCLA, CWA, OPA			$583,000.00	No
6/23/2004	CERCLA			$190,000.00	No
10/6/2010	CERCLA			$50,000.00	No
	CERCLA				
7/19/1996	CERCLA			$19,464.72	No
7/19/1996	CERCLA			$113,868.61	No
7/19/1996	CERCLA			$133,333.34	No

Name	State	Web Site Link(s)	Consent Decree/ Settlement Docs Link(s)
United Heckathorn NPL Site (Lauritzen Channel, Parr Channel, Richmond Harbor, San Francisco Bay) – Parr Group	CA		Parr Group: https://www.cerc.usgs.gov/ orda_docs/DocHandler. ashx?task=get&ID=660
Upper Arkansas River/California Gulch NPL Site	CO	https://www.cerc.usgs.gov/orda_ docs/CaseDetails?ID=37 http://www.fws.gov/mountain -prairie/nrda/LeadvilleColo /CaliforniaGulch.htm	Various (see below):
Upper Arkansas River/California Gulch NPL Site – U.S. BOR	CO		U.S. Bureau of Reclamation: https://www.cerc.usgs.gov/ orda_docs/DocHandler. ashx?task=get&ID=149
Upper Arkansas River/California Gulch NPL Site – ASARCO	CO		ASARCO: https://www.cerc.usgs.gov/ orda_docs/DocHandler. ashx?task=get&ID=147
Upper Arkansas River/California Gulch NPL Site – Newmont	CO		Newmont: https://www.cerc.usgs.gov/ orda_docs/DocHandler. ashx?task=get&ID=148
Valley Forge NHP Asbestos Release	PA	https://www.cerc.usgs.gov/ orda_docs/CaseDetails?ID=978	https://www.cerc.usgs.gov/ orda_docs/DocHandler. ashx?task=get&ID=1161
Vermont Asbestos Group Mine Site (G-I Holdings Bankruptcy)	VT	https://www.cerc.usgs.gov/orda_ docs/CaseDetails.aspx?ID=201	http://www.cerc.usgs.gov/ orda_docs/DocHandler. ashx?task=get&ID=503
Vertac NPL Site	AR	https://www.cerc.usgs.gov/ orda_docs/CaseDetails?ID=8	http://www.adeq.state.ar.us/ downloads/webdatabases/ legal/cao/lis_files/97-176.pdf See United States v. Vertac Chemical Corp., Nos. LR-C-80-109, -110, LR-C-87-833 (756 F. Supp. 1215) (E.D. Ark. February 4, 1991)
Vieques/AFWTA	PR		
W.R. Grace and Company, Inc./ Wayne Interim Storage NPL Site	NJ	https://www.cerc.usgs.gov/ orda_docs/CaseDetails?ID=944	https://www.cerc.usgs.gov/ orda_docs/DocHandler. ashx?task=get&ID=690

Date	Federal Statute(s)	NRD Assessment Costs (Past)	NRD Assessment Costs (Future)	NRD Restoration Payments	PRP/RP Implemented NRD Projects (Cost Projection if Provided)
7/19/1996	CERCLA			$133,334.33	No
	CERCLA				
10/26/2006	CERCLA			$300,000.00	No
8/29/2008	CERCLA			$10,000,000.00	No
8/29/2008	CERCLA			$10,500,000.00	No
3/30/2010	CERCLA			Not specified	
9/24/2009	CERCLA			$850,000.00	No
8/7/1997	CERCLA, CWA			$1,000,000.00	Yes [not specified]
	CERCLA				
4/29/1999	CERCLA			$270,000.00	No

Name	State	Web Site Link(s)	Consent Decree/ Settlement Docs Link(s)
Waste, Inc. Landfill Site (Trail Creek)	IN	https://www.cerc.usgs.gov/ orda_docs/CaseDetails?ID=923	https://www.cerc.usgs.gov/ orda_docs/DocHandler. ashx?task=get&ID=673
Wayne Reclamation & Recycling/Wayne Waste Oil Site	IN	https://www.cerc.usgs.gov/ orda_docs/CaseDetails?ID=924	Various (see below):
Wayne Reclamation & Recycling/Wayne Waste Oil Site – Active Products	IN		Active Products: https://www.cerc.usgs.gov/ orda_docs/DocHandler. ashx?task=get&ID=674
Wayne Reclamation & Recycling/Wayne Waste Oil Site – De Minimis	IN		De Minimis: https://www.cerc.usgs.gov/ orda_docs/DocHandler. ashx?task=get&ID=675
Wellwood [M/V]	FL		http://www.gc.noaa.gov/gc-cd/ well-cd.pdf
West Kingston Town Dump/URI Disposal Area NPL Site	RI	https://www.cerc.usgs.gov/ orda_docs/CaseDetails?ID=175	https://www.cerc.usgs.gov/ orda_docs/DocHandler. ashx?task=get&ID=454
West Site/Hows Corner NPL Site	ME	https://www.cerc.usgs.gov/ orda_docs/CaseDetails?ID=1015	https://www.cerc.usgs.gov/ orda_docs/DocHandler. ashx?task=get&ID=1298
Westchester [M/V] Oil Spill	LA	https://www.cerc.usgs.gov/ orda_docs/CaseDetails?ID=1011	https://www.cerc.usgs.gov/ orda_docs/DocHandler. ashx?task=get&ID=272 http://www.gc.noaa.gov/gc-cd/ cd-westr.pdf
Weyerhauser Plymouth Wood Treating Site (Albemarle Sound)	NC	https://www.cerc.usgs.gov/orda_ docs/CaseDetails?ID=1036 https://casedocuments.darrp.noaa. gov/southeast/albemarle_sound/ admin.html	Funding & Participation Agreement: https:// www.cerc.usgs.gov/ orda_docs/DocHandler. ashx?task=get&ID=368
Whitewood Creek NPL Site	SD	https://www.cerc.usgs.gov/orda_ docs/CaseDetails.aspx?ID=900	https://www.cerc.usgs.gov/ orda_docs/DocHandler. ashx?task=get&ID=1510
Wide Beach Development NPL Site	NY	https://www.cerc.usgs.gov/ orda_docs/CaseDetails?ID=280	https://www.cerc.usgs.gov/ orda_docs/DocHandler. ashx?task=get&ID=1067
Woodstock Municipal Landfill NPL Site	IL	https://www.cerc.usgs.gov/orda_ docs/CaseDetails.aspx?ID=62	https://www.cerc.usgs.gov/ orda_docs/DocHandler. ashx?task=get&ID=212

Date	Federal Statute(s)	NRD Assessment Costs (Past)	NRD Assessment Costs (Future)	NRD Restoration Payments	PRP/RP Implemented NRD Projects (Cost Projection if Provided)
9/10/1999	CERCLA	$3,500.00		$599,500.00	No
	CERCLA				
7/20/1992	CERCLA			$151,034.52	No
Unknown	CERCLA			$24,000.00	No
12/22/1986	Not specified			$3,000,000.00	No
3/9/2009	CERCLA			$9,936.83	Yes [not specified]
11/4/2009	CERCLA	$59,427.00		$70,161.00	No
4/6/2003	OPA	$934,014.66	$76,434.00		Yes [not specified]
10/12/2006	CERCLA				
7/13/1999	CERCLA	$500,000.00	$500,000.00	$4,300,000.00	No
3/22/1996	CERCLA			$57,974.00	No
10/31/2007	CERCLA			$967,000.00	No

Name	State	Web Site Link(s)	Consent Decree/ Settlement Docs Link(s)
World Prodigy [M/V]	RI	https://www.cerc.usgs.gov/ orda_docs/CaseDetails?ID=173	
Wyckoff/Eagle Harbor NPL Site	WA	http://www.cerc.usgs.gov/orda_ docs/CaseDetails?ID=219 https://darrp.noaa.gov/ hazardous-waste/eagle-harbor	https://www.cerc.usgs.gov/ orda_docs/DocHandler. ashx?task=get&ID=565 https://darrp.noaa.gov/sites/ default/files/case-documents/ psr.pdf
Yaworski Waste Lagoon NPL Site	CT	https://www.cerc.usgs.gov/orda_ docs/CaseDetails.aspx?ID=42 http://www.fws.gov/newengland/ Contaminants-NRDAR-restoration_ projects-yaworski.htm	https://www.cerc.usgs.gov/ orda_docs/DocHandler. ashx?task=get&ID=663
Yellow River Wastewater Discharge/ AgriProcessors – Iowa Turkey Products	IA	https://www.cerc.usgs.gov/orda_ docs/CaseDetails.aspx?ID=969	https://www.cerc.usgs.gov/ orda_docs/DocHandler. ashx?task=get&ID=678
Yeoman Creek Landfill NPL Site	IL	https://www.cerc.usgs.gov/orda_ docs/CaseDetails.aspx?ID=63	https://www.cerc.usgs.gov/ orda_docs/DocHandler. ashx?task=get&ID=213
Zoecon/Rhone Poulec NPL Site/ Starlink Logistics, Inc./ 1990 Bay Road Site	CA	https://www.cerc.usgs.gov/orda_ docs/CaseDetails.aspx?ID=1040	https://www.cerc.usgs.gov/ orda_docs/DocHandler. ashx?task=get&ID=138

Date	Federal Statute(s)	NRD Assessment Costs (Past)	NRD Assessment Costs (Future)	NRD Restoration Payments	PRP/RP Implemented NRD Projects (Cost Projection if Provided)
	OPA				
8/29/1994	CERCLA			Half of the liquidation proceeds	No
8/11/2000	CERCLA			$40,000.00	No
1/7/2005	CERCLA; CWA			$20,000.00	No
4/10/2007	CERCLA	$300,000.00			No
12/18/2009	CERCLA	$12,764.20			No

Table of Cases

Index